FINANCIAL INVESTIGATION and FORENSIC ACCOUNTING

George A. Manning, C.F.E., E.A.

CRC Press
Boca Raton   London   New York   Washington, D.C.

Library of Congress Cataloging-in-Publication Data

Manning, George A.
Financial investigation and forensic accounting / by George A. Manning.
    p. cm.
    Includes bibliographical references.
    ISBN 0-8493-0435-0 (alk. paper)
    1. White collar crime investigation—United States. 2. Forensic accounting—United States. 3. Fraud investigation—United States.
I. Title.
    HV8079.W47M35 1999
    364. 16′3—dc21
    for Library of Congress   99-21263
                                                                   CIP

Visit the CRC Press Web site at www.crcpress.com

© 2000 by CRC Press LLC

No claim to original U.S. Government works
International Standard Book Number 0-8493-0435-0
Library of Congress Card Number 99-21263
Printed in the United States of America   4 5 6 7 8 9 0
Printed on acid-free paper

Preface

Forensic accounting can be defined as the science of gathering and presenting financial information in a form that will be accepted by a court of jurisprudence against perpetrators of economic crime.

Economic crimes have increased dramatically in recent years. This becomes evident in viewing newspaper reports which, on an almost daily basis, report of economic crimes committed in communities across the country. One can read of a person embezzling funds from a bank or company; a political person accepting kickbacks for political favors; a "con artist" who swindles people out of money by fraudulent schemes; or a person selling illegal products (drugs, alcohol, and tobacco).

Law enforcement personnel, in recent years, have become more aware of "white collar" crimes. However, they have lacked the training and expertise in combating such crimes. This is particularly true for small police departments. The law enforcement community, today, is better trained at combating violent or personal behavior crimes, but now has the responsibility to expand its knowledge and expertise into the economic crimes area. In order to do this, law enforcement must receive further education and training. Many police departments, both small and large, focus their resources on violent crimes. Since many detectives don´t have an accounting background, they often fail to use financial information to support their case. This is particularly true in organized crime and drug-trafficking cases. Congress and some states have enacted laws for law enforcement to use financial information to support their cases. Some large police departments have employed accountants to help law enforcement develop financial information, but they are relatively few. One South Florida police department with over 2,000 sworn officers has only 1 accountant and he is swamped with cases. Some police departments will contract an accountant for a case, but this is rare.

The accounting profession is beginning to change from examination for "irregularities" to examination for fraud on part of employees and management. This change, of course, has resulted in a change of audit procedures to encompass external third party inquiries as well as internal audit procedures. Financial institutions and credit reporting agencies are becoming more involved with business organizations´ financial affairs by requiring more disclosures. They are developing more techniques to uncover potential fraudulent schemes by developing profiles, which will identify perpetrators before huge losses are incurred by other businesses.

The cooperation of accountants and law enforcement has now become not just important, but imperative. Accountants must know what financial data are admissible in a court of law. The criminal investigator must learn how to use financial information to enhance his or her case.

The following illustration gives an example of what the results can be when law enforcement personnel do not have the training and knowledge to use financial information.

A police department in South Florida obtained a search warrant for a car dealership suspected of dealing in drugs. The officers went in and discovered large amounts of cocaine, money, jewelry, precious metals, and financial files. The police officers confiscated the cocaine, money, jewelry, and precious metals, but left the financial files behind. In a forfeiture hearing, the defendants claimed that the jewelry and precious metals did not belong to them and provided witnesses who testified that the jewelry and precious metals were being held on consignment. The court ruled in favor of the defendants and several days later, the defendants got on a flight out of the country with the jewelry and precious metals in their possession. It was later learned that the jewelry and precious metals were purchased from various vendors in the city. The estimated cost of the jewelry and precious metals was $1,800,000. The drug traffickers removed their laundered money out of the country by buying jewelry and precious metals since no Treasury Currency and Monetary Instrument Reports (CMIR) were required at the time. The police would not have lost the jewelry and precious metals if they had confiscated the financial records, which clearly showed how the defendants purchased the commodities.

Accountants, in both public practice and industry, must recognize financial crimes at an early stage and document such crimes for judicial prosecution. Most accountants don't recognize fraud. Business people don't recognize fraud schemes until it is too late. The following illustration shows how a business became a victim even when advised of the situation.

A major supplier of appliances had a policy of granting liberal credit terms to new businesses. A new appliance store took advantage by ordering a nominal number of appliances. The new store regularly ordered appliances at an increasing rate using the liberal credit terms. The controller noticed that the rate of increase was above normal. The management of the supplier disregarded the controller's concern. After about nine months, the new store placed an $800,000 order and since the new store paid its bills on time, the order was shipped. The management of the new store received the $800,000 order and the next day shipped its entire inventory to another location some 300 miles away. When the supplier sent notices to the new store for payment, the notices first came back marked "unclaimed" and later came back marked "moved with no forwarding address." When the supplier sent collectors out to the new store, they found the building empty. The new storeowners disposed of the inventory for $1,500,000 and the supplier suffered a loss of $800,000, which took them five years to recover by raising the prices by 10 percent. The supplier unsuccessfully sued the new store. Law enforcement would not proceed against the storeowners because they concluded that the new storeowners were merely bad businessmen. Actually, law enforcement did not know how to prosecute this kind of crime.

The purpose of this book is twofold. First, it should be used as a reference guide by law enforcement and accountants. This book is written so the reader can find specific issues and how to investigate and present them in a court of law. Second, it can be used as a textbook in training both law enforcement and accountants in the field of fraud examination and forensic accounting.

This book is focused upon practical, everyday use by both law enforcement and accountants. Theory is also addressed, but is explained more in terms of everyday use. Another objective is to make accountants familiar with law enforcement and the law; and make law enforcement familiar with the importance of financial information in both civil and criminal cases. It has been made very clear that when a team of both accountants and criminal investigators team up, they rarely lose a criminal case. Also, they learn the interrelationships and the needs of each other.

A trend across this country today is the declining budgets of law enforcement agencies at all levels of government. At the same time, violent crime is on the increase and is expected to increase much more in the future. Public opinion today is for law enforcement to go after violent criminals. Violent crime is on television every day, but white-collar crimes are rarely reported. If this trend continues, then law enforcement will be unable to provide the personnel and other resources to investigate white-collar criminals. The Federal Bureau of Investigation (FBI) reported a few years ago that violent crime makes up 95 percent of all cases, while white-collar crime only makes up 5 percent. Yet, the white-collar crime is responsible for 95 percent of the financial losses suffered by victims.

The security industry has had a tremendous growth in recent years. It has created a great demand for security locks, various types of alarms, and security guards. Private investigation firms have also shown a tremendous growth, particularly in matters relating to civil litigations, searching for hidden assets, and tracing funds. Some law enforcement agencies have retained private fraud examiners in their investigations. If this trend continues, and the outlook is that it will, fraud examiners will be in greater demand in the future. Fraud examiners have a bright future ahead.

The Author

George A. Manning, CFE, EA is currently working as a fraud examiner, forensic accountant, and expert/summary witness for the Internal Revenue Service (IRS). He has a Bachelor in Business Administration (BBA) from the University of Miami (Florida) and a Master of Science in Criminal Justice Administration from Lynn University, Boca Raton, Florida. He is a Certified Fraud Examiner and is enrolled to practice before the Internal Revenue Service (Enrolled Agent). He has worked with various federal, state, and local law enforcement agencies. He has 14 years experience in the forensic accounting field.

Acknowledgment

A special and most heartfelt thanks to my wife, Lois. Her sacrifices, made to allow me the time and freedom to do my research and writing, are greatly appreciated. She also spent many hours in the library researching and gathering material for the book and performing secretarial duties.

TABLE OF CONTENTS

Exhibits

Tables

Figures

Economics of Crime

1

Introduction

The effects of crime act upon the economy in two primary ways. Microeconomics deals with the effect on individuals and businesses. Macroeconomics deals with the effect on the national and international economies. Individuals and businesses can easily understand the effect of crime in their everyday activities. However, most individuals and businesses have difficulty understanding the effect of crime on the national and international levels.

Microeconomics

This segment of economics deals with individuals and businesses. The primary effect is the direct loss of money or property. In most cases, the dollar amount of money or property can be determined after the commission of the crime. In other cases, this may not be true. The loss to the local community can be enormous when considering the final result.

Arson

This crime can affect both the victim and the insurance company. If the victim has no casualty insurance coverage, then the business or individual will undoubtedly be put out of business or home if the owners do not have the capital to rebuild. If the victim has insurance, then the insurance company has to pay the claim. If the casualty is caused by the victim in order to collect insurance, then the insurance company can refuse to pay and the victim will normally suffer the loss. In either case, one or the other, or both, will realize a loss of property or money.

Bankruptcy Fraud

This crime affects the creditors of a business. They ship goods to a customer with the expectations of receiving payment on agreed terms. The customer diverts the goods elsewhere and doesn't make the payment. The creditor suffers a loss of not only the cost of the merchandise, but also the gross profits. For small businesses, this can be devastating. They are usually unable to recover the losses. For larger businesses, they pass the loss on to other customers by raising their prices which could take weeks, months, or even years to recover.

Bribery

Businesses that pay kickbacks or bribes have to compensate by increasing their prices or contracts. Normally, businesses that pay kickbacks or bribes will charge more for their goods and services than other businesses in that particular industry. If the industry is controlled by organized crime, then a business may be forced to move elsewhere or go out of business.

Loan Sharking

The borrower pays interest at a very high rate. Usually, the interest is so high that the borrower can never get the principal reduced. As a result, the loan shark may use violence against the borrower which, in turn, results in the borrower getting further behind on his payments because of additional bills, e.g., medical expenses. In the case of organized crime, the borrower may be forced to commit some other act, usually economic, which will either repay the lender or help the lender to get some economic advantage.

Credit Card Fraud

Most stolen credit cards are stolen before they reach the intended customer, although many credit card numbers are stolen by store cashiers. In some cases, credit cards are counterfeited, sometimes using legitimate numbers. Stolen credit cards are used to purchase merchandise which is fenced to an illegitimate vendor. The vendor in turn, sells the merchandise for cash. The card holder is usually out the purchases made before he realizes his losses. Even after he discovers that his card is stolen, he still suffers a loss, usually $50 after the credit card company is notified. One organized crime group ships the goods overseas for resale. Credit card companies report that they lose multiple millions of dollars through credit card fraud. This is the primary reason they charge high interest rates of 14 to 18 percent or higher in some states.

Mail-Order Operations

This crime occurs when a customer sends money in to a mail-order house for the purchase of merchandise and the mail-order house does not send the merchandise, but just "pockets" the money. This is called a "boiler room operation." Some states have required licensing of telemarketers. This has not prevented or deterred these operations, however, it has made it somewhat easier to track down corrupt telemarketers by law enforcement.

Skimming/Embezzlement

Skimming involves the diversion of business receipts from the business, in effect, stealing from the business and the government. The owner of the business is usually trying to hide money from either the tax collector or a partner. Embezzlement is the stealing of money from the employer. The economic loss is the amount of funds diverted or stolen.

Stock Manipulation

Stock manipulation is the transfer of stock, between related entities or people, in order to increase the market value. When the value is high, normally far above the market value, the stock is sold to other investors. Later, the value of the stock or bond drops to the actual market values. The investor later suffers a loss measured by the cost less the amount realized when sold.

Narcotics

The use of narcotics by consumers has devastating effects at both the micro- and macroeconomic levels. This section deals with the microeconomic level. First, narcotic use diverts the consumer's funds for narcotics instead of everyday living expenses. The narcotic user becomes addicted which drives the user to want to buy more. After a time, the narcotic user will use all his resources to purchase the illegal substance. "Crack cocaine" is one narcotic which will do this in a relatively short time. There is no such thing as a casual drug user. The narcotic user will eventually do anything to get funds to purchase more narcotics. The user's job performance drops and absenteeism increases. Eventually, the user will lose his job. In some instances, he will steal from his employer and may get caught. Narcotics users would rather pay for narcotics than living expenses. When they lose their jobs, they resort to borrowing and stealing from others.

The street pusher, who sells the narcotics to the consumer, is usually a user himself. If not, the pusher is trying to make money in order to get out of his economically-depressed state. Street pushers have been found to be as young as 12 years old. In recent years, organized crime organizations like to have kids do their drug pushing because children don't serve time in jail or correctional centers. Secondly, elementary, middle, and high schools are easy markets for drugs.

The drug kingpins reap the major profits from drug trafficking. They usually don't use or possess any drugs. They control and direct the shipments and distribution of drugs. A major part of the profits goes to the drug kingpin. This, in effect, causes the wealth of a community to become concentrated from the many to the few. In small communities, this can be readily evident by observing who the wealthy people are in the community and by their occupation or business ventures. In metropolitan areas, this is not so evident because of the intermingling of wealthy people from both legal and illegal business ventures.

Local Industries

In the local community, organized crime operates many businesses, legal and illegal. Organized crime likes to operate local businesses in the legal arena of the following:

a. Construction
b. Waste removal
c. Garment industry
d. Food processing, distribution, and retailing
e. Hotels
f. Liquor retailing and wholesaling
g. Entertainment
h. Motor vehicle sales and repairs
i. Real estate
j. Other cash-oriented businesses

These businesses are attractive for three reasons. First, illegal profits can be laundered through a legitimate business. Second, profits can be skimmed by various methods. Last, if a monopoly can be obtained in the area, then organized crime can get higher prices for their products and services. This results in greater profits.

Construction

Organized crime likes the construction industry, particularly in major metropolitan areas, because profits can be received through "ghost" employees, extortion, and control of materials. For contractors to get jobs, they must employ "ghost" (nonexistent) employees, pay kickbacks, and pay higher prices for raw materials. All of these costs are passed down to the consumer in the form of higher prices for goods and services, higher rents, higher taxes, and other costs.

Waste Removal

Organized crime affects the waste removal industry by either controlling the labor or the dumping sites. Labor unions are a favorite target for organized crime since gains can be achieved from exploiting labor. Workers are mostly uneducated and make easy targets. Dumping sites are either owned by organized crime, who charge excessive charges, or waste is simply dumped at unsuspecting sites without the permission or knowledge of the property owners.

Motor Vehicle Sales and Repairs

Organized crime becomes involved with motor vehicles in many ways. First, vehicles are stolen and transported to other states where they are sold to unsuspecting customers. Second, repair shops are used to selling parts from stolen cars that were previously obtained from "chop" shops. These parts are sold at "new" part prices.

Cash Businesses

Organized crime particularly targets cash businesses, e.g., bars, restaurants, hotels, package stores, and convenience stores. First, illegal profits can be easily laundered through cash businesses. Second, they are susceptible to skimming and embezzlement. People who do not like to pay taxes particularly like cash businesses since records are not usually kept.

Macroeconomics

Macroeconomics deals with the national and international levels.

National

The magnitude of organized crime, as measured by its income, continues to be of much debate. James Cook, *Forbes Magazine* (1980), estimated that organized crime is a large and growing part of the national economy. He estimated that its income was over $150 billion annually.

Cook based his estimate on gross criminal income by types of activity taken from various original sources. However, Peter Reuter (1983) believed Cook's estimates were too high by a factor of four. Cook asserted that organized crime was the second largest industry in the U.S. during 1979.

The Wharton School of Economics conducted an independent study of the income of organized crime using new data sources on the number of persons engaged in organized criminal activities and on the average income of people involved with criminal organizations. The data was collected from law enforcement agencies and from a sample of 100 IRS tax cases involving members of criminal organizations. Wharton estimated that gross receipts ranged from a high of $106.2 billion to a low of $65.7 billion. It also estimated that net income ranged from a high of $75.3 to a low of $46.6 billion.

Wharton indicates that organized crime is a major industry. Wharton's income estimate of $47 billion in 1986 equals 1.13 percent of the U.S. gross national product (GNP). They estimated that organized crime employs at least 281,487 people as members and associates with the estimated number of crime related jobs ranging to over 520,000.

Prior studies did not examine the impact of criminal activities on the other segments of the economy. The legitimate industry segments showing greatest involvement by organized crime include:

- Construction
- Waste removal
- Garment industry
- Food processing, distribution, and retailing
- Legalized gambling
- Hotels
- Bars
- Liquor retailing and wholesaling
- Entertainment
- Business and personal services
- Motor vehicle sales and repairs
- Real estate
- Banking
- Various other wholesale and retail businesses

Manufacturing and mining operations are the only major industries that do not appear to be heavily infiltrated. A major concern with organized crime involvement in these industries is that threats and intimidation may be used to limit competition and obtain excessive profits. The measurable result of such activities is higher prices. Taxes are not paid on much of the income generated by organized crime; implicitly, this results in higher taxes being imposed on the incomes of other citizens to make up for this loss in tax revenues. Based on the lower level estimate of organized crime income ($29.5 billion) and the assumption that taxes are not paid on 60 percent of this criminal income, it is estimated that personal taxes on other citizens were $6.5 billion higher than would be the case if all organized crime income were taxed.

The net economic cost per year of higher prices and a higher tax burden on ordinary citizens due to organized crime was estimated using Wharton's Long-Term Model of the U.S. economy as follows:

- A reduction in total output of $18.2 billion (1986 dollars)
- A loss of 414,000 jobs
- An increase in overall consumer price levels of 0.3 percent
- A reduction in per capita disposable income of $77.2 billion (1986 dollars)

The unpaid taxes combined with higher prices would cause:

- A reduction in total output of $17.4 billion (1986 dollars)
- A loss of 394,000 jobs
- An increase in overall consumer price levels of 0.3 percent
- A reduction in per capita disposable income of $72.54 billion

Most studies often used in organized crime do not actually relate to organized crime. Most of the income estimates are for all types of criminal activity and include much more than organized crime. The other common characteristics of most studies is a focus on illegal activities, especially drugs and gambling. Less attention is paid to the other side of organized crime: its involvement in legitimate businesses and labor unions. As a result, part of the income of organized crime is not counted and part of its impact on society, through its infiltration of the legitimate economy, is missed. It is known that organized crime involvement in the legitimate economy is increasing. Previous studies were used and updated. In some cases, new data were obtained and used for the 1986 report to the President's Commission on Organized Crime (Table 1-1).

Table 1-1 Estimates of Organized Crime Income By Type of Crime

CRIME	OC SHARE (%)	TOTAL CRIMINAL NET INCOME (BILLIONS) LOW	HIGH
Heroin	100	.509	14.903
Cocaine	100	1.392	23.711
Marijuana	100	.518	14.093
Loansharking	100	.619	13.411
Illegal gambling	42	1.878	1.878
Prostitution	20	.000	5.675
Theft (personal)	20	.583	1.207
Shoplifting and employee theft	50	2.099	4.000
Trucking cargo	100	.026	.955
Air cargo	100	.032	.037
Railroad cargo	100	.010	.038
Bank robbery	0	.000	.000
Business robbery	0	.000	.000
Nonresidential burglary	0	.000	.000
Fraud arson	50	.005	.400
Bank fraud	0	.000	.000
Counterfeiting	30	.018	.018
Cigarette smuggling	100	.154	.311
TOTAL		8.077	80.637

International

Macroeconomics deals not only with national economic policies, but also with the international economic arena. This section deals with the international impact of organized crime. International organized crime is almost solely involved in narcotics trafficking, however, this is changing. Basic narcotic substances are produced in one country and exported to another country where they are sold for huge profits. A lot of the huge profits are returned to the country where the narcotic substances are produced. These profits are not only used to acquire wealth, but also to acquire power which can be almost as great as the government itself.

Cocaine

Cocaine production has a great impact on South and Central American countries. Coca plants are grown, harvested, and sold to the drug lords who produce coca paste. They not only produce the coca paste, but sometimes carry the production down to pure cocaine powder. The cocaine is shipped to other countries, principally the United States, where it is sold. The profits are then smuggled back to the country of origin where they are invested in the local economy.

Mexico. Mexico has become, in recent years, the largest supplier of cocaine and marijuana to the United States. The United States has complained to the Mexican government that they are not doing enough to stop the drug trafficking and has even accused their law enforcement agencies of corruption. It was not until the brutal murder of Enrique Camarena, a U.S. Drug Enforcement Agent (DEA), in February 1985 that the Mexican government began getting some "heat." However, it was not until the murder of Excelsior columnist Manuel Buendia who was shot and killed, that the Mexican government began to take action. In June 1990, the Mexican government finally acted, arresting Chief of Domestic Intelligence Jose Antonio Zorrilla Perez and four other members of the National Security Directorate, a combination of the Central Intelligence Agency (CIA) and the FBI. Prosecutors charged that Perez killed Buendia because the reporter learned Perez was protecting top drug traffickers. The allegations of drug trafficking or protection involved a former defense minister, two brothers of the governor of Baja California Sur, and the cousin of a former president. Also arrested was a drug kingpin known as the godfather, Miguel Angel Felix Gallardo. It is well known that drug profits went not only to these officials, but to others who have not been identified. Mexico has provided a classic case that drug profits corrupt public officials at all levels.

Costa Rica. Even though Costa Rica is not a producer of cocaine, it does have means to be an attractive "money launderer" of cocaine profits. In addition, it serves as a transshipment point from South America to the United States. The United States warned Costa Rican officials of their position of being a "laundering alternative." A Costa Rican commission, in 1988, concluded that drug traffickers influenced all three branches of the government. Former government officials were accused of links to drug traffickers and some were charged and arrested. A drug trafficker, Roberto Fionna, who previously was able to get legal residence through his political connections was arrested.

Guatemala.   Guatemala is a big producer of opium poppies (the raw material for heroin) and a transshipment point for cocaine bound for the United States. Mexican drug traffickers, who are in alliance with left wing guerrillas to protect growers of poppies, control large geographical areas. This resulted in the Guatemalan police's refusal to enter the areas. In recent years, Guatemala has become active in cocaine production and corruption is increasing.

Honduras.   Honduras is an important transshipment point for Colombian cocaine. It is also a growing center for money laundering. In 1989, Honduran authorities arrested Juan Ramon Mata Ballesteros, a cocaine kingpin, and expelled him to the United States. This has sparked anti-government and anti-American demonstrations. The corruption of public officials is not countrywide, but has been limited to area- or district-level military officials.

Panama.   Prior to the December 1989 U.S. invasion of Panama, General Manuel Noreiga was indicted by U.S. district courts for drug trafficking and money laundering. Top Panamanian military officers were living far above their means. This source of wealth was from drug trafficking or money laundering. It was alleged that General Manuel Noreiga had stashed $200 million in various bank accounts. It was discovered when the Bank of Credit and Commerce International was seized by U.S. law enforcement agents in the United States that nearly half of the assets in the Panamanian branch belonged to General Noreiga. The United States invaded Panama in December 1989. The findings have not been fully disclosed at this time, however, newspaper accounts have indicated that corruption was very widespread.

Bolivia.   Hundreds of thousands of Bolivians are involved in growing, making, or distributing cocaine. Drugs account for $300 to $500 million in the economy. Exports total only $600 million from legal goods or services. Vast areas of Bolivia are not patrolled by the police so that traffickers are able to fly cocaine to Colombia or Brazil without any interference.

Corruption is rampant. The right-wing government installed by the military in 1980 was backed by drug traffickers. The Bolivian Interior Minister is under indictment in Miami on drug trafficking charges.

Brazil.   Brazil is a vast country with unguarded borders and underpaid police, therefore, alarming increases in drug shipments and processing operations have resulted. Colombian cartel bosses have for many years spent vacations there and began their work in the jungles as far back as 1984. The growing of coca is greatly increasing. It is expected that Brazil will become a major coca producer in the years ahead.

Ecuador.   This country is a minor producer of coca. However, it is becoming an important center for drug trafficking and money laundering. Shipments to the United States and Europe from Ecuador have had cocaine hidden in various merchandise such as handicrafts, canned goods, and wood products. Officials have reported that Colombian drug traffickers launder from $200 to $400 million through Ecuador every year. Newspapers have expressed concern about the corruption of government officials by drug cartels. In one case, two judges signed an order for the release of a drug trafficker from jail. The judges fled when people made an outcry. One judge was captured with about $20,000 in cash. The other judge and drug trafficker are still at large.

Peru.   The most potent coca plants are produced in Peru. Most of the coca plants are grown in the Huallaga Valley which is northeast of Lima. This area is controlled by Colombian cocaine producers and distributors. In addition, the drug traffickers have formed an alliance with the guerrillas, The Shining Path, to unite their effort to seize power in the area. The area has become so violent that government officials are unable to appear in the region. It is estimated that there are at least one to two killings a day as a result of narcotics trafficking. Cocaine brings from $700 million to $1.2 billion every year to the Peruvian economy, while legal exports bring in $2.5 billion.

Colombia.   This country has become the cocaine industry processing and exporting center. Most of the raw materials come from remote areas of Peru and Bolivia. There are two areas where major drug traffickers have formed cartels. One is located in Medellin and the other in Cali. The Medellin cartel has gained more prominence than the Cali cartel, however, they have been known to work together in many aspects. These cartels have gained such wealth, influence, and power that they have considerable control over the affairs of Colombia in both political and economic matters. After the killing of a presidential candidate in Colombia, the Colombian government declared war against the Colombian drug cartels. As the war against the drug cartels escalated, the Colombian government began to make raids and seizures of cartel members' property. One piece of property which was owned by Gonzalo Rodriguez Gacha covered one city block. The mansion was almost entirely constructed of marble and had gold fixtures in the bathrooms with toilet paper that was designed with nude women on each sheet. Even lesser men of authority had equivalent estates. Gacha was finally cornered and shot to death. The other cartel members fled to the jungles. The cartel members still control much of the economy and exercise political power. Yet, one can read on an almost daily basis that the Colombian government is still actively involved in a "war" with the drug cartels. It is believed that the cartel attacked the Justice Building and killed many of the country's top judges. Many bombings are attributed to the cartels. In essence, this is a country under siege.

Bahama Islands.   The Bahama Islands are ideal as a way station between South and Central America and the United States. It is estimated that over half of the cocaine shipments from South America go through the Bahama Islands. Corruption in high office has surfaced for many years. One convicted drug trafficker testified in South Florida that he paid Prime Minister Lynden O. Pindling $100,000 per week. Prime Minister Pindling has been the subject of many federal grand jury investigations and official inquiries in the Bahama Islands; however, Pindling has never been charged in the United States and corruption proceedings in the Bahama Islands are rare. Bahamian police have been cooperative in the anti-drug activities. Yet, many U.S. law enforcement officers confirm that the Bahamian police are being corrupted by drug traffickers. They take bribes from drug traffickers and at the same time inform on some of them.

Cuba.   Fidel Castro prosecuted seven high-ranking officials for helping the Medellin cartel leader Pablo Escobar ship cocaine to Florida. Four of the conspirators were executed. This is the first time Castro acknowledged any official involvement in cocaine trafficking. In

1982, the U.S. Attorney's office indicted two members of the Central Committee of the Cuban Communist party for marijuana trafficking in Miami. A former Panamanian official testified before Congress that Castro mediated a dispute between General Manuel Noriega and the Medellin cocaine cartel.

Mideast.   The Middle East is a source of morphine base for the Sicilian and U.S. Mafia. Most of this morphine base comes from Turkey, Lebanon, and Pakistan. The impact on the local economies of these countries is limited so far, however, some currency is pumped into their economy. On the other hand, no reliable economic data is available. Other criminal activities in this area involve gun and weapon smuggling and sales, exploiting of foreign labor, smuggling of various consumer goods, and white slavery.

Sicily.   Like Colombia, Sicily has become a country under siege by organized crime known as La Cosa Nostra. The Sicilian Mafia had a governing commission, which was created by the American Mafia leader, "Lucky" Luciano. But unlike their American counterparts, they began to fight among themselves. The Corlenesse Family began to get the upper hand. One family head, Thomasa Buscetta, had to leave Sicily and flee to Brazil. The principal activity of the Sicilian Mafia was the control of the heroin trade. They imported the morphine base from Turkey and other mideastern countries. They processed the morphine base into heroin using French chemists. The heroin was smuggled into the United States where it was sold on the street. The profits were enormous. The money was smuggled back to Sicily and Switzerland through Bermuda. The Sicilian Mafia began to control Sicily. Judges and police were killed; in fact, anyone who tried to investigate their activities was killed. They had control of the economy. With the capture and trial of Buscetta, Sicilian authorities began taking back control, yet, today the Sicilian authorities are still battling the Mafia using military tactics against their heroin-trafficking activities.

Far East.   There are various organized crime organizations in the Far East. In Japan, there is the "Yakuza." In China, there are the "Triads" with a long history spanning many centuries. In Indochina, there are various criminal organizations. One of the major producers of heroin is a place called the "Golden Triangle" which encompasses an area around Laos, Cambodia, and Burma. All Asian criminal organizations are involved in drug production and trafficking, extortion, protection rackets, armed robberies, burglaries, gambling, prostitution, and slavery. Prostitution has grown to massive proportions in Thailand in recent years with acquired immunodieficiency syndrome (AIDS) and other sexually transmitted diseases on the rise. In various parts of the countryside, criminal groups control the local government or have become the local government as provincial lords.

Cost Reality

The cost of crime on the economy in the United States is now at a staggering height. The outlook does not look any better. There is no real compensation for emotional and social harm done to members of a society by criminal acts. The average citizen would be shocked to know the actual costs. There are no consolidated figures as to the total cost of crime.

However, if all the various costs were compiled into a consolidated figure, then they would surely be enormous. The cost of crime involves the following elements:

1. Law enforcement. This encompasses the cost of training and maintaining a police department and all of its support staff, equipment, and buildings.
2. Crime prevention. This involves all the community programs that try to help prevent crime. Some common programs are "Crime Stoppers," school programs, and various other programs sponsored by local community tax dollars.
3. Drug prevention and rehabilitation. This involves both public and private financing. Both government and private organizations offer programs to prevent and rehabilitate drug and alcohol offenders. This costs both the taxpayers and the patients.
4. Incarceration. Taxpayers spend a large amount of money to house, supervise, train, feed, clothe, and provide medical care for inmates in a jail or detention center.
5. Courts. The cost of operating and maintaining the court system costs the taxpayers many tax dollars. It involves judges, court reporters, clerks, and buildings.
6. Prosecutors. The cost of employing prosecutors and their staff, buildings, and all of the associated costs of operating and maintaining them is enormous, especially, in large metropolitan areas.
7. Public defenders. Many defendants are not able to afford defense attorneys, therefore, the taxpayers must foot the bill. This bill includes costs of defense attorneys, their staff, and all the costs of operation and maintenance.
8. Hospitalization. Medical cost for criminals, victims, and those involved in the justice system is a significant item. The increase in AIDS and other diseases made this cost even more of an "attention-getter."
9. Businesses. Businesses suffer losses when customers or employees steal from them. They have to raise prices or lay off employees because of theft.
10. Insurance companies. Individuals and businesses that have insurance file claims for losses that they suffer from crime. This, in turn, causes insurance companies to raise premiums to individuals and businesses.

The cost of crime, as you can see, is very high. Some people say that some types of crime do not cost society. You can see that it does cost society. Let's take an example of a simple case. A bookmaker takes bets from his bettors. It is illegal in his area. The bettors are not forced to place bets. They place wagers because they want to "place their money where their mouth is." Most bettors are middle-class workers. The bookmaker pays off the winners and collects from the losers. When law enforcement makes an arrest after a considerable time of investigation, they must put the bookmaker in jail. The bookmaker usually posts bond or bail and is out after a short period of time. The bookmaker claims poverty and must retain a public defender. The case goes to trial and the bookmaker is found guilty. He is sentenced to 60 days in the county jail.

The cost to society is high. First, bettors use money that could be used for living expenses. The taxpayers pay the investigators' salaries and all supporting staff to investigate the bookmaker. In addition, it costs the taxpayer to try the bookmaker in court. Judges and their staff draw salaries and submit expenses. It costs to house the bookmaker in jail. The taxpayer has to pay for food and medical costs while the bookmaker is in jail. Also, jailers and correction officers must be paid wages and benefits to guard the bookmaker while he is in jail. The taxpayer pays for the detention facilities. The public defender must be paid from public funds. One can see that it costs society in "dollar" terms, even though there is no violence.

Summary

The economic costs of crime affect both the individuals and the community. They also affect national governments. In some instances, governments are controlled or manipulated by criminal organizations. Some national economies are dependent upon illegal activities, i.e., drugs, in order to survive. One important factor to remember is that there is no victimless crime. Crime costs everyone either directly or indirectly.

Financial Crimes

2

Introduction

There are many types of financial crimes. Some of these crimes can be solved in a short period of time while others will take long periods of time. The time required directly relates to the complexity of the crime. Complex financial crimes consume large amounts of time to gather sufficient financial records to support a conviction. However, all financial crimes have one common factor: greed. Most people are honest and trustworthy when the temptation is not present. There are three factors that are present in financial crimes. The first factor is that something of value must be present. The second factor is that an opportunity to take something of value without being detected must be present. Last, there must be a perpetrator who is willing to commit the offense.

The most common financial crimes are shown below. The Federal Statutes are shown for those crimes that are federal offenses. Many financial crimes are not directly an offense at the federal level, but may indirectly become an offense. Federal statutes place some state crimes under federal jurisdiction when the criminal crosses state line(s).

Arson

Arson is defined in law as the malicious and willful burning of another person's dwelling, house, or outhouse. The crime is not primarily concerned with the resulting property damage, but rather with the danger to which the occupants of the dwelling were exposed by the criminal act. Dwelling has a broad definition of encompassing any building. Setting fire to timberlands, prairies, or grasslands is a statutory offense. The burning must be willful or malicious to be arson. A person who burns a dwelling while committing a felony, such as burglary, is guilty of arson regardless of the absence of any intent to set the fire or to destroy the house. It is essential to the crime of arson that there be an actual burning of some part of the property. Mere scorching, smoking, or discoloration of the building without any charring, destruction, or actual burning is not sufficient to be a crime of arson. Arson is considered a felony in all states. Arson of any federal installation, structure, and personal property is prohibited by Federal Statute 18 USC 81 (United States Code).

Bankruptcy

The prime characteristic of bankruptcy fraud is the hiding or nondisclosure of assets. This leaves little or no means of recovery by creditors. This is called "bust out". "Bust outs" have become more prevalent in recent years, especially, in high inventory turnover businesses. This crime usually requires identification of inventory purchased, sold, and "carted" off. Inventory is usually shipped to the enterprise premises. Afterwards, it is transported to another enterprise premise, which is controlled by the same principals. There, it is sold and the profits are diverted to the principals. Normally, a corporate shield will be in place to hide the principals involved in the scheme. Organized crime will take over a business not to keep it alive and healthy, but to force the company into bankruptcy after making a quick cash profit. Individuals commit bankruptcy fraud by not disclosing or hiding assets from the trustee.

Bankruptcy is primarily a federal crime under 18 USC 151 through 157. It prohibits any debtor from concealing assets, making false oaths or claims, or bribery of any custodian, trustee, marshal, or other officer of the court charged with the control or custody of property (18 USC 152). It prohibits any person who knowingly or fraudulently appropriates any property to a person's own use, embezzles, spends, or transfers any property or secrets or destroys any document belonging to the estate of the debtor (18 USC 153). It is bankruptcy fraud if a person devises or schemes to defraud creditors (18 USC 157).

Bribery

This is a crime of offering and acceptance of money or favors for some kind of preferential treatment or to influence another party for such treatment whether in public service or private business. A problem in investigating bribery or kickbacks is the difficulty in tracing it back through books and records if they exist at all. If the payment is uncovered, a problem arises as to locating who actually received the payment. To constitute this crime, the item of value must be given with the intent of influencing official conduct. The acceptance of a gift without corrupt prior intent is not bribery. The offense of bribery includes both the acts of offering or giving and the accepting or receiving, thereby rendering the giver as well as the receiver criminally liable. The offeror is guilty even if the bribe is refused. It is not required that the act for which the bribe was given be accomplished. Federal Statute 18 USC 201 prohibits anyone to directly or indirectly, corruptly give, offer, or promise anything of value to any public official or person with intent to:

1. Influence any official act
2. Influence such public official to commit or aid in committing, or allowing, any fraud, or make opportunity for such commission on the United States
3. Induce such public official or person to do or omit to do any action in violation of lawful duty

Loan Sharking

Loan sharking is the lending of money at higher rates than the law allows. Many people get involved with loan sharks. Gamblers borrow in order to pay gambling losses; narcotics users borrow to purchase drugs; and businessmen borrow when legitimate credit channels are closed. Loan sharks menace both white- and blue-collar workers as well as small and large corporations. Employees have agreed to disclose corporate secrets, leave warehouses unlocked, steal securities, ship stolen goods, and pass along information about customers, which sets the business up for burglaries. Officers of both small and large corporations are forced to turn over control of their companies to organized crime.

Loan sharking is identified as Extortionate Credit Transactions under federal statutes as well as many state statutes (18 USC 891 through 894). The elements of extortionate credit transactions are as follows:

1. The extension of credit would be unenforceable through civil judicial processes against the debtor.
2. The extension of credit was made at a rate of interest in excess of 45 percent per annum.
3. The extension of credit was collected or attempted to be collected by extortionate means.
4. The interest or similar charges exceeded $100.

Loan sharks' funds come from organized crime lieutenants that charge rates of 5 to 6 percent per week. The lieutenant has to pay from 1 to 3 percent per week. Sometimes the rates to the public reaches 20 percent weekly. This is called a 6 for 5 loan, which means for every $5 borrowed, $6 is required to be paid weekly. The loan shark is usually more interested in getting interest than principal. When the borrower defaults on the loan, the loan shark resorts to force against the borrower or his family so that a borrower hesitates to report his dilemma to the authorities.

Credit Card Fraud

Credit card fraud is a multimillion dollar business, which hurts business and the public. Most credit card fraud is controlled by organized crime. The scheme is a classic pattern. Credit cards are stolen, fenced, and sent elsewhere. Generally, the credit cards are stolen before the credit card holder is able to report its disappearance, or before the issuing company is able to warn its subscribers of the theft so that they can refuse to honor them. Credit cards are often obtained in the following ways:

1. Credit cards are stolen in the delivery process.
2. Credit cards are stolen in the printing process or duplicated.
3. Credit cards are stolen when returned to the issuer when they are refused or were undeliverable.
4. Credit cards are sometimes stolen on the street like cash or checks.
5. Business employees deliberately "forget" to return credit cards to their customers.
6. Credit cards are counterfeited.
7. Credit card numbers are copied from legitimate customers and used to make purchases.

A person who, with intent to defraud the issuer or a person or organization providing money, goods, services, or anything else of value, uses a credit card, for the purpose of obtaining money, goods, services, or anything of value, without the consent of the card holder is committing credit card fraud. This is fraud by the customer. Credit card fraud is also committed by businesses. Federal Statutes 15 USC 1644 as well as many state statutes prohibit the fraudulent use of credit cards. The federal statute prohibits:

1. The use of credit cards by any person who knowingly uses or conspires to use any counterfeit, fictitious, altered, forged, lost, stolen, or fraudulently obtained credit cards to obtain money, goods, services, or anything of value aggregating $1,000 or more.
2. The transportation or attempt to transport in interstate or foreign commerce any counterfeit, fictitious, altered, forged, lost, stolen, or fraudulently obtained credit card knowing it to be same.
3. Anyone, who knowingly receives, conceals, uses, or transports money, goods, services or anything of value from the use of credit cards.
4. Anyone who knowingly furnishes money, property, services, or anything of value through the use of fraudulent credit cards.

This federal statute prohibits anyone to receive, give, or transport goods, services, and other consideration through fraudulent credit card use. In addition, it prohibits actual fraudulent use of credit cards.

Prostitution and Pandering

Prostitution is the selling of oneself or another for purposes of sexual intercourse, debauchery, or other immoral acts for monetary gain. A panderer, usually called a pimp, is one who solicits clients for a prostitute. Clients usually pay in cash, which is shared between the prostitute and the pimp. Organized crime is often involved. Credit cards have become acceptable. This is especially true in operations called escort services. Records are usually not maintained for very long. There are two types of prostitutes. Those called "street walkers" are one type, while "call girls" are the other type. "Street walkers" get this name because they walk along the street soliciting clients. "Call girls" use referrals from friends, associates, and pimps. Many call girls rely upon repeat clients. Many prostitutes steal from clients. Organized crime makes huge profits from prostitution.

Most states have statutes which prohibit prostitution and pandering. Federal Statute 18 USC 2421 prohibits anyone who transports any individual in interstate or foreign commerce with the intent that such individual engage in prostitution or in any sexual activity. Section 2422 prohibits anyone to persuade, induce, entice, or coerce any individual to travel interstate to engage in prostitution or any sexual activity. Section 2423 prohibits the transportation of minors to travel interstate for prostitution or sexual activity. A minor is defined as anyone under 18 years of age.

Fencing

This involves the purchase of stolen goods from a thief. In general, this involves organized crime figures stealing large quantities of goods, usually from hijacked trucks, ships, or planes and distributing and selling the merchandise.

1. Federal Statute 18 USC 2113(c) prohibits anyone who receives, possesses, conceals, stores, barters, sells, or disposes of any property or money or anything of value which has been taken or stolen from a bank, credit union, or savings and loan association.
2. Federal Statute 18 USC 2114(b) prohibits anyone who receives, possesses, conceals, stores, barters, sells, or disposes of any property or money or anything of value which has been taken or stolen from the U.S. Postal Service.

The federal statutes are limited to the fencing of personal property that is stolen from government control or financial institutions.

Mail-Order Operations

These operations involve fraudulent schemes of advertising products in the media such as magazines, newspapers, radio, or television. Customers send money to the mail-order house. The mail-order house keeps the money, but does not ship the merchandise. This is called a "boiler room" operation. Sometimes, operators use high pressure telephone solicitors who call and persuade the potential buyer with phrases like "You'll miss out on this great deal if you don't buy now" or they might say "This deal is too good to pass up." The most common characteristic in this kind of fraud is that you can't reach them later because the telephone is disconnected or the address is no longer valid. There are three basic federal statutes which address this type of fraud. They are as follows:

1. Federal Statute 18 USC 2325 prohibits anyone from conducting a plan, program, promotion, or campaign to induce someone to purchase goods or services or participate in a contest or sweepstakes through the use of the telephone.
2. Federal Statute 18 USC 1341 prohibits anyone to scheme or defraud anyone by obtaining property or any means of false or fraudulent pretenses, representations, or promises through the use of mail service by the U.S. Postal Service.
3. Federal Statute 18 USC 1343 prohibits anyone to scheme, defraud, or obtain money or property by means of false pretenses, representations, or promises through the use of wire, radio, or television communication in interstate or foreign commerce.

Pornography

This industry includes production, distribution, and sale of sex novels, magazines, photographs, stag films, and other sex-related items. Most of these items can be purchased in adult bookstores. Manuscripts are purchased from individuals for a minimal price and sent to a printing firm for large-volume printing. In the case of video or film, the master negatives or tapes are purchased from a producer and put into mass production. The books, videos, and films are sold to adult bookstores through "shell" corporations for legal insulation. Payments are not always paid to the printing and production firms once the books, videos, and films are delivered.

Organized crime usually doesn't directly own the retail adult bookstores. When they do own these stores, they hire employees to actually operate the stores for a salary. In some areas where adult bookstores are illegal, hard-core material is generally sold "under the counter" and only to those customers who are not suspected to be law enforcement officers.

Another attraction of the adult bookstores is the peep show. This is a viewing machine where a customer can see a stag video or film. Each film or video is usually 12 minutes in length and the customer is required to drop a quarter for every 12 minute segment. Federal Statute 18 USC 2251 prohibits any person to employ, use, persuade, induce, entice, or coerce any minor to engage in or transport any minor in interstate with the intent to have such minor engage in sexually explicit conduct for the purpose of producing any visual depiction of such conduct. Federal Statute 18 USC 2258 prohibits the importation of child pornography.

Gambling

Gambling attracts organized crime. Large gambling operations require a staff to run such an operation. Organized crime, in large cities, controls gambling operators. Gambling involves betting on sports events, lotteries, off-track racing, large dice games, and illegal casinos. Most large gambling operations have a sophisticated organization that ranges from the operator who takes bets from customers through people who pick up money and betting slips, to people in charge of particular areas or districts, to the main office or bank. The profits move through channels so complex that even most people working for the organization do not know the identity of the leader. The use of telephone systems has kept the bookmaker remote from the district or area management.

Independent bookmakers have joined organized crime operations for the following reasons:

1. Organized crime syndicates have resources for backing all bets so the independent operator doesn't hedge his bets or re-insure bets through a "layoff" operation.
2. Independent operators can handle more bettors.
3. Bookmakers don't need to work on the streets taking bets.
4. Bookmakers no longer have to handle many telephone bets, which could alert police.
5. Bookmakers have legal services and connections available to them.
6. Bookmakers have territorial assignment, which minimizes conflicts with other bookies.

Federal Statute 18 USC 1955 prohibits anyone who conducts, finances, manages, supervises, directs, or owns all or part of an illegal gambling business. The gambling activities must also be illegal under state law or any political subdivision and involve five or more people. It does not apply to gambling activities, i.e., bingo, lottery, or similar games of chance by an exempt organization as defined by the Internal Revenue Code, Section 501(c), if no part of the gross receipts inures to the benefit of a private member or employee of the organization.

Bettors usually do not know the location of the betting operation, but the bookmaker advises the bettor of the telephone numbers at which bets can be placed. The bettor is later contacted by telephone for collection and payment. The bookie usually makes 10 percent before paying off winners, expenses, and commissions to runners and solicitors.

Projections of income should be based upon gambling records seized by law enforcement on the number of days of operations shown in the records. Bookmakers do not keep records for any great length of time; usually about one or two weeks. Gains from this activity will usually require an indirect method of proving income.

Skimming/Embezzlement

Skimming is the act of diverting business receipts to one's own personal use. Officers or owners of the business enterprise can only do this. Embezzlement is diverting funds or receipts of the business by an employee. Cash businesses such as bars, nightclubs, grocery stores, laundromats, coin-operated machines, and liquor stores are very susceptible to both skimming and embezzlement. In most cases, funds skimmed or embezzled usually can't be traced from the business enterprise to the individuals. An indirect method of proving income is usually required. Federal Statute 18 USC 641 prohibits any person who embezzles, steals, purloins, or knowingly converts to his use or the use of another without proper authority, sells, conveys, or disposes of any record, voucher, money, or anything of value that belongs to the United States or any department or agency thereof.

Labor Racketeering

Labor unions provide many methods for illicit gains.

1. Kickbacks from employers for favorable contracts and labor peace are common as is extortion.
2. The unions can provide a vehicle for embezzlement. Organized crime syndicates use excessive or fictitious salaries or expenses; nonworking associates; or personal work done by union officers or employees. Professional or legal services are used to benefit union officials or employees. Sometimes they make donations to organizations for benefit of union officials or employees.
3. Welfare and pension funds provide vehicles for kickbacks from insurance agents and organized crime investments and loans.

The audit program and techniques are many and varied when dealing with union racketeering.

There are various federal statutes which deal with the various facets of labor racketeering. They are as follows:

a. Federal Statute 18 USC 1027. This section prohibits a pension plan administrator from making false statements or concealing facts or information relating to pension plans that are covered by the Employee Retirement Income Security Act of 1974 as amended.
b. Federal Statute 18 USC 664. This section prohibits any person who embezzles, steals, or unlawfully or willfully abstracts or converts to his own use or the use of another, any money, funds, securities, premiums, credit, property, or other assets of any employee welfare benefit plan or employee pension benefit plan.

    c.   Federal Statute 18 USC 1954. This section prohibits any administrator, officer, trustee, custodian, counsel, agent, or employee to offer, accept, or solicit any fee, kickback, commission, gift, loan, money, or anything of value with the intent to influence any action or decision with respect to employee pension or benefit plans. Also, it is unlawful for anyone to offer, solicit, kickback, give any commission, gift, loan, money, or anything of value to influence the action or decision of a plan administrator, trustee, and others.

Stock Fraud and Manipulation

Some criminals use stock and bond fraud schemes to make illicit gains. They use counterfeit stock certificates as collateral on loans. They set up dummy corporations to sell worthless stock in "boiler room" operations. A legitimate corporation can be taken over and sold back and forth between insiders so as to highly inflate the market price of the stock. Then the stock is sold at highly-inflated prices, the company would be abandoned and the stock allowed to drop to the correct market value. Stock and bond fraud is a complex and sophisticated area. An extremely detailed investigation and analysis is required. The investigation requires analysis of transactions before, during, and after the scheme to determine the trends.

    The federal statutes that deal with securities fraud are as follows:

    a.   Federal Statute 18 USC 513. This section prohibits anyone from making, uttering, or possessing counterfeit securities of any state, political subdivision, or organization.
    b.   Federal Statute 18 USC 2314. This section prohibits the transporting, transmitting, or transfer of securities when anyone knows that the securities have been stolen, converted, or taken by fraud.

Narcotics

The sale of narcotics is structured like a well-organized, large corporation. It involves numerous people from all levels. The large amount of profits and the international connections necessary for long-term narcotic supplies can only be supplied by an organized crime organization. There are various types of narcotics which come from various parts of the world. Heroin comes from Turkey in the Middle East and the "Golden Triangle" in Southeast Asia. Cocaine comes from Central and South America. Synthetic drugs are made in the United States and Canada. Organizations involved in distribution are loosely knit for the most part and involve individuals from all walks of life. The profits from narcotics are enormous. Federal statutes which address drug trafficking are listed under Title 21 of the United States Code (USC). The principal sections are as follows:

- Section 848. Continuing Criminal Enterprise is any person who occupies a position of organizer, supervisor, or any management position with five or more other people who engage in illegal drug manufacturing, distribution, and sale, and obtains substantial income or resources.

- Section 858. This section prohibits anyone who manufactures or transports any material including chemicals that create a substantial risk to human life.
- Section 860. This section prohibits the manufacturing and/or sale of controlled substances in or near schools and colleges within 1,000 feet.
- Section 952. This section prohibits the importation of controlled substances.

Racketeering

Racketeering, in the past, has been hard to define. In 1968, when the Omnibus Control and Safe Street Act was passed, it defined racketeering as any unlawful activity by members of a highly-organized, disciplined association engaged in supplying illegal goods and services. In 1970, Congress passed the Racketeer Influenced and Corrupt Organization statute (RICO) which has become the centerpiece of federal and most state laws proscribing organized criminal activity. A pattern of racketeering activity requires at least two acts of racketeering activity. Racketeering activity means almost any illegal act such as gambling, murder, kidnapping, robbery, and drug trafficking. It encompasses any individual, organization, corporation, or union or group of associated individuals. RICO was not used very much until the late 1970s and the early 1980s when many organized crime figures were indicted and convicted of racketeering. When the conviction rates soared, district and U.S. attorneys became more aggressive. Now, RICO indictments are becoming more common. However, convictions are not increasing as much as the indictments. The major reason is the lack of evidence, particularly in the form of financial data. The RICO act provides for the use of financial data in prosecutions and forfeitures. Section 1963 of Title 18 reads as follows:

> In lieu of a fine otherwise authorized by this section, a defendant who derives profits or other proceeds from an offense may be fined not more than twice the gross profits or other proceeds. (b) Property subject to criminal forfeiture under this section includes (1) real property including things growing on, affixed to, and found in land; and (2) tangible and intangible personal property, including rights, privileges, interests, claims, and securities.

Clearly, financial data is a major element in these criminal cases. In some instances, the gross profits are more than the net assets of the criminal or the criminal enterprise. In other cases, the fines or penalties are less than the gross profits of the illegal enterprise. This will put any criminal enterprise out of business if there is a conviction since forfeitures are based on gross profits instead of fines and penalties.

Continuing Criminal Enterprise

This is defined by Federal Statute 21 USC 848. Many states have adopted variations of this statute as well. It defines continuing criminal enterprise as any person who commits three or more felonies with five or more other persons with respect to whom such person occupies a position of organizer, a supervisory position, or any other position of management and who obtains substantial assets or resources from these acts is guilty of engaging in continuing criminal enterprise. The elements of this offense are as follows:

1. A person has committed three or more felonies.
2. The person is in a supervisory capacity.
3. The person has five or more people working for him in some illegal capacity.
4. The person has acquired substantial assets or financial resources.

Title 21 USC 855 repeats the fines as stated in Title 18 USC 1963:

In lieu of a fine otherwise authorized by this section, a defendant who derives profits or other proceeds from an offense may be fined not more than twice the gross profits or other proceeds.

Nonprofit Organization Fraud

This type of fraud is primarily a tax fraud even though other types of fraud are also committed. In some cases, the victims do not know that they have been defrauded, while in other cases, the victims suffer both great financial and emotional losses. The Internal Revenue Service, as well as many state laws, allow various types of organizations to operate without paying taxes, obtaining permits and licenses, and to be exempt from various laws and regulations. Religious institutions, social clubs, paternal organizations, and various charities operate to help or benefit its members or the community in which it operates. These nonprofit organizations are very beneficial to members and the community, however, there are individuals who operate or control these organizations for their own benefit. It is illegal for individuals to operate these nonprofit organizations for their sole benefit. As a case in point, bingo operations are legal in most states when it benefits the nonprofit organization that is sponsoring it. However, some bingo operations are conducted for the sole benefit of operators, which is illegal. Social clubs operate bars and restaurants for the benefit of its club members. However, some social clubs operate for profit, which benefits the operators.

Corrupt Churches

Churches and other religious organizations are exempt from federal and state taxes. These organizations don't pay property, sales, or income taxes. However, there are individuals and criminal organizations that like using a church "cover" to obtain profits and gains for their own benefit. There are three facets of an abusive church. First, the church appears to be an attractive group of motivated, high-principled Christians or other religious sect. They want to talk to you. They want you to be part of their church. The rank and file of its membership sees the second facet. It is a facet of discipline and authority. The word of the leader is law. No questioning is allowed. The leader is always demanding more from you; more commitment to the church or group, more obedience to the leader's directives, more financial sacrifices, more separation from friends and family, more adulation of the leader. Its inner core of leadership sees the third facet. It is a facet of excess. The leader, his immediate family and his inner, favored group lead a life of open or secret extravagance. The signs of a corrupt church are as follows:

1. The church is God's special, and perhaps only, true church on earth at this time. You may be called upon to make great sacrifices now, but they will be worth it, because to not join the church is to miss out on your chance to be in God's face or favor.
2. The human leader is the link to God. He is the most important person on earth. His interpretation of the Bible or similar religious literature is the only correct one. The leader never wants any criticism. He denounces any criticism as the product of a negative attitude.
3. The leadership attempts to control your personal life. The leader sets forth his own rules and regulations. You are told what to eat, what to wear, how to live, whom to marry, when to divorce, and how to raise your children.
4. The member is no longer responsible for his/herself. The leader tells the member what is right and wrong. The member has no mind or conscience of his own. The member becomes confused by contradictory attitudes and strives to subjugate himself to the church.
5. The church is the only reality. True spirituality and obedience to God are found only in this church. The rest of society is Satan's world of vanity and deceit. The member will find himself less able to function "in the world," but more at home "in the church." The member will move to church headquarters, live in church accommodations, work for a church-owned business, spend spare time in church activities, and be friends with only church members. The member's life is totally consumed by the church.
6. The church is isolated. They only want to build and maintain membership, improving its image in society, and gratifying the whims of the leadership. The church wants to keep its financial affairs secret. The church does all it can to avoid newspaper reporters so that they won't publish "gross lies and distortions."
7. The church is a prison. Once in the church, the member is a captive. If the member leaves the church, he leaves behind his financial security, home, job, and family.

This type of crime usually comes under the Federal Civil Rights Laws, which are listed in Sections 241 through 248 of Title 18, USC.

Burglary

Burglary is defined as the breaking and entering of a dwelling place or habitation of another with the intent to commit a felony therein. The statutory offense of burglary includes homes, trains, automobiles, barns, business establishments, storehouses, public buildings, telephone coin boxes, and boats. It is the intent of the perpetrator in the breaking and entering to commit a felony. Without such intent, the mere breaking and entering may only be a civil trespass and not punishable as a crime. Breaking does not necessarily require physical damage to or any destruction of property. It is the breaking of the secureness rather than any physical violence to the property itself. It is breaking when an intruder unlocks a door, opens a window, or removes screening or a window pane. If a person has permission to enter a building and then commits a felony inside, he has not committed burglary because there was no "breaking" in order to make entry. Constructive breaking is made when an entry has been obtained by trickery, fraud, threats, intimidation, or conspiracy. If entry is achieved as the result of a pretense of a business or social call, passage may be deemed to be "breaking" for purposes of committing burglary. Burglary requires "entry" into the dwelling as well as breaking. Burglars steal property for the purpose of selling the property to unsuspecting customers. Pawnshops are an ideal place to sell stolen property. However, the burglar cannot sell too much stolen property without the pawnshop owner becoming suspicious. Organized crime groups set up businesses for the purpose of selling stolen property. There are various federal statutes which involve burglary. These burglary statutes basically involve property either belonging to the United States or are in possession of the United States. The more common federal statutes are as follows:

1. Federal Statute 18 USC 2112. This prohibits anyone to rob or attempt to rob personal property belonging to the United States.
2. Federal Statute 18 USC 2113. This prohibits anyone from robbing banks and other financial institutions.
3. Federal Statute 18 USC 2114. This prohibits anyone from robbing any postal service employee.
4. Federal Statute 18 USC 2115. This prohibits anyone from robbing any postal facility.
5. Federal Statute 18 USC 2116. This prohibits anyone from robbing any car, steamboat, or vessel assigned to carry mail service.

Forgery and Uttering

Forgery is the false making or material alteration, with the intent to defraud, of any writing to the prejudice of another person's rights. The intent to defraud is the very essence of the crime of forgery. It is immaterial that the alteration or false writing in fact deceived no one. It is not necessary to show that any particular person was intended to be defrauded. A general intent to defraud is sufficient and it is not limited to the possibility of obtaining money or other property. Forgery may be committed by writing in ink or pencil, by typewriter, printing, engraving, or even pasting one name over another name. It has been frequently held that every such crime must contain at least the following two elements:

1. The signature was not made by the hand of the person whose signature it purports to be.
2. Another wrongfully made the signature.

It is not necessary that the entire instrument be fictitious, nor is it required that the forged document contain incorrect statements. The act of making a forged instrument in its entirety is distinct from the act of altering an instrument already made, although both acts are forgeries. A forgery can be committed even though the name alleged to be forged is in fact a fictitious one. Signing a fictitious name to a check with intent to defraud is forgery even when the check is made payable to cash. It is not necessary that the forged signature resemble the genuine one. Forgery may be committed by a person signing his own name where it appears that his name is the same as that of another person and he intends his writing to be received as that of such other person. Generally, a mere immaterial change or alteration, which does not affect the legal liability of the parties concerned with the instrument involved, does not constitute a forgery.

Uttering is the offering of a forged instrument, knowing it to be such, with the intent to defraud. It is immaterial whether such offer is accepted or rejected. A defendant may be guilty of uttering a forged instrument even though he was not the actual forger. The offense is complete when one knowing it is forged, with the representation by work or action that it is genuine, offers a false instrument. In this sense, the words utter and publish have frequently been held to be synonymous as used in forgery statutes. Specific instances of uttering or publishing have been held to include:

1. Exhibiting a forged license to teach as evidence of a right to receive compensation
2. Depositing a forged check to one's own account
3. Delivering a forged note to satisfy a debt
4. Procuring the probate of a forged will
5. Using a forged instrument in judicial proceedings

The federal statutes, which deal with forgery and uttering, are as follows:

1. Federal Statute 18 USC 472. Prohibits uttering counterfeit obligations or securities of the United States.
2. Federal Statute 18 USC 496. This section prohibits any forgeries, counterfeits, or falsely alters any writing made or required to be made in connection with the entry or withdrawal of imports or collection of customs duties.
3. Federal Statute 18 USC 473. This prohibits anyone from dealing in counterfeit obligations of the United States.
4. Federal Statute 18 USC 482. This prohibits any forgeries, counterfeits, or falsely alters any obligations or securities of foreign banks or corporations.
5. Federal Statute 18 USC 478. Prohibits any forgeries or counterfeits any bond, certificate, obligation or other security of any foreign government.
6. Federal Statute 18 USC 1542. Prohibits anyone who falsely makes, forges, counterfeits, mutilates, or alters any passport.
7. Federal Statute 18 USC 1546. Prohibits anyone who forges, counterfeits, alters or falsely makes any immigrant or nonimmigrant visa, permit, border crossing card, alien registration receipt card, or other documents.
8. Federal Statute 18 USC 2314. Prohibits anyone who transports in interstate or foreign commerce any falsely made, forged, altered, or counterfeit securities, tax stamps, traveler's checks, or tools to be used in making, forging, or counterfeiting any securities.

Larceny

The crime of larceny is the wrongful taking and carrying away of personal property of another person without his consent and with the intent to deprive the owner, thereof, of such property permanently. Many states divide larceny into two grades: grand larceny and petit larceny. The distinction between the two is usually based solely on the value of the appropriated property. In some states, the crime of larceny is known as theft and stealing.

There is no separate offense for each article taken at the same time. Similarly, stealing property at the same time and from the same place belonging to different owners constitutes only one offense of larceny since there is but one act of taking. Where separate items of property are stolen from different owners at different times, of course, separate larcenies have taken place. In order to be a proper subject of larceny, the item taken by a defendant must conform to the following conditions:

1. It must be capable of individual ownership.
2. It must be personal rather than real property.
3. It must be of some intrinsic value, although it is not necessary that it have any special, appreciable or market value.
4. It must have corporeal existence, regardless of its value to the owner who has had it. If it is not capable of a physical taking, then it is not a subject of larceny.

Animus furandi, the intent to deprive the owner permanently of the property taken, is an essential element of larceny. In order to indicate such intent, it has generally been held that the item of personal property must be taken from the possession of the owner or possessor into the possession of the thief and be carried away by him. There is no larceny when a person takes property temporarily with the intent of returning it later to the owner. The intent must be to deprive the owner permanently of his property. In order to constitute robbery as distinguished from larceny, either force or fear must be used by the thief. There is a distinction between owning something and having it in one's possession. Ownership is legal title, possession is physical control. Ownership and possession are regarded as synonymous in the crime of larceny. A taking in jest or mischief is not deemed to be larceny, particularly when such taking is done openly in the presence of numerous witnesses. The federal statutes, which deal with embezzlement and theft, are listed in Title 18, Sections 641 through 668.

Robbery

Robbery is the unlawful taking of any property from the person or in the presence of another by the use of force or intimidation. The offenses of assault and larceny are deemed to be essential elements of the crime of robbery. Robbery is a felony. The elements of this crime include:

1. A felonious taking.
2. The use of actual or constructive force.
3. No consent by the victim
4. Personal property of any value.
5. An intent by the perpetrator to deprive the owner permanently of his property.

A person is not guilty of robbery in forcibly taking his own property from the possession of another. It is not necessary to the crime of robbery that the property is taken from the actual owner. A robbery may be committed by a taking from the person having only care, custody, control, management, or possession of the personal property. It is vital to the crime of robbery that the taking of the property be accomplished by the use of force, fear, or intimidation. The degree of force or violence is immaterial if it is enough to compel a person to give up his property against his will.

The federal statutes that address robbery are as follows:

1. Federal Statute 18 USC 1951. This prohibits interference with commerce by threats or violence.
2. Federal Statute 18 USC 2113. This prohibits robbery of banks and other financial institutions.
3. Federal Statute 18 USC 2119. This prohibits robbery of motor vehicles with the intent to cause death or serious bodily harm in interstate or foreign commerce.

Tax Evasion

The federal and state governments have laws that make it a felony for those who willfully attempt to evade or defeat any tax. The crime of willful tax evasion is completed when the false or fraudulent return is willfully and knowingly filed. Tax evasion must be proved by an affirmative act. The willful failure to collect or pay over what is taxed is a felony. It, likewise, must be proved by an affirmative act. The net worth, nondeductible expenditure method is the one mostly used by the Internal Revenue Service and states with individual income tax laws. These methods have been approved by the Supreme Court. This method is explained in a later chapter. Voluntary disclosures by taxpayers of intentional violation of tax laws prior to the initiation of an investigation does not ensure that the government will not recommend criminal prosecution. There is no requirement that returns be made under oath. The law merely requires that returns contain a declaration that they are made under the penalties of perjury. Perjury is considered a felony. Any person who willfully delivers or discloses any list, return, account, statement, or other document that is known to be fraudulent or to be false is committing a crime. The federal government classifies this as a misdemeanor, however, many states classify this as a felony. The taxpayer is responsible for the correctness of any return filed, even if he pays a preparer. If the preparer has willfully prepared a false return, then he/she can be criminally prosecuted.

1. Federal Statutes 26 USC 7201 through 7216 deal with the various types of criminal tax law violations.

Bank Frauds

Bank frauds encompass both customers and employees of banks. Bank frauds relate to the passing of bad checks, fraudulent loans, and check kiting. Officers or employees usually embezzle funds from the bank through various schemes. Customers defraud banks by writing bad checks or presenting false documents to obtain funds. Federal Statue 18 USC 1344 defines bank fraud as anyone who knowingly executes or attempts to execute a scheme to defraud a financial institution. It involves obtaining any of the moneys, funds, credits, assets, securities, or other property owned by or under the custody or control of a financial institution by means of false or fraudulent pretenses, representations, or promises. The financial institution does not have to suffer a loss. A person only has to submit false documents.

Restraint of Trade

Restraint of trade is a violation by corporate decision-makers on behalf of their organizations. The major federal statute involved is the Sherman Antitrust Act of 1890. It was designed to curb the threat to competitive, free enterprise economy posed by the spread of trusts and monopolies to combine or form monopolies. There are three principal methods of restraint of trade:

1. Consolidation, so as to obtain a monopoly position
2. Price fixing to achieve price uniformity
3. Price discrimination, in which higher prices are charged to some customers and lower ones to others

For those corporate decision-makers, restraint of trade makes sense in that the less competition it has and the greater control over prices, the larger the profits. However, small and independent businesses will lose business and the public at large will face higher prices and loss of discretionary buying power. The most common violations are price fixing and price discrimination.

Government Contract Fraud

There are many federal statutes that involve fraud against the government for products and services. They can be classified into the following categories:

1. Fraudulent billing for products and services
2. Providing faulty or inferior products or services
3. Providing substituted products
4. Overcharging on government contracts

Corporate Raiding

Corporate raiding involves individuals or organizations that take over business entities for the purpose of exploiting the business assets for gains. These corporate raids may be for the control of the industry or for personal gains. Generally, corporate raiding involves either violations of the Sherman Antitrust Act or a combination of other offenses, e.g., embezzlement, pension fraud, bankruptcy fraud, or stock fraud or manipulation.

Extortion

This crime involves the threat by an individual to another for money. It is usually committed by organized crime organizations in areas where they operate, but they don't have control of the market on this type of crime. Many of the federal statutes address extortion. Federal Statutes 18 USC 871 through 880 address extortion by or to federal employees.

Coupon Fraud

This crime usually involves individuals who operate a business. The business operator collects various coupons and submits them to either a clearinghouse or to the company that issued them for refunds or rebates on products that bogus customers have submitted when purchasing products from the business. This is primarily a state crime, but the federal statutes for mail fraud would normally apply in this type of case.

Money Laundering

Money laundering is a criminal offense under Federal Statute 18 USC 1956. It has made it a crime for individuals or business entities to launder gains from illegal activities through various methods and schemes. Money laundering activities encompass:

1. Transporting money and other money instruments offshore
2. Purchasing various intangible and intangible properties with large sums of cash
3. Depositing large sums of cash into various financial institutions
4. Maintaining bank accounts offshore with large balances

Medicare and Medicaid Fraud

This crime involves various health care providers who submit claims to the government programs for services and products that were either not provided or overcharged for those services or products. Federal Statute 18 USC 286 makes any conspiracy or claim against the government a crime. It states:

> Whoever enters into any agreement, combination, or conspiracy to defraud the United States, or any department or agency, thereof, by obtaining or aiding to obtain the payment or allowance of any false, fictitious, or fraudulent claim, shall be fined under this title or imprisoned not more than 10 years, or both.

Repair and Maintenance Fraud

Maintenance and repair attracts swindlers who prey on consumers because typical consumers find it necessary to maintain or repair things that they own, but do not usually have the time, resources, or know-how to do for themselves. The best opportunities for fraud in maintenance and repair involve expensive products and those so sophisticated or specialized as to be beyond the technical expertise of most consumers. Automobiles, electrical appliances, and home maintenance items are the most susceptible. Home maintenance is especially common. Federal Statute 18 USC 286 is used to prosecute those elements that submit false, fictitious, or fraudulent claims to the United States.

Computer Thefts

Computer crime is viewed as a means of crime rather than a type of crime. As an instrument of crime, the computer may be used to victimize individuals, one's own company, competitive companies, the government, the public at large, or even other countries. Computers are involved in the following ways:

1. Submitting false claims to employers or government agencies
2. Embezzling funds from one's employer or financial institution
3. To manipulate stock and bond prices
4. Deleting information that may be harmful if made known
5. Deleting information that would interrupt day-to-day business activities
6. Selling company secrets or software

Federal Statute 18 USC 1030 deals with computer fraud and related activities. It prohibits:

1. Accessing government computers without authorization that requires protection against unauthorized disclosure
2. Intentionally accessing financial institution or card issuer records without authorization
3. Accessing government computers of any department or agency without authorization
4. Accessing a government computer to defraud the government
5. Transmission of a program, information, code, or command to cause damage to a computer system, network, information, data, or program used in interstate commerce or communications

Insider Trading

It is a crime under federal and state statutes for corporate officers or employees of companies who trade their stocks or bonds on the various exchanges when they have knowledge of their company's internal activities. The Securities Exchange Act of 1933, as amended, prohibits this kind of conduct. Indictments for insider trading are usually returned under both 18 USC 1341 and 15 USC 77(x).

Corporate Fraud

Corporate fraud involves crimes committed by organizations or to organizations in the following areas:

1. Stealing company secrets by employees for gain
2. Stealing company secrets by corporate organizations often called corporate espionage
3. Copyright and patent infringements
4. The production, distribution, and sale of harmful food or drug products to the public

It is not a federal crime for an employee or organization to steal secrets from a business organization, unless the theft deals with interstate or foreign commerce (18 USC 2315).

Copyright fraud is a violation under 18 USC 2319. The production, distribution, and sale of harmful food or drug products to the public are governed by various sections of Title 21, USC. In 1906, Congress passed the Federal Food and Drug Act which was the first step in declaring it illegal to manufacture or introduce into the market any adulterated or misbranded food or drug. Congress further expanded this in 1938, when they passed the Food, Drug, and Cosmetic Act. This expanded to cover areas of cosmetics and other health devices.

Swindlers

Swindlers are confidence artists who rely on the principal of getting something for nothing. They do this through a system of persuasion. First, they must find a victim. Second, they gain the confidence of the victim. Third, they convince the victim to depart with something, usually their money on some enterprise. Fourth, they get rid of the victim through consolation and not by fear. There are many hundreds of variations. It may take a "con artist" only a short period of time to fleece a victim or it may take a long period of time. Federal Statute 18 USC 1341 prohibits swindlers from using the postal service to defraud or obtain money by means of false or fraudulent pretenses, representations, or promises. Federal Statute 18 USC 1343 prohibits swindlers from using wire, radio, or television to defraud or obtain money by means of false or fraudulent pretenses, representations, or promises.

Conspiracy

A person who agrees, combines, confederates, or conspires with another person to commit any criminal offense is committing a felony. Usually, the punishment for conspiracy is related to the type of crime that the person is conspiring to commit. The person does not have to commit the offense, but only agree or plan to commit the offense. The offense does not have to take place. The most commonly used federal conspiracy charges revolve around 18 USC 1962, 1951, and 241.

Principal

A principal is anyone who commits any criminal offense or aids, abets, counsels, hires, or otherwise procures such offense to be committed or attempts to be committed. The person does not actually or constructively have to be present at the time of the commission of such offense (18 USC 2).

Accessory

A person can be an accessory either before the fact or after the fact. An accessory is anyone who gives an offender any aid, knowing that he had committed a felony. Normally, an accessory after the fact aids the criminal with intent to escape detection, arrest, or trial. The primary element is that the accessory has knowledge that a person committed an offense (18 USC 3).

Kidnapping

Kidnapping means forcibly, secretly, or by threat confining, abducting, or imprisoning another person against his will and without lawful authority, with intent to:

1. Hold for ransom or reward or as a shield or hostage
2. Commit or facilitate commission of any felony
3. Inflict bodily harm upon or to terrorize the victim or another person
4. Interfere with the performance of any governmental or political function

Under Federal Statutes 18 USC 1201 through 1204, kidnapping is a capital offense.

Theft

Theft is normally defined as any person who obtains or uses, or endeavors to obtain or to use the property of another with intent to, either temporarily or permanently, deprive the owner. Many states have placed various degrees of theft from petit to grand theft, which is usually based upon the value of the property taken. In addition, many states address theft to particular types of theft. The most common are shoplifting, hijacking, trade secrets, utilities and cable theft, dealing in stolen property, mortgage or loan fraud, cheating, misleading advertising, and many others (see the sections on larceny, burglary, and robbery). Sections 2311 through 2322, 18 USC, address theft of various kinds of property which cross state lines.

Child Support

Many states have laws which make it a crime for a person to misuse child support payments, whether from another person or by any government agency. A person shall be deemed to have misapplied child support funds when such funds are spent for any purpose other than necessary and proper home, food, clothing, and the necessities of life, which expenditure results in depriving the child of the above-named necessities. Some states require public welfare agencies to give notice of these provisions at least once to each payee of any public grant for the benefit of any child and shall report violations to the proper authorities.

The failure to pay legal child support obligations with respect to a child who resides in another state is a violation under 18 USC 228.

Counterfeiting

Counterfeiting is the act of imitating something genuine so as to defraud someone. Most people think of counterfeiting in terms of printing money or forging coins that are false. However, both federal and state statutes provide criminal sanctions for imitating or publishing or tendering anything with the intent to utter and pass something as true. Counterfeiting can encompass money, contracts, merchandise, documents, licenses, certificates, or any document or property. Sections 470 through 513, 18 USC, deal with many kinds of counterfeiting under federal statutes. Also, 18 USC 2320 prohibits trafficking in counterfeit goods or services.

Bad Checks

Most states have statutes which prohibit anyone from giving checks, drafts, bills of exchange, debit card orders, and other orders on banks without first providing funds in or credit with the depositories on which the same are made or drawn to pay and satisfy the same. It usually includes any person who, by act or scheme, cashes or deposits any item in a bank or depository with intent to defraud. Bad checks and drafts are prohibited from purchasing goods and services with the intent to defraud any person, firm, or corporation.

The issuing of bad checks comes under the Bank Fraud Statute 18 USC 1344.

False Statements

Federal Statute 18 USC 1001, as well as many state statutes, prohibit anyone from giving false information to any law enforcement or official in the performance of their duties. Title 18 USC 1001 reads:

> Whoever, in any manner within the jurisdiction of any department or agency of the United States and knowingly and willfully falsifies, conceals, or covers up by any trick, scheme, or device a material fact, or makes false, fictitious, or fraudulent statements or representations, or makes or uses any false writing or document knowing the same to contain any false, fictitious, or fraudulent statement or entry, shall be fined under this title or imprisoned not more than five years, or both.

Misprison of Felony

Federal Statute 18 USC 4 defines a misprison of felony as:

> Whoever, having knowledge of the actual commission of a felony cognizable by a court of the United States, conceals and does not, as soon as possible, make known the same to some judge or other person in civil or military authority under the United States, shall be fined under this title or imprisoned not more than three years, or both.

The key element in this offense is that one, having knowledge of an offense, must take an affirmative act of reporting the crime.

Summary

There are many federal statutes which cover a wide variety of crimes, most of which are financially related. States and possessions of the United States have the same or similar laws. A fraud examiner must know the state or federal statute that is being violated in order to examine and gather evidence to support a conviction. The fraud examiner should study the appropriate statute and determine the elements of each offense, then he should see if the evidence supports each one of the elements required to sustain a conviction.

Offshore Activities

3

Introduction

Organized crime organizations, as well as individuals, have taken their illegal gains to offshore countries. Legitimate businesses have been using offshore countries for many years to avoid taxes and preserve capital. These countries which offer various business services, especially to multinational corporations, are called "tax havens." International businessmen know that countries have different tax systems. This disparity may constitute tax havens in relation to a particular operation or situation as compared with the tax treatment given to the identical taxable event in another country's tax system. Hence, "tax haven" is a relative concept. As mentioned in our economic chapter, organized crime and individual illegal operations pay no taxes on their income, therefore, tax havens become very attractive vehicles for hiding their untaxed income from both tax authorities and law enforcement.

Tax Haven Characteristics

Tax havens have many common characteristics which make them ideal for both multinational businesses and criminal organizations. These characteristics are explained below.

Taxes

Countries fall into one of five categories when it comes to tax systems:

1. Countries which impose virtually no direct taxes
2. Countries which impose tax at relatively low rates
3. Countries which impose tax only on domestic source income
4. Countries whose tax treaties can be used as a conduit
5. Countries granting special tax privileges

Organized crime, of course, prefers Categories 1 and 2. The primary function is to eliminate the connecting factor between the taxing jurisdiction and the taxpayer or taxable event. The principal connecting factors for individuals are residence, domicile, and citizenship. For companies, the connecting factors are management and control, owner-ship, place of incorporation, and location of registered office. An important connecting factor is the center of economic interests and the presence of a permanent establishment. Therefore, organized crime tries to eliminate any connecting factors from the taxable events (profits from narcotics trafficking, gambling, loansharking, and more), and the taxpayer (a crime figure of any level).

Exchange Control

The exchange control system of a country is a body of statutory and administrative regulations, which has an objective of control over a country's liquid resources abroad and the international movement of currency owned by its residents. Both organized crime and multinational companies seek countries which have little or no exchange controls. This affords them the ability to easily and quickly transfer funds without any interference.

Banking

Many international banking takes place offshore. Most of the world's banks have oper-ations in tax havens. Tax haven countries have enacted various laws and set up regulatory agencies to control banking activities. Banks offer the same type of services in tax havens as they do in other countries, however, branch offices of international banks in tax havens have the ability to move funds swiftly and have better expertise in handling international transactions. Nonresident banks are only licensed to serve clients who are not tax haven residents.

Bank Secrecy

Secrecy is an important element in tax havens. The banker is required to keep the cus-tomer's affairs secret. In some tax havens, breaches of bank secrecy is a criminal violation, however, there are specific exemptions where the banker is discharged. Organized crime cherishes tax havens with bank secrecy laws. This gives them the ability to further hide the illegal gains.

Stability

Political and economic stability are important factors. Neither businessmen nor organized crime organizations want to do business with any country that is not politically and economically stable.

Communications

Communications are another factor in selecting a tax haven. Some tax havens are small islands which have limited communication and transportation facilities. The Colombian cartels have used small islands as transshipment points. These transshipment points require good communications. The Colombian drug cartels have installed sophisticated communication equipment and facilities on small islands in the Caribbean. Organized crime requires good communication facilities so that illegal gains can be transferred by wire quickly and easily.

Corruption

International businessmen don't want to establish operations in a tax haven country in which public officials are corrupt. This would require them to make payoffs and kickbacks to public officials, which in turn reduces their profits. On the other hand, organized crime has the opposite view. They want to make payoffs and kickbacks so the public officials will look the "other way" and won't interfere with their operations. For organized crime, this is a small price of doing business.

Tax Haven Countries

The following countries are classified as tax havens because they seek business and promote themselves as tax havens. In addition, criminals and organized crime elements look to these countries for ways of money laundering and concealing their illegal gains.

Andorra

This principality is located in the heart of the eastern Pyrenees, between France and Spain. It is a principality covering 468 square kilometers in mountainous terrain. It lacks adequate transportation since there is no airline or train service. Roads can be clogged for hours. It has a president, who is elected by the general counsel or parliament. The parliament members, called ""Consellers General," are elected. There are no taxes on income, capital, and duties although they do have a property tax imposed by the local *Comu* (a parish) each year. The official language is Catalan, but French and Castilian is in daily use. English is understood in banks and public offices. The French franc and the Spanish peseta are both everyday currencies. There are no exchange controls or monetary authority. The telephone system is tied to both the Spanish and French systems so it is possible to dial out through either country. Generally, the service is efficient and costs are similar to those of neighboring countries. The postal system is supplied by the French and Spanish postal services which provide their own stamps. They generally follow Roman law, however, in many instances, they follow the Napoleonic Code. The main industry is tourism, which sells duty-free goods to its neighboring residents. There are three types of business entities that can be formed and operate in Andorra:

a. A Collective Society (SRC), essentially a partnership. There are no capital require-ments, however, one partner must be a native Andorrian.
b. A Societat Anonima (SA), essentially a large corporation. There must be real capital investment of 5 million in pesetas or equivalent with no more than 10 shareholders.
c. A Societate De Responsibilitat Limitada (SL), essentially a small corporation. There must be real capital investment of 3 million pesetas or equivalent with no less than 3 shareholders.

A foreign national cannot own more than one third interest in any Andorrian company. Foreign nationals use Andorrians as trustees or nominees. Bank accounts can be opened in any amount and in any currency. Breach of bank secrecy is a criminal offense. Every bank offers a numbered account facility.

Bahama Islands

The Bahama Islands are located off the Florida east coast. They consist of 700 islands, of which only about 40 are inhabited. They are part of the British Commonwealth, however, independence was established on July 10, 1973. There are no income, sales, capital, estate, or inheritance taxes. The islands have property taxes, which is assessed at 1 to 3 percent on nonresidents. Most of the Bahama Islands' revenue comes from custom duties. The islands have exchange control to conserve foreign currency resources of the Bahama Islands and assist in the balance of payments. Exchange controls on nonresidents are nonexistent. The Bahamian dollar is used, which is tied to the U.S. dollar. There is good transportation and communications to both the United States and Europe. There are many branch offices of international banks in both Nassau and Freeport. The Bahama Islands have strict bank secrecy laws. No banker can disclose a customer's affairs without an order from the Supreme Court of the Commonwealth of the Bahama Islands. The legal system is based upon English common law rules of equity with a parliamentary form of government consisting of the senate and house assembly. The Queen of England is the head of state and is represented by the governor general. The governor general appoints the senate and prime minister. A Bahamian company can be formed with minimum formalities. For companies wanting to do business in the Bahama Islands, there are various types of licenses that need to be obtained. For nonresidents, only a resident agent is required to be in the Bahama Islands. The officers and directors of a Bahamian company can hold meetings anywhere. Directors can be as few as one, but two is better. Nominees can be used as directors and shareholders. However, all directors' names and addresses are to be registered in the public register.

Barbados

This country is an island in the Caribbean chain. It was a British colony until 1966 at which time it gained its independence, however, it remains part of the British Common-wealth. Its official language is English. The Barbados dollar is tied to the U.S. dollar at the rate of US$1 = BDS$2. They have an Exchange Control Authority, however, it does not control companies operating in the offshore sector. Under the Offshore Banking Act, the affairs of nonresident customers are not to be disclosed. Share warrants are permitted. The names and addresses of beneficial owners of shares must be made to the Central Bank. The Central Bank keeps them confidential, although it is not a criminal violation for government officials or employers to reveal such information. Barbados has a tax information exchange agreement with the United States. There are many international bank branches in Barbados. Transportation and communication from Barbados to the United States and Europe are good. There are regularly scheduled flights. Income tax is imposed on domestic income for both individuals and corporations. Foreign income is not taxed, except on residents. There are no capital gains or inheritance taxes. Barbados also imposes withholding taxes on income derived within the country. Barbados has tax treaties with the United Kingdom, United States, Canada, Denmark, Norway, Sweden, and Switzerland. Barbados has a parliamentary form of government consisting of a senate and house of assembly. It follows the English common law and law of equities. The Companies Act allows for flexibility in forming, operating, and winding up or transfer-ring the domicile of a company. Single shareholder and director companies are allowed.

Board meetings can be held both within and outside Barbados. Shareholder anonymity can be achieved by the following:

a.   Using nominees
b.   Using foreign trusts
c.   Using share warrants (a form of bearer stock)

Bermuda

This country is located in the middle of the Atlantic Ocean about halfway between the United States and Europe. It is a self-governing colony of the British Commonwealth. Transportation and communication are very good to both the United States and Europe. The official language is English. Bermuda has exchange control authority on local residents. However, offshore companies and individuals can maintain bank accounts in the currency of the country that they choose. The government has restrictions on who can incorporate and do business there. There are no income, capital gains, or withholding taxes. Nominees can be used to safeguard real beneficial owners. There are many branches of international banks on the island. Bermuda has its own monetary authority and dollar, which can be converted into any currency of choice. The legal system is based upon English common law. The Companies Act allows for the formation of "exempt" companies, which are corporations that do not operate on the island. These exempt companies are not taxed, but must maintain an office in Bermuda. An auditor located on the island must audit the books every year. There must be at least three shareholders. The shareholders must be registered in company registers which are open to the public. Nominees can be used as shareholders.

Cayman Islands

The Cayman Islands are located between Cuba and the Yucatan Peninsula. They are a British colony. The official language is English. Transportation and communication to the United States and Europe are very good. There are no income, capital gains, estate, and inheritance taxes. Income is derived from import duties. The currency is the Cayman dollar which is pegged to the U.S. dollar at CI$1 = US$1.20. There are many branches of international banks on the island. The Cayman Islands have bank secrecy laws. There are criminal penalties on government officials and professionals who make unauthorized disclosure of customer's accounts. The British government signed an agreement with the United States to prevent drug traffickers from enjoying benefits of the Cayman Islands laws in 1984. The law provides a mechanism for obtaining evidence in federal court proceedings through the Attorney General of the United States and the Cayman Islands. The procedure must be strictly complied with and cannot be used in any other case or for any other purpose. There are no currency exchange controls. The Cayman Islands are politically and economically stable. The Islands have a substantial trade surplus with the outside world. Employment and standard of living are very high. The Islands have direct dial telephone, telecopier, cable, and telex links. The postal service is efficient with air courier services available to virtually all parts of the world. The Companies Act provides for "exempt" corporations. These are corporations that do not operate on the island. An exempt corporation must have one meeting a year on the island. It must also have at least one director. The company register is not open for public inspection.

Costa Rica

This country is located in Central America. The official language is Spanish, but English is used in commercial practice. The country has a democratic form of government and no military forces. The national currency is the colon. There is exchange control on the colon, however, there is no control of funds transferred into a Costa Rican account and maintained in a foreign currency account. The banks are required by law to maintain secrecy regarding the affairs of their customers. There are income, capital gains, and withholding taxes. Costa Rican law provides for foreigners to reside in Costa Rica, especially those on retirement income. The pensioned resident must reside in Costa Rica for at least six months per year. In addition, the pensioned resident can travel on a Costa Rican passport called a "Passport of Convenience." Organized crime figures like this characteristic because they can go directly to Costa Rica when things get "hot" in the United States. They, in turn, can travel to other countries using a Costa Rican passport instead of a United States passport. Costa Rican law establishes four different legal capacities in which people can engage in business. These are as follows:

   a.   Individual Enterprise with Limited Liability, regarded as an individual
   b.   Collective Company, similar to partnership in common law countries
   c.   The Limited Partnership, a partnership that has limited liability
   d.   Stock Corporation or Chartered Company, a corporation

The Stock Corporation can be formed with two or more incorporators. A single person may be the only shareholder. A Stock Corporation can issue "bearer" shares of stock. This allows the shareholder that wants to keep his/her identity from being known ensured of secrecy regarding the investment. The bearer stock must be paid in full, otherwise the shares must be registered with the Public Registry.

Liechtenstein

This country is located between Switzerland and Austria. It became an independent state in 1719 by the union of two Imperial Baronies of Vaduz and Schellenberg. It obtained full independence in 1806 when it joined the Confederation of the Rhine that was founded by Napoleon. After World War I, Liechtenstein drifted away from Austria, with whom a customs union had existed, toward Switzerland. Liechtenstein joined the Swiss customs area and the Swiss franc became the country's official currency. The official language is German, but English is used in the economic sectors. It has a democratic form of government. It has taxes on income, property, estate, gift, motor vehicles, and alcoholic beverages. There are no currency exchange laws or regulations. It does permit bearer securities, bonds, and stock. It has bank secrecy laws. Bankers are forbidden to disclose a customer's financial affairs. Transportation and communications are good. Peculiar to Liechtenstein is its law relating to associations of persons and the company without juridical personality, which is codified in the Laws on Persons and Companies (PGR Code). The PGR Code provides for a number of different kinds of corporate associations. The focal point of these legal forms, with their tax advantages, lies in holding companies and domiciliary enterprises. Holding companies and domiciliary enterprises are tax law concepts designating enterprises operating in Liechtenstein, which are liable for capital and revenue taxes. These forms include:

a. Companies limited by shares
b. Private limited companies
c. Establishments
d. Trust enterprises
e. Foundations

The PGR Code also provides for the limited partnership with a share capital, the company limited by quota shares, associations, cooperative associations and others, and companies without juridical personality. The PGR Code contains only a few mandatory provisions. The features of the holding company and domiciliary enterprise with their own juridical personality are as follows:

a. The name and references to their legal form may be entered into public register in a foreign language.
b. One member of the board of directors must be a Liechtenstein citizen residing within the principality and also be a lawyer.
c. They are exempt from property, income, and revenue tax and subject to only capital tax at a beneficial rate.
d. There must be a representative (registered agent) residing in the principality.

The Establishment is an autonomous fund with its own juridical personality and for whose commitments only the resources of the undertaking are liable. It has no members, or shareholders or participants of any other kind and no capital distributed in share form, acknowledging only beneficiaries, i.e., persons who draw economic advantage from it. The Establishment is referred to as Anstalt. The Establishment may be authorized to issue its own shares in which case it comes closer to becoming a corporation. The founders of an Anstalt may be natural persons or juridical entities with residence in Liechtenstein or abroad. The founders must draw up and sign articles in written form that contain the following:

a. Company name including the designation Anstalt
b. The establishment's domicile, objects and capital, the powers of its supreme governing body
c. The appointment of bodies for management and supervision
d. The principles for preparing financial statements
e. The form in which notices are published

The objective of the Anstalt must indicate whether the business will engage in commercial activities or investment or management of assets. The capital may be expressed in foreign currency, but must be at least Fr 30,00 or equivalent. The bearer of the founder's rights constitutes the establishment of a supreme body. The supreme body can:

a. Appoint or dismiss the board of directors and auditors
b. Determine the signing powers of management
c. Approve the financial statements
d. Change the articles or by-laws
e. Determine beneficiaries and their rights
f. Appoint or dismiss the legal representative

The Establishment's beneficiaries are the people to whom the profit and benefit of the Establishment accrue; who are entitled to the income, the individual assets, and the eventual liquidation proceeds. Unless third parties are nominated as beneficiaries, the law assumes that the bearer of the founder's rights is the beneficiary.

Netherland Antilles

This country is located off the coast of Venezuela. It is dominated and controlled by the Netherlands. The Netherlands Antilles is also part of the European Economic Community. These islands have their own island government. The official language is Dutch, however, English, German, French, and Spanish are used. The monetary unit is the Netherlands Antilles guilder. It is pegged to the U.S. dollar at $1.79 per one guilder. Identity of shareholders is not available for public inspection until all issued shares of stock have been fully paid up. Income tax is imposed only on income derived within the Netherlands Antilles. Currency exchange is only imposed on individuals and corporations doing business within the Netherlands Antilles. Transportation and communications are very good. The government does not mandate bank secrecy, however, it is banker's custom to regard their customers' affairs as confidential. A Limited Liability Company (NV) is allowed to issue "bearer" shares, but they must be fully paid. Shareholder meetings must be held in the Netherlands Antilles, but proxy can represent them. It requires two or more people to incorporate. The managing director, "directeur," must be a resident of the island. He serves as the registered agent. Financial reports are required to be filed with the Commercial Registry if the corporation has issued 1) bearer shares exceeding 50,000 guilders, 2) shares or bonds on a stock exchange, and 3) the corporation borrows from third parties. Auditors are required to audit the financial statements. Only auditors from the Netherlands Antilles can be used.

Panama

This country is located in Central America, north of Colombia. The official language is Spanish. Transportation and communication are excellent. It is supposed to have a democratic form of government, however, it has had dictators during the past several decades. The United States military invaded Panama in December 1989 and removed General Manuel Noriega. The currency of Panama is the balboa, however, since there is no balboa currency, the U.S. dollar is circulated and accepted as the medium of exchange. Panama has income taxes, but they are imposed at the provincial level. Income derived outside Panama is not taxed. There are no currency exchange controls in Panama. There are no bank secrecy laws, but customs has its bankers to regard their customers' affairs as confidential. A corporation can be formed by as few as two people and be of any nationality or domicile. "Bearer" shares can be issued. The full names and addresses of directors must be recorded in the Public Registry Office. Every corporation must have a resident registered agent, which is generally some lawyer in Panama. There is no requirement for general or special meetings of shareholders or directors. The directors can be of any nationality or domicile. There must be three directors. They do not have to be shareholders.

Switzerland

This country is located in the heart of Europe. Switzerland has three official languages: German, French, and Italian. English is not used for official documents, but is used in official correspondence. This is a democratic country. The currency is the Swiss franc. Transportation and communication to and from Switzerland is excellent. The banks guard their customers' financial accounts. Switzerland has income, estate, capital gains, and inheritance taxes on residents. There are no currency exchange controls. The substantive law of Switzerland is codified. The civil and commercial codes are applicable throughout Switzerland. While the law is based on federal and cantonal legislation, court decisions and precedents play an important role. Foreign nationals can open numbered bank accounts in most banks. Switzerland does have double taxation treaties with many countries including the United States. Three or more individuals or companies can form a Swiss corporation. Their nationality and residence doesn't matter. The corporation must have a minimum capital of Fr 50,000 and deposit of Fr 20,000. They can have either ordinary shares or preference shares. Both classes of stock can be bearer or registered shares. Shareholders can use nominees. Shareholder names are not allowed to be identified to third parties or fiscal authorities. Auditors in Switzerland must audit the financial statements. They can only release their results to directors and shareholders as a group. The registered agent must be a resident of Switzerland and his/her name is published in the Commercial Gazette.

Aruba

Aruba is an island nation, situated approximately 12 miles off the coast of Venezuela in South America. Its capital is Oranjestad; its population totals about 65,000 inhabitants. Aruba is a small island measuring 19.6 miles long and 6 miles across at its widest point. Until January 1, 1986, Aruba together with Curacao and some small islands formed part of the federation, which formed the country of the Netherlands Antilles. On that date, it acquired a separate status. Aruba has a parliamentary democracy with a governor representing the Queen of the Netherlands. The parliament consists of 21 members that are elected by universal suffrage. The Aruba legal system of civil and penal law is a copy of the Dutch legal system; a system derived from Roman law. The basic laws are the Civil Code (Burgerlijk Wetboek) and the Commercial Code (Wetboek van Koophandel). Besides these two principal codes, there are numerous laws, regulations, and directives. As Aruba is part of the Kingdom of the Netherlands, all laws are in Dutch. The Arubian florin (or guilder) is divided into 100 cents. The Arubian florin is tied to the U.S. dollar at a rate of Af. 1.79. Papianmento is the native language; however, Dutch is the official language. Most professional advisors speak English fluently. Dutch, English, and Spanish are widely spoken. French and German are also spoken. Professionals have mostly had either a Dutch or a North American education. Aruba is an associate member of the European Economic Community (EEC). Aruba has excellent communications on the island. Automatic international communications is possible with most countries in the world. Telegraphic communication services are provided by SETAR, a government-owned company. There is also a data communications system through which several data networks in the United States and Europe are accessible.

The country has excellent telephone, telex, and cable communications as well as daily connections by air with major cities in the United States, Latin America, and Europe. There are a number of reputable international and local banks to service the financial needs of the tax haven sector. There are also many law firms, accounting firms, and trust companies established in Aruba. With the termination of its treaty base in 1988, the Aruban government passed legislation for zero tax offshore company facilities in Aruba. Aruba is an attractive tax haven in the Caribbean and Central America region because of political stability. All legal and natural persons, carrying on a business enterprise in Aruba, are subject to a number of obligations to provide the tax inspector's office with certain information. Numbered bank accounts are not permitted in Aruba. In order to open a bank account, one normally has to prove one's identity, or, if the bank account is for a legal entity, a certificate of the Chamber of Commerce must be lodged.

There are two kinds of limited companies in Aruba, the Naamloze Vennootschap (N.V.) and the Aruba Vrijgestelde Vennootschap (A.V.V.) or "Aruba Exempt Company." Prior to the introduction of the Aruba Exempt Company (A.E.C.) all limited companies were NV's. There are many similarities between N.V. and A.V.V., but also fundamental differences. In general it can be said that the Aruban zero tax company (A.V.V.) has a more modern corporate structure than the Aruban N.V. The Aruban zero tax company provides an attractive vehicle for international tax planning because of the absence of taxes, relatively low cost of formation and maintenance, the flexibility of its corporate structure and the absence of red tape and regulatory restrictions. Aruba Exempt Company may not conduct business activities in Aruba other than those which are necessary in connection with the maintenance of its office in Aruba. The company is also prohibited from conducting banking, insurance, or any other activity which would make it a creditor of a financial institution under Aruban law. This rule applies regardless of whether the activities are conducted in or outside Aruba. The required minimum capital is Afl. 10,000, which is approximately $5,600 in U.S. currency. The company must be registered in the Commercial Register, which is open to the public. It contains the names and other personal data about the directors and legal representatives. There are no currency exchange controls for A.E.C. companies or foreign nationals and companies.

Cyprus

Cyprus has been an independent Republic since 1960. It was previously a British colony. Cyprus is a member of the United Nations, British Commonwealth, and the Council of Europe. In 1974, part of the island was occupied by Turkish forces and remains occupied. This study does not relate to the area under Turkish occupation. The legal system is mainly based upon English common law and equity. English case law is widely followed. The official language is Greek, but English is widely spoken and used especially in court, government offices, and businesses. The economy, after the Turkish invasion in 1974, has recovered and has surpassed its pre-1974 standard of living. Foreign investments are increasing, mainly in the industrial and tourist sectors. Political and economic stability is now rated as good. The Cyprus pound is divided into 100 cents; it is subject to fluctuation. Cyprus is not in the sterling area. There are very good air and sea communications. It has excellent telecommunications facilities with automatic connections to 69 countries and automatic telex communications to 148 countries. Cyprus is rated among the top five countries with excellent automatic telecommunications. A satellite earth station started operating in 1980. There are also marisat, facsimile, and datel services. Secrecy laws bind banks. Banks do not have numbered accounts. The geographical position, the climatic conditions, the availability of local skilled personnel, and the low cost of living make Cyprus a very suitable place from which to manage offshore activities, especially for the Middle East. Cyprus has Double Taxation Agreements with 18 countries, which includes the United States. Cyprus has an income tax on individuals and companies who operate on the island. Income earned offshore is not taxable. There are exchange controls for local residents and companies who do business in Cyprus. All foreign incorporated companies are nonresident. Foreign companies who do not have business in Cyprus are free from exchange control. Only local lawyers with a minimum of two shareholders can form corporations. There can be two classes of stock. Bearer shares are prohibited. Shareholders names must be filed with the Registrar of Companies, however, nominees can be used.

Gibraltar

Gibraltar is a British Crown Colony situated at the southern end of the Iberian Peninsula. The legal system is based upon English law using both common law and Acts of Parliament. The official language is English and all official documents are produced in English. The legal tender consists of currency notes of the Gibraltar government. United Kingdom currency is also legal tender. Gibraltar notes are not easily convertible outside Gibraltar. There are no currency exchange controls. There are no double taxation treaties and no provisions for exchange of information with any other country. There are excellent communication facilities and bank facilities. A corporation formed in Gibraltar can be exempt from submitting annual account to the Commissioners of Income Tax, but must apply for exemption. The corporation can remain exempt so long as no one is a resident of Gibraltar or the United Kingdom. It can issue bearer shares of stock, but must be paid in full. Identity of a person or persons applying for exemption must be kept secret.

Guernsey

This is an island nation off the coast of England about 108 miles south of Southampton and about 40 miles from France. It is a British possession, but has its own legal system and government. Committees of the state generally administer public services and departments. Their law is customary law of the Duchy which dates back to the Normandy customary law. The customary law of Normandy is nowadays significant in matters of succession and real property. In taxation and commercial legislation, English Acts are followed, especially in matters of investor protection. The United Kingdom negotiated special terms upon accession to the Treaty of Rome within the framework of Article 227 of the Treaty as amended by the Treaty of Accession. The arrangements, which are set out in Protocol Number 3 of the Treaty of Accession, have the effect of retaining fiscal independence of Guernsey and freedom from the imposition of duties and levies, in particular, value-added tax. There is no requirement upon Guernsey to adopt Community fiscal, commercial or economic policies. English is the official language, however, many laws have been enacted in French. Many law firms and staff are fluent in French and English. The currency is sterling and both English and local notes are circulated freely. The economy of Guernsey is based upon horticulture, tourism, finance, and light industry. Guernsey is dependent upon communications. They have stable links with the United Kingdom, Jersey, and continental Europe. Telecommunications and postal services are cheaper than mainland services and are available at most professional offices and banks. There is no local legislation enacted relating to secrecy of information, but English common law which imposes a duty upon a bank and bank personnel to maintain secrecy is applicable. Nominee and numbered account facilities are available. The Double Taxation Agreements with Jersey and the United Kingdom do provide for exchange of information, but only to the revenue authority of those jurisdictions respectively. Guernsey has a low income tax of 20 percent on any income that is derived or remitted to Guernsey. A company or individual is liable for income taxes if they are resident for a year or conduct substantial parts of their business there. An individual is a resident if he spends more than 182 days in Guernsey. There are no exchange controls on the island. At least seven people must form a corporation. Their names, addresses, nationalities, and domiciles are filed with the law officer of the crown in court only on Thursdays. Annual reports are required to be sent to the Greffier no later than January 31 of each year. These reports must identify shareholders and their respective holdings. Annual meetings must be held in Guernsey.

Hong Kong

Hong Kong is situated on the southeast coast of China, 90 miles southeast of Canton and 40 miles east of the Portuguese province of Macau. The total land area is 404 square miles. The estimated population in 1987 was about 5.6 million of which 98 percent were Chinese. Great Britain and the People's Republic of China signed an agreement in 1984 which allowed Hong Kong to revert back into the control of China on July 1, 1997. This joint agreement provided for Hong Kong to remain a separate customs territory after June 30, 1997. Hong Kong has experienced dynamic economic growth since the end of World War II. Hong Kong is the third largest financial center in the world after New York and London. The Hong Kong government has a policy of nonintervention on the financial sectors. English common law and rules of equity apply in Hong Kong to the extent that they are applicable to local circumstances. English acts have force in Hong Kong by virtue of their own terms, or by an order of the legislative council of Hong Kong. Chinese and English are the official languages of Hong Kong. Most important documents are published in both languages and are required in many instances. There is no central bank in Hong Kong, but Hong Kong currency notes are issued by two commercial banks. On June 6, 1972, the Hong Kong government decided to quote the Hong Kong dollar in terms of the United States dollar. Hong Kong is not a tax haven, per se, but an area with a low tax structure. There are no residence or nationality restrictions regarding the ownership of real estate in Hong Kong. There are no exchange controls or restrictions in force. Banks and their personnel maintain secrecy as a matter of custom and not by law. Hong Kong has not entered into any double taxation agreements with other countries. Transportation and communication are some of the best in the world. There are regularly scheduled flights to and from Hong Kong to most of the major cities around the world. A corporation can be formed with no less than two subscribers. It can have different classes of stock. Nominees can be used to hide true identities of shareholders. There are no nationality or residency requirements, nor any requirements to disclose beneficial interests. Annual returns must be filed with the Registrar of Companies which must disclose the shareholders of the company. Minutes of shareholder meetings must be kept in Hong Kong and be open to inspection. Director's meetings can be held anywhere in the world and are not open to inspection. At least two directors must be shareholders.

Isle Of Man

The Isle of Man lies in the Irish Sea and forms part of the British Isles but not the United Kingdom. It is a possession of the British Crown, but remains self-governing. The island is within the European Economic Community as far as free trade in agriculture and industrial products are concerned, but is outside the community for all other aspects of the Treaty of Rome. There are scheduled flights to and from London, Manchester, Liverpool, Glasglow, and Blackball. There are also regularly scheduled ferries to Liverpool and Heysham. There are normal telephone and telex services available worldwide. The currency is the pound sterling, which the government issues through the Isle of Man Bank, Ltd. English, Scottish, and Manx notes are all in circulation. There are about 30 international banks which have branches on the island. They offer a wide range of services. There is a Double Taxation Treaty of mutual disclosure with the United Kingdom. Bank secrecy is a matter of custom and not of law. There is an income tax on resident individuals and associations and nonresidents whose income is derived from the Isle of Man. There are no gift, estate, capital gains, or stamp duty (document tax) on the island. There are no exchange controls on the island. Two or more people can form a private corporation. The corporation must keep a register of all shareholders. For residents outside the Isle of Man, this register is called a "dominion register." All corporations must have two directors and also hold shares. Annual reports are required which must show the names, addresses of shareholders, and their registered office. A registered office must be located on the island.

Jersey

Jersey is the largest of the Channel Islands that are situated in the English Channel. It is 103 miles south of Southampton and 14 miles from the coast of France. The business center is in St. Helier. There is a busy passenger and cargo port at St. Helier providing services to England, France, and the other islands. There are frequent and regular air services to London, Paris, and other airports in the United Kingdom, France, and Ireland. Jersey has a long history of political and economic stability. The currency is the sterling. Jersey does not like the term "tax haven." It prefers to be known as a finance center and has the attitude of maintaining respectability and protection of investors dealing on the island. There are no exchange controls. There is no legislation on secrecy of information or bank secrecy, but bankers and professional advisors can use numbered bank accounts and nominees. There is a 20 percent income tax on resident individuals and businesses which has remained constant since 1940. English and French are the official languages. Most legal firms maintain principals and staff fluent in French and can translate French into English. There are many international banks on the island. Three or more people are required to form a corporation. At least nine shares must be issued and paid up. The share capital can be in any currency. There are no nationality or residence requirements for shareholders. However, a register of shareholders must be kept at the registered office and be available for public inspection. There is no requirement to disclose nominee holdings. Annual reports reflecting names and addresses of shareholders are required to be filed with the Company Registry.

Liberia

The Republic of Liberia was established in 1847 and has enjoyed independence and a stable, free enterprise economy since its formation. The official language of commerce and government is English. The United States dollar is legal tender. There are no currency regulations or exchange controls. There are excellent transportation and communication facilities. Liberia has several of the most modern seaports in the world. There are no bank secrecy laws. Secrecy is a matter of custom and not law. Liberians are subject to the Liberian Internal Revenue Code. Liberia has a tax law that attracts incorporation of Liberian companies by foreign investors. Corporations that qualify are not required to file income tax returns. Liberian corporations do not incur income tax liability in Liberia if not more than 25 percent of the stock is owned by residents and the company does not carry on operations in Liberia. Anyone can form a corporation in Liberia. A single person can form a corporation. It can issue "bearer" stock if fully paid. Only the registered agent must be present in Liberia. No annual reports are required to be filed with any government agency. Shareholders and directors meetings can be held any place in the world.

Luxembourg

The Grand Duchy of Luxembourg is situated in western Europe lying between Belgium, France, and Germany. The capital city, also called Luxembourg, is the government, business, and financial center. Transportation is good since it is in easy reach of all of Europe's road, rail, and air services. It is also linked directly to the northern European seaports through the river Moselle and the European canal system. Communication is also good with direct dialing with most of Europe and the United States. Luxembourg has developed a sophisticated banking sector. There are more than 115 international banks operating in Luxembourg. In recent years, Luxembourg has become a center for Eurobond issues. Luxembourgish is the spoken language. French, German, and English are widely used in official and business circles. French is used in administration while many laws still exist in German. The currency is the Luxembourg franc, currently on par with the Belgium franc which is also legal tender in Luxembourg. Luxembourg has no central bank although the Luxembourg Monetary Institute has been created which is entitled to issue 20 percent of money in circulation and rediscount bills held by Luxembourg Banks. The laws are based upon the Code Napoleon and the legal system has much in common with Belgium and France. It is common practice in Luxembourg for registered companies to issue bearer bonds or shares which can be held or deposited anywhere in the world. Bank secrecy with numbered accounts is normal and respected. It is governed by civil law. Luxembourg has double taxation treaties with fifteen countries under which information may be exchanged. The United States is one of those countries. Holding companies are the most commonly used in Luxembourg. The ordinary holding company pays no corporation, income, capital gains, wealth, withholding, or liquidation taxes. Exchange control regulations are in effect with the Central Bank in Brussels. Local banks are entrusted with the control of financial transactions based upon the directives of the Central Bank in Brussels.

Montserrat

Montserrat is an island east of Puerto Rico and the United States Virgin Islands. The island is a dependent territory of the United Kingdom with an appointed governor by the British government. The island has a history of political stability. The legal system is based upon the common law of England. The local and official language is English. The economy is based upon agriculture, light industry, and tourism. Tax incentives are available for new business enterprises on the island. The eastern Caribbean dollar is the official currency, although the United States dollar and the sterling are circulated. The EC$ is tied to the US$ and is fully convertible. The government has provided incentives for businesses to operate on the island. It offers incentives of tax holidays and duty-free imports. The Confidential Information Ordinance, 1985, provides heavy penalties for unauthorized revealing of information. Montserrat has double taxation treaties through the extension of some of the United Kingdom treaties with the governments of Canada, Denmark, Japan, New Zealand, Norway, Sweden, and Switzerland. Two local banks, Barclays and the Royal Bank of Canada, do not permit numbered accounts although there are no legal bars against them. Corporations can be formed under the provisions of the International Business Companies Ordinance, 1985. It provides that only one subscriber is necessary. There are no restrictions on the transfer of shares, number of shareholders, or debentures. The Memorandum of Association must include the name of the company, which must contain "Limited," a registered office in Monserrat, purpose, authorized capital, and number of shares. A registered office must be maintained on the island. Annual reports must be filed with the Registrar of Companies for private companies, but none are required for international business companies. Bearer stock is allowed provided that it is paid in full. Annual meetings of shareholders and directors can be held anywhere in the world. All international business companies are specifically exempted from exchange control. Monserrat is part of the eastern Caribbean banking network. There are good transportation facilities, both air and sea. Communication facilities are also good.

Recently, a volcano erupted on the island, which sent many residents fleeing to neighboring islands. The British government has asked for the remaining residents to move off of the island, since it is expected that the volcano will erupt again. This island may become deserted which will leave its tax haven status in doubt.

Nauru

The smallest country in the world, Nauru became an independent sovereign state on January 31, 1968 and subsequently an associate member of the British Commonwealth. It is in the center of the Pacific basin, being located about equidistant from Sydney, Australia to the southwest and from Hawaii to the northeast. Nauru has close educational links with Australia. Nauru has a democratic government with elected parliament and president. It has a well-developed and efficient civil service and judicial system. Air Nauru, the airline of Nauru, connects Nauru with Australia, Fiji, Hong Kong, Manila, Honolulu, and other Pacific Islands on a regular basis, usually twice a week. Nauru is well connected through a satellite in order to render telephone, cable, telex and facsimile services to and from the principal cities of various countries, including the United States. The official currency of Nauru is the Australian dollar, which is freely convertible into different currencies. Nauru designed legislation with the intent to provide facilities for tax planners. It wants to help entrepreneurs both new and existing to generate and mobilize their resources for economic expansion. At the same time, it guards against fraud on creditors, investors, depositors, and shareholders. It offers full freedom for entrepreneurs to establish holding and trading companies, but does not hesitate to terminate the corporate existence of those corporations which carry out fraudulent business within or outside Nauru. Corporations offer the following advantages:

a.   Minimum formation time (24 hours)
b.   Low formation costs
c.   Minimum pre- and post-incorporation legal formalities
d.   Low capitalization
e.   Freedom to issue bearer shares
f.   Complete secrecy of operations
g.   Anonymity of promoters

A resident secretary is required by statute. Shares must be stated in Australian currency. There are some exceptions. Annual reports are required to be filed with the Registrar. The reports only require the names of directors, secretaries, and registered agents.

Nevis

This Caribbean Island lies east of Puerto Rico and west of Montserrat. It is a democratic country that is part of the British Commonwealth. Britain is responsible for external affairs and defense. Nevis is part of the Federation of St. Kitts and Nevis. The judicial commonwealth of the privy council of Great Britain is the court of ultimate jurisdiction and consists of members from the House of Lords. The official language is English. Nevis is self-sufficient in food production, but has a trade deficit. The government is seeking diversification through expansion of tourism, fisheries, light manufacturing, and offshore financial activities. The currency is the eastern Caribbean Currency dollar (EC$). It is pegged to the U.S. dollar at EC$2.70 = US$1. The EC$ is not an internationally-traded currency. The adoption of the Nevis Business Corporation Ordinance, 1984, signified the government's commitment to become a modern tax haven. The ordinance provided that the Nevis Business Corporation conduct no commercial business on the island. Corporations can be formed in 24 hours. The government adopted the Confidential Relationships Act, 1985, which is applicable to Office of the Registrar of Companies and professionals engaged in related services, financial and otherwise. There are no treaties respecting information exchange. Numbered bank accounts are not available through Nevis banks. Corporations formed under the Nevis Business Corporation Ordinance are not subject to exchange controls. Exchange controls on EC$ are in effect when exchanged for foreign currency. Transportation and communications are good. There are regularly scheduled flights to other major islands in the Caribbean basin. Only two people are required to form a corporation. The Articles of Incorporation must show the names and addresses of the incorporators and the initial directors. Bearer stock is authorized, but must be paid in full. There must be three directors who can be of any nationality or domicile. There is no requirement to show the names of subsequent shareholders or directors. Shareholders and directors meetings can be held anywhere in the world. A registered agent is required to be a resident of the island. Most corporations use Corporate Services Company on Charlestown, Nevis, as the registered agent. No annual reports are required to be filed.

Turks and Caicos Islands

The Turks and Caicos Islands lie about 100 miles north of Haiti and the Dominican Republic. They are a British crown colony under the jurisdiction of the British government. The British government appoints the governor. The legal system is based upon British common law. Ultimate appeal is the privy council sitting in London. English is both the official and spoken language. The U.S. dollar is the official currency in the islands. The Turks and Caicos Islands government enacted the Companies Ordinance, 1981, to establish the islands as a major offshore center. The government has a strong desire to attract offshore financial and business activity. The principal banks on the islands are Barclays Bank International and the Bank of Nova Scotia. There is no central bank. The economy is based primarily on tourism, offshore business, and fishing. There is good transportation and communications. There are regularly scheduled flights to the United States and other islands. Direct-dial service is available on the islands. Bank secrecy is a matter of custom and not of law. The Turks and Caicos Islands have no income, capital gains, corporate, sales, property, withholding, payroll, inheritance, gift, or estates taxes. The islands get most of their revenue from import duties. The Turks and Caicos Islands enacted the Narcotic Drug Ordinance, 1986, under which the Attorney General of the United States may certify to the attorney general of the Turks and Caicos Islands that certain documents and testimony are needed for grand jury investigation of narcotics offenses. The islands can compel both public and private sources to comply with requests. The islands don't want to become a haven for drug traffickers. An "exempt" company is one that does not operate on the islands. An exempt corporation can be formed with as few as one shareholder. The corporation can be formed without going to the islands. Annual reports are not required. It does not have to hold either shareholder or director meetings. A registered agent is required to be on the island. Identities of shareholders and directors are not shown in public records. Bearer shares can be issued.

Vanuatu

Vanuatu is an independent democratic republic. It was formally called the New Hebrides when it was part of the British Commonwealth. Vanuatu lies east of Australia. English and French are widely used, together with Bislama. Bislama is the official language. The official currency is the Vatu which is linked to Special Drawing Rights (1 SDR = 110 VT). In 1985, 106 VT = $1.00 U.S. Exempt companies under Vanuatu law are secret companies and breach of that secrecy can entail fines and imprisonment. There are no taxes on income and capital, thus, there are no double taxation treaties with other countries. Number accounts are not available in Vanuatu. It can take only three days to two weeks to set up a company. "Exempt" companies are not allowed to do business in Vanuatu. Every company is required to keep a register of members, directors, officers, and proper books of account on the island. Annual reports are required to be filed every year. For exempt companies, these records and reports are to be kept secret. It is against the law for any government official to disclose this information. An auditor and registrar are required for all companies to be on the island. Exempt companies are not required to have an auditor, but must have a registrar. Shareholders and directors names of an exempt company are not available to the public. There are no income or capital gains taxes on the island. There are no exchange controls. Bank accounts can be kept in foreign currency.

British Virgin Islands

These islands lie just east of Puerto Rico in the Caribbean basin. They consist primarily of four islands: Torola, Anegada, Virgin Gorda, and Jost Van Dyke. The main and largest city is Road Town. The official and common language is English. The British Virgin Islands are a part of the British Commonwealth. The British government appoints the governor. Its main industry is tourism. Transportation is good. There are regularly scheduled flights to Puerto Rico, Miami, and other eastern Caribbean islands. Communications are also good. There is direct-dial telephone service to Puerto Rico and other countries. Sterling is the main currency, however, U.S. dollars are also accepted. There are no exchange controls. There is no central bank. There are no income, capital gains, gift or estate taxes. The primary source of revenue is import duties. The government encourages foreign investment and capital. Banking and finance in the islands are the same as those in the Turks and Caicos Islands. The legal system is the same for the British Virgin Islands as it is for the Turks and Caicos Islands. An international business company is a corporation that does no business on the islands. A single individual can incorporate in the British Virgin Island. Bearer stock is allowed, but must be paid in full. Annual reports for exempt companies do not reflect names and addresses of shareholders or directors. A registered agent is required and is a resident in the islands. Shareholder and directors meetings can be held anywhere in the world.

Fraud Indicators

Fraud examiners will invariably come across offshore entities when examining organized crime elements with international connections. The fraud examiner should become familiar with the country of origin as well as the type of entity. An entity that is located in a "tax haven" country should be examined very closely. Indicators of fraudulent offshore entities are as follows:

1. No payments. The offshore entity either lends or invests funds in the United States. However, there are no interest or dividend payments going out.
2. Not U. S. registered. The offshore entity is not licensed to do business in the United States. A check with the Secretary of State Bureau of Corporations of any particular state shows that the corporation or business entity is not registered or licensed to conduct business in the state. Failure for the foreign entity to register with the state bars any legal recourse or remedy. What company would loan or invest funds without having some legal recourse if the capital provided is not protected?
3. Failure to file tax returns. The offshore entity does not file federal or state tax returns. In general, income derived in the United States by foreign entities is taxable at both federal and state levels.
4. No place of business. The entity does not have any place of business in either the country of origin or the United States. This will clearly show that the offshore entity is a means of concealing ownership of illegal funds.

Finance, investment, insurance companies, and trusts are the most common types of entities used to launder illegal gains from illegal activities through offshore companies.

Summary

The fraud examiner should pay close attention to foreign individuals and entities that are located offshore. Attention is particularly necessary when foreign individuals and entities are located in "tax haven" countries that have bank secrecy laws or customs. Many tax haven countries have treaties whereby a prosecutor can obtain information. In some countries, records of legal entities are public and are freely available. However, bank records are not available and will require some judicial proceeding to obtain them. Some of the tax haven countries cooperate with international law enforcement agencies, particularly in the drug-trafficking area. Official requests can be made, but should go through the Department of State. The fraud examiner should study the country's legal system and find out what records are available and how to obtain them. Records that fall in the public domain can be obtained by a consular officer and certified by him/her for use in federal or state courts. Various federal law enforcement agencies, i.e., Customs, FBI, and DEA have liaison offices in many countries. These representatives can help obtain information for law enforcement. For instance, they can see if a foreign corporation has a going business in the country of origin. They can secure public information and interview witnesses. For local law enforcement agencies, these resources should be utilized. All tax haven countries that allow bearer stocks and bonds require that they be paid in full before they are issued. When these bearer stocks and bonds are found in the course of searches, these securities have the same value as money. Depending upon the circumstances, these securities can be exchanged for cash.

Evidence

4

Introduction

Forensic accountants must gather evidence to support an investigation of a financial crime that too often takes much time and effort to gather and compile. The objective of this chapter is to show the forensic accountant what evidence is admissible in both civil and criminal court proceedings. The Federal Rules of Evidence (FRE) are used in this chapter, therefore, forensic accountants should check with local prosecutors to ensure these rules are applicable to state and local courts.

Evidence

Evidence is all means by which an alleged matter of fact is established or disproved. A forensic accountant can obtain documents and statements which show that a bank account has increased substantially. This is an evidentiary fact from which an inference may be drawn relative to the ultimate or principal fact, namely, that the subject was involved in a profitable activity. Evidence is legally admissible in court under the rules of evidence because it tends to support or prove a fact. Evidence is distinguished from proof in that the latter is the result or effect of evidence.

Direct evidence is that which proves the existence of the principal or fact without any inference or presumption. It is direct when those who have actual knowledge of the facts by means of their senses swear to the very facts in dispute. It may take the form of admissions or confessions made in or out of court.

Circumstantial evidence is that which tends to prove the existence of the principal fact by inference. The courts recognize the use of circumstantial evidence as a legitimate means of proof. It involves proving several material facts, which, when considered in their relationship to each other, tend to establish the existence of the principal or ultimate fact. Violations involving willful intent are provided by circumstantial evidence. It is the only type of evidence generally available to show such elements of a crime such as malice, intent, or motive, which exists only in the mind of the perpetrator of the act. Circumstantial evidence may be as convincing as direct evidence. Sometimes, a jury may find that it outweighs conflicting direct evidence.

Evidence may also be classified as oral, documentary, and real. Evidence may be presented orally through witnesses or by the submission of records or other physical objects. Oral testimony consists of statements made by living witnesses under oath. Documentary evidence consists of writings such as judicial and official records, contracts, deeds, and less formal writings such as letters, memorandums, and books and records of private persons or organizations. Maps, diagrams, and photographs are classified as documentary evidence.

Real or physical evidence relates to tangible objects or properties that are admitted in court or inspected by a trier of facts, such as a knife or pistol. Evidence must be relevant, material, and competent in order for it to be admissible in court.

Relevancy

Relevancy relates evidence in some manner to the principal fact. It implies a traceable and significant connection. It is sufficient if it constitutes one link in a chain of evidence or if it relates to facts that would constitute circumstantial evidence that a fact in issue did or did not exist. Rule 401 defines relevant evidence as "Evidence having any tendency to make the existence of any fact that is of consequence to the determination of the action more probable or less probable than it would be without the evidence." Rule 402 provides that "All relevant evidence is admissible, except as otherwise provided by the Constitution of the United States, by Act of Congress, or by other rules prescribed by the Supreme Court pursuant to statutory authority. Evidence, which is not relevant, is not admissible."

Investigators should obtain all facts that relate to the case. They should never omit any significant facts because of doubt regarding relevance. There are no set standards for relevancy because facts vary from case to case and judges have wide discretion in determining what evidence is relevant. Also, investigators should not omit evidence because of doubt as to its materiality or competency.

Materiality

Evidence is material if it is essential to the subject matter in dispute as to affect the outcome of a trial, or to help establish the guilt or innocence of the accused. This definition is included in the definition of relevancy.

Competency

Evidence must not only be relevant and persuasive, but also legally admissible. Relevant evidence may be incompetent and, hence, inadmissible because it is hearsay or not the best evidence. Evidence, such as documents, is competent if it was obtained in a manner, in a form, and from a source proper under the law.

Limited Admissibility

Evidence may not be admissible for one purpose, but does not preclude its use for another. A piece of evidence may not be admissible as independent proof of a principal fact and still may be admitted to corroborate another fact.

Hearsay

Hearsay has been defined as evidence, which does not come from the personal knowledge of the witness, but from of what he has heard others say or document prepared by others. Hearsay is secondhand evidence and is not admissible in court. An investigator's testimony that payees of corporate checks were for personal expenses of the subject, an officer of the corporation, is inadmissible as hearsay (Greenberg Rule). The personal nature of the payments should be proven through the subject's own records or others as to his admission, or testimony of the third parties.

Cross-examination is essential as a test of the truth of the facts offered. It provides an opportunity to test the credibility of the witness, his observations, memory, bias, prejudice, and possible errors. It subjects the witness to the penalties of perjury and may eliminate deliberate or unintentional misstatements of what he has been told.

Admissions and Confessions

An admission is not considered to be hearsay. An admission may be defined as a statement or act of a party, which is offered in evidence against him. It also may be defined as a prior oral or written statement or act which is inconsistent with his position in the pleadings or at trial. Admissions can be used either as evidence of facts or to discredit a party as a witness. They can be used only as to facts, not as to matters of law, opinion, or hearsay. A confession is a statement of a person that he is guilty of a crime.

Exceptions to Hearsay Rule

The courts have made certain exceptions to the hearsay rule. The exceptions are based on two principal reasons: necessity for use and probability of trustworthiness. The necessity rule usually comes into being from the unavailability of the person who made the statement to appear or testify. The court would, thereby, be deprived of evidence that is important in the decision of an issue. The evidence must also have the probability of truthfulness that will substitute for cross-examination. Evidence that meets the above standards is admissible as an exception to the hearsay rule. Other exceptions are as follows:

Business Records, Public Records, and Commercial Documents
Records containing entries made in the regular course of business, as well as marriage, baptismal, and similar certificates are admissible without testimony of the person who made the entries, if some witness properly identifies them. Public records made by an officer, in the performance of his duties, are also admissible after proper authentication.

Expert and Opinion Testimony
Expert opinions are the conclusions of a person who has been qualified as an expert in his field; they are admitted to aid the jury in its deliberations. Opinions of laymen may also be admitted into evidence under certain circumstances, e.g., handwriting recognition and

physical condition. Another example is that a police officer may give his opinion concerning the speed of an automobile. The basis for permitting this is that the police officer has specialized experience beyond that of the ordinary person, which would qualify him to give his opinion in the matter.

Reputation

A defendant in a prosecution may offer witnesses to testify as to his good reputation in the community where he lives. Such evidence is competent because it may tend to generate a reasonable doubt of his guilt. The evidence should be restricted to the character trait in issue and should bear an analogy to the nature of the charge. For instance, a witness for the defendant in a bribery case may be asked, on direct examination, if he knows the defendant's general reputation for peacefulness would be improper. The witnesses must confine their testimony to general reputation and may not testify about their own knowledge or observation of the defendant, or about his specific acts or courses of conduct. Once the defense has raised the issue of character, the prosecution may offer evidence of bad reputation in rebuttal of character testimony. Rule 405 provides that "On cross-examination, inquiry is allowable into relevant specific instances of conduct."

Records of Documents Affecting an Interest in Property

If a document affecting an interest in property, e.g., deed, is recorded in a public record and an applicable statute authorizes the recording of documents of that kind in that office, the record of such document may be admissible as proof of the original recorded document and its execution and delivery by each person by whom it purports to have been executed (FRE 803(114)).

Mental and Physical Condition

Contemporaneous or spontaneous declarations of a person may be admissible to prove his mental or physical condition. While such statements carry more weight when made to a physician for purposes of treatment, they may be competent even if made to family members or to other persons. Thus, a trial court in a fraud case might admit a lay witness's testimony that he heard the defendant complain of severe headaches and inability to concentrate just before preparing his alleged false travel expense voucher.

Excited Utterance (also known as "Spontaneous Declaration")

This has been defined as a "Statement relating to a startling event or condition made while the declarant was under the stress or excitement caused by the event or condition," (Rule 803.2). The trustworthiness of such statements lies in their spontaneity, for the occurrence must be startling enough to produce a spontaneous and unreflected utterance without time to contrive or to misrepresent.

Excited utterances may be made by participants or by bystanders, and a person who made or heard such statements may testify about them in court.

Recorded Recollection

A memorandum or record about which a witness once had knowledge, but at the time he is called to testify has insufficient recollection to enable him to testify fully and accurately, may be used in court. It must be shown, however, that the memorandum or record was made or adopted by the witness when the matter was fresh in his memory and reflects his knowledge correctly. If admitted, the memorandum or record may be read into evidence, but may not itself be received as an exhibit unless offered by an adverse party (Rule 303.5).

Absence of Entry

The FRE also provides for an exception to the hearsay rule with respect to evidence of the absence of an entry in records kept in the regular course of business and absence of a public record or entry if the matters were of a kind in which the business or public office ordinarily made and preserved a record. It must be shown that a diligent search of the records has been made and the evidence may be ruled inadmissible if "The sources of the information or other circumstances indicate trustworthiness," Rules 308.7 and .10.

Hearsay Exceptions: Declarant Unavailable

The following exceptions to the hearsay rule relate to situations in which the declarant (person who made the statements) is unavailable for the trial. For example, if he has died, has disappeared, is mentally or physically incapacitated, is beyond the jurisdiction of the court, or is exempted by ruling of the court on the ground of privilege concerning the subject matter of his statement.

Former Testimony

Testimony given as a witness at another hearing of the same or a different proceeding, or in a deposition taken in compliance with law in the course of the same or another proceeding, if the party against whom the testimony is now offered (in a criminal proceeding) had an opportunity and similar motive to develop the testimony by direct, cross- or redirect examination (Rule 804(b)(1)). Testimony and evidence in civil proceedings can be used later on in criminal proceedings.

Statement Against Interest

A statement against interest relates to an oral or written declaration by one not a party to the action and not available to testify. It must be shown that such statement was, at the time of its making, so far contrary to the declarant's pecuniary or proprietary interest, or so far tended to make invalid a claim by him against another, that a reasonable person in his position would not have made the statement unless he believed it to be true. For example, in order to establish that a defendant paid off a large debt with currency on a certain date, the government may prove the payment through an entry in the personal diary of the deceased creditor. The diary could be identified by a relative of the deceased as having been found among his papers after his death (Rule 804(b)(3)). Some courts have extended this rule to include statements against penal interest.

Dying Declarations

Dying declarations are statements made by the victim of a homicide who believes that death is imminent. To be admissible, such statements must relate only to facts concerning the cause for and circumstances surrounding the homicide charged. They are admitted from the necessities of the case to prevent a failure of justice. Furthermore, the sense of impending death is presumed to remove all temptation of falsehood. The statements may be admitted only in a murder trial, or under Rule 804(b)(2), in a civil proceeding.

Documentary Evidence

Documentary evidence is evidence consisting of writing and documents as distinguished from oral evidence.

Best Evidence Rule

The best evidence rule, which applies only to documentary evidence, is that the best proof of the contents of a document is the document itself. The best evidence rule, requiring production of the original document, is confined to cases where it is sought to prove the contents of the document. Production consists of either making the writing available to the court or opposing counsel. Facts about a document other than its contents are provable without its production. For example, the fact that a sales contract was made is a fact separate from the actual terms of the contract and may be proven by testimony alone.

The best evidence rule has applied essentially to documents. Modern techniques of storing data have made its expansion to include computers, photographic systems, and other new developments. In the Rule 1001, writings and recordings are defined as "Letters, words, or numbers, or their equivalent, set down by handwriting, typewriting, printing, or their equivalent, set down by handwriting, typewriting, printing, photostatting, photographing, magnetic impulse, mechanical or electronic recording, or other form of data compilation." The original of a writing or recording is defined as "The writing or recording itself or any counterpart intended to have the same effect by a person executing or issuing it."

Certain documents, such as leases, contracts, or even letters, which are executed "signed" on more than one copy are all considered originals. Any one of the copies may be produced as an original.

Application of Best Evidence Rule

When an original document is not produced and its absence is satisfactorily explained, secondary evidence which could consist of testimony of witnesses or a copy of writing, will be received to prove its contents. Unavailability of the original document is a question to be decided by the trial judge, just as he decides all questions regarding admissibility of evidence.

The reason for the rule is to prevent fraud, mistake, or error. For example, the testimony of an investigator as to the contents of a sales invoice will be excluded unless it is shown that the invoice itself is unavailable. If the document is unavailable, the investigator's testimony is admissible even though the person who prepared the invoice is available to testify. The best evidence rule will not be invoked to exclude oral testimony of one witness merely because another witness could give more conclusive testimony.

Secondary Evidence

All evidence that does not meet the best evidence rule is classified as secondary evidence and is a substitute for better evidence. Secondary evidence may be either the testimony of a witness or a copy of a document. There is no settled rule for which one of these is a higher degree of secondary evidence. Secondary evidence of any nature may be admitted in court. There must be evidence of the present or former existence of an original document. It must be established that the original has been destroyed; destruction provable by an eyewitness. The party proving the document must have used all reasonable means to obtain the original, that is, he must have made such diligent search as was reasonable under the facts. Some cases have specifically set the rule that search must be made in the place where the document was last known to be, or inquiry must be made of the person who last had custody of it. In every case, the sufficiency of the search is a matter to be determined by the court. If a document is offered as secondary evidence, it must be shown to be a correct copy of the original to be admissible.

When the original document has been destroyed by the party attempting to prove its contents, secondary evidence of the contents will be admitted if the destruction was in the ordinary course of business, or by mistake or even intentionally, provided it was not done for any fraudulent purpose.

With respect to an original document in the possession of an opponent, Rule 1004 provides that the original is not required and that other evidence of the contents is admissible. If, at the time the original was under the control of the party against whom offered, the party was put on notice by the pleadings or otherwise that the contents would be subject to proof at the hearing and that the party does not produce the original at the hearing.

Admissibility of Specific Forms of Documentary Evidence

Records of regularly conducted (business) activity. Rule 803(6) states "A memorandum, report, record, or data compilation, in any form, of acts, events, conditions, opinions, or diagnoses, made at or near the time by, or from information transmitted by, a person with knowledge, if kept in the course of regularly conducted business activity, and if it was the regular practice of that business activity to make the memorandum, report, record, or data compilation, all as shown by the testimony of the custodian or other qualified witness, unless the source of information or the method or circumstances of preparation indicate lack of trustworthiness, is admissible." The term "business" as used in this paragraph includes business, institution, association, profession, occupation, and call of every kind, whether or not conducted for profit.

The above rule permits showing that an entry was made in a book maintained in the regular course of business without producing the particular person who made the entry and having him identify it. For example, in proving a sale, an employee of the customer may appear with the original purchase journal and cash disbursement book of the customer and testify that these were books of original entry showing purchases by the customer even though the witness is not the person who made the entries.

Regular Course of Business

This rule relies on records made under circumstances showing no reason or motive to misrepresent the facts. As stated by the courts "The rule contemplates that certain events are regularly recorded as 'routine reflections of the day-to-day operations of the business so that the character of the records and their earmarks of reliability import trustworthiness'." For example, the rule is applied to bank records under the theory that the accuracy of the records is essential to the very life of the bank's business.

The fact that a record has been kept in the regular course of business is not enough to make it admissible. The rules of competency and relevancy must still be applied. If a ledger is offered in evidence to prove entries posted from a journal which is available, the journal itself, as the book of original entry, should be produced.

If it is the practice to photograph, photostat, or microfilm the business records mentioned above, such reproductions, when satisfactorily identified, are as admissible as the original. Also, enlargements of the original reproductions are admissible if the original reproductions are in existence and available for inspection under the direction of the court. This rule is particularly helpful in connection with bank records because of the common practice of microfilming ledger sheets, deposit tickets, and checks.

Photographs, Photostats, and Microfilmed Copies

Photographs, photostats, and microfilmed copies of writings not made in the regular course of business are considered secondary evidence of the contents, generally inadmissible if the original can be produced and no reason is given for failure to produce it. The same rule is usually applied where the original is already in evidence and no reason has been given for offering the copy. However, notes of the advisory committee regarding the Federal Rules of Evidence indicate an intent to liberalize the rule with respect to photostat copies to the extent that such copies may be admitted in evidence in absence of a showing of some reason for requiring the original (Rule 1003).

A photographic or photostat reproduction of a document may be admitted after evidence has been produced that the original cannot be obtained and that the reproduction is an exact and accurate copy. This principle has been followed where the original was in the hands of the defendant and the government could compel its production. It has further been held that a photograph of a promissory note taken because the writing was becoming faded and illegible was admissible in place of the illegible original.

When photostats of documents are obtained during an investigation, they should be initialed on the back, after comparison with the original, by the one who made the photostat or by the investigator who obtained the document which was photostatted. The date of such comparison should be noted following the initial. The source of the original document should be set out on the reverse of the photostat, or on an initialed attachment or memorandum relating to each photostat or group of photostats covered by the one memorandum. This procedure will ensure proper authentication at a trial.

Transcripts

Transcripts are copies of writings. They are admissible as secondary evidence. The investigator should insure proper authentication for their admission in court when the original documents are not available. The investigator should compare any transcript with the original and certify it. The certification should show the date of the transcript, the author, where it originated, and the source. Each page should be identified to show that it forms part of the whole or is a partial.

Charts, Schedules, and Summaries

Charts, schedules, and summaries prepared by a summary/expert witness can be placed in evidence if they are summaries of evidence previously admitted in court. Charts, summaries, and schedules have been permitted in the jury room to aid in the jury's deliberations. Schedules may be used to summarize specific business transactions, i.e., the accumulated cost of a construction project after the introduction of the pertinent records and testimony. Prejudicial headings or titles should be avoided, e.g., "false claims."

Notes, Diaries, Workpapers, and Memorandums

Notes, diaries, workpapers, and memorandums made by auditors and accountants are not considered evidence. Auditors and accountants can use them on the witness stand or prior to testifying as an aid to recollection, or they may be introduced into evidence by the adverse party if they constitute impeaching evidence. Any documents used by a witness are subject to inspection by opposing counsel.

Proving Specific Transactions

It is not sufficient to rely on documents and recorded entries. Documents and recorded entries are not facts, but are a written description of the event. Witnesses will have to testify about the transaction and authenticate the documents. This is called the Greenberg Rule. The investigator must interview the party of the transaction to insure the documents or entries substantiate the circumstances. The witness may have additional facts or documents relating to the transaction or other transactions. Vendors should be questioned as to all transactions and any other information. Sellers and agents should be questioned as to the details of the transactions for possible nominees and nonexistent parties. Complete documentation and witness interviews should be obtained for each and every transaction as much as possible.

Official Records

The provisions of the Federal Rules of Evidence and rules of criminal and civil procedure cover the admissibility of official public records and copies or transcripts, thereof, in federal proceedings.

Authentication of Official Records

Evidence must be authenticated in order to establish its reliability. It must be shown that a certain document actually is an official record of a particular state or local government. Document authenticity does not mean it will be admissible in court.

Admissibility of Official Records

The admissibility of official records and copies is provided by the Federal Rules of Evidence. Rule 1005 states "The contents of an official record, or of a document authorized to be recorded or filed and actually recorded or filed, including data compilations in any form, if otherwise admissible, may be proven by copy, certified as correct in accordance with Rule 902 or testified to be correct by a witness who has compared it with the original." If a copy, which complies with the foregoing, cannot be obtained by the exercise of reasonable diligence, then other evidence of the contents may be given. Under this rule, there is no requirement that the original be introduced.

Rule 902 provides that extrinsic evidence of authenticity is not required for certain types of documents, including public documents under seal, certified copies of public records, newspapers and periodicals, trade inscriptions and the like, or labels purporting to have been affixed in the course of business and indicating ownership, control, or origin, and commercial papers and related documents to the extent provided by general commercial law. This does not mean that the documents will be admitted.

A method of authentication of copies of federal records is set forth in the Federal Rules of Civil Procedure, which is made applicable to criminal cases by Rule 27 of Federal Rules of Criminal Procedure. Authentication of a copy of a government record under these rules would consist of a certification by the officer having custody of the records and verification of the official status of the certifying officer by a federal district judge over the seal of the court.

State and Territorial Statutes and Proceedings

The admissibility of copies of legislative acts of any state, territory, or possession of the United States and of court records and judicial proceedings is provided for in the United States Code 28 USC 1738 as follows:

> Such acts, records, and judicial proceedings or copies thereof, so authenticated, shall have the same full faith and credit in every court within the United States and its territories and possessions as they have by law or usage in the courts of such state, territory, or possession from which they are taken.

The procedures for authentication of the above records are recited in the same section of the code.

Nonjudicial records or books kept in any public office of any state, territory, or possession of the United States, or copies thereof, are made admissible by the United States Code 28 USC 1739 and given full faith and credit upon proper authentication. Rules 901 and 902 provide procedures for authentication of the documents covered in this section.

Chain of Custody

"Chain of custody" is an expression that is applied to consecutive custodians of the physical items or documents. Documents or other items used in a crime are generally admissible in court. The judge must be satisfied that the writing or other item is in the same condition as it was when the crime was committed. The witnesses through whom the document or other item is sought to be introduced must be able to identify it as being in the same condition as when it was recovered. Investigators must identify and preserve in original condition all evidentiary matter that may be offered into evidence.

Identification of Seized Documentary Evidence

In order for a seized document to be admissible as evidence, it is necessary to prove that it is the document that was seized and that it is in the same condition as it was when seized. Since several persons may handle it in the interval between the seizure and the trial of the case, it should be adequately marked at the time of seizure for later identification. Its custody must be shown from that time until it is introduced in court.

An investigator who seizes documents should at once identify them by some markings so that he can later testify that they are the documents seized and that they are in the same condition as they were when seized. The investigator should put his initials and the date of seizure on the back of each document, or put the document into an envelope and write a description and any other identifying information on the face of the envelope and seal the envelope.

Constitutional Provisions

The principal constitutional limitations relating to investigative techniques are the Fourth, Fifth, and Sixth Amendments to the U.S. Constitution and similar provisions in the state constitutions.

The Fourth Amendment

The Fourth Amendment provides:

> The right of the people to be secure in their persons, houses, papers, and effects, against unreasonable searches and seizures, shall not be violated, and no warrants shall issue, but upon probable cause, supported by oath or affirmation, and particularly describing the place to be searched and the persons or things to be seized.

This protection is given to corporations as well as individuals.

The Fifth Amendment

The relevant part of the U.S. Constitution's Fifth Amendment provides:

> No person shall be compelled in any criminal case to be a witness against himself, nor shall he be deprived of life, liberty, or property without due process of law.

This privilege is given only to individuals, not to corporations.

The Sixth Amendment

The relevant part of the U.S. Constitution's Sixth Amendment states:

> In all criminal prosecutions the accused shall enjoy the right to have the assistance of counsel for his defense.

Statutory Provisions

Statutes can be passed permitting financial investigations if they are within constitutional guidelines. Challenges to financial investigations have been litigated primarily in federal courts, particularly tax-related cases. Therefore, federal court decisions are based on the federal constitution and statutes, most of which deal with tax cases.

Court Decisions

U.S. Supreme Court decisions are based on the U.S. Constitution, which are binding on state courts and officers. Federal court decisions relating to federal statutes are not directly binding on state officers since they operate under state statutes. But state statutes must conform to federal statutes either directly or indirectly; so the rulings on similar provisions are quite relevant on how the state courts can interpret its statutes.

Access to Books and Records

Federal and many state statutes provide that certain auditors can examine a subject's books and records and summon subjects (including third party witnesses) to come before them to give testimony or bring records. The Fourth Amendment prohibits illegal search except for probable cause. The Fifth Amendment prohibits self-incrimination. If the federal and state auditors request these records in the normal course of their business, then this does not violate the Fourth or Fifth Amendment. If the subject voluntarily submits to the auditor's request, then this is not a violation of his Fourth or Fifth Amendment rights. However, if the auditor requests these records for a criminal investigator without the suspect's knowledge, then this is a violation of the suspect's Fourth Amendment rights (*United States v. Nicholas J. Tweel*, 550 F2d 297).

Some courts and state statutes permit certain regulatory searches to be made without warrants, but these regulatory searches cannot be used in criminal cases.

Privileged Relationships

The rule on privileged communications is based on common law and the legislature's belief that it is necessary to maintain the confidentiality of certain communications. It applies only to those communications which relate to a unique relationship. They must have been made in confidence and not in the presence of third parties unless the speaker has a privileged relationship with the third party. Common law has granted the privilege to the following relationships:

1. Husband — Wife
2. Attorney — Client
3. Ordained clergyman — Parishioner
4. Physician — Patient
5. Reporter — Source
6. Accountant — Client (not recognized in federal courts in criminal cases)

Only the holder of a privilege or someone authorized by him can assert a privilege. The privilege can be waived if he fails to assert it after having notice and an opportunity to assert it. He also waives it if he discloses a significant part of the communication or if the communication is made in the presence of a third party whose presence is not indispensable to the conversation. The presence of a secretary or an interpreter would not abolish the privilege.

The client holds the attorney-client privilege, not the lawyer, and the privilege does not terminate at the client's death. The communication is protected only if its purpose was related to legal consultation. An exception is where the attorney was consulted for the purpose of aiding in the perpetration of a crime or fraud or for the giving of business advice.

Foreign Evidence

Evidence from foreign countries is admissible in federal courts. Some criminal elements operate on an international level. Therefore, it is important that foreign countries, when known, be asked for assistance and cooperation. In most cases, foreign governments will cooperate and give assistance as necessary. The United States has many mutual assistance, extradition, and tax treaties. As a general rule, only high tax countries have tax treaties with other high tax countries. Tax haven countries will not provide financial information in criminal or civil tax cases. Some tax haven countries will provide financial information in nontax criminal cases. However, the requesting country must certify that the evidence provided will not be used for tax purposes.

Foreign Public Documents

Foreign public documents are admissible in federal courts when properly attested and certified. Also, a secretary of an embassy or legation, consul general, consul, or consular agent of the United States may make a final certification. If reasonable opportunity has been given to all parties to investigate the authenticity and accuracy of official documents, the court may, for good cause shown, order that they be treated as presumptively authentic without final certification or permit them to be evidenced by an attested summary with or without final certification. Foreign public records are the most easily obtained since public access is readily obtained.

Foreign Documents

Title 18 USC 3491 provides that any book, paper, statement, writing, or other document, or any portion thereof, of whatever character and in whatever form, as well as any copy thereof, equally with the original, which is not in the United States shall, when certified, be admissible in evidence in any criminal action or proceeding in any court of the United States. This clearly shows that foreign documents, when property certified, are admissible in criminal cases.

Consular Officers Commission

U.S. consular officers are responsible for taking oral or written interrogatories of witnesses in foreign countries. They are also tasked with the authority of authenticating foreign documents that will be used in any criminal proceeding. The court shall make provisions for the selection of foreign counsel to represent each party to the criminal action. Selection of foreign counsel shall be made within 10 days prior to taking testimony. Foreign counsel does not represent the United States. If the consular officer has an interest in the outcome of the criminal action or proceeding, or has participated in the investigation or preparation of evidence, then the consular officer is disqualified from taking oral or written interrogatories (18 USC 3492).

Deposition on Foreign Documents

Title 18 USC 3493 provides that the consular officer shall caution and swear in testimony as to the whole truth. The witness testimony shall be reduced to writing by the consular officer or by some person under his personal supervision. Every foreign document shall be annexed to such testimony and subscribed by each witness for the purpose of establishing the genuineness of such document. The consular officer shall obtain an interpreter if needed.

Foreign Records

The rules for admission of foreign documents are about the same as domestic documents. Foreign records of regularly conducted activity, or a copy of such record, shall be admissible as evidence provided that such document is authenticated as being genuine.

Foreign Witnesses

If a person is held in custody in a foreign country which is needed in the United States in a criminal proceeding, the Attorney General shall request the foreign country to temporarily transfer that person to the United States for the purpose of giving testimony. The personal shall be returned to the foreign country when the task is finished. If a treaty or convention is in effect with the foreign country, then the terms of the treaty or convention shall be adhered.

Awareness

The forensic accountant should always be aware of the rules of evidence. Evidence obtained improperly is inadmissible, thus, becomes worthless. The following checklist should help in verifying compliance with the rules of evidence:

1. Chain of Custody. Is a log of evidence obtained maintained and who has had access to the evidence?
2. Witnesses. Are interview memorandums, depositions, and more maintained for each witness? Also, are name, addresses, and contact telephone numbers maintained for each witness?
3. Physical Evidence. Is physical evidence properly secured? Only copies of documents should be used for marking and not originals.
4. Diary. The fraud examiner should maintain a diary showing dates of interviews, when and where evidence was obtained, and a description of work performed.
5. Notes. All interview notes should be kept and not destroyed.
6. Expenses. All expenses should be documented. If informants are paid, then some type of receipt should be obtained. Informants can initial a diary entry or appointment book.

In the Chapter 14: Accounting and Auditing Techniques, there is a recommended witness list that can be maintained on a computer database. This witness list will help the forensic accountant in keeping track of witnesses and evidence. It can also help the prosecutor in planning and scheduling of witnesses for trial.

Summary

Both fraud examiners and law enforcement must have some knowledge of the rules that allow evidence into court. No prosecutor wants evidence that is not admissible. If inadmissible evidence is entered into court then the defendant has grounds on appeal to get his conviction thrown out. The Supreme Court, under its "exclusionary rule," will overturn convictions when inadmissible evidence is introduced in court. Evidence must be properly guarded and handled. Any defacing or alteration of evidence will make the evidence inadmissible. Evidence can only be obtained in a legal manner. Security procedures should be set up and followed in order to preserve evidence. Without evidence, there is no case. Evidence from any part of the world is admissible provided that it is obtained in a proper and legal manner.

Net Worth Theory

5

Introduction

The Internal Revenue Service was the first to use the Net Worth Method. . According to Section 61, Internal Revenue Code, all taxpayers are to report all taxable income. When taxpayers do not report all their taxable income, the IRS devised the Net Worth Method to determine the amount of unreported taxable income. The IRS acknowledges that this method is appropriate in cases where the taxpayer accumulates vast amount of assets. It is not useful in cases where the taxpayer has little or no assets and spends all his income on "lavish" living. When Congress passed the RICO Act in 1970, it expanded the use of the Net Worth Method to organized crime.

Tax Use

The Net Worth Method is preferred by the Justice Department and was used as far back as 1931 on Alfonso Capone (2 USTC 786) by the IRS. The Net Worth Method is not an accounting method, but is a method of proof by circumstantial or indirect evidence. The IRS attempts to establish an "opening net worth" which is defined as assets less liabilities. It then proves increases in the taxpayer's net worth for each succeeding year during the period under examination. The taxpayer's nondeductible personal expenditures less nontaxable income are added to each year's increase in net worth. This is compared to income reported and any differences is considered to be unreported income. The following chart (Table 5-1) is presented to illustrate the theory.

Table 5-1 Tax Net Worth Theory

Year One	Year Two
Assets	Assets
Less: Liabilities	Less: Liabilities
Equals: Net Worth	Equals: Net Worth
	Less: Net Worth Year One
	Equals: Net Worth Increase
	Add: Nondeductible Expenditures
	Less: Nontaxable Income
	Equals: Corrected Taxable Income
	Less: Reported Taxable Income
	Equals: Unreported Taxable Income

RICO Use

The above theory relates to tax purposes. The use in RICO and other economic crime cases requires a different set of principals and a different presentation. The basic theory in a RICO Net Worth Method is similar to the tax method. The basic objective is different. In a RICO Net Worth Method, the objective is to determine the amount of illegal income. Like the tax purpose Net Worth Method, the RICO Net Worth Method is defined as assets less liabilities. It proves increases in net worth for each succeeding year. The subject's personal expenditures are added to each succeeding year's increase in net worth. This gives the gross income. The legal income is subtracted to determine the amount of illegal income derived. The following chart (Table 5-2) is presented to illustrate the theory.

Table 5-2 RICO Net Worth Theory

Year One	Year Two
Assets	Assets
Less: Liabilities	Less: Liabilities
Equals: Net Worth	Equals: Net Worth
	Less: Net Worth Year One
	Equals: Net Worth Increase
	Add: Personal Expenses
	Equals: Legal Income
	Less: Legal Income
	Equals: Illegal Income

History

The first Net Worth case was *Alfonso Capone v. United States* (2 USTC 786). The U.S. Supreme Court heard the first Net Worth case in 1943 with *United States v. Johnson* (43-1 USTC 9470). In the Johnson case, the Supreme Court approved its use as a potent weapon in establishing taxable income from undisclosed sources when all other efforts failed. Since then the Net Worth Method has been widened. Until now it is used in run of the mill cases, regardless of the tax deficiency involved. The Supreme Court has denied certiorari because the cases involved were only questions of evidence and presented no important questions of law. The Court of Appeals had serious doubts regarding the implications of the Net Worth Method. In 1954, the Supreme Court granted certiorari in four cases. One of these was *M.L. Holland v. United States* (54-2 USTC 9714), the High Court pointed out the dangers that must be kept in mind in order to assure adequate appraisal of facts in individual cases. These dangers include:

a. Cash hoard. A favorite defense is the existence of substantial cash on hand. The defense is that the cash is made up of many years of savings which, for various reasons, were hidden and not expended until the prosecution period. Obviously, the government has great difficulty in refuting such a contention. However, this can be overcome when the emergence of hidden savings also uncovers a fraud on the taxpayer's creditors. Also, taxpayers frequently give lead to agents indicating specific sources of his cash on hand. This forces the government to run down all such leads in face of grave investigative difficulties; still, a failure to do so might jeopardize the position of the taxpayer.

b. Assumptions. The method requires assumptions among which is the equation of unexplained increases in net worth with unreported taxable income. It may be those gifts, inheritances, loans, and the like that account for newly acquired wealth. Base figures have a way of acquiring an existence of their own independent of the evidence which gave rise to them. Therefore, the jury needs the appropriate guarding instructions.

c. Poor memory or business judgment. The taxpayer may be honest, yet, is unable to recount his financial history. The Net Worth Method could tend to shift the burden of proof from the government to the taxpayer. The taxpayer would then be compelled to come forward with evidence which could lend support to the government by showing loose business methods or apparent evasiveness.

d. Books and records. When the government uses the Net Worth Method and the books and records of the taxpayer appear correct on their face, an inference of willful tax evasion could be inferred which might be unjustified, where the circumstances surrounding the deficiency are as consistent with innocent mistakes as with willful violation. On the other hand, the very failure of the books to disclose a proved deficiency might include deliberate falsification.

e. Taxpayer's statements. The prosecution, in many cases, relies on the taxpayer's statements made to revenue agents in the course of their investigation. When revenue agents confront the taxpayer with an apparent deficiency, the revenue agent may be more concerned with a quick settlement than an honest search for the truth. The prosecution may pick and choose from the taxpayer's statements relying on the favorable portion and throwing aside that which does not bolster the taxpayer's position. An investigation must not only obtain inculpatory evidence, but also exculpatory evidence.

f. Time periods. The statute defines the offenses by individual years. While the government may be able to prove with reasonable accuracy an increase in net worth over a period of years, it often has great difficulty in relating that income sufficiently to any specific prosecution year. Unless the increase can be reasonably allocated to the appropriate tax year, the taxpayer may be convicted on counts of which he is innocent.

The Supreme Court also added that the trial courts should approach these cases in full realization that the taxpayer may be ensnared in a system which is hard for the defendant to refute. Charges should be especially clear and formal in instructions as to the nature of the Net Worth Method, the assumptions on which it rests, and the inferences available to both sides.

The main thrust of the Net Worth Method since the Holland case is that the Net Worth Method can be used against the ordinary average citizen without criminal affiliations. It may also be used to show that the taxpayer's books do not reflect true income, or to corroborate specific adjustments in the agent's report. For the revenue agents, they must make an effort to seek the truth rather than try to get quick settlement to close the case.

Since the Holland case, there have been many court decisions which affect either the net worth presentation or the source of such item on the net worth. Some of the court decisions should be kept in mind when preparing a Net Worth Statement. They are as follows:

Burden of Proof

Jacobs v. United States (54-1 USTC 9704) states that the burden of proof rests with the taxpayer in rebutting a Net Worth Method, especially, when he does not keep required books and records.

Cash on Hand

In *W. Epstein* (57-2 USTC 9797), the government used cash-on-hand figures which came from financial statements submitted by the taxpayer to his bank and reports to Dun and Bradstreet. On the other hand, the courts have ruled that the IRS may not determine that the taxpayer had no cash on hand at the beginning of a specified period merely because the taxpayer made no affirmative showing to the contrary (*Thomas*, 56-1 USTC 9449, and *L. Fuller*, 63-1 USTC 9248).

Family Group

In *William G. Lias* (56-2 USTC 9817), the court approved a consolidated net worth of family members, where the taxpayer had no permanent books and refused to furnish financial statements. From the combined taxable income, agents deducted income reported or adjusted for the other members of the family group and treated the balance as taxable income of the taxpayer.

Cost of Living

In *H. G. Leach* (36 TCM 998), the court allowed the use of cost of living data supplied by the Bureau of Labor Statistics, but adjustments were made to reflect the size of the taxpayer's family and their geographical location. This is a civil case, it can't be used in a criminal case. It can be inferred that this data can be used in civil RICO cases as well. So far, it has not been tried.

Corroboration

In *Daniel Smith v. United States* (54-2 USTC 9715), the court determined that the government, in a criminal case, must corroborate a defendant's opening statement of net worth. The use of the taxpayer's tax returns which shows poor financial history prior to the prosecution period is corroboration of the defendant's opening net worth. However, in *Greenberg v. United States* (61-2 USTC 9727), a criminal case, the agent prepared a check spread and made the assumption that all expenditures were personal in nature. Further, no records or admissions of the defendant corroborated the agent's testimony, nor did any payee or other third party testify. This case pointed out that the use of check spreads or any other method used must be corroborated by third parties and not the agent's conclusions or assumptions.

RICO Use

Congress, since the Holland case, has enacted new laws and amended others in order to fight organized crime and drug kingpins. The Comprehensive Crime Control Act of 1984 and the Anti-Drug Abuse Act of 1986 have now forced the use of the Net Worth Method to be used in nontax cases. In civil cases, the Net Worth Method is used to identify assets for seizure and forfeiture. In criminal cases, the Net Worth Method is used to show the amount of financial benefit derived from some illegal activity. Under 18 USC 371, the prosecution can obtain a conviction under the Conspiracy section to defraud the United States government. In *Klein v. United States* (355 US 924), the conspiracy to defraud the United States by impeding, impairing, obstructing, and defeating the lawful functions of the Department of the Treasury in the collection of taxes was upheld. No proof of financial loss to the government was necessary.

U.S. Attorneys, as well as state attorneys, whose states have adopted or copied U.S. Title 18 laws, have been obligated to rely on the Net Worth Method in proving both their civil and criminal cases. Title 18 USC 1963(a)(b), Racketeering Influenced Corrupt Organizations, provides the following:

> ... In lieu of a fine otherwise authorized by this section, a defendant who derives profits or other proceeds from an offense may be fined not more than twice the gross profits or other proceeds. (b) Property subject to criminal forfeiture under this section includes: (1) Real property including things growing on, affixed to, and found in land; and (2) Tangible and intangible personal property, including rights, privileges, interests, claims, and securities.

The Net Worth Method provides prosecutors the precise means of determining the illegal gains and, at the same time, identifying the assets and expenditures. For prosecutors to get twice the gross profits, one must first determine the amount of the gross profit. The Net Worth Method, from an accountant's point of view, provides a complete snapshot of a person's financial affairs over a specified period of time.

Continuing Criminal Enterprises

Congress, in addition to the RICO act, passed the Continuing Criminal Enterprise Act (CCE). This act was passed by Congress to combat drug trafficking. Title 21 USC 848 defines Continuing Criminal Enterprise as being any person, in concert of five or more people, who occupies a position of organizer and supervisory position who obtains substantial income or resources. The alternative fine is "A defendant who derives profits or other proceeds from an offense may be fined not more than twice the gross profits or other proceeds (21 USC 855)." It is clear from this statute that prosecutors can use the Net Worth Method of proving illegal gains and identifying assets for forfeiture.

Connection

In *United States v. J.C. Pate Jr.*, the Court of Appeals, 11 Circuit, made a ruling in a drug forfeiture case. To demonstrate the substantial connection between property and illegal drug transaction in forfeiture action, the government is not required to show the relationship between property and a specific drug transaction. However, the claimant can meet his burden of proof in civil forfeiture proceedings to establish by a preponderance of evidence that the property is not subject to forfeiture either by rebutting the government's evidence that property represents proceeds of illegal drug activity or by showing that the claimant is an innocent owner without knowledge of the property's connection with illegal drug activities. In order to establish probable cause for forfeiture under Section 881(a)(6), the government must show that "A substantial connection exists between the property to be forfeited and an illegal exchange of a controlled substance." The government's burden of demonstrating probable cause requires "Less than prima-facie proof, but more than mere suspicion." The Net Worth Method is considered one of the best methods of showing the relationship between illegal gains and the related asset acquisitions if properly prepared and documented.

When Use is Required

The Net Worth Method should be used in tax cases when one or more of the following conditions prevail:

a. Subject maintains no books and records.
b. Subject's books and records are not available.
c. Subject's books and records are inadequate.
d. Subject withholds books and records.

A taxpayer's keeping of accurate records does not prevent the use of the Net Worth Method. The government can still use the method to either confirm or deny the taxpayer's declarations. It can be used in either organized crime and illegal activities or in general fraud cases. The Net Worth Method can be used as a primary means of proving taxable income or it can be used to corroborate or test the accuracy of reported taxable income.

The Net Worth Method should be used in RICO cases when one or more of the following conditions prevail:

a. The target acquires a large amount of assets.
b. The target spends beyond his means.
c. The target is a high level drug trafficker where most, if not all, witnesses against him are drug distributors for him.
d. Illegal income needs to be determined in order to determine the forfeiture amount.

Theory

When the determination has been made to use the Net Worth Method, the questions of how to prepare and present items on the Net Worth Schedule arise. The following guidelines are provided.

As a general rule for tax Net Worth Method purposes, items on the Net Worth Schedule should be treated in the manner prescribed for tax purposes. Only cost figures should be used. Market values can be used, but only in extreme or unusual circumstances or if the tax law and regulations require it.

As a general rule for RICO Net Worth Method purposes, the source and use of the Funds principle is to be applied. Only cost figures should be used. Market values cannot be used unless they relate, either directly or indirectly, to the source and use of funds. No phantom figures are to be used. Phantom figures are defined as accounting entries for amortization, depreciation, and depletion allowances. These figures do not reflect the use of funds and, therefore, cannot be used.

Cash on Hand

You must anticipate this particular problem and show that the taxpayer had no large sum of cash for which he or she was not given credit. Consequently, it is important that you interview the taxpayer early in the investigation to tie down a maximum cash accumulation. You should attempt to obtain the following:

a.   The maximum amount claimed to be on hand at the end of each year from the starting point through the present.
b.   How it was accumulated (from what sources).
c.   Where it was kept and in what denominations.
d.   Who had knowledge of it?
e.   Who counted it?
f.   When and where it was spent.

All of the above information is necessary to establish the consistency and reliability of the taxpayer's statements. Usually, no direct cash-on-hand evidence is available, but statements made as to the sources, amount, and use of funds can be corroborated or refuted with circumstantial evidence.

Examples of evidence, which may tend to negate the existence of a cash hoard, include:

a.   Written or oral admissions of the taxpayer to investigating officers concerning a small amount of cash on hand
b.   Financial statements prepared by the taxpayer showing a low net worth and/or cash on hand
c.   Compromises of overdue debts by the taxpayer
d.   Foreclosure proceedings against the taxpayer
e.   Collection actions against the taxpayer
f.   Tax returns (or no returns) evidencing little or no income in prior years
g.   Loan records
h.   Consistent use of checking and savings accounts

It may be possible to reconstruct the taxpayer's cash on hand from prior earning records. If cash on hand for an earlier period can be reasonably established, income earned from that period to the starting point could be used to establish a maximum available cash on hand.

The problem for cash on hand or cash hoard is the same for both RICO Net Worth Method purposes as it is for tax Net Worth Method purposes. However, for tax purposes, the agent is more likely to interview the taxpayer, while for RICO Net Worth Method purposes, the investigator will either not want to interview the target or will not be able to do so because of some legal or safety reason.

Cash in Banks

The main problem here can be whether to use the bank statement balances or use the book balances. Either can be used, however, if book balances are used then bank reconciliations must be provided as well. Whether book balances are used or bank balances are used, you must be consistent in its use. One cannot use book balances for one year and the bank balance the next. Bank balances can be used from some bank accounts while book balances can be used for other bank accounts. Each bank account must use a consistent method.

Inventory

Taxpayers tend to understate their inventories by using various devices. Large profits can be made by stealing or fencing stolen goods. This is particularly true in business "bust outs" when a taxpayer purchases inventory on credit at one location and transports the inventory to another location where it is sold off, leaving the creditors holding the bag. A problem arises in correcting continuing understatements of inventory. The resulting increase in closing inventory in a closed year creates a deficiency that could not be corrected due to the statute of limitations. A possible remedy in this situation is IRC 481 regarding changes in method of accounting. The agent should verify inventory in stock. IRM 424(10) provides the minimum tests to be made. In using the RICO Net Worth Method, it is unlikely that the investigator can verify inventory. The investigator might be able to verify inventory from surveillance photographs, if a surveillance was done. Otherwise, the investigator will have to use some other method of determining inventory, usually from witness testimony or by computation based upon a constant gross profit percentage.

Accounts/Loans Receivable

Normally, the investigator can confirm and verify receivables whether using the RICO or tax Net Worth Methods by third party contact. Problems arise in this area where related parties are involved, especially if they are subjects of the investigation, whether it be individuals, partnerships, or corporations. Remember, a receivable on the taxpayer's books must be a payable on the other and the amounts must agree for both principal and interest.

Intercompany Transfers

Shareholders can invest in multiple corporations and partnerships. These corporations or partnerships can transfer funds or goods between each other. Whether it is for tax or RICO Net Worth Method purposes, these transfers should be ignored as to the individual net worth. The additional investment in a particular corporation should be reflected on the individual net worth. Whatever the corporation or partnership does with the money is a matter of the entity. In the case of partnerships and Sub S corporations, basis reverts back to the original entity that received the funds from the individual.

Sole Proprietorship

The tax Net Worth Method only requires that the assets and liabilities of the sole proprietor be shown. The RICO Net Worth Method requires not only the assets and liabilities of the sole proprietorship, but also the income and expenses. For RICO Net Worth Method purposes, the problem lies in converting the sole proprietorship into a fund statement. Remember, all depreciation, amortization, and depletion expenses must be reversed out. Only cash expenses should be shown. If the sole proprietorship keeps it books on the accrual method, then the assets, liabilities, income, and expenses should be shown on the individual networth after adjustments for accountant's depreciation, amortization, and depletion deductions.

Exchanges

Individuals, at times, will pay for expenses of another person. In turn, the other person will pay the individual back. The reverse is that another person will give the individual funds to pay for expenses of the other person. There are two ways of showing this situation. First, the expenses can be shown as an expenditure and the reimbursements can be shown as a source (nontaxable in the tax Net Worth Method) of income. The last method is to show the receipts as a receivable and any reimbursements shows a decrease in the receivable.

Securities

Subjects have a tendency to report to financial institutions the fair market value instead of the cost. For the Net Worth Method purposes, only cost figures can be used. Another problem to face with securities is how the subject acquired the securities by means other than by direct purchase. The basis must be firmly established and any doubts should be made in favor of the subject. Drug traffickers use commodities to launder their money. Commodities such as gold and platinum and securities such as bearer bonds can be transported much easier than hauling around cash. Also, they are easier to convert back into currency. This is where Currency Transaction Reports and IRS 8300s should be obtained, if possible, and examined for leads.

Personal Property

Actual cost figures must be used in reflecting personal property, i.e., cars, boats, furniture, jewelry, etc., instead of fair market values. The cost of cars, boats, and airplanes can be determined from state and federal agencies, whereas, the costs of other personal property cannot be determined unless the investigator discovers it from a canceled check or some other source by chance. Surveillance of the subject to expensive stores will be very helpful. Also, the proceeds from disposition of nontraceable personal property is hard to trace unless the subject deposits a check into his bank account. The main thrust here is to fully document nontraceable personal property by third party confirmation. The county tax assessor's office maintain files for tangible personal property which are used in business operations. These tangible personal property tax returns show costs of personal property used in business operations.

Real Property

Real estate must be reported at cost instead of fair market value. However, real estate is probably the most easy to verify because these records are easily accessible at the county records department. In Florida, the state document stamps are charged by set rates upon the purchase price of the real property. In addition, the tax assessor is supposed to assess real property at two thirds of the market value. The problem with real property records is that sometimes they are difficult to read from microfilm and, if real property is transferred by quitclaim deed, no purchase price is reflected from the document stamps. Quit-claim deeds are usually between related parties.

Cash Value Insurance

The subject sometimes has life insurance which has cash values (called Whole Life Policies). The subject has access to these cash values and can withdraw by either borrowing or canceling the policy. The investigator will have to break down the premium between cash value and insurance expense for both RICO and tax Net Worth Method purposes. This information can readily be obtained from the insurance company.

Subchapter S Corporation

Subchapter S corporations are treated differently from Chapter C corporations for tax purposes. In Chapter C corporations, the investigator picks up his net cash investment in the corporation. In Sub S corporations, the investigator picks up not only the net cash investment, but also makes allowances for any income and losses attributed to the subject from such entity, but never below zero (no negative basis). For RICO Net Worth Method purposes, the Sub S corporation is treated the same as for Chapter C corporations which is net cash investment in the corporation. This is definitely an item that will have a different effect from a RICO Net Worth Method and a tax Net Worth Method.

Partnership

Partnerships are treated similar to Subchapter S corporations. The investigator picks up his net cash investment plus makes allowances for subject's share of income and losses. However, the subject can have a negative basis, but only to the extent at which the taxpayer is at risk. Nonrecourse financing is considered not at risk and, therefore, cannot be used in having a negative basis. For RICO Net Worth Method purposes, only net cash investment is considered. This is another item that will have a different effect from RICO to tax Net Worth Method.

Prepaid Insurance

The problem here is whether to reflect prepaid insurance or any other expense for that matter as an asset and show a write-off in subsequent periods or just reflect one lump sum expenditure. Since the subject can cancel the insurance before its expiration, prepaid insurance should be capitalized and later amortized based upon potential refund of premium for tax Net Worth Method purposes. However, for RICO Net Worth Method purposes, prepaid insurance should be expensed in the year incurred. Phantom costs, such as amortized costs, are not to be recorded in subsequent years on RICO Net Worth Schedules.

Controlled Foreign Corporations (CFE)

For tax Net Worth Method purposes, the agent should pick up not only the net cash investment, but also the taxpayer's share of net income. For RICO Net Worth Method purposes, only the subject's net cash investment should be used. Another problem that arises in foreign corporations is the effect of foreign exchange rates. Gains and losses from foreign exchange rates will have to be reflected for both tax and RICO Net Worth Method computations. On RICO Net Worth Schedules, gains are identified sources and losses are identified expenses.

Accounts Payable

Accounts payable is used for accrual taxpayers only. A problem can arise when payables are from related persons or entities which are not on the accrual basis. For RICO Net Worth Method purposes, accounts payable are not used, since this would defy the fund concept which RICO Net Worth Methods are based upon. However, if the subject has a sole proprietorship with inventory and cost of sales, then accounts payable will have to be used on the RICO Net Worth Schedule.

Credit Cards

In a net worth, credit card balances are shown as a liability, and the total charges are reflected in the personal expenditure section. One problem that could arise at year end is when charges are made, but do not show up until the subsequent period. There is sometimes a lag as long as two or three months. Also, the charges have to be confirmed and differentiated as to what is personal or business, especially for those credit cards that have a widespread use. Another method of presentation is where no liability is reflected on the net worth and only the payments are reflected to the credit card company as a personal expenditure. The agent still has the problem of distinguishing between business and personal use. Credit cards cannot be ignored because the funds spent can be enormous. The problem with credit cards is the same for both tax and RICO Net Worth Method purposes. Whether you use the total charges and ending liability presentation or the total payment expenditure presentation, you must be consistent with only one presentation. For RICO purposes, there is really no need to distinguish between business and personal charges since they are just expenditures. The agent, however, must distinguish between expense and asset.

Deferred Gains

This item comes about when the taxpayer reports sales on the installment method or is allowed to use the installment method to report a gain. For tax Net Worth Method purposes, the agent will have to set up a deferred gain in the liability section of the Net Worth Schedule and recognize the gain in subsequent periods based upon receipts. For RICO Net Worth Method purposes, deferred gains are not recognized in subsequent periods. They are recognized in full when they are incurred.

Prepaid Interest

This item comes about from installment loan contracts. The installment loan is recorded by bank with principal, interest, and other charges combined. Interest should be recognized the same way the bank recognizes the interest income. It should be noted that when the installment method is paid off early, the bank uses a different method of rebating the interest (called the rule of 78) from the method used in computing the interest. The IRS issued a ruling that the rule of 78s cannot be used in computing interest expense by the taxpayer. For RICO Net Worth Method purposes, prepaid interest is not capitalized and later amortized. Prepaid interest is expensed in the year incurred.

Contributions

Cash contributions is treated the same for both tax and RICO Net Worth Method purposes. In the case of noncash contributions, tax Net Worth Method computations reflect the fair market value, but not more than the original cost. For RICO Net Worth Method computations, only cost figures should be used.

Capital Gains and Losses

Capital gains and losses are treated differently for tax Net Worth Method purposes vs. RICO Net Worth Method purposes. For tax Net Worth Method purposes, losses are limited to $3,000 per year. This will result in an asset called deferred capital losses. For capital gains prior to 1987, the gain will be recognized, but a portion of the gain called 1202 deduction will be shown as nontaxable income. The RICO Net Worth Method must recognize the gains and losses in full during the period incurred.

Ira and Keogh Accounts

People are increasingly funding Individual Retirement Accounts (IRA) and Keogh Plans for self-employed individuals. The contributions to these plans are tax deductible and the interest and dividend incomes are tax free. On tax Net Worth Method computations, these retirement plans should be reflected as an asset and the interest and dividend income should be reflected as nontaxable income. On RICO Net Worth Method computations, these retirement plans should be reflected as an asset and the income appropriately recognized as legal income.

Personal Living Expenses

There are other expenses that should be considered in doing a net worth computation whether for tax or RICO Net Worth Method purposes. These expenses should be identified as early as possible and records obtained. They are as follows:

a. Food and outside meals
b. Home and other repairs
c. Utilities, i.e., electric, water, waste, etc.
d. Telephone charges and payments as well as toll calls (toll calls can help tie the target to other individuals as well as offer leads for additional financial information)
e. Vacation and/or trips
f. Alimony
g. Child support
h. Property taxes
i. Medical expenses including health insurance
j. Educational expenses

    k. Moving expenses
    l. Gifts
    m. Federal and state income taxes
    n. Personal bad debts

Various Income Items

There are income items that should be kept in mind. Some items will have different effects on net worth computations from tax vs. RICO Net Worth Method purposes. The RICO Net Worth Method will probably use income items that the tax Net Worth Method will either not use or present differently. Some of these items are as follows:

    a. Tax exempt interest
    b. Social Security benefits
    c. Unemployment compensation
    d. Dividend exclusion
    e. Life insurance proceeds
    f. Inheritance
    g. Disability income
    h. Two-wage earner deduction
    i. Educational assistance
    j. Military allowances
    k. Casualty insurance proceeds

Civil vs. Criminal

In tax Net Worth Method cases, there usually are differences between the criminal case and the civil case. The primary reason is the civil agent is trying to establish a tax deficiency, while the criminal agent is trying to show intent to defraud the government. The criminal agent has to interview and have witnesses testify about various income and expenditure items. The civil agent does not have to obtain very many witnesses since deductions are the responsibility of the taxpayer and not the government. The following items will inevitably reflect differences between criminal and civil agents' reports.

    a. Dividend vs. reduction in capital investment in corporations
    b. Interest vs. loan
    c. Personal expenditures (civilly, taxpayer must prove deductions; criminally, the government must prove deductions)
    d. Basis of assets, i.e., auto basis on trade-ins

    The RICO Net Worth Method computation is used for both criminal and civil purposes. There should be little or no differences. The only differences that might appear in RICO Net Worth Method cases are items that were not admitted in criminal court because they were unknown at the time, just wasn't introduced, or the hearsay rules forbid their use in criminal proceedings, but not in civil proceedings. Otherwise, there should be no difference in technical issues.

Defenses

Whenever using any indirect method to determine correct taxable income or to determine the amount of illegal gain from an illegal enterprise, the defendant will have various defenses. Some of the more common defenses are as follows:

a. Cash on hand. This is the cash hoard story. The defendant claims to have accumulated wealth in years prior to the prosecution years.

b. Loans. The defendant testifies that the sudden wealth came from somebody or entity as loan proceeds. In some cases, the lender doesn't have the resources to make any loans to the defendant. This is common with loans from relatives, family members, and closely-held corporations.

c. Gifts. The defendant claims to have received gifts from family members, relatives, or friends. The investigator should verify whether the donor has the resources to make such a gift to the defendant.

d. Inheritance. When the defendant claims inheritance(s) as a sudden source of wealth, the investigator should check probate court records. If the inheritance is very large, it could expose the defendant for possible estate tax fraud if no estate tax returns were filed, whether for federal or state purposes.

e. Innocent bystander. The defendant could claim to be an innocent bystander where money was left in their possession while another person was on the run.

f. Agent or nominee. Defendants like to deny ownership and place assets in nominees or alter egos. The investigators should determine whether the nominee or alter ego has the resources to acquire the assets (the issue of nominees and alter egos are addressed in a later chapter).

g. Possession. The defendants may claim that they are an agent for an anonymous person, or that they are unaware the goods were in their possession.

h. Jointly-held assets. The defendant may claim that the other party purchased the jointly-held assets. The investigator should confirm with the other party that the transaction purchased the jointly-held asset. If the other party purchased it, then the asset should not be shown on the Net Worth Schedule.

i. Overstated inventories. The defendant may claim that the inventory or other assets are overstated. The investigator should confirm with subject (if permitted), employees, and records, or some covert means as available.

j. Failure to account for other sources of funds. The defendant may not be able to account for all sources of income. It is the duty of the investigator to check all possible sources of income.

k. Commodities. The subject claims the purchase of commodities, i.e., gold, silver, auto parts, etc., that were accumulated prior to the prosecution years. The investigator has the difficult job of confirming this claim.

Remember, particularly in criminal cases, whether for tax or RICO Net Worth Method purposes, the burden of proof is placed on the government when a net worth method is used. In the Holland case, the Supreme Court said that the government is responsible for the following burdens of proof:

1. The opening net worth must be established with reasonable certainty. This includes verification of subject's admissions.
2. There must be significant signs that there is a likely source of taxable income and refute nontaxable sources for tax Net Worth Method purposes. In RICO Net Worth Method cases, it is evident that all sources of any legal income should be identified.
3. If the subject offers any leads of income, they must be investigated and accepted or refuted.

In RICO Net Worth Method cases, the defendant will use the same defenses as in tax Net Worth Method cases. The tendency in RICO Net Worth Method cases is to try to introduce more legitimate income or disclaim ownership of various assets. Organized crime figures and high-level drug traffickers have the pattern of using nominees or agents to hide their assets and illegal income. The investigator, in these situations, has to determine if the agent or nominee has the ability to acquire assets or generate that kind of legal income.

Summary

The Net Worth Method, whether for RICO or tax purposes, is a very powerful tool. It tends to place the burden upon the defendant to disprove once introduced into evidence. The examiner or investigator has a tedious job of locating, obtaining, analyzing, and preparing a Net Worth Schedule. The examiner has to pay close attention to all the details presented in a Net Worth Schedule. All the issues should be identified and resolved.

Expenditure Theory

6

Introduction

The Internal Revenue Service was also the first to use the Expenditure Method. The Expenditure Method is a derivation of the Net Worth Method, which has been used since the early 1940s. Like the Net Worth Method, the Expenditure Method is used to determine the amount of unreported taxable income. This method is appropriate in cases where the taxpayer does not accumulate assets, but spends all his income on "lavish" living. When the RICO Act of 1970 was passed, the Expenditure Method was expanded to encompass organized crime figures.

Tax Use

The Expenditure Method is a method of proof by circumstantial or indirect evidence. The IRS establishes the total expenditures, less total nontaxable sources to arrive at adjusted gross income. Exemptions and itemized deductions are subtracted to arrive at corrected taxable income. This is compared to the reported taxable income to arrive at any unreported taxable income. The following chart (Table 6-1) is presented to illustrate the theory.

Table 6-1 Tax Expenditure Theory

	Year
Total	Expenditures
Less:	Total Nontaxable Source
Equals:	Adjusted Gross Income
Less:	Itemized/Standard Deduction
Less:	Exemptions
Equals:	Corrected Taxable Income
Less:	Reported Taxable Income
Equals:	Unreported Taxable Income

RICO Use

Like the Net Worth Method, the Expenditure Method is used in RICO and other economic crime cases. In a RICO case, the basic objective is to determine the amount of illegal income. The RICO Net Worth Method is defined as total expenditures less legal sources to derive at illegal income. The RICO Expenditure does this for each succeeding year. The following chart (Table 6-2) is presented to illustrate the theory.

Table 6-2 RICO Expenditure Theory

	Year
Total	Expenditures
Less:	Legal Sources
Equals:	Illegal Income

History

The Expenditure Method came into use in the early 1940s. Since then, it has been used more frequently than the Net Worth Method. There are various reasons for this. First, it is more easily prepared. Second, it is easier to explain to a jury in a trial. The Expenditure Method has not been ruled upon directly by the U.S. Supreme Court. One reason is that the Expenditure Method is a derivation of the Net Worth Method. Any accountant can take a net worth computation and convert it to an expenditure computation and vice versa. The Supreme Court in its decisions in net worth cases has referred to the Net Worth and Expenditure Method. This alone implies that the Supreme Court approves of the Expenditure Method. As such, the rules, which the Supreme Court outlined in net worth cases, apply to expenditure cases.

The Internal Revenue Service has been using the Expenditure Method against the ordinary average citizen. It can be used to show that the taxpayer books do not reflect true income or to corroborate specific adjustments. Revenue agents are sometimes using the Expenditure Method by using figures on the tax return even before beginning their examinations or contact with the taxpayer. Revenue agents call this Expenditure Method the "T" account. The "T" account method is actually the Expenditure Method in which sources of income are reflected on the left side of a spreadsheet. The expenditures are shown on the right side of the same spreadsheet. If the right side of the spreadsheet, the expenditure side, is greater than the left side, the income side, then the revenue agent will suspect that the taxpayer has unreported taxable income.

The tax court and some district courts have, on occasions, disapproved of the Expenditure Method. The primary reason is that the Internal Revenue Service failed to establish the amount of funds available at the beginning of the taxable years in question. Like the Net Worth Method, the prosecution has to show that the taxpayer does not have a cash hoard or other convertible assets prior to the prosecution years.

RICO Use

The Expenditure Method, like the Net Worth Method, can be used in the prosecution of organized crime figures and drug kingpins. The primary use in organized crime figures and drug kingpins is to show the amount of illegal income. When the illegal income is determined by the Expenditure Method, the prosecution can recommend the fine. Unlike the Net Worth Method, the Expenditure Method does not identify the assets the defendant has accumulated. It only identifies the assets acquired in any specific year. It does not mean that the defendant still has those assets. The Expenditure Method can identify sales and disposition of assets, but only in the year of disposition. Assets can be destroyed or abandoned and the investigator may not learn of it right away. In addition, assets can be disposed of after the years under examination or investigation.

When Use is Required

The Expenditure Method should be used in tax cases when one or more of the following conditions prevail:

a. Taxpayer maintains no books and records.
b. Taxpayer's books and records are not available.
c. Taxpayer's books and records are inadequate.
d. Taxpayer withholds books and records.
e. Taxpayer has no visible or identifiable assets.

The Expenditure Method should be used in RICO cases when one or more of the following conditions prevail:

a. The target doesn't seem to acquire assets.
b. The target spends beyond his means (lavish living).
c. The target is a high level "kingpin" where most, if not all, witnesses against him are convicted criminals.
d. Illegal income needs to be determined in order to determine the fine or forfeiture amount.

Theory

When the determination has been made to use the Expenditure Method, then the questions of how to prepare and present items on the Expenditure Method arises. The following guidelines are provided.

As a general rule for tax Net Worth Method purposes, items on the Expenditure Schedule should be treated in the manner prescribed for tax purposes. Only cost figures should be used. Market values can be used, but only in extreme or unusual circumstances or if the tax law and regulations require it.

As a general rule for RICO Net Worth Method purposes, the source and use of funds is to be applied. Only cost figures should be used. Market values cannot be used unless they relate, either directly or indirectly, to the source or use of funds. No phantom figures are to be used. Phantom figures are defined as accounting entries for amortization, depreciation, and depletion allowances. Also, earnings and profits from partnerships and corporations are not to be used. These figures do not reflect the use of funds and, therefore, should not be used.

The Expenditure Method treats assets and liabilities different from the treatment of assets and liabilities on the Net Worth Method. Assets and liabilities are shown on the Expenditure Method during the period that they are acquired or disposed of. Accumulated or ending balances are not shown on the Expenditure Method. Those items that are presented in a different manner are discussed below.

Cash on Hand

The net worth method reports the amount of cash on hand at year end. The Expenditure Method reports either the increase or decrease in cash on hand from one year to the next. However, the same rules apply as to the determination of cash on hand for each year under investigation as well as prior years. The cash hoard defense applies to the Expenditure Method as well as the Net Worth Method. If the subject has or claims cash hoard, then the cash hoard will decrease over the periods under investigation.

Cash in Bank

The Expenditure Method reports either the increase or decrease of cash in the bank rather than the bank or book balances. Whether the book balances or bank balances are used, the use must be consistent. You cannot use book balance increases or decreases in one year and the bank balance in a subsequent year. This applies to both tax and RICO Net Worth Method purposes. Increases and decreases in bank accounts can be used using the bank balances for one account and the book balances in another account.

Inventory

The Expenditure Method has the same presentation problems as the Net Worth Method. Except in the Expenditure Method, the inventory is stated by the increase or decrease in ending inventory balances. It is suggested that the investigator determine the inventory balance, determine the increase or decrease by subtracting the beginning and ending inventory balances for the period.

Intercompany Transfers

Intercompany transfers should be ignored on the individual Expenditure Schedule. Only the initial investment should be accounted for on the individual Expenditure Schedule. What the corporation or partnership does with funds has no effect on the individual Expenditure Schedule.

Sole Proprietorships

The net changes in assets and liabilities should be reflected on the individual Expenditure Schedule, whether tax or RICO Net Worth Method is used. The income and expenses should be reflected on the RICO Expenditure Schedule. The examiner will have to make adjustments to eliminate any phantom figures (accountant's depreciation, amortization, and depletion allowances). The tax Expenditure Method does not reflect the income and expenses of a sole proprietorship since they relate to net income or loss to derive adjusted gross income.

Exchanges

Both the tax and RICO Net Worth Method should reflect exchanges identically. This means that payments to or on behalf of other people should be reflected as an expenditure. Any reimbursements should be reflected as a source of funds. For the tax Net Worth Method this source of receipts should be reflected as a nontaxable source of income. Another method of reflecting exchanges is to show the net effect of exchanges. This applies to both tax and RICO Net Worth Methods. If the net effect is an expenditure, then this should be shown in the Expenditure Section. If the net effect is a source, then it should be shown as a source of funds. In RICO cases, this is a source of receipts.

Accounts/Loans Receivable

The Expenditure Method shows the increases or decreases in the accounts and loans receivable. It does not show the year-end balances. The investigator has the same problems in the Expenditure Method as in the Net Worth Method. The year-end balances must be confirmed before the differences can be determined. The related party issue in this area is the same as the Net Worth Method. The increase or decrease in loans and accounts receivable on the subject's books must correspond to the opposite increase or decrease on the related party books. The examiner must determine if related party loans are bona-fide. The related party may not be able to make large loans.

Subchapter S Corporation

Like the tax Net Worth Method purposes, the Expenditure Method accounts for the total earnings or losses plus any contributions less any withdrawals for the period. The Net Worth Method only shows the beginning and ending balances for the period. For RICO Expenditure Method purposes, the Expenditure Method accounts for the net change during the period as to the subject's cash investment. Earnings and losses are not accounted for in the RICO Expenditure Method. Regular corporations are treated the same for both RICO and tax Net Worth Method purposes. The net changes in cash investment for the period is reflected on the expenditure computation.

Partnership

The tax Expenditure Method accounts for the total earnings or losses plus any contributions less any withdrawals for the period. Negative changes can be reflected for both RICO and tax Expenditure Method purposes. However, for tax Expenditure Method purposes, the negative changes will not be allowed if the taxpayer is not at risk on loans that the partnership has acquired.

Credit Cards

The net change in credit card balances is reflected on the Expenditure Method if the total charges are shown on the Expenditure Schedule. It is easier for both the examiner or investigator to reflect the net cash payments to the credit card companies than to reflect total charges and changes in credit card balances. For tax Expenditure Method purposes, the payments for business expenses has to be separated from personal expenses. This can be extremely difficult. Interviews of witnesses or the subject will have to be done to determine the nature of the expenditures. The best evidence on credit card payments is to see how the taxpayer paid for the credit cards. If they come from his personal bank accounts, then it is obvious that they are personal expenses. If paid from a business account, then it implies that they are for business purposes. This can leave the investigator open for debate between both counsels. For RICO Expenditure Method purposes, this is not an issue.

Other Assets

The net change in assets is reflected on the Expenditure Method, whether tangible or intangible or real or personal property. In tax cases, the expenditure will reflect a decrease in intangible assets such as prepaid interest and insurance. In RICO cases, prepaid items are not recognized since they don't exist. Prepaid items on an RICO Expenditure Schedule are expensed in the year incurred.

Loans and Mortgages Payable

The Expenditure Method shows only the receipt of the funds borrowed (source of funds) during the period and the total payments (application of funds) made during the period. Loan proceeds should not be netted out with loan repayments. This can be confusing for the jury.

Income and Expenses

Income and personal living expenses are reflected the same way for expenditure computations as it is for net worth computations, actual disbursement of funds. This applies to both tax and RICO Expenditure Method purposes. The tax Expenditure Method recognizes only nontaxable sources of income. Expenses are recognized when paid for cash basis taxpayers and when incurred for taxpayers on the accrual method. The RICO Expenditure Method recognizes all personal income and expenses of the subject when received or paid. However, if the subject has a sole proprietorship that is on the accrual method of accounting, then the income and expenses should be recognized when incurred along with the changes in accounts payable.

Deferred Gains

Deferred gains are not recognized on the RICO Expenditure Method. Gains are recognized in full when incurred. For tax Net Worth Method purposes, deferred gains are recognized by showing an acquired liability. Since this is an adjustment to arrive at adjusted gross income, it will be reflected on the Expenditure Schedule as a nontaxable source.

Depreciation, Amortization, and Depletion

Depreciation, amortization, and depletion are not recognized on the RICO Expenditure Schedule since these are accountant's figures that do not relate to the use of funds. In tax cases, depreciation, amortization, and depletion allowances are shown as a current liability, but not as a personal living expense. The Internal Revenue Code and regulations govern the amount that can be claimed.

Controlled Foreign Corporations (CFC)

For tax Expenditure Method purposes, the investigator should pick up the net cash investment plus the taxpayer's income and loss for the period. For RICO Expenditure Method purposes, only the subject's net cash investment for the period should be used. These net investment figures should be in U.S. currency. Any gains and losses should be reflected in other sections of the Expenditure Schedule. This applies to both tax and RICO Net Worth Method purposes. However, for tax Net Worth Method purposes, losses will be limited to the loss limitation rules.

IRA and Keogh Accounts

On tax Expenditure Schedules, Individual Retirement Accounts and Keogh plan contributions should show the amount of the contributions plus earnings for the period. Earnings for the period are reflected as nontaxable sources. For RICO Expenditure Method purposes, the plan contributions are shown as an expenditure plus any earnings. However, the earnings for the period are reflected as a source of income.

Capital Gains and Losses

There are differences between the tax Expenditure Method and the RICO Expenditure Method. For tax Expenditure Method purposes, capital losses are not recognized on the expenditure computation because they are used as adjustments to arrive at an adjusted gross income. However, losses in excess of the amount allowed to be deducted during the period should be shown as an intangible asset expenditure. This intangible asset is reduced by the amount of loss allowed in subsequent years. For RICO Expenditure Method purposes, both gains and losses are recognized for the period in the appropriate section, income or expense. In addition, the recovered costs are to be reflected in the source section. In RICO cases, it is easier to show the gross proceeds from the sale of capital assets as a source, and reflect the cost of the asset as an expenditure.

Civil vs. Criminal

Like the Net Worth Methods, the Expenditure Methods have the same issues. Like the Net Worth Methods, the expenditure methods will have to solve the same issues in somewhat the same manner. In tax cases, there will be differences between criminal and civil cases. This is due primarily to the degree of proof required in criminal cases, which is greater than in civil cases. In tax civil cases, issues can become more technical than in criminal cases. In RICO cases, there should be little or no differences. Any difference usually relates to the admissibility during criminal proceedings or later discovery of additional items.

Defenses

The defenses for the Expenditure Method, whether tax or RICO, are the same as for the Net Worth Method. In criminal cases, the burden of proof is the responsibility of the government when the expenditure method is used. The cash hoard or conversion of old assets is the most used defense in the expenditure method. Any defense will have to be investigated and refuted. The Expenditure Method will have to use the same investigative techniques to refute any cash hoard or asset conversion as used in the Net Worth Method. Defense attorneys use the same defenses in both Expenditure and Net Worth Method cases.

Summary

Like the Net Worth Method, the Expenditure Method is also a powerful tool. It also tends to place the burden upon the defendant to disprove once introduced into evidence. The examiner or investigator has a tedious job of locating, obtaining, analyzing, and preparing an Expenditure Schedule. The examiner has to pay close attention to all the detail presented in an Expenditure Schedule. All the issues must be identified and resolved. The principal difference between the Expenditure and Net Worth Methods is the presentation of assets and liabilities. The Expenditure Method only reflects assets and liabilities that are obtained or disposed of during a period.

Scenario Case

7

Case

This case problem is designed to acquaint the reader with how to put together a Net Worth Computation Schedule, an Expenditure Computation Schedule, and a Tracing Schedule for Title 26 USC (Income Tax) and for Title 18 USC (Racketeering). It is designed to show the theories and objectives. It illustrates these objectives and addresses the most common problems and issues that forensic accountants will encounter.

This case is based upon real-life incidents. The material for this case is divided into two parts for the purpose of showing the importance of both financial information and nonfinancial information and their interrelationships. The first section, Financial Data, will provide you with financial data for use in your various computational schedules. The second section, Intelligence, will provide you with information about the subject's activities and dealings. This section also has some financial information, but is not generally admissible in court because the Federal Rules of Evidence disallow it.

This case scenario is used to prepare four schedules using the theory for both tax and RICO purposes. The following chapters will explain in detail and provide the schedules for the following:

a. Net Worth Schedule for tax purposes
b. Net Worth Schedule for RICO purposes
c. Expenditure Schedule for tax purposes
d. Expenditure Schedule for RICO purposes

The tax laws and regulations are the basis for computing a tax Net Worth or Expenditure Schedule. The objective is to determine the amount of unreported taxable income. The funds principal is the underlying guide in preparing the RICO Net Worth or Expenditure Schedules. No amortization, depreciation, or depletion allowances are allowed in a RICO Net Worth or Expenditure Schedule. The objective is to determine the amount of illegal income and identify forfeitable assets. The subsequent chapters show how these schedules should appear and the explanations as to how they were arrived for each type of schedule.

Financial Data

Search Warrant Data

Investigators conducted an authorized search warrant on John Doe's residence on December 31, 19X3. During this search, the following items were discovered and seized:

a. Cash found in a floor safe, $50,000
b. Two kilos of cocaine (the wholesale value at time of search warrant was $25,000 per kilo)
c. Bank statements in the name of John Doe from Barclays Bank of London, England

  The statement transactions are given below in British pounds (BL). At the time of deposits, the exchange rate was US$1.00 to BL$2.00.

Date	Deposits	Withdrawals	Balance	Interest
1/28/X1	1,000,000		1,000,000	
2/10/X1	1,000,000		2,000,000	
3/15/X1	2,000,000		4,000,000	
3/30/X1			4,120,000	120,000
5/1/X1		2,000,000	2,120,000	
6/30/X1			2,203,600	83,600
7/2/X1		2,203,600	-0-	

d. Ten gold bullion bars were found at his residence in a hidden compartment in the kitchen cabinets (market value at time of seizure is $20,000 per bar).

Public Records

During the investigation, the following data were discovered in county public records.

a. Public records show John Doe purchased his residence at 100 Alpha Street. The Warranty Deed shows purchase was on 1/30/X1. The document stamps paid on the purchase were $1,500. Document stamps are based upon $5 per thousand. A mortgage was recorded along with the Warranty Deed. The mortgage shows John Doe obtained a mortgage for $250,000. The mortgage states monthly payments of $1,000 per month plus interest at 10 percent per annum due commencing 3/1/X1. The mortgage is Panama Mortgage Company, a foreign corporation (Panama Republic).
b. On 5/8/X1, John Doe purchased an apartment building on 100 Bravo Street. The Warranty Deed shows document stamps paid were $20,000. Document stamps were paid on a purchase price of $5 per thousand. A mortgage was recorded at the same time by Florida Mortgage Corp., a domestic corporation. The principal amount was $2,000,000. Monthly payments are $10,000 per month plus interest until the mortgage is paid commencing 6/1/X1. Interest rate is 10 percent.

Life Insurance

John Doe purchased a life insurance policy for $10,000 on 6/30/X1. The policy is for $1,000,000 with John Doe's mother as beneficiary. This is a whole life policy. Doe paid five years at one time. The policy shows the cash value as follows based upon annual installments of $2,000:

Date	Value
19X1	$ -0-
19X2	2,000
19X3	3,000
19X4	5,000

Home Improvements

John Doe purchased furniture and fixtures for his house. Receipts obtained show the following purchases from vendors:

Description	Amount	Date
Furniture	$50,000	2/2/X1
Cabinets	20,000	2/3/X1
Paintings	20,000	3/1/X1
Fixtures	10,000	4/1/X1
Pool and Tennis Court	100,000	7/1/X1
Appliances	20,000	9/1/X2
Electronic Equipment	100,000	9/1/X2
Security System	50,000	2/1/X3

Corporations

A check with the State Bureau of Corporations shows that John Doe is owner of the following entities. All these entities were formed on 10/1/X1.

a. Lounge Doe, Inc. — A Florida Corporation
b. Doe Kwik Stop, Inc. — A Florida Corporation
c. Real Property Co., Ltd. — A Florida Partnership

Individual Tax Returns

The individual tax returns were obtained on John Doe. They show the following data:

Description	19X0	19X1	19X3
Wages	$ 10,000	$190,000	$200,000
Sole Proprietor			(250,000)
Doe Lounge Inc. Dividend		100,000	
Doe Kwik Stop, Inc.		(25,000)	175,000
Real Property Co., Ltd.		(100,000)	(30,000)
Rental Property Sch E		(70,000)	(30,000)
Adjusted Gross	$ 10,000	$ 95,000	$ 65,000
Deductions:			
Standard	$ 3,000		
Mortgage Interest		$ 25,000	$ 22,600
Property Taxes		5,000	5,000
Exemptions	2,000	2,000	2,000
Taxable Income	$ 5,000	$ 63,000	$ 35,400
Tax Liability	500	15,750	7,000
Refund in 19X1	500		
Refund in 19X2		79,250	
Withholding	$ 1,000	$ 95,000	$150,000

John Doe filed a schedule C for his sole proprietorship with the returns that he filed. John Doe did not file his tax return for 19X2. This business sells women's clothes. Suzy Que runs the business after she leaves her bank job. John Doe does not manage the business, but frequently checks the business operations. The tax return and financial statements provide the following information:

A. Balance Sheet Presentation

Balance Sheet	19X2	19X3
Cash in Bank	$ 20,000	$ 10,000
Accounts Receivable	10,000	20,000
Inventory	140,000	50,000
Business Assets	150,000	150,000
Accum. Depreciation	(30,000)	(60,000)
Total	$290,000	$170,000
Accounts Payable	$ -0-	$50,000
Bank Loan Payable	100,000	80,000
Capital	700,000	800,000
Accumulated Earnings	(560,000)	(760,000)
Total	$290,000	$170,000

B. Income Statement Presentation

Income	19X2	19X3
Sales	$ 80,000	$440,000
Beginning Inventory	$ -0-	$140,000
Purchases	180,000	130,000
Total Inventory	$180,000	$270,000
Ending Inventory	140,000	$ 50,000
Cost of Sales	$ 40,000	$220,000
Gross Profit	$ 40,000	$220,000

Overhead Expenses		
Advertising	$ 80,000	$ 40,000
Depreciation	30,000	30,000
Interest	10,000	8,000
Insurance	50,000	50,000
Professional Fees	25,000	25,000
Office Expenses	30,000	10,000
Rent Expense	50,000	50,000
Repairs	20,000	10,000
Supplies	30,000	10,000
Taxes	50,000	40,000
Utilities	40,000	40,000
Wages	120,000	150,000
Miscellaneous	15,000	7,000
Total	$550,000	$470,000
Net Loss	$510,000	$250,000

The business has a part-time bookkeeper, Betsy Low, who maintains the books. The bookkeeper prepares all the various journals (cash receipts, disbursements, payables, receivables, and purchases). Mr. I. M. Balance, CPA, prepares the individual tax returns for John Doe. In addition, he does a certified audit of the sole proprietorship that is known as

"Suzy's Women's Clothes." The bookkeeper does the bank reconciliations, but they are reviewed by I. M. Balance, CPA.

C. Rental Income Schedule: Depreciation is based upon the straight-line method over 15 years

Description	19X2	19X3
Rental Receipts	$200,000	$450,000
Interest Expense	120,000	180,000
Property Taxes	20,000	40,000
Insurance	20,000	40,000
Maintenance	10,000	20,000
Depreciation	100,000	200,000
Total	$270,000	$480,000
Net Loss	($ 70,000)	($ 30,000)

Lounge Doe, Inc.

The corporate tax returns and financial statements were obtained. This is a calendar year corporation. The corporate records were also obtained and they substantiate the tax return figures.

A. Balance Sheet Presentation

Description	19X1	19X2	19X3
Cash	$ 10,000	$ 50,000	$ 40,000
Inventory	500,000	400,000	300,000
Personal Property	500,000	500,000	500,000
Real Property	1,000,000	1,000,000	1,000,000
Accum. Depreciation	(50,000)	(200,000)	(350,000)
Land	500,000	500,000	500,000
Organization Cost	1,000	900	800
Total Assets	$2,461,000	$2,250,900	$1,990,800
Accounts Payable	$1,000	$50,000	$ 40,000
Shareholder Loan	2,435,000	2,435,000	2,134,900
Stock	5,000	5,000	5,000
Retained Earnings	20,000	(239,100)	(189,100)
Total	$2,461,000	$2,250,900	$1,990,800

B. Income Statement Presentation

Income	$1,070,100	$ 891,000	$1,400,100
Cash Expenses	100,000	150,000	300,000
Depreciation	50,000	150,000	150,000
Amortized Costs	100	100	100
Inventory:			
Beginning	-0-	500,000	400,000
Purchases:	1,300,000	750,000	800,000
Ending	500,000	400,000	300,000
Cost of Sales	800,000	850,000	900,000
Total Costs	$ 950,100	$1,150,100	$1,350,100
Net Income (Loss)	$ 120,000	$(259,100)	$ 50,000

Examination of the corporate books and records reveal that the corporation purchased a boat for $100,000 on 11/1/X1. It is not used for business purposes.

Doe's Kwik Stop, Inc.

The corporate records were obtained for this corporation. The corporate tax return shows that Doe's Kwik Stop, Inc. is a Subchapter S corporation.

A. Balance Sheet Presentation

Description	19X1	19X2	19X3
Cash	$ 20,000	$ 20,000	$310,100
Inventory	50,000	60,000	70,000
Personal Property	500,000	500,000	500,000
Accum. Depreciation	(50,000)	(200,000)	(350,000)
Prepaid Insurance	10,000	5,000	-0-
Organization Cost	1,100	1,000	900
Total Assets	$531,100	$386,000	$531,000
Accounts Payable	$ 50,000	$ 60,000	$ 30,000
Shareholder Loan	501,100	396,000	396,000
Stock	5,000	5,000	5,000
Retained Earnings	(25,000)	(75,000)	100,000
Total	$531,100	$386,000	$531,000

B. Income Statement Presentation

	19X1	19X2	19X3
Income	$ 275,100	$ 405,100	$1,000,100
Cash expenses	100,000	150,000	400,000
Amortized Insurance	-0-	5,000	5,000
Amortized Organization	100	100	100
Depreciation	50,000	150,000	150,000
Inventory:			
Beginning	-0-	50,000	60,000
Purchases	200,000	160,000	280,000
Ending	50,000	60,000	70,000
Cost of Sales	150,000	150,000	270,000
Total Expenses	$ 300,100	$455,100	$825,100
Net Income (Loss)	$(25,000)	$(50,000)	$175,000

Real Property Ltd.

The partnership records were obtained. The partnership records are summarized below. John Doe has a 50 percent partnership interest and contributed equally.

A. Balance Sheet Presentation

Description	19X1	19X2	19X3
Cash	$ 10,000	$ 10,000	$ 30,000
Building	10,000,000	10,000,000	10,000,000
Accum. Depreciation	(250,000)	(750,000)	(1,250,000)
Land	2,000,000	2,000,000	2,000,000
Total Assets	$11,760,000	$11,255,000	$10,780,000

Description	19X1	19X2	19X3
Mortgage	$ 7,900,000	$ 7,500,000	$ 7,000,000
Capital	3,860,000	3,755,000	4,890,000
Total	$11,760,000	$11,255,000	$10,780,000

B. Capital Account Analysis

Beginning	$ -0-	$ 3,860,000	$ 3,755,000
Contributions	4,060,000	-0-	85,000
Net Loss	(200,000)	(105,000)	(60,000)
Ending Balance	$ 3,860,000	$ 3,755,000	$ 3,780,000

C. Income Statement Presentation

Rental Income	$ 330,000	$ 1,285,000	$ 1,300,000
Depreciation	250,000	500,000	500,000
Interest	200,000	750,000	700,000
Taxes	10,000	40,000	40,000
Insurance	20,000	50,000	60,000
Maintenance	50,000	50,000	60,000
Total Expenses	$ 530,000	$ 1,390,000	$1,360,000
Net Loss	($ 200,000)	($ 105,000)	($ 60,000)

Bank Accounts

John Doe's bank accounts were obtained from First National Bank. The following is a summary of those accounts:

A. Checking Account

Date	Deposits	Withdrawals	Balance	Interest
12/31/X1	$5,010,000	$5,000,000	$ 10,000	
12/31/X2	600,000	560,000	50,000	
12/31/X3	200,000	150,000	100,000	

B. Savings Account

Date	Deposits	Withdrawals	Balance	Interest
12/31/X1	$ 100,000	$ -0-	$ 110,000	$10,000
12/31/X2	400,000	-0-	550,000	40,000
12/31/X3	50,000	-0-	650,000	50,000

Credit Card

John Doe's credit card records were obtained. The following is a summary of this account:

Date	Charges	Payments	Balance
12/31/X1	$ 30,000	$ 30,000	$ -0-
12/31/X2	100,000	70,000	30,000
12/31/X3	180,000	160,000	50,000

All charges were for personal living expenses for both himself and his girlfriend.

Living Expenses

Various vendor's records were obtained as to John Doe's personal living expenses. They are summarized below:

Description	19X1	19X2	19X3
Utilities	$10,000	$10,000	$20,000
Telephone	30,000	40,000	45,000
Insurance	5,000	10,000	10,000
Church Donations	-0-	10,000	50,000

Automobiles

John Doe purchased a Mercedes Benz for $80,000 in 19X1. He put $30,000 down and financed the remainder with the First National Bank. In 19X2, John Doe purchased a Toyota for $18,000. He put $10,000 down and financed the remainder with the First National Bank. Records for both cars were obtained from the sellers. The following summarizes these transactions:

Description	19X1	19X2
Mercedes Benz	$80,000	
Toyota		$18,000
Financed Amount	50,000	8,000
Finance Charge	10,000	2,000
Monthly Payments	1,000	200
Term	60 months	50 months
Paid During the Year	9,000	1,200

Rental Property

Records were obtained for John Doe's rental property for 19X2. I. M. Balance, CPA, had these records in his possession. They are summarized below:

Description	19X2
Rental Receipts	$400,000
Interest Expense	190,000
Property Taxes	40,000
Insurance	40,000
Maintenance	20,000
Depreciation	200,000
Total Expenses	$490,000
Net Loss	$ 90,000

Individual Retirement Accounts

John Doe opened several Individual Retirement Accounts at First National Bank. One for Suzy Que and the other for himself. The bank records show the following:

A. For John Doe

Year	Deposits	Interest	Balance
19X2	$2,000	$ 200	$ 2,200
19X3	2,000	400	4,600

B. For Suzy Que

Year	Deposits	Interest	Balance
19X2	$2,000	$ 200	$ 2,200
19X3	2,000	400	4,600

Trusts

John Doe set up trust accounts for his parents, two brothers, and sister at First National Bank during 19X3.

Parents	$100,000	
Brothers (2)	100,000	each
Sister	100,000	

The trust funds pay for the brothers' college tuition and books.

Earnings

The Unemployment Bureau was contacted about the earnings of Suzy Que. They provided the following data:

Date	Bank	Que Clothes	Total
19X1	$13,000	$ -0-	$13,000
19X2	14,000	50,000	54,000
19X3	15,000	70,000	85,000

Securities

John Doe purchased 100 shares of ABC stock for $10,000 on 6/30/X2. Three months later Doe sold the stock for $12,000. On 9/30/X2, Doe purchased 10 shares of XYZ stock for $12,000. Two months later, the XYZ stock was sold for $9,000.

Property Taxes

The county tax collector's office provided records on property taxes assessed and collected from John Doe on his personal residence at 100 Alpha Street. The records show that John Doe paid $5,000 in 19X1 and $5,000 in 19X3. John Doe is delinquent on his property tax bill for 19X2 of $5,000.

Intelligence

Background

John Doe is 24-year-old young man. He dropped out of high school during his sophomore year. He held only menial jobs as a boat mechanics' helper. He never married, but dated many girls on a regular basis. Even though he had no formal training in boat mechanics, he became fairly good at fixing boat engines, especially diesel engines. He was born in Cuba and came to the United States with his parents, two brothers, and a sister. In high school, he smoked marijuana and sold it to fellow high school students. His father is a medical doctor who worked as a laboratory technician until he became certified in this country in 19X4. His mother also worked as a laboratory technician until she got certified as a registered nurse in 19X4. His two brothers, who are older, are attending college. One brother is studying to become a civil engineer and the other is studying to become a dentist. Doe's sister is still in high school.

Commodities

Investigators observed John Doe on 6/30/X1 going into a jewelry store with a black attaché case. He stayed in the store for about 30 minutes and came out with his black attaché case. The investigators went into the store after Doe drove away. The store manager told the investigators that Doe purchased 10 bars of gold bullion for $100,000 in cash. The store owner was very reluctant to talk about this transaction.

Offshore Mortgage

Investigators in Panama did a check on Panama Mortgage Company. They discovered that the corporation was a registered corporation. The registered agent was a law firm. The law firm would not give any information about the corporation. The president and director of the corporation were shown on public records. When the investigators checked out the address of the president and director, they found only a vacant lot in Panama.

Offshore Bank

A formal request was issued to Scotland Yard, London, England for bank records from Barclays Bank of London. The British authorities sent the records to the United States. An examination of these records showed that John Doe deposited cash in the British bank. The funds were later sent by wire transfer to the Panama National Bank in Panama. Banks in Panama did not give any banking information because of the banks rules or confidentiality.

Surveillance

During a surveillance, it was observed that John Doe and Ramon Calderone were having dinner at the luxury club, Tootie, on 12/22/X0. Ramon Calderone is a well-known drug kingpin from Colombia. Calderone has been arrested five times, but the charges were dropped because the witnesses were found floating in the Miami River.

Corporate Check

Bureau of Corporations shows that Real Estate, Ltd., a partnership, has only two partners, John Doe and Ramon Calderone. Panama Mortgage Company has no registered agent in the United States. It is not even registered to do business in any state of the United States.

Girl Friend

John Doe met a girl, Suzy Que, on 2/28/X1 at the First National Bank where she worked as a teller. She was seen regularly with John Doe at various nightclubs, sporting events, and shopping malls. Shortly after John Doe purchased the house on 100 Alpha Street, Suzy moved in with John. She drove her own car until John purchased the Toyota for her. She drove the Toyota exclusively. Suzy continued working at the First National Bank. Friends said that she used cocaine regularly after meeting John Doe. In 19X2 and 19X3, after leaving her bank teller job, Suzy Que operated the Suzy's Women's Clothes business. Suzy hired and supervised employees, however, John Doe was frequently at the business and controlled all the finances. When Suzy Que traveled with John Doe, Ms. Betsy Low, the bookkeeper, would manage the business. Betsy Low kept the books. She maintained all journals, ledgers, and prepared a trial balance each month. John Doe never told Suzy Que about his drug-trafficking activities. She only assumed that John Doe was a legitimate businessman because of all of the business activities that John Doe controlled. She never overheard any conversations of John Doe's illegal activities.

Currency Transaction Reports

A check of currency transaction reports revealed that First National Bank filed no reports for John Doe or any of his businesses. Also, there were no payments to Panama Mortgage Company for the mortgage on the residence by either personal checks, wire transfers, cashier's checks, or money orders.

Wiretap

During an authorized wiretap of Doe's residence during the last two months of 19X3, it was discovered that Doe was talking with Ramon Calderone in Colombia about a large shipment of cocaine by ship from Colombia to the Bahama Islands. Doe was to pick up the cocaine by his boat while the ship was docked in Freeport, Bahama Islands. Two weeks later, Doe and Que, along with two unidentified couples, got on the boat for the weekend. U.S. Customs intercepted the boat on the way back to the United States, but no drugs were found.

Telephone Records

The telephone toll records were obtained from the telephone company on John Doe's home telephone. These records covered the period of 1/1/X1 through 12/31/X3. They reflected the following data. Also, the telephone company provided the subscribers information.

Telephone Number	Number of calls	Subscriber	Country
809-XXX-XXX1	33	(A) Residence	Bahama Islands
809-XXX-XXX2	20	Barclays Bank	Cayman Islands
809-XXX-XXX3	18	Central Bank	Barbados
809-XXX-XXX4	6	Central Bank	Jamaica
809-XXX-XXX5	65	Central Bank	Bahama Islands
011-41-1-XXXXXA	2	Credit Swiss	Switzerland
011-44-1-XXXXXB	8	Barclays Bank	England
011-57-4-XXXXXC	24	R. Calderone	Colombia
011-507-XXXXXD	10	Panama Bank	Panama
011-599-8-XXXXXE	36	Panama Bank	Netherlands Ant.
011-34-3-XXXXXF	18	(B) Residence	Spain
011-34-3-XXXXXG	12	Central Bank	Spain

(A) Residence in the name of John Doe

(B) Residence in the name of Ramon Calderone

Bahama Islands Banks

A request to the Bahamian authorities was made as to the property in the Bahama Islands and for banking information from the Central Bank. They provided the following:

a. The residence in the Bahama Islands was purchased on 7/1/X2 for U.S. $100,000. It was a four-bedroom, three-bath house on Blue Lagoon Cay. The house is recorded in the name of Suzy Que. There are no liens. The house has excellent dockage facilities along with a small guesthouse.

b. The Bahamian authorities obtained the following bank records along with other information regarding the bank account. The bank account at Central Bank is held under the name of Transshipment, Ltd. The corporate officers and directors are John Doe and Suzy Que. The corporation was formed on 6/1/X2 in Freeport, Grand Bahama. The bank account is summarized as follows:

Date	Description	Deposits	Checks	Balance
6/1/X2	Cash	$2,000,000		$2,000,000
6/30/X2	Cash	1,000,000		3,000,000
7/1/X2	Blue Lagoon Realty		$ 110,000	2,890,000
7/10/X2	Calderone		1,500,000	1,390,000
10/1/X2	Cash	5,000,000		6,390,000
10/30/X2	Wire Calderone		2,000,000	4,390,000
3/1/X3	Cash	10,000,000		14,390,000
3/10/X3	Wire Calderone		6,000,000	8,390,000
3/31/X3	Cayman Islands		2,000,000	6,390,000
3/31/X3	Barbados		2,000,000	4,390,000
3/31/X3	Spain		1,000,000	3,390,000
3/31/X3	Switzerland		1,000,000	2,390,000
3/31/X3	Panama		500,000	1,890,000
3/31/X3	Aruba		370,000	1,520,000
3/31/X3	Bank charges		20,000	1,500,000
3/31/X3	Jamaica		1,000,000	500,000
10/1/X3	Cash	8,000,000		8,500,000
10/10/X3	Spain		4,500,000	4,000,000
12/1/X3	Panama		3,500,000	500,000

Barbados Banks

A request to the Barbados authorities was made as to the banking information from their Central Bank. The account is titled to John Doe. Suzy Que can also sign on the account. They provided the following information:

Date	Description	Deposits	Checks	Balance
3/31/X3	Bahama Islands	$2,000,000		$2,000,000
3/31/X3	Bank fees		$ 10,000	1,990,000
12/31/X3	Interest	199,000		2,189,000

Spanish Banks

A formal request to the Spanish authorities was made for banking information from their Central Bank. Transshipment, Ltd. holds the account. The officer is John Doe. They provided the following information:

Date	Description	Deposits	Checks	Balance
3/31/X3	Bahama Islands	$1,000,000		$1,000,000
6/30/X3	Interest	100,000		1,100,000
6/30/X3	Bank charges		$ 10,000	1,090,000

The Spanish authorities also provided additional information. The Central Bank of Spain has an account for Ramon Calderone. In addition, Calderone owns a residence on the Coast at Costa Del Sol. Calderone paid $2,000,000 for the residence, which has seven bedrooms, four baths, a three-car garage, swimming pool, and dock space for two yachts. The residence has two guest houses and servant quarters for eight servants.

Cayman Island Banks

A request to the Cayman Island authorities was made for banking information from Barclays Bank plus any other information that they could provide. The account is titled under John Doe with Suzy Que as a signatory on the account. They provided the following data:

Date	Description	Deposits	Checks	Balance
3/31/X3	Bahama Islands	$2,000,000		$2,000,000
6/30/X3	Interest	200,000		2,200,000
6/30/X3	Bank charges		$20,000	2,180,000
9/30/X3	Interest	210,000		2,390,000
9/30/X3	Bank charges		20,000	2,370,000
12/31/X3	Interest	230,000		2,600,000
12/31/X3	Bank charges		20,000	2,580,000

Swiss Banks

The Swiss authorities provided the following information in response to a formal request. The account is held under Transshipment, Ltd. John Doe is shown as president.

Date	Description	Deposits	Checks	Balance
4/1/X3	Bahama Islands	$1,000,000		$1,000,000
12/10/X3	Panama	3,000,000		4,000,000
12/20/X3	Aruba		$2,000,000	2,000,000
12/31/X3	Interest	100,000		2,100,000
12/31/X3	Bank fees		10,000	2,090,000

Aruba Banks

Authorities in Aruba provided the following data. The bank account is listed under Doe Holding NV. John Doe is shown as president and Suzy Que is treasurer and secretary.

Date	Description	Deposits	Checks	Balance
4/4/X3	Bahama Islands	$ 370,000		$ 370,000
4/4/X3	Jamaica	100,000		470,000
4/10/X3	Schmidt Mgt. Co		$ 20,000	450,000
6/30/X3	Bank fees		10,000	440,000
12/20/X3	Switzerland	2,000,000		2,440,000
12/31/X3	Interest	150,000		2,590,000
12/31/X3	Schmidt Mgt. Co		25,000	2,565,000

Jamaican Banks

The bank records from Jamaica were obtained. The account is only in John Doe's name. These records reflected the following:

Date	Description	Deposits	Checks	Balance
3/31/X3	Bahama Islands	$1,000,000		$1,000,000
4/3/X3	Aruba		$ 100,000	900,000
4/3/X3	Boat Repair Shop		100,000	800,000
4/10/X3	Montego Hotel		20,000	780,000
4/10/X3	Gulf Oil		500	779,500
12/31/X3	Interest	7,500		787,000
12/31/X3	Bank fees		1,000	786,000

Accountant

I. M. Balance, CPA, prepares all the various tax returns for John Doe including his corporations and partnerships. I. M. Balance did not suspect John Doe of being a drug trafficker or money launderer. John Doe periodically brought all of his various records to Mr. Balance except for the sole proprietorship. Mr. Balance went to "Suzy's Women's Clothes" store in order to perform his certified audit. He performed the entire audit tests and analysis that were required under Standard Audit Procedures. Mr. Balance had the records for John Doe's apartment building for 19X2. He had in his possession all the records required to complete John Doe's individual tax return for 19X2, but failed to complete this return. His excuse was that he simply forgot to prepare the individual tax return for 19X2. Investigators had no evidence that Mr. Balance helped John Doe in laundering his illegal profits. In fact, Mr. Balance believed that John Doe was a young and successful businessman who would adhere to his advice. Doe was friendly and personable to Mr. Balance. Doe would give small gifts to Mr. Balance at Christmastime.

RICO Net Worth Solution

8

Introduction

The following solution and explanations relate to the scenario case problem as presented in the previous chapter. The solution and explanations are based upon RICO Net Worth principals in this chapter.

Principals

The RICO Net Worth is based upon the fund principal. Funds involve the use of cash, either directly or indirectly. As mentioned earlier, there is no amortization, depreciation, or depletion allowances allowed in a RICO Net Worth. Cash spent for asset purchases and expenses are recognized immediately. Cash spent to reduce liabilities and some income items are recognized indirectly. In the case of liabilities, the liability balance is shown instead of the payments for the liability. However, the payments can be determined by subtracting the ending balance from the beginning balance. In the case of some income, such as wages, the gross wages are shown as income and the various withholdings are shown as an expense.

Problem

The following Net Worth Schedule shows how each item in the scenario problem is presented. In addition, an explanation of why it is presented in this manner is explained after the Net Worth Schedule. The explanation section will refer to the line items on the Net Worth Schedule.

RICO Net Worth Schedule

The next several pages present a RICO Net Worth Schedule (Table 8-1). The first section of the Net Worth Schedule is entitled "Assets." These are items that can be forfeited in case of conviction or civil ruling. The next section is "Liabilities." These are claims upon the assets by creditors. They have prior claims on these assets if secured. The liabilities are subtracted from the total assets. This will give the net worth of the subject. This net worth is compared to find the increase from one period to the next. The following section entitled "Business Expenses," shows the business expenses from the sole proprietorship. The next section is

"Personal Expenses." This is the cost which the subject incurs in everyday living. The last section is "Legal Income" or "Identified Income." This reflects the subject's legal sources of funds. When the personal expenses and the business expenses are added to the net worth increase less the legal income or identified income sources then the amount of unexplained income is derived. Under federal law, this is the amount of illegal income. The fine and forfeiture can be calculated at twice this amount.

Table 8-1 RICO Net Worth Schedule
John Doe Net Worth Schedule Title 18 - RICO

Description	19X0	19X1	19X2	19X3
		Assets		
1. Cash on hand	$ -0-	$ -0-	$ -0-	$ 50,000
2. Cocaine: 2 kilos				50,000
3. First National Bank checking		10,000	50,000	100,000
4. First National Bank savings		110,000	550,000	650,000
5. Business cash in bank			20,000	10,000
6. Accounts receivable			10,000	20,000
7. Inventory			140,000	50,000
8. Business assets			150,000	150,000
9. Security system				50,000
10. Electronic equipment			100,000	100,000
11. Appliances			20,000	20,000
12. Fixtures		10,000	10,000	10,000
13. Furniture		50,000	50,000	50,000
14. Cabinets		20,000	20,000	20,000
15. Paintings		20,000	20,000	20,000
16. Pool and tennis court		100,000	100,000	100,000
17. 100 Alpha Street		300,000	300,000	300,000
18. 100 Bravo Street		4,000,000	4,000,000	4,000,000
19. Gold bullion: 10 bars		100,000	100,000	100,000
20. Lounge Doe, Inc.		2,440,000	2,440,000	2,440,000
21. Doe Kwik Stop, Inc.		506,100	401,000	401,000
22. Real Property, Ltd.		2,030,000	2,030,000	2,072,500
23. Mercedes Benz		80,000	80,000	80,000
24. Toyota sedan			18,000	18,000
25. IRA—John Doe			2,200	4,600
26. IRA—Suzy Que			2,200	4,600
27. Bahama Islands residence			110,000	110,000
Total Assets	$ -0-	$9,776,100	$10,723,400	$10,980,700
		Liabilities		
28. FNB—Mercedes loan	$ -0-	$ 51,000	$ 39,000	$ 27,000
29. FNB—Toyota loan			8,800	6,400
30. Credit card			30,000	50,000
31. Accounts payable				50,000
32. Fla. Mortgage Co.		1,930,000	1,810,000	1,690,000
33. Business bank loan			100,000	80,000
Total Liabilities	$-0-	$1,981,000	$1,987,800	$1,903,400
Net Worth	$-0-	$7,795,100	$8,735,600	$9,077,300
Net Worth Increase		$7,795,100	$ 940,500	$ 341,700

Table 8-1 RICO Net Worth Schedule
John Doe Net Worth Schedule Title 18 - RICO

Description	19X0	19X1	19X2	19X3
Business Expenses				
34. Purchases			$ 180,000	$ 130,000
35. Inventory change			(-140,000)	90,000
36. Cost of sales			40,000	220,000
37. Advertising			80,000	40,000
38. Interest on loan			10,000	8,000
39. Insurance			50,000	50,000
40. Professional fees			25,000	25,000
41. Office expenses			30,000	10,000
42. Rent expense			50,000	50,000
43. Repairs			20,000	10,000
44. Supplies			30,000	10,000
45. Taxes and licenses			50,000	40,000
46. Utilities			40,000	40,000
47. Wages			120,000	150,000
48. Miscellaneous			15,000	7,000
Total Business Expenses		$ -0-	$ 560,000	$ 660,000
Personal Expenses				
49. Fla. Mortgage Co. interest	$ 200,000	$ 188,000	$ 176,000	
50. Utilities	10,000	10,000	20,000	
51. Telephone	30,000	40,000	45,000	
52. Insurance	5,000	10,000	10,000	
53. Life insurance	10,000			
54. Interest—Car loans	10,000	2,000		
55. Income tax withheld	95,000		150,000	
56. Property taxes	5,000		5,000	
57. Credit card charges	30,000	100,000	180,000	
58. Church donations		10,000	50,000	
59. Trust funds			400,000	
60. Loss—XYZ stock		3,000		
Total Personal Expenses	$ 395,000	$ 363,000	$1,036,000	
Total Expenses	$ 395,000	$ 923,000	$1,696,000	
Legal Income				
61. Wages/salaries	$ 190,000	$ -0-	$200,000	
62. Dividends	100,000			
63. Rental income	30,000	113,000	170,000	
64. Gain—ABC stock		2,000		
65. IRA—interest Doe		200	400	
66. IRA—interest Que		200	400	
67. Tax refunds	500	79,250		
68. Sale—XYZ stock		9,000		
69. Business income		80,000	440,000	
Total Legal Income	$ 320,500	$ 283,650	$ 810,800	
Illegal/Unidentified Income		$ 7,869,600	$ 1,579,850	$ 1,226,900

Cash on Hand

In this case, cash on hand is based upon the currency found at John Doe's residence during the execution of the search warrant (Table 8-1, line 1). There are tax cases that state there must be cash on hand figures. Cash on hand must be established as much as possible. There are various methods to determine cash on hand. One method is to check on bank deposits shortly after year end. Any cash deposits can be shown as cash on hand at year end. Another method is to show the difference between cash deposits and checks to cash during the year. Another method is to use the cash on hand figure used on personal financial statements to creditors. If there is no cash on hand at year end, then the investigator must present some evidence that the subject has no possible cash on hand.

Cocaine: 2 Kilos

In this situation, the market value of cocaine is used (Table 8-1, line 2). This is a situation where market values are used. The main reason is that no receipts will be available. However, it is well known that the subject purchased the cocaine. There were no facilities discovered that demonstrated that the cocaine was manufactured there. This means that the subject had to purchase the cocaine. Since the suspect is a subject of a drug investigation, then the suspect is in the business of reselling cocaine, thus a wholesaler. The Drug Enforcement Agency, as well as some local law enforcement agencies, keep records of the market values of drugs on a weekly, monthly, and yearly basis, by type of drug. In trial, an expert who keeps statistics on drug market values will have to testify on this issue.

Bank Accounts

The bank balances are used in this schedule for the personal bank accounts and the book balance is used for the business account (Table 8-1, lines 3, 4, and 5). The personal bank accounts require no need for a bank reconciliation schedule if only the expenses, asset purchases, and liability payments are based solely upon checks that clear the bank during the year. Since there are two bank accounts, a year-end confirmation should be made to see if funds from one account are transferred to the other account for asset purchases, liability payments, and personal expenses, overlapping years. This is not the case here. The business bank account is based upon what is recorded in the books. A bank reconciliation will be needed for this bank account.

Accounts Receivable

The accounts receivable is an asset of John Doe. Sole proprietorship assets are assets of the individual since the sole proprietor has accepted title and personal liability (Table 8-1, line 6). In criminal cases, the fraud examiner will have to confirm these accounts receivables, or else have the customer testify in court that the receivable is his/her personal liability.

Inventory

Inventory of the sole proprietorship is an asset of John Doe since he has title and personal liability (Table 8-1, line 7). The key problem with inventory is determining the proper quantity and costs. It is preferred to use the sole proprietor's quantity and costs unless there is other evidence that would show something different. In this case, the sole proprietor's quantity and costs are used.

Business Assets

The business assets of the sole proprietorship are assets of John Doe since he has title and personal liability (Table 8-1, line 8). These assets are recorded at costs.

Security System

The purchase of this asset is recorded at the purchase price paid (Table 8-1, line 9).

Electronic Equipment

These assets are recorded at cost (Table 8-1, line 10).

Appliances

These assets are also recorded at cost (Table 8-1, line 11).

Fixtures

These assets are likewise recorded at cost (Table 8-1, line 12).

Furniture

These assets are recorded at cost (Table 8-1, line 13).

Cabinets

These assets are recorded at cost (Table 8-1, line 14).

Paintings

These assets are recorded at cost (Table 8-1, line 15).

Pool and Tennis Court

These assets are recorded at cost (Table 8-1, line 16). If the subject is making periodic payments for the construction of these assets, then a payment schedule will have to be obtained from the vendor to show the total costs. Remember, only the cost incurred for the period should be reflected on the schedule. Subsequent period costs will be added on as they are incurred.

100 Alpha Street

The purchase of the house is recorded at cost (Table 8-1, line 17). In this case, public records are used to determine the cost. However, the closing agent can be contacted for the closing statement which can also be used. The Best Evidence Rule should be followed whenever possible.

100 Bravo Street

The purchase of this apartment is recorded at cost (Table 8-1, line 18). Public records are used to determine the cost. The closing statement can be obtained from the closing agent which will show the exact cost including any closing costs.

Gold Bullion: 10 Bars

The 10 gold bars are recorded at cost (Table 8-1, line 19). The market value is given at the time of seizure. If the cost was not known, then the market value would be used.

Commodities, such as gold, are becoming more prevalent in money laundering. In this case, the market value is much higher than the original costs. The date of purchase should also be known. If the date is not known, then the market value would be used, but only for the period discovered. If the market value and year discovered are used, then the defense would have the burden of proof to show otherwise. If the defense does present such evidence, then the cost(s) and purchase date should be used.

Lounge Doe, Inc.

The net investment in this corporation is to be used (Table 8-1, line 20). This is normally a positive balance, but there are occasions when the net cash investment is negative. This can happen when the shareholder withdraws more out than his investment. Corporate assets belong to the corporation and not the shareholder. In this case, the corporation has a boat that is not used in the ordinary course of business. The boat might be used in illegal activities; if so, law enforcement can seize the boat. If the shareholder is caught in illegal activities, the shareholder's stock can be forfeited. The corporation then can be dissolved and the assets sold, or the corporation can be operated by a court-appointed trustee and later sold. Generally, the United States Marshal Service is responsible for seized assets.

Doe Kwik Stop, Inc.

The net investment is this corporation is to be used (Table 8-1, line 21). Its tax status has nothing to do in a RICO computation. The net investment should take into consideration capital stock, additional paid in capital, and loans from shareholder. If the corporation has loans to shareholders, then they should be subtracted from the other investment accounts.

Real Property, Ltd.

This is a partnership in which the subject has a half interest (Table 8-1, line 22). Like corporations, the net investment is used for the partner's interest only. The other partner(s) interest is not considered. Partnership assets belong to the partnership. If the assets of the partnership can be identified to the partner under investigation, then they can be severed from the partnership. In this case, the partners have an undivided interest in the assets, of real property, therefore, it can not be severed.

Mercedes Benz

This automobile is recorded at cost (Table 8-1, line 23). One problem that can arise with vehicles is trade-ins. The car dealer will allow a trade-in allowance for an old car against the purchase of a new car. This trade-in allowance will have to be accounted for. The cost of the old automobile should be subtracted from the trade-in allowance. This will give a profit or loss which will have to be recognized on the Net Worth Schedule. The purchase price will be recognized in full for the new automobile. Even though there is no cash exchanging hands, funds have been used. This is a good example of the use of funds where cash is not used.

Toyota Sedan

This automobile is also recorded at cost (Table 8-1, line 24). Even though Suzy Que is driving the car, it is still charged to Doe because he paid for it. Even if the car is registered to Suzy Que, John Doe purchased it, therefore, he should be charged for it. In essence, John Doe made a gift to Suzy Que. Another method of presentation is to show the car purchase as a gift in the expenditure section of the Net Worth Schedule instead of an asset of John Doe. The vehicle is a forfeitable asset since Suzy Que has involvement in the money laundering activities, even though not realizing it.

IRA—John Doe and Suzy Que

Individual retirement account(s) (IRA) and Keogh plans should be shown as assets (Table 8-1, lines 25 and 26). The earnings from these accounts should also be shown in the source of income schedule and added to the asset account.

Residence—Bahama Islands

The cost of foreign real estate should be shown at cost (Table 8-1, line 27). If the property is acquired in currency other than United States dollars, any loss or gain on the conversion will also have to be recognized.

First National Bank Auto Loans

These are two bank installment loans (Table 8-1, lines 28 and 29). Installment loans are presented as a liability. Period balances are shown at the end of each period. When these liabilities are incurred, they include both the principal and interest. For RICO Net Worth purposes, the interest is charged off to expense in the year incurred.

Credit Card

Balances owed on credit cards can be shown as a liability at period end (Table 8-1, line 30). The charges are shown as an expense for the period. This is an example of where the use of funds is shown indirectly. The use of funds is reflected by subtracting the liability balance from the total charges for the period. If there is a beginning liability balance, it will have to be taken into account. Another method of recognizing credit card payments is to only show the payments as an expenditure and ignore the total charges and ending liability balances.

Accounts Payable

Liabilities of a sole partnership are personal liabilities since the proprietor is personally liable. Accounts payables are claims by vendors for the business purchases (Table 8-1, line 31). In criminal cases, the fraud examiner should confirm the accounts payable, or else each vendor will have to testify as to their accounts receivable from the subject.

Florida Mortgage Co.

Mortgage balances are shown at period end (Table 8-1, line 32). There is only one major issue to speak of in this area, and that is proper recognition of year end balances. The test of mortgage balances is to subtract the interest from the total payments. This gives the amount of principal payments which reduce the mortgage balance. The escrow payments, if any, must be subtracted from the mortgage payments before the computation for principal payments is done.

Accumulated Depreciation

Accumulated depreciation is not used in RICO Net Worth computations. It must be remembered that there are no depreciation, amortization, or depletion allowances allowed in RICO Net Worth computations.

Business Bank Loan

Loans made to a sole proprietorship are personal liabilities. John Doe acquired a bank loan to help finance his business. This is a personal liability and is presented the same way as other personal liabilities (Table 8-1, line 33).

Business Expenses

The business expenses that are paid or accrued (if on the accrual basis of account) are to be added to the increase in net worth. These are period expenses which must be recognized during the period incurred whether paid or accrued in this case (Table 8-1, lines 34, and 37 through 48).

Inventory Changes

This account relates to the changes in inventory (Table 8-1, line 35). If inventory goes up, then this account will have a negative amount to reduce purchases (as shown on line 34). If inventory decreases as shown for 19X3, then this account will have an increase. These increases and decreases will directly relate to the changes in inventory balances (as shown on line 7). This inventory change account has two purposes. First, it accounts for the changes in inventory. Second, it explains the composition of the cost of sales. The combination of purchases and inventory changes make up the cost of sales account.

Cost of Sales

The cost of sales accounts for the sale of goods sold is composed of purchases and changes in inventory (Table 8-1, line 36). This is an expenditure for each period.

Florida Mortgage Co.

As explained previously, this is the interest portion of the mortgage payment (Table 8-1, line 49). This is a period expense which must be recognized during the period incurred.

Utilities

This is a period expense which must be recognized during the period paid (Table 8-1, line 50).

Telephone

This is a period expense which must be recognized during the period paid (Table 8-1, line 51).

Insurance

This is a period expense which must be recognized during the period paid (Table 8-1, line 52).

Life Insurance

This is a period expense which must be recognized during the period paid (Table 8-1, line 53). This is a prepaid expense. Prepaid expenses are generally shown as assets. For RICO purposes, this is recognized as an expense in the year paid. For forfeiture purposes, this is an asset that can be seized.

Interest

This is interest paid for the two installment loans (Table 8-1, line 54). This is the total interest for the life of the loans. For RICO purposes, the interest charged is recognized during the period incurred. In this case, the interest was incurred when the loan was obtained. Even though the interest is over a period of time beyond the current period, it is only recognized during the period incurred. It is not capitalized and amortized, instead, it is expensed in the year incurred.

Income Tax Withheld

This is a period expense which must be recognized during the period paid (Table 8-1, line 55). Even though there is a refund in later years, the fact that the income tax is withheld makes it a period expense in the period incurred. Refunds will be recognized in the period received as an identified source of funds.

Property Taxes

These are period expenses which must be recognized during the period incurred (Table 8-1, line 56). In this case, the tax return figures are used. These can be admissible in a court of law, but it is advisable to get the property taxes confirmed with the local tax collector.

Credit Card Charges

These are period expenses which must be recognized in the period incurred (Table 8-1, line 57). This is a situation where the actual charges are shown as an expense. In the case of a criminal trial, the vendors will each have to testify unless there is a stipulation to the charges made. Otherwise, the alternative solution is to show the payments made to the credit card company, which results in no credit card liability. The problem of distinguishing between business and personal use is not necessary in this case. If a corporation pays for part or all of the personal credit card balance, then these payments should be ignored.

Church Donations

These are period expenses that are recognized in the period paid (Table 8-1, line 58).

Trust Funds

These are period expenses that are recognized in the period paid (Table 8-1, line 59).

Loss—XYZ Stock

This is a period expense that is recognized in the period incurred (Table 8-1, line 60).

Wages/Salaries

These are period income items (Table 8-1, line 61). Wages and salaries are reported at the gross amounts. The various withholding items are reported as personal expenses.

Dividends

These are period income items which are reported for the period received (Table 8-1, line 62).

Rental Income

This is period income which is reported for the period earned (Table 8-1, line 63). It must be noted that these figures reflect net cash flow. Depreciation is not reflected in this net income figure. For RICO purposes, the net income that is shown on a tax return or financial statement for rental property should be adjusted by adding back any amortized and depreciation expenses. The prosecutor may want the forensic accountant to present all of the income and expenses on the Net Worth Schedule instead of net figures.

Gain—ABC Stock

Gains on the sale of capital assets, such as stock, bonds, commodities, and other properties, are reported on the RICO Net Worth Schedule (Table 8-1, line 64). Gains are computed by subtracting the original costs from the gross proceeds received. This is an identified source of receipts.

Interest

Earnings from savings are income for the period earned and available (Table 8-1, lines 65 and 66). When interest is credited to the savings account, it is recognized in the source of funds section of the Net Worth Schedule. Interest may actually be earned in a prior period, but if it is not credited to the account then it is not recognized.

Tax Refunds

This is a source of funds for the period (Table 8-1, line 67) which must be recognized. Many people file tax returns in which income tax was withheld in the prior period, but a refund is due to overpayment of the tax liability. When the subject files a tax return, it is, in essence, a claim for the excess payment.

Sale—XYZ Stock

The proceeds from the sale of capital assets, such as stocks, bonds, commodities, and other properties, are also reported on the RICO Net Worth Schedule (Table 8-1, line 68), provided they are not reinvested into other assets. If they are reinvested into other assets, then the other assets will be reflected on the asset section of the Net Worth Schedule. If they are not reinvested, then this is a source of funds which must be recognized in the source of funds section in the Net Worth Schedule.

Business Income

Gross receipts from a sole proprietorship are income to the individual owner (Table 8-1, line 69). Gross receipts are income to the proprietor whether or not all of it is collected when the proprietor is using the accrual method of recognizing income. This is the case here. When accruing sales income, there is a related account called "accounts receivable." The accounts receivable is actually gross receipts which have not been collected. If any part of the accounts receivable is determined to be uncollectable, then it should be reduced to the collectible amount and a business expense created called "bad debts" which is the amount of uncollectable accounts receivable.

Illegal Income

After adding the net worth increases, personal and business expenses, and subtracting legal or identified income, illegal income or unidentified income is derived. In presenting this case to the jury, the words "unidentified income" should be used instead of "illegal income" since the defense will object and be sustained on the grounds of "leading" the jury or "invoking" a verdict.

Offshore Evidence

The scenario problem shows many offshore transactions. You will note that these transactions are not used except for one exception. Many countries have bank secrecy laws which provide heavy criminal and civil penalties for any violations. However, certain types of records can be used if they are provided to the general public.

In this case, the real property acquired in the Bahama Islands by John Doe is public record in the Bahama Islands. The United States Embassy or Consulate in the Bahama Islands can obtain certified copies of documents and present them in court. Many countries have various treaties with the United States. Tax treaties are not in existence with "tax haven" countries. However, there are many treaties with countries, including tax haven countries, that will provide information and assistance in criminal cases other than tax cases. For instance, Switzerland will provide financial information in a criminal case, i.e., drug trafficking, but will not provide financial information in a criminal tax case. Swiss authorities, like many other tax haven countries, will require that the United States not use financial information for criminal tax cases even if obtained for other criminal charges. Introducing bank records, or other nonpublic records, from a foreign country has other problems.

The principal problem is obtaining a witness from a foreign country to introduce records into court. Foreign nationals do not like to come to the United States and testify in a criminal case. Second, the government (federal or state) must bear the expense of bringing these foreign nationals to the United States. In some instances, foreign nationals want fees and expenses.

Offshore Records

In this scenario, it will be assumed that witnesses will be obtained to introduce evidence into court. John Doe, as well as Suzy Que, has financial transactions offshore in various countries. If offshore evidence is obtained and properly introduced into court, then the Net Worth Schedule will be modified as follows (Table 8-2):

Table 8-2 RICO Net Worth Schedule Adjustments for Offshore Activities

Description	19X1	19X2	19X3
Illegal/Unidentified Income	$ 7,869,600	$ 1,579,850	$ 1,226,900
Assets			
70. Transshipment, Ltd.:			
71. Bahamian bank account		4,390,000	500,000
72. Spanish bank account			1,090,000
73. Swiss bank account			2,090,000
74. Barbados bank account			2,189,000
75. Cayman Islands bank account			2,580,000
76. Jamaica bank account			786,000
77. Doe Holding, NV			2,565,000
Total Additional Assets	$- 0-	$4,390,000	$11,800,000
Net Worth Increase	$ -0-	$4,390,000	$ 7,410,000
Expenses			
78. Barbados bank charges	$ -0-	$-0-	$ 10,000
79. Cayman Islands bank charges			60,000
80. Jamaica bank charges			1,000
81. Jamaica travel expenses			120,500
82. Wires to Calderone		3,500,000	6,000,000
83. Spanish bank charges			10,000
84. Aruba bank charges			10,000
85. Bahama Islands bank charges			20,000
86. Schmidt Mgt. Co.			45,000
Total Offshore Expenses	$ -0-	$3,500,000	$6,276,500
Identified Income			
87. Interest income—Cayman			$ 640,000
88. Interest income—Spain			100,000
89. Interest income—Swiss			100,000
90. Interest income—Aruba			150,000
91. Interest income—Jamaica			7,500
Total Identified Income	$ -0-	$-0-	$997,500
Illegal/Unidentified income	$ 7,869,600	$9,469,850	$13,915,900

Transshipment, Ltd.

Transshipment, Ltd. is a Bahama Islands Corporation. It is registered in the Bahama Islands. It does no business in the United States. However, it has opened up bank accounts in Spain and Switzerland as well as in the Bahama Islands. One can see that this is an entity that is used for laundering illegal income since it does not have the normal business expenses.

First, it receives funds in cash which are used to pay for drug shipments. These funds are, obviously, smuggled out since there are no CMIR reports. Calderone is a supplier of drugs. For trial purposes, witnesses will have to be introduced that will confirm this fact. Witnesses are hard to come by since they are sometimes found deceased. The profits are transferred to other countries: Cayman Islands, Barbados, Aruba, Panama, Jamaica, and Switzerland. Transshipment, Ltd. has no financial statements or tax returns prepared.

Therefore, the only financial information about this corporation is the bank balances in the various bank accounts (Table 8-2, lines 70 through 73, 82, 83, 85, 88, and 89).

Barbados Bank Account

John Doe opened up a bank account in Barbados. He put Suzy Que on the account by having her be a signatory on the account (Table 8-2, lines 74 and 78). This is a personal bank account that can be used on the Net Worth Schedule. However, a witness from Barbados will have to testify in court that John Doe opened and maintained the account. It is easy to see that this bank account is used for money laundering. The only expenses in this account are bank charges. The only income is interest income.

Cayman Islands Bank Account

John Doe opened a bank account in the Cayman Islands (Table 8-2, lines 75, 79, and 87). These funds came from the Bahamian bank account by wire transfer. In reality, this is an investment account since it is an interest bearing account and no funds have been withdrawn except for service charges by the bank.

Jamaican Bank Account

John Doe opened a bank account in Jamaica. John Doe used this account to pay for expenses (Table 8-2, lines 76, 80, 81, and 91). It does not earn any interest, but, in fact, has paid for expenses while John Doe was in Jamaica. The vendors for those expenses would have to testify before they could be used on the Net Worth Schedule.

Doe Holding, NV

Aruba is part of the Netherlands Antilles. It comes under Dutch control. John Doe formed this corporation along with his girlfriend, Suzy Que. Doe Holding, NV is basically an entity that is used to conceal his illicit income. The only expenses are bank charges and fees for maintaining this corporation. The only asset of this corporation is the bank account (Table 8-2, lines 77, 84, 86, and 90).

Tax Net Worth Solution

9

Introduction

The following solution and explanations relate to the scenario problem as presented in Chapter 7. The solution and explanations are based upon tax Net Worth principals.

Principals

The tax Net Worth is based upon the Federal Income Tax laws and regulations. The Federal Tax Code defines a few concepts. One concept is gross income. Gross income means income from whatever source unless specifically exempt. Adjusted gross income is another concept. It means gross income less specified deductions. Some of these deductions are individual retirement account contributions, Keogh plan contributions, alimony payments, capital losses, and others. Taxable income is another concept which involves subtracting exemptions, itemized deductions, or standard deductions from adjusted gross income. The tax Net Worth Schedule is based upon these concepts. The first objective in a tax Net Worth is to establish, if the person filed an individual Federal Income Tax Return, corrected adjusted gross income. After corrected adjusted gross income is determined, then corrected taxable income must be determined. Some itemized deductions have limitations which are based upon adjusted gross income. Medical expense is one example of a deduction which has limitations on the amount deductible based upon adjusted gross income. Corrected taxable income is determined by subtracting exemptions and itemized or standard deductions from corrected adjusted gross income.

Problem

The following Net Worth Schedule shows how each item in the scenario problem is presented. An explanation of why it is presented in the manner shown is explained after the Net Worth Schedule. The explanation section will refer to the line item on the Net Worth Schedule.

Tax Net Worth Schedule

The next several pages present a tax Net Worth Schedule (Table 9-1). The first section is "Assets." Assets are items that have future value and can be levied against if additional tax is due. The next section is "Liabilities." These are the claims by creditors against the assets. They have priority if secured. The "Liabilities" are subtracted from the "Assets" to derive the net worth. This is compared from one period to the next to derive increases. The next section is "Personal Living Expenses." This reflects the taxpayer's cost of living. The next section is "Nontaxable Income." This is income, derived from sources, that is not taxed. When the net worth increase is added to personal living expenses less nontaxable income, then adjusted gross income is derived. To arrive at taxable income, exemption(s) and itemized deductions or standard deductions are subtracted from adjusted gross income. This corrected taxable income is compared to reported taxable income, if taxpayer filed a return, for the net increase.

Cash on Hand

Cash on hand is based upon the currency found at John Doe's residence during the execution of a search warrant (Table 9-1, line 1). There are many tax cases, which state that there must be cash on hand figures. Cash on hand must be established as precisely as possible, whenever possible. There are various methods to determine cash on hand. One method is to check on bank deposits shortly after year-end. Any cash deposits can be shown as cash on hand at year-end. Another method is to show the difference between cash deposits and checks to cash during the year. Yet, another method is to use the cash on hand figures used on personal financial statements to creditors. If there is no cash on hand at year-end, then the investigator must present some evidence that the taxpayer has no possible cash on hand.

Cocaine: 2 Kilos

The market value of cocaine is used (Table 9-1, line 2) since no receipts will be available. There were no facilities discovered that the cocaine was manufactured there. This means that the taxpayer had to purchase the cocaine for resale. The Drug Enforcement Administration, as well as some local enforcement agencies, keeps records of the market values of drugs on a weekly, monthly, and yearly basis, by type of drug. In trial, an expert who keeps statistics on drug market values will have to testify on this issue.

First National Bank Accounts

The bank balances are used in this case (Table 9-1, lines 3 and 4). This requires no need for a bank reconciliation schedule. Since there are two bank accounts, a year-end confirmation should be made to see if funds from one account are transferred to the other account, overlapping years. This is not the case here.

Business Cash In Bank

This bank account is based upon book balances (Table 9-1, line 5). The sole proprietorship is kept on the accrual method of accounting. When books are kept on the accrual method of accounting, then the book balances are used. There are various reasons. First, there are books and records kept on each transaction, which show the appropriate time of occurrence. Second, timing differences are eliminated. If a loan is made to the bank, then the book balance of the loan will be recognized instead of the bank balance, which would be higher since they received the payment in the subsequent year. Book balances will reflect

Table 9-1 Tax Net Worth Schedule
John Doe Net Worth Schedule Title 26, Tax

Description	19X0	19X1	19X2	19X3
Assets				
1. Cash on hand	$ -0-	$ -0-	$ -0-	$ 50,000
2. Cocaine: 2 kilos				50,000
3. FNB checking		10,000	50,000	100,000
4. FNB savings		110,000	550,000	650,000
5. Business checking			20,000	10,000
6. Accounts receivable			10,000	20,000
7. Inventory			140,000	50,000
8. Business assets			150,000	150,000
9. Security system				50,000
10. Electronic equipment			100,000	100,000
11. Appliances			20,000	20,000
12. Fixtures		10,000	10,000	10,000
13. Furniture		50,000	50,000	50,000
14. Cabinets		20,000	20,000	20,000
15. Paintings		20,000	20,000	20,000
16. Pool and tennis court		100,000	100,000	100,000
17. 100 Alpha Street		300,000	300,000	300,000
18. 100 Bravo Street		4,000,000	4,000,000	4,000,000
19. Gold bullion: 10 bars		100,000	100,000	100,000
20. Lounge Doe, Inc.		2,440,000	2,440,000	2,440,000
21. Doe Kwik Stop, Inc.		481,100	326,000	501,000
22. Real Property, Ltd.		1,930,000	1,877,500	1,890,000
23. Mercedes Benz		80,000	80,000	80,000
24. Toyota sedan			18,000	18,000
25. IRA—Doe			2,200	4,600
26. IRA—Que			2,200	4,600
27. Residence—Bahama Islands			110,000	110,000
28. Prepaid interest		8,500	8,260	5,780
Total Assets	$ -0-	$ 9,659,600	$ 10,504,160	$ 10,903,980
Liabilities				
29. FNB—Mercedes loan	$-0-	$ 51,000	$ 39,000	$ 27,000
30. FNB—Toyota loan			8,800	6,400
31. Credit card			30,000	50,000
32. Accounts payable				50,000
33. Accumulated depreciation		100,000	330,000	560,000
34. Fla. Mortgage Co.		1,930,000	1,810,000	1,690,000
35. Business bank loan			100,000	80,000
Total Liabilities	$ -0-	$2,081,000	$ 2,317,800	$ 2,463,400
Net Worth	$ -0-	$7,578,600	$ 8,186,360	$ 8,440,580
Net Worth Increase		$7,578,600	$607,760	$ 254,220
Personal Living Expenses:				
36. Fla. Mortgage Co. interest		$ 200,000	$188,000	$ 176,000
37. Utilities		10,000	10,000	20,000
38. Telephone		30,000	40,000	45,000
39. Insurance		5,000	10,000	10,000

continued

Table 9-1 Tax Net Worth Schedule
John Doe Net Worth Schedule Title 26, Tax

Description	19X0	19X1	19X2	19X3
40. Life insurance		10,000		
41. Interest-Mercedes loan		1,500	2,000	2,000
42. Interest-Toyota loan			240	480
43. Income tax withheld		95,000		150,000
44. Property taxes		5,000		5,000
45. Credit cards		30,000	100,000	180,000
46. Church donations			10,000	50,000
47. Trust funds				400,000
Total Personal Expenses		$ 386,500	$ 360,240	$ 1,038,480
Nontaxable Income:				
48. IRA—interest—Doe			2,200	2,400
49. IRA—interest—Que			2,200	2,400
50. Tax refunds		500	79,250	
Total Nontaxable Income		$ 500	$ 83,650	$ 4,800
Adjusted Gross Income		$ 7,964,600	$ 884,350	$ 1,287,900
Itemized Deductions		206,500	200,240	233,480
Exemptions		2,000	2,000	2,000
Corrected Taxable Income		$ 7,756,100	$ 682,110	$ 1,052,420
Reported Taxable Income		63,000	0	285,400
Increase		$ 7,693,100	$ 682,110	$ 767,020

proper account balances throughout the business accounts. Third, bank reconciliations will normally be available to prove out the book balances of accounts. This not only applies to the bank account but also related accounts, i.e., accounts receivable, accounts payable, loans, capital accounts, and more.

Accounts Receivable

Even though this is a business asset, it is an asset of the individual since assets of a sole proprietorship are individually owned (Table 9-1, line 6). Accounts receivable is an amount owed to the individual by customers of the sole proprietorship. This is an intangible asset of the individual, in this case, John Doe.

Inventory

This is an asset of the individual owner of the sole proprietorship (Table 9-1, line 7). This is an asset that is hard to prove, especially, if the business has many product lines. If the business takes inventory at year-end, then this inventory quantity and value should be used, especially if done by independent parties. If inventory is not taken, then the inventory value should be estimated as closely as possible to its costs. One method of doing this is the gross profit method which uses a fairly constant cost of sales percentage based upon either the business mark-ups or industry average that will force out inventory values at year-end.

Business Assets
Business assets of a sole proprietorship are assets of the individual that owns the business (Table 9-1, line 8). These assets should be recorded at cost, especially when they are recorded in the books and records at cost, which is normal for keeping business books and records. This will have a contra asset account called accumulated depreciation. This account will be addressed in a later paragraph.

Security System
The purchase of this asset is recorded at the purchase price (Table 9-1, line 9).

Electronic Equipment
These assets are recorded at cost (Table 9-1, line 10).

Appliances
These assets are also recorded at cost (Table 9-1, line 11).

Fixtures
These assets are likewise recorded at cost (Table 9-1, line 12).

Furniture
These assets are recorded at cost (Table 9-1, line 13).

Cabinets
These assets are recorded at cost (Table 9-1, line 14).

Paintings
These assets are recorded at cost (Table 9-1, line 15).

Pool and Tennis Court
These assets, likewise, are recorded at cost (Table 9-1, line 16). If the taxpayer is making periodic payments for the construction of these assets, then a payment schedule will have to be obtained from the contractor to show the total costs. Remember, only the cost incurred during the period should be reflected on the schedule. Subsequent period costs will be added on as they are incurred.

100 Alpha Street
The purchase of the house is recorded at cost (Table 9-1, line 17). In this case, public records are used to determine the cost. However, the closing agent can be contracted for the closing statement which can also be used. Remember, the Best Evidence Rule should be used when possible.

100 Bravo Street
The purchase of this apartment building is recorded at cost (Table 9-1, line 18). Public records are used to determine cost. The closing statement can be obtained from the closing agent who will show the cost including any closing costs.

Gold Bullion: 10 Bars

The 10 gold bars are recorded at cost (Table 9-1, line 19). The market value is given at the time of seizure. If the cost is not known, then the market value would be used. The market value is higher than the original cost in this case. If the market value and year discovered are used, then the defense would have the burden of proof to show otherwise. If the defense does present such evidence, then their costs and purchase date should be used.

Lounge Doe, Inc.

The net investment in this corporation is to be used (Table 9-1, line 20). This is normally a positive balance, but there are occasions when the net cash investment can be negative. This can happen when the shareholder withdraws out more than his investment. Corporate assets belong to the corporation and not the shareholder. This corporation has a boat that is not used in the ordinary course of business. The boat might be used in illegal activities. However, the boat cannot be depreciated on the corporate books for tax purposes.

Doe Kwik Stop, Inc.

This is a Subchapter S Corporation (Table 9-1, line 21). The Net Worth Schedule not only uses the shareholder's net cash investment, but also must take into consideration any accumulated earnings or losses the corporation has during the period. The Sub S Corporation is not a taxable entity. Instead, the earnings and losses are passed on to the individual shareholders on a pro rata basis. The total net cash investment, earnings, and losses are shown on the Net Worth Schedule, but never below zero.

Real Property, Ltd.

This is a partnership in which the taxpayer has half interest (Table 9-1, line 22). Like the Sub S corporation, partnership is a nontaxable entity. Any earnings or losses are passed through to the partner based upon the partner's interest. The total net cash investment, earnings, and losses are shown on the Net Worth Schedule. This can be negative only to the extent that the partner is at risk for his share of the liabilities.

Mercedes Benz

This automobile is recorded at cost (Table 9-1, line 23). One problem that can arise with vehicles is accounting for trade-ins. The car dealer will allow a trade-in allowance for an old car against the purchase of a new car. This trade-in allowance is used to reduce the purchase price. For tax purposes, the trade-in allowance is used to determine the gain or loss of the old car by subtracting the net basis (cost less any accumulated depreciation) from the trade-in allowance. The gain or loss on the old car will be subtracted (gains) or added (losses) to the cost of the new car. This is referred to as like-kind exchanges.

Toyota Sedan

This automobile is also recorded at cost (Table 9-1, line 24). Even though Suzy Que is driving the car, it is still charged to Doe because he paid for it. Even if the car is registered in Suzy Que's name, if John Doe purchased it, then he should be charged for it. Another method of presenting the car purchase is a gift in the personal expenditure section of the Net Worth Schedule instead of an asset of John Doe.

IRA—John Doe and Suzy Que

Individual Retirement Accounts (IRA) and Keogh Plans should be shown as assets (Table 9-1, lines 25 and 26). The earnings from IRA's and Keogh Plans are nontaxable. One method of presentation is to show, as an asset, the total contributions and earnings. The earnings for the period will be reflected in the nontaxable source of income. The other method of presentation is to show, as an asset, the total accumulated contributions and ignore the accumulated earnings. Either method is acceptable, however, the former is preferred since it shows the actual fund(s) in the account.

Residence—Bahama Islands

The cost of foreign real estate should be shown at cost (Table 9-1, line 27). If the property is acquired in currency other than United States dollars, then a conversion will have to be made. Any loss or gain on the conversion will also have to be recognized. Since this would be an adjustment to gross income, it would not be recognized on the tax Net Worth Schedule.

Prepaid Interest

Installment loans have the characteristic of computing interest for the life of the loan and adding it to the principal balance. For tax purposes, the interest can only be recognized over the period of the loan (Table 9-1, line 28). This will result in a deferred expense account called prepaid interest. It is shown in the asset section of the Net Worth Schedule. Each subsequent year, a pro rata portion is written off to the personal expenditure section. In addition, it is shown again as an itemized deduction, if deductible.

First National Bank Auto Loans

There are two bank installment loans (Table 9-1, lines 29 and 30). Installment loans are presented as a liability. Period balances are shown at the end of each period. When these liabilities are incurred, they include both the principal and interest.

Credit Card

Balances owed on credit cards can be shown as a liability at period end (Table 9-1, line 31). The charges are shown as a personal expenditure for the period. Another way of presenting credit cards is to show only the amount paid to the credit card company as a personal expenditure. Either method can be used, but they must be used consistently.

Accounts Payable

Accounts payables are liabilities of the sole proprietor (Table 9-1, line 32). Liabilities of a sole proprietor are liabilities of the individual since the individual is personally liable.

Accumulated Depreciation

Accumulated depreciation balances has to be shown on the Net Worth Schedule (Table 9-1, line 33). This is a liability on the grounds that this is a potential liability. The federal tax laws and regulations require the recovery of accumulated depreciation as ordinary taxable income to the extent of any gain recognized on the sale of the depreciable asset.

Florida Mortgage Co.

Mortgage balances are shown at period end (Table 9-1, line 34). The mortgage payments include principal and interest. In many cases, mortgage payments also include escrow payments to cover property taxes and insurance. If this is the case, a corresponding asset for escrow balances will have to be reflected on the Net Worth Schedule.

Business Bank Loan

Loans from financial institutions by a sole proprietor are individual loans (Table 9-1, line 35). The individual is personally liable for the business bank loan, therefore, it is a personal liability.

Florida Mortgage Co. Interest

This is the interest portion of the mortgage payments (Table 9-1, line 36). This is shown as both a personal expenditure and as an itemized deduction.

Utilities

This is a period expense which must be recognized during the period paid as a personal expenditure (Table 9-1, line 37).

Telephone

This is also a period expense that must be recognized during the period paid as a personal expenditure (Table 9-1, line 38).

Insurance

This is a period expense that must be recognized during the period paid (Table 9-1, line 39). It also must be kept in mind that medical insurance premiums can also be deducted as an itemized deduction.

Life Insurance

Life insurance is normally a period expense (Table 9-1, line 40). However, in the case of whole life policies which have surrender or cash values, life insurance policies should reflect the cash value as an asset and the noncash value as an expense. This solution has treated the whole life policy as an expense.

Interest Amortized

This is the pro rata portion of the prepaid interest (Table 9-1, lines 41 and 42). This is shown as a current period expense. In addition, it can be used as an itemized deduction.

Income Tax Withheld

This is a period expense (Table 9-1, line 43). Even though this is a personal expenditure, there won't be any payments found for this expense in the taxpayer's possession. The employer pays this expense out of the taxpayer's gross wages and salaries. In addition to the income tax withholding, FICA tax (Social Security contributions) is also withheld and should be reflected as a personal expense. The FICA tax was not presented in this problem.

Property Tax

This is a period expense (Table 9-1, line 44). Property taxes must be recognized only in the period when paid. Sometimes, taxpayers will pay their property taxes for two years in one year.

Credit Card Charges

These are period expenses (Table 9-1, line 45). This presentation shows the total charges made during the period. It does not show the payments to the credit card company. For trial purposes, the vendors who accepted the credit card charges will have to introduce these into court. The alternative method is to introduce the credit card record custodian as to the payments received from the taxpayer. A problem can arise if any of the charges made were for business expenses. If any charges were made for business expenses, then they will have to be subtracted from the total charges or the total of the payments.

Church Donations

These are period expenses (Table 9-1, line 46). In addition to being shown on the personal expenditure section, they are also used as an itemized deduction.

Trust Funds

These are period expenses (Table 9-1, line 47). The key question in this situation is whether the trust is a viable instrument. Sometimes, trusts are set up to cover up a taxpayer's own funds. If this is the case, then the trust fund should be shown as the taxpayer's asset.

Loss—XYZ Stock

This is a period expense. For tax purposes, losses on stock are not recognized since this is a capital asset. Losses on sale of capital assets are not recognized on the net worth computation. The main reason is that this is an adjustment to derive adjusted gross income. The purpose of the tax Net Worth Schedule is to derive adjusted gross income and not gross income. Therefore, it is not shown on the tax Net Worth Schedule.

IRA Interest

The interest earned on Individual Retirement Accounts and Keogh plans is not taxable (Table 9-1, lines 48 and 49). As explained previously, if these accounts are shown in the asset section with both earnings and contributions, then the interest earned for the period will have to be shown as a nontaxable source of income.

Tax Refunds

Tax refunds are nontaxable sources (Table 9-1, line 50). This Net Worth Schedule reflects the total taxes paid as a personal expenditure and refunds as a source of nontaxable income. However, it can be shown at net. It is better to show it separately in order to disclose both.

Itemized Deductions

Itemized deductions or the standard deduction is allowed to reduce adjusted gross income to derive at taxable income. The Federal Income Tax Code allows certain expenses to be deducted. The primary ones are medical expenses, interest expenses, charity contributions, certain taxes, and some other miscellaneous expenses. In this solution, itemized deductions are the total personal expenditures for interest (mortgage and amortized interest), church donations, and property taxes. Limitations on these deductions, which are built in the Federal Income Tax Code, have been ignored in this problem. The itemized deductions are delineated below:

Description	19X1	19X2	19X3
Fla. Mortgage Co. interest	$200,000	$188,000	$176,000
Interest—Mercedes	1,500	2,000	2,000
Interest—Toyota		240	480
Property taxes	5,000		5,000
Church donations		10,000	50,000
Total	$206,500	$100,240	$233,480

Exemptions

Exemptions are an income tax concept. The amount of these exemptions varies from year to year. For the sake of simplicity, $2,000 per exemption is used in this case.

Offshore Evidence

The scenario problem has many offshore assets and transactions. These assets and transactions cannot be used on the Net Worth Schedule unless witnesses are available to introduce them into court. There are exceptions. One exception is the introduction of public records from a particular country. In this case, the Bahama Islands' real property is public record and can be introduced into court. The United States Embassy or Consulate in the Bahama Islands can obtain certified copies of documents and present them into court records. Bank records cannot be introduced into court since many countries have bank secrecy laws which provide heavy criminal and civil penalties for any violations. Also, many "tax haven" countries will not allow bank records for criminal or civil tax trials in the United States. Another problem of introducing nonpublic records is obtaining a witness from a foreign country. Foreign nationals do not like to come to the United States and testify in a criminal case. The government (federal and state) must bear the expense of bringing these foreign nationals to the United States.

Offshore Records

Now, it will be assumed that witnesses will be obtained to introduce evidence into court. John Doe and Suzy Que have assets and financial transactions in various countries. If the offshore evidence is properly obtained and introduced into court, then the Net Worth Schedule will be modified (Table 9-2).

Transshipment, Ltd. Bank Accounts

Transshipment, Ltd. is a Bahamian Corporation. Since corporate books and records were not kept, then the bank accounts are assets of the corporation as well as the capital, which is the shareholder's equity. The corporation does not do any business, therefore, it is a "shell" corporation. Transshipment, Ltd. has bank accounts in three foreign countries (Table 9-2, lines 51 through 53).

Table 9-2 Tax Net Worth Adjustments for Offshore Activities
John Doe Net Worth Schedule Title 26, Tax

Description	19X1	19X2	19X3
	Assets		
Transshipment, Ltd:			
51. Bahamian bank account	$ -0-	$ 4,390,000	$ 500,000
52. Spanish bank account			1,090,000
53. Swiss bank account			2,090,000
Personal Accounts:			
54. Barbados bank account			2,189,000
55. Cayman Islands bank account			2,580,000
56. Jamaica bank account			786,000
57. Doe Holding NV bank account			2,565,000
Total Additional Assets:	$-0-	$4,390,000	$11,800,000
Net Worth Increase	$ -0-	$4,390,000	$ 7,410,000
Expenses:			
58. Barbados bank charges			10,000
59. Cayman Islands bank charges			60,000
60. Jamaica bank charges			1,000
61. Jamaica travel expenses			120,500
Total Expenses	$ -0-	$ -0-	$ 191,500
Previous Corrected Income	$ 7,756,100	$ 682,110	$1,052,420
Corrected Taxable Income	7,756,100	5,072,110	8,653,920
Reported Taxable Income	63,000	-0-	285,400
Increase	$ 7,693,100	$ 5,072,110	$ 8,368,520

Bank Accounts

These are assets of John Doe (Table 9-2, lines 54 through 56). Bank balances are used instead of book balances. These accounts are in three different countries, two of which are tax haven countries. In tax cases, tax haven officials, whether bank or government, will not cooperate in tax matters. However, these records can be used if found during a search. The Jamaican bank account was used to pay expenses while in that country. The other two accounts were used only to park his illegal gains. In all probability, the government will not be able to seize these funds. The corporate bank accounts are also assets of John Doe.

Doe Holding, NV

Aruba is part of the Netherlands Antilles which is under Dutch control. Doe Holding, NV is a Netherlands Antilles corporation that was formed by John Doe and Suzy Que. The only asset of this corporation is the bank account (Table 9-2, line 57). The corporation has no business activities. The funds are capital contributions by John Doe. This is a "shell" corporation.

Bank Charges

These are period expenses (Table 9-2, lines 58 through 60). Record custodians will have to introduce these records into trial court unless the defense will stipulate. This can be a problem if the foreign witnesses refuse to testify. Another problem area is the conversion of foreign currency into United States currency. Bank charges on corporate accounts are not shown since this would be a corporate expense. However, they could be shown in this case based upon the fact that these corporations were only "shells." Assets of "shell" corporations are in reality assets of the individual(s) who is (are) being concealed by corporate identity.

Travel—Jamaica

This is a period expense (Table 9-2, line 61). This could be classified as either a vacation trip or a business trip. A vacation trip is a personal expense and should be reflected on the Net Worth Schedule. If this is a business trip, then this is not reflected on the Net Worth Schedule if it is part of a sole proprietorship. As an employee or officer of a corporation, it can be classified as a personal expense, but later on can be deducted as an itemized deduction with limitations. However, if the business trip is to facilitate drug-trafficking activities, then this is not an allowable business expense per the Federal Income Tax Code. Thus, it then becomes a personal expense.

RICO Expenditure Solution

10

Introduction

The following solution and explanations relate to the scenario problem as presented Chapter 7. The solution and explanations are based upon the RICO (Racketeer Influenced and Corrupt Organization) Expenditure principles.

Principles

The RICO Expenditure Method is based upon the fund principle. Funds involve the use of cash either directly or indirectly. There is no amortization, depreciation, or depletion allowances allowed on a RICO expenditure schedule. Unlike the RICO Net Worth Method, the RICO Expenditure Method, by its nature, shows the use of funds more directly than indirectly. It is also easier to explain to a jury of laymen. One disadvantage of the Expenditure Method is that it does not list the accumulated assets and liabilities. Assets are only reflected when they are purchased. Liabilities are only shown when they are acquired. It also only shows the amount of payment on liabilities and not the balances.

Problem

The following Expenditure Schedule shows how each item in the scenario problem is presented. An explanation follows the Expenditure Schedule, which explains why the item is presented in this manner. The explanation section will refer to the line item on the Expenditure Schedule.

RICO Expenditure Schedule

The following presents a RICO Expenditure Schedule (Table 10-1). The first section deals with the expenditure side. The second section deals with the identified or legal source of income. The difference between the total expenditures and the total sources of identified receipts gives the amount of income derived from unidentified sources. Whether the Expenditure Method or the Net Worth Method is used, the bottom line should be the same. An Expenditure Schedule can be converted to a Net Worth Schedule and vice versa.

Table 10-1 RICO Expenditure Schedule
John Doe Expenditure Schedule Title 18, RICO

Description	19X1	19X2	19X3
Asset Purchases			
1. Cash on hand	$ -0-	$ -0-	$ 50,000
2. Cocaine: 2 kilos			50,000
3. Gold bullion: 10 bars	100,000		
4. FNB—checking	10,000	40,000	50,000
5. FNB—savings	110,000	440,000	100,000
6. Business cash in bank		20,000	(10,000)
7. Accounts receivable		10,000	10,000
8. Inventory		140,000	(90,000)
9. Business assets		150,000	
10. 100 Alpha Street	300,000		
11. 100 Bravo Street	4,000,000		
12. Furniture	50,000		
13. Cabinets	20,000		
14. Paintings	20,000		
15. Fixtures	10,000		
16. Pool and tennis court	100,000		
17. Appliances		20,000	
18. Electronic equipment		100,000	
19. Security system			50,000
20. Lounge Doe, Inc.	2,440,000		
21. Doe's Kwik Stop, Inc.	506,100	(105,100)	
22. Real Property, Ltd.	2,030,000		42,500
23. Mercedes Benz	80,000		
24. Toyota sedan		18,000	
25. IRA—John Doe		2,200	2,400
26. IRA—Suzy Que		2,200	2,400
27. Residence—Bahama Islands		110,000	
Total Asset Purchases	$ 9,776,100	$ 947,300	$ 257,300
Acquired Liabilities			
28. Fla. Mortgage Co.	$70,000	$120,000	$120,000
29. Loan—Mercedes	9,000	12,000	12,000
30. Loan—Toyota		1,200	2,400
31. Business bank loan			20,000
Total Acquired Liabilities	$79,000	$ 133,200	$ 154,400
Business Expenses			
32. Inventory purchases		180,000	130,000
33. Inventory changes		(140,000)	90,000
Total Business Expenses	$ -0-	$ 40,000	$ 220,000
Business Expenses			
34. Advertising		$80,000	$40,000
35. Interest—bank loan		10,000	8,000
36. Insurance		50,000	50,000
37. Professional fees		25,000	25,000
38. Office expenses		30,000	10,000
39. Rent expense		50,000	50,000
40. Repairs		20,000	10,000
41. Supplies		30,000	10,000

Table 10-1 RICO Expenditure Schedule
John Doe Expenditure Schedule Title 18, RICO

Description	19X1	19X2	19X3
42. Taxes		50,000	40,000
43. Utilities		40,000	40,000
44. Wages/salaries		120,000	150,000
45. Miscellaneous		15,000	7,000
Total Business Expenses	$ -0-	$ 520,000	$ 440,000
Personal Expenses			
46. Fla. Mortgage Co. interest	$200,000	$188,000	$176,000
47. Life insurance	10,000		
48. Income tax withheld	95,000		150,000
49. Property taxes	5,000		5,000
50. Credit card charges	30,000	70,000	160,000
51. Utilities	10,000	10,000	20,000
52. Telephone	30,000	40,000	45,000
53. Insurance	5,000	10,000	10,000
54. Church donations		10,000	50,000
55. Interest—Mercedes	10,000		
56. Interest—Toyota		2,000	
57. Trust funds			400,000
58. Loss—XYZ stock		3,000	
Total Personal Expenses	$ 395,000	$ 333,000	$1,016,000
Identified Receipts			
59. Fla. Mortgage Co.	$2,000,000		
60. Loans—autos	60,000	$10,000	
61. Accounts payable			$50,000
62. Income tax refunds	500	79,250	
63. IRA interest—Doe		200	400
64. IRA interest—Que		200	400
65. Dividends	100,000		
66. Wages/salaries	190,000		200,000
67. Rental income	30,000	113,000	170,000
68. Gain—ABC stock		2,000	
69. Sales—XYZ stock		9,000	
70. Business income		80,000	440,000
71. Business bank loan		100,000	
Total Receipts	$2,380,500	$393,650	$860,800
Illegal/Unidentified Income	$ 7,869,600	$ 1,579,850	$ 1,226,900

Cash on Hand

Cash on hand is based upon the currency found at John Doe's residence during the execution of the search warrant (Table 10-1, line 1). Cash on hand should be established as much as possible for each period. Cash on hand should show the addition to or decrease of funds for the period and not the ending balance.

Cocaine: 2 Kilos

The market value of cocaine is used in this solution (Table 10-1, line 2). This is a situation where market values are used. The primary reason is that receipts will not be available. It is well known that the subject purchased the cocaine. There were no facilities discovered that the cocaine was manufactured there. This implies or suggests that the subject purchased the cocaine. The Drug Enforcement Agency and other local law enforcement agencies keep statistics on the market values of drugs, both retail and wholesale, on a regularly periodic basis.

Gold Bullion: 10 Bars

The 10 gold bars are recorded at cost (Table 10-1, line 3). The market value at the time of the search warrant is higher than the original cost. If the cost and date of purchase is not known, then the market value and time of discovery can be used. If market value is used, then the burden of proof is placed upon the defense to establish cost and date of purchase.

Cash in Banks

Increases or decreases in bank balances are reflected in this schedule (Table 10-1, lines 4, 5, and 6). The increase or decrease in bank balances can be based upon either the book changes or the bank changes. Whatever method is used, it must be used consistently for each bank account. It is suggested that a better way of presenting the changes in bank balances is to show the ending balance on the Expenditure Schedule and subtract the beginning balance. First it shows the jury where and how the figures were obtained. Also, it helps confirm the change computations. In this case, the personal bank accounts use the bank balances while the business account is based upon book balances. The business bank account is kept and reconciled on a monthly basis and is used as a basis for keeping the cash receipts and disbursement journals. Also, the sole proprietorship uses the accrual method of accounting while the personal expenses and receipts are based upon the cash method of accounting.

Accounts Receivable

Accounts receivable from a sole proprietorship is a personal asset of the individual owner (Table 10-1, line 7). The Expenditure Method requires only changes be reflected on the Expenditure Schedule. A suggested way of presenting the changes in accounts receivable balances is to show the ending balance on the Expenditure Schedule and subtract the beginning balance. It shows the jury from where and how the figures were obtained by relating them to the financial statements or tax returns that are introduced into evidence.

Inventory

Inventory from a sole proprietorship is a personal asset of the individual owner (Table 10-1, line 8). The Expenditure Method requires only changes be reflected on the Expenditure Schedule. This also can be presented by showing the ending balances less the beginning balances so the jury can find how the figures were derived.

Business Assets

Assets purchased for use in the business of a sole proprietorship are assets of the individual owner (Table 10-1, line 9). Business assets are recorded at cost for the period purchased.

100 Alpha Street

The purchase of the house is recorded at cost (Table 10-1, line 10). In this case, public records are used to determine the cost. However, the closing statement from the closing agent can be used which would also show additional closing costs. The Best Evidence Rule requires the original document(s) to be produced instead of copies.

100 Bravo Street

The purchase of the apartment building is recorded at cost (Table 10-1, line 11). Public records are used to determine the cost. The closing statement can be used which would show additional closing costs charged by the closing agent.

Furniture

The furniture is recorded at cost for the period purchased (Table 10-1, line 12).

Cabinets

Cabinets are recorded at cost for the period purchased (Table 10-1, line 13).

Paintings

Paintings are recorded at cost for the period purchased (Table 10-1, line 14).

Fixtures

Fixtures are recorded at cost for the period purchased (Table 10-1, line 15).

Pool and Tennis Court

These assets are recorded at cost for the period purchased (Table 10-1, line 16). If there were subsequent purchases or additional costs, these costs would be shown for the period incurred and not the accumulated balances.

Appliances

Appliances are recorded at cost for the period purchased (Table 10-1, line 17).

Electronic Equipment

These assets are recorded at cost for the period purchased (Table 10-1, line 18).

Security System

This asset is recorded at cost for the period purchased (Table 10-1, line 19).

Lounge Doe, Inc.

This investment is recorded at the net cash investment for the period (Table 10-1, line 20). This can be either a positive or negative change. A negative change means the subject withdrew more funds than what was invested into the corporation. The boat is a corporate asset and not the shareholder.

Doe Kwik Stop, Inc.

Investment in this corporation is also recorded at the net cash investment for the period (Table 10-1, line 21). Its tax status has nothing to do with a RICO investigation. The net investment, like any other corporation, should take into consideration capital stock; additional paid in surplus and loans from and to shareholder. If the corporation has made any loans during the period to the shareholder, then they should be subtracted from the other investment accounts.

Real Property, Ltd.

Investment into this partnership by the partner is recorded at the net cash investment (Table 10-1, line 22). The partner's shares of liabilities are not considered in this computation. The other partners interest is not considered. Partnership assets belong to the partnership and not the partners. If the partners assets can be identified separate from the other partners, then they can be severed for forfeiture purposes, but not for Expenditure Method purposes. In this case, the partners have an undivided interest in the assets, specifically real property. The partner's interest cannot be severed in this situation. Another problem arises when one partner either contributes or withdraws assets out of proportion of his partnership interest. These out-of-proportion contributions or withdrawals should be reflected in the Expenditure Schedule.

Mercedes Benz

This car is recorded at cost during the period purchased (Table 10-1, line 23). A problem can arise if another car was a trade-in for this one. Like the Net Worth Method, the trade-in allowance will have to be accounted for in the same manner as in the net worth computation. In essence, the gain or loss on the old car will increase or decrease the cost of the new car.

Toyota Sedan

This vehicle is also recorded at cost during the period purchased (Table 10-1, line 24). The car is charged to John Doe if he paid for it. This vehicle can be shown either as a gift or as an asset purchase.

Individual Retirement Accounts

Contributions to Individual Retirement Accounts and Keogh plans should be shown for the period (Table 10-1, lines 25 and 26). These accounts will also have earnings for the period. There are two ways of presenting these accounts on the Expenditure Schedule. One is to show only the contributions and ignore the earnings altogether. The other way is to show the contributions plus the earnings. The earnings would be reflected as a source of income for the period.

Bahama Islands Residence

This asset should be shown at cost for the period acquired (Table 10-1, line 27). One problem involved in this case is the possible conversion from foreign currency to U.S. currency. Any gain or loss on the conversion will have to be recognized. In this case, the Bahama Islands accept U.S. currency as well as their own currency in their everyday economy. Thus, no conversion is necessary in this case.

Florida Mortgage Co.

The proceeds from a mortgage should be shown on the Expenditure Schedule as a source of funds (Table 10-1, line 28). The payments to the mortgage company should be shown as an application of funds. Mortgage payments usually include principal and interest. Many times, escrow payments are included to cover property taxes and insurance. A breakdown of these payments will have to be made as to both principal and interest. If escrow payments are included in the mortgage payments then a breakdown of escrow payments will have to be made. The breakdown of the mortgage payments can be done on a supporting schedule. Any closing costs should be expensed for the period.

Installment Loans

The proceeds from installment loans should be shown as a source of funds for the period obtained (Table 10-1, lines 29 and 30). The payments to these installment loans should be reflected as an application of funds. A problem arises when the bank adds the interest to the principal balance. The interest is for the whole period of the loan which normally extends beyond the current period. In this situation, the interest is recognized at the same period the loan proceeds are recognized. This interest is not capitalized and later amortized. It is expensed in the period the loan was incurred.

Business Bank Loan

Payments on a loan are classified as expenditure of funds (Table 10-1, line 31). This is a business loan from his sole proprietorship. A loan from a sole proprietorship is a personal loan since the sole proprietor is solely liable for the loan.

Inventory Purchases

The purchases of inventory for a sole proprietorship are expenditures by the individual owner (Table 10-1, line 32). These expenditures are classified as personal expenditures even though they are for resale in a business. Assets of a sole proprietorship, whether used personally or for resale, belong to the individual.

Inventory Changes

This account is used to show the changes in inventory as it affects the cost of sales (Table 10-1, line 33). The total purchases, plus or minus the changes in inventory, compose the total cost of sales of inventory that is sold. When inventory increases, the inventory change account decreases because part of the purchases have not been sold. When the inventory decreases, the inventory change account increases because part of the inventory has been sold in addition to the purchases that have been made during the period.

Business Expenses

The expenses of operating a sole proprietorship are considered personal expenditures (Table 10-1, lines 34 through 45). When the sole proprietorship uses the accrual method of accounting, all business expenses are recognized when incurred whether or not they have been paid. Any outstanding liabilities will be recognized as a source of funds. This will offset the expenses that are not paid.

Florida Mortgage Co.

This is the interest portion of the mortgage payments to Florida Mortgage Company (Table 10-1, line 46) which was paid during the period.

Life Insurance

This is an expense during the period incurred (Table 10-1, line 47). This expenditure is recognized during the period paid. It is not amortized over the period for which the premium covers.

Tax Withholdings

These are period expenditures (Table 10-1, line 48). Even though a refund is made in later years, withholding is recognized during the period incurred. The employer pays withholding during the year from the employee's salaries and wages. Thus, it is a personal expenditure even though it was not paid directly by the employee.

Property Taxes

These are expenses for the periods involved (Table 10-1, line 49). It should be kept in mind that expenditures are recognized during the period paid and not when incurred.

Credit Card Charges

These are expenses for the periods involved (Table 10-1, line 50). This case shows only the amount of funds paid to the credit card company and not the charges made against it. The Expenditure Method normally uses the payments to the credit card company instead of the charges. However, the expenditure method can use credit card charges, but this is offset in the source of funds by the change in the liability to the credit card companies.

Utilities

This is also an expense for the period involved (Table 10-1, line 51).

Telephone

This is an expense for the period incurred (Table 10-1, line 52).

Insurance

This is also an expense for the period involved (Table 10-1, line 53).

Church Donations

These are expenditures for the period involved (Table 10-1, line 54).

Installment Loan Interest

This is an expense for the period incurred (Table 10-1, lines 55 and 56). It is not capitalized and amortized over the term of the loan. It is expensed during the year the loans were incurred. The interest relates to an installment loan where the bank charges interest for the term of the loan and adds it to the principal borrowed.

Trust Funds

These are expenditures for the period involved (Table 10-1, line 57). Trust(s) should be examined closely because there may be funds set aside for the contributor. In this case, the trust funds are set aside for the benefit of the subject's relatives and not the subject.

Stock Losses

These are expenses for the period (Table 10-1, line 58). Losses on the sale of assets are recognized as an expenditure during the period the loss was incurred.

Accounts Payable

Accounts payable is a personal liability of the sole proprietor (Table 10-1, line 61). The purpose of this account is to offset the purchases of goods and services that have not been paid. This remaining liability is actually a source of funds for goods and services that are not paid for the sole proprietorship. The sole proprietor is the subject of investigation. The Expenditure Schedule should show the change in the liability and not the balance.

Income Tax Refunds

These are a source of funds during the period received (Table 10-1, line 62).

IRA Interest

This is a source of funds for the period when credited to the accounts (Table 10-1, lines 63 and 64). Also, the earnings should show up as an application to the contributions made for the period.

Dividends

Corporate distributions, called dividends, should be recognized during the period received (Table 10-1, line 65).

Wages/Salaries

Earnings from employment should be recognized when received or reported for the period received or declared (Table 10-1, line 66). Any withholding should be recorded as an expenditure for the period paid or reported.

Rental Income

Earnings from rental income are solely based upon the net funds either received or paid for the period (Table 10-1, line 67). Any "phantom" figures are to be removed from the earnings or losses shown on the appropriate financial statements. Rental income should be shown only as the net cash flow from earnings. Any asset payments or liability reductions will be reflected on the Expenditure Schedule for those respective line items.

Stock Gains

Gains from the sale of capital assets will be shown on the Expenditure Schedule as a source of fund (Table 10-1, line 68) even if the gains are reinvested into other capital assets.

Stock Sales

The sale of XYZ stock is the proceeds which recovers the original cost (Table 10-1, line 69). Any gains or losses will be recognized separately. If the proceeds from the sales were reinvested into other capital assets, then this recovery of cost would not be recognized as a source of funds. The application side would show the purchase of other assets.

Business Income

This is the gross receipts of the sale of goods and services from a sole proprietorship (Table 10-1, line 70). Income from a sole proprietorship is income to the individual. This sole proprietorship's income is based upon the accrual method of accounting. As shown above, the sole proprietor has accounts receivable. Accounts receivable is the amount of gross receipts at year-end that has not been collected.

Offshore Evidence

The scenario problem shows many offshore assets and financial transactions. Offshore transactions are generally not admissible in court. However, there are some exceptions. Public records in foreign countries are admissible when properly certified. The Bahama Islands residence in this case is one example. Land transfer records are open to the public in the Bahama Islands, as well as, many other countries. Bank records are not public and, in many countries, improper disclosure can result in criminal and civil actions. Some "tax haven" countries' bank records are not allowed in criminal or civil tax cases, however, by treaty agreements, other countries will provide bank records in other criminal cases, i.e., racketeering, drug trafficking, or other criminal activities. One major problem in admitting foreign, nonpublic records is obtaining witnesses to introduce them into court. Government budgets may not allow the travel expenses of the witnesses. Many foreign nationals do not like to testify in court, especially if they feel that they can be charged for aiding and abetting.

Offshore Records

It is now assumed that witnesses will be obtained to introduce evidence into court. This offshore evidence, as you will see, has a material effect on the Expenditure Method. The RICO Expenditure Schedule (Table 10-2) would be modified as follows:

Table 10-2 RICO Expenditure Schedule Adjustments for Offshore Activities John Doe Expenditure Schedule Title 18, RICO

Description	19X1	19X2	19X3
Illegal/Unidentified Income	$ 7,869,600	$ 1,579,850	$ 1,226,900
Assets			
72. Transshipment, Ltd.			
73. Bahamian bank account		$4,390,000	$(3,890,000)
74. Spanish bank account			1,090,000
75. Swiss bank account			2,090,000
76. Barbados bank account			2,189,000
77. Cayman Islands bank account			2,580,000
78. Jamaica bank account			786,000
79. Doe Holding, NV			2,565,000
Total Additional Assets	$-0-	$ 4,390,000	$ 7,410,000
Expenses			
80. Barbados bank charges			$10,000
81. Cayman Islands bank charges			60,000
82. Jamaica bank charges			1,000
83. Jamaica Travel Expenses			120,500
84. Wires to Calderone	$ -0-	$3,500,000	6,000,000
85. Spanish bank charges			10,000

Table 10-2 RICO Expenditure Schedule Adjustments for Offshore Activities
John Doe Expenditure Schedule Title 18, RICO

Description	19X1	19X2	19X3
86. Aruba bank charges			10,000
87. Bahama Islands bank charges			20,000
88. Schmidt Mgt. Co.			45,000
Total Offshore Expenses	$ -0-	$ 3,500,000	$ 6,276,500
Identified Income			
89. Interest income—Cayman Islands			$640,000
90. Interest income—Spain			100,000
91. Interest income—Swiss			100,000
92. Interest income—Aruba			150,000
93. Interest income—Jamaica			7,500
Total Identified Offshore Income	$ -0-	$ -0-	$997,500
Illegal/Unidentified Income	$ 7,869,600	$ 9,469,850	$13,915,900

Assets

The assets consist primarily of changes in the various offshore bank accounts (Table 10-2, lines 72 through 79). In 19X3, the bank account in the Bahama Islands under the alter ego of Transshipment, Ltd. had a decrease in the account. This is a source of funds, therefore, the negative amount. The other accounts, whether under a corporate name or individual, show an increase in the accounts, thus an application of funds.

Expenses

This section records the disbursements made from the various bank accounts that have been identified (Table 10-2, lines 80 through 88). Mr. Calderone received a large part of the funds by wire transfer. These payments are probably for drug purchases. Wire transfers are a quick and easy way of disbursing funds. Some charges are for bank fees. Doe had some personal expenses since he paid for a hotel and other expenses in Jamaica. The payments to Schmidt Management Co. are for the formation of Doe Holding, NV, a foreign corporation. If this were an active corporation, these expenses would be capitalized on the corporate books. It would not be considered a personal expenditure. Expenditures on a "shell" corporation are considered personal expenses.

Income

The identified income from offshore activities is from interest income from his savings accounts (Table 10-2 lines 89 through 93). Those accounts held under corporate names are identified as his personal income since those offshore corporations are only "shells." "Shell" corporations are just a way of hiding income from authorities.

Tax Expenditure Solution

11

Introduction

The following solution and explanation relate to the scenario problem as presented in Chapter 7. The solution and explanations are based upon the tax Expenditure principles.

Principles

The tax Expenditure Method is based upon the Federal Income Tax laws and regulations. The Federal Tax Code defines a few concepts. One concept is gross income. Gross income means income from whatever source unless specifically exempt. Adjusted gross income is another concept. It means gross income less specified deductions. Some of these deductions are individual retirement account contributions, Keogh plan contributions, alimony payments, and others. Taxable income is another concept which involves subtracting exemptions, itemized deductions, or standard deductions from adjusted gross income. These principles are the same for both the Net Worth Method and the Expenditure Method. The first objective in a tax Expenditure Method is to establish adjusted gross income or corrected adjusted gross income if the taxpayer filed a tax return. After adjusted gross income is determined, then taxable income or corrected taxable income must be determined. Some itemized deductions have limitations, which are based upon adjusted gross income. Medical expenses are an example of a category of deductions which has limitations on the amount deductible based upon adjusted gross income. Whether the user is applying the Net Worth Method or the Expenditure Method, the bottom line should be the same as is shown in these examples.

Problem

The following Expenditure Schedule shows how each item in the scenario problem is presented. An explanation of why it is presented in the manner shown is explained after the Expenditure Schedule. The explanation section will refer to the line items on the Expenditure Schedule.

Tax Expenditure Schedule

The Expenditure Schedule is shown below. Each line item is numbered. After the Tax Expenditure Schedule (Table 11-1), an explanation of each line item is presented. The first section shows all the expenditures by the taxpayer. The second section shows all nontaxable source of income or receipts. Adjusted gross income is determined by subtracting nontaxable income from the total expenditures. From adjusted gross income, exemptions and itemized deductions or standard deduction is subtracted to arrive at corrected taxable income (if taxpayer previously filed). This is compared to what the taxpayer reported for possible increases. The explanations refer to the line item on the Expenditure Schedule.

Table 11-1 Tax Expenditure Schedule
John Doe Expenditure Schedule Title 26, Tax

Description	19X1	19X2	19X3
Expenditures			
1. Cash on hand	$ -0-	$ -0-	$ 50,000
2. Cocaine: 2 kilos			50,000
3. Gold bullion: 10 bars	100,000		
4. FNB checking	10,000	40,000	50,000
5. FNB savings	110,000	440,000	100,000
6. Business bank account		20,000	(10,000)
7. Accounts receivable		10,000	10,000
8. Inventory		140,000	(90,000)
9. Business assets		150,000	
10. 100 Alpha Street	300,000		
11. 100 Bravo Street	4,000,000		
12. Furniture	50,000		
13. Cabinets	20,000		
14. Paintings	20,000		
15. Fixtures	10,000		
16. Pool and tennis court	100,000		
17. Appliances		20,000	
18. Electronic equipment		100,000	
19. Security system			50,000
20. Lounge Doe, Inc.	2,440,000		
21. Doe Kwik Stop, Inc.	481,100	(155,100)	175,000
22. Real Property, Ltd.	1,930,000	(52,500)	12,500
23. Mercedes Benz	80,000		
24. Toyota sedan		18,000	
25. IRA—Doe		2,200	2,400
26. IRA—Que		2,200	2,400
27. Residence—Bahama Islands		110,000	
28. Fla. Mortgage Co.	70,000	120,000	120,000
29. Loan—Mercedes Benz	9,000	12,000	12,000
30. Loan—Toyota sedan		1,200	2,400
31. Prepaid interest	8,500	1,760	
32. Interest—Fla. Mortgage Co.	200,000	188,000	176,000
33. Bank loan—business			20,000
34. Life insurance	10,000		
35. Income tax withheld	95,000		150,000
36. Property tax	5,000		5,000

Table 11-1 Tax Expenditure Schedule
John Doe Expenditure Schedule Title 26, Tax

Description	19X1	19X2	19X3
37. Credit card charges	30,000	70,000	160,000
38. Utilities	10,000	10,000	20,000
39. Telephone	30,000	40,000	45,000
40. Insurance	5,000	10,000	10,000
41. Church donations		10,000	50,000
42. Interest—Mercedes	1,500	2,000	2,000
43. Interest—Toyota		240	480
44. Trust funds			400,000
Total Expenditures	$10,125,100	$ 1,310,000	$ 1,575,180
Nontaxable Sources			
45. Fla. Mortgage Co.	$2,000,000		
46. Loan—Mercedes benz	60,000		
47. Loan—Toyota sedan		$10,000	
48. Business bank loan		100,000	
49. Accounts payable			$50,000
50. Income tax refunds	500	79,250	
51. IRA—Doe		2,200	2,400
52. IRA—Que		2,200	2,400
53. Depreciation	100,000	230,000	230,000
54. Prepaid interest		2,000	2,480
Total Nontaxable Sources	$ 2,160,500	$ 425,650	$ 287,280
Adjusted Gross Income	$ 7,964,600	$ 884,350	$ 1,287,900
Itemized Deductions	206,500	200,240	233,480
Exemptions	2,000	2,000	2,000
Corrected Taxable Income	$ 7,756,100	$ 682,110	$ 1,052,420
Reported Taxable Income	63,000	-0-	285,400
Increase	$ 7,693,100	$ 682,110	$ 767,020

Cash on Hand

Cash on hand is based upon the currency found at John Doe's residence during the execution of the search warrant (Table 11-1, line 1). Cash on hand should be established as much as possible for each period. Cash on hand should show the addition to or the use of funds for the period and not the ending balance.

Cocaine: 2 Kilos

Market value of cocaine is used in this solution (Table 11-1, line 2). This is a situation where market values are used. The primary reason is that receipts will not be available. It is well known that the taxpayer purchased the cocaine. There were no facilities discovered that the cocaine was manufactured there. This implies or suggests that the taxpayer purchased the cocaine. The Drug Enforcement Agency and other local law enforcement agencies keep statistics on the market value of drugs on a regular periodic basis.

Gold Bullion: 10 Bars

The 10 gold bars are recorded at cost (Table 11-1, line 3). The market value at time of the search warrant is higher than the original cost. If the cost and date of purchase is not known, then the market value and time of discovery can be used. If market value is used, then the burden of proof is placed upon the defense to establish cost and date of purchase. The defense is not going to do this since it would be an admission by the defendant.

First National Bank Accounts

Increases or decreases in bank balances are reflected in this section (Table 11-1, lines 4 and 5). The increase or decrease in bank balances can be based upon either the book changes or the bank balance changes. Whatever method is used, it must be used consistently. It is suggested that a better way of presenting the changes in bank balances is to show the ending balances on the expenditure schedule and subtract the beginning balance. It shows the jury from where and how the figures were obtained. Also, it helps confirm the change computations.

Business Cash in Bank

This bank account is based upon change in book balances (Table 11-1, line 6). The sole proprietorship keeps its books on the accrual method of accounting. The accrual method of accounting recognizes income and expenses when incurred and not when received or paid. The changes in book balances are used because, first, books and records are kept of each transaction, which shows their appropriate time of occurrence. Second, timing differences are eliminated. Third, bank reconciliations will normally be available to prove out the book balances of accounts. In this case, the changes in bank balances increase during one year and decrease the subsequent year.

Accounts Receivable

Assets of a sole proprietorship are assets of the individual since he has title and personal liability (Table 11-1, line 7). The expenditure method recognizes the net changes in these assets. Accounts receivable is an intangible asset which accounts for funds owed by customers to the sole proprietor, John Doe.

Inventory

Inventory is an asset of the sole proprietor, John Doe (Table 11-1, line 8). He has title and personal liability for inventory. The expenditure method recognizes only the net changes during the period. In this case, inventory increased for the first year and decreased the following year.

Business Assets

These assets are property of John Doe, the sole proprietor, since he has title (Table 11-1, line 9). The Expenditure Method only recognizes acquisitions and dispositions during the period.

100 Alpha Street

The purchase of the house is recorded at cost (Table 11-1, line 10). In this case, public records are used to determine the cost. However, the closing statement from the closing agent can be used which would also show additional closing costs.

100 Bravo Street

The purchase of the apartment building is recorded at cost (Table 11-1, line 11). Public records are used to determine the cost. The closing statement can be used which would show additional closing costs charged by the escrow agent.

Furniture

The furniture is recorded at cost for the period purchased (Table 11-1, line 12).

Cabinets

Cabinets are recorded at cost for the period purchased (Table 11-1, line 13).

Paintings

Paintings are recorded at cost for the period acquired (Table 11-1, line 14).

Fixtures

Fixtures are also recorded at cost for the period purchased (Table 11-1, line 15).

Pool and Tennis Court

These assets are recorded at cost for the period purchased (Table 11-1, line 16). If there were subsequent purchases or additional costs, these costs would be shown for the period incurred and not when the contract was signed. Only period costs should be shown and not accumulated balance.

Appliances

Appliances are recorded at cost for the period acquired (Table 11-1, line 17).

Electronic Equipment

These assets are recorded at cost for the period purchased (Table 11-1, line 18).

Security System

This asset is also recorded at cost for the period acquired (Table 11-1, line 19).

ABC Stock Purchase

This intangible asset is recorded at cost for the period purchased. The cost is reflected on the Expenditure Schedule. However, this asset was sold during the period. Any gain or loss will not be recognized on the Expenditure Schedule since this is an adjustment to arrive at adjusted gross income.

Lounge Doe, Inc.

This investment is recorded at the net cash investment for the period (Table 11-1, line 20). This can be either a positive or negative change. A negative change means the taxpayer withdrew more funds than what was invested into the corporation during the period. The boat is a corporate asset. The corporation is taxed upon its income and not the shareholder. The net investment should take into consideration capital stock; additional paid in surplus, and loans from the shareholder. If the corporation has made any loans to the shareholder, then they should be subtracted from the other investment accounts.

Doe Kwik Stop, Inc.

This is a Sub S Corporation (Table 11-1, line 21). Like taxable corporations, the Expenditure Schedule should reflect the net cash investment from all accounts, but, in addition, the earnings and losses for the period. Sub S corporations are not taxed, but the earnings and losses are passed on to the shareholders. It should also be noted that Sub S corporations cannot have a negative balance. Losses on Sub S corporations are limited to the shareholder's investment.

Real Property, Ltd.

Investment into this partnership by the partner is recorded at the net cash investment plus any earnings less any losses for the period (Table 11-1, line 22). The other partner's interest is not considered. Partnership assets belong to the partnership and not the partners. If the partner's assets can be identified separately from the others, then they can be severed. The partnership is not a taxable entity. The partner can have a negative basis provided that the partner is at risk for his share of the partnership liabilities. The Expenditure Method only recognizes the changes in the partnership investment for the period and not year-end balances.

Mercedes Benz

This car is recorded at cost during the period purchased (Table 11-1, line 23). A problem can arise if another car was traded-in for this one. Like the Net Worth Method, the trade-in allowance will have to be accounted for in the same manner. In essence, the gain or loss on the old car will increase or decrease the cost of the new car.

Toyota Sedan

This vehicle is also recorded at cost during the period purchased (Table 11-1, line 24). The car is charged to John Doe since he paid for it. This vehicle can be shown either as a gift or as an asset purchase. Since the car is financed and John Doe is probably making the payments, then this vehicle should be shown as an asset.

IRA Accounts

Contributions to Individual Retirement Accounts and Keogh plans should be shown for the period (Table 11-1, lines 25 and 26). These accounts will also have earnings for the period. Contributions to these plans are an adjustment to arrive at adjusted gross income. The earnings are nontaxable until withdrawn. Therefore, there are two ways to present these items. One is to completely ignore them altogether. The issue in this case would be whether the taxpayers have an asset that they can access. The other way of presenting this issue is to show the contributions and earnings and later back out the earnings and contributions as a nontaxable source.

Bahama Islands Residence

This asset should be shown at cost for the period acquired (Table 11-1, line 27). One issue involved in this case is the possible conversion from foreign currency to United States currency. Any gain or loss on the conversion is not recognized since this would be an adjustment to arrive at adjusted gross income.

Florida Mortgage Co.

The proceeds from a mortgage should be shown on the Expenditure Schedule as a non-taxable source of funds (Table 11-1, line 28). The payments to the mortgage company should be shown as an application of funds. Mortgage payments usually include principal and interest. Many times, escrow payments are included to cover property taxes and insurance. A breakdown of these payments will have to be made as to both principal and interest. If escrow payments are included in the mortgage payments then a breakdown of the escrow payments will have to be made as to changes in the escrow balance, property taxes, and insurance paid for the period.

Automobile Loans

The proceeds from installment loans should be shown as a source of funds for the period obtained (Table 11-1, lines 29 and 30). The payments to these installment loans should be reflected as an application of funds. A problem arises where the bank adds the interest to the principal balance. The interest is for the whole period of the loan which normally extends beyond the period. In this situation, the interest is shown as an expenditure. The interest is amortized over the period of the loan and is later shown as an itemized deduction. For the initial year that the loan was obtained, the prepaid interest is divided up between the current year's expense and the unamortized expense.

Prepaid Interest

This is the unamortized portion of the interest charged by the bank on installment loans (Table 11-1, line 31). This interest is amortized over subsequent periods. It is shown as an expense and later as an itemized deduction, if deductible.

Mortgage Interest

This is the interest portion of the mortgage payments to Florida Mortgage Company (Table 11-1, line 32) which was paid during the period. This same amount will also be shown on the itemized deduction schedule.

Business Loan Payment

This is a principal payment on a business loan. (Table 11-1, line 33) This payment reduces the principal of the loan. The tax Expenditure Schedule only recognizes the payments made to principal balance and does not reflect loan balances. Since the loan is for a business, Suzy's Women's Clothes, the interest is not recognized. Interest is not a personal expense, but a business expense. Adjusted gross income determines net business income.

Life Insurance

This is an expense for the period incurred (Table 11-1, line 34). It is not amortized over the period for which the premium was incurred. If this were a medical insurance premium, then an itemized deduction would be made in subsequent years, subject to limitations. Prepaid medical insurance should be treated the same way as prepaid interest on installment loans.

Income Tax Withheld

This is a period expenditure (Table 11-1, line 35). Even though a refund is made in later years, withholding is recognized during the period withheld.

Property Tax

This is an expense for the period involved (Table 11-1, line 36). In addition, this expenditure is also an itemized deduction.

Credit Card Charges

These are expenses for the period involved (Table 11-1, line 37). This case shows only the amount of funds paid to the credit card company and not the charges made against it. The expenditure method uses the payments to the credit card company instead of the charges. If the credit card has charges for business expenses, then payments for these expenses will have to be subtracted from the payments. Business expenses are ignored for tax purposes.

Utilities

This is an expense for the period involved (Table 11-1, line 38).

Telephone

This also is an expense for the period involved (Table 11-1, line 39).

Insurance

This is an expense for the period involved (Table 11-1, line 40).

Church Donations

These are expenses for the period involved (Table 11-1, line 41). In addition, these are itemized deductions which are subject to limitations.

Installment Loan Interest

This is an expenditure for the period (Table 11-1, lines 42 and 43). This is the portion of interest charged by the bank that is expensed for the period. It also is used as an itemized deduction. In subsequent periods, the interest is shown as an expense and as a possible itemized deduction. Another way of presenting the future amortized interest and itemized deduction is not to show it at all.

Trust Funds

These are expenses for the period involved (Table 11-1, line 44). Trusts should be examined closely because they may be funds that the contributor can obtain access.

XYZ Stock Loss

Losses on the sale of capital assets, such as stock in this case, are an adjustment to arrive at adjusted gross income. Therefore, losses are ignored in this case.

Mortgage Proceeds

The mortgage proceeds from Florida Mortgage Company are a nontaxable source of funds (Table 11-1, line 45). The gross proceeds should be recognized as a source of funds. Any closing costs should be expensed or added to the cost of the real property.

Automobile Loans

The installment loans for the purchase of automobiles are shown as a nontaxable source of funds (Table 11-1, lines 46 and 47). Installment loans should be shown with both principal and interest charged for the term of the loans. The interest for the loan term will offset the initial loan balance with a charge to prepaid interest. For subsequent years, the prepaid interest will be amortized as an expenditure for the period. Installment loan payments are shown on the expenditure side of the Expenditure Schedule.

Business Bank Loan

John Doe, the sole proprietor, borrowed funds from the bank (Table 11-1, line 48). Even though this is a business loan, John Doe is personally liable. This is a nontaxable source of funds which should be recognized when received.

Accounts Payable

Accounts payable of a sole proprietorship is a liability of the individual (Table 11-1, line 49). The individual is personally liable for business payables of sole proprietorship. The Expenditure Method recognizes the net changes in this account for the period.

Income Tax Refunds

This is a source of funds during the period received (Table 11-1, line 50). This should be shown as a nontaxable source.

IRA Accounts

As explained earlier, if this is to be shown as an expenditure for the period, then it has to be offset by a nontaxable source of funds. The purpose is to arrive at adjusted gross income (Table 11-1, lines 51 and 52). When preparing an individual tax return, this is an adjustment to gross income in order to arrive at adjusted gross income.

Depreciation

This is considered a nontaxable source of funds for the period (Table 11-1, line 53). This does not deal with the source of funds. It is considered a "phantom figure" for RICO purposes. For tax purposes, it is considered a source of funds on the grounds that this is a potential liability. The federal laws and regulations require the recovery of depreciation as ordinary taxable income to the extent of any gain recognized on the sale of the depreciable asset. Depreciation, amortization, and depletion charges for the current period are recognized not the accumulated balances.

Prepaid Interest Reduction

Installment loans have been recorded with prepaid interest for the term of the loan (Table 11-1, line 54). The tax Expenditure Method requires this prepaid interest to be capitalized and amortized over the term of the loan. During subsequent years, the prepaid interest account will be reduced by the amount of interest recognized for the period. This reduction of the prepaid interest account is a source of funds and becomes an expense for the period. The expense was recognized above (Table 11-1, lines 42 and 43).

Itemized Deductions

Itemized deductions or standard deductions are allowed to reduce adjusted gross income to derive at taxable income. The Federal Income Tax Code allows certain expenses to be deducted. The primary ones are medical expenses, interest expenses, certain taxes, charity donations, and some other miscellaneous expenses. In this solution, itemized deductions are the total of personal expenditures for interest (mortgage and amortized interest), church donations, and property taxes. Limitations on these deductions, which are built in the Tax Code, have been ignored in this problem. The itemized deductions are identified below:

Description	19X1	192X	19X3
Interest—Fla. Mortgage Co.	$200,000	$188,000	$176,000
Interest—Mercedes	1,500	2,000	2,000
Interest—Toyota		240	480
Property taxes	5,000		5,000
Church donations		10,000	50,000
Total	$206,500	$200,240	$233,480

Exemptions

Exemptions are an income tax concept. The amount of these exemptions varies from year to year. For the sake of simplicity, $2,000 per exemption is used in this case.

Offshore Evidence

This scenario problem shows many offshore assets and financial transactions. Offshore transactions are generally not admissible in court. However, there are some exceptions. Public records in foreign countries are admissible when properly certified. The Bahama Islands residence in this case is one example. Land transfer records are open to the public in the Bahama Islands as well as in many other countries. Bank records are usually not public and in many countries improper disclosure can result in criminal and civil actions. Some "tax haven" countries' bank records are not allowed in criminal or civil tax cases. One major problem in admitting foreign nonpublic records is obtaining a witness to introduce them into court. Government budgets may not allow the travel expenses of the witness. Many foreign nationals do not like to testify in court, especially if they feel that they can be charged for aiding and abetting.

Offshore Records

Now, it will be assumed that witnesses will be obtained to introduce evidence into court. This offshore evidence, as you will see, has a material effect on the tax Expenditure Method. The tax Expenditure Schedule (Table 11-2) will be modified.

Table 11-2 Tax Expenditure Schedule Adjustments for Offshore Activities
John Doe Expenditure Schedule Title 26, Tax

Description	19X1	19X2	19X3
Previous Corrected Income	$ 7,756,100	$ 682,110	$1,052,420
Expenditures:			
55. Bahamian bank account		$4,390,000	$(3,890,000)
56. Spanish bank account			1,090,000
57. Swiss bank account			2,090,000
58. Aruba bank account			2,565,000
59. Barbados bank account			2,189,000
60. Cayman Islands bank account			2,580,000
61. Jamaican bank account			786,000
62. Barbados bank account			10,000
63. Cayman Islands bank charges			60,000
64. Jamaican bank charges			1,000
65. Jamaican Travel Expenses			120,500
Corrected Taxable Income	$ 7,756,100	$ 5,072,110	$ 8,653,920
Reported Taxable Income	63,000	-0-	285,400
Increase	$ 7,693,100	$ 5,072,110	$ 8,368,520

Doe Holding, NV

The net cash investment in this foreign corporation for the period is reflected on the Expenditure Schedule (Table 11-2, line 58). The fees paid to Schmidt Management Co. are for the creation of this corporation. Thus, this is a corporate expenditure. The Expenditure Method shows the net cash investment for the period. Like any offshore transaction, it must be shown in U.S. currency and any gain or loss on the conversion must also be recognized. The tax Expenditure Schedule does not recognize any gains or losses on currency exchange since they are an adjustment to arrive at adjusted gross income.

Offshore Bank Charges

These expenses are recognized during the period paid (Table 11-2, lines 62 through 64). The main issue in these expenditures is the conversion of foreign currency to U.S. currency. This problem does not address this issue.

Jamaica Travel

This is an expenditure for the period (Table 11-2, line 65). Expenditures are recognized only during the period paid.

Transshipment, Ltd.

This is a Bahamian corporation. Its only assets and capital are the bank accounts set up by the sole shareholder (Table 11-2, lines 55 through 57). The Spanish and Swiss banks were interest-bearing accounts since they were credited with interest income. This income is an adjustment to arrive at adjusted gross income. Therefore, it is ignored. Since some expenditures cannot be specifically identified, other than those that are transferred to other bank accounts, only the changes in the bank balances are used. The Bahamian bank account shows payments going to Calderone who is a known drug trafficker, however, he cannot be used as a witness. The reason should be obvious. He wouldn't testify without self-incrimination.

Foreign Bank Accounts

Changes in bank balances are recognized as sources or expenditures of assets, principally cash (Table 11-2, lines 59 through 61). If the bank account balances go up, as it does here, this is an application of funds. If the bank account balances goes down, then it is a source of funds.

Organized Crime

12

Definition

Both the judicial and legislature have had disputes in defining organized crime. In 1967, the Administration of Justice defined organized crime as "A society that seeks to operate outside the control of the American people and their government. It involves thousands of criminals working within structures as large as those of any corporation." The McClellan Committee, following highly publicized investigations, increased public awareness of organized crime as a pervasive social force and prompted federal legislative action. However, they did not sufficiently emphasize the importance and roles of groups other than the La Cosa Nostra in American organized crime. In 1968, Congress passed into law the first major organized-crime bill, The Omnibus Crime Control and Safe Streets Act. This act defined organized crime as the unlawful activities of the members of a highly-organized, disciplined association engaged in supplying illegal goods and services including, but not limited to gambling, prostitution, loan-sharking, narcotics, labor racketeering, and other unlawful activities. In 1970, Congress passed the Racketeer Influenced and Corrupt Organization Statute (RICO), which has become the centerpiece of federal law proscribing organized criminal activity. RICO defines racketeering activity as any act or threat involving murder, kidnapping, gambling, arson, robbery, bribery, extortion, dealing in narcotic or dangerous drugs, or other denominated crime. A pattern of racketeering activity requires at least two acts of racketeering activity.

Organized crime is the collective result of the commitment, knowledge, and actions of three components: the criminal groups each of which has at its core persons tied by racial, linguistic, ethnic, or other bonds; the protectors, persons who protect the group's interests; and specialist support, persons who knowingly render services on an ad hoc basis to enhance the group's interests.

Criminal Group

The criminal group is a continuing, structured collective of persons who utilize criminality, violence, and a willingness to corrupt in order to gain and maintain power and profit. The characteristics of the criminal group are continuity, structure, criminality, violence, membership based on a common denominator, a willingness to corrupt, and a power/profit goal.

The criminal group carries out its purpose over a period of time. The group operates beyond the lifetime of individual members and is structured to survive changes in leadership. At different times, activities are focused, organized, and controlled in various ways. Group members work to ensure that the group continues and their interests are subordinate to those of the group.

The criminal group is structured as a collection of hierarchically-arranged, interdependent offices devoted to the accomplishment of a particular function. It can be highly structured or fluid. It is distinguishable and ordered in ranks based on power and authority.

Membership is the core in a criminal group that is restricted and based on a common trait, such as ethnicity, race, criminal background, or common interest. Potential members of a criminal group are closely scrutinized and required to prove their worth and loyalty to the criminal group. Membership in most instances requires a lifetime commitment to the group. The rules of membership include secrecy, a willingness to commit any act for the group, and intent to protect the group. In return for loyalty, the criminal group member receives benefits from the group, including protection, a certain prestige, an opportunity for economic gain, and, perhaps most importantly, a sense of belonging.

Criminality

Organized crime is aimed at the pursuit of profit along well-defined terms. The criminal group relies on continuing criminal activity to generate income. Some groups engage in a range of illegal activities while others limit themselves to one central activity. Some criminal groups are involved in legitimate business activities in order to skim or launder profits and increase its power.

Violence

Violence and the threat of violence are an integral part of the criminal group. Both are used to control and protect against both members of the group who violate their commitment and those outside the group to protect it and maximize its power. Members are expected to commit, condone, or authorize violent acts.

Power/Profit Goal

Members of a criminal group are united in that they work for the group's power and ultimately its profit. Political power is achieved through the corruption of officials. The group's structure and the fear it instills through the use of violence manifests power. The criminal group maintains power through its association with the criminal protectors which defend the group and its profits.

Protectors

The protectors are a complement of corrupt public officials, attorneys, and businessmen, who individually or collectively protect the criminal group through abuses of status and/or privilege and violation of law. Protectors include lawyers, judges, politicians, financial advisors, financial institutions, and businesses in the United States and worldwide. As a result, the criminal group is insulated from both civil and criminal government actions. Protectors are members of organized crime. The success of organized crime is dependent upon this buffer which helps to protect the criminal group from civil and criminal action.

Specialist Support

The criminal group and protectors rely on skilled individuals or specialists to assist in the attainment of group goals. These individuals do not share a continuing commitment to the group's goals. They are, nonetheless, considered part of organized crime.

Groups

There will be little lasting benefit in disabling the La Cosa Nostra if other groups successfully claim its abandoned criminal franchises. If progress is to be made, the perspective of organized crime must be on not only the current groups, but also their possible successors and the protectors of organized crime.

La Cosa Nostra

The La Cosa Nostra (This Thing of Ours) has been the largest, most extensive, and most influential crime group in this country for more than a half century. Today, it must share some of the criminal enterprises that it once thoroughly dominated with newer crime groups. The La Cosa Nostra (LCN) undertakings range from heroin trafficking to storefront numbers operations and from extortion by violence to sophisticated infiltration of legitimate businesses. The LCN is so formally organized, so broadly established, or so effective, that it can demand a portion of the proceeds of other crime groups.

Background And Structure

The basic territorial unit with the LCN is the family, known as a borgata. The name does not imply any blood relationship. The LCN families total about 1,700 members, with a concentration in the northeastern United States. About one half the strength is in the five New York families. The number of formal members represents only a small portion of the criminal network by which the organization survives and prospers.

Nearly all the LCN families around the country fall under the authority of the "national commission," established by Salvatore "Lucky" Luciano in 1931. The exception is the New Orleans family, the longest established LCN group, which is independent of the commission in most matters. The commission traditionally has consisted of the bosses or acting bosses from the five New York families and bosses from several of the more important families around the country. Besides the five New York bosses, the LCN commission currently includes bosses from Buffalo, Chicago, Detroit, and Philadelphia.

The national commission regulates joint ventures between families, intervenes in family disputes, approves the initiation of new members, and controls relations between the U.S. and Sicilian branches of the LCN. In 1964, electronic surveillance by the FBI recorded a conversation in which Sam DeCavalcante, boss of the New Jersey family, discussed the commission's intervention in a leadership struggle within New York's Joseph Profaci family. While the commission has precedence in issues that affect the overall conduct of LCN and its families, lesser rights are still reserved for the individual families, such as what they do, who they kill, and who they do business with, as explained by informant James Fratianno, a former member of the Los Angeles LCN group.

Not all LCN families have equal power. Those in the West are less formally organized, and their leadership is less easily identified. Law enforcement has speculated that power within LCN is gravitating to Chicago. The five New York families influence activities as far west as Chicago, while the midwestern and western families are believed to report to the boss of the Chicago LCN family. Angelo Lonardo, a former Cleveland underboss, has testified that Chicago dominates over midwestern families, while the Cleveland LCN family reports to New York. Ken Eto, a former associate of the Chicago family, has stated that the Cleveland family is subordinate to the Genovese family in New York.

The structure of a LCN family typically consists of the following positions:

Boss. He is head of the family. He does not participate in the day-to-day activities of the organization, but is supposed to receive a cut from every income source. He usually has his own legitimate and illegitimate businesses.

Underboss. He assists the boss. Usually he is being groomed to succeed the boss, but succession is not automatic. There is only one underboss per family.

Consiglieri. Literally, the "counselor," assists the boss, but has no leadership authority. He is generally an older, experienced member who can advise family members. Usually only one per family.

Capo. Caporegima, or captain. Supervisors of the family's day-to-day criminal operations; represents the family among the soldiers they oversee. A capo gains his position by proving his ability as an "earner," one earns a great deal of profit for the family. They may have there own legitimate and illegal ventures and retain part of the income paid by their soldiers before passing it on to the leadership. The number of capos in a family depends on the size of the family.

Soldier. The basic rank in the family. Sometimes known as a "wiseguy" or "button", or a "made man." The last term refers to any formal member of the LCN, one who has undergone the initiation ritual. To be "made," a man must be of Italian ancestry.

Associates. An informal position, yet one that is crucial to the family. An associate need not be of Italian descent; he is someone whose skills or position make him of value to the organization. Some are used as soldiers while others are more distantly connected. The FBI has estimated for every formal member of the LCN there are ten criminal associates who cooperate with members and share their enterprise.

Protectors. Among any family's associates is a support network of "protectors." These are corrupt public officials, bankers, lawyers, accountants, and other professionals who protect the criminal group from governmental action, both civil and criminal. Angelo Lonardo has described the role of Milton Rockman, who acted as a conduit for cash skimmed from Las Vegas casinos for several midwestern families, "We all belonged to the same organization. He always took care of the labor movement and financial movement, but he was a member of the organization, but he wasn't a member of the family."

LCN structure usually insulates the boss from the crimes committed by soldiers in his family. Often he receives money derived from illegal enterprises which he did not organize and about which he has no real knowledge.

Activities

The true nature of LCN is derived from the lowest and the uppermost elements of its overall structure. The existence of the commission, the highest level of authority, makes the American LCN an organized crime group in every sense of the definition, a cartel with national oversight, and it is the soldier who makes the organization such a truly predatory creation.

The soldier is Italian and male. Typically, he already has a background in burglary and robbery before he is considered for membership. Except in unusual circumstances, a candidate for membership cooperates with family members in some criminal tasks as part of a testing process; he may be asked to participate in a murder, at least as an accomplice. Before he is accepted as a member, his name will be circulated around the family. In New York, other family bosses will review the name. Associates do part of the screening with contacts in law enforcement.

To be a "made" member of the LCN requires a sponsor. This is no casual relationship since the sponsor's life may be in jeopardy if the initiate later turns "sour." The candidate vows that the organization will be foremost in his life, and acknowledges that only death will release him from the oath. One immediate effect of his new status is that among other members, he will now be referred to as "a friend of ours," while associates and outsiders are referred to as "a friend of mine" when one member introduces them to another.

Martin Light, an attorney close to the LCN and serving a sentence for a drug conviction, testified on January 29, 1986 and stated that prospective members are watched from childhood on, judged on their toughness and ability, and on their respect for superiors. Their willingness to "do the right thing" may be to share criminal profits with family leaders, to risk a jail term for refusal to testify before a grand jury, or to plead guilty to a crime actually committed by more important figures in the family. It is to follow unquestioningly the self-perpetuating practices of a most secret and exclusive criminal society. Rank in the LCN is strictly observed. Dealings between families always involve members of equal rank; an underboss will deal only with his counterpart in another organization. Within a given family, the boss deals exclusively with his consiglier and underboss from which the captain gets his orders. Each captain has a "crew" of several soldiers who are affiliated with him for life, each soldier has a "crew" of several soldiers who are affiliated with him for life, and each soldier has a "crew" of nonmember associates, some of whom may be Italian, prospects for initiation some day. Thus, several buffers are created between the lowest and the topmost levels of the family.

The soldier is the lowest ranking formal member of the organization, but he commands respect and fear on the street. Light testified that Gregory Scarpa, a soldier of the Colombo family, would not allow anyone to do anything without getting his permission, even down to double-parking.

Even as the captains and the family leadership reap the fruits of the soldier's aggressiveness and respect, they are also engaged in large-scale crime that requires the full influence and capital of the family. Even a partial recounting of LCN criminal activities is a virtual catalogue of organized crime: drug trafficking, illegal gambling, extortion, theft, fraud, prostitution, loansharking, labor racketeering, embezzlement, money laundering, bribery, bombing, hijacking, kidnapping, auto theft, arson, kickbacks, burglary, smuggling, and forgery.

There are regional differences. In the Northeast, labor racketeering and infiltration of the construction trades are among the LCN primary activities, while firearms trafficking is common in the north central region. The Bruno family in Philadelphia seems to be more heavily involved than other families in trafficking of methamphetamines. Forgery and arson are prominent in the southern and western regions.

Intelligence reports in the Argent Corporation Skimming case that gambling is the largest source of income for the midwestern LCN groups which are supported by the recent trail of family leaders from Chicago, Kansas City, Milwaukee, and Cleveland. It is also reported in the conviction of Carl Deluna and others in a similar 1983 skimming case involving the Tropicana Casino in Las Vegas, in the 1985 bookmaking convictions of Caesar DeVarco and others in Chicago, and the guilty pleas entered by Kansas City LCN figures, Anthony and Carlo Civella, on gambling charges in 1984. Chicago is considered one of the few cities where prostitution is controlled by the LCN.

The New Orleans family of Carlos Marcello generates most of its income by infiltrating legitimate businesses and gains most of its power through political influence. New Orleans serves as an example for other LCN families which in recent years have infiltrated legitimate businesses, including liquor and food purveyors, restaurants, construction, banking, vending, jewelry, meat packing, sanitation and toxic waste disposal, import/export, tobacco, laundry, and many others.

Prosecutions and Their Effect

During the 1980s, the leadership in 17 of 24 LCN families was indicted or convicted. In 1984, organized crime indictments totaled 2,194, involving predominantly LCN members and associates. One of the most valuable tools for prosecutors has been the Racketeer Influenced Corrupt Organization Act (RICO). Signed into law in 1970, RICO recognizes the true institutional nature of organized crime.

Professor Howard Abadinsky believes that the arrest of a single capo or even a boss does not disrupt the entire organization because family power is decentralized. He further adds that imprisonments may serve as the equivalent of forced retirement, allowing younger members to move into authority.

Ronald Goldstock, head of the New York Organized Crime Task Force, oversees the families move from active crime into financing crime by others such as importing heroin or backing numbers operations.

Working law enforcement has a different view. The imprisonment of LCN bosses has brought to power a generation of inexperienced leaders who have not been fully groomed for responsibility and who do not subscribe to the old customs of loyalty and secrecy, producing an organization that is more vicious, less skillful at crime, and less bound by honor and heritage than their predecessors. Financial ties are more easily broken than obligations of honor and loyalty. Numerous cases against LCN figures have hinged on the testimony of their former colleagues.

Sicilian Faction

An important new development is the disclosure of an element of the Sicilian LCN that is operating in the United States. Its existence was revealed almost simultaneously during a 1984 investigation of a heroin smuggling ring known as the "Pizza Connection" which involved Sicilian LCN crime boss Gaetano Badalamente, and by the testimony of Tommaso Buscetta, a high-level Sicilian LCN figure who has become a witness for prosecutors in Italy and the United States. It has been held that Sicilian members were bound to the American LCN families. It is now apparent that while Sicilian and American groups may cooperate in some crime, there is, in fact, an independent Sicilian organization in the United States.

The LCN in Italy has undergone several periods of severe repression including a purge by Mussolini in the 1920s. American groups became safe havens for Sicilian members during these periods of difficulty. During the 1920s, formative Sicilian members fled to the United States. Among them were Joseph Bonanno, Carlo Gambino, Stefano Maggadino, and Joseph Profaci, men who were among the leadership of U.S. organized crime during the next 40 years.

There appears to have been a short break in relations between the two groups around 1950. In 1957, American LCN leaders Lucky Lucciano, Joe Bananno, Carmine Galante, and Frank Garofalo met in Palermo with Sicilian leaders including Tommaso Buscetta and Gaetano Badalamente. One of the products of that meeting was the formation of a Sicilian commission similar to the one instituted by Lucciano in 1931. Unlike the U.S. commission, the first Sicilian commission included soldiers, not bosses, and dissolved in 1962.

In the early 1960s, the Italian LCN again came under intense pressure from police as a result of murderous factional conflict. Scores of LCN members in Italy were arrested and tried. LCN members fled to the United States, Canada, and South America. Law enforcement experts naturally assumed that the new arrivals would be absorbed into existing families. However, these expatriates remained loyal to their original families in Sicily and formed the nucleus of an independent LCN group in the United States.

Sicilian leaders established a second national commission, this one headed by Badalamente, Stefano Bontade, and Salvatore Reina. Around the end of 1977, Badalamente was expelled from his seat under pressure from the faction based in the Corleone area and went into exile, fearing for his life. Friction between the Corleonese group and Badalamente's organization resulted in what has become known in Italy as La Grande Guerra, The Great War. More than 500 LCN members and associates died in this conflict between 1980 and 1983, as Badalamente attempted to regain his position. Eventually, the Corleone faction prevailed with Michele Greco as head of the commission. The Corleone faction has held exclusive rights in the Sicilian LCN to drug trafficking since 1981. Under the Corleonesi, the heroin industry in Sicily was taken from individual LCN members and supervised by family bosses. An elaborate smuggling network supplied morphine base from Afghanistan, Pakistan, and Iran to Sicilian processing labs, from which it was shipped via Spain or Switzerland, most often, to the United States and the Sicilian LCN faction in place here.

Michele Greco went into hiding in 1982 when Italian police made mass arrests of LCN figures following a series of murders of judges, prosecutors, and police. In 1984, Greco was sentenced to life imprisonment for the assassination of Palermo Judge Rocco Chinnici. On February 20, 1986, Greco was arrested at a farmhouse near Palermo and was bound over for trial with 467 suspected LCN members. Tommaso Buscetta became an informant for prosecutors in Italy and the United States after two of his sons, a son-in-law, two brothers, and two nephews died in La Grande Guerra. He was a key witness against Greco and the others.

Sicilian Operations in the United States.   The number of Sicilian LCN members in this country is not known. However, they are believed to be concentrated mainly in the northeastern United States. They apparently operate without geographical restrictions. There has been little friction between U.S. families and Sicilian members in this country, which suggests that working agreements are in effect. In the "Pizza Connection" case, it has been documented that Sicilian members supplied heroin to an American LCN faction headed by Salvatore Catalano, capo of the Bonanno family. Since the early 1970s the Sicilians have been one of the principal suppliers of southeast Asian heroin in this country. They moved into the trade after the end of the French Connection, through which American LCN interest controlled the flow of Turkish heroin into this country. In 1977, authorities of the United States, France and Italy began assembling evidence of the Sicilian network. In 1980, Italian police discovered two labs in Palermo capable of processing up to 50 kilos of heroin per week.

The Sicilian LCN in this country has generated enormous amounts of cash that must be laundered through its drug-trafficking operations. Members have bought into businesses in which illicit proceeds may be hidden along with the legitimate cash flow. The Sicilians have used investment schemes involving commodity futures and a courier system for transporting bulk currency out of the United States to banks in the Bahama Islands and Bermuda which would then transfer the funds to commercial accounts overseas. Sicilian members have also purchased large amounts of real estate. The property can be resold for its true value and the proceeds are considered legitimate.

Outlaw Motorcyle Gangs

When they first appeared, outlaw motorcycle gangs were a disenchanted anomaly within the general contentment of the postwar U.S. groups of young men. Newly returned soldiers formed motorcycle clubs and rejected normal civilian lifestyles. In the next few years, their behavior was boisterous and rebellious. Today, there are 800 to 900 outlaw motorcycle gangs, ranging in size and sophistication from loosely organized single chapters to gangs with dozens of chapters in the United States and foreign countries. During the 1970s, at least four outlaw motorcycle gangs, Hell's Angels, the Outlaws, the Bandidos, and the Pagans, evolved into full organized crime groups. Together, their member chapters reach across the continental United States into Europe and Australia. They engage in almost every conceivable crime, including murder, extortion, and highly involved drug-trafficking schemes. They have been known to cooperate with LCN figures.

In addition to these four gangs, several other outlaw motorcycle groups are active in the United States. They include the Sons of Silence (Midwest and Great Lakes region), the Vagos (Los Angeles and Mexico), the Peacemakers (southeastern United States), and the Dirty Dozen (Arizona and the Southwest). None of these groups, however, is thought to have achieved the status of true organized crime groups.

Background

Today's outlaw motorcycle gangs are secretive and closely knit groups, selective about their membership. The gangs usually require that a member introduce a prospective recruit to the group. During a probationary period, the recruit's loyalty and willingness to commit crime are tested.

The symbol of membership in an outlaw motorcycle gang is its "colors," usually a sleeveless denim or leather jacket with embroidered patches sewn on the back. The patches display a gang logo, sometimes slogans or initials. There may be "rockers" that identify the name of the gang member's most prized possession. They represent the foremost commitment of his life, his commitment to the gang and its criminal lifestyle.

Part of that lifestyle, common to most outlaw motorcycle gangs, is the member's outrageous treatment of the women who associate with them. Women are held to be less important than the gang itself and the gang member's motorcycle. In some cases, women are used to generate income through prostitution and topless dancing as well as for the transportation of drugs and weapons. Some gangs regard women as "club property," available for the gratification of all the members. Others are considered the property of individual members.

Members of outlaw motorcycle gangs refer to themselves as "1 percenters," in reference to the estimate by the American Motorcycle Association that outlaw motorcyclists comprised less than 1 percent of the motorcycling population.

Membership

No firm figures of gang membership exist. The estimated membership is 3,100 in the four gangs as follows:

Hell's Angels:	800 (150 worldwide)
Outlaws:	500
Bandidos:	900
Pagans:	900

Every gang has a coterie of associates, followers, and aspiring members. Some associates may include their conspirators in the manufacture and distribution of chemical drugs such as methamphetamines. It is estimated that there are 10 "hangers-on" for every full member. In 1985, the FBI listed 16 major crimes typical of outlaw motorcycle gangs. These include illegal drugs, murder, extortion, kidnapping, arson, robbery, bombings, and receiving stolen property.

Structure

The leadership hierarchy of an outlaw motorcycle gang chapter generally consists of a president, vice president, secretary-treasurer, and sergeant of arms, usually elected for specific terms. However, informal "leaders" also emerge and often exercise more control than the elected officers. Chapters usually are gathered into regional groups which support the national organization. The national organization is frequently headed by a "mother club," which may be either an original chapter or a national ruling body in which each member supervises several chapters. The national president may be the actual leader or simply a spokesman for the gang.

Hell's Angels

The Hell's Angels' ties to LCN are well established. Informants have corroborated reports that members of the Cleveland chapter were involved in contract killings and drug trafficking for the Licavoli LCN family. Associations between members of the Hell's Angels and the Genovese crime family have been identified. In Troy, New York, Hell's Angels members are known to have a relationship with an associate of the Buffalino LCN family.

As is true of most organized crime groups, the Hell's Angels must launder their illicit income before it can be used legitimately. When income exceeds the immediate needs of the members, it is invested. The West Coast faction has been especially active in buying legitimate businesses including motorcycle and automobile services, catering operations, bars and restaurants, antique stores, landscaping operations, and machine shops. The faction has recently acquired large parcels of acreage in the California "gold country," a foothill area of the Sierra Nevada mountains, east of Sacramento. The gang's only discernible weakness is that its members are easily identified by their "colors." However, some members are abandoning their outlaw image, wearing business suits and driving luxury cars, in essence, becoming an outlaw motorcycle gang without motorcycles. The gang's strengths are many. It is institutionally wary of authority and uses sophisticated methods to protect itself from surveillance. Some clubhouses are fortified with elaborate electronic and physical security systems. Gang members do extensive background checks on prospective members, often using female associates, who have been placed in positions with government services, and law enforcement agencies to assist them.

The Outlaws

Founded in the late 1950s in the Chicago area, the Outlaws are an international group with chapters in Canada and Australia. The group's territory which is divided into four or five regional areas, each with a president, runs mainly through the midwestern United States. Outlaw territory includes Michigan, Illinois, western New York, Ohio, western Pennsylvania, and parts of Oklahoma, Arkansas, and Kentucky. It also reaches into North Carolina, Georgia, and Florida. The Outlaws are intense rivals of the Hell's Angels in those areas where the two gang's territories overlap. Like the Hell's Angels, the individual chapters of the Outlaws are independent and may cooperate with one another when mutually beneficial. The Outlaws are considered less criminally sophisticated than some chapters of the Hell's Angels, but perhaps even more violent.

The Outlaws are heavily involved in the production and distribution of methamphetamines. The group's strength in the midwestern border states has allowed it to smuggle "Canadian Blue" valium into the United States while its chapters in Florida have made use of cocaine and marijuana smuggling outlets from South America.

The Outlaws have a record of involving their women associates in crime. Their general treatment of those women, who are typically regarded as gang property, borders on slavery. Women are used in drug transactions to insulate members from arrest and are put to work as masseuses, prostitutes, and topless dancers in bars controlled by the gang. Some women are said to have been sold from one member to another. Besides trafficking in illegal drugs, the Outlaws are known to be involved in extortion, armed robbery, rape, mail fraud, auto theft, and witness intimidation. Their reputation for violence is strong. The Outlaws have had at least some contact with the LCN families. Clarence Michael Smith, a member of the Tampa, Florida chapter, was convicted of the murder of Robert Collins in New Orleans. Collins had testified against a nephew of Carlos Marcello, the LCN boss in New Orleans.

Bandidos

The Hell's Angels and the Outlaws were already well-established gangs when Donald Chambers organized the Bandidos, also known as "the Bandido Nation," in 1966 in Houston. The Bandidos are about a decade behind the Hell's Angels in their development, but are quickly catching up. The mother chapter is in Corpus Christi although the powerbase is believed to be in Rapid City, South Dakota. The mother chapter's territories reach throughout the Southwest, through the Rocky Mountain region, and into Washington State. It has strength in Louisiana, Arkansas, and Mississippi.

The Bandidos are involved in a wide variety of crimes. A former female associate said that the Outlaws in Florida began supplying cocaine to the Bandidos as early as 1978.

Many have been arrested for offenses involving dynamite and explosives. Massage parlors and escort services are among their favorite business enterprises.

Since 1979, the Bandidos have undergone several changes in leadership. The founding president, Donald Chambers, was convicted of a double murder and began serving a life term in 1979. Ronald Hodge succeeded him, but stepped down in 1982. Leadership was then passed to Alvin Frakes, who has recently died of cancer, and the presidency may have reverted to Hodge.

Pagans

The Pagans have no international connections. They are considered second only to the Hell's Angels in criminal sophistication, and the strength of their internal structure is unmatched by any of the other three major gangs. Its territory is mainly in the mid-Atlantic region. The original chapter was formed in Price George's County, Maryland in 1959. Since then, the mother chapter was moved to Marcus Hook, Pennsylvania and then to its current location of Suffolk County, New York.

The Pagans' mother chapter is unique among outlaw gangs because it functions like a board of directors or a ruling council. Each member of the mother chapter is responsible for a certain geographic area and has authority over chapters in that area, a system similar to the La Cosa Nostra's national commission.

Prison Gangs

In the last 20 years, some groups in United States prisons have evolved into self-perpetuating criminal gangs. Several operate both in and out of prison and have taken on the characteristics of true organized-crime associations. Prison gangs engage in narcotics and weapons trafficking, extortion, robbery, and murder. Members released from prison remain in the gang, often providing support and enforcement for the organization inside.

The Department of Justice has identified 114 different gangs, not all of which are formally organized. A close examination of the 114 gangs yielded five that appear to meet the criteria of an organized crime group, the Mexican Mafia, La Nuestra Familia (Our Family), the Aryan Brotherhood, the Black Guerrilla Family, and the Texas Syndicate. All five operate in more than one state. In all five, either murder or the drawing of blood are prerequisites for membership.

Mexican Mafia

In 1957, members of the Mexican-American youth gangs were incarcerated at the Deuel Vocational Institute in Tracy, California. They banded together, at first for self-protection, but soon began to control such illicit activities as homosexual prostitution, gambling, and narcotics. They called themselves the Mexican Mafia out of admiration for LCN. The group spread throughout California and into the federal prison system because of gang member transfers. The group recruited heavily from among the most dangerous and violent Mexican-American prisoners. A general and a few "godfathers" direct the activities of captains, lieutenants, and "soldados." Prospects must be sponsored for membership and must be approved by vote of other members. They are required to kill without question, which gives the gang a constant pool of potential contract killers.

Since 1968, the Mexican Mafia has been in a constant feud with La Nuestra Familia, another Mexican-American gang whose members are primarily from rural areas of central

California. The feud began when La Nuestra Familia attempted to take over heroin trafficking inside the California prison system. By 1972, 30 prisoners had died in prison as a result of the feud.

The Mexican Mafia's allies in the feud have been the white supremacist prison group, the Aryan Brotherhood, with whom they cooperate in prison contract killings as well as in robberies and illicit drug transactions on the outside.

La Nuestra Familia

Originally formed in 1967 as a Latin cultural organization in Soledad prison, La Nuestra Familia began to sell protection to others that had been victimized by the Mexican Mafia. Soon the group moved into the extortion rackets that their rivals had monopolized. In 1975, the gang began establishing "regiments" outside prison, using Fresno County, California as a home base.

The gang's organizational structure consists of a single "general" with supreme power, captains, lieutenants, and soldados. Rank is usually achieved by the number of "hits" in which a member is involved.

La Nuestra Familia is allied closely with the Black Guerrilla Family.

Aryan Brotherhood

San Quentin prison in California was the origin of the group first known as the "Diamond Tooth Gang," now the Aryan Brotherhood, a white, Nazi-oriented gang dominated by members and associates of outlaw motorcycle gangs. The Aryan Brotherhood (sometimes known as the A-B's) has branches in prisons around the country, but seems most active in state prisons in California, Arizona, Wisconsin, Idaho, and throughout the federal prison system.

Its typical crimes include robberies and extortion of inmate's families outside prison as well as offenses commonly associated within the walls; extortion, protection schemes, and crimes of intimidation and violence.

A commission and a governing council rule the group. Members advance in the ranks through acts of violence.

Black Guerrilla Family

George Jackson, a former member of the Black Panther party, founded the Black Guerrilla Family in San Quentin in 1966. It is the most politically oriented of the five major prison gangs and often follows a Maoist philosophy.

The goal of the gang is cultural unity and the protection of black prison inmates. Many members formerly belonged to the Black Liberation Army, the underground organization responsible for the October 1981 robbery of a Brinks armored truck, during which a guard and two New York police officers were killed. New recruits for the prison organization frequently have belonged to black street gangs. They join the prison gang to share its criminal profits, which has led to a split between a political faction and the moneymaking faction.

The gang's ruling structure consists of a single leader (known as a chairman or supreme commander), a central committee, and a very loose ranking of soldiers.

Texas Syndicate

A third major Mexican-American prison gang is the Texas Syndicate. It was formed in California's Folsom prison in 1974. Its founders were all from Texas. They banded together for mutual protection and soon became known for their swift retaliation against any opposition. As gang members were released from California, they returned to their home state. Many were soon rearrested and imprisoned in Texas. Today, the Texas Syndicate is the largest gang in that state's prison system.

The gang is active in drug trafficking, contract murders, assaults, and intimidation within the prison. Members take a life oath and are more secretive than most prison gangs.

Under the leader is a chain of command similar to that of most prison gangs. The Texas Syndicate is known to be exceptionally violent, frequently assaulting or killing non-members and prison staff. They have no working relationship with other prison gangs.

Chinese Organized Crime

Secret Chinese criminal societies known as Triads were originally formed as resistance groups to the Chiang Dynasty which ruled China from the early seventeenth century until 1912. Triads flourished in Hong Kong and Taiwan through the 1950s and 1960s, controlling many important police posts in Hong Kong until the early 1970s.

Now, members of the Triads in Hong Kong and Taiwan are living in the United States. They have formed Triad-like crime groups in major American cities and are active in drug trafficking, illegal gambling, and loansharking, among other sophisticated criminal offenses. They operate through youth gangs under the direction of established Chinese businessmen and community leaders. They cooperate with LCN families and maintain close ties to criminal associates in Hong Kong, Taiwan, Thailand, and the People's Republic of China.

History And Background

With the end of the Chiang Dynasty, Dr. Sun Yat Sen, who had been a Triad member, called for the disbanding of the secret societies in 1912. Many nationalists heeded Sun's appeal, some moved into government posts. Criminal elements filled the vacated positions in the Triads.

General Chiang Kai Shek, also a former Triad member, enlisted a number of the groups in his fight against communism. All Triads were politically oriented. Many took advantage of lawless conditions in China to expand their organized criminal activities, and some Triads made open agreements with Japanese occupational forces in order to continue their illegal enterprises.

Many Triad members fled China in 1949 after the collapse of the Nationalist China government. A large group followed Chiang to Taiwan, others sought refuge in Hong Kong reinforcing an already strong Triad presence in that British Colony. When Kuomingtang and Nationalist China armies retreated to Burma and Thailand, they established an important foothold in the Golden Triangle and began to supply the Hong Kong Triads with opium and heroin. That connection continues today. The drugs are now shipped out of Hong Kong to the United States, Canada, Australia, and northern Europe.

Triad members in Hong Kong developed extortion rackets, illegal gambling, drug trafficking, prostitution, loansharking, and other criminal trades. Despite frequent and bloody territorial battles, they thrived almost unhindered after compromising and corrupting police and local officials. During an anticorruption drive in 1970, five former sergeants in the Hong Kong police, known as the "Five Dragons," fled the country carrying as much as $1 million each. One of the associates of the Five Dragons was Eddie Chan, now a businessman in New York's Chinatown and a leader of the On Leong Tong there.

Triads based in Taiwan were allowed to continue operating on the condition that they support the anti-communist stand of General Chiang and his exiled government. Thus, Taiwan-based Triads and their affiliates in other countries are known as "right hand" groups, a political reference. They have been involved in political intelligence gathering and, at least once in this country, in the assassination of political opponents.

"Left Hand" Triads, many based in Hong Kong, maintain working relationships within the People's Republic of China. For example, the Kung Lok Triad, a Hong Kong group, has ties to officials of the Peoples Republic of China.

After more than 200 years of an underground existence, the Triads developed an intricate secret structure with arcane designations and ceremonies, many of which survive today. Various offices in the organization are identified by numbers, each beginning with the digit "4," a reference to the ancient Chinese belief that the world is surrounded by four seas. The leader of a Triad group is given number 489. Second-tier leaders, each with specific duties, are known by the number 432 (messenger or liaison) and 438 (incense master or recruiter). Lower ranking officers are designated as 426 (organizer or enforcer) or 415 (an expert on administration and finance). Ordinary members are given the number 49. Initiation rituals include the beheading of a chicken (intimating the fate of a member who betrays the group), the mingling of blood by members and initiates, and the recitation of 36 loyal oaths.

Triad Groups and Tongs

As early as the nineteenth century, Chinese immigrants in America had formed benevolent associations known as "Tongs," a term that loosely means "meeting hall." Today, many Tongs are national organizations with chapters in cities that have large Chinese communities. Tongs function as business associations, ethnic societies, and centers of local politics.

However, there is a sinister aspect of many Tongs. Several of the largest and most respected are used as fronts for vicious Chinese organized crime groups that prey mainly on Chinese immigrants and Chinese-Americans. Tong members direct gang enterprises that include extortion, illegal gambling, narcotics trafficking, robbery, and "protection" schemes for prostitution and pornography. Among the prominent Tongs associated with Chinese organized crime are the On Leong Tong, headquartered in New York; the Hip Sing, also New York based; and the Hop Sing, with headquarters and operations on the West Coast.

The Tong members, who supervise Chinese criminal groups, frequently are Triad members with Triad designations. The 426 is the street-level leader of the gang. Gang members are Chinese males in the late teens and twenties. They are often chosen specifically for their youth and malleability and on the further assumption that the justice system is lenient with young offenders whose criminal records, in this country, are negligible or nonexistent.

A secret commission witness identified as 426, designating his position as captain and enforcer in a Chinese crime gang in the United States, described in a deposition how, as a teenager, he had been inducted into a Triad group while in Hong Kong. He told how he left Hong Kong to avoid prosecution and came to North America where he eventually joined a Triad chapter. Later, he was active in a New York group that included Triad members among its leadership. The gang functioned as a criminal arm of a major national Tong and was involved in narcotics, extortion, and murder, often drawing on its ties with a Triad group in Hong Kong. He described international collaboration between branches of Triad groups on such matters as intimidation of witnesses, assassinations, and the importation of heroin from sources in the Golden Triangle and sometimes through mainland China.

Chinese Crime Groups in New York

Chan Tse-Chiu, also known as Eddie Chan, is president of the On Leong Tong in New York. He has been president of the national organization which has chapters throughout the United States. Currently, he is its honorary national president. Chan is also a former Hong Kong police sergeant who served in the post during the era of the "Five Dragons." According to several sources, he is also the supervisor of a street gang known as the Ghost Shadows, a national crime group with chapters in several cities and with intimate ties to the On Leong Tong.

In New York and elsewhere, the Ghost Shadows engage in narcotics trafficking, loan-sharking, illegal gambling, and extortion rackets. At one time, the gang was led by Nicky Louie, whose influence in the group was such that he attempted to wrest control from Eddie Chan. Loyalists from Ghost Shadow groups in Boston and Chicago sided with the Louie faction in the gang war that resulted when Chan ordered the murder of his rival. Eventually, Louie and his coterie fled to Chicago. Eight assassins from the Chan faction of the New York Ghost Shadows were dispatched to Chicago. A car they used was eventually traced back to the rental account of On Leong Tong officials in Chicago. Louie was critically wounded in an ambush at On Leong Tong headquarters in Chicago. He survived, but his driver was killed.

As a part of a negotiated settlement, Nicky Louie was allowed to retire. Eddie Chan and the On Leong Tong retained control of the Ghost Shadows and their criminal enterprises.

The other major association in New York's Chinatown is the Hip Sing Tong, with headquarters located on Pell Street. Its leader is 75-year-old Feilo Chat, known as "Benny Ong," "Uncle Seven," or "Uncle Benny." Ong is an immigrant and gang member who served 17 years in prison for a homicide and was released in 1952. Today he is among the most visible members of the Chinese community in New York with significant business holdings throughout Manhattan.

The criminal arm of the Hip Sing Tong is the Flying Dragons whose activities include extortion, illegal gambling, and narcotics trafficking. A truce with the On Leong Tong in the 1960s secured Hip Sing's hold on Pell Street and the nearby area.

Violence Among Chinese Crime Groups

In New York, rivalries among newer groups have resulted in three massacres of associations in the early 1980s. On December 23, 1983, members of the White Tiger's group were ambushed at a bar. Eleven people, most of them White Tiger's recruits, were killed and wounded. On September 4, 1977, at the Golden Dragon restaurant in San Francisco's Chinatown, five innocent people were murdered. The restaurant was a favorite of the gang, known as the Hip Sing Boys. They killed 5 people and seriously wounded 11 others. None of the victims were gang members since the Wah Ching and the Hip Sing boys had fled when they noticed the gunmen approaching.

In addition to New York, Chicago, and San Francisco, Chinese organized crime groups have a strong presence in Monterey Park, California; Boston, Massachusetts; and many other U.S. cities.

The Hong Kong Summit

During the early 1980s, the principal leaders of Chinese organized crime in North America, or their representatives, met in Hong Kong to discuss a possible détente between major rival groups. Those in attendance included Kis Jai (Peter Chin), leader of the New York Ghost Shadows under Eddie Chan; Vincent Jew, west coast leader of the Wah Ching; Danny Mo (Danny Mo Sui Chen), the operational leader of the Kung Lok Triad in Canada; and Stephen Tse, leader of the Ping On gang from Boston, who is also believed to be a former associate of the 14K Triad in Hong Kong.

The meeting resulted in a recognition of territories and an agreement to assist one another when necessary. The participants "burned the yellow paper," a ritual that symbolizes brotherhood and the start of a new venture. Later, the principals formed a joint venture, the Oriental Arts Promotion Company, by which they have attempted to monopolize the U.S. bookings of Chinese-speaking entertainers from Hong Kong and Taiwan.

Canada: The Kung Lok Triad

The international scope of the Chinese crime gangs is evident in the Canadian chapter of the Hong Kong-based Triad, Kung Lok. This group undertakes the standard range of crimes against Chinese Canadians and is considered active in Toronto, Montreal, Ottawa, Vancouver, Hamilton, and other metropolitan areas. The Kung Lok is a more traditional Triad establishment. Its members in Canada undergo the same ritual initiation as those in Hong Kong.

There is constant traffic of Kung Lok members among Canada, the United States, and various Caribbean locations, particularly Santo Domingo. In the early 1980s, Kung Lok established an illegal gambling house on Division Street in New York through agreement with the Hip Sing and the On Leong Tong. Lau Wing Kui, deported leader of Kung Lok in Canada, owns an interest in at least one casino in Santo Domingo and has interests in several other Hong Kong gambling establishments. It is believed that the Kung Lok members carry large sums of cash out of Canada to be laundered at the Santo Domingo casino before the money is brought to the United States. Kung Lok has members in the United Kingdom and Europe who act on orders of the Hong Kong leadership, giving them a worldwide capability to intimidate witnesses directly or through threats against the witness's family in any area where Kung Lok members operate.

Vietnamese Gangs

In the first eight years after the Communist China victory in Vietnam, about 650,000 Indochinese immigrated to the United States. Among them were criminals with backgrounds in drug trafficking, extortion, and prostitution. Many criminals assumed the identities of deceased Vietnamese who had no arrest records.

Small bands of these criminal refugees formed in resettlement camps. Later, they formed gangs in Vietnamese communities around the United States. There are seven cities in California with active Vietnamese gangs, four gangs in Texas, three in Louisiana, two in Alabama, and one in each of the following states: Washington, Colorado, Florida, Massachusetts, New York, Pennsylvania, Oregon, Virginia, and Hawaii.

In some cases, the groups are little more than street gangs. Others conduct sophisticated criminal schemes, extortion, gambling, and drug trafficking that require organization and discipline. Police report that there is at least informal communication between gangs. Also, they are extremely mobile. There is evidence of networking among gangs, i.e. Vietnamese fugitives in California finding sanctuary in New Orleans. Vietnamese gangs are known to cooperate with other Asian crime groups.

Generally, Vietnamese gangs confine themselves to communities of other Vietnamese who are particularly susceptible to extortion. The immigrant victims are reluctant to testify because they do not believe police will protect them from retribution.

Japanese Organized Crime

With membership as high as 110,000 in as many as 2,500 associated gangs, the Japanese Yakuza may be the largest organized-crime group in the world. The Yakuza originated in sixteenth and seventeenth century Japan where feudal lords maintained stables of Samurai warriors. Stronger national government in Japan subsequently made many regional warriors superfluous, and they allied themselves both with the ruling Shogunate and with dissident villages. Eventually, the vagabond warriors became known as "Yakuza," a gambling term for numbers that are worthless or losers. The name evolved into an expression for "outlaw," with a connotation of respect based on fear. Through the next three centuries, the status of the Yakuza fluctuated depending on the strength of the national government.

Immediately after World War II, immense social and economic changes in Japan meant opportunity for organized crime, particularly in black markets. The Yakuza prospered, adding pornography, narcotics, and systematic racketeering to their illicit enterprises while expanding into entertainment, sports, labor unions, and corporate affairs. Their enforcement tactics became brutal. Police and media in Japan referred to Yakuza as "Boryokudan," or "violent gang." Many street gangs associated with the Yakuza began to mimic American outlaw motorcycle gangs. Others imitated the dress and style of Prohibition-era gangsters, as interpreted by U.S. moviemakers.

Japanese police designate seven major groups of Yakuza. The largest is "Yamaguchi Gumi," with an estimated membership of 10,000 which has a hierarchical structure resembling that of the LCN family in this country. There is a single "Kaicho" (chairman), who has advisors without command authority. "Wakato" control several deputies, beneath them are lieutenants who manage numerous "soldiers," or "wakai shu."

The other six major groups, with more elaborate structures, are confederations of smaller gangs that have combined to increase their power. These alliances control criminal activities in assigned territories. The most powerful and the most important rival of Yamaguchi Gumi is the alliance known as "Sumiyoshi Rengo" with an estimated strength of 8,000 to 15,000 members.

Whatever the internal arrangement of the organization, a Yakuza member's status is determined by his efficiency as an "earner," one who passes profits to his higher-ups. The more elevated his position the more money he receives from below, although his obligations remain to those still above him. It is a highly-competitive system calculated to maintain pressures for production. Yakuza members, particularly those in the lower echelons, are encouraged to find new enterprises with which to satisfy the constant demand from above. Loyalty to superiors is considered paramount. A Yakuza member who has angered his supervisor may apologize by amputating a finger or finger joint from his own hand, then presenting it to the offended party as a gesture of sincerity.

The Yakuza groups are active in drug trafficking, primarily smuggling amphetamines from the United States into Japan. They also supply a lucrative Japanese market for firearms which are strictly regulated in that nation. A handgun that sells for $100 to $200 here may be worth $1,000 in Japan, and a single round of ammunition might sell for $12 to $15.

Yakuza enforcers are sometimes used by the boards of large corporations in Japan to keep order at open stockholder meetings, a practice known as "sokaiya." Strong-arm gang members discourage potentially embarrassing questions by stockholders. Also, the reverse occurs when a minority faction, perhaps affiliated with Yakuza interests, wishes to intimidate the board or majority. Physical violence is not uncommon.

Yakuza in the United States

The Yakuza has been mainly involved in obtaining contraband for shipment to Japan. However, recent intelligence has shown that they are involved with factions of the LCN in East Coast gambling operations catering to wealthy Japanese businessmen. For at least 20 years, the Yakuza members have invested illegal earned profits in U.S. businesses. Recently, Yakuza interests have increased in legitimate businesses, massage parlors, and pornography. Three Yakuza groups, the Yamaguchi Gumi, Sumiyoshi Rengo, and Toa Taui Jigyo Kumiai are currently active in southern California. In recent years, the Yakuza has bought shares of major corporations and has started the function of "sokaiya," corporate intimidation. Also, the Yakuza has infiltrated legitimate businesses. In so doing, they have employed business practices that American companies cannot do because of fear of being prosecuted for antitrust violations or illegal business practices. However, the Yakuza have been getting away because prosecutors haven't developed their case to the extent necessary to obtain a conviction.

Asian Characteristics.   Asians, citizens and criminals, have some common characteristics that a fraud examiner should be aware of as follows:

A. Authority. Asians do not view law enforcement as servants of the community. In Asia, law enforcement was set up to protect rulers and their parties and not protect and serve the community. Asian citizens are reluctant to report crimes when they become victims. This is due to no belief in or understanding of the criminal justice system as well as fear of retaliation by the criminals. Many Asians feel that the American justice system doesn't impose punishment to fit the crime.

B. Asset Hiding. Asians have created their own underground currency by trading in commodities. They invest their cash into gold and precious stones, particularly, diamonds, rubies, and jade. They prefer to keep their valuables in their homes or businesses rather than use banking services. They invest heavily into "taels" since they can be easily hid and exchanged. (A tael is a standard Chinese measurement that measures $3\frac{3}{4}$ by $1\frac{1}{2}$ inches and weighs one troy ounce. It is a 24-carat piece and gold prices determine its market value.) Asian immigrants will invest in taels until they have enough to acquire their own business. Asians will launder their illegal profits by investing in legitimate businesses. This underground currency helps them avoid paper trails and evade taxes. Asian immigrants will work "under the table" and even collect public subsistence while accumulating their wealth.

C. Credit Unions. Asians have organized together to form an informal "credit union." These self-help programs consist of 10 to 20 people who are mostly women. They are organized for definite periods and have regularly-scheduled meetings. Members are required to invest specific amounts of money at each meeting. When cash holdings are ample, members bid for the cash. The highest bidder receives the funds.

The bidder must repay the loan back with interest over a specific time. This allows the funds to be available to another member. These informal credit unions have no official recognition and usually involve large amounts of cash. They can also lend themselves to the organizer to rig bids or abscond with the cash. Asian credit unions are known by the following names:

HUI	Vietnamese
GAE	Korean
CHO WUI	Chinese
TANA-MOSHI	Japanese

D. Corruption. Most Asians believe that all government officials have a price. "Payoffs" in Asian countries are very common. They are a way of life and are considered to be an additional tax by Asian businessmen. Payments begin small and build up from there. They start out as "free lunches" and build up to cash payments out of the cash register. Any government official who accepts any gift will soon learn that the Asian businessman has announced in the community that he has a "friend down-town" that can cut through "red tape" or can provide protection.

Warning: Due to this belief, government officials should never accept any gifts or gratuities from any Asian businessmen, not even a cup of coffee or tea.

Cuban Organized Crime

Since 1959, over one million Cuban refugees have arrived in the United States. Most have come seeking political freedom and the opportunity to build productive lives. But from the first wave of refugees in 1959 to the latest, a criminal minority of Cubans has found ground for illegal enterprises that are as ambitious and sophisticated as any before seen in this country.

There have been three periods of mass Cuban immigration to the United States.

a. First, immediately before and after the fall of the Batista regime until Fidel Castro halted emigration in 1959.
b. Second, between 1965 and 1972 during the Camarioca boatlift "freedom flotilla," prompting the Family Reunification Program under which more than 250,000 Cubans migrated to the United States.
c. Finally, between April 21 and November 10, 1980, during a boatlift from Mariel Harbor, bringing nearly 125,000 new Cuban refugees to the United States.

By far, the greatest concentration of criminals was in the Mariel Harbor exodus, with nearly 2 percent of those arriving in the United States having been classified as prostitutes, criminals, drug addicts, or vagrants. Because of this minority, the term "Marielito" has come to imply a criminal or undesirable; referring specifically to the career criminals who left Cuba during the 1980 boatlift.

There are differences between the criminals who immigrated in the first two waves and those who came in the 1980 Mariel boatlift. Criminal syndicates founded by the earlier arrivals tend to be more extensive, more highly structured, and more closely associated with other criminal groups, especially the La Cosa Nostra, than those of the Marielitos.

While the established groups have partly built their criminal fortunes on less violent crimes, mainly on forms of gambling, the newcomers have shown a propensity for killing, kidnapping, and street crime. The differences may partly be attributed to the fact that for more than 20 years, while early arrivals were busy establishing themselves, the later arrivals were in primitive prisons and hospitals, and in a brutal underworld subculture. There is evidence that the established Cuban syndicates have begun using Marielitos in their criminal enterprises, so these distinctions may soon become less clear. Nevertheless, the present differences between them are great enough so that the two groups are treated separately in this report.

There are two established groups in the United States which are known as the La Compania or The Corporation. The La Compania is involved in drug trafficking and gambling. Illegal gambling, particularly bolita or policy lotteries, are widely accepted by Cubans. While La Cosa Nostra controls most lotteries and bookmaking in Cuban communities, many of those operations have come under the control of the Cuban groups.

The most prominent emerging Cuban gambling cartel is The Corporation, headed by Jose Miguel Battle. This group's annual profit was estimated to be between $45 and $100 million in 1984. Battle, known as Jose Miguel Vargas, Miguel Blasquez, Rafael Franco Tesona, "Don Miguel," and "El Gordon" was a soldier in the Batista army and was a Havana policeman until the fall of the Batista regime. After Cuba collapsed, Battle fled to Miami and joined the Brigade 2506 (the Bay of Pigs landing group). After the failed invasion, Battle returned to Miami and founded the first Cuban controlled gambling organization. The group grew through police and political corruption.

In the late 1960s, Battle moved his operations to New York City and Union City with the help of Joseph Zicarelli and Santo Trafficante. He began to take over existing operations there by violent means.

By the early 1970's, Battle's group collected bets from most of the Hispanic bodegas and bars in New York and New Jersey. Zicarelli and James Napoli, soldiers of the Genovese crime family, helped negotiate a settlement by which Battle agreed to pay a percentage of his earnings to the La Cosa Nostra and lay off some of his betting action. The Corporation's records show that the group grossed in excess of $2 million on a weekly basis. Battle and The Corporation have amassed assets valued at several hundred million dollars. The Corporation owns or controls Union Management and Mortgage Company, the Union Finance Company, the Union Financial Research Company Inc., Union Travel and Tours, and El Zapotal Realty Inc., all in South Florida.

During the 1970s, Battle was convicted on RICO gambling charges. He fled to Madrid, Spain, after receiving an 18-month sentence. He served 13 months in prison after he was arrested trying to re-enter the United States by way of Costa Rica. Battle received prison sentences totaling 34 years for a concealed weapon charge and murder of a former associate, Ernest Torres.

In 1982, Battle and several key associates, including Abraham Rydz, moved to Florida. Battle, his wife, son, and Rydz, bought various real estate properties totaling $1,115,000 on which they paid $805,000 in cash. On April 8, 1983, the New York Port Authority police found $439,000 cash in luggage belonging to Rydz and Battle's son, Jose Battle Jr., after the two men resisted search of their carry-on baggage while boarding a flight to Miami. On December 3, 1984, British Customs authorities at Heathrow Airport in London detained several associates of The Corporation, whose itinerary included stops in the Bahama Islands, Switzerland, and Spain, with a return to Miami. Between them they possessed $450,000 in U.S. currency. In all, cash seizures from members of the groups have totaled about $43 million.

The enormous cash flow was laundered through a complex web of influence in mortgage and lending companies. The Capitol National Bank in Manhattan received huge deposits of The Corporation's gambling receipts. The bank was also the largest redeemer of food stamps from the north New Jersey bars.

A task force, in June 1985, arrested 16 people, including 11 present or former Puerto Rican bank officials. In Operation Greenback, Puerto Rico uncovered a scheme by members of The Corporation to launder hidden income by the purchase of winning tickets in the legal Puerto Rican lottery. Members of The Corporation would privately buy the winning ticket from the owner, paying a premium price in "dirty" cash from the gambling operation. A $125,000 ticket, for example, would be bought for $150,000. The money then would be deposited without being traced to the source.

The La Compania was formed in the early 1960s. Its primary purpose was to import cocaine, heroin, and marijuana. The group is estimated to have about 125 members with a connecting group in Los Angeles. The La Compania has branches in New York, Las Vegas, Texas, Arizona, New Jersey, and Tijuana, Mexico. After more than 20 years, the Cuban group have produced large amounts of capital which is invested in businesses, real estate, and banks.

Marielito Crime Gangs

The Mariel boatlift had its genesis on April 1, 1980 when a small band of Cubans in a city bus attempted to gain political asylum by crashing the gates of the Peruvian Embassy. One Cuban guard at the gate accidentally killed another guard while trying to stop the bus. Fidel Castro was enraged and publicly announced the removal of all guards from the gates. Within days, over 10,000 people had crowded into the embassy grounds, requesting political asylum. Eventually, Castro allowed them to be flown out of the country. This group and the majority of those who followed later included primarily decent and working-class people who genuinely sought liberty. Castro proclaimed the refugees to be the scum of Cuban society. When the exodus continued, he tried to prove his description by forcibly including convicts, hard core criminals, prostitutes, and the mentally ill among those who left by boat from Mariel.

The career criminals who came to the United States during the Mariel boatlift are commonly known as "Marielitos." Some have formed crime gangs, including large drug-trafficking rings and some formally organized groups with operations in several different cities. They have cooperated with longer-established Cuban crime groups as collectors and enforcers in drug or gambling operations. Gangs of Marielitos have assisted Colombian drug smuggling organizations, and least once, the LCN family used a Marielito as a hired killer.

There has been an unprecedented wave of violent crime among Cubans since their arrival in this country. Increased homicide rates in several locales are directly attributable to Mariel criminals. Homicide rates in Hialeah, Florida, increased from 12 to 43 from 1980 to 1981, most involved Marielitos. Marielitos are involved in robbery, burglary, rape, counterfeiting, bookmaking, auto theft, shoplifting, extortion, and prostitution, but are mostly involved in cocaine trafficking along with murders.

The profile of the Mariel career criminal is specific and unique. He is generally male, in his 30s, poorly educated, superstitious, with a good physique and poor personal hygiene. Many are former military conscripts who have served in Angola or Central

America, thus, there is a good chance that the Marielito is familiar with automatic weapons and knowledgeable in guerrilla warfare. Commonly, the Marielito's body is marked with scars which he often reveres as emblems of battle. Some are self-inflicted or the result of religious rituals.

Over 90 percent of the convicted Mariel refugees have a tattoo somewhere on their bodies. In Cuban society, tattoos are a sign of disgrace. Mariel tattoos are often intricate, displaying patron saints, names, words, or arcane symbols. A display of five dots on the web of the hand between the thumb and forefinger identifies a pickpocket or delinquent.

The Marielitos are members of Afro-Cuban religious cults which explains the aberrant behavior. The cult is called "Santeria" which is imbued with qualities of Christian saints and various African deities. Its antithesis is the practice of Leader Palo Mayombe. Criminals honor the god of hunting, Ochosi, who is believed to guarantee freedom from incarceration, which leads them to take risks or perform acts they would normally avoid.

Another Afro-Cuban sect is the Abaqua cult with origins in Cuban prisons. It is considered as much a fraternal order as a religious society. Members wear an arrow-shaped tattoo in the web of the hand.

In five years, the Marielitos formed two large gangs. The Abaqua Cult and the Mariel Bandidos are both located in the Washington, D.C. area and have memberships as high as 500 to 1,000. Other groups are located in Las Vegas, New York, and Los Angeles. Intermediate size groups have appeared in other states, primarily dealing in illicit narcotics. They form small, loosely structured, highly-mobile gangs that disband after the criminal task has been completed. Its members then drift to other cities. Investigation has been difficult because the gangs are so fluid and difficult to identify. The new gangs have earned a share in drug trafficking. They are crude in their approach, but established crime groups may supply the necessary sophistication.

Colombian Cocaine Cartels

About 75 percent of the cocaine consumed in the United States comes from Colombia. There are at least 20 Colombian drug rings. These rings are centered in two major cities, Medellin and Cali. Most of the drug rings are centered in Medellin. Medellin is the second largest city in Colombia. Their members and workers handle every phase of production from manufacture, distribution, finance, and security. Each function is separate from the other, thus, the loss of one member or group does not threaten the entire group. The rings can quickly adapt to outside pressure while continuing to pursue the goal of maximum production for maximum profit. The rings' influence is broad. They use foreign banks and tax havens in the Caribbean and Europe. Colombian traffickers are ruthless in pursuit of profit and use violence to protect their enterprises. The cocaine trade in South America is in a state of flux. The Medellin cartel has been hit hard by aggressive enforcement and interdiction strategy and is in a state of disarray and confusion. Some smaller traffickers have collapsed or moved their operations to neighboring countries. Concentration of resources by the Colombian government upon the Medellin cartel, however, has allowed other groups to consolidate and to grab a larger share of the market.

It is estimated that the Cali cartel has taken over 70 percent to 80 percent of the Medellin cartel's business. The Colombian government has indicted many bankers and lawyers in recent years for money-laundering cartel profits. The best known case is Banco de Occident, which is based in the western city of Cali where the bank was indicted for laundering millions for the late drug kingpin Gonzalo Rodriguez Gacha. The U.S. Drug Enforcement Agency found Gacha's bank records in an oil drum. Fabio Ochoa and his sons were indicted in the United States. Ochoa, after the Colombian government indictments, built his own jail. He stayed in the jail for awhile, then later escaped. Ochoa is considered to be one of the wealthiest men in the world. He lives a very lavish lifestyle. The Colombian government found that Ochoa has his own army of mercenaries which are trained by former Israeli military. Prior to the Colombian government crack down with U.S. aid, the drug lords in Medellin controlled most of the countryside. It is believed that the communist rebels in the country tried to blackmail the drug lords by kidnapping family members. This backfired on them. The drug lords had more wealth and firepower. This later resulted in the communist rebels and the drug lords to form an alliance. The Colombian drug lords have expanded their operations to other surrounding countries. They have established sophisticated communication and transportation networks from South America to the United States and Europe.

Irish Organized Crime

The Irish syndicate lost much of their territory and influence to Sicilian groups during prohibition. However, they are still active in New York and Philadelphia by accommodation with the LCN.

Irish organized crime is in the hands of three groups. Jimmy Bolger, a reputed killer, bank robber, and drug trafficker controls one. The second is the McLaughlin gang. The third is headed by Howard Winter who is involved in drug trafficking, hijacking, loan-sharking, and contract murder on behalf of the Angiulo branch of the Patriarca LCN family in New England.

The three gangs have divided Boston into territories. Howard Winter's gang controls the docks and Local 25 of the International Brotherhood of Teamsters. The Irish share their income with the Angiulo group in North Boston.

In New York, the Irish gang is known as the Westies. The group is lead by James Coonan. Like Boston, the New York gang is closely connected with the LCN interests. Their overall impact on New York is insignificant, however, its influence is considerable in the entertainment industry.

Russian Organized Crime

There have been three waves of Russian immigration to the United States. It has been speculated that the Soviet Union attempted to empty their prisons and rid their undesirables from 1971 and 1980 as Castro did in 1980.

The first indication of Russian organized crime was when a gang from the Odessa region began to perpetrate a con game against other Russians living throughout the United States. The group became known as the "Potato Bag Gang" because victims who believed they had bought a sack of gold coins actually received only a bag of potatoes.

The Russian gangs have become more sophisticated. The American Express Company estimated that it lost $2.7 million to Russian organized-crime groups during the first nine months of 1984. The gangs are loosely structured without formal hierarchy. Many are formed on the basis of regional backgrounds. The gang members are described as intelligent, professional criminals. Extortion appears to be the most frequent crime among Russian gangs. The Russian immigrant community is also a target of insurance fraud and con games. There are reports that Russian gangs in New York are linked to the Genovese family. Police suspect that Genovese family member Evsei Agron was murdered by the LCN because of a territorial conflict. Russian communities in this country are closed and suspicious of police.

Canadian Organized Crime

There are three major factions in Canadian organized crime which are active around the border region. In addition, members of Canadian crime groups have begun to concentrate in South Florida in an apparent expansion of both the scope and the base of their criminal enterprises.

The Vincent Cotroni crime family was identified during the 1960s and is an affiliate of the Bonanno LCN family in New York. Two Cotroni members from Montreal were convicted on drug conspiracy charges involving associates of Carmine Galante, a Bonanno capo. Today, the Cotroni group is headed by Santos "Frank" Cotroni and is engaged in drug trafficking.

Nine brothers control the French Canadian Dubois gang in Quebec Province. Four brothers are currently in prison. In 1985, Jean Paul Dubois headed the gang. Its main activity is drug trafficking.

Johnny McGuire, a one-time labor racketeer, has been called "The Canadian Jimmy Hoffa." Today, the crime group headed by McGuire works its own rackets and cooperates with other groups in smuggling drugs, guns, and stolen cars into Canada.

In 1963, Pasquale Cuntrera, boss of the Siciliana family, left Italy. He went to Caracas, Venezuela, where in 1964, he established, with the approval of the Cupola, the base of the Siciliana family. The most known members of the Siciliana family living in Canada are Nicolo Rizzuto, Vito Rizzuto, Paolo Renda, Giuseppe Lopresti, and Agostino Cuntrera. The Rizzutos have very close ties with the Gambino, Bonanno and DeCavalcante families in the United States. The year 1973 marked the beginning of the feud for control of criminal activities in Canada between Cotroni and Rizzuto families. Nicolo Rizzuto achieved his goal by killing Paolo Violi, underboss of the Cotroni family, and Francesco and Rocco Violi, Paolo's brothers. In 1984, Nicolo Rizzuto took control of all criminal activities in Canada after the death of Vincenzo Cotroni. In 1988, Nicolo Rizzuto was convicted in Caracas, Venezuela, for cocaine trafficking. His son, Vito Rizzuto, became the boss of the family. The Rizzuto crime family controls most of the gambling operations in Canada. Gambling consists of bookmaking, video poker machines, and casino operations. The Rizzuto crime family is also involved in narcotics, extortion, corruption, and money laundering.

Canadian organized crime groups have considerable presence in Florida; finding their customers and victims among both Floridians and the nearly one million Canadians who visit Florida. They engage in drug trafficking, loansharking, bookmaking, and smuggling stolen automobiles.

In Florida, Canadian gangs are close to points of supply for cocaine. The trade in handguns smuggled to Canada is also lucrative since weapons are easily available in Florida. Canadian crime groups have heavily invested in Florida business and real estate particularly beachfront property. In some cases, they obtained the property after intimidating legitimate buyers. Two Gambino family members who had been trying to open pizza restaurants in what apparently was Canadian-claimed territory were murdered and were found dead in the trunk of their car in Dade County, Florida. Since 1982, there have been a number of bombings involving pizza parlors in South Florida.

Jamaican Posse

The Jamaican Posses are a growing group of bold and dangerous individuals who traffic in large quantities of firearms and narcotics. There are about 40 posses operating in the United States, Great Britain, Canada, and the Caribbean with an estimated 10,000 members. These illegal activities are increasing along with the propensity for violence. They are attributed to be responsible for over 1,000 homicides nationwide. About 1976, two large violent groups emerged on the island of Jamaica: the Reatown Boys and the Dunkirk Boys. The Reatown Boys consisted of people from Reatown, Jamaica, most of who became known as the "Untouchables." They were loyal to the People's National Party. They later became known as the Shower Posse. The Dunkirk Boys became known as the Spangler Posse. They were aligned to the Jamaica Labor Party. The larger posse is the Shower Posse. They distribute drugs on a wholesale and street level in many large cities in the United States. Most of the Jamaican posses believe in a doctrine called Rastafarian. The original thrust was for improvement of conditions in Jamaica and eventual migration of Black people back to Africa, specifically Ethiopia. The most universal beliefs are as follows:

a. Rastafarian is the living God.
b. Ethiopia is the black man's home.
c. Repatriation is the way of redemption for black men.
d. The ways of the white man are evil.

Other doctrines, which are not universally adhered to on an individual basis, are as follows:

a. Eating pork is forbidden.
b. The "herb" marijuana or ganja is a gift of God who enjoined us to smoke it.
c. Beards and long hair are enjoined on men; it is a sin to shave or cut the hair.
d. Alcohol is forbidden, together with gambling.

When they recognize Emperor Selassie as God, they make a vow or pledge accepting the laws and decrees of conformance. Not all Rastafarians are criminals and not all Jamaicans are Rastafarians.

The Jamaican posses have a proclivity for violence seldom seen in other organized crime groups. They have little regard for public safety or human life. The posses violence can be directed at members of their own groups, rival groups, or others who may interfere with their drug territories. Age and sex present no barrier to their acts of violence. They have killed women, children, friends, and relatives. The Jamaican posse members have the following general traits:

a. They are usually well armed with high-powered weapons.
b. They will confront and kill police.
c. They use extensive surveillance methods.
d. They have disregard for innocent bystanders.

e. They use extensive aliases and false identification.
f. They use females to transport narcotics, weapons, and make weapon purchases.

In recent years, the Jamaican posses have begun establishing working relationships with other organized-crime groups. The La Cosa Nostra (LCN) is working with the Jamaican posses, along with the Colombian cartels. Posse members have been known to steal credentials of police officers, federal agents, military officers, and intelligence officers. They have developed their own slang based upon the existing elements of the English language. The Rastafarian language comes with a whole new vocabulary of "I" words which express their individualism. The word for "myself" is "I self," and "ourselves" is "I n I self." This new language is used as follows:

a. To prepare cover stories.
b. To identify true believers.
c. To plan criminal acts.
d. To appear to not know English.

Posses members are highly mobile with tremendous access to false identification. Weapons are a mark of manhood. High-quality weapons are a status symbol. In some posses, assaults or murders are used as membership requirements.

Posses members lack many of the sophisticated money-laundering methods. Most posses prefer to avoid direct use of traditional financial institutions. They smuggle most of their proceeds out of the United States. They use wire transfer companies by structuring their transactions. Higglers are street merchants in Jamaica. Higglers travel to the United States and purchase merchandise for resale in Jamaica, using posse funds. The goods are sold in Jamaica and the money is given to the posses. The Jamaicans use friends, relatives, and other "straw" purchasers to hide the true ownership of property. They like to use women's names in leasing cars, apartments, and obtaining other items. They have in recent years obtained small businesses, mostly cash sales operations, i.e., restaurants, grocery stores, nightclubs, record stores, boutiques, and garages.

Israeli Mafia

During the 1980s, the Israeli Mafia has been discovered operating in the United States. They are involved primarily in narcotics trafficking. They use business fronts to launder their profits. Most Israeli Mafia members were born in a Middle East country and immigrated to Israel where vast cultural and language difficulties were experienced. Many were not able to assimilate into the Israeli culture. Most of the criminal elements were born in an Arab Country, within a poor economic situation. The Israeli National Police arrested and incarcerated many for criminal activity. Numerous Israelis left Israel for other countries in order to pursue a lifestyle of criminality. It should be noted that if the criminals remained in Israel, their prospect for financial success would be limited since Israel and its populace are not financially prosperous. In the United States, the Israeli Mafia are close-knit. They have ties to the heroin trade in the Middle East and Southeast Asia and to the cocaine trade with ties to Colombia, Peru, Brazil, and Mexico. Besides drug trafficking, the Israeli Mafia are involved in other criminal activities of extortion, fencing stolen property, and various kinds of fraud. They use the following methods of disguise:

a. They use one another's address on official documents, particularly drivers licenses and vehicle registrations. The true resident would deny any knowledge of anyone listed on any document.
b. The inclusion or omission of the Hebrew word "Ben" in their last name. This word means "son of."
c. The Hebrew alphabet is phonetic and there is usually only one way of spelling a word or name. When translating a Hebrew name into the Roman alphabet, mistakes, whether intentional or unintentional, can occur in the spelling. The phonetic word of Levy can be translated into Levey, Levi, Levie, Leve, Leive, etc. These variations of spelling can provide numerous legitimate documents that can be used for identification purposes.

In the past, Israeli members maintained a low profile and a pretentious lifestyle. They met in small social clubs and drove old vehicles. Recently, members are driving luxury vehicles, smartly attired, wear expensive jewelry, and frequent luxury cabarets.

Gypsies/Travelers

The gypsies are people from Eastern Europe who have distinct coloring and body structure. The travelers are people from Ireland and the British Isles who have Caucasian coloring and cast. Both groups are involved in the same type of criminal activity of home invasions, shoplifting, store diversions, fortune telling, and jewelry store operations. The gypsies are dark-skinned with black or brown eyes, black hair, and are usually short and stocky. They like to wear colorful clothing. The gypsies are small in number in the United States and seem to remain on the lower economic scale. The travelers, on the other hand, have become much more prosperous. They are scattered throughout the United States, but the larger clans are concentrated in or around North Augusta and Defilade, South Carolina. Other clans are located near Memphis, Tennessee, and Ft. Worth, Texas. Their numbers are estimated to be around 6,000 individuals. The travelers live in a closed society. They do not socialize with nontravelers and discourage marriage outside the clan. Travelers get together about four times a year. At all other times, they are traveling and engaging in fraud and criminal activities. Men are the primary workers and head of the family. The travelers prefer to operate in rural areas. The European gypsies prefer to work urban areas because they can blend in with many cultural groups, targets of opportunity are more available, and they get assistance from other gypsy groups. The gypsies and travelers like to seek the elderly because:

a. They may live alone.
b. They are easily intimidated.
c. The make poor witnesses due to failing eyesight and memory capability.
d. They keep large sums of cash in their homes
e. They cannot physically make home repairs or improvements.

Both the travelers and the gypsies are mostly involved in consumer fraud. Their primary operations center on:

a.   Painting. The basic element here is giving an exaggerated estimate for the job using cheap grades of paint, poor quality due to thinning, and poor workmanship.
b.   Roof repair. They use poor materials and workmanship. In addition, they will drive their victim to the bank to get cash for a discount.
c.   Home repairs/service. They will pose as termite or building inspectors to advise people of bad conditions. They offer to do the repairs for an exaggerated fee. When the work is done, the quality is poor or the work was not even done. This is also used to get into people's homes for the purpose of canvassing and stealing valuables and money.
d.   Auto body repairs. Travelers look for dented automobiles. When found, they offer to repair it for a low fee. After repairs are done, they will attempt to inflate the price.
e.   Selling tools. The travelers like to sell cheap tools at inflated prices at flea markets, highway intersections, and even door to door.
f.   Social security/health scam. Here, two travelers pose as social security workers or health department workers. They offer to give a free physical to the victim. While one traveler is keeping the victim's attention, the other traveler is stealing money and valuables from the house.
g.   Recreational vehicle sales. The traveler purchases poorly constructed RVs. They sell these vehicles at two to three times their cost. These RVs are not inspected or approved by many states that have established standards of construction and safety requirements.

The principal characteristics of the travelers are as follows:

a.   Workers. The men do most of the work.
b.   Vehicles used. The travelers use late model pickup trucks. There are no business names or advertising shown on the trucks.
c.   Housing on the road. The travelers usually stay in family-oriented motels, campgrounds, and trailer parks.
d.   Group size. They usually travel in groups of 3 to 5 vehicles with 10 to 15 people.
e.   Travel. Travelers spend 40 to 70 percent of their time engaged in nomadic activity.
f.   Identification. Travelers will have many sets of identification from different states. Identification should be checked with vehicle registration.

Haitian Organized Crime

Members of Haitian organized crime are not highly organized. They operate in gang fashion. For the most part, they are not highly educated. Many are illegal aliens in the United States. Even though they are not highly educated and are loosely organized, they are becoming very effective as being an organized crime group. In South Florida and elsewhere, they are successful in robberies, home invasions, and thefts. Since Haiti is a poor country, criminal groups have specialized in stealing bicycles, mopeds, small motorcycles, and economy automobiles. They steal these items and ship them back to Haiti for resale. The U.S. Customs, in the late 1980s, boarded a ship leaving Miami with a destination of Port-au-Prince, Haiti. On the ship, there were 20,000 bicycles. They found that all of the bicycles were stolen. For the Haitian gang, these bicycles were pure profit. Their intent was to ship the stolen bicycles to Haiti where they would be sold. The disturbing aspect of the Haitians is that they are increasing their sophistication. This is because of their association with the Jamaican posses and other criminal organizations. Since most cannot speak English very well, they have become limited in what they can do.

Nigerian Organized Crime

The Nigerian criminal elements operate out of three clans. Two clans are Christians while the other is Muslim. The Nigerians are highly educated. Many have Master of Arts, Master of Science, and doctorate degrees. Nigeria was a British Crown Colony until 1960 when it obtained its independence. Nigerians speak English with a British accent. This makes it easier for them to obtain employment and assimilate into American society. The Nigerians are principally involved in drug trafficking and various fraud schemes. The Nigerians have cost the credit card companies millions of dollars in losses. They apply to credit card companies using people's names with good credit standing. The cards are sent to an address different from the true person. They use the card to the maximum credit limit. The goods are then sent to Nigeria for resale. The address where the card is sent is only rented for a short time, usually three to five months. The Nigerians move to another rented dwelling. They use false identification or other people's identification, obtained in business establishments that require identification or the use of credit cards. Sometimes, from reading the local newspapers, they will use prominent people's names. Nigerians are involved in many fraud schemes. They get low-income housing when they don't qualify. They are involved in food stamp fraud and other government programs. Nigerians are also involved in narcotics trafficking, principally, heroin, which is imported from Africa and the Middle East. They can be violent, but generally are not, except in their drug-trafficking operations. One unique characteristic of Nigerians is that they will deny any wrong doing even when caught "red-handed." They never admit to any crime.

Palestinian Organized Crime

Members of Palestinian organized crime are involved in fraud and weapons smuggling. They like to use convenience stores for fronts. They are involved in cashing checks for high fees and paying cash for food stamps at half the face value. Most of their business establishments are located in economic depressed areas. Profits are used to obtain various kinds of weapons for shipment to the Middle East. The Palestinians sponsor other Palestinians into this country. The new arrivals are set up in a convenience store. They repay their sponsor from their profits. They keep two sets of books, one for the sponsor, which is kept correctly, and the other set for government-reporting purposes. The second set of books does not show all their income. It does not show the payments to the sponsor or the skimmed receipts. Weapons are purchased or stolen and shipped to the Middle East. There, they are sold to various terrorist groups. They will cooperate with the Israeli Mafia if profits are available.

Organized Crime Patterns

Organized crime groups have a pattern of four stages of development.

Tactical Crimes

Most criminals start their career at this stage. It's labeled tactical because local law enforcement will have to use tactical methods of detecting. The most common crimes in this category are as follows:

a. Arson
b. Assault
c. Bribery
d. Burglary
e. Corruption
f. Extortion
g. Hijacking
h. Murder
i. Robbery

Illegal Business Activities

When criminal groups become more organized with a leadership structure, they move into more illegal enterprises. The most common criminal enterprises are as follows:

a. Counterfeiting
b. Frauds
c. Gambling
d. Illegal alcohol
e. Loan sharking
f. Narcotics
g. Prostitution
h. Protection rackets
i. Smuggling
j. Stolen property

Legitimate Business

When criminal groups have developed a good organizational structure, they turn to legitimate businesses to disguise their profits and to appear respectable in the community. At the same time, they must obtain a business that lends itself to hiding their illegal profits without attracting attention to law enforcement and tax authorities. The most common businesses used by organized criminal groups are as follows:

a. Auto agencies
b. Factoring
c. Food products
d. Garment manufacturing

e.   Juke boxes and video machines
f.   Liquor distributors and sales
g.   Night clubs and bars
h.   Trade unions and associations
i.   Trucking
j.   Vending machines
k.   Waste collections

Big Business

When retaining lawyers and accountants, sophisticated criminal groups get involved in larger businesses. They do this mostly to obtain respectability in the community and to launder their illegal gains. The most common businesses are:

a.   Banking
b.   Construction
c.   Credit cards
d.   Entertainment
e.   Hotel and motels
f.   Insurance
g.   Labor
h.   Mortgages
i.   Real estate
j.   Securities

The fraud examiner will be involved in the last three stages. Each stage will require different investigative and audit techniques. Stage two requires more investigative techniques than audit techniques, while stage four requires much more auditing techniques than investigative techniques. The more complex the enterprise, the more time required to uncover the fraud.

Trial Preparation and Testimony

13

Definition

A forensic accountant will sooner or later have to prepare and testify in a court of law. The basic function of a forensic accountant is to present accounting data that are admissible in a court of law, and the purpose of this book is to prepare an accountant to present accounting data in a court of law. The word *forensic* means anything that is admissible in a court of law or open to public debate.

Types of Trials and Hearings

The forensic accountant will have to testify in some kind of legal proceeding, whether for the prosecution or defense in a criminal case or for the plaintiff or respondent in a civil case. The complexity of any case will depend on the issues raised. Some cases will only require a small amount of time to study and testify regarding, whereas others will require many hours of study and testifying. In any case, the forensic accountant's testimony will provide the basis for the judge's rulings. The forensic accountant will normally be called to testify in the following types of legal proceedings:

Criminal Trials

The forensic accountant will normally testify about the defendant's net worth and expenditures, whether for the prosecution or defense. This will require alot of time to study and testify in court. Other cases involve tracing funds and assets.

Civil Trials

The forensic accountant will normally testify about the plaintiff or respondent's financial status. Most cases usually involve income tax litigation or divorce asset division and/or the ability to make alimony and/or child support payments. The time required will depend upon the complexity of the case.

Hearings

The forensic accountant will testify before a judge. No jury will be present. In criminal cases, the testimony will be aimed at the defendant's financial position or financial affairs. A bond hearing is common example of this kind of hearing. In civil cases, the forensic accountant will testify about the plaintiff's or respondent's financial condition or ability to pay a claim.

Deposition

The forensic accountant will give testimony about some issue that involves litigation between two parties. There is no judge or jury present. Only opposing attorneys and a court reporter are present.

Sworn Statement

In this case, the forensic accountant will give a sworn statement about a particular issue(s). There is no judge or jury present. This is a one-sided situation. The sworn statement is given in response to questions asked by attorneys for their client or the government.

Preparation

As soon as the forensic accountant finds that he/she will be testifying, he/she should begin preparing for the witness chair. Regardless of the role, the following steps should be taken:

1. First, discuss with the attorney what is expected, how your testimony is to be used, and when you will be expected to testify.
2. Review all available documents pertaining to the issue(s) being litigated.
3. Discuss your testimony with the attorney and what line of questioning will be used to develop the case and give the attorney a general idea of how you will respond to those questions.
4. Consider what the opposing counsel's approach will be and the areas they will most likely probe during cross-examination.

Testimony

Expert/Summary Witness

An expert witness is a person skilled in some art, science, profession, or business or who has experience or knowledge in relation to matters that are not commonly known to the ordinary person. (See Federal Rules of Evidence, Rule 702, 28 USCA.) The ordinary witness testifies to facts, that is, what the witness has seen, heard, or othewise observed. The expert witness expresses an opinion or answers hypothetical questions based on facts presumably in the record. It should be kept in mind that for expert witness testimony it is entirely within the province of the jury to determine the weight given to such opinions. The jurors are not bound by the opinion of experts.

Duties and Responsibilities

The forensic accountant has various responsibilities and duties during a judicial proceeding:

1. In criminal cases, review the prosecution memorandum.
2. In criminal cases, review the indictment (if the case was presented to a grand jury) or the information (if the charges were filed by the federal or state prosecutor), which sets forth the specific allegations of the criminal act.
3. Review the anticipated evidence available to prove or disprove the indictment or information in criminal cases or to support or deny the plaintiff or respondent position in a civil case.
4. Check the mathematical accuracy of the accounting data that are to be presented in court, whether criminal or civil.
5. Advise the attorney of the potential accounting or technical problems.
6. Determine the clearest manner to present your testimony in terms that the jury of lay persons will understand.
7. Prepare tentative summary computations, based upon the evidence that is expected to be admitted.
8. Supply to the attorney whom you are assisting a written a statement of your qualifications as a forensic accountant and/or a current résumé.
9. Testify only to those matters that are admitted by the court into evidence, whether by testimony or documents or by stipulation.
10. Take notes about evidence that is admitted and prepare a list of documentary exhibits of both sides, whether a criminal or civil case.
11. Alert the attorney to any evidence that has been overlooked. It is important that all evidence necessary to support your testimony has been admitted.
12. Allow enough time to check your computations and review witnesses testimony. You should be sure to make copies of those computations for the jury, court, and counsel.

The Do's

To be a good witness, there are things that you should do or observe:

1. Speak up so that the jury, judge, stenographer, opposing counsel, and all other parties to the case can hear you.
2. Define technical terms and put them into a simple language so the jury, judge, and counsel can understand them.
3. In testifying, refer to the exhibit number or some other identification. When indicating or pointing to an object in the exhibit, you should describe what you are referring to so that the court stenographer can make an accurate and complete record of your testimony.
4. Take enough time in answering questions to gather your thoughts and give an accurate and brief answer. If you are asked to give an opinion and feel that you do not have enough facts or enough time to form an intelligent expert opinion, so inform the court. The jury is impressed with such frankness on the part of the witness.

5. Always have adequate notes available so that you can testify regarding all of the details.
6. Walk to the witness stand with even steps.
7. When taking the oath, hold your right hand high with fingers straight and look at the officer administering the oath. When the officer finishes the oath, you should answer "I do" in a loud voice so that all in the courtroom can hear. Do not act timid.
8. Think before you speak.
9. When one of the lawyers calls "Objection" or the court interrupts, stop your answer immediately and wait until the court gives its ruling.
10. Be fair and frank.
11. If you make a mistake, or a slight contradiction, admit it and correct it. Do not tie yourself up in knots trying to cover up some slip of speech or memory.
12. Keep your temper! Be firm, but flexible.
13. If you cannot answer yes or no, say so.
14. If you don't know or can't remember, say so.
15. Avoid mannerisms of speech.
16. "Do you want this jury to understand..?" Listen closely to a question that begins that way. If you do not want the jury to understand it that way, make clear what you want them to understand.
17. Never try to be a "smart" witness.
18. Express yourself well, using simple technical language that the jury, judge, and attorneys can understand.
19. Be brief. Just answer the question and stop.
20. During the recess do not carry on any conversation with other witnesses or parties to the controversy. You should stand aloof from everyone except the attorney who retains you to testify.
21. Wait until the entire question is asked before answering.
22. On cross-examination, don't look at the attorney who retains you.
23. Keep your hands away from your mouth or face.
24. Be serious and businesslike during recesses and on the witness stand.
25. Stay away from opposing counsel, defendant or plaintiff, and his or her witnesses.
26. Be available and answer promptly when called to testify.

The Don'ts

The following items are things that you should not do:

1. Don't discuss the case in the corridors.
2. Don't chew gum.
3. Don't memorize any of your testimony.
4. Don't nod or shake your head to indicate yes or no.
5. Don't make any public display of elation or disappointment over the outcome of the case after the verdict has been rendered.
6. Don't volunteer any information.
7. Don't show any emotion about proceedings, such as disbelief or astonishment.
8. Don't allow yourself to get caught in the trap of a defense counsel asking you to answer a question by either "yes" or "no." Some questions cannot be answered this way, and you should so state to the court and jury and ask for permission to explain your answer.

9. Don't get caught by such snares as "Did you ever discuss this with anyone?" Of course, you did, and, if asked, you should name the people, the lawyers, the parties to the suit.
10. Avoid "horseplay" in corridors. Don't be noisy.

Cross-examination will be your most difficult time on the witness stand. Opposing counsel will attempt to confuse you, discredit you, and destroy the value of your testimony.

Trial Presentation

In presenting financial information in a trial, whether civil or criminal, the following steps should be followed to get the maximum effect.

1. Before trial, set up net worth or other schedules with all items expected to go to trial listed. Do not list any references until the items have been admitted into evidence. This serves as a control to ensure that everything that must be entered is entered.
2. As a summary witness, before going on the stand, take a recess of 4 hours, more or less, to go over all items on the schedule(s) to be presented.
3. In trial, try to get the attorney to present witnesses in the following order.
   a. Custodian of records
   b. Case investigators
   c. Likely source of income witnesses
   d. Finally, the summary witness

This order serves to help the summary witness in several ways.

First, it gets all documentary evidence in first whereby the summary witness can have time to double-check computations and review the evidence.

Second, it impresses on the the jury that the defendant has been involved in illegal activities and financial effect of these activities.

Summary

The basic rule for the fraud examiner and investigator is to testify truthfully in court. His or her demeanor should be professional. Fostering cooperation with the attorney can be greatly beneficial. Communication between the attorney and other fraud examiners or investigators can enlighten you, as well as those around you on the case. The fraud examiner and investigators should expect to work long hours during the trial. Most of the work is done outside the courtroom, not in it. The fraud examiner should be very familiar with the case. If not, the fraud examiner should study the case files at least a week before the trial begins. The fraud examiner or investigator may not go to trial on the case for many months or years after he or she worked the case. In those instances, the fraud examiner and investigator must refamiliarize themselves with the case.

Accounting and Audit Techniques 14

Introduction

The forensic accountant must identify what accounting techniques and audit programs to use and when to use them. Criminal elements will use whatever means they can to cover up their acts. Organized crime groups use teams of lawyers and accountants to "legitimatize" their illegal income. Such use of professionals necessitates sophisticated accounting techniques to uncover the schemes. This, in turn, requires more time, funding, and personnel. Individuals can also develop highly sophisticated fraudulent schemes. This chapter identifies the more common accounting techniques and audit programs that the forensic accountant can use to uncover fraudulent schemes used by criminals.

Net Worth and Expenditure Methods

In previous chapters, the Net Worth and Expenditure Methods have been discussed in detail in regard to how to prepare and present them in a court of law. The forensic accountant should also know *when* to use them. These methods are very powerful tools in both civil and criminal cases and are most appropriate when the subject's lifestyle appears to be much higher than known or probable sources of income. An extreme example would be a person who lives in a $100,000 house and drives an expensive automobile, but works at a fast food restaurant earning close to the minimum wage or is not working at all. These methods are particularly applicable to organized crime figures, narcotics traffickers, and other racketeering activities. In these cases, most of the witnesses against the leaders are usually convicted criminals. The best defense often is to attack the credibility of these witnesses, and, at times, the defense wins a not guilty verdict when there is insufficient corroboration. The Net Worth and Expenditure Methods help corroborate the testimony of witnesses whose credibility could be attacked by showing the income they paid the leaders and how the leaders disposed of the funds.

Tracing

This accounting technique involves the flow of funds. It shows the flow of funds from bank to bank, from entity to entity, from person to person, or a combination of each. This technique can be used in cases involving organized crime or individuals. Its primary purpose is to identify illegal funds and trace them to the beneficiary in criminal or civil cases. In civil cases, its purpose is to trace funds from a source to the end receiver. Table 14-1 illustrates a tracing schedule. It should be noted that the sources initially identified are greater than what the end beneficiary receives. The courts have ruled that it is not necessary to establish the exact amount, but, rather, that the end receiver received funds from an illegal source over an established time period. This accounting technique is very useful in money-laundering cases, regardless of the illegal activity. The tracing schedule in Table 14-1 uses the Scenario Problem, Intelligence Section.

It should be noted in Table 14-1 that Transshipment Ltd. bank account was used to purchase real estate in the Bahama Islands; however, the offsetting "In" is not shown. This is because funds did not go to another bank account. Also, the transfer from the Trans-shipment Ltd. bank account in Switzerland goes to the Doe Holdings bank account in Aruba. This example shows the subject making another step in transferring funds before it reaches its final destination. Funds can go through many bank accounts and entities before reaching the final destination.

Check Spreads

Check spread is an accounting method that should be used when the subject uses checking accounts. In a forensic accounting situation, the use of check spreads is different from the normal accounting practices. The forensic accountant must have the following information in performing a check spread.

1. **Date.** The date of the check must be recorded. The date the check cleared the bank is not necessary. The main purpose is to determine the intent of the subject, which would be the date the subject wrote the check.
2. **Payee.** The name of the payee must be shown. This identifies the person or entity that is supposed to receive the funds.
3. **Check number.** The check number identifies the instrument that is paying the payee. It is useful in that it can identify the specific payment made. It shows in numerical order the payments made to any individual or entity. It serves as a good reference to identify specific transactions.
4. **Amount.** This shows the amount of funds used or given to an individual or entity. This serves as evidence in showing the cost of a purchase whether an asset, expense, or a reduction in a liability.
5. **Bank from.** The purpose of this is to show what bank account this expenditure was made from. The subject could have more than one bank account and usually does. This identifies which bank account the subject is using. This can be the specific bank account number or can be a code that identifies a bank account which is listed elsewhere.

Table 14-1 Tracing Schedule of John Doe

Date	Description	Bahama Islands Transshipment Ltd		Cayman Islands Transshipment Ltd		Barbados John Doe	
		In	Out	In	Out	In	Out
6/1/X2	Cash	$2,000,000					
6/30/X2	Cash	1,000,000					
7/1/X2	Blue Lagoon Realty[a]		$110,000				
10/1/X2	Cash	5,000,000					
3/1/X3	Cash	10,000,000					
3/31/X3	TRF Cayman Islands		2,000,000	$2,000,000			
3/31/X3	TRF Barbados		2,000,000			$2,000,000	
				Spain Transshipment		**Switzerland Transshipment**	
		In	Out	In	Out	In	Out
3/31/X3	TRF Spain		1,000,000	1,000,000			
3/31/X3	TRF Switzerland		1,000,000			1,000,000	
12/10/X3	TRF Switzerland		3,000,000			3,000,000	
12/20/X3	TRF Switzerland To Aruba						2,000,000
				Aruba Doe Holding		**Jamaica John Doe**	
		In	Out	In	Out	In	Out
3/31/X3	TRF Aruba		370,000	370,000			
4/04/X3	TRF Jamaica		1,000,000			1,000,000	
4/4/X3	TRF Aruba		100,000	100,000			
4/3/X3	Boat Repair Shop						100,000
4/10/X3	Montego Bay Hotel						20,000
4/10/X3	Gulf Oil						500
10/1/X3	Cash	8,000,000					
12/20/X3	TRF Switzerland			2,000,000			
				Panama			
		In	Out	In	Out		
3/31/X3	TRF Panama		500,000	500,000			
12/1/X3	TRF Panama		3,500,000	3,500,000			
	Total	$26,000,000	$14,480,000				
	Balance	$11,520,000					

[a] Bahama Islands Residence.

6. **Bank to.** This should show the bank account where the check was deposited — in other words, the ultimate payee's bank account. This can show the specific bank account number or can use a code that identifies the bank account. This field is mostly used for payments made to other bank accounts or entities that are controlled by the subject.

7. **First endorsement.** The first person or entity who endorses the check should be shown. It is possible and sometimes common that the person to whom the check is made payable is not the person or entity who receives the check. The check could be made payable to a "John Smith" but the check goes into account called "ABC

Corporation" with John Smith's signature. Also, the check could be cashed by someone who is not John Smith. Therefore, the person or entity who endorses the check can be very important.

8. **Second endorsement.** The payee or first person receiving the check may give it to a second person who will endorse the check. Attention should be focused on the second endorsement. This may be a kickback or diversion of funds. The ultimate receiver of the funds should be fully identified regarding any relationships with the company or person providing the funds.

9. **Account.** The purpose of this field is to group similar transactions. It can be used to group transactions for a particular type of expenditure or to group for a particular purpose. Account means purpose. For trial presentation, the forensic account may use "Purpose" as the heading so the jury of laypeople can understand it.

10. **Note.** This field is used to show any memos or notes shown on the check. It also can be used to record any peculiarities on the check, such as different amounts between the figure amount and the written amount.

11. **First signatory.** This field should show the person who is the primary signatory on the check. This can be important in determining who has control over the bank account.

12. **Second signatory.** This field should show the second person who has cosignatory authority over the checking account. This person has some degree of control over the bank account.

If the investigator or analyst records this information on a computer using a database, then various printouts can be produced. The check spread can be sorted by the above fields. This will show patterns of activities. Check spreads also can offer more leads that will need to be further investigated. Also, they provide data that will be used for the net worth or expenditure schedules.

Deposit Spreads

This is an accounting method that should be used when the subject uses checking accounts. The previous section deals with the disbursements from the checking account, and this section deals with the receipts into the checking account. The use of deposit spreads is different from other accounting practices. The forensic accountant should have the following information in a deposit spread.

1. **Date.** The date of the deposit is recorded here. The date shows the time period when the funds are received by the bank.

2. **Source.** The source shows from whom the funds were received. For cash deposits, the source would not be known unless the subject kept other records to show who paid the funds to the subject.

3. **Amount.** This shows the amount of funds received by the individual or entity. This amount should only show the deposited items and not the total.

4. **Bank.** The purpose here is to show into what bank account the deposit was made. The subject could have more than one bank account and usually does. This identifies

into which bank account the subject made the deposit. This can be the specific bank account number or a code that identifies a bank account which is listed elsewhere.

5. **Account.** The purpose of this field is to group similar transactions. It can be used to group transactions for a particular type of deposit or for a specific purpose. Account means purpose.

6. **Reference.** This field should list the number of the item deposited, usually the check number of the check or draft being deposited.

7. **Number of items.** Many times deposits contain more than one deposited item. Each item in the deposit should be recorded separately. In order to connect all items in the deposit, this field will give the total items in the deposit. The date will be the same for each item in the deposit.

8. **Note.** This field should be used as a memo. The memo can record what was noted on the deposited item or it can be used to record odd things about the item.

If the investigator or analyst uses a computer, then various printouts can be produced. The deposit spread can be sorted by the above fields. Sorting deposited items by any of the above fields will disclose patterns and offer more leads that will need to be investigated. Also, they provide data that will be used in the net worth or expenditure schedules.

Credit Card Spreads

Credit card spreads should be used when the subject uses credit cards frequently. Credit cards are being used more and more these days. Some criminals use stolen credit cards to make purchases which are later fenced. Other criminals use credit cards legally. In either case, credit card transactions should be analyzed. They are also important in that they show where a subject has been geographically. The fraud examiner should prepare a credit card spread by using the following fields.

1. **Date.** The date should be the date of the transaction and not the date the credit card transaction was processed.

2. **Vendor.** The vendor is the company that sold the merchandise or provided the service to the credit card holder. The vendor may be a valuable witness in trial, especially if it is a large transaction.

3. **Credit card number.** This field should show the credit card account number or a code which will identify the specific credit card account on a separate listing.

4. **Amount.** This field shows the amount of the charge.

5. **Reference number.** The reference number should be the charge slip number. This is found on either the credit card statement or the charge slip.

6. **Signer.** This should record the person who actually signed the charge slip. There are occasions where more than one person can sign on a credit card. Sometimes there is no signature, but a statement stating "on file." This is common on mail orders. For criminal cases, the on-file slip should be obtained from the vendor to confirm that the subject signed for the purchase.

7. **Account.** The purpose of this field is to group similar transactions. It can be used to group transactions either by type or purpose.
8. **Note.** This field is used to record any unusual characteristics of the transactions.

Access to a computer can be very helpful. The credit card data can be sorted by the above fields. This will show patterns in transactions and can offer leads that can be followed up. Credit card transactions are useful in showing subjects' whereabouts over time if they use the credit cards a lot. The data from credit card transactions can be used on the Net Worth and Expenditure schedules.

Gross Profit Analysis

An accounting method that is useful in cases of money-laundering or skimming operations is the gross profit analysis. The subject will acquire a legitimate business. Normally, this business will be one that takes in cash. In a skimming operation, the subject will withdraw money from the business. The funds will not reach the business bank account, but are diverted to personal use. In a money-laundering operation, illegal funds will be added to legitimate funds and put through the business bank account. The amount of funds that are either skimmed out or added in can be determined by finding out the cost of merchandise purchased and the normal sales price or markup. The following steps should be used to determine the amount of funds either skimmed out or laundered through the business.

1. The normal markups or sale prices should be determined. If there is more than one product with different markups, then each product markup will have to be determined.
2. The next step is to determine the amount of merchandise purchased for each period under investigation. Product lines should be separated according to the different markup rates.
3. The markup rate for each product is applied to product costs. This will give the gross proceeds that should be generated from the sale of the products.
4. Once the gross sales have been determined for all products for the period, then a comparison is made with the funds deposited into the business bank account(s). If the sales figures are higher than the bank deposits, then the difference indicates the amount of funds skimmed out of the business. If the sales figures are lower than the bank deposits, then this would indicate the amount of funds laundered through the business.

A suggested gross profit schedule is presented in Figure 14-1.:

	PRODUCT A	PRODUCT B	PRODUCT C
	Cost of Sales	Cost of Sales	Cost of Sales
Divide:	C/S Rate	C/S Rate	C/S Rate
Equals:	Gross Sales	Gross Sales	Gross Sales
Less:	Deposits	Deposits	Deposits
Equals:	Skimmed/	Skimmed/	Skimmed/
	Laundered	Laundered	Laundered
	Income	Income	Income

Figure 14-1 Gross profit analysis schedule.

In the figure, the cost of sales rate is the percentage of cost of goods sold to the sales price for those goods. The gross profit method is used in bookmaking cases. It is called the "Commission" or the "Vig" method and will be explained later.

Witness List

The use of either the Net Worth or Expenditure Methods in either criminal or civil cases will require many witnesses, most of whom will be records custodians. It is common to have anywhere from 100 to 200 record custodians in an average case. Keeping track of these witnesses can be very unwieldy. It is suggested that a computer database be used with the following fields:

1. **Name.** The full name of the individual.
2. **Firm.** The name of the company where the individual works as the record custodian. In case one individual is unable to testify, then another person in the company can replace the initial individual.
3. **Street.** Street address, not a post office box number.
4. **City.** The municipality where the firm is located.
5. **State.** The state where the company is located.
6. **Home telephone.** This might be necessary if the records custodian is not at work.
7. **Business telephone.** The telephone number of the company where the records custodian can be reached or a replacement if needed.
8. **Witness number.** The number as assigned by the attorney handling the case.
9. **Exhibit number.** The number assigned by the attorney handling the case.
10. **Exhibit description.** A brief description of what the documents are in the case.

The computer can sort this data by any of the fields mentioned. It normally takes a records custodian about 15 minutes to testify and introduce the documents. It is better for opposing counsels to stipulate rather than subpoena records custodians. If the records custodians have to be subpoenaed, then this data can be used not only to contact the witnesses, but also to help in scheduling them for the appropriate court date and time.

Bank Deposit Method

Another indirect method of determining income, whether tax or RICO, is called the bank deposit method. In tax cases, this is referred to as the bank deposit expenditure method which is more apt. The IRS and state tax authorities have used this method for many years. It has not been used in RICO cases, primarily because it is not known by many fraud examiners or investigators. Also, it requires that the subject uses bank accounts to a great extent. This method is very useful for a subject who operates only one business, whose only source of income seems to be the one source; and whose business is a cash-type business, where receipts are received in cash.

Theory

When a subject has income from an undisclosed source, the use of the bank deposit method is justified. Under the bank deposit method, the subject's gross receipts are determined by adding total bank deposits, business expenses paid in cash, capital items purchased in cash, personal expenses paid in cash, and cash accumulations not deposited in any bank account. For tax purposes, this is compared with gross income reported on tax returns. For RICO purposes, this is compared with identified income. The difference is the amount of unreported taxable income or illegal income. When this method is employed, each item of income and expense must be examined regarding the source of funds and their subsequent use. This method is similar to the Expenditure Method as discussed in Chapter 6.

Schedule

To illustrate this method in more detail, Figure 14-2 is presented. The "total income" should be compared with the total identified income for RICO purposes and with the total gross income reported on the tax return for tax purposes. The difference will be either illegal income or unreported taxable income. The schedule in Figure 14-2 accounts for cash-basis as well as the accrual-basis businesses.

1. Total Deposits:
   a. Business checking: $_____
   b. Personal checking: _____
   c. Savings account(s):   _____
   Total Deposits $_____
2. Plus: Cash Expenditures:
   a. Business expenses $_____
   b. Personal expenses   _____
   c. Capital purchases   _____
   Total Cash Expenditures $_____
3. Less: Total Checks Written:
   a. Bank balances 1/1/XX $_____
   b. Total deposits for year   _____
   Less:c. Bank balances 12/31/XX   (_____)
   Total Cash Expenditures $_____
   TOTAL RECEIPTS $_____
4. Less: Nonincome Items:
   a. Transfers $_____
   b. Redeposits   _____
   c. Loans   _____
   d. Gifts   _____
   Total Nonincome Items $_____
   TOTAL INCOME RECEIPTS $_____
5. Accrual Adjustments:
   a. Accounts Receivable — add increase $_____
   b. Accounts Receivable — less decrease   _____
   c. Accounts Payable — less increase   _____
   d. Accounts Payable — add decrease   _____
   Total Accrual Adjustment $_____
6. TOTAL INCOME $_____

Figure 14-2 Bank Deposit Method.

Telephone

The fraud examiner should be aware of telephone calls. Telephone calls will help identify personal contacts and associates of the subject. They are also one of the subjects expenses. If the subject is a heavy telephone user, then this could be a major expenditure. This is particularly true with bookmakers who rely on the telephone for their business. Law enforcement will sometimes use a court-authorized wire tap or pen register. A pen register is only a listing of telephone numbers of calls that are either received or made by the subject. The fraud examiner will have to establish a database that will identify telephone contacts. This database should contain at least the following fields:

1. **Date.** This is the date the telephone call is received or sent.
2. **Caller.** This field should identify the person who is making the call. It could be either the subject or another person.
3. **Receiver.** This field should identify the person who receives the call. This could be the subject or another person.
4. **Sender number.** This field should identify the telephone number of the person making the call. This could be the subject or another person.
5. **Receiver number.** This field should identify the telephone number of the person receiving the call. This could be the subject or another person.
6. **Time.** This field should show the time the call is either received or made.
7. **Length.** This field should show the length of the call in minutes as a minimum.

Telephone calls will usually not identify assets or expenses, but they can identify leads to assets or expenses. Either the telephone company or a cross reference guide can identify telephone subscribers. The subscribers can later be interviewed about their relationships with the subject. It will be difficult for the subject to deny knowing a person who is called frequently by the subject.

Flowcharts

There are many kinds of flowcharts that the fraud examiner can use. In many cases, the fraud examiner will probably use many kinds of flowcharts in the same case. The flowcharts most commonly used by fraud examiners are as follows:

1. **Organizational.** This flowchart identifies the chain of command or lines of authority. In organized criminal groups, this is an important tool to be used during the investigation and in court as evidence. An example is shown in Figure 14-3.
2. **Chronological.** A chronology of events that shows people, transactions, dates, and events can be very useful. Its primary purpose is to identify a pattern. Once a pattern is established, then the fraud examiner or investigator can project future events. The best tool in this case is to use a calendar showing the dates of particular events.
3. **Matrix.** A matrix is a grid that shows relationships among a number of entities. This is most commonly used with telephone numbers and physical contacts, i.e., meetings. An example is shown in Figure 14-4.

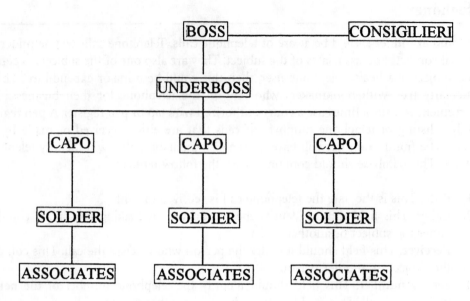

Figure 14-3 Organizational flowchart.

	1	2	3	4	5	
	6	7	8	9	1	
	2	8	9	1	2	
	-	-	-	-	-	
	6	7	8	9	5	
	4	3	2	1	5	
	6	7	8	9	1	
	2	3	4	5	6	TOTAL
162-6462	X	1	3	3	8	15
278-7373	3	X	1	5	8	17
389-8284	5	3	X	2	2	12
491-9195	8	2	6	X	1	17
512-5516	1	8	2	10	X	21
TOTAL	17	14	11	20	18	82

Figure 14-4 Telephone matrix.

4. **Operational.** This type of flowchart shows the flow of operations (Figure 14-5). This kind of flowcharting is used by public accountants and various governmental auditors to examine internal controls. Its purpose is to illustrate the flow of documents through various departments within an organization. Internal controls are compromised when an individual or department has too much involvement in the processing of a receipt of income or payment of an expense.

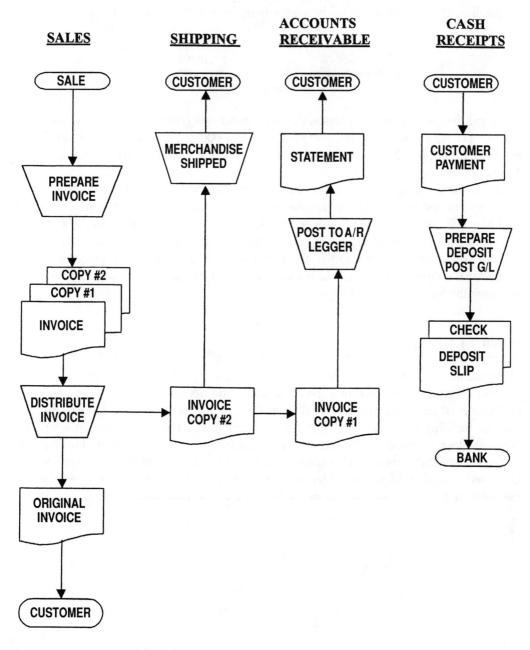

Figure 14-5 Operational flowchart.

Commission/Percentage Method

The percentage method of computing income is used primarily in sports bookmaking cases. Its primary objective is to determine income (gross receipts) earned from operations. It is generally referred to as the "Vig" method (vigorish). For cases involving only football and basketball, this percentage method is often called the 4.54 method since the percentage is 4.5454. It is determined by the following example. Let us say that Miami and Atlanta are playing. The bookmaker takes bets equally on both sides (balances the books).

	Miami	Atlanta
Total wagers placed	$10,000	$10,000
Add the vigorish/juice rate	1,000	1,000
Total amount at risk by the bettors	$11,000	$11,000

Regardless of who wins or losses, the bookmaker will collect $11,000 from losers and pay out $10,000 to winners. He, therefore, has a $1,000 gross profit (commission). This $1,000 divided by $22,000 (total wagers of $11,000 + $11,000) at risk by bettors equals 4.5454 percent.

In the case of baseball and hockey bets, the bets are based on odds which will require a different computation. If the bookmaker is using a 10-cent line, the 5 percent of the total base bets will approximate the gross profit. Base bet as used here refers to the stated bet without regard to the odds. For example, if the Los Angeles Dodgers play the Atlanta Braves and the line is 160 Los Angeles, then the stated wager of $100 on Los Angeles means that the bettor is risking $160 against the bookmaker's $100. The $100 is the base bet. The odds are normally based upon a 5 to 6 ratio.

When to Use

The forensic accountant should use as many of these accounting techniques as possible, whether or not they are used in a trial. The check and deposit spreads are the basic tools of any forensic accountant or fraud examiner. They are the starting point of an examination and the building blocks to reach the final summary. The credit card spread is another building block in those cases where the subject uses credit cards. These accounting techniques also provide leads to other financial information and establishes connections with other people and entities. The subject's connections are a key to any fraud case. They are the building blocks for indirect methods, e.g., Net Worth and Expenditure Schedules.

Summary

The forensic accountant has many tools that can be used, depending upon the circumstances of each case. Some tools may not be needed. If the subject has no bank accounts, then the check and deposit spreads would not be necessary. To summarize, these tools are:

1. Tracing schedule
2. Check spread
3. Deposit spread
4. Credit card spread
5. Gross profit analysis
6. Witness list
7. Bank deposit method
8. Telephone matrix
9. Organizational chart
10. Operational flowchart
11. Commission/percentage method (use for bookmakers only)

Sources of Information

15

Introduction

The investigator, whether involved in a criminal or civil case, has the monumental task of obtaining the information needed to put a case together. The subject of the investigation will not usually provide financial information and documents. This is particularly true in criminal cases. Therefore, investigators have to turn to third parties to obtain the financial information necessary to put their cases together. Some investigators, especially novice ones, do not know where to go to find financial information and documents. It can be surprising that financial information, in many cases, can be obtained fairly easily; however, in other cases, financial information cannot be obtained. It is imperative for the investigator to know where to get the financial information needed to put cases together.

The objective of this chapter is to help investigators identify third parties from which they can obtain the financial information and/or documents to put their case together. Some sources will give the information upon oral or written request, whereas others require service of a subpoena. Yet, there are some sources that cannot give out information or documents unless authorized by a court of law. It is therefore necessary for the investigator to know what the sources require to obtain financial information and/or documents from them.

Codes

In this chapter each source of information has a code that identifies who may obtain the information and/or documents. These codes are explained as follows:

1. GP — General Public. This information is available to the general public. This means anyone can obtain this information. An example of this is county public records, which show ownership of real property, mortgages, judgments, tax liens, and many other items.
2. LE — Law Enforcement. This information is available only to law enforcement agencies.
3. CO — Court Order. This information can only be obtained by court order of either a state or federal court.
4. LP — Limited Public Access. This information is available only to members of the organization. Examples are credit-reporting agencies and financial institutions.

Federal Departments

This section covers the various federal agencies and departments that can supply information for the investigator's case.

Description	Code	Information Available
Department of Defense	LE	Personnel records for civilian and military personnel, i.e., pay, training, service locations
Defense Investigative Service	LE	Background investigations, security clearances
Department of Energy	LE	Background investigations, personnel records
U.S. Attorney	LE/CO	Prosecution of federal violations, indictments from grand juries, trial and hearing records. Court orders are required for grand jury records
U.S. Border Patrol	LE	Information related to investigations of aliens and smuggling and apprehension of illegal aliens
Drug Enforcement Agency	LE	Information on drug criminals; monitoring of sales of legal and illegal drugs; drug company data
Federal Bureau of Investigation	LE	Information on investigations of federal laws in jurisdiction; also, various records, i.e., fingerprints, U.S. property
U.S. Immigration and Naturalization Service	LE	Information on registered and unregistered aliens in United States; some financial information
Office of International Affairs	LE	Information gained from formal requests to foreign governments for information through diplomatic channels
U.S. Marshal Service	LE	Investigations and arrests relating to bond defaults, escapes, parole, and probation
U.S. Department of Labor	LE	Investigations of labor violations, labor unions, and pension plans
Federal Probation Office	LE	Information on current federal probationers and parolees
U.S. Postal Service	LE	Investigations on postal law violations, mail fraud, and mailing obscene material
U.S. Department of State	LE	Passport information, visa fraud, terrorism, diplomatic motor vehicle registrations
U.S. Coast Guard	LP	Documentation of vessesl over five net tons used in commercial operations; investigations of high-seas crimes
Federal Aviation Administration	LP	Aircraft title history, aircraft owners, pilot and aircraft information
Bureau of Alcohol Tobacco and Firearms	LE	Information on violations of firearms, explosives, bombs, liquor; files on firearm dealers
U.S. Customs Service	LE	Information on customs violations, smuggling activity, theft of shipments, CMIR data bank
Internal Revenue Service	CO	Information on tax law violations; various tax returns and reports
U.S. Secret Service	LE	Information on counterfeiting, forgery, altering government checks, currency, and bonds
Treasurer of the United States	LE	Photostats of government checks
Interstate Commerce Commission	LE	Information on individuals and companies engaged in interstate commerce
Securities and Exchange Commission	PL	Securities violations files, corporate officers and directors; quarterly bulletins; certified financial statements of corporations
Federal Courts	GP	Records of civil and criminal cases; also claims, bankruptcy and tax cases

State Agencies and Departments

This section covers agencies and departments within state governments that can provide information for an investigator's case. It must be kept in mind that each state does not title its particular agency or department the same as another state. This section uses the State of Florida as its model. Therefore, investigators in another state will have to compare the State of Florida with their comparable state agency or department.

Description	Code	Information Available
Department of Agriculture and Consumer Services	LE	Issuance of permits and inspections of amusement rides, public fairs, expositions, carnivals, bazaars, and celebrations
Division of Animal Industry	LE	Investigation and enforcement of livestock, livestock and farm equipment thefts, livestock movement
Division of Consumer Services	GP	Information on inquiries and complaints against businesses; infromation on businesses and products
Division of Forestry	LE	Investigations of fire and theft of forest and timber
Division of Public Assistance	LP	Investigations of fraud by recipients and state employees of welfare programs
Medicaid Fraud Control Unit	GP	Investigations of fraud by nursing homes, hospitals, pharmacies, etc.
Division of Banking	GP	Information on charter and regulation of state financial institutions
Division of Finance and Insurance	GP	Information on licensing, regulation of mortgage brokers' finance company, money orders, traveler's checks, home improvement financing offers
Division of Securities	GP	Information on security dealers, agents, and advisors; national index of agents and dealers; corporate applications
Division of Alcoholic Beverages and Tobacco	LP	Information on beverage and cigarette wholesalers, retailers
Bureau of Land Sales	GP	Registration records on developers
Division of Pari-Mutuel Wagering	GP	Information on track employees, concessions, owners of racing animals
Division of Corrections, Bureau of Admission and Release	LE	Information on current and former prisoners, parole, and probation people
Department of Education	LP	Investigations of violations of ethics and law by people holding teaching certificates
Department of Environment Regulation	LE	Information on all companies involved in hazardous materials
Game and Fresh Water Fish Commission	LE	Information on wildlife law violations
Department of Health and Rehabilitative Services	LE	Information on state mental hospitals and patients
Child Support Enforcement	LE	Information on parents who stop paying child support
License and Certification	GP	Licenses of all health care facilities, day care centers, family planning clinics; investigations of state law violations
Office of Vital Statistics	GP	Records of birth, death, marriage, and divorce
Division of Drivers	LE	Driver's licenses and driving record data; photographs of drivers in some states

continued

Description	Code	Information Available
Bureau of Records and Training	LP	Copies of all accident reports in state
Division of Motor Vehicles, Bureau of Licensing and Enforcement	LP	Licenses on manufacturers, importers, distributors of all motor vehicles including mobile homes
Bureau of Title and Lien Services	LP	Records of titles, liens, and owner information
Department of Insurance and Treasurer	LP	Information on insurance agents, adjusters, bail bondsmen
Division of Consumer Services	GP	Records of complaints, fines, legal actions on unethical business practices
Bureau of Insurer Company Regulation	LP	Information on insurance companies and officers
Division of Insurance Fraud	LE	Investigations of fraudulent claims and activities involving companies, agents, and adjusters
Division of State Fire	LP	Licenses of dealers, users, and manufacturers of explosives; investigations of arson, fires, and explosives
Department of Labor and Employment Security	GP	Information on public and private labor organizations in state
Department of Law Enforcement	LE	Investigations and records of criminals, intelligence trends; supplies services for local law enforcement
State Medical Examiner	LE	Investigations and determination of cause of death
Florida Intelligence Center	LE	Intelligence on criminals; supports local law enforcement
Attorney General	LP	Investigations of consumer complaints
Department of Lottery	LP	Information on retail applications and lottery winners of $600 or more
Department of Natural Resources, Florida Marine Patrol	LE	Investigations of salt water violations; interdiction of narcotics smuggling on waters
Bureau of License and Motor Boat Registration	LP	Information on boat titles and data
Licenses and Permits Section	LP	Licenses for seafood dealers, dredge fill permits, commercial fishermen, and trolling permits
Division of Recreations and Parks	LE	Records of state law violations on state lands
Parole Commission	LE	Information on parole status, release dates, and conditions
Department of Professional Regulation	LP	Information on occupations regulated by boards
Professional Boards	LP	Accountancy
		Acupuncture
		Architecture and interior design
		Auctioneers
		Barbers
		Chiropractic
		Construction industry
		Cosmetology
		Electrical contractors
		Geologists
		Funeral directors
		Hearing aids
		Landscape architects
		Land Surveyors

Description	Code	Information Available
		Massage
		Medical (physicians)
		Nursing homes
		Occupational therapists
		Opticianary
		Optometry
		Osteopathy
		Pharmacy
		Physical therapists
		Pilots
		Professional engineers
		Podiatry
		Psychological services
		Real estate
		Respiratory therapists
		Veterinary medicine
Department of Revenue	LE/CO	State tax returns and information (subpoena only)
Department of State Division of Corporations	GP	Information on corporations (profit and nonprofit)
Division of Elections, Bureau of Election Records	GP	Information forms filed by state public officials and some state employees
Department of Transportation, Bureau of Weights	LE	Information on trucking violations and their drivers
Aerial Surveys Section	GP	Aerial photos of the entire state

County and Municipal Agencies

This section covers departments and agencies within the county and municipal governments that can provide information for an investigator's case. Not every county or municipality has the same departments and agencies. Some counties and municipalities have departments and agencies that others do not have. Also, they do not title their departments and agencies the same. This is true even in the same state. Therefore, the investigator will have to inquire of each county or municipality the names of its particular departments.

Description	Code	Information Available
Aviation Department	GP	Information on airline companies and license to operate
Building and Zoning	GP	License and permit applications, names of contractors, and identification of owner and place of construction
Clerks of the Circuit and County Courts	GP	Court records on both criminal and civil cases
Library	GP	Various reference material and copies of old books, magazines, and newspapers
Environmental Services	GP	Licenses and other data on hazardous waste
Utilities	GP	Billings and payments of various utilities, i.e., water, waste, electric, and gas
Sheriff's Office or Police Department	LE	Arrests, accidents, gun permits, towed or repossessed autos, traffic violations

continued

Description	Code	Information Available
Licenses	GP	Various licenses, i.e., fishing, hunting, etc. Marriage Occupational Dog and cat
Health Department	GP	License, inspections, and other data on businesses
Voter Registration	GP	Data on people registered to vote; political affiliations
State/District Attorney	LE	Detailed information on criminals and criminal activities
Public Records	GP	Detailed information on real estate, mortgages, liens, judgments, and various other items
Tax Assessor/Collector	GP	Records of personal and real property tax assessments and collections
Schools	LP	Records of students; sometimes medical and other personal information
Social or Welfare Services	LP	Records of recipients of welfare and other social programs
Personnel Departments	LP	Records on employees
Purchasing and Procurement	LP	Records on vendors, contracts, etc.

Business Records

Businesses maintain records that can help in supplying data for a financial case. In most cases, it is one of the important sources of obtaining financial information. The following is a general listing of the types of businesses that can supply financial data.

Description	Code	Information Available
Abstract and Title Companies	GP	Provide records of real estate transactions, title policies, escrow files, maps, and plats
Bonding Companies	LP	Investigative and other records on persons or firms; financial statements; identity of person on bond
Credit Reporting Agencies	LP	Data on people's loan history, bank accounts, employment, insurance, and other credit actions
Department Stores	LP	Credit files and charge account records
Detective Agency	LP	Investigative files, evidence and identifying information on clients and other parties
Fraternal, Veterans, Labor, Social, Political Organizations	LP	Membership, dues, location, and history of members
Hospitals	LP	Payments; entry and release dates
Hotels and Motels	LP	Identity of guests, phone calls, credit cards, payments, forwarding address and date
Insurance Companies	LP	Applications, assets being insured, ledger cards, dividends, cash values, claims, refunds, and cancellations
National Credit Card Companies	LP	Applications, charge uses and payments, i.e., travel and entertainment, goods, and services
Telephone Companies	LP	Local directories, toll call charges and payments, list of numbers called and calling numbers
Transportation Departments	LP	Passenger list, fares paid, destinations, departure and arrival times and dates

Description	Code	Information Available
Public Utility Companies	LP	Charges and payments, service address, hookup and disconnect dates
Automobile Dealers and Manufacturers	LP	Franchise agreements, dealers financial records, car sales, trade-ins, and service records
Brokerage Companies	LP	Monthly statements, amount and date of purchase and sale of securities, market values, and types of security and accounts
Banks and Other Financial Institutions	LP	Name, address, occupation, source of deposits and expenditures, signatures, wire transfers, safe deposit box, letters of credit

Reference Materials

There are other sources of information that can be obtained by just going to the local library. The library is a source of financial information as well as biographical profiles. The following are some of the more common references that can be used in helping develop a case.

Description	Code	Information Available
American Almanac of Jobs and Salaries	GP	Salary and wages by industry and region
Dun and Bradstreet Reference Book	GP	Financial and other information about various public companies
Encyclopedia of Associations	GP	Names, addresses, and types of organizations
Funk And Scott Index of Corporations and Industries	GP	Names, addresses, stock issues, and summary of financial data
Funk and Scott International Index	GP	Data about companies located offshore
Moody's Bank and Finance Manual	GP	Data about various financial institutions
Moody's Industrial Manual	GP	Data about various manufacturers in the United States
Standard and Poor's Register of Corporations, Directors, Executives	GP	Data about various publicly held companies, biographical summaries of officers and directors
Thomas Register of American Manufacturers	GP	Data about various U.S. manufacturing companies
Better Business Bureau	GP	Complaints against businesses and owners
Newspapers and Magazines	GP	Index to issues by topic and names

International

Evidence from foreign countries is admissible in federal courts when it is properly authenticated. Title 18 USC 3494 provides the procedures necessary to certify foreign documents for admission in federal criminal cases. Title 18 USC 3492 provides that testimony of foreign witnesses may be taken by oral or written interrogatories. Many law enforcement officers and prosecutors, federal and state, feel that records from foreign countries are not obtainable. This is not true in every case. Some countries have various records more available than do others. This section identifies those records that are available by country. It must be kept in mind that there are federal procedures that must be followed in obtaining foreign evidence in criminal cases. Treaties sometimes provide procedures that must be followed, such as in Japan. Direct contact is forbidden. Also, proper certification must be obtained and the chain of custody properly maintained in criminal cases. Another problem in obtaining foreign evidence is whether the records are centralized or decentralized. Centralized records mean that these records are located in one location. Decentralized records are located at various locations. International records that are public are shown below and identified as either centralized (CEN) or decentralized (DEC).

Country	Location	Type of Record
Anguilla	CEN	Court records
	CEN	Wills
	CEN	Commercial register
	CEN	Corporation charter
	CEN	Land transfer records
	CEN	Birth records
	CEN	Death records
	CEN	Marriage records
	CEN	Company records
	CEN	Company bylaws
	CEN	Company financial statements
Antigua	CEN	Court records
	CEN	Wills
	CEN	Patents
	CEN	Trademarks
	CEN	Copyrights
	CEN	Corporation charter
	CEN	Land transfer records
	CEN	Birth records
	CEN	Death records
	CEN	Marriage records
	CEN	Other public records
	CEN	Company bylaws
Argentina	CEN	Court records
	CEN	Patents
	CEN	Trademarks
	CEN	Copyrights
	CEN	Commercial register
	CEN	Corporation charter
	CEN	Land transfer records
	CEN	Birth records
	CEN	Death records
	CEN	Marriage records
	CEN	Public company records
	CEN	Company bylaws
	CEN	Public company financial statements
Australia	DEC	Court records
	DEC	Wills
	CEN	Patents
	CEN	Trademarks
	DEC	Commercial register

Country	Location	Type of Record
	DEC	Corporation charter
	DEC	Land transfer records
	DEC	Company records
	DEC	Company bylaws
	DEC	Company financial statements
Austria	CEN	Patents
	CEN	Trademarks
	CEN	Copyrights
	DEC	Commercial register
	DEC	Corporation charter
	DEC	Land transfer records
	DEC	Birth records
	DEC	Death records
	DEC	Marriage records
	CEN	Company financial statements
	DEC	Company bylaws
	DEC	Alien registration (U.S. only)
Bahama Islands	CEN	Court records
	CEN	Wills, patents, trademarks, and copyrights
	CEN	Corporation charter
	CEN	Land transfer records
	CEN	Birth, death, marriage records
	CEN	Company records and bylaws
Bahrain	CEN	Court records
	CEN	Corporate charter
	CEN	Commercial register
	CEN	Land transfer records
	CEN	Birth, death, marriage records
	CEN	Bank and credit information
	CEN	Other public records
	CEN	Alien registration (U.S. only)
Bangladesh	DEC	Court records
	CEN	Patents and trademarks
	CEN	Commercial register
	CEN	Corporate charter
	CEN	Land transfer records
	CEN	Birth and marriage records
	CEN	Company bylaws and financial statements
Barbados	CEN	Court records
	CEN	Wills, patents, trademarks and copyright records
	CEN	Corporation charter
	CEN	Land transfer records
	CEN	Birth, death, marriage records
	CEN	Other public records
	CEN	Company bylaws
Belgium	DEC	Court records
	CEN	Patents and trademarks
	CEN	Commercial register
	DEC	Corporation charter
	DEC	Land transfer records
	DEC	Company bylaws, records, financial statements
Belize	CEN	Court records
	CEN	Patents and trademarks

continued

Country	Location	Type of Record
	CEN	Commercial register
	CEN	Corporation charter
	CEN	Land transfer records
	CEN	Company bylaws
Bermuda	CEN	Court records
	CEN	Wills, patents, trademarks, and copyrights
	CEN	Corporation charter
	CEN	Land transfer records
	CEN	Birth, death, marriage records
	CEN	Credit information
	DEC	Other public records
	CEN	Company records
Bolivia	DEC	Court records
	CEN	Patents and trademarks
	DEC	Copyrights
	CEN	Commercial register
	CEN	Corporation charter
	CEN	Land transfer records
	CEN	Birth, death, marriage records
	CEN	Public company records
	CEN	Public company bylaws and financial statements
Brazil	DEC	Court records
	CEN	Patents, trademarks, copyrights
	DEC	Commercial register
	DEC	Corporation charter
	DEC	Land transfer records
	DEC	Birth, death, marriage records
	CEN	Public company bylaws and financial statements
British Virgin Islands	CEN	Court records
	CEN	Wills, patents, trademarks, and copyrights
	CEN	Corporation charter
	CEN	Birth, death, marriage records
	CEN	Other public records
	CEN	Company bylaws
Brunei	CEN	Court records
	CEN	Patents, trademarks, and copyrights
	CEN	Commercial register
	CEN	Corporation charter
	CEN	Land transfer records
	DEC	Birth, death, marriage records
	CEN	Company by-law and financial statements
Burma	DEC	Court records
	DEC	Wills
	CEN	Patents, trademarks, copyrights
	CEN	Commercial register
	CEN	Corporation charter
	DEC	Land transfer records
	DEC	Birth, death, marriage records
	CEN	Alien registration (U.S. only)
	CEN	Company records, bylaws, and financial statements
Canada	DEC	Court records
	DEC	Wills
	CEN	Patents
	DEC	Commercial register

Country	Location	Type of Record
	DEC	Corporation charter
	DEC	Land transfer records
	DEC	Company bylaws
Cayman Islands	CEN	Court records
	CEN	Wills, patents, trademarks, and copyrights
	CEN	Land transfer records
	CEN	Birth, death, marriage records
	DEC	Other public records
Channel Islands-Jersey	CEN	Court records
	CEN	Wills, patents, trademarks
	CEN	Commercial register
	CEN	Corporation charter
	CEN	Land transfer records
	CEN	Birth, death, marriage records
	CEN	Company records and bylaws
Channel Islands-Guersey	CEN	Court records
	CEN	Wills, trademarks
	CEN	Commercial register
	CEN	Corporation charter
	CEN	Land transfer records
	CEN	Birth, death, marriage records
	CEN	Company records, bylaws
Channel Islands-Alderney	CEN	Court records
	CEN	Wills
	CEN	Corporation charter
	CEN	Land transfer records
	CEN	Birth, death, marriage records
	CEN	Company records, bylaws
Chile	CEN	Court records
	CEN	Wills, patents, trademarks, and copyrights
	CEN	Corporation charter
	CEN	Commercial register
	CEN	Land transfer records
	DEC	Birth, death, marriage records
	CEN	Credit information
	CEN	Public company records, bylaws, and financial statements
Colombia	DEC	Court records
	DEC	Wills
	CEN	Patents, trademarks, copyrights
	DEC	Commercial register
	DEC	Corporation charter
	DEC	Land transfer records
	DEC	Birth, death, marriage records
	DEC	Credit information
	DEC	Other public records
	DEC	Alien registration (U.S. only)
	DEC	Company records, bylaws, and financial statements
Cooks Islands	CEN	Court records
	CEN	Land transfer records
	CEN	Birth, death, marriage records

continued

Country	Location	Type of Record
	CEN	Alien registration (U.S. only)
	CEN	Company records and bylaws
Costa Rica	CEN	Court records
	CEN	Wills, patents, trademarks, and copyrights
	CEN	Commercial register
	CEN	Corporation charter
	CEN	Land transfer records
	CEN	Birth, death, marriage records
	CEN	Credit information
	CEN	Company bylaws
	CEN	Alien registration (U.S. only)
Cyprus	CEN	Patents and trademarks
	CEN	Corporation charter
	CEN	Birth, death, marriage records
	CEN	Other public records
	CEN	Company records
	CEN	Company bylaws and financial statements
Denmark	DEC	Court records
	CEN	Patents, trademarks, copyrights
	CEN	Commercial register
	CEN	Corporation charter
	DEC	Land transfer records
	DEC	Birth, death, marriage records
Dominican Republic	CEN	Corporation charter
	CEN	Land transfer records
	CEN	Birth, death, marriage records
	CEN	Other public records
Egypt	CEN	Patents, trademarks, and copyrights
	CEN	Commercial register
	CEN	Corporation charter
	CEN	Land transfer records
	CEN	Birth, death, marriage records
	CEN	Other public records
	CEN	Company bylaws, and financial statements
Fiji	CEN	Court record
	CEN	Wills, patents, trademarks, and copyrights
	CEN	Commercial register
	CEN	Corporation charter
	CEN	Land transfer records
	CEN	Company bylaws
Finland	DEC	Court records (limitations)
	DEC	Wills
	CEN	Patents and trademarks
	CEN	Commercial register
	DEC	Corporation charter
	DEC	Land transfer records
	CEN	Company bylaws and financial statements
France	CEN	Patents, trademarks and copyrights
	CEN	Commercial register
	CEN	Corporation charter
	CEN	Company bylaws and financial statements
Germany	DEC	Court records
	CEN	Patents and trademarks
	DEC	Commercial register

Country	Location	Type of Record
	DEC	Corporation charter
	DEC	Land transfer records
	DEC	Credit information
	CEN	Other public information
	DEC	Company bylaws and financial statements
Gibraltar	CEN	Court records
	CEN	Wills, trademarks, and copyrights
	CEN	Commercial register
	CEN	Corporation charter
	CEN	Land transfer records
	CEN	Birth, death, marriage records
	CEN	Company bylaws and records
Greece	DEC	Court records
	DEC	Wills, patents, trademarks
	CEN	Copyrights
	DEC	Land transfer records
	DEC	Birth, death, marriage records
	DEC	Company bylaws and financial statements
Grenada	CEN	Court records
	CEN	Wills, patents, trademarks, and copyrights
	CEN	Corporation charter
	CEN	Land transfer records
	CEN	Birth, death, marriage records
	CEN	Other public records
	CEN	Company bylaws
Guatemala	CEN	Corporation charter
	CEN	Land transfer records
	CEN	Birth, death, marriage records
	CEN	Credit information (limited)
	CEN	Other public records
	CEN	Company records and bylaws
Haiti	DEC	Court records
	CEN	Patents, trademarks and copyrights
	CEN	Corporation charter
	CEN	Land transfer records
	CEN	Birth, death, marriage records
	CEN	Company records and bylaws
Honduras	CEN	Court records (limitations)
	CEN	Wills, patents, trademarks, and copyrights
	CEN	Commercial paper
	CEN	Corporation charter
	CEN	Land transfer records
	CEN	Birth, death, marriage records
	CEN	Other public records
	CEN	Company records and bylaws
Hong Kong	DEC	Court records
	CEN	Wills, patents, trademarks, and copyrights
	DEC	Commercial register
	DEC	Corporation charter
	CEN	Land transfer records
	DEC	Birth, death, marriage records
	CEN	Credit information
	DEC	Other public records

continued

Country	Location	Type of Record
	DEC	Company bylaws
Iceland	DEC	Court records
	CEN	Patents and trademarks
	CEN	Commercial register
	CEN	Corporation charter
	CEN	Land transfer records
India	CEN	Patents, trademarks and copyrights
	CEN	Commercial register
	DEC	Corporation charter
	CEN	Birth and death records
	CEN	Other public records
	CEN	Company bylaws
Indonesia	DEC	Court records
	CEN	Wills, patents, trademarks, and copyrights
	CEN	Commercial register
	DEC	Land transfer records
	DEC	Birth, death, marriage records
	DEC	Other public records
Ireland	CEN	Wills, patents, trademarks, and copyrights
	CEN	Commercial register
	CEN	Corporation charter
	CEN	Land transfer records
	CEN	Birth, death, marriage records
	CEN	Other public records
	CEN	Company records, bylaws, and financial statements
Isle Of Man	CEN	Court records
	CEN	Commercial register
	CEN	Corporation charter
	CEN	Land transfer records
	DEC	Birth, death, marriage records
	CEN	Company records and bylaws
Israel	DEC	Court records
	DEC	Wills
	CEN	Patents, trademarks and copyrights
	CEN	Commercial register
	CEN	Corporation charter
	DEC	Land transfer records
	CEN	Company records, bylaws, and financial statements
Italy	DEC	Court records
	DEC	Wills
	CEN	Patents, trademarks and copyrights
	DEC	Commercial register
	DEC	Corporation charter
	DEC	Land transfer records
	DEC	Birth, death, marriage records
	DEC	Company records, bylaws, and financial statements
	DEC	Bankruptcy judgments
	DEC	Movie production records
Jamaica	CEN	Court records
	CEN	Patents and trademarks
	CEN	Commercial register
	CEN	Corporation charter
	CEN	Land transfer records
	CEN	Birth, death, marriage records

Country	Location	Type of Record
	CEN	Company records, bylaws, and financial statements
Japan	CEN	Court records
	CEN	Patents, trademarks and copyrights
	DEC	Commercial register
	CEN	Corporation charter
	DEC	Land transfer records
	DEC	Birth records
	CEN	Company bylaws and financial statements
Jordan	CEN	Patents, trademarks, and copyrights
	CEN	Commercial register
	CEN	Corporation charter
	CEN	Land transfer records
	CEN	Birth, death, marriage records
Kenya	DEC	Court records
	CEN	Patents, trademarks, and copyrights
	CEN	Commercial register
	CEN	Corporate charter
	CEN	Land transfer records
	DEC	Birth, death, marriage records
Korea	DEC	Court records
	DEC	Commercial register
	DEC	Corporation charter
	DEC	Birth, death, marriage records
	CEN	Company bylaws and financial statements
Kuwait	CEN	Wills, copyrights
	CEN	Commercial register
	CEN	Corporation charter
	CEN	Land transfer records
	CEN	Birth, death, marriage records
	CEN	Company records and by laws
Lebanon	CEN	Land transfer records
	CEN	Birth, death, marriage records
	CEN	Company records, bylaws, and financial statements
Liberia	DEC	Court records
	CEN	Wills
	DEC	Patents, trademarks and copyrights
	DEC	Commercial register
	CEN	Corporation charter
	DEC	Land transfer records
	DEC	Marriage records
Liechtenstein	CEN	Patents, trademarks and copyrights
	CEN	Commercial register
	CEN	Birth, death, marriage records
	CEN	Other public records
Luxembourg	CEN	Patents, trademarks, and copyrights
	CEN	Commercial register
	CEN	Corporation charter
	DEC	Land transfer records
	DEC	Birth, death, marriage records
	CEN	Other public records
	CEN	Company records, bylaws, and financial statements
Malaysia	CEN	Patents, trademarks, and copyrights
	CEN	Commercial register

continued

Country	Location	Type of Record
	CEN	Corporation charter
	CEN	Land transfer records
	CEN	Birth, death, marriage records
	CEN	Company records and bylaws
Malta	CEN	Court records
	CEN	Patents, trademarks and copyrights
	CEN	Commercial register
	CEN	Land transfer records
	CEN	Birth, death, marriage records
Mexico	CEN	Patents, trademarks and copyrights
	CEN	Commercial register
	CEN	Corporation charter
	DEC	Land transfer records
	CEN	Birth, death, marriage records
	CEN	Company records
Monaco	CEN	Patents and trademarks
	CEN	Commercial register
	CEN	Corporation charter
	CEN	Land transfer records
	CEN	Company bylaws
Nauru	CEN	Wills, patents, trademarks
	CEN	Land transfer records
	CEN	Birth, death, marriage records
Nepal	DEC	Court records
	CEN	Commercial register
	CEN	Corporation charter
	CEN	Company records
Netherlands	CEN	Patents, trademarks and copyrights
	CEN	Commercial register
	CEN	Corporation charter
	CEN	Land transfer records
	DEC	Birth, death, marriage records
	DEC	Company bylaws and financial statements
Netherlands Antilles	CEN	Court records
	CEN	Wills, patents, trademarks, and copyrights
	CEN	Corporation charter
	CEN	Land transfer records
	CEN	Birth, death, marriage records
	CEN	Other public records
	CEN	Company records and bylaws
New Zealand	DEC	Court records
	DEC	Wills, patents, and trademarks
	DEC	Commercial register
	DEC	Corporation charter
	DEC	Land transfer records
	DEC	Credit information
	DEC	Company records, bylaws, and financial statements
Norway	DEC	Court records
	CEN	Patents and trademarks
	DEC	Commercial register
	DEC	Corporation charter
	DEC	Land transfer records
	CEN	Birth, death, marriage records
	CEN	Register of ships

Country	Location	Type of Record
	DEC	Register of chattel, fishing vessels, and aircrafts
Oman	CEN	Commercial register
	CEN	Bank information
Pakistan	CEN	Patents, trademarks and copyrights
	DEC	Corporation charter
	DEC	Land transfer records
	CEN	Credit information
	DEC	Other public records
	CEN	Company records
	DEC	Company bylaws and financial statements
Panama	CEN	Court records
	CEN	Wills, patents, trademarks, and copyrights
	CEN	Corporate charter
	CEN	Land transfer records
	CEN	Birth, death, marriage records
	DEC	Other public records
	CEN	Company bylaws
Paraguay	CEN	Court records
	CEN	Wills, patents, trademarks, and copyrights
	CEN	Commercial register
	CEN	Corporation charter
	CEN	Land transfer records
	CEN	Birth, death, marriage records
	CEN	Company records, bylaws, and financial statements
Peru	DEC	Court records
	CEN	Wills, patents, trademarks, and copyrights
	CEN	Commercial register
	DEC	Corporation charter
	DEC	Land transfer records
	DEC	Birth, death, marriage records
	CEN	Public company records, bylaws, financial statements
Philippines	CEN	Patents, trademarks, and copyrights
	CEN	Commercial register
	CEN	Corporation charter
	DEC	Land transfer records
	CEN	Company bylaws
Poland	CEN	Patents and trademarks
	DEC	Commercial register
Qatar	CEN	Commercial register
Romania	CEN	Patents and trademarks
	DEC	Land transfer records
St. Kitts-Nevis	CEN	Court records
	CEN	Wills, patents, trademarks, and copyrights
	CEN	Corporation charter
	CEN	Land transfer records
	CEN	Birth, death, marriage records
	CEN	Other public records
	CEN	Company bylaws and financial statements
St. Vincent	CEN	Court records
	CEN	Wills, patents, trademarks, and copyrights
	CEN	Corporation charter
	CEN	Land transfer records
	CEN	Birth, death, marriage records

continued

Country	Location	Type of Record
	CEN	Other public records
	CEN	Company bylaws
Western Samoa	CEN	Court records
	CEN	Wills, patents, trademarks
	CEN	Commercial register
	CEN	Corporation charter
	CEN	Land transfer records
	CEN	Birth, death, marriage records
	CEN	Alien registration (U.S. only)
	CEN	Company records and bylaws
Saudi Arabia	CEN	Trademarks and copyrights
	CEN	Commercial register
	CEN	Corporation charter
	CEN	Company bylaws
Singapore	CEN	Court records
	CEN	Wills, patents, trademarks, and copyrights
	CEN	Commercial register
	CEN	Corporation charter
	CEN	Land transfer records
	CEN	Birth, death, marriage records
	CEN	Company records and bylaws
Solomon Islands	CEN	Court records
	CEN	Wills, patents, trademarks
	CEN	Commercial register
	CEN	Corporation charter
	CEN	Land transfer records
	CEN	Birth, death, marriage records
	CEN	Company bylaws and financial statements
South Africa	CEN	Court records
	CEN	Wills, patents, trademarks, and copyrights
	CEN	Commercial register
	CEN	Corporation charter
	CEN	Land transfer records
	CEN	Birth, death, marriage records
Spain	DEC	Patents, trademarks, and copyrights
	DEC	Commercial register
	DEC	Corporation charter
	DEC	Land transfer records
	DEC	Birth, death, marriage records
	DEC	Company bylaws
Sri Lanka	CEN	Patents, trademarks and copyrights
	CEN	Commercial register
	CEN	Corporation charter
	DEC	Land transfer records
	DEC	Other public records
	CEN	Company records and bylaws
Sudan	CEN	Court records
	CEN	Commercial register
	CEN	Corporation charter
	CEN	Land transfer records
	CEN	Marriage records
	CEN	Credit information
	CEN	Company bylaws
Sweden	DEC	Court records

Country	Location	Type of Record
	CEN	Patents and trademarks
	CEN	Commercial register
	CEN	Corporation charter
	DEC	Land transfer records
	DEC	Birth, death, marriage records
	CEN	Company bylaws and financial statements
Switzerland	CEN	Patents, trademarks and copyrights
	CEN	Commercial register
	CEN	Corporation charter
	CEN	Land transfer records
	CEN	Birth, death, marriage records
	DEC	Credit information
	CEN	Other public records
Syria	CEN	Commercial register
	CEN	Corporation charter
	CEN	Land transfer records
	CEN	Birth, death, marriage records
	CEN	Company records, bylaws, and financial statements
Thailand	DEC	Court records
	DEC	Patents, trademarks, and copyrights
	DEC	Commercial register
	DEC	Corporation charter
	DEC	Land transfer records
	DEC	Birth, death, marriage records
	DEC	Company records, bylaws, and financial statements
Trinidad and Tobago	CEN	Court records
	CEN	Patents, trademarks and copyrights
	CEN	Corporation charter
	CEN	Land transfer records
	CEN	Birth, death, marriage records
	DEC	Other public records
	CEN	Public company records
Tunisia	CEN	Court records
	CEN	Trademarks and copyrights
	DEC	Commercial register
	DEC	Corporation charter
	DEC	Land transfer records
	DEC	Birth, death, marriage records
	DEC	Company bylaws
Turkey	CEN	Patents and trademarks
	CEN	Commercial register
	CEN	Land transfer records
Turks and Caicos Islands	CEN	Court records
	CEN	Corporation charter
	CEN	Land transfer records
	CEN	Birth, death, marriage records
	CEN	Other public records
	CEN	Company records and bylaws
United Kingdom	DEC	Court records
	CEN	Patents and trademarks
	CEN	Commercial register
	CEN	Corporation charter
	CEN	Birth, death, marriage records

continued

Country	Location	Type of Record
	CEN	Other public records
	CEN	Company bylaws
Uruguay	CEN	Court records
	CEN	Wills, patents, trademarks, copyrights
	CEN	Commercial register
	CEN	Corporation charter
	CEN	Land transfer records
	CEN	Birth, death, marriage records
	CEN	Company records, bylaws, and financial statements
Vanuatu	DEC	Court records
	CEN	Patents, trademarks, and copyrights
	CEN	Land transfer records
	DEC	Birth, death, marriage records
Venezuela	CEN	Patents, trademarks and copyrights
	CEN	Commercial register
	CEN	Corporation charter
	CEN	Land transfer records
	CEN	Birth, death, marriage records
	CEN	Company bylaws
Yugoslavia	CEN	Patents and trademarks
	DEC	Commercial register
	DEC	Land transfer records
	DEC	Birth, death, marriage records

Definitions

The terms shown above have different meanings from one country to another. Commercial register can mean nothing more than the name and address of a company in some countries while it could mean a whole biographical sketch in an other country. Company records have different meanings from one country to another. Company financial statements imply complete financial statements are available; this may not be the case in every country. Some countries only require selected financial information, i.e., inventory, sales, net profit, etc. Tax return information is not available unless a treaty is in effect. Banking information is not public record in any country. In some countries, banking information is prohibited by law to be disclosed to any party or governmental body.

Summary

For the investigator, knowing where to find financial information is very important. This is particularly true during the initial phase of developing a case. During the initial phase the investigator should get as much information as possible. A lot of information can be obtained from various public sources, which can determine if the investigator has a possible subject or case. From that point, the investigator can concentrate on the most likely subject by obtaining more information from more difficult sources. Some information is easy to get by just simply asking, whereas other information may require administrative subpoenas or court orders. Remember, the more information that is obtained, the better. Sometimes, only one or two pieces of information can either make or break the case.

Wagering and Gambling

16

Introduction

Gambling, in its various forms, is illegal in most states. In many cases, organized crime groups control illegal gambling. Gambling has become more complicated by the fact that many states have instituted state lotteries to obtain additional revenue without raising taxes. However, organized crime groups have tied their operations to various state lotteries. In this chapter, the most common gambling activities are discussed. Their terminology and record keeping will be discussed in detail. The gambling activities that will be addressed are as follows:

Sports Bookmaking. The section below explains the terminology and how sports bookmaking operates. Baseball, basketball, football, and hockey are the primary sports involved in sports bookmaking.

Bingo. Bingo halls are illegal in most states; unless they are operated by and for the benefit of charitable organizations.

Lotteries. Lotteries are number games, policy, and similar types of wagering. The operator of the lottery pays a prize if the selected numbers appear or are published in a manner understood by the parties. State-operated lotteries require participants to pay a certain amount for selected numbers. If the numbers are chosen, then the participants win a percentage of the "pot." In illegal lotteries — sometimes called "bolito" — prizes are paid in the range of $400 to $600 to $1.

Pari-Mutuel Wagering. Many states have various racetracks where betting on a race or sporting event is legal. Jai Alai is a sporting event. Races usually encompass dog and horse events.

Sports Bookmaking

This form of gambling involves placing bets on sports events, principally, baseball, basketball, football, and hockey. Professional and collegiate teams are subjects of bettors. This form of gambling is based upon credit of the bettor. The bettor calls the bookmaker — commonly called "bookie" — and places a bet. If the bettor loses, then he or she pays the bookie the amount of the bet plus a commission, usually 10 percent, at a collection site. If the bettor wins, then the bettor collects the amount of the bet at the same collection site. The collection site is designated in advance.

Elements

The elements of a bookmaking case are as follows:

1. *In The Business.* The person is engaged in the business of wagering when evidence is located on the premises. This is easily established when law enforcement conducts surveillances, wiretaps, search warrants, etc. In some states, the mere fact that gambling paraphernalia is present puts the person in the business of gambling or wagering.
2. *Volume.* The volume of wagers means the size of the gross receipts. Records are normally destroyed after a week since settlement takes place once a week. The bookie destroys all records except for the amount outstanding on open accounts.
3. *Period of Operation.* The period of the operation relates to the length of time the operation was conducted. This could range from weeks to years. Direct evidence may not be available, but rather a preponderance of the evidence may be sufficient to establish the length of time.

Federal Law

Federal law prohibits illegal gambling under Title 18, Section 1955. The Internal Revenue Code, under Section 4401, imposes an excise tax on certain gambling activities. This excise tax is usually 2 percent of the gross wagers including vigorish.

Federal law provides:

a. Whoever conducts, finances, manages, supervises, directs or owns all or part of an illegal gambling business shall be fined not more than $20,000 or imprisoned not more than five years, or both.

b. Illegal Gambling Business means a gambling business which:

1) Is a violation of the law of a State or political subdivision in which it is conducted.

2) Involves five or more persons who conduct, finance, manage, supervise, direct or own all or part of such business; and

3) Has been or remains in substantially continuous operation for a period in excess of thirty days or has gross revenue of $2,000 in any single day.

c. If five or more persons conduct, finance, manage, supervise, direct or own all or part of a gambling business, and such business operates for two or more successive days; then for the purposes of obtaining warrants for arrests, interceptions, and other searches and seizures, and probable cause that the business receives gross revenue in excess of $2,000 in any single day shall be deemed to have been established.

d. This section shall not apply to any bingo game, lottery, or similar game of chance conducted by an organization exempt from tax under paragraph (3) of subsection (c) of Section 501 of the Internal Revenue Code of 1954, as amended, if no part of the gross receipts derived from such activity inures to the benefit of any private shareholder, member, or employee of such organization except as reimbursement for actual expenses incurred by him in the conduct of such activity.

Terms

The following list of commonly used sports bookmaking terms should be a reference guide for use in wagering investigations. It identifies and explains bookmaker's language.

Dime bet — A wager of $1,000.

Dollar bet — A wager of $100.

Fifty cent bet — A wager of $50.

Four dollar bet — A wager of $400.

Quarter bet — This may be a bet of $25 or, at times, $2,500. The bettor's betting pattern or a checkup can be used to establish which definition applies.

Nickel bet — A wager of $500.

Bettor balance sheet — A list of amounts due to and from bettors. Usually amounts due from bettors are designated by a minus sign (–) and amounts payable to bettors are designated by plus sign (+).

Bettor list — This is the bookmaker's list of bettors, which includes name, number, one or more telephone numbers, and address. The bettor list can be used as a witness list, if necessary.

Bettor number — The number assigned to a bettor for identification.

The book — This usually refers to the physical location from which the bookmaker is operating.

Bookmaker or Bookie — This is the person who for his or her own account accepts wagers on sporting events and charges vigorish on the bettor's losses. Bookmakers may also have others who accept wagers for them.

Busted out — This refers to a bettor who is "bankrupt." In other words, the bettor is unable to pay off.

Buy a half point — A wager placed on which the bettor purchases an extra half-point advantage over the normal line by laying 6 to 5 odds.

Check a figure or checkup — The function of comparing the bettor's computation of the amount due to or from the bettor with the amount computed by the bookie. If the amount stated by the bettor agrees with the bookie's figure, then there is no problem.

Checkup sheet — Another term for bettor balance sheet.

Cheese bet — A combination bet on the straight line and the over–under line on a given game. The Braves and Dolphins are playing. If the Braves are a three point favorite, or –3, and the over–under line is 30, then there are four combinations that make up a cheese bet: (1) the Braves +3, over 30; (2) the Braves +3, under 30; (3) the Dolphins –3, under 30; and (4) the Dolphins –3, over 30. A winning $100 wager would return $300 to the bettor. The bettor would usually have at risk $110 or $120 depending on the bookie with whom the bettor bet.

Dog — The team expected to lose a sporting event.

Favorite — The team expected to win a sporting event.

Half-time bet — A wager placed during the period between the first and second half of a game. Normally, a bettor must lay 6 to 5 odds on such bets. Most bookies limit half-time lines for betting to games carried on local television.

In a circle — This refers to a "homemade" or uncertain line on which the size bet the bookmaker will accept is restricted. In some cases, it refers to buying a half-point.

Juice — This is another term for vigorish, which is the commission charged to losers.

Lay off — This is a wager placed from one bookmaker to another bookmaker to reduce the bookmaker's amount of risk on a given game. If the bookmaker receives bets of $10,000 on team A of a sports event and $1,500 on team B, then the bookmaker will place a bet of $8,500 on team B with another bookmaker to balance the books.

Line — A number of points given to place two opposing teams on equal footing. Adjustments may be made to influence betting on one team over the other. In baseball, hockey, and boxing, the line is expressed in terms of odds. If the odds are expressed as 8 to 5 in favor of team A, then the bookmaker dealing a "ten percent" line will require the bettor to place $165 against the bookmaker's $100 should the bettor place a bet on team A. A bettor wishing to bet the "dog," team B, will place $100 at risk against the bookmaker's $155. A bookmaker dealing a "twenty cent" line will require $170 against the bookmaker's $100 on the favorite and place $150 at risk against the bettor's $100 on wagers placed on the "dog."

Line sheet — A schedule of sporting events to be played with the line and changes in the line penned in.

Markup — This is the same as vigorish or juice.

Middled — This is a situation where a drastic change has been made in the line and the final score is such that it falls between two different lines used on the same game and bettors have placed bets that win on each of two teams.

Mule — This is a bettor who has lost. The bettor has incurred a betting liability and refuses to pay.

Off the board — A game, for various reasons, that a bookie will not accept wagers on. Therefore, the bookie takes it "off the board."

Over–under bet — A wager placed on either over or under the total points expected to be scored in a given game. Some bookies treat a score that is exactly the same as the over–under line as a loss on the part of the bettor. Some bookies will treat a score that is exactly the same as the over–under line as a push and no one wins.

Parlay bet — This is a combination bet on a series of teams at the normal line. All teams must win. A winner parlay bet returns to the bettor more than the amount the bettor has at risk but less than the true odds. The true odds of a three-team parlay winning are more than 8 to 1. The amount a bettor will win on a winning $100 three-team parlay bet is usually around $500 to $600. Normally, the more teams bet in a parlay bet, the greater the percentage disadvantage to the bettor.

Percentage — This is the same as vigorish or juice.

Phone man — An employee or owner/bookmaker, who provides betting lines and accepts wagers over the telephone in a bookmaking operation. A phone man is often referred to as a bookmaker or bookie.

Pick or **pick it** — A game that is considered a toss-up. Both teams have an equal chance on a bet at pick. No points are given.

Post — These are notations of the approximate amount of wagers received on each team of a given name. Such notations are primarily made for the purpose of attempting to avoid accepting substantially more in wagers on one team over the other. The bookmaker can change the line and make wagers less desirable and become more desirable for the other team. However, care must be exercised to avoid making a large change. A large change could place the bookmaker in a position to "get middled."

Push — A tie bet based on the line. A bettor bets on team A at +3. The final score is 21 on team A, and 18 on team B. When the score is adjusted for the line, the effective score is 21 on team A, and 21 on team B, or a tie. No one wins.

Settle — The act of paying or receiving amounts won or lost.

Settlement sheet — The same as the bettor balance sheet.

Sharp — A knowledgeable bettor.

Square — A novice bettor.

Straight bet — A bet placed on a single team at the normal line.

Tax — This is the same as vigorish or juice.

Taxable bet — Total amount at risk including any charge or fee incident to the placing of a wager.

Teaser bet — A combination bet on a series of teams with extra points added to the line depending on the number of teams in the teaser bet. Usually 6 points (half points are rounded in favor of the bookie) are added to the normal line of each team on a two-team teaser, 10 points to a three-team teaser, 12 points to a four-team teaser, etc. Some bookies may vary from this pattern and permit a total number of additional points to be spread among the teams as desired by the bettor.

To the game — A wager placed by a bettor on a baseball game with regard to whether the scheduled pitcher starts the game.

To the pitcher — A wager placed by a bettor on a baseball game predicted on the scheduled or a certain pitcher starting the game.

Vigorish — This is the bookmaker's markup to provide a profit margin. Normally, the markup is 10 percent; that is, if a bettor places a wager of $100 and loses, the bettor must pay $110. If the bettor wins, he or she wins $100. Half-time bets are normally at 6 to 5 odds or 20 percent. Some bookmakers will permit a bettor to place a wager on a game with an extra $1/2$ point advantage, if the bettor will lay 6 to 5 odds. Sometimes, the bookmaker will require 6 to 5 odds. In the case of baseball, if the bookmaker is dealing a 10-cent line, there will be a $10 spread between the amount a bettor must place at risk on a stated bet of $100, if the bettor bets on the favorite team, than what the bettor can expect to receive if he or she bets on the underdog. If the true odds on a game between team A and team B is 8 to 5 in favor of team B, and if a bettor places a stated bet of $100 on team B, the bettor must pay $165 to the bookmaker if he or she loses; the bettor will receive $100 if the bettor wins. Conversely, if the bettor places a stated bet of $100 on team A and wins, the bettor will win only $155; the bettor must pay $100 if the bettor loses. The spread on a 20-cent line would be $20 on a stated bet of $100. The bookmaker would state the line at team B minus 65 or team A minus 165. At times when the odds reach approximately 2 to 1, runs may be given rather than the foregoing.

With a hook — The adding of half a point to the line, i.e., "3 with a hook" means $3^1/_2$.

Teams

Sports betting encompasses professional and collegiate teams. The sports most commonly used for wagering are baseball, basketball, football, and hockey. The following paragraphs list the teams and their hometowns by sport.

1. **Professional Baseball.** Professional baseball teams are grouped into two leagues — American and National. The two leagues with the teams are listed below:

American League

Team Name	Location
Anaheim Angels	Anaheim, CA
Baltimore Orioles	Baltimore, MD
Boston Red Sox	Boston, MA
Chicago White Sox	Chicago, IL
Cleveland Indians	Cleveland, OH
Detroit Tigers	Detroit, MI
Kansas City Royals	Kansas City, MO
Minnesota Twins	Minneapolis, MN
New York Yankees	Bronx, NY
Oakland A's	Oakland, CA
Seattle Mariners	Seattle, WA
Tampa Bay Devil Rays	Tampa, FL
Texas Rangers	Arlington, TX
Toronto Blue Jays	Toronto, Ontario

National League

Team Name	Location
Arizona Diamondbacks	Phoenix, AZ
Atlanta Braves	Atlanta, GA
Chicago Cubs	Chicago, IL
Cincinnati Reds	Cincinnati, OH
Colorado Rockies	Denver, CO
Florida Marlins	Miami, FL
Houston Astros	Houston, TX
Los Angeles Dodgers	Los Angeles, CA
Milwaukee Brewers	Milwaukee, WI
Montreal Expos	Montreal, Quebec
New York Mets	Flushing, NY
Philadelphia Phillies	Philadelphia, PA
Pittsburgh Pirates	Pittsburgh, PA
St. Louis Cardinals	St. Louis, MO
San Diego Padres	San Diego, CA
San Francisco Giants	San Francisco, CA

2. **Professional Basketball.** Professional basketball only has one league, the National Basketball Association. The teams are as follows:

National Basketball Association

Team Name	Location	Team Name	Location
Atlanta Hawks	Atlanta, GA	Denver Nuggets	Denver, CO
Boston Celtics	Boston, MA	Detroit Pistons	Pontiac, MI
Charlotte Hornets	Charlotte, NC	Golden State Warriors	Oakland, CA
Chicago Bulls	Chicago, IL	Houston Rockets	Houston, TX
Cleveland Cavaliers	Richfield, OH	Indiana Pacers	Indianapolis, IN
Dallas Mavericks	Dallas, TX	Los Angeles Clippers	Los Angeles, CA

Team Name	Location	Team Name	Location
Los Angeles Lakers	Inglewood, CA	Portland Trail Blazers	Portland, OR
Miami Heat	Miami, FL	Sacramento Kings	Sacramento, CA
Milwaukee Bucks	Milwaukee, WI	San Antonio Spurs	San Antonio, TX
Minnesota Timberwolves	Minneapolis, MN	Seattle Super Sonics	Seattle, WA
New Jersey Nets	E. Rutherford, NJ	Toronto Raptors	Toronto, Canada
New York Knicks	New York, NY	Utah Jazz	Salt Lake City, UT
Orlando Magic	Orlando, FL	Vancouver Grizzlies	Vancouver, Canada
Philadelphia 76ers	Philadelphia, PA	Washington Bullets	Landover, MD
Phoenix Suns	Phoenix, AZ		

3. **Professional Football.** There are two major professional football leagues, the National Football League and the Canadian Football League. The two leagues along with their teams are listed below.

National Football League

Team Name	Location	Team Name	Location
Atlanta Falcons	Suwanee, GA	Minnesota Vikings	Eden Prairie, MN
Arizona Cardinals	Tempe, AZ	New England Patriots	Foxboro, MA
Baltimore Ravens	Baltimore, MD	New Orleans Saints	New Orleans, LA
Buffalo Bills	Orchard Park, NY	New York Giants	E. Rutherford, NY
Carolina Panthers	Charlotte, NC	New York Jets	New York, NY
Chicago Bears	Chicago, IL	Oakland Raiders	Oakland, CA
Cincinnati Bengals	Cincinnati, OH	Philadelphia Eagles	Philadelphia, PA
Cleveland Browns	Cleveland, OH	Pittsburgh Steelers	Pittsburgh, PA
Dallas Cowboys	Dallas, TX	St. Louis Rams	St. Louis, MO
Denver Broncos	Denver, CO	San Diego Chargers	San Diego, CA
Detroit Lions	Pontiac, MI	San Francisco 49ers	Redwood City, CA
Green Bay Packers	Green Bay, WI	Seattle Seahawks	Kirland, WA
Indianapolis Colts	Indianapolis, IN	Tampa Bay Buccaneers	Tampa, FL
Jacksonville Jaguars	Jacksonville, FL	Tennessee Titans	Nashville, TN
Kansas City Chiefs	Kansas City, MO	Washington Redskins	Washington, DC
Miami Dolphins	Miami, FL		

Canadian Football League

Team Name	Location	Team Name	Location
British Columbia Lions	Surrey, British Columbia	Ottawa Rough Riders	Ottawa, Ontario
Calgary Stampeders	Calgary, Alberta	Saskatchewan Roughriders	Regina, Saskatchewan
Edmonton Eskimos	Edmonton, Alberta	Toronto Argonauts	Toronto, Ontario
Hamilton Tiger-Cats	Hamilton, Ontario	Winnepeg Blue Bombers	Winnepeg, Manitoba
Montreal Alouettes	Montreal, Quebec		

4. **Professional Hockey.** There is only one hockey league. This is the National Hockey League. The teams are as follows:

National Hockey League

Team Name	Location	Team Name	Location
Atlanta Thrashers	Atlanta, GA	Buffalo Sabres	Buffalo, NY
Boston Bruins	Boston, MA	Calgary Flames	Calgary, Alberta

continued

Team Name	Location	Team Name	Location
Carolina Hurricanes	Morrisville, NC	New York Islanders	Uniondale, NY
Chicago Blackhawks	Chicago, IL	New York Rangers	New York, NY
Colorado Avalanche	Denver, CO	Ottawa Senators	Kanata, Ontario
Columbus Blue Jackets	Worthington, OH	Philadelphia Flyers	Philadelphia, PA
Dallas Stars	Dallas, TX	Phoenix Coyotes	Phoenix, AZ
Detroit Red Wings	Detroit MI	Pittsburgh Penguins	Pittsburgh, PA
Edmonton Oilers	Edmonton, Alberta	Quebec Nordiques	Charlesbourg, Quebec
Florida Panthers	Sunrise, FL	San Jose Sharks	San Jose, TX
Hartford Whalers	Hartford, CT	St. Louis Blues	St. Louis, MO
Los Angeles Kings	Inglewood, CA	Tampa Bay Lightning	Tampa, FL
Mighty Ducks	Anaheim, CA	Toronto Maple Leafs	Toronto, Ontario
Minnesota Wild	St. Paul, MN	Vancouver Canucks	Vancouver, BC
Montreal Canadiens	Montreal, Quebec	Washington Capitals	Landover, MD
Nashville Predators	Nashville, TN	Winnepeg Jets	Winnipeg, Manitoba
New Jersey Devils	E. Rutherford, NJ		

5. **Collegiate Football.** Many colleges have football teams. The colleges and universities are members of the National Collegiate Athletic Association (NCAA). The NCAA makes the rules for collegiate football. The college teams that are used most often by bookmakers are the universities or colleges listed below:

Team	University/college	Team	University/college
Air Force	Air Force Academy	Florida A&M	Florida A&M University
Akron	Akron State College	Florida	University of Florida
Alabama	University of Alabama	Florida State	Florida State University
Albright	Albright University	Fresno	Fresno University
Arizona	University of Arizona	Fullerton	Fullerton State College
Arizona State	Arizona State University	Georgia Tech	Georgia Institute of Technology
Arkansas	University of Arkansas	Georgia	University of Georgia
Army	U.S. Military Academy	Harvard	Harvard University
Auburn	Auburn University	Hawaii	University of Hawaii
Ball State	Ball State College	Holy Cross	Holy Cross University
Baylor	Baylor University	Houston	University of Texas
Bethune-Cookman	Bethune-Cookman College	Illinois	University of Illinois
Boston College	Boston College	Indiana	University of Indiana
Brigham Young	Brigham Young University	Iowa	University of Iowa
Brown	Brown University	Iowa State	Iowa State University
Cal	California University	Kansas	University of Kansas
Central Florida	University of Central Florida	Kansas State	Kansas State University
Carroll	Carroll College	Kent State	Kent State University
Chicago	University of Chicago	Kentucky	University of Kentucky
Cincinnati	University of Cincinnati	Wake Forest	Wake Forest College
Citadel	Citadel Military Academy	Lafayette	Lafayette College
Clemson	Clemson University	Las Vegas	University of Nevada, Las Vegas
Colgate	Colgate College	L.A. Tech	Los Angeles Institute of Technology
Colorado	University of Colorado	Lehigh	Lehigh University
Colorado State	Colorado State University	Louisiana	Louisiana State University
Columbia	Columbia University	Louisville	Louisville University
Cornell	Cornell University	Maryland	University of Maryland
Dartmouth	Dartmouth College	Memphis State	Memphis State University
Duke	Duke University	Methodist	Southern Methodist University
East Carolina	University of E. Carolina	MIT	Massachusetts Institute of Technology

continued

Team	University/college	Team	University/college
Miami Hurricanes	University of Miami, Florida	South Carolina	South Carolina University
Miami	University of Miami, Ohio	Southern Cal	University of Southern California
Michigan	University of Michigan	S.W. Louisiana	S.W. Louisiana University
Michigan State	Michigan State University	Stanford	Stanford University
Minnesota	University of Minnesota	Syracuse	Syracuse University
Mississippi	University of Mississippi	Temple	Temple University
Missouri	University of Missouri	Tennessee	University of Tennessee
Navy	U.S. Naval Academy	Texas	Texas A&M University
Nebraska	University of Nebraska	Texas-El Paso	University of Texas, El Paso
Nevada	University of Nevada	Texas Tech	Texas Institute of Technology
New Mexico	University of New Mexico	Toledo	University of Ohio, Toledo
North Carolina	University of North Carolina	Tulane	Tulane University
North Carolina State	North Carolina State University	Tulsa	Tulsa University
Northwestern	Northwestern University	Utah State	Utah State University
Notre Dame	Notre Dame University	Vanderbilt	Vanderbilt University
Ohio	University of Ohio	VMI	Virginia Military Academy
Ohio State	Ohio State University	UCLA	University of California, Los Angeles
Oklahoma	University of Oklahoma	Utah	University of Utah
Oklahoma State	Oklahoma State University	Virginia	University of Virginia
Old Miss	Mississippi State University	Virginia Tech	Virginia Institute of Technology
Oregon	University of Oregon	Wake Forest	Wake Forest University
Oregon State	Oregon State University	Washington	George Washington University
Penn	University of Pennsylvania	Washington	University of Washington
Penn State	Pennsylvania State University	Washington State	Washington State University
Pitts	University of Pittsburgh	Wesleyan	Wesleyan University
Princeton	Princeton University	West Virginia	West Virginia University
Purdue	Purdue University	W. Michigan	W. Michigan University
Rice	Rice University	Wisconsin	University of Wisconsin
Rutgers	Rutgers University	Wyoming	University of Wyoming
San Diego State	San Diego State University	Yale	Yale University
San Jose State	San Jose State University		

Baseball

Baseball is more complicated for a person to learn. In baseball, there are two lines, the "money line" and the "western line." There are also "totals," or "over and under," on each game. The money line is also called "the pitcher's line" because the price of the favorite depends on who is pitching or it is called the "dime line" because there is a "10 dollar" difference between the "favorite price" and the "underdog price". When a player bets the money line the pitcher must pitch, both of them, or there is no action (or no bet). The only time a bettor receiving the money line has a bet is on the occasion that one of the two pitchers on the list does not pitch when the bettor states before the bet that the bettor wants action on the plays. Action means if a pitcher did not go, then the bettor would have a bet at an adjusted price according to the strength of the new pitcher. The following chart illustrates all possible money lines and what the bet would be on the favorite and the underdog in terms of $100.

Possible Money Line		Bet	Win
Favorite	−110	110	100 On favorite
Underdog	Even	100	100 On underdog
Favorite	−115	115	100 On favorite
Underdog	+105	100	105 On underdog
Favorite	−120	120	100 On favorite
Underdog	+110	100	110 On underdog
Favorite	−125	125	100 On favorite
Underdog	+115	100	115 On underdog
Favorite	−130	130	100 On favorite
Underdog	+120	100	120 On underdog
Favorite	−135	135	100 On favorite
Underdog	+125	100	125 On underdog
Favorite	−140	140	100 On favorite
Underdog	+130	100	130 On underdog
Favorite	−145	145	100 On favorite
Underdog	+135	100	135 On underdog
Favorite	−150	150	100 On favorite
Underdog	+140	100	140 On underdog
Favorite	−155	155	100 On favorite
Underdog	+145	100	145 On underdog
Favorite	−160	160	100 On favorite
Underdog	+150	100	150 On underdog
Favorite	−165	165	100 On favorite
Underdog	+155	100	155 On underdog
Favorite	−170	170	100 On favorite
Underdog	+160	100	160 On underdog
Favorite	−175	175	100 On favorite
Underdog	+165	100	165 On underdog
Favorite	−180	180	100 On favorite
Underdog	+170	100	170 On underdog
Favorite	−185	185	100 On favorite
Underdog	+175	100	175 On underdog
Favorite	−190	190	100 On favorite
Underdog	+180	100	180 On underdog
Favorite	−200	200	100 On favorite
Underdog	+185	100	185 On underdog
Favorite	−210 [a]	210	100 On favorite
Underdog	+190	100	190 On underdog
Favorite	−220	220	100 On favorite
Underdog	+200	100	200 On underdog
Favorite	−230	230	100 On favorite
Underdog	+210	100	210 On underdog
Favorite	−240	240	100 On favorite
Underdog	+220	100	220 On underdog
Favorite	−250	250	100 On favorite
Underdog	+230	100	230 On underdog
Favorite	−260	260	100 On favorite
Underdog	+240	100	240 On underdog

[a] You should notice that 210 or more becomes a $20 difference instead of
10. This is done so the bookmaker's vigorish/juice stays the same rate.
When there is no favorite or pick, then both teams are the same or shown
as Favorite 105 and Underdog 100. Also, note that the favorite always
uses the minus sign while the underdog uses the plus sign.

You can understand how baseball betting works by going through an example. A sports line service provides the line on the Mets vs. Cincinnati as:

Mets   -160
Cincinnati

The Mets are the favorite because the price and the minus (–) sign are by the name. The Mets are minus 160. This means that for every $100 a person wants to win on the Mets, then the bettor must risk $160. If the bettor bets on the Mets for $100 and loses, then the bettor owes the bookmaker $160. If the bettor wins, then the bookmaker owes the bettor $100. The bookmaker's bettor sheet would show:

Team	Vigorish	Bet	Win
Mets	−60	160	100

The team column tells what team the bettor is placing the bet on to win. The vigorish column tells the bookmaker what amount of vigorish/juice that the bookmaker is expected to win. The bet column is the amount wagered by the bettor. This is the full amount the bettor will have to pay the bookmaker if the bettor loses. The win column shows the amount that the bookmaker will owe the bettor if the bettor wins.

Using the same line and teams, the bettor places a wager on the underdog, Cincinnati. The underdog is always $100 less than the favorite, or +150. Here, the bettor is risking $100 to make $150. The bookmaker's bettor sheet would show:

Team	Vigorish	Bet	Win
Cincinnati	+50	100	150

Now, let us go through another example but with a different bet amount. The bettor wants to place a wager on the Mets for 300. The bookmaker's bettor sheet would show:

Team	Vigorish	Bet	Win
Mets	−60	480	300

This requires computation on the part of the bookmaker. The calculation is based upon the line of 160 to 100. So the bettor wants 300. This corresponds to $100 \times 3 = 300$. The bet would be $160 \times 3 = 480$. The bettor risks 480 to win 300. This rule also applies to the other team. If the bettor wants to place 300 on Cincinnati, since it is the underdog, the computation changes as follows:

Team	Vigorish	Bet	Win
Cincinnati	+50	300	450

The win column will show the amount the bettor would win. It is computed by $150 \times 3 = \$450$. The bet column is based upon the ratio of $100 \times 3 = \$300$.

The basic rule, from the examples above, is that it is impossible to win more on a favorite than you are betting. It is impossible to bet more on an underdog than the bettor can win.

A parlay is picking two or more teams to win their games. A parlay is for a set amount that the bettor wants. If the bettor wins, the bookmaker must figure it out by the prices (vigorish or juice). In a parlay, all teams must win; otherwise, the bettor loses. The following examples illustrate a parlay.

The line for two games are

Mets	−160
Cincinnati	150
Los Angeles	−120
Miami	110

The bettor places a wager of $200 parlay on Mets and Miami. The bookmaker's bettor sheet would show the following:

Team	Vigorish	Bet	Win
Mets	−60		
Miami	+10	200 Parlay	

You should notice that the Mets is a favorite, while Miami is the underdog. Remember, all teams in a parlay must win before the bettor can win. If one team loses and the other wins, the bettor loses. In this example, if both teams win, then the bettor wins the following by the rules shown above.

Team	Vigorish	Bet	Win
Mets	−60	320	200
Miami	+10	200	220
Total			420

If one or both of the teams loses, then the bettor has to pay the bookmaker the following:

Team	Vigorish	Bet	Win
Mets	−60	320	200
Miami	+10	220	240
Total		540	

A "round robin" is a group of two team parlays written in a shorter and easier way. A round robin must have at least three teams. The three-team round robin is the same as three two-team parlays. To illustrate a round robin and a three two-team parlay, the following example is given.

The line is given below on three games.

Mets	−160	Los Angeles	−120	Boston	−140
Cincinnati	150	Miami	110	Braves	130

The round robin must have at least three teams. The bettor calls the bookmaker and places a 200 round robin wager as follows:

Team	Vigorish	Bet	Win
Mets	–60		
Miami	+10		
Boston	–40	200 Round robin	

Notice two teams are favorites while one team is an underdog. In a three two-team parlay, it would appear on the bookmaker's bettor sheet as follows:

Team	Vigorish	Bet	Win
Mets	–60		
Miami	+10	200 Parlay	
Mets	–60		
Boston	–40	200 Parlay	
Miami	+10		
Boston	–40	200 Parlay	

For the bettor to win, all teams must also win. If any team loses, then the bettor loses. In a round robin, the bettor would win the amount shown below when all teams win.

Team	Vigorish	Bet	Win
Mets	–0	320	200
Miami	+10	200	220
Boston	–40	280	200
Total			620

If the bettor loses, the bookmaker would collect the following:

Team	Vigorish	Bet
Mets	–60	320
Miami	+10	200
Boston	–40	280
Total		800

Bettors will also make wagers based upon points either over or under the line. When points are placed on either over or under the line, then the bets change to only three possible combinations. They are

    120 to 100
    110 to 100
    100 to 100 or even money

These three combinations are called flat, over, or under. These are defined as:

Flat (F) When the total line is flat, the bettor goes either over (O) or under (U); the bettor must lay 110 to win 100. Flat has no favorite.

Over (O) When the total line is favored over (O), the bettor must bet 120 to 100, because the over (O) is the bookmaker's favorite. If he goes under (U), then the bet is 100 to 100, because the bettor is going against the bookmaker's favorite.

Under (U) When the total line is favored under (U) and the bettor wagers under, then the bettor must lay 120 to 100, because the under is the favorite. If the bettor wagers over, the bettor lays 100 to 100 because the bettor is going against the favorite.

As an example, let us assume the same example as before. The line is

Mets	−160
Cincinnati	150

The bettor wants the Mets at over the eighth for $200. The bookmaker's sheet would show:

Team	O/U	Bet	Win
Mets	O 8	240	200

This shows that the bettor must pay $120 if the bettor loses, or the bettor wins $100. Now, let us assume that the bettor wagers the Mets under the eighth for $200. The bookmaker's sheet should reflect:

Team	O/U	Bet	Win
Mets	U 8	200	200

In this instance, the favorite is the Mets. Therefore, the odds are 100 to 100 or even money. Now, let us assume that the bookmaker has no favorite. This is called a flat. In other words, there is no favorite or underdog. In a nonfavorite situation, the odds are always 110 to 100. The bettor calls and wagers 8 points under for 200. The bookmaker's tally sheet will show:

Team	O/U	Bet	Win
Mets	U 8	220	200

If the bettor wins, then the bettor receives $200. If the bettor loses, then the bettor pays $220. The points, both over and under, can have $1/_2$ points. Many bookmakers use the minus (−) sign to represent a half point, sometimes called half run. Example:

$$7- = \text{seven and a half runs}$$

The bettor calls up and wants to put 7− on the Mets for $300. The line is

Mets	−160	7− U
Cincinnati	150	

The bettor, in this illustration, wants $7^1/_2$ points under on the Mets for $300. The bookmaker's tally sheet should show:

Team	Bet	Win
Mets U 7–	360	300

In this illustration, the bettor must lay 120 to 100 since the team is the bookmaker's favorite. When the bettor places bets in a parlay or round robin using points and half points (runs), then the bookmaker's tally sheet would probably look like this, using $100:

Line		Team	Bet	Win
Mets	−160	Mets U 8 U	120	100
Cincinnati	150			
Los Angeles	−120	Miami O 7– F	110	100
Miami	110			
Boston	−140	Boston U 6 O	100	100
Braves	130			

The line is shown here as reference; otherwise, it would not be reflected on the bookmaker's sheet. In the above example, the Mets is given as eight runs for under. This is the book-maker's favorite. In the Miami O 7- F, the bookmaker has no favorite or underdog. In the Boston U 6 O, the bettor is betting opposite the bookmaker. This is called an even bet. The rule of thumb is, when the bettor places bets in favor of the bookmaker's choice, then this is a favorite bet. When the bettor places a bet opposite of the bookmaker's choice, then this is an even bet. When the bettor places a bet that is neither a favorite nor an underdog to the bookmaker, then this is a flat.

When the bookmaker does not know who is pitching in a game, then the bookmaker will have four prices or odds. The bookmaker's sheet would read like the following example.

Team	Pitcher	Odds	Odds	Odds	Odds
SF Giants	Swan, Reuschel	PS-S	−8	G-S	G-R
Braves	P. Smith, Glavine	20	R-PS	35	15

The price is on the line that is the bookmaker's favorite. Above or below the price (odds) is the pitchers. When a bettor calls, the bookmaker would say Braves P. Smith is −20 over Swan, but Giants Reuschel is −8 over P. Smith, and Braves Glavine is 35 over Swan and −15 over Reuschel.

If the bettor does not care who pitches and places a bet, using the odds above, for $1,000 on SF Giants, then the bookmaker's tally sheet would show the following breakdown.

Team	Price	Pitcher	Bet	Win
Giants	+10	PS-S	1000	1100
	−08	R-PS	1080	1000
	+25	G-S	1000	1250
	+05	G-R	1000	1050

If the bettor places a bet on Braves double header (two games by the same teams) with no pitcher identified, then the bookmaker's tally sheet would show the following:
This bet would apply to both games.

Team	Price	Pitcher	Bet	Win
Braves	−20	PS-S	1200	1000
	−02	R-PS	1020	1000
	−35	G-S	1350	1000
	−15	G-R	1150	1000

Using the same teams and odds, the bettor places a bet on the Giants Reuschel, but does not care who pitches against him, for $100. The bookmaker's tally sheet would reflect:

Team	Price	Pitcher	Bet	Win
Giants	−08	PS	108	100
	+05			

The bettor could change his or her odds or price on game 2 of a double hitter. The bettor bets on the Braves for $200. The tally sheet would show:

Team	Price	Pitcher	Bet	Win
Braves	−20	PS-S	240	200
	−02	R-PS	204	200
	−35	G-S	270	200
	−15	G-R	230	200

The bettor wants the Braves if Swan pitches for $1,000. Swan is the Giants pitcher. The tally sheet would show:

Team	Price	Pitcher	Bet	Win
Braves	−20	PS	1200	1000
(Swan)	−35	G	1350	1000

This section has given a summary of how baseball sports betting works.

Football

Football only involves a point spread and a total. All bets are 110 to 100 odds. The only time a football bet is not 110 to 100 is when a player buys a half point or plays a gimmick. Like baseball, football has favorites and underdogs. Teams with minus (−) points are always the bookmaker's favorite, those with plus (+) points are always the underdog, and a pick or even game has no favorite. The point spread can also have half points. The bookmaker gives the bettor the favorite team, the point spread (expressed in minus points), and the total. Example:

$$
\begin{array}{ll}
\text{Phoenix} & \text{5 And 41} \\
\text{49ers} & \text{3 And 39}
\end{array}
$$

For every $100 a bettor places to win on a football game, the bettor must risk $110 or 10 percent. The 10 percent is called the juice or vigorish, which the bookmaker earns. The bookmaker's tally sheet will always have as a minimum the bettor's number, team, point spread, and the amount of the bet. Example:

Team	Points	Bet
Buffalo	−30	500 Favorite
Dolphins	+3	400 Underdog

A parlay is picking two or more teams to win. A parlay is a set amount. How much the bettor wins depends on how many teams the bettor puts in the parlay. The bettor must win all picks in order for the parlay to win. One loser will cause the whole parlay to lose. The bettor tells the bookmaker that the bettor wants a $100 parlay on the 49ers and Miami. The tally sheet would read

Team	Points	Bet
49ers	−3	
Miami	+4	100 P

The bettor would win $260 or $100 × 2.6 = $260.

The bettor can use not only points but total as well. Example:

Team	Points	Bet
Rams	−6	
Denver	O 41	1,000 P

The bettor would win $2,600 or $1,000 × 2.6 = $2,600. This is based upon the odds of 13 to 5 or amount times 2.6.

The odds are set by the bookmaker for parlays and round robin bets. These are normally as follows, but the bookmaker can change them.

Team	Odds	
2	13–5	or amount times 2.6
3	6–1	or amount times 6
4	10–1	or amount times 10
5	15–1	or amount times 15

In a three-team parlay, the bettor wants the Rams, Denver, and Dolphins under for $300. The tally sheet would read

Team	Points	Bet
Rams	−2	
Denver	U 39	
Dolphins	−5	300 P

The bettor would win $1,800 or $300 × 6 = $1,800. The odds are 10 to 1.

A round robin is a group of two-team parlays playing three games. The bettor wants $100 round robin on the Rams, Denver, and the Dolphins for $100. The tally sheet reads

Team	Points	Bet
Rams	+6	
Denver	+2	
Dolphins	+5	100 RR

Notice, the bettor is betting on the underdog. A round robin would be the same as writing three parlays as follows:

Team	Points	Bet
Rams	+6	
Denver	+2	100 P
Rams	+6	
Dolphins	+5	100 P
Denver	+2	
Dolphins	+5	100 P

A round robin has

> Three-team round robin has three two-team parlays
> Four-team round robin has six two-team parlays
> Five-team round robin has 10 two-team parlays

The only time a football bet is not 110 to 100 odds is when a bettor wants to buy a $1/_2$ point in the bettor's favor; then it will cost the bettor 120 to 100 odds.

If the bettor is betting a favorite and wants a $1/_2$ point, then this $1/_2$ point spread will be lower by $1/_2$ point.

Team	Points	Bet	Win
Denver	−2	120	100

If the bettor is betting on an underdog and wants to purchase a $1/_2$ point; the spread will go up by $1/_2$ point.

Team	Points	Bet	Win
Dolphins	+2−	240	200

This bet is figured out by taking the amount times 1.2 equals 240.

A bettor can also buy $1/_2$ points on totals.

> Ô is just like buying on a flaw
> U is just like buying on a dog

Denver is 40. The bettor wants to buy a $1/_2$ point and go over for 300. The bettor gets the total at 39–.

Team	Points	Bet	Win
Denver	Ô 39–	360	300

The bettor wants to buy a $1/_2$ point and go under for 500. The total goes up to 40–.

Team	Points	Bet	Win
Denver	U 40–	600	500

Note: The only time the 120 to 100 odds on buying a $^1/_2$ point change is when the customer is buying off a round robin. It then costs the bettor 125 to 100, or the amount times 1.25.

Note: The bettor can buy a full point; however, it will cost him 140 to 100, or the amount times 1.4.

Teaser bets are *only* used in the sport of football. Bookmakers get many teaser bets. Most bookmakers use the following chart.

No. Of Team	6 Points	6 points	7 Points
2	100–100	110–100	120–100
3	100–180	100–160	100–150
4	100–300	100–250	100–200
5	100–450	100–400	100–350

There are 12 possible combinations for a teaser using the above chart. The breakdown is as follows:

Team and Points	Odds
2 teaser 6	100–100
2 teaser 6–	110–100
2 teaser 7	120–100
3 teaser 6	100–180
3 teaser 6–	100–160
3 teaser 7	100–150
4 teaser 6	100–300
4 teaser 6–	100–250
4 teaser 7	100–200
5 teaser 6	100–450
5 teaser 6–	100–400
5 teaser 7	100–350

Teasers are gimmicks that offer to give the bettor another betting choice in which the bookmaker allows the bettor to add points to the bettor's team's point spread for a certain price. The bettor wants a two-team teaser for 6 points for 100 on Denver at –3 and the Dolphins at +5.

Team	Points	Teaser Points	Points Used
Denver	–3	6	+3
Dolphins	+5	6	+11

The bettor wants a two-team teaser, 7 points for 400 using Denver and the Dolphins. The points are Denver –3- and the Dolphins –3.

In this case, the bettor is using points of +3- on Denver and +4 on the Dolphins. The bookmaker's tally sheet would read as follows:

Team	Points	Bet	Win
Denver	+3–	480	400
Dolphins	+4	480	400 Teaser

In a three-team teaser, the bookmaker's tally sheet would read as follows:

Team	Points	Bet	Win
Denver	+2–		
Dolphins	$-^1/_2$		
Dallas	+2	200	360

Basketball

Basketball is identical to football. If fraud examiners know football, then they will know basketball since the rules are the same. The point spread is the line, which is rated to equal betting action on each team of a game. A total is based upon an average of total points scored. Like football, basketball odds are 110 to 100.

Lottery

Lottery is a game of chance whereby bettors place bets on numbers that are randomly selected from some identified, independent source. In some areas, this form of betting is called "bolito." In essence, the bettor picks a two- or three-digit number at random and places a bet of $1.00 or more with a writer. If the bettor's number is selected, then the bettor wins anywhere from $30.00 to $600.00 depending upon the digits and betting volume.

Terminology

Lottery operators and bettors have their own terminology. These terms are defined as follows:

Add back — An outstanding previous week's balance from a writer or ribbon. This amount is added back to the net of the current week's summary.

Bag man or **Pick-up man** — A person who picks up monies generated from lottery activity from ribbons and/or writers or carries out funds needed to cover hits.

Banker — One who directs, finances, controls, and receives the final profit from a lottery.

Box bet — A wager placed on any permutation of given three-digit numbers. Normally, such wagers are divisible by 3 and/or 6. For example, a 48¢ box bet on number 123 is the equivalent of an 8¢ bet of the numbers 123, 132, 213, 231, 321, and 312.

Call sheets — A list of writers and/or ribbons, the time or times they are to be called for their lottery, and their telephone number or numbers.

Combination bet — A six-way number, or a box number. Sometimes it is a three-way number. Different terms are used in various localities.

Cut number — A number on which the payout rate is reduced. Cut numbers can be used to discourage betting on a number or series of numbers.

High money — Gross wagers prior to being reduced by a given commission.

Highs — A list of numbers on which wagers exceeding "X" dollars have been accepted.

Hit — A wager placed on the winning number.

Layoff — A bet placed by one lottery bank to another lottery bank to reduce the risk of substantial loss should a number on which a bank has a substantial amount of betting hit. For example, lottery A has a total of $100 on number 601. At a payout rate of 400 to 1, if number 601 was the winning lottery number, payouts on that number would total $40,000. A lottery, especially a smaller lottery, may not wish to carry this potential loss and may place a bet itself with another lottery. For example, a $50 layoff would reduce the potential payout to $20,000.

Low money — This is gross wagers after being reduced by a given commission. For example, a writer receives $100 in gross wagers and is to receive a $25 commission. High money would be $100 and low money would be $75.

Numbers lottery bet — This is a wager placed on a series of numbers, usually two- or three-digit numbers, the winning number of which is determined by a relatively random set of events.

Office or telephone relay station — This is a location from which a person accumulates such items as wagers, hits, outstanding balances due from or to the writers, and other financial records of a lottery.

Overlook — This is a bet placed on a winning on a prior lottery day that was overlooked; i.e., the lottery operation had to go back to records for the prior lottery day to ascertain if the bettor had placed a bet on the winning number and it failed to pay.

Ribbon — This is a person who supervises or receives wagers from writers and forwards such wagers. A ribbon may be a writer also. A ribbon may also be an adding machine tape.

Six-way number — This is any three-digit number from 000 through 999 in which none of the numbers is the same. There are six permutations of these numbers. For example, the numbers 1, 2, and 3 can be arranged as 123, 132, 231, 213, 321, and 312.

Stock and bonds lottery — This is a three-digit lottery in which the winning number is determined from the published results of trading on the New York Stock Exchange. Wagers can be placed on any one of 1,000 numbers from 000 through 999. The first two digits of the winning number are determined from the $100,000 and the $10,000 digits of the total bond sales on a given day, and the third digit is determined from the 10,000 digit of units traded on the New York Stock Exchange.

Straight or triple number — This is any three-digit number from 000 through 999 in which all three digits are the same.

Three-way number — This is any three-digit number from 000 through 999 in which two of the three digits are the same. There are three permutations of these numbers. For example, the numbers 1, 1, and 2 can be arranged 112, 121, and 211.

Two-digit lottery — This is any lottery on which wagers on two-digit numbers 00 through 99 are accepted. The winning number may be derived from any one of several random sources. For example, the winning number for the "Wednesday, Puerto Rico" is published in the Pittsburgh Courier. "The Saturday Dog" is determined from the results of pari-mutuel payoffs on certain races at a given dog track. The "Sunday Nighthouse" is determined by a drawing from a bag containing 100 numbered bolita balls, etc.

Wall number — This is a wager on a lottery number, which is to be repeated for an extended period of time. For example, on a week wall bet, the wager would be repeated each day of a given week. A wall bet may be placed for 2 days or may extend through an indefinite period of time. This term varies by locality. For example, in the Mid-Atlantic Region, it is referred to as "Keep in."

Lottery Operations

Figure 16-1 shows the structure of a lottery organization.

1. **Banker.** The banker is the person who directs, finances, controls, and receives the final profit. In many cases, the banker does not participate in the day-to-day operations; relying instead on the office manager. The banker usually receives 10 percent of the gross receipts as the profits from the operations. If the banker does not have an office manager, then the banker will participate actively in the day-to-day operations. In this case, the banker's commission will be 20 to 30 percent.

2. **Office Manager.** The office manager accumulates the wagers, hits, outstanding balances due from or to the writers, and other financial records of the lottery. The office manager provides the cutoff time for writers to call in their final bets. This prevents writers from including winning numbers in the tally. The office manager will have collectors who collect from ribbons and writers and make payouts. The office manager directs and controls the collectors.

3. **Writer.** The writer takes the bets and money from the bettors and reports to the office manager the total bets placed and funds collected. The writer pays the collector the money owed to the banker less the commission. If the writer has to pay a winning number and does not have the funds to do so, then the collector will provide the funds from the office manager. Writers in large operations are known as "ribbons" The writers usually earn a commission of 25 percent. In large operations, ribbons may have writers reporting to them in which they pay them a commission, usually 5 to 7 percent.

Lottery Examples

The following examples illustrate both two-digit and three-digit lotteries. An explanation follows the illustration.

Two-Digit Lottery

The following is an illustration of a two-digit lottery that a ribbon/writer has taken from the bettors:

Bettor	Number	Bet
Bill	12	$1
Chuck	78/	1
Dan	44	1
198	67	1
134	23/	1*

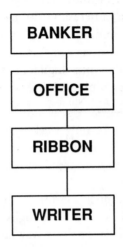

Figure 16-1 Lottery organization chart.

Bill placed a wager of $1.00 on number 12. Chuck placed a bet of $1.00 on number 78. This is a box bet since Chuck wants number 78 and 87. Dan placed a bet of $1.00 on 44. This is a straight number since both digits are the same. Bettor 198 has placed a straight bet on 67 for $1.00. The bettor is not identified by name, but by a number assigned to the bettor. Bettor 134 placed a box bet on number 23 for $1.00. The box numbers are 23 and 32. Bettor 134 is a winner and will receive $30 to $40 on a $1.00 bet. If this were not a box bet, then the bettor would receive $40 to $60. The writer will usually circle the number that is the winner on the tally sheet and trace the number back to the bettor's sheet.

   The writer will summarize the bets for the ribbon or office manager as illustrated below:

Number	Bets
00	130
01	450
02	300
03	180
04	250
//	//
23*	210
//	//
98	100
99	50
Total	$18,500

In this case, the winning number is 23 and 32 for box bets. The total amount of wagers placed on this number is $210.00. The writer collected a total of $18,500 from all bettors. If the payout is $30 and $40 to 1, then the writer would have the following accounting:

Gross Bettor Income	$18,500
Payouts:	
110 @ $30.00	3,300
200 @ $40.00	8,000
Commission earned (25 percent)	4,625
Net due officer manger	**$ 2,575**

The 110 @ $30.00 is for box bettors, while 200 @ $40.00 is for straight bettors. It should be noted that some two-digit lottery operations do not allow box bets.

Three-Digit Lottery

The following illustrations shows how a three-digit lottery operates at the ribbon/writer level.

Bettor	Number	Bet
Bill	235	$1
Chuck	111	1
148/	121	1
160/	365	1

Bill has placed a straight bet on number 235 for $1.00. Chuck has placed a bet of $1.00 on 111, which is a triple number where all three digits are the same. Bettor 148 placed a box bet on number 121 for $1.00. This is a three-way number since two of the three digits are the same. In a box bet, the bettor would win on numbers 121, 112, and 211. Bettor 160 placed a box bet on number 365 for $1.00. This is a six-way number. There are six permutations of this number that are 365, 635, 563, 356, 536, and 653.

The ribbon/writer would summarize the bets for the office manager as follows:

Number	Bets
111	230
121	120
235/*	210
300	200
310/	280
365	180
465	312
535	295
678	286
//	//
879/	195
978	233
Total	$98,000

The winning number is 235. Bettors who made straight or box bets would win on this number. The bettor who placed a box bet on 235, 253, 532, 523, 325, and 352 would win. The bettor who made a straight bet, 235, would usually win $400.00 to $1.00, while those bet on a box would normally win $300.00 to $1.00. The box bets are called cut numbers since they pay out less than a straight bet.

The ribbon/writer would account for his business activity as follows:

Gross Bets Collected	$98,000
Payouts:	
$400 @ 90	36,000
$300 @ 120	36,000
Commission (20%)	19,600
Net due office manager	**$ 6,400**

In this scenario, the writer/ribbon collected $98,000 in gross bets. The writer had to pay out $36,000 to straight bettors, those who bet three- or six-way numbers. The payout to box bettors was $36,000. The writer/ribbon gets a commission of $19,600 since the commission is 20 percent. The balance of $6,400.00 goes to the officer manager or banker.

The ribbon/writer can estimate the average payouts as follows:

$$\frac{(\$400 \times \text{No. of winners}) + (\$300 \times \text{No. of winners})}{1,000} = \text{Average Payout}$$

or

$$\frac{(\$400 \times 90) + (\$300 \times 120)}{1,000} = \frac{36,000 + 36,000}{1,000}$$

or

$$\frac{(72,000)}{1,000} = 720 \text{ to } 1$$

Bingo

Bingo is a game of chance where the bettor matches random numbers between 0 and 75 in groups of 15 on a randomly selected card where it forms a straight line that is either vertical, horizontal, or diagonal. The bingo card has random numbers going five across and five down the card, totaling 25 numbers. Usually the center box has no number, but is called a free space. The word *Bingo* denotes the group of numbers 0 through 75 as follows:

Letter	Numbers
B	0–15
I	16–30
N	31–45
G	46–60
O	61–75

When the random selected numbers form a straight line, whether vertical, horizontal, or diagonal, the winner calls out "Bingo." The winner receives funds of either a fixed amount or a percentage of the gross receipts that are received by the "house." An example of a winning bingo card is shown in Figure 16-2. The house calls the numbers that are winners for one player: 6, 18, 50, and 71. The center box has no number and is considered a free space (FS).

Tax Exempt

Many nonprofit organizations hold bingo games in order to raise funds. Neither the federal nor state governments tax these profits. Legitimate charities use the profits for their needs. However, organized crime and other criminal groups use bingo halls for personal profit. Many states allow bingo halls and parlors for charity. However, it is unlawful to operate bingo halls for personal profit. Criminal groups sometimes get around this "loophole" by giving charities funds ranging from $200 and up per week. The profits are skimmed from the operations after expenses have been paid.

B	I	N	G	O
1	19	40	49	**71**
4	22	31	**50**	73
12	17	**FS**	53	69
10	**18**	42	47	66
6	29	39	58	75

Figure 16-2 Winning Bingo Card.

Variations

There are three basic variations of playing bingo games. These types of bingo games are "paper," "grind," and "lightning." Besides the normal way of getting numbers in a straight row, players must play games that get numbers that form various patterns, i.e., X, H, O, 8, 7, E, F, etc., or "black-out" or "coverall" in which every block must be covered. Also, there are bingo games that have "highlighted" numbers which must be called before the player wins. There usually is no pattern for the "highlighted" or predetermined numbers.

Paper Bingo

In paper bingo, bingo cards are printed on disposable paper. They come in various sizes. One bingo card can be printed on a small sheet or multiple bingo cards, called "faces," on a single sheet. Multiple sheets are often put together to form a package that is sold to customers so that they can play multiple games. Players also purchase ink dabbers for use in playing bingo games. The ink dabbers are used to mark called numbers on the bingo faces. The players throw away the sheets after a winner has been called, and use another sheet for the next game. In most cases, more than one game can be played on a single sheet. Bingo halls purchase these sheets from suppliers who produce these sheets in various sizes. The suppliers have a standard method of billing and identifying the bingo supplies. As an example, a bingo hall receives the bill shown in Figure 16-3 for bingo supplies.

Description	Quantity	Total Costs
3 on V padded (1–9000) Olive	1 case	$11.50
3 on V padded (9–18000) Purple	2 cases	36.00
6 on 5 up (1–9000) BN,GY,BK,PL,RD	1 set	84.15
12 on 5 up (1–9000) BN,GY,BK,PL,RD	5 sets	420.75
12 on 10 up (9–18000) SBL,SOR,SGN,SYW,SPK,BL,OR,GN,YW,PK	1 set	153.00
15 on 20 up (6001–9000) Double SBL,SOR,SGN,SYW,SPK,BL,OR,GN,YW,PK	5 sets	292.00
18 on 20 up (18001–27000) SBL,SOR,SGN,SYW,SPK,BL,OR,GN,YW,PK	2 sets	306.00

Figure 16-3 Sample Bingo Paper Invoice.

Figure 16-3 shows that a bingo hall purchased seven different products. The meanings of these products are explained below:

1. 3 on V padded. There are three faces on a single sheet. The V means vertical. The faces are arranged from top to bottom. Padded means that they are all single sheets. The 1–9000 says that there are 9,000 faces in a case. The sheets are all olive in color.
2. 3 on V padded. There are three vertical faces on a single sheet. The 9–18000 means there are 9,000 faces in a case with a series ranging from 9001 to 18000. The color is purple.
3. 6 on 5 up. There are six faces on a sheet with three down and two across. 5 up means that there are five sheets in the set. A player can play five bingo games. The series ranges from 1 to 9000. Each sheet in the set has a different color. This allows bingo operators to make each player use the same color.
4. 12 on 5 up. There are 12 faces on a sheet with three down and four across. 5 up means that there are five sheets in the set with different colors.
5. 12 on 10 up. There are 12 faces on a sheet with three down and four across. 10 up means that there are 10 sheets in the set with different colors.
6. 15 on 20 up. Here, there are 15 faces on a sheet with three down and five across. 20 up means that there are 20 sheets in the set with different colors.
7. 18 on 20 UP. This set has 18 faces on a sheet with three down and six across. 20 up means that there are 20 sheets in the set with different colors.

Bingo operators and suppliers use the following guide to determine the number of faces per set and booklet, and the number of booklets in an order.

Faces = up times series
Booklets = series divided by on
Faces per book = up times on

Paper bingo terms. Bingo operators and suppliers define the following terms:

Series — The number of faces contained in a single set. This is usually 9,000. In large sets, it is 3,000. The total series is 1 to 63,000.

Face — The individual bingo card containing 24 numbers plus a consecutively numbered center free space.

On — The number of bingo faces per sheet.

Cut — The direction a sheet of faces will be cut from a master sheet. A cut may be square, horizontal, or vertical.

Up — The number of sheets in a booklet.

Off-cut
Faces that cannot be cut from the master sheet in the desired "on." If the master sheet is a 24 on vertical and the order is a 9 on sheet, the result will be two 9 on-cuts that equal 18 faces and an off-cut of six faces, which totals 24 faces from the 24 on vertical sheet.

Bingo paper sales.   Bingo halls that sell paper usually does so in various size packages. The prices of each packages vary according to size. The package sizes can be composed of only one bingo product or a combination of bingo products. For internal control or fraud examination, the gross sales can be determined by use of the gross profit method of determining income. This can be done by computing the number of bingo products sold times the sales price. This will give the amount of the gross proceeds that were collected. The gross profit can be determined by taking the gross proceeds and subtracting the direct costs. The direct costs is the cost of the bingo products and the prize money paid out. To illustrate the computation of gross income, the following example is given.

A Bingo Hall sells the following packs to customers.

	Cost	Prize
A - 3 on V	$20.00	$50.00
12 on 10 up		
B - 6 on 2 up	$35.00	$75.00
12 on 10 up		
C - 3 on V 2 up	$50.00	$100.00
15 on 10 up		

The 12 on 10 up is the common product for packs A and B. It has a series of 1 to 9000. The number of booklets in a series is 9,000/10 = 900 booklets. The 15 on 10 up is the main product for pack C. It has a series of 1 to 9000. The number of booklets in this series is 9,000/10 = 900 booklets.

Inventory shows 100 booklets of 12 on 10 up were sold and 20 booklets of 15 on 10 up were sold. The gross receipts are computed as shown below.

12 on 10 up ($20 + $35 = $55/2 = 22.50 × 100)	$2,250.00
15 on 10 up ($50 × 20)	1,000.00
Total Sales	$3,250.00

The 3 on V and 6 on 2 up are excluded from the computation since they are part of the packages sold. However the cost of these products should be part of the cost of sales.

Prize payouts.   The principal cost of sales is the prize money that is paid out. Using the above example, the cost of sales is computed as follows:

Prize ($50 + $75 + $100 = $225/3)	$75.00
The number of games in the session	× 12
Total prize payouts	$900.00

The cost of the paper sold is computed on a prorated basis:

12 on 10 up (100/900 × $153.00)	$17.00
15 on 10 up (20/900 × $180.00)	+ 4.00
Cost of packages sold	$21.00

It should be observed that the 3 on V and the 6 on 2 up should be added to the computation above. It is omitted in this case since the amount sold and on hand is not given.

The gross profit from this bingo hall session is computed as follows:

Gross proceeds from sales	$3,250
Prize payouts	900
Cost of paper bingo sheets	21
Total cost of sales	921
Gross profit	$2,329

Grind Bingo

Grind bingo uses reusable bingo cards. Grind bingo usually is played faster than paper bingo. Grind bingo has cards of one or more colors. The card colors determine both the price for the cards and the prize payouts. Example:

Blue cards — cost 50¢ each but pay out $10.00
Brown cards — cost 75¢ each but pay out $20.00
Red cards — cost $1.00 each but pay out $25.00
Gold cards — cost $2.00 each but pay out $200.00

The player obtains a bag of chips. When a number is called, the player puts a chip on the number called. When bingo is called, the winner receives the prize money for that game based on the type of card that the player got. The player places money in front for the operator to collect before the game begins. The money placed in front is dependent upon the color and the number cards the player is using, e.g., $0.50 for blue cards, $0.75 for brown cards, etc.

Grind bingo income.   Grind bingo income is determined simply by multiplying the average number of players times the average number of games per day times the average income per game. The key elements in determining gross income are the following:

1. The number of players during each game.
2. The number of games being played during the session. This usually averages about 20 to 26 games per hour.
3. The amount of funds collected from the floor based upon the average type (color) of cards being played.

This type of bingo is more labor intensive since it requires each set of tables to have a "floor" person to collect the coins. However, the "floor" person has to turn in a tally sheet and the coins to the manager after each game or session. This type of bingo is often called "ten cent bingo." Grind bingo callers must call the letter and the number, i.e., B five, I twenty, N thirty-three, and etc. These types of bingo halls are generally found in lower-income neighborhoods since the costs to play seem low. In actuality, it costs the players almost the same as paper bingo.

Lightning Bingo

Lightning bingo is about the same as grind bingo, except that it uses cards that have some "highlighted" numbers. Players use a reusable card and play with coins. The players must get the highlighted numbers to win. The caller does not call out the letters, but only the numbers. It is called "lightning bingo" since the games only last about 10 to 15 seconds. Gross proceeds for lightning bingo are computed the same way as for grind bingo. In many states, this form of bingo is illegal since it does not call out letters and is classified as a numbers racket.

Pari-Mutuel Wagering

Pari-mutuel wagering is gambling at various types of racetracks or sporting events. The types of racetracks used usually involve dog, car, and horse races. Jai alai is the most common sport for pari-mutuel wagering. Many states have legalized pari-mutuel wagering on either racing or sporting events or both. Like other types of gambling activities, pari-mutuel wagering has its own terminology. "Pari-mutuel" means each player is competing against another player, and not against the track.

Terminology

Understanding the terms of pari-mutuel wagering will help the examiner understand the mechanics of pari-mutuel wagering. The following are the most common terms used:

Across the board — Three equal wagers placed on one animal to win, to place, and to show.

Boxing — The bettor selects any number of animals (three or more) in a race. If the selections finish one, two, and three in any order, the bettor wins. In a Quinella box, if any two selections finish one and two in any order, the bettor wins.

Breakage — The difference between true mutuel odds and lesser, rounded amounts given to winning players. Breakage usually is divided between track and state.

Chalk — A term which refers to the favorite in a race.

Closing odds — The odds displayed on the tote board after wagering closes.

Coupled — Two or more animals belonging to the same owner.

Daily double — A wager whereby the bettor must select the winners of two consecutive races, usually the first and second races, prior to the first race.

Daily triple — A wager whereby the bettor must select the winners of three consecutive races.

Entry — Two or more animals in a race owned by the same person(s) or trained by the same trainer are termed an "entry" and coupled as a single betting unit; a bet on one coupled horse is a bet on all horses it is coupled with.

Exacta — A wager that a bettor wins when the better selects the first and second place finishers in a race in exact order.

Field — An animal grouped with other animals as a single betting interest in races where the number of starters exceeds the number of betting interests the tote system of the track can handle; a bet on one field animal is a bet on all animals in the mutuel field.

Handicapping — Studying race histories to select the best wagering options.

Handle — The total amount wagered on a race or on a day's races.

Hedging — The art of covering the original bet by placing an additional wager to cover the potential loss of the first. An example would be buying a $2 place or show ticket to insure a $2 win bet.

In-the-money — Finishing first, second, or third.

Minus pool — In pari-mutuel betting, a situation in which so much money is bet on an animal (usually to show) that the pool is insufficient after the take and breakage to pay holders of winning tickets the legal minimum odds of 1 to 10 or 20. The track is required to make up the difference from its own funds.

Morning line — The track handicapper's estimate of the probable odds for each animal at post time.

Mutuel field — A grouping of animals as a single betting interest in races where the number of starters exceeds the number of betting interests the track tote system can handle; a bet on one field animal is a bet on all mutuel field animals.

Odds on — Odds that are less than even money ($1 to $1).

Off-the-board — Failure to finish first, second, or third (in the money).

On the nose — A bet that an animal will win.

Overlay — An underbet animal, a good value.

Parlay — A wagering format that allows each player to compete against the other players rather than against the track.

Perfecta — To win this wager, the animals must finish first and second in the exact order of finish.

Pick-3 — A bettor wins when the bettor selects the winners of three consecutive races on one ticket, which the bettor must buy before the first of the three races begins.

Pick-6 — A bettor wins when the bettor selects the winners of six consecutive races on one ticket, which the bettor must buy before the first of the six races begins. If no one correctly picks all six winners, half the pot will be paid to patrons correctly picking the most winners, and the other half will "carry over" to the pick-6 pool on the next racing day.

Place — A bettor wins when the bettor's selection finishes first or second.

Pool — The total amount of money wagered on any one type of bet (win pool, show pool, exacta pool, etc).

Quinella — A bettor wins when the bettor selects two animals finishing first and second in a race, regardless of order.

Show — A bettor wins when the bettor's selection finishes first or second or third.

Superfecta — A bettor wins when the bettor's selection finishes first, second, third, and fourth in the exact order of finish.

Takeout — The percentage of betting pools taken out by the state and the racetrack, with the track putting its share of the takeout toward race purses and expenses. It also means the withholding on winning tickets over $5,000, which are turned over to the IRS.

Totalizator (tote) — The system of computers and electronic components tied to the pari-mutuel ticket issuing machines that calculates the odds to $1 and computes the various winning payoffs.

Tote board — An electronic board in the infield displaying approximate odds, amounts bet, track condition, post time, time of day, result of race, inquiry or objection sign if a foul is claimed, running time, and payoff prices.

Trifecta (triple) — A wager in which the winning bettor picks the first three finishers of a race in exact order.

Wheel — To make an exotic wager (e.g. exacta or daily double) using a single "key" animal with the balance of the field (in the case of an exacta) or all the animals in the other race (in the case of a daily double).

Win — A bettor wins when his selection finishes first.

Odds and Payoff

The following chart is the odds on dogs or horses and the payoff to winners based on a $2.00 bet.

Odds	Payoff	Odds	Payoff	Odds	Payoff
1–5	$2.40	9–5	$5.60	8–1	$18.00
2–5	2.80	2–1	6.00	9–1	20.00
1–2	3.00	5–2	7.00	10–1	22.00
3–5	3.20	3–1	8.00	12–1	26.00
4–5	3.60	7–2	9.00	15–1	32.00
1–1	4.00	4–1	10.00	20–1	42.00
6–5	4.40	9–2	11.00	30–1	62.00
7–5	4.80	5–1	12.00	40–1	82.00
3–2	5.00	6–1	14.00	50–1	102.00
8–5	5.20	7–1	16.00	99–1	200.00

Ten Percenting

Ten percenting is illegal at both the federal level and in most states. Ten percenting is a scheme whereby the true winner of a bet sells the winning ticket to another person for a ten percent fee, thus the term *ten percenting*. The true winner of the winning ticket does not want the track to file a W-2G with the IRS. If the winning ticket pays off over $5,000, then the track is required to withhold 28 percent from the winnings. A ten percenter takes the winning ticket to the track teller. The ten percenter fills out the W-2G, collects the winnings; keeps 10 percent of the winnings, and gives the balance to the true winner. In the case of winning tickets that require income tax withholding, the ten percenter gives the true winner the balance of the winnings after the income tax withholding and the ten percenter's 10 percent have been deducted. The IRS only requires W-2Gs to be filed when the winnings exceed $1,000. The ten percenter collects losing tickets off the track floor; gathering enough losing tickets to offset the winnings. If there is income tax withholding, the ten percenter files an individual income tax return to claim the winnings offset by the losses, which results in an income tax refund.

Indicators

There are many indicators that show a person may be ten percenting at the tracks:

1. A very large amount of winnings from any particular track that requires the filing of W-2Gs.
2. A very large amount of winnings from any particular track with only "take out" (withholding of income tax) W-2Gs.
3. The bettor presents losing tickets that show two or more tickets with the same date and time. Some tracks use systems that do not show the times on the tickets; however, the tracks can provide data regarding when the tickets were purchased.
4. The bettor presents losing tickets from different tracks that were purchased on the same date only minutes apart. That the tracks are miles apart means that it was impossible to go from one track to the other within the time frame.
5. The bettor presents losing tickets from the same teller. The teller history for that day shows a series of tickets being purchased in sequence in which none is a winning ticket. The bettor does not have all of the sequential tickets that were purchased in a series (multiple tickets purchased at once).
6. The bettor has a full-time job, but presents tickets that show the bettor was at the track all day when in fact the bettor was at work.
7. The bettor provides losing tickets in such quantity that it is impossible to purchase in any 1 day.
8. The bettor's losing tickets do not show any constant pattern. Bettors usually have a pattern of betting.
9. The bettor has no other sources of income but W-2Gs.
10. The bettor does not complete the W-2G form correctly. Ten percenters sometimes use false social security numbers, or false names, or both. Sometimes they use other people's names and social security numbers.
11. The bettor has a lot of winnings from one track, but has large losses from another track.
12. The bettor has a criminal past of illegal gambling. Criminals who are involved in gambling activities go from one form of gambling to another when they hear or feel that law enforcement is looking into a particular type of illegal gambling.
13. A cash-flow schedule of the winning and losing tickets is prepared. If the bettor does not have any other sources of funds, then any negative cash balances clearly indicate that the bettor is a ten percenter. No one can have negative cash on hand.

More than one of these indicators should be present before an examiner considers the bettor a ten percenter. If many of these indicators are present, then the bettor is a ten percenter. However, for item 13; this clearly shows by itself that the bettor is a ten percenter since no one can have negative cash on hand.

Violation

For federal purposes, as well as in many states, ten percenting is illegal. It is illegal in that taxes are not properly reported. The true winner is not paying the income taxes on the winnings, both federal and state. The ten percenter is not paying taxes on the winnings either. Anyone who signs W-2G signs the form under penalties of perjury; which is also a felony. The signer of the W-2G also declares, "no other person is entitled to any part of these payments." In essence, the ten percenter is committing two felony counts, i.e., tax evasion and making a false statement. Each signed W-2G form is a separate felony count.

Gambling

Many people gamble in various ways. Some of the common methods were discussed above because these are either illegal or can be illegal based upon circumstances. Some gamblers, as described in the movies, play various kinds of card games. Card games are basically illegal in most states if they involve betting, but because most card games are privately held, law enforcement does not get involved unless something brings it to its attention, i.e., extortion, murder, organized crime, loan sharking, etc. Many states now have lotteries. Those states use the profits from lotteries to help finance education, roads, and other types of services. Private lottery operations are illegal in all states. Bingo is legal in most states provided that it benefits charitable organizations. Organized crime groups get involved in illegal gambling. In some areas, they control illegal gambling operations. People who try to set up a gambling operation in an area controlled by organized crime can find themselves at odds, to say the least. Illegal gambling offers organized crime groups the ability to skim huge profits.

Fraud Prevention for Consumers 17

Introduction

There are many precautions that the consumer can take to prevent fraud. There is an old cliché that goes "an ounce of prevention is worth a pound of cure." This is particularly true in the area of crime. If consumers will take the appropriate steps and procedures to prevent fraud, then their loses can be nonexistent or minimal. In many cases, fraud can be prevented by making appropriate inquires while more investigative procedures are required in other cases. It should be stressed here that taking all precautions that can be taken does not guarantee that consumers will not become victims; however, it will reduce the chances. There are many "con" artists, who, despite all precautions, can "take your shoes while you're standing in them." Therefore, the procedures and precautions taken to prevent fraud do not guarantee anyone from being a fraud victim. It is also not true that all people or businesses are in the business of committing fraud.

Consumers

Consumers are vulnerable to many kinds of fraud schemes. These fraud schemes range from small car repairs to large investment schemes. Statistics shows that the elderly, women, and minorities are victimized the most. However, in recent years, practically everyone has become vulnerable to fraud schemes. Even well-educated and knowledgeable people have become victims. "Con" people are very personable and friendly. The following paragraphs describe the more common fraud schemes that consumers will face. It should be remembered that the "consumer should beware." One advertiser said an "educated consumer is the best customer;" however, it can be said, "an educated consumer has the best defense against becoming a fraud victim."

Automobile Purchases

There are automobile dealerships that operate in both an unethical manner and fraudulently. An auto dealer will advertise a particular vehicle for a certain price. When the consumer goes to look at this particular vehicle, the salesperson says that it is out of stock and will try to direct the consumer to another model, which usually costs more. Using high-pressure sales tactics, the salesperson will get the consumer to purchase the more expensive car. This is true for both new and used car dealerships. If you have decided upon a particular vehicle that you want, then you should inquire when this model will become available. If the model will not become available anytime soon, then you should walk out and ignore any salesperson's "deals." In the case of a used car dealership, you should ask the salesperson if a mechanic of your own choosing could inspect and test the car. If the salesperson denies your request, then you should not waste your time in looking at the car. Most likely, the vehicle is a lemon. If the salesperson approves your request, then retain a mechanic that will check the vehicle out, and follow the mechanic's advice to purchase or not. If you are going to finance the vehicle, it is recommended that you arrange for your own financing in advance. Most finance companies, banks, etc., will approve vehicle loans up to certain dollar amounts. The car dealerships have made arrangements with particular finance companies in which they will get a "rebate." These financing arrangements will charge higher interest rates on the vehicle loans so that they can cover these rebates. These arrangements are not illegal.

Business Investment

Many people are losing their jobs because of economic conditions, "downsizing" of companies, and a whole host of other reasons. Many people are looking to acquire or start up their own business. The problem of starting up your own business is having the necessary capital and knowledge to do so. Many investors will turn to a business broker who can offer a wide range of existing businesses that are for sale. The broker may be legitimate but the prospective business may not be. Business owners will try to inflate the books to show higher sales and profits in order to entice someone to buy when, in fact, the business is operating at a loss. Some owners will go so far to say that they are taking out funds that are not recorded on the books. They'll even brag about it. This is an indication of fraud, both as to federal and state taxes and to the prospective buyer. An established business is a better investment than to start a business from scratch; however, an established business could be a worse investment than starting from scratch. This is particularly true if the buyer does not know what to look out for or how to evaluate the prospective business. The following guidelines are provided.

1. **Financial statements.** The prospective buyer should obtain financial statements for not only the current year but also the past 4 years as a minimum. In addition, tax returns should be obtained for the last 3 years. These financial statements and tax returns should be analyzed to determine the trends and conditions of the business. "Are sales increasing each year? Are assets remaining steady or increasing? Is inventory increasing with sales?" Further auditing procedures are explained in Chapter 23. If the buyer does not know how to analyze and audit the statements, then an accountant should be retained to do so. The accountant's fees will be much less than the possible loss the buyer could incur by acquiring a bad business.

2. **Bank statements.** The prospective buyer should obtain the bank statements for at least the past 2 years along with the current year. The deposits should be compared with the gross receipts reported on the tax returns and the financial statements. Explanations

should be sought for any large differences, especially when inventory, liabilities, and assets do not increase.

   3. **Observation.** The prospective buyer should visit the business location on various occasions. The purpose is to see what the customer traffic is in the business and if the assets and inventory exist as purported on the financial statements.

   4. **Purchase price.** The seller will always ask more than the business is worth. When businesses have been in existence for many years, owners will have a personal attachment and concern for whoever takes over. Therefore, they will want much more than what the business is worth. As a prospective buyer, you will want to acquire the business at a reasonable price. As a general guideline, the prospective buyer should acquire the business based upon the following formula:

a.   Net worth of the business.
b.   Add to the net worth the accumulated depreciation and amortization.
c.   Add any shareholder loans (this item shows up as an outside liability).
d.   This gives the total equity by the owner.
e.   Add the yearly officer salaries and bonuses.
f.   Add the yearly profits based upon the time frame in which you plan to finance part of the purchase.
g.   This gives the purchase price that the prospective buyer should pay for the business.

The profits can be considered the goodwill of the business. If the business is acquired solely for cash, then goodwill can be paid based upon the net profits of the business. However, goodwill should not be paid for more than 5 years of profits. If there are no profits, then there is no goodwill.

   From the seller's point of view, business owners should not expect that they could get more than what the above formula shows. However, the seller will have to evaluate the buyer when the seller is going to take a note or payment plan for part of the purchase price. The seller will have to evaluate the prospective purchaser in the following ways:

1.   Payment of note. Can the business pay off the note without any hardship to the buyer? If the formula described above is followed, then the business can pay off the note. It should be noted that the prospective buyer's only source of income would be the business.
2.   Buyer. The buyer should be investigated if a note is part of the purchase price. The following questions should be answered.
   a. Does the prospective buyer have any expertise in this type of business? If not, how much time will the prospective buyer require for training? Some training is required to give the prospective buyer some knowledge of the operations. He/she will have to know the vendors and their policies, banking relationships, employees, regular customers, and the policies and procedures the business has been following.
   b. What is the character and integrity of the prospective buyer? References should be checked. Sellers should be wary of references with answering machines. County records should be checked for any criminal or civil actions. Also, previous employers should be contacted regarding job performance and character.

c. What is the credit rating of the prospective buyer? A credit report should be obtained from the credit bureau. It will show promptly the prospective buyer's record of paying off debts. If the prospective buyer has a record of delinquent payments, then the seller can expect the same.

Accountants

Many people go to accountants for various purposes. Among those purposes are to prepare their tax returns, accounting advice and services, management advice, and audits for their business. However, there are some accountants who are unscrupulous. In tax return preparation, they will decrease income, or increase deductions, or both. The taxpayer gets a large refund. When the IRS or other taxing authority audits the taxpayer, the taxpayer has to repay the shortage along with penalties and interest. The penalties and interest can double or even triple the original tax liability. Only Certified Public Accountants (CPA) and Enrolled Agents (EA) are allowed to represent taxpayers before the IRS and most other taxing authorities. These individuals have the appropriate training and experience. There are many individuals and companies that prepare tax returns that are not qualified to represent taxpayers. There are some national chains that have offices across the country. Some of these national chains offer 6-week courses to train their tax preparers. When these tax preparers complete the course they think that they have become tax "experts." This is ironic in that it takes nearly 6 months to train revenue agents in the Federal Tax Code and Regulations. The major problem with "nonlicensed" accountants is that they are negligent due to incompetence, whereas "licensed" tax preparers, who have the appropriate training and education, sometimes prepare fraudulent tax returns to obtain higher fees. The taxpayer thinks that the accountant is very good since the taxpayer is getting a refund larger than usual. Taxpayers should consider the following factors when having their tax returns completed.

1. Fees. The charges for services should be known before engaging the accountant. Fees are charged either by the number of forms to be completed or by the time required to complete the returns.
2. License. If the taxpayer has a complex return, then a CPA or EA should be retained since they have the training and experience. Also, the CPA or EA can represent the taxpayer in an audit. Higher-income and complex tax returns tend to be audited more than simple returns.
3. Check return. Taxpayers should review their own returns before signing and sending off. Remember, the taxpayer provided the information to the preparer; therefore, the taxpayer should compare the information provided with the information on the return to see if they match. Taxpayers should keep in mind that they are responsible for the accuracy of the return and not the accountant.

People who have their own business retain an accountant for various services, principally, preparing various federal and state tax returns, periodic financial statements, and management advice. The greater use of the services leads to greater contact, reliance, and trust on the accountant. However, the accountant may be a crook. There are many cases where the accountant has absconded with client's funds. The following precautions should be followed to prevent this:

1. The accountant should never be a signatory on any bank account.
2. All tax returns should be signed and mailed in by the taxpayer and not by the accountant.
3. The accountant should not have any custodial control over any personal or business assets.
4. Investments proposed by the accountant should be reviewed by someone else, i.e., a certified financial planner. Accountants are trained to evaluate past performance, not future expectations. Financial planners are trained to evaluate investments in terms of future returns.
5. The accountant should not be retained as trustee for any estate or trust. However, the accountant should be used to prepare tax returns and financial statements. This serves as a way to oversee the affairs of a trustee.

Attorneys

Fraud that is committed by attorneys usually falls into two areas. The first area is overcharging the client for services. The second area is a violation of trust where the attorney outright steals from the client. Some unscrupulous attorneys, in conjunction with doctors, operate an "ambulance-chasing" scam. In personal injury cases, lawyers are paid on contingent fees. This means the lawyer and the client agree that the fee will be based on a percentage of the settlement or court award in the case. If no settlement or court award is made, the lawyer will not be paid. This type of law practice requires a high volume of cases to insure a steady cash flow. Lawyers running personal injury "mills" are not anxious to engage in litigation. They rely on the insurance company's desire to settle quickly; to avoid the expense a company must absorb by going to court to fight a claim. The lawyer will entice accident victims to cooperate by promising a big "payday" from the insurance company. The big payday often never arrives for the victim, since medical fees, runner fees, and contingency fees may be deducted before the victim gets his or her share. Some ambulance-chasing lawyers blatantly rip off their clients by forging the signature of the victim on the insurance company check. Even if the victims discover their lawyers cheated them, they are reluctant to report fraud, since they too may have conspired to defraud the insurance company or appear to have done so. The consumer, therefore, should take the following measures in dealing with personal injury cases:

1. Consumers should consult their own doctors as to the extent of the injuries before consulting a lawyer.
2. Consumers should obtain a complete statement of all the charges and evaluate their reasonableness.
3. Consumers should discuss and obtain a copy of the engagement contract from the attorney.
4. Instead of using a doctor the lawyer recommends, consumers should use their own doctor. It is almost certain that the doctor's fees by the lawyer-recommended doctor would be above those normally charged by others.

5. Consumers should ask their local or state consumer affairs departments about any complaints or disciplinary actions against the lawyer. County public records should be searched for any lawsuits against the lawyer. A large number of complaints or lawsuits is an indication of an unscrupulous attorney.

6. Ambulance-chasing lawyers use people called "runners" to obtain business. The "runners" will approach victims soon after the accident, sometimes at the scene. They will give a lawyer's business card and urge the victim to call a certain attorney. They also promise big "paydays." This is a clear sign of an attorney that the consumer will want to avoid.

The second area of fraudulent lawyers is the position of trust. The client is relying on the attorney to handle certain financial matters. The attorney, in handling these financial matters, embezzles the funds of the client. This happens a lot in areas of real estate sales, probating an estate, and performing trustee duties. This can be done very blatantly or very clandestinely. Few attorneys actually take their client's funds and flee; however, many attorneys will pad expenses, overcharge fees, and inflate bills. The client should then review these expenses before taking the final settlement.

Bankers

Bankers can be thieves in various ways. First, they can embezzle funds from the bank using various schemes. Second, they can overcharge for their services. One way to steal from customers is to provide encoded deposit slips for their own account instead of for the customer's account. Many banks have tried to prevent this by not having deposit slips displayed in the lobby. However, some customers will not have any deposit slips and will ask their banker for them. The banker then gives them some with an encoded account number not belonging to the customer. The customer makes a deposit, but the funds go to the banker. When customers make deposits using "counter" deposit slips, they should check the encoded number on the bottom to see if it matches their account number on their checks.

Bankers also overcharge for obtaining a bank loan. In the case of car and boat loans, they will inflate the expenses of obtaining an appraisal for the used car or boat. In recent years, this has been a common practice in granting home equity loans. Also, bankers charge a high rate of interest or large "points" for customers obtaining home equity loans. Points are bank fees for processing loan applications, principally, real estate loans. Customers should be wary of points over 4 percent. Home mortgages should not be more than 3 points over the prime rate. The prime rate is what banks charge their preferred customers. This is published daily in most newspapers across the country.

With the advent of automatic teller machines (ATMs), unscrupulous bankers have been able to embezzle funds from customer accounts. The banker can get "pin" numbers if the bank's internal controls are deficient. Also, they can obtain duplicate cards, by alleged customer request. The banker, with duplicate ATM cards and pin numbers, can access the customer's account and withdraw funds. To prevent this, customers should review and reconcile their bank statements every month; otherwise, these withdrawals by the banker will go undetected.

Credit Cards

With the widespread use of credit cards, credit card fraud has become an easy source of income for criminals. Some bank credit cards, i.e., Visa and MasterCard, can be used at ATM machines for cash withdrawals. However, most credit card thieves will not have access to "pin" numbers. Credit card thieves are usually organized and have more than one person involved. Some credit cards are stolen from the mail at some point before the customer receives them. Other thieves obtain the credit card or the numbers where the customer has made a purchase. The thieves use the customer's number or credit card to make additional purchases. The goods purchased are fenced to a store or through a store that the thieves control, or hocked at a pawnshop. Some business establishments will make additional charges on customer's credit cards for services or purchases not rendered. Counterfeiting credit cards is becoming more prevalent. For the credit card holder, the following precautions should be followed:

1. If you have applied for a credit card, the credit card company will notify you of approval and approximately when the credit card will be sent. If you have not received the credit card by the time frame specified, then you should make inquiries about it.
2. When making purchases, you should always obtain a copy of the charge slip and any carbon paper used. You never rely on the business establishment to destroy the carbon paper. The carbon paper shows your account number and expiration date, which can be used to make purchases.
3. When making purchases, you should ensure that you get your credit card returned to you.
4. You should always review your statements for the charges made, and ask yourself, "Did I make this charge?" Even if you are not sure, you should make inquiries to the credit card company. You should save your card receipts and compare them with your billing statements. Report promptly and in writing any questionable charges to the card issuer.
5. You should notify the credit card company if you get a statement for a credit card that you do not have. Also, it is advisable to notify your local police about this.
6. You should never pay a fee when applying for a credit card. There are "boiler room" operators who advertise that they can obtain a credit card even if you have bad credit or no credit. For them to get a customer a credit card, they require that the applicant submit an application and a "processing" fee of anywhere from $100 and up. In some states, this processing fee is illegal. Applicants will find that they will not get a credit card and that they are out the fee.
7. You should sign your new cards as soon as they arrive.
8. You should carry your cards separately from your wallet. Also, you should keep a record of your card numbers, their expiration dates, and the phone number and address of each company in a secure place.
9. You should avoid signing a blank receipt, whenever possible. Draw a line through blank spaces above the total when you sign card receipts.
10. You should obtain and destroy all carbons and incorrect receipts.
11. You should notify card companies in advance of a change of address.

12. You should never lend your card to anyone.
13. You should never leave cards or receipts lying around.
14. You should never put your card number on a postcard or on the outside of an envelope.
15. You should never give your number over the phone unless you are initiating a transaction with a company you know is reputable. If you have questions about the company, then check with your local consumer protection office or Better Business Bureau before ordering.

Boat Purchases

Boat dealers operate in the same manner as automobile dealers. The rules that apply to automobiles, as explained earlier, also apply to boats. For large used boats, banks require a "hull" appraisal and certification by an appraiser. The prospective buyer should make inquiries with various appraisers in the area about fees for such hull certifications. In some cases, the banks inflate the appraiser's fee.

Contractors

Many people either want to build their "dream" house or remodel their current house. This involves building a house from the ground up or adding a room addition, reroofing, installing new windows and doors, or remodeling a room. Many people will buy new homes that were built by a land developer in a planned community. The contractors who commit fraud do so by either overcharging or by using inferior materials, and usually both. Consumers usually will call a contractor listed in the Yellow Pages of the telephone directory or may be solicited over the telephone. Telephone solicitors are more prone to being scam artists. Also, their prices are usually high. Land developers will build a model for customers to inspect before their house is built. The model will usually be built to local building codes and with high-grade material; however, the buyer's house will be built using inferior materials and poor workmanship. There are danger signs that the consumer should be aware of in order to prevent being a victim:

1. *Advertisements.* The consumer should check listings in the telephone directory. The consumer should obtain business cards and contract proposals. Many states require a contractor license number on all advertisements.
2. *Down payment.* The consumer should never make a large down payment. Down payments should never be more than 25 percent of the total contract price. If the contract is being financed, the down payment should never be more than what the finance company or bank requires.
3. *Partial payment.* In case of large jobs or building a whole house, partial payments should equal the amount of costs incurred by the contractor.
4. *Permits.* The contractor should always get the permits required. No one else should get permits. If the consumer obtains the permits, then it leaves the consumer liable for anything that goes wrong, including an injury to an employee. Small jobs do not always require a permit, but you should contact your local building department

for specific requirements. The contractor should post the permit before starting the job. Most states require building permits to be posted before the job is started.

5. *Proposal and contract.* The consumer should always get a proposal and contract in writing. No written agreement means no legal recourse.

6. *Insurance.* The contractor in most states is required to have insurance. Consumers should obtain a copy of their insurance binder before the work begins.

7. *Payments.* The consumer should always pay by check and not cash. The check should always be payable to the company and not the individual.

8. *Licenses.* The contractor should have both an occupational and a state contractor's license.

9. *References.* The contractor should be willing to provide references regarding his reputation, abilities, experience, and knowledge. Consumers should see previous work done and ask previous customers their likes and dislikes.

10. *License board.* The consumer should call the state licensing board to see if the contractor is actually licensed. There are some unlicensed contractors who use another contractor's license number.

11. *"Bird-dogging."* In the case of large remodeling jobs or house construction, the consumer should retain a person who knows the construction industry, to act as an inspector during the course of the construction. The "inspector" should report only to the consumer.

12. *Bids.* Consumers should always get three bids for any contracting job. They should be sure that the contractors are bidding for the same job for comparison purposes. A bid for apples cannot be compared with a bid for oranges. Also, the consumer should never pay for a bid.

13. *Identification.* The consumer should ask for and get identification of the contractor or principals of the company. This should be done at the time of signing the contract. This will be helpful to law enforcement if the contractor skips town before the job is finished.

14. *Complaints.* The consumer should file complaints with local and state regulators and/or consumer affairs offices. They can act quickly in remedying the situation if notified early. Some state regulators have police powers, thus can take appropriate action on the consumers behalf.

Doctors

There are unscrupulous doctors who commit fraud in various ways. One common way is overbilling for services to insurance companies. This is particularly true in automobile accidents, Medicare or Medicaid, and worker's compensation claims. Another way is charging for tests that were not performed either to the insurance company or the individual. Still another is selling prescription drugs that are not needed by the patient.

The patient should take the following steps to help prevent overcharges.

1. The patient should check the local physician referral service for a recommended doctor.
2. Once the patient has located a physician, then the patient should check public records for any lawsuits. This should show any malpractice or financial lawsuits.
3. The patient should ask for fee schedule up-front before seeing the doctor.

4. The patient should inspect the bill for services. If there are charges for services that the patient feels were not performed, then inquiries should be made with the doctor.
5. When a doctor bills the insurance company for services, then the patient should review the bill upon receipt and notify the insurance company of any possible overcharges. Remember, inflated or nonperformed services mean higher insurance premiums because the insurance company has to pay higher claims.

These rules apply not only to doctors, but also to dentists, chiropractors, opticians, and other health care professionals. Hospital bills should definitely be examined since many hospitals will overcharge for services for people with health insurance to make up the losses for nonpaying patients.

Patients who purchase prescription drugs when there is no need put the doctor and patient at risk of being detected by law enforcement for drug possession and/or drug trafficking.

Insurance

Although most insurance agents are reputable, some unscrupulous agents may pocket premiums or use high-pressure tactics to gain a large commission. Three of the more common agent schemes follow:

1. **Pocketing.** In pocketing schemes, the agent issues a binder indicating the customer is insured against specific losses but never forwards the customer's premium payments to the insurance company. The signs of an unscrupulous agent are

a. The agency employs a large number of support staff and has only one licensed agent (who is frequently absent).
b. The insured, uneducated, young, or otherwise "high-risk," are usually the main victims.
c. The agent only accepts premium payments in cash or money orders.
d. No policy is received or provided.

2. **Sliding.** The term "sliding" means the art of including additional coverage with that requested by the consumer. The extra charges are hidden in the total premium. Since the consumer does not know about the extra charges, claims against that coverage are practically nonexistent, and the profits for the agent are astounding. Since many consumers do not read their insurance policies, the crime may go undetected. Coverage that is easy to slide is motor club memberships, accidental death, and travel accident policies, which carry premiums of less than $100 per year. The indicators of sliding are

a. The "breakdown of coverage" provided by the agent lists coverage in addition to that requested.
b. Insurance applications and other forms are quickly shuffled in front of the consumer, and a signature is required on each.
c. The agent offers a "package deal" which includes accidental death, travel accident, or motor coverage.

3. **Twisting.** Twisting is nothing more than the replacement of existing policies with new ones, where the primary reason for doing so is to enrich the agent. Commissions are higher on first-year sales; therefore, the consumer will pay more in premiums for less coverage. The signs of twisting are

a. The agent suggests the policy, which is less than 1 year old, be replaced with a new and "better" one.
b. When the consumer declines replacement coverage, the agent employs high-pressure tactics.

Insurance companies, either with or without the agent's knowledge and cooperation, offer policies to consumers with the intent of not providing coverage. Most states have insurance regulatory agencies, some with enforcement authority. These insurance companies usually sell their products through boiler-room operations or direct mail. Their advertisements will usually show premiums below the industry average for the area. All types of insurance are affected, i.e., auto, life, health, and business. The consumer should take the following precautions:

1. The consumer should check with the state insurance commission that the insurance company is registered or licensed. The consumer should never purchase a policy with an unlicensed insurance company.
2. The consumer should consult an insurance advisory service, i.e., Best. These advisory services evaluate the insurance company regarding its product lines, premiums, and claims. It also rates insurance companies from bad to good based upon their financial conditions and stability. The consumer should check these insurance advisory services as to the company's financial condition and compare the premium rates with other insurance companies. Most libraries have these advisory services, usually in their reference section.

Stockbrokers

Unscrupulous stockbrokers perpetrate fraud by either selling worthless securities or by buying and selling their clients' securities. Stockbrokers get commission on both sales and purchases of securities. Securities consist of stocks, bonds, or mutual funds. Commodity brokers, like stockbrokers, buy and sell various kinds of commodities for their clients. They also get commissions on both sales and purchases. Fraud schemes used by both stock and commodity brokers follow.

Clients' Accounts

Some investors will allow their stockbroker, or their commodity broker, to buy and sell securities for them without consultation. This is not a good practice for the investor. It gives the broker a "blank" check. The broker will sell and purchase securities for the investor. Most of the time, the sales will result in losses. The broker will get a commission on both sales and purchases. Investors will finally learn that their investment has been depleted. When investors open up a "margin" account, they automatically allow the broker to liquidate their account when they fall below the margin requirements. Margin refers to the amount of funds required to be deposited with the broker. The Federal Reserve Board of Governors sets the margin requirements and changes them from time to time. The Securities and Exchange Commission (SEC) is responsible for investigation and enforcement. These margin requirements are set at a percentage of the purchase price of securities. Unscrupulous brokers will sell securities or commodities to earn a commission and tell investors that they fell below the margin requirements. These brokers do not notify or give the investor time to meet the margin requirements. The investor should take the following preventive measures.

1. Do not allow the broker to buy and sell without consulting the investor.
2. Investors should advise the broker to contact the investor when margin requirements have to be met, if using margin accounts.
3. Investors should keep track of the market prices of their securities. A brokerage statement, which is provided each month, gives the market values of their securities. Investors should review these brokerage statements very closely.
4. Investors should check with the SEC that the broker is licensed. Brokers must be licensed with the SEC as well as with state authorities.
5. Investors should ask for and check out references of the broker regarding his or her character, integrity, and professional abilities.
6. Investors should check public records regarding any lawsuits or criminal actions against the broker.

Worthless Securities

Unscrupulous brokers, both stock and commodities, will sell worthless or phony securities to investors. In the 1980s, there were many corporate mergers. For one corporation to buy out another corporation, the purchasing corporation had to issue bonds. These bonds came to be called "junk" bonds since personal or real property did not secure them. The interest rate was very high, sometimes, as high as 18 percent or more. Issuers found that they could not pay the interest on the bonds since the profits were not high enough to cover the interest expense. The issuing corporation had to declare bankruptcy. This led to the bondholders losing their investment. Some brokers will sell securities to investors knowing that they are on the verge of bankruptcy or in bankruptcy. Some brokers will even sell false or stolen securities to investors. These are some instances of fraud by brokers. Another area of stock and commodity fraud is selling securities at artificially inflated prices, which the broker has created. This requires collusion between two or more investment companies. The stocks or commodities are traded between cooperating members, which drives the stock value up on the over-the-counter securities market. It is then sold to the public. These securities can be either registered or nonregistered. This results in large profits by boosting the value of the shares to artificially high levels. Organized crime engages in the purchase, promotion, and sale of numerous securities. These sales are made through various boiler-room operations, which are controlled by these individuals. Even though stock and commodity fraud and manipulation is complex and sophisticated, there are steps that can be taken to prevent becoming a victim:

1. The investor should never purchase securities from telephone solicitors. Invariably, these are false securities.
2. The investor should examine registration statements, which are available to the public. Title 15 USC 77(f) requires registration of securities with the SEC if they are sold by mail or in interstate commerce. Section 77(g) and (aa) prescribe the contents of registration statements.
3. The investor should always obtain a prospectus. Law specifically prescribes the contents and timing of the prospectus. The investor should read these prospectuses and evaluate the risk of purchasing these securities.
4. Bonds should be purchased based upon the current interest rates. Bonds showing high rates of returns should be either avoided or investigated further. Further investigation should encompass the collateral of the bonds, the ability of the issuer to redeem the bonds, and the market value of the collateral at a minimum.
5. The stock market quotes should be reviewed over the past 2 or more years for any security or commodity. The investor needs to evaluate the trend for this security or commodity. If there is an upward swing in market value during a short period of time, usually less than a year, then the investor should try to determine the reason. If the security or commodity did not have increased earnings or dividends, then this is a danger sign of stock manipulation and the stock should not be purchased.
6. The investor should find out if the issuer of the stock or bond is in bankruptcy or reorganization under the federal bankruptcy law. This can be determined by either calling another investment firm or consulting any of the investment services at a local library.
7. There are investment advisory services, i.e., Standard and Poor's, and Moody's, which publish information about the company or commodity. This information encompasses earnings, dividends, market values and trends, assets, net worth, and management profiles. In addition, they have a rating system which evaluates the security or commodity from bad to good investment potential. The investor should consult these investment advisory services.

Telemarketing

Telemarketing is a fast growing business. Many telemarketers are legitimate; however, there are many fraudulent ones. The scheme involves selling products or services that are not delivered. Telemarketing is referred to as a boiler-room operation. It involves hiring telephone solicitors who call customers using high-pressure sales tactics. The customer orders the product or service and makes payment in advance. Either the product or service is not provided or an inferior product or service is provided. In most cases, these products or services cost more than what is available in local stores. There are many variations. In one scheme the telemarketer tells customers that they have won a prize, but, in order to receive it, they must send in money for shipping, handling, or taxes. The customer sends in the money, but either receives an inferior product or does not receive any product. The unscrupulous telemarketer will make misrepresentations about products or services. This is evident in such statements as "the best deal or investment ever made" or "it's too good to be true." When contacted by a telemarketer, the consumer should follow these guidelines:

1. If the telemarketer is "pushy" in using high-pressure sales tactics, then hang up the telephone. The consumer should treat the telemarketer as an obscene telephone caller.
2. Some states have passed laws requiring telemarketers to be licensed or registered. The consumer should obtain identification of telemarketers, as well as information about the company that they represent.
3. If the deal sounds too good to be true, then you can be assured that it is not good. So, if telemarketers make claims about their product or service that in any way seem too good to be true, do not order it.
4. Some products or services are forbidden to be sold over the telephone in many states. It is unlawful to sell fraudulent securities using the telephone or mail. Some states have laws against certain professions of soliciting customers by mail or telephone, i.e., accounting, legal, and medical.
5. The consumer should compare prices of products and services that the telemarketer is selling to the same products and services in the local area. In many cases, the products and services cost more than what the local merchants provide. Shipping and handling charges should be considered when ordering from telemarketers. These drive up the costs.
6. It is advisable to use a credit card for making a purchase. It provides the ability for the consumer to have the credit card company cancel the charge, provided that it is done within 30 days from date of purchase. Also, U.S. Postal Regulations require that the company ship the goods within 30 days. However, consumers should review their monthly credit card statements for any possible charges by the company at a later date or for fraudulent use of their credit card number at another location.
7. The consumer should make inquiries with the Better Business Bureau or the state consumer affairs department about any complaints about the company.

Mail Order

Many consumers receive "junk" mail, which solicits them to purchase goods through the mail. Consumers can also see advertisements on television and in the newspapers. Most advertisements are done by legitimate businesses; however, there are unscrupulous mail-order houses. Mail-order houses operate like fraudulent telemarketers, except they lack the element of direct communication. It also allows the consumer to make inquiries about the product and company before placing the order. The consumer should take the following steps:

1. The consumer should compare mail-order prices of products and services with those in the local area. Shipping and handling charges should be considered since they can drive up the total costs of the product.
2. If the product or service sounds too good to be true, then do not order it.
3. The consumer should make inquiries with the Better Business Bureau or the state consumer affairs department about any complaints or about the company's existence. Some states require an out-of-state company to be registered in that state before it can do business in that state.
4. Local merchants should be consulted about special ordering products that are not generally available. In some cases, local merchants can obtain the product or service at lower costs than by direct mail.

5. If the product is not received within 30 days, then the consumer should call the company and find out the status. If consumers get no satisfactory response, then they should notify the U.S. Postal Inspection Office near them.
6. The consumer should keep in mind that some products are not allowed to be shipped through the mail. This is particularly true for dangerous or flammable products. Also, illegal products, such as illegal drugs and pornographic material, are not allowed to be mailed.

Religious/Nonprofit Organizations

There are religious cults and nonprofit organizations that exist for the purpose of committing fraud. There are many criminals who will either call on the telephone or approach a victim on the street. They ask the person to contribute to their particular cause or organization. These causes or organizations either do not exist or are only fronts. Many criminals will claim that their organizations are tax exempt. Nonprofit organizations, except for religious organizations, must apply to the IRS to get a tax exemption. The consumer can call or write to the IRS and find out if a particular nonprofit organization is tax exempt. If it is not tax exempt, then any contributions made are not tax deductible. The United Way is an organization that conducts campaigns to raise funds for various charitable organizations. The United Way can provide contributors a list of tax exempt organizations that need donors.

Religious organizations present a different problem. By federal statute, religious organizations (churches, synagogues, temples, etc.) are tax exempt. This is due to the Constitution, which separates church and state. There are various evangelists who prey upon people's emotions and feelings so that they will open their pocketbooks. Some religious leaders try to control member's lives. They become cults. The danger signs of a corrupt religious organization are as follows:

1. The leaders claim to be the only true church.
2. The leaders never accept criticism and denounce any criticism as a negative attitude.
3. The leaders attempt to control a person's life. They then start to tell members what to wear, give, where to work, play, and what to do or say.
4. The leader tells the member what is right and wrong.
5. The religious organization is mostly isolated from the rest of the world. It's only contact is to improve its image to outsiders and recruit new members.
6. The religious organization wants to keep its financial affairs secret. The leadership lives a high lifestyle.

Summary

The consumer should observe the following rules:

1. Remember, if the deal seems too good to be true, it probably is.
2. Investigate the company and/or product being offered. The local library is an excellent source.

3. Never purchase any product or service from anyone who solicits you whether by telephone, Internet, mail, or in person.
4. Never give anyone control over any part of your financial affairs unless you really know the person or company.
5. Keep your checks, credit cards, and ATM cards in a safe place and separate them from other things or valuables. Never give account numbers over the telephone, Internet, or solicitors unless YOU contacted them.
6. Review all bank statements, credit card statements, and brokerage statements for accuracy.

Fraud Prevention for Businesses

18

Introduction

There are many precautions that businesses can take to prevent fraud. If businesses, like consumers, will take the appropriate steps and procedures to prevent fraud, then their losses can be nonexistent or minimal. In some cases, fraud can be prevented by just making appropriate inquiries. In other cases, implementing proper internal controls can help prevent fraud. It should be stressed that taking all the precautions that can be taken does not guarantee that businesses will not become victims; however, it will reduce the chances. There are many "con" artists, who, despite of all the precautions taken, can "take your shoes while you are standing in them."

Business

Businesses can be victims of fraud in several areas:

1. Customers
2. Employees
3. Vendors and suppliers
4. Worker's compensation claims
5. Surety bonds

Businesses should be aware of fraud that is committed by these groups. If fraud by any of the groups is uncovered, then prosecution should be initiated. Failure to prosecute only encourages more fraud. Large corporations and many medium and small companies do not like to prosecute since they rationalize that it could hurt their image. This is not so. Many of the consumer frauds also apply to businesses, i.e., insurance, legal and accounting, banking, construction, repairs, etc. Therefore, the preventative measures discussed in Chapter 17 apply to businesses as well. Fraud issues that especially concern businesses are addressed here.

Customers

Shoplifting is the most common fraud committed by customers. It involves customers walking out of the business establishment with the merchandise either open in their hands or concealed in bags or undergarments. Detecting shoplifting can be done by observing or detecting customers in some manner. However, some customers commit fraud in other ways. The two principal methods, in addition to shoplifting, are known as the "refund" method and the "bust-out" artist.

Refund Method

The refund method of committing fraud is becoming more prevalent. This has been used by organized crime groups in recent years in "fencing" stolen property. The customer purchases merchandise on one day and returns it later, for various reasons, for a refund. The customer later brings in more merchandise using a receipt, either forged or the same old receipt, for another refund. The second or subsequent refund claim usually involves merchandise that is stolen or purchased from another store. Organized crime groups use it to fence stolen property. If done often enough, law enforcement agencies may believe that the business establishment is owned or controlled by organized crime. In the case of large chain stores, if internal controls are not implemented and followed, then this scheme can become enormous which will result in losses. For the business to prevent such a scheme, the following precautions are recommended.

1. When making a refund, the cashier should take back the original receipt and match it up with the refund slip. This will prevent the customer from reusing the purchase slip.
2. The business should establish a policy that is posted for both customers and cashiers to follow. This policy should not allow refunds after 30 days. No refunds should be allowed for some small consumer items, e.g., paper products, shoes, pencils, pens, flashlight batteries, cleaning agents, etc.
3. For merchandise that has serial numbers or some specific identification, which requires some detailed accounting, returned merchandise should be matched with sales records to find if they were the same goods that were sold by comparing this identification.
4. For refunds that are made by credit card credit slips, account numbers should be analyzed to identify customers with excessive refunds. Excessive refunds should be gauged to the number of refunds made to the same customer within 1 month. Names and credit card account numbers should be scrutinized. Some fraudulent customers will use more than one credit card.

Most refund fraud will usually involve merchandise that involves low dollar prices. The principal target of refund fraud is almost solely on retailers. Wholesalers and manufacturers are rarely victims.

"Bust-Out" Artists

Businesses that extend credit to customers become easy victims of credit fraud. They ship goods to a customer with the expectation of getting paid in the normal 30 days or sooner with a discount. However, payment is never received. Letters requesting payment are sent. Telephone calls are made only to find out that the telephone has been disconnected or is not operating. This usually happens within a month after shipment of merchandise. The credit manager finds the business premises empty. Inquiries about the business are to no avail. The credit manager reports back that the business is nonexistent and the merchandise is gone. The company controller then has to write off the accounts receivable to bad debts. This causes the company to have a loss or a reduction of earnings on its financial statements. For some companies, this can be devastating. It could even cause the company to close up shop. This kind of fraud is called bust-out. There are many bust-out artists around that make a living at doing this kind of fraud. The surprising part of all this is that the company does not pursue the bust-out artist. The LCN, called the Mafia, and other organized crime groups have been doing this for years. They have become experts in this field.

The extent of business credit fraud is not known. The primary reason for this is that businesses do not report such losses, nor do they pursue criminal prosecution. It is estimated by the National Association of Credit Management that businesses lose tens to hundreds of thousands of dollars. They also have records of people who have operated credit frauds for many years. Measures that can be taken to prevent this kind of fraud follow:

1. The sales department should not control the credit department. The credit department should make the final decision based upon its inquiries about the creditor. Remember, it is better to have unsold inventory than to have a bad debt write-off.

2. The company should obtain and study a credit report. The credit manager should call up all previous creditors. However, the credit manager should be cautious of references in the same geographical area, as well as post office boxes and private mailboxes since this indicates "singers" (phony references).

3. Businesses should call better business bureaus and/or local or state consumer affairs departments about any complaints and how many. It is a danger sign if there are complaints registered.

4. Bust-out artists like to have rush orders. This is a ploy to get shipment before a full credit check is made.

5. Credit managers should be wary of unsolicited orders. Bust-out artists try to obtain as many suppliers as possible. They usually want orders shipped immediately without any credit checks.

6. Credit managers should be wary of references located around the country. There is a strong danger sign if the references turn out to be answering machines or answering services.

7. Increases in orders are a danger sign. The bust-out artist sometimes buys small and gradually increases the orders. In the beginning the bust-out artist pays promptly, or pays slower on each order. The bust-out artist tries to gain confidence before the last and largest order is made.

8. Credit managers should be careful of business names that are almost identical to a well-known and highly credit-worthy corporation. The address given may even be on the same street as that of the reputable concern.

9. The customer's business comes under new management, the change of ownership is not publicly announced, and the identity of the new owners is obscure. This is a danger sign.

10. The company should be wary of orders unrelated to the usual line (like a grocery store ordering jewelry as door prizes) during the business's busy season or the customer's off-season.

11. The customer orders increased quantities that are contradictory to the seasonal nature of the customer's business.

12. Financial statements of the customer are unaudited, unverified, and appear inconsistent or unusual. A cash flow should be done to see if the cash balances agree. Also, ratios should be checked to see if they are consistent. Vertical and horizontal analysis should be performed on the financial statements. If the company is new, it will not have multiperiod financial statements. Therefore, industry statistics and other data should be compared to see if they are consistent.

13. If racketeers or those with criminal records have been installed in positions of importance in a customer being serviced, then credit should not be extended.

14. Credit managers should be wary of abnormal numbers of credit inquiries. Bust-out artists attempt to order from as many companies as possible. The credit manager should be alert to other legitimate references that tell the manager of receiving many inquiries. Credit inquiry rates indicate a strong danger sign.

15. The credit manager should check the background of the principals. The business must know with whom it is dealing. Credit reports and other financial information should be obtained on the principals, their backgrounds, and businesses they have operated in the past.

16. Front men are used by organized crime groups. Organized crime uses front men because they have clean backgrounds. The credit manager must determine if the front men have the capital to start or control the business. Also, do the front men have the experience, education, and knowledge to operate such a business successfully?

17. Payments are made on time at first. As purchases are made, the payments become slower and sometimes these checks begin to bounce. When the checks begin to bounce, this is a danger sign. Credit should then be terminated. This is especially true when orders are also increasing.

Employee Fraud

Employee theft and embezzlement are the most common forms of fraud in businesses. Most employees are not dishonest when they are first hired. They only become dishonest when the opportunity becomes available. Fraud only occurs when three elements come together:

1. Items of value
2. A perpetrator
3. Opportunity

These elements will equal fraud. There are three basic areas where businesses can take steps to help prevent fraud by employees:

1. Hiring
2. Working environment
3. Establishing and maintaining internal controls

Hiring

Hiring honest employees is the first step. Screening prospective employees can do this. Personnel managers should implement and maintain a thorough selection process. The prospective employee should be screened regarding both character traits and financial stability. Obtaining the following information can do this:

    1. **Application.** The business should obtain a complete application and/or résumé from the prospective employee. The application and résumé should contain:

a. Full name. The applicant's full name should be obtained along with any and all aliases and nicknames.
b. Identification data. This should consist of date of birth, social security number, and driver's license number. If the applicant is a resident alien, then the INS alien number, country of origin passport number, and the country should be recorded.
c. History. This should contain work history back to the age of 21. The work history should show the name, address, and manager's name of each company who employed the applicant. Any gaps of employment should be questioned and explanations obtained.
d. Character references. The prospective employee should give a minimum of three character references. These character references should not be former employers or relatives.
e. Relatives. A listing of close relatives should be obtained. This includes spouse, parents (both applicant and spouse), children (with dates of birth), and brothers and sisters (with ages or dates of birth).

    2. **Character examination.** The business should have prospective employees take a personal (psychological) character examination. This is strongly urged for prospective employees applying for positions of trust.

    3. **References.** The prospective employee character and employment references should be checked. For character references, personnel managers should make inquiries about the applicant's moral values. Pastime activities should be identified. Character references should be examined regarding the extent of their association with the applicant. The applicant's former employers should be examined regarding job performance and skills, reason for leaving the past employer, and punctuality.

    4. **Drug test.** The applicant should be examined for any signs of drug or alcohol abuse. Many employees commit fraud because of drug or alcohol abuse. They need the funds to support such habits.

5. **Credit history.** The applicant's credit history should be obtained. This will show the applicant's financial history and current status. An applicant with a high debt service has a potential of committing fraud. Also, question whether the applicant can live off the income the employer expects to pay him or her.

6. **Public records.** Public records should be examined to check if the applicant has any criminal or civil actions on file. Traffic infractions should not be considered unless the applicant is applying for a driver's position. Also, real and personal property that is owned by the applicant should be identified in public records.

The above information will help the employer evaluate the applicant in terms of fraud potential. It will supply information about the applicant in case the applicant commits fraud. This information will help law enforcement track a fraudulent employee. It will also help in civil tort cases. Subjecting the applicant to such scrutiny will discourage some dishonest individuals from applying and will inform those hired that fraud will not be tolerated.

Working Environment

Once an employee is hired, then an environment should be created that will discourage dishonesty. Treating employees fairly can do this. Employers also can provide amenities that do not cost very much. They can implement policies that will discourage employees from being dishonest. Internal controls and physical security procedures can be maintained to discourage theft. All of these environmental controls are discussed below:

1. **Amenities.** The business should have amenities that will benefit the employee. These include such things as clean rest rooms, a decent break room, parking space, and clean work space.

2. **Ethical standards.** The business has to promote and display good ethical and moral standards. These standards must be equally applied to employees, managers, and officers. These ethical and moral standards should be applied to employees, vendors and suppliers, and customers alike.

3. **Performance evaluation.** Job performance goals should be high, but not unrealistic. Employees should be encouraged to perform to the best of their abilities. If a business sets unrealistic goals, this will force employees and managers to lie or cheat. Outstanding employees and managers should be rewarded for their performance. Incentives. such as bonuses, time off, stock options, etc., should be made available. These awards should be based upon performance. Different employees will perform differently. Greater performance should result in greater rewards.

4. **Benefits.** The employer should provide various benefits, which should be available to officers, managers, and employees alike. Health insurance, disability insurance, retirement, stock options (if publicly-held company) should be made available. Small companies are not financially able to provide many of these benefits at their expense; however, they can make them available to employees at the employees' expense (payroll deductions). Even if the employee has to pay (through payroll deductions) for these benefits, it can be a boost to employee morale and performance. Most employees, especially in hard economic times, want security. If a business has to downsize for whatever reason, then it is up to management to advise the employees. In some cases, particularly for small businesses,

management should solicit the cooperation of employees to reduce the downsizing. Employees should be considered an asset to the business and not an expense.

Establishing and Maintaining Internal Controls

Internal controls.   Management should implement and maintain internal controls. Internal controls mean more than just establishing administrative procedures. They should include assuring that employees take vacations, making periodic rotations, and providing training for different assignments. Remember, the more responsibilities that an employee can take on, the more valuable the employee becomes to the business. However, a business should not rely too heavily on any one or two employees for a particular assignment. Internal controls should also encompass security procedures. Change or rotation of guards should be made periodically. Lunch boxes, handbags, etc. should be inspected if suspicion dictates before managers and employees leave the business site. Access to various areas should be limited to only employees who work in the area. This is especially true for computers. Work areas should be locked after hours. Access to keys should be limited to appropriate personnel.

Internal auditors.   For medium and large businesses, internal auditors should be employed to act as "watchdogs." They should insure compliance with company policies and procedures. Internal auditors should be hired by and report to the board of directors. Management should not have any control over internal auditors. Many corporate fraud cases involve upper management who can control internal auditors by directing them away from the area where the fraud is being committed.

Employee Theft

Employee theft usually involves the following schemes:

1. Cash register thefts
2. Payroll falsification
3. Issuing fraudulent refunds
4. Kickbacks
5. Embezzlement
6. Lapping schemes
7. Check kiting

These schemes will not be discussed here, since they are explained in more detail in Chapter 23. However, prevention is the primary key to preventing fraud by employees. If items of value and the opportunity do not exist, then employee fraud will be minimal or nonexistent.

Vendors and Suppliers

A third source of fraud upon businesses is by vendors and suppliers. In this scenario, the business is basically the consumer. Chapter 17 addressed the various areas where the consumer can be defrauded. These apply to businesses as well; however, businesses face additional areas. These are addressed below.

Kickbacks

Kickbacks come in various guises. In each case, they involve an employee(s) and a vendor or supplier. One scheme involves the sale of unreported inventory, which is sold and the proceeds shared by the vendor and employee. The other scheme involves the business paying a vendor or supplier for inventory at inflated prices and the employee receiving a portion of the excess payment back. Internal controls can help prevent these schemes; the key indicators are as follows:

1. The same vendor is constantly used.
2. The current vendor has prices higher than other vendors in the same line.
3. Inventory reveals goods in stock that cannot be accounted for in existence.
4. Payments to vendors show more than one endorsement.
5. Manager or purchasing agent has excessive debts.
6. Purchasing agent or manager does not take any vacation time.
7. Only photocopies of invoices are provided.

Worker's Compensation

Worker's compensation fraud is the most common fraud committed. What usually begins as a minor injury on the job develops into a golden opportunity for an early retirement, a paycheck without having to work, or an income supplemented from the insurance company. False information is presented to the worker's compensation carrier. The report describes the claimant as totally or partially disabled and either unable to work at all, or only able to work part time. In many cases, these schemes are enhanced with the assistance of an unscrupulous doctor who, for an extra fee, provides false diagnosis of the claimant's condition and fabricates medical records for phony treatments. Greedy claimants have collected worker's compensation benefits and still work at full- or part-time jobs elsewhere. Some claimants use another name or alias. Worker's compensation claims cause businesses to pay higher rates for worker's compensation insurance. Therefore, fraud is perpetrated on both the business and the insurance carrier. The indicators are

1. The employee has a history of prior worker's compensation claims.
2. Injuries are soft-tissue kinds.
3. The employee claims to be incapacitated but is seen engaging in activities that require full mobility.

Surety Bonds

Surety and performance bonds guarantee that certain events will or will not occur. A performance bond guarantees the completion of a construction project, whereas a surety bond protects the public against damages sustained on a construction project. Certain insurance agents specialize in this kind of market and earn an excellent income. Others use the bond market to generate a far greater income by issuing worthless bonds. In this scheme, the unscrupulous salesperson manufactures worthless paper, which is issued to the consumer, usually for high-risk coverage. This might include bridge construction, building demolition, fireworks displays, transportation or storage of explosives, or other potentially hazardous situations. The agent issues the bonds in hopes that no claims will be made.

If a claim is made, the agent pays the claim with available funds, uses delay tactics, or skips out. The indicators of fraudulent agents are

1. No bond or endorsements are received from the agent.
2. The bond is a photocopy or the bond papers bear no company watermark.
3. The agent requests payments by cash, money order, or cashier's check made payable to the agent or to a company other than the insurance carrier.
4. Checks are returned, having been cashed or deposited to the agent's personal account.
5. The insurance company allegedly issuing the coverage is not authorized to sell insurance in the state or is unknown to the state insurance department.

Banks

Criminals like to target banks for various fraud schemes since that is where the money is located. Also, insiders cause many bank frauds. Banks offer many types of services. Each of these services is an area that criminals can target for fraud. The Federal Deposit Insurance Corporation (FDIC) has identified the following danger signs:

1. **Loan participations.** The danger signs in this area are as follows:

a. Excessive participation of loans among closely related banks, correspondent banks, and branches or departments of the lending bank;
b. Absence of a formal participation agreement;
c. Poor or incomplete loan documentation;
d. Investing in out-of-territory participation;
e. Reliance on third-party guarantees;
f. Large paydown or payoff of previously classified loans;
g. Some indication that there may be informal repurchase agreements on some participations;
h. Lack of independent credit analysis;
i. Volume of loan participations sold is high in relation to the size of the bank's own loan portfolio;
j. Evidence of lapping of loan participations (for example, the sale of loan participation in an amount equal or greater than, and at or about the same time as, participation that has matured or is about to mature);
k. Disputes between participating banks over documentation, payments, or any other aspect of the loan participation agreements.

2. **Secured lending — Real Estate and Other Types of Collateral**

a. Lack of independent appraisals;
b. Out-of-territory loans;

c. Evidence of land flips (a land flip is a process in which individuals or businesses buy and sell properties among themselves, each time inflating the sales price to give the appearance of rapidly increasing property values; the mortgage amounts increase with each purchase until, in many cases, the amounts of the mortgages greatly exceed the actual values of the mortgaged property);

d. Loans with unusual terms and conditions;

e. Poor or incomplete documentation;

f. Loans that are unusual considering the size of the bank and the level of expertise of its lending officers;

g. Heavy concentration of loans to a single project or to individuals related to the project.

h. Concentrations of loans to local borrowers with the same or similar collateral that is located outside the bank's trade area;

i. Asset swaps (sale of real estate or other distressed assets to a broker at an inflated price in return for favorable terms and conditions on a new loan to a borrower introduced to the bank by the broker; the new loan is usually secured by property of questionable value and the borrower is in a weak financial condition; borrower and collateral are often outside the bank's normal trade area);

j. Failure to consider the risk of decline in collateral value.

3. Insider Transactions

a. Financing the sale of insider assets to third parties;

b. From a review of personal financial statements, evidence that an insider is lending the insider's own funds to others;

c. Improper fees to major shareholders;

d. Frequent changes of auditors or legal counsel;

e. Unusual or unjustified fluctuations in insider's or officer's personal financial statements or statements of their interests;

f. Frequent appearances of suspense items relating to accounts of insiders, officers, and employees;

g. An insider's borrowing money from someone who borrows from the bank;

h. Purchase of bank assets by an insider;

i. A review of the bank's fixed assets or other asset accounts revealing that the bank owns expensive artwork, expensive automobiles, yachts, airplanes, or other unusual items that are out of character for a bank of its size and location;

j. A review of the bank's expense accounts revealing expenditures for attorney's fees, accountant's fees, broker's fees, and so forth, that do not appear to correspond to services rendered to the bank or that appear unusually high for services rendered;

k. Heavy lending to the bank's shareholders, particularly in conjunction with recent capital injections;

l. A large portion of the insider's bank stock that has been pledged to secure debts to other financial institutions;

m. An insider who has past due obligations at other financial institutions;

n.   An insider is who receiving all or part of the proceeds of loans granted to others;
o.   An insider is who receiving special consideration or "favors" from bank customers (for example, an insider may receive favorable lease terms or favorable purchase terms on an automobile obtained from a bank customer).

4. Credit Card and Electronic Funds Transfer

a.   Lack of separation of duties between the card-issuing function and the issuance of a personal identification number (PIN);
b.   Poor control of unissued cards and PINs;
c.   Poor control of returned mail;
d.   Customer complaints;
e.   Poor control of credit limit increases;
f.   Poor control of name and address changes;
g.   Frequent malfunction of payment authorization system;
h.   Unusual delays in receipt of cards and PINs by customers;
i.   A bank that does not limit amount of cash that a customer can extract from an ATM in a given day;
j.   Evidence that customer credit card purchases have been intentionally structured by a merchant to keep individual amounts below the "floor limit" to avoid the need for transaction approval.

5. Wire Transfers

a.   Indications of frequent overrides of established approval authority and other internal controls;
b.   Intentional circumvention of approval authority by splitting transactions;
c.   Wire transfers to and from tax haven countries;
d.   Frequent large wire transfers to persons who do not have an account relationship with the bank;
e.   In a linked financing situation, a borrower's request for immediate wire transfer of loan proceeds to one or more banks where the funds for brokered deposits originated;
f.   Large or frequent wire transfers against uncollected funds;
g.   Wire transfers involving cash where the amount exceeds $10,000;
h.   Inadequate control of password access;
i.   Customer complaints and frequent error conditions.

6. Offshore Transactions

a.   Loans made on the strength of a borrower's financial statement when the statement reflects major investments and income from businesses incorporated in tax haven countries;
b.   Loans to offshore companies;
c.   Loans secured by obligations of offshore banks;

d. Transactions involving an offshore "shell" bank whose name may be very similar to the name of a major legitimate institution;

e. Frequent wire transfers of funds to and from tax haven countries;

f. Offers of multimillion dollar deposit at below market rates from a confidential source to be sent from an offshore bank or somehow guaranteed by an offshore bank through a letter, telex, or other "official" communication;

g. Presence of telex or facsimile equipment in a bank where the usual and customary business activity would not appear to justify the need for such equipment.

7. Third-Party Obligations

a. Incomplete documentation;

b. Loans secured by obligations of offshore banks;

c. Lack of credit information on third-party obligor;

d. Financial statements reflect concentrations of closely held companies or businesses that lack audited financial statements to support their value.

8. Corporate Culture Ethics

a. Absence of a code of ethics;

b. Absence of a clear policy on conflicts of interest;

c. Lack of oversight by the bank's board of directors, particularly outside directors;

d. Absence of planning, training, hiring, and organizational policies;

e. Absence of clearly defined authorities and lack of definition of the responsibilities that go along with authorities;

f. Lack of independence of management in acting on recommended corrections;

9. Miscellaneous

a. Indications of frequent overrides of internal controls or intentional circumvention of bank policy;

b. Unresolved exceptions of frequently recurring exceptions on exception reports;

c. Out-of-balance conditions;

d. Purpose of loan not recorded;

e. Proceeds of loan used for a purpose other than purpose recorded;

f. A review of checks paid against uncollected funds indicating that a customer is offsetting checks with deposits of the same or similar amount and maintaining a relatively constant account balance, usually small in relation to the amount of activity and the size of the transactions.

Summary

The best things that businesses can do to prevent fraud are

1. Establish and adhere to high moral and ethical standards by management.

2. Prosecute any employee who commits fraud. Failure to do so will only encourage other employees to do the same.
3. Establish and adhere to internal controls.
4. Install and use various detection devices for customer-oriented business. Restrict access to only certain employees where customers and other employees have no business or need to be.

Money Laundering

19

Introduction

Money laundering was not considered a crime until the 1980s when Congress passed a series of laws that made it a crime. Organized crime groups have laundered gains from illegal activities for many years. However, it was not until the 1980s that laws were passed to address the money-laundering activities. Fraud examiners are called upon to unravel various money-laundering schemes. There are many accounting and auditing techniques that can be used to detect these schemes, and the fraud examiner should be well versed in their use.

Definition

Money laundering is defined as "washing" proceeds to disguise their true source. The source of these proceeds can be from either legal or illegal activities. The things that a money launderer wants to accomplish are to move money, reduce its volume, and change its character to allow for spending or investing, while sheltering it from detection and taxation. All of these actions are forms of money laundering. While it comes up quite often in drug trafficking, it is not limited to that area. It also comes up in bookmaking, loan sharking, skimming business receipts, and many other areas.

History

Congress began a long series of steps to combat money laundering. The first step was the passage of the Bank Secrecy Act in 1970. Its purpose was to identify money launderers and tax evaders. To do this, the Act required the following:

1. **Form 4789.** This form (Exhibit 19-1) is to be filled out by financial institutions that report currency transactions exceeding $10,000 to the Treasury Department, thus its name Currency Transaction Report. Financial institutions are broadly defined and have been expanded since. Some of these institutions that are defined as financial institutions follow:

Form **4789**

Currency Transaction Report

(Rev. October 1995)

▶ Use this 1995 revision effective October 1, 1995.

Department of the Treasury
Internal Revenue Service

▶ For Paperwork Reduction Act Notice, see page 3.   ▶ Please type or print.

(Complete all parts that apply—See instructions)

OMB No. 1545-0183

1   Check all box(es) that apply:

a ☐ Amends prior report   **b** ☐ Multiple persons   **c** ☐ Multiple transactions

Part I   **Person(s) Involved in Transaction(s)**

Section A—Person(s) on Whose Behalf Transaction(s) Is Conducted

2 Individual's last name or Organization's name	3 First name	4 M.I.

5 Doing business as (DBA)	6 SSN or EIN

7 Address (number, street, and apt. or suite no.)	8 Date of birth M M D D Y Y

9 City	10 State	11 ZIP code	12 Country (if not U.S.)	13 Occupation, profession, or business

14   If an individual, describe method used to verify identity:

a ☐ Driver's license/State I.D.   **b** ☐ Passport   **c** ☐ Alien registration   **d** ☐ Other _____

e Issued by: **f** Number:

Section B—Individual(s) Conducting Transaction(s) (if other than above).

If Section B is left blank or incomplete, check the box(es) below to indicate the reason(s):

a ☐ Armored Car Service   **b** ☐ Mail Deposit or Shipment   **c** ☐ Night Deposit or Automated Teller Machine (ATM)

d ☐ Multiple Transactions   **e** ☐ Conducted On Own Behalf

15 Individual's last name	16 First name	17 M.I.

18 Address (number, street, and apt. or suite no.)	19 SSN

20 City	21 State	22 ZIP code	23 Country (if not U.S.)	24 Date of birth M M D D Y Y

25   If an individual, describe method used to verify identity:

a ☐ Driver's license/State I.D.   **b** ☐ Passport   **c** ☐ Alien registration   **d** ☐ Other _____

e Issued by: **f** Number:

Part II   **Amount and Type of Transaction(s). Check all boxes that apply.**

26 Cash In $ _____ .00   **27** Cash Out $ _____ .00   **28** Date of Transaction   M M D D Y Y

29 ☐ Foreign Currency _____ (Country)   **30** ☐ Wire Transfer(s)   **31** ☐ Negotiable Instrument(s) Purchased

32 ☐ Negotiable Instrument(s) Cashed   **33** ☐ Currency Exchange(s)   **34** ☐ Deposit(s)/Withdrawal(s)

35 ☐ Account Number(s) Affected (if any):   **36** ☐ Other (specify)

Part III   **Financial Institution Where Transaction(s) Takes Place**

37 Name of financial institution	Enter Federal Regulator or BSA Examiner code number from the instructions here. ▶ [ ]

38 Address (number, street, and apt. or suite no.)	39 SSN or EIN

40 City	41 State	42 ZIP code	43 MICR No.

Sign Here ▶

44 Title of approving official	45 Signature of approving official	46 Date of signature M M D D Y Y
47 Type or print preparer's name	48 Type or print name of person to contact	49 Telephone number ( )

Cat. No. 42004W   359   Form **4789** (Rev. 10-95)

Exhibit 19-1 Form 4789.

Form 4789 (Rev. 10-95)

Multiple Persons
(Complete applicable parts below if box 1b on page 1 is checked.)

Part I   Person(s) Involved in Transaction(s)

Section A—Person(s) on Whose Behalf Transaction(s) Is Conducted

2 Individual's last name or Organization's name	3 First name	4 M.I.

5 Doing business as (DBA)	6 SSN or EIN

7 Address (number, street, and apt. or suite no.)	8 Date of birth M M D D Y Y

9 City	10 State	11 ZIP code	12 Country (if not U.S.)	13 Occupation, profession, or business

14   If an individual, describe method used to verify identity:
   a ☐ Driver's license/State I.D.   **b** ☐ Passport   **c** ☐ Alien registration   **d** ☐ Other ....
   e Issued by: **f** Number:

Section B—Individual(s) Conducting Transaction(s) (if other than above).

15 Individual's last name	16 First name	17 M.I.

18 Address (number, street, and apt. or suite no.)	19 SSN M M D D Y Y

20 City	21 State	22 ZIP code	23 Country (if not U.S.)	24 Date of birth M M D D Y Y

25   If an individual, describe method used to verify identity:
   a ☐ Driver's license/State I.D.   **b** ☐ Passport   **c** ☐ Alien registration   **d** ☐ Other ....
   e Issued by: **f** Number:

Part I   Person(s) Involved in Transaction(s)

Section A—Person(s) on Whose Behalf Transaction(s) Is Conducted

2 Individual's last name or Organization's name	3 First name	4 M.I.

5 Doing business as (DBA)	6 SSN or EIN

7 Address (number, street, and apt. or suite no.)	8 Date of birth M M D D Y Y

9 City	10 State	11 ZIP code	12 Country (if not U.S.)	13 Occupation, profession, or business

14   If an individual, describe method used to verify identity:
   a ☐ Driver's license/State I.D.   **b** ☐ Passport   **c** ☐ Alien registration   **d** ☐ Other ....
   e Issued by: **f** Number:

Section B—Individual(s) Conducting Transaction(s) (if other than above).

15 Individual's last name	16 First name	17 M.I.

18 Address (number, street, and apt. or suite no.)	19 SSN

20 City	21 State	22 ZIP code	23 Country (if not U.S.)	24 Date of birth M M D D Y Y

25   If an individual, describe method used to verify identity:
   a ☐ Driver's license/State I.D.   **b** ☐ Passport   **c** ☐ Alien registration   **d** ☐ Other ....
   e Issued by: **f** Number:

continued

Exhibit 19-1 (continued) Form 4789.

Paperwork Reduction Act Notice.—The requested information has been determined to be useful in criminal, tax, and regulatory investigations and proceedings. Financial institutions are required to provide the information under 31 U.S.C. 5313 and 31 CFR Part 103. These provisions are commonly referred to as the Bank Secrecy Act (BSA) which is administered by the U.S. Department of the Treasury's Financial Crimes Enforcement Network (FinCEN).

The time needed to complete this form will vary depending on individual circumstances. The estimated average time is 19 minutes. If you have comments concerning the accuracy of this time estimate or suggestions for making this form simpler, we would be happy to hear from you. You can write to the **Internal Revenue Service,** Attention: Tax Forms Committee, PC:FP, Washington, DC 20224. **DO NOT** send this form to this office. Instead, see **When and Where To File** below.

Suspicious Transactions

This Currency Transaction Report (CTR) should NOT be filed for suspicious transactions involving $10,000 or less in currency OR to note that a transaction of more than $10,000 is suspicious. Any suspicious or unusual activity should be reported by a financial institution in the manner prescribed by its appropriate federal regulator or BSA examiner. (See Item 37.) If a transaction is suspicious and in excess of $10,000 in currency, then both a CTR and the appropriate referral form must be filed.

Should the suspicious activity require immediate attention, financial institutions should telephone 1-800-800-CTRS. An Internal Revenue Service (IRS) employee will direct the call to the local office of the IRS Criminal Investigation Division (CID). This toll-free number is operational Monday through Friday, from approximately 9:00 am to 6:00 pm Eastern Standard Time. If an emergency, consult directory assistance for the local IRS CID Office.

General Instructions

Who Must File.—Each financial institution (other than a casino, which instead must file Form 8362 and the U.S. Postal Service for which there are separate rules), must file Form 4789 (CTR) for each deposit, withdrawal, exchange of currency, or other payment or transfer, by, through, or to the financial institution which involves a transaction in currency of more than $10,000. Multiple transactions must be treated as a single transaction if the financial institution has knowledge that (1) they are by or on behalf of the same person, and (2) they result in either currency received (Cash In) or currency disbursed (Cash Out) by the financial institution totaling more than $10,000 during any one business day. For a bank, a business day is the day on which transactions are routinely posted to customers' accounts, as normally communicated to depository customers. For all other financial institutions, a business day is a calendar day.

Generally, financial institutions are defined as banks, other types of depository institutions, brokers or dealers in securities, money transmitters, currency exchangers, check cashers, issuers and sellers of money orders and traveler's checks. Should you have questions, see the definitions in 31 CFR Part 103.

When and Where To File.—File this CTR by the 15th calendar day after the day of the transaction with the IRS Detroit Computing Center, ATTN: CTR, P.O. Box 33604, Detroit, MI 48232-5604 or with your local IRS office. Keep a

copy of each CTR for five years from the date filed.

A financial institution may apply to file the CTRs magnetically. To obtain an application to file magnetically, write to the IRS Detroit Computing Center, ATTN: CTR Magnetic Media Coordinator, at the address listed above.

Identification Requirements.—All individuals (except employees of armored car services) conducting a reportable transaction(s) for themselves or for another person must be identified by means of an official document(s).

Acceptable forms of identification include a driver's license, military, and military/dependent identification cards, passport, state issued identification card, cedular card (foreign), non-resident alien identification cards, or any other identification document or documents, which contain name and preferably address and a photograph and are normally acceptable by financial institutions as a means of identification when cashing checks for persons other than established customers.

Acceptable identification information obtained previously and maintained in the financial institution's records may be used. For example, if documents verifying an individual's identity were examined and recorded on a signature card when an account was opened, the financial institution may rely on that information. In completing the CTR, the financial institution must indicate on the form the method, type, and number of the identification. Statements such as "known customer" or "signature card on file" are not sufficient for form completion.

Penalties.—Civil and criminal penalties are provided for failure to file a CTR or to supply information or for filing a false or fraudulent CTR. See 31 U.S.C. 5321, 5322 and 5324.

For purposes of this CTR, the terms below have the following meanings:

Currency.—The coin and paper money of the United States or any other country, which is circulated and customarily used and accepted as money.

Person.—An individual, corporation, partnership, trust or estate, joint stock company, association, syndicate, joint venture or other unincorporated organization or group.

Organization.—Person other than an individual.

Transaction in Currency.—The **physical** transfer of currency from one person to another. This does not include a transfer of funds by means of bank check, bank draft, wire transfer or other written order that does not involve the physical transfer of currency.

Negotiable Instruments.—All checks and drafts (including business, personal, bank, cashier's and third-party), money orders, and promissory notes. For purposes of this CTR, all traveler's checks shall also be considered negotiable instruments. All such instruments shall be considered negotiable instruments whether or not they are in bearer form.

Specific Instructions

Because of the limited space on the front and back of the CTR, it may be necessary to submit additional information on attached sheets. Submit this additional information on plain paper attached to the CTR. Be sure to put the individual's or organization's name and identifying number (items 2, 3, 4, and 6 of the CTR) on any additional sheets so that if it becomes separated, it may be associated with the CTR.

Item 1a. Amends Prior Report.—If this CTR is being filed because it amends a report filed

previously, check Item 1a. Staple a copy of the original CTR to the amended one, complete Part III fully and only those other entries which are being amended.

Item 1b. Multiple Persons.—If this transaction is being conducted by more than one person or on behalf of more than one person, check Item 1b. Enter information in Part I for one of the persons and provide information on any other persons on the back of the CTR.

Item 1c. Multiple Transactions.—If the financial institution has knowledge that there are multiple transactions, check Item 1c.

PART I - Person(s) Involved in Transaction(s)

Section A must be completed. If an individual conducts a transaction on his own behalf, complete Section A; leave Section B BLANK. If an individual conducts a transaction on his own behalf and on behalf of another person(s), complete Section A for each person; leave Section B BLANK. If an individual conducts a transaction on behalf of another person(s), complete Section B for the individual conducting the transaction, and complete Section A for each person on whose behalf the transaction is conducted of whom the financial institution has knowledge.

Section A. Person(s) on Whose Behalf Transaction(s) Is Conducted.—See instructions above.

Items 2, 3, and 4. Individual/Organization Name.—If the person on whose behalf the transaction(s) is conducted is an individual, put his/her last name in Item 2, first name in Item 3 and middle initial in Item 4. If there is no middle initial, leave Item 4 BLANK. If the transaction is conducted on behalf of an organization, put its name in Item 2 and leave Items 3 and 4 BLANK.

Item 5. Doing Business As (DBA).—If the financial institution has knowledge of a separate "doing business as" name, enter it in Item 5. For example, Johnson Enterprises DBA PJ's Pizzeria.

Item 6. Social Security Number (SSN) or Employer Identification Number (EIN).—Enter the SSN or EIN of the person identified in Item 2. If none, write NONE.

Items 7, 9, 10, 11 and 12. Address.—Enter the permanent street address including zip code of the person identified in Item 2. Use the Post Office's two letter state abbreviation code. A P.O. Box should not be used by itself and may only be used if there is no street address. If a P.O. Box is used, the name of the apartment or suite number, road or route number where the person resides must also be provided. If the address is outside the U.S., provide the street address, city, province, or state, postal code (if known), and the name of the country.

Item 8. Date of Birth.—Enter the date of birth. Six numerals must be inserted for each date. The first two will reflect the month of birth, the second two the calendar day of birth, and the last two numerals the year of birth. Zero (0) should precede any single digit number. For example, if an individual's birth date is April 3, 1948, Item 8 should read 04 03 48.

Item 13. Occupation, Profession, or Business.—Identify fully the occupation, profession or business of the person on whose behalf the transaction(s) was conducted. For example, secretary, shoe salesman, carpenter, attorney, housewife, restaurant, liquor store, etc. Do not use non-specific terms such as merchant, self-employed, businessman, etc.

Exhibit 19-1 (continued) Form 4789.

Form 4789 (Rev. 10-95)

Item 14. If an Individual, Describe Method Used To Verify.—If an individual conducts the transaction(s) on his/her own behalf, his/her identity must be verified by examination of an acceptable document (see **General Instructions**). For example, check box **a** if a driver's license is used to verify an individual's identity, and enter the state that issued the license and the number in items **e** and **f**. If the transaction is conducted by an individual on behalf of another individual not present or an organization, enter N/A in item 14.

Section B. Individual(s) Conducting Transaction(s) (if other than above).—Financial institutions should enter as much information as is available. However, there may be instances in which Items 15-25 may be left BLANK or incomplete.

If Items 15-25 are left BLANK or incomplete, check one or more of the boxes provided for Item 15 to indicate the reason(s).

Example: If there are multiple transactions that, if only when aggregated, the financial institution has knowledge the transactions exceed the reporting threshold, and therefore, did not identify the transactor(s), check box **d** for Multiple Transactions.

Items 15, 16, and 17. Individual(s) Name.—Complete these items if an individual conducts a transaction(s) on behalf of another person. For example, if John Doe, an employee of XYZ Grocery Store makes a deposit to the store's account, XYZ Grocery Store should be identified in Section A, and John Doe should be identified in Section B.

Items 18, 20, 21, 22, and 23. Address.—Enter the permanent street address including zip code of the individual. (See Items 7, 9, 10, 11, and 12.)

Item 19. SSN.—If the individual has an SSN, enter it in Item 19. If the individual does not have an SSN, enter NONE.

Item 24. Date of Birth.—Enter the individual's date of birth. See the instructions for item 8.

Item 25. If an Individual, Describe Method Used To Verify.—Enter the method by which the individual's identity is verified (see **General Instructions** and Item 14).

PART II - Amount and Type of Transaction(s)

Complete Part II to identify the type of transaction(s) reported and the amount(s) involved.

Items 26 and 27. Cash In/Cash Out.—In the spaces provided, enter the amount of currency received (Cash In) or disbursed (Cash Out) by the financial institution. If foreign currency is exchanged, use the U.S. dollar equivalent on the day of the transaction.

If less than a full dollar amount is involved, increase that figure to the next highest dollar. For example, if the currency totals $20,000.05, show the total as $20,001.00.

Item 28. Date of Transaction.—Six numerals must be inserted for each date. (See Item 8.)

Determining Whether Transactions Meet the Reporting Threshold

Only cash transactions that, if alone or when aggregated, exceed $10,000 should be reported on the CTR. Transactions shall not be offset against one another.

If there are both Cash In and Cash Out transactions that are reportable, the amounts should be considered separately and not aggregated. However, they may be reported on a single CTR.

If there is a currency exchange, it should be aggregated separately with each of the Cash In and Cash Out totals.

Example 1: A person deposits $11,000 in currency to his savings account and withdraws $3,000 in currency from his checking account.

The CTR should be completed as follows: Cash In $11,000 and no entry for Cash Out. This is because the $3,000 transaction does not meet the reporting threshold.

Example 2: A person deposits $11,000 in currency to his savings account and withdraws $12,000 in currency from his checking account.

The CTR should be completed as follows: Cash In $11,000, Cash Out $12,000. This is because there are two reportable transactions. However, one CTR may be filed to reflect both.

Example 3: A person deposits $6,000 in currency to his savings account and withdraws $4,000 in currency from his checking account. Further, he presents $5,000 in currency to be exchanged for the equivalent in French francs.

The CTR should be completed as follows: Cash In $11,000 and no entry for Cash Out. This is because in determining whether the transactions are reportable, the currency exchange is aggregated with each of the Cash In and the Cash Out amounts. The result is a reportable $11,000 Cash In transaction. The total Cash Out amount is $9,000 which does not meet the reporting threshold; therefore, it is not entered on the CTR.

Example 4: A person deposits $6,000 in currency to his savings account and withdraws $7,000 in currency from his checking acount. Further, he presents $5,000 in currency to be exchanged for the equivalent in French francs.

The CTR should be completed as follows: Cash In $11,000, Cash Out $12,000. This is because in determining whether the transactions are reportable, the currency exchange is aggregated with each of the Cash In and Cash Out amounts. In this example, each of the Cash In and Cash Out totals exceed $10,000 and must be reflected on the CTR.

Item 29. Foreign Currency.—If foreign currency is involved, check Item 29 and identify the country. If multiple foreign currencies are involved, identify the country for which the largest amount is exchanged.

Items 30-33.—Check the appropriate item(s) to identify the following type of transaction(s):

30. Wire Transfer(s)

31. Negotiable Instrument(s) Purchased

32. Negotiable Instrument(s) Cashed

33. Currency Exchange(s)

Item 34. Deposits/Withdrawals.—Check this item to identify deposits to or withdrawals from accounts, e.g., demand deposit accounts, savings accounts, time deposits, mutual fund accounts or any other account held at the financial institution. Enter the account number(s) in item 35.

Item 35. Account Numbers Affected (if any).— Enter the account numbers of any accounts affected by the transaction(s) that are maintained

at the financial institution conducting the transaction(s). If necessary, use additional sheets of paper to indicate all of the affected accounts.

Example 1: If a person cashes a check drawn on an account held at the financial institution, the CTR should be completed as follows: Indicate Negotiable Instrument(s) Cashed and provide the account number of the check.

If the transaction does not affect an account, make no entry.

Example 2: A person cashes a check drawn on another financial institution. In this instance, Negotiable Instrument(s) Cashed would be indicated, but no account at the financial institution has been affected. Therefore, item 35 should be left BLANK.

Item 36. Other (specify).—If a transaction is not identified in Items 30-34, check Item 36 and provide an additional description. For example, a person presents a check to purchase "foreign currency".

Part III - Financial Institution Where Transaction(s) Takes Place

Item 37. Name of Financial Institution and Identity of Federal Regulator or BSA Examiner.—Enter the financial institution's full legal name and identify the federal regulator or BSA examiner, using the following codes:

FEDERAL REGULATOR OR BSA EXAMINER	CODE
Comptroller of the Currency (OCC)	1
Federal Deposit Insurance Corporation (FDIC)	2
Federal Reserve System (FRS)	3
Office of Thrift Supervision (OTS)	4
National Credit Union Administration (NCUA)	5
Securities and Exchange Commission (SEC)	6
Internal Revenue Service (IRS)	7
U.S. Postal Service (USPS)	8

Items 38, 40, 41, and 42. Address.—Enter the street address, city, state, and ZIP code of the financial institution where the transaction occurred. If there are multiple transactions, provide information on the office or branch where any one of the transactions has occurred.

Item 39. EIN or SSN.—Enter the financial institution's EIN. If the financial institution does not have an EIN, enter the SSN of the financial institution's principal owner.

Item 43. MICR Number.—If a depository institution, enter the Magnetic Ink Character Recognition (MICR) number.

Signature

Items 44 and 45. Title and Signature of Approving Official.—The official who reviews and approves the CTR must indicate his/her title and sign the CTR.

Item 46. Date the Form Was Signed.—The approving official must enter the date the CTR is signed. (See Item 8.)

Item 47. Preparer's Name.—Type or print the full name of the individual preparing the CTR. The preparer and the approving official may not necessarily be the same individual.

Items 48 and 49. Contact Person/Telephone Number.—Type or print the name and telephone number of an individual to contact concerning questions about the CTR.

362   *Printed on recycled paper*

Exhibit 19-1 (continued) Form 4789.

a. Banks and trust companies
b. Thrift institutions
c. Brokers and dealers in securities
d. Pawnbrokers
e. Currency exchangers
f. Check-cashing stores
g. Auto dealers
h. Real estate businesses
i. U.S. Postal Service money orders
j. Issuers, sellers, or redeemers of money orders, traveler's checks, and cashier's checks
k. Transmitters of funds
l. Telegraph companies
m. Casinos
n. Loan companies

The financial institution must file this form within 15 days from the date of the transaction. Also, the financial institution must retain copies or maintain a log of the transaction for 5 years. Currency is defined to include coins or paper of the United States or any other country, but not negotiable instruments.

2. **Form 4790.** Any person who transports cash or bearer instruments into or out of the United States requires this form (Exhibit 19-2). The title of this form is Report of International Transportation of Currency or Monetary Instruments (CMIR). The CMIR is to be filed at the time of entry or departure from the United States with U.S. Customs. Monetary instruments are defined, as amended, to include:

a. U.S. and foreign coin and currency
b. Bearer-negotiable instruments (personal checks, business checks, bank checks, cashier's checks, promissory notes, and money orders)
c. Bearer stock and securities

Transportation is defined to include physical mailing and shipping as well as carrying.

3. **Form 90-22.1.** This form (Exhibit 19-3) requires a person to report any transaction with a foreign financial institution. This form is titled Report of Foreign Bank and Financial Accounts (FBAR). Accounts with domestic branches of foreign banks are exempt from this requirement. The report requires the aggregation of separate accounts regardless of whether they are located in one or more foreign countries. This form is required to be filed by June 30 of each calendar year with respect to foreign financial accounts exceeding $10,000 during the previous calendar year. This requirement is in addition to the block on IRS Form 1040, Schedule B.

In 1984, Congress passed the Deficit Reduction Act, commonly known as the Tax Reform Act of 1984. Congress added Internal Revenue Code Section 6050I to enable the IRS to discover unreported income, from legal or illegal sources, by identifying taxpayers involved in large cash transactions. Section 6050I requires information returns to be filed

(U.S. Customs Use Only)		DEPARTMENT OF THE TREASURY UNITED STATES CUSTOMS SERVICE	Form Approved OMB No. 1515-0079

Control No.

31 U.S.C. 5316; 31 CFR 103.23 and 103.25

▶ Please type or print.

REPORT OF INTERNATIONAL TRANSPORTATION OF CURRENCY OR MONETARY INSTRUMENTS

▶ This form is to be filed with the United States Customs Service

▶ For Paperwork Reduction Act Notice and Privacy Act Notice, see back of form.

Part I FOR INDIVIDUAL DEPARTING FROM OR ENTERING THE UNITED STATES

1. NAME (Last or family, first, and middle)	2. IDENTIFYING NO. (See instructions)	3. DATE OF BIRTH (Mo./Day/Yr.)
4. PERMANENT ADDRESS IN UNITED STATES OR ABROAD		5. OF WHAT COUNTRY ARE YOU A CITIZEN/SUBJECT?
6. ADDRESS WHILE IN THE UNITED STATES		7. PASSPORT NO. & COUNTRY
8. U.S. VISA DATE	9. PLACE UNITED STATES VISA WAS ISSUED	10. IMMIGRATION ALIEN NO. (If any)

11. CURRENCY OR MONETARY INSTRUMENT WAS: (Complete 11A or 11B)

A. EXPORTED		B. IMPORTED	
Departed From: (City in U.S.)	Arrived At: (Foreign City/Country)	From: (Foreign City/Country)	At: (City in U.S.)

Part II FOR PERSON SHIPPING, MAILING, OR RECEIVING CURRENCY OR MONETARY INSTRUMENTS

12. NAME (Last or family, first, and middle)	13. IDENTIFYING NO. (See instructions)	14. DATE OF BIRTH (Mo./Day/Yr.)
15. PERMANENT ADDRESS IN UNITED STATES OR ABROAD		16. OF WHAT COUNTRY ARE YOU A CITIZEN/SUBJECT?
17. ADDRESS WHILE IN THE UNITED STATES		18. PASSPORT NO. & COUNTRY
19. U.S. VISA DATE	20. PLACE UNITED STATES VISA WAS ISSUED	21. IMMIGRATION ALIEN NO. (If any)

22. CURRENCY OR MONETARY INSTRUMENTS DATE SHIPPED DATE RECEIVED	23. CURRENCY OR MONETARY INSTRUMENTS ☐ Shipped To ▶ ☐ Received From ▶	NAME AND ADDRESS	24. IF THE CURRENCY OR MONETARY INSTRUMENT WAS MAILED, SHIPPED, OR TRANSPORTED COMPLETE BLOCKS A AND B. A. Method of Shipment (Auto, U.S. Mail, Public Carrier, etc.) B. Name of Transporter/Carrier

Part III CURRENCY AND MONETARY INSTRUMENT INFORMATION (SEE INSTRUCTIONS ON REVERSE)(To be completed by everyone)

25. TYPE AND AMOUNT OF CURRENCY/MONETARY INSTRUMENTS		Value in U.S. Dollars	26. IF OTHER THAN U.S. CURRENCY IS INVOLVED, PLEASE COMPLETE BLOCKS A AND B. (SEE SPECIAL INSTRUCTIONS)
Coins...........................	☐ A. ▶	$	A. Currency Name
Currency........................	☐ B. ▶		
Other Instruments (Specify Type) ___	☐ C. ▶		B. Country
(Add lines A, B and C).................	TOTAL AMOUNT ▶	$	

Part IV GENERAL - TO BE COMPLETED BY ALL TRAVELERS, SHIPPERS, AND RECIPIENTS

27. WERE YOU ACTING AS AN AGENT, ATTORNEY OR IN CAPACITY FOR ANYONE IN THIS CURRENCY OR MONETARY INSTRUMENT ACTIVITY? (If "Yes" complete A, B and C) ☐ Yes ☐ No

PERSON IN WHOSE BE-HALF YOU ARE ACTING ▶	A. Name	B. Address	C. Business activity, occupation, or profession

Under penalties of perjury, I declare that I have examined this report, and to the best of my knowledge and belief it is true, correct and complete.

28. NAME AND TITLE	29. SIGNATURE	30. DATE

(Replaces IRS Form 4790 which is obsolete)

Customs Form 4790 (043093)

continued

Exhibit 19-2 Form 4790.

GENERAL INSTRUCTIONS

This report is required by Treasury Department regulations (31 Code of Federal Regulations 103).

Who Must File.--Each person who physically transports, mails, or ships, or causes to be physically transported, mailed, shipped or received currency or other monetary instruments in an aggregate amount exceeding $10,000 on any one occasion from the United States to any place outside the United States, or into the United States from any place outside the United States.

A TRANSFER OF FUNDS THROUGH NORMAL BANKING PROCEDURES WHICH DOES NOT INVOLVE THE PHYSICAL TRANSPORTATION OF CURRENCY OR MONETARY INSTRUMENTS IS NOT REQUIRED TO BE REPORTED.

Exceptions.--The following persons are not required to file reports: (1) a Federal Reserve bank, (2) a bank, a foreign bank, or a broker or dealer in securities in respect to currency or other monetary instruments mailed or shipped through the postal service or by common carrier, (3) a commercial bank or trust company organized under the laws of any State or of the United States with respect to overland shipments of currency or monetary instruments shipped to or received from an established customer maintaining a deposit relationship with the bank, in amounts which the bank may reasonably conclude do not exceed amounts commensurate with the customary conduct of the business, industry, or profession of the customer concerned, (4) a person who is not a citizen or resident of the United States in respect to currency or other monetary instruments mailed or shipped from abroad to a bank or broker or dealer in securities through the postal service or by common carrier, (5) a common carrier of passengers in respect to currency or other monetary instruments in the possession of its passengers, (6) a common carrier of goods in respect to shipments of currency or monetary instruments not declared to be such by the shipper, (7) a travelers' check issuer or its agent in respect to the transportation of travelers' checks prior to their delivery to selling agents for eventual sale to the public, nor by (8) a person engaged as a business in the transportation of currency, monetary instruments and other commercial papers with respect to the transportation of currency or other monetary instruments overland between established offices of banks or brokers or dealers in securities and foreign persons.

WHEN AND WHERE TO FILE:

A. Recipients.--Each person who receives currency or other monetary instruments shall file Form 4790, within 30 days after receipt, with the Customs officer in charge at any port of entry or departure or by mail with the Commissioner of Customs, Attention: Currency Transportation Reports, Washington DC 20229.

B. Shippers or Mailers:--If the currency or other monetary instrument does not accompany the person entering or departing the United States, Form 4790 may be filed by mail on or before the date of entry, departure, mailing, or shipping with the Commissioner of Customs, Attention: Currency Transportation Reports, Washington DC 20229.

C. Travelers.--Travelers carrying currency or other monetary instruments with them shall file Form 4790 at the time of entry into the United States or at the time of departure from the United States with the Customs officer in charge at any Customs port of entry or departure.

An additional report of a particular transportation, mailing, or shipping of currency or the monetary instruments, is not required if a complete and truthful report has already been filed. However, no person otherwise required to file a report shall be excused from liability for failure to do so if, in fact, a complete and truthful report has not been filed. Forms may be obtained from any United States Customs Service office.

PENALTIES.--Civil and criminal penalties, including under certain circumstances a fine of not more than $500,000 and imprisonment of not more than five years, are provided for failure to file a report, supply information, and for filing a false or fraudulent report. In addition, the currency or monetary instrument may be subject to seizure and forfeiture. See section 103.47, 103.48 and 103.49 of the regulations.

DEFINITIONS:

Bank.--Each agent, agency, branch or office within the United States of a foreign bank and each agency, branch or office within the United States of any person doing business in one or more of the capacities listed: (1) a commercial bank or trust company organized under the laws of any state or of the United States; (2) a private bank; (3) a savings and loan association or a building and loan association organized under the laws of any state or of the United States; (4) an insured institution as defined in section 401 of the National Housing Act; (5) a savings bank, industrial bank or other thrift institution; (6) a credit union organized under the laws of any state or of the United States; and (7) any other organization chartered under the banking laws of any state and subject to the supervision of the bank supervisory authorities of a state.

Foreign Bank.--A bank organized under foreign law, or an agency, branch or office located outside the United States of a bank. The term does not include an agent, agency, branch or office within the United States of a bank organized under foreign law.

Broker or Dealer in Securities.--A broker or dealer in securities, registered or required to be registered with the Securities and Exchange Commission under the Securities Exchange Act of 1934.

IDENTIFICATION NUMBER.--Individuals must enter their social security number, if any. However, aliens who do not have a social security number should enter passport or alien registration number. All others should enter their employer identification number.

Investment Security.--An instrument which: (1) is issued in bearer or registered form; (2) is of a type commonly dealt in upon securities exchanges or markets or commonly recognized in any areas in which it is issued or dealt in as a medium for investment; (3) is either one of a class or series or by its terms is divisible into a class or series of instruments; and (4) evidences a share, participation or other interest in property or in an enterprise or evidences an obligation of the issuer.

Monetary Instruments.--Coin or currency of the United States or of any other country, travelers' checks, money orders, investment securities in bearer form or otherwise in such form that title thereto passes upon delivery, and negotiable instruments (except warehouse receipts or bills of lading) in bearer form or other in such form that title thereto passes upon delivery. The term includes bank checks, travelers' checks and money orders which are signed but on which the name of the payee has been omitted, but does not include bank checks, travelers' checks or money orders made payable to the order of a named person which have not been endorsed or which bear restrictive endorsements.

Person.--An individual, a corporation, a partnership, a trust or estate, a joint stock company, and association, a syndicate, joint venture or other unincorporated organization or group, and all entities cognizable as legal personalities.

SPECIAL INSTRUCTIONS:

You should complete each line which applies to you. Part II.--Line 22, enter the exact date you shipped or received currency or monetary instrument(s). Line 23, check the applicable box and give the complete name and address of the shipper or recipient. Part III.--Line 26, if currency or monetary instruments of more than one country is involved, attach a schedule showing each kind, country, and amount.

PRIVACY ACT AND PAPERWORK REDUCTION ACT NOTICE

Pursuant to the requirements of Public Law 93-579 (Privacy Act of 1974), notice is hereby given that the authority to collect information on Form 4790 in accordance with 5 U.S.C. 552a(e)(3) is Public Law 91-508; 31 U.S.C. 5316; 5 U.S.C. 301; Reorganization Plan No. 1 of 1950; Treasury Department No.165, revised, as amended; 31 CFR 103; and 44 U.S.C. 3501.

The principal purpose for collecting the information is to assure maintenance of reports or records where such reports or records have a high degree of usefulness in criminal, tax, or regulatory investigations or proceedings. The information collected may be provided to those officers and employees of the Customs Service and any other constituent unit of the Department of the Treasury who have a need for the records in the performance of their duties. The records may be referred to any other department or agency of the Federal Government upon the request of the head of such department or agency.

Disclosure of this information is mandatory. Failure to provide all or any part of the requested information may subject the currency or monetary instruments to seizure and forfeiture, as well as subject the individual to civil and criminal liabilities.

Disclosure of the social security number is mandatory. The authority to collect this number is 31 CFR 103.25. The social security number will be used as a means to identify the individual who files the record.

The collection of this information is mandatory pursuant to 31 U.S.C. 5316.

Statement Required by 5 CFR 1320.21: The estimated average burden associated with this collection of information is 10 minutes per respondent or recordkeeper depending on individual circumstances. Comments concerning the accuracy of this burden estimate and suggestions for reducing this burden should be directed to U.S. Customs Service, Paperwork Management Branch, Washington DC 20229, and to the Office of Management and Budget, Paperwork Reduction Project (1515-0079), Washington DC 20503.

---

*U.S. GPO: 1993-343-023/80734   Customs Form 4790 (043093)(Back)

Exhibit 19-2 (continued) Form 4790.

Department of the Treasury TD F 90-22.1 10/92 SUPERSEDES ALL PREVIOUS EDITIONS	REPORT OF FOREIGN BANK AND FINANCIAL ACCOUNTS For the calendar year 19 Do not file this form with your Federal Tax Return	Form Approved: OMB No. 1505-0063 Expiration Date: 9/95

This form should be used to report financial interest in or signature authority or other authority over one or more bank accounts, securities accounts, or other financial accounts in foreign countries as required by Department of the Treasury Regulations (31 CFR 103). You are not required to file a report if the aggregate value of the accounts did not exceed $10,000. Check all appropriate boxes. SEE INSTRUCTIONS ON BACK FOR DEFINITIONS. File this form with Dept. of the Treasury, P.O. Box 32621, Detroit, MI 48232.

1. Name (Last, First, Middle)	2. Social security number or employer identification number if other than individual	3. Name in item 1 refers to ☐ Individual ☐ Partnership ☐ Corporation ☐ Fiduciary
4. Address (Street, City, State, Country, ZIP)		

5. ☐ I had signature authority over one or more foreign accounts, but had no "financial interest" in such accounts (see Instruction J.) Indicate for these accounts:

(a) Name and social security number or taxpayer identification number of each owner _____

(b) Address of each owner _____

(Do not complete item 9 for these accounts)

6. ☐ I had a "financial interest" in one or more foreign accounts owned by a domestic corporation, partnership or trust which is required to file TD F 90-22.1 (See Instruction L). Indicate for these accounts.

(a) Name and taxpayer identification number of each such corporation, partnership or trust _____

(b) Address of each such corporation, partnership or trust _____

(Do not complete item 9 for these accounts)

7. ☐ I had a "financial interest" in one or more foreign accounts, but the total maximum value of these accounts (see Instruction I) did not exceed $10,000 at any time during the year. (If you checked this box, do not complete item 9).

8. ☐ I had a "financial interest" in 25 or more foreign accounts. (If you checked this box, do not complete item 9.)

9. If you had a "financial interest" in one or more but fewer than 25 foreign accounts which are required to be reported, and the total maximum value of the accounts exceeded $10,000 during the year (see Instruction I), write the total number of those accounts in the box below:
Complete items (a) through (f) below for one of the accounts and attach a separate TD F 90-22.1 for each of the others.
Items 1, 2, 3, and 10 must be completed for each account.

Check here if this is an attachment. ☐

(a) Name in which account is maintained	(b) Name of bank or other person with whom account is maintained
(c) Number and other account designation, if any	(d) Address of office or branch where account is maintained

(e) Type of account. (If not certain of English name for the type of account, give the foreign language name and describe the nature of the account. Attach additional sheets if necessary.)

☐ Bank Account   ☐ Securities Account   ☐ Other (specify)

(f) Maximum value of account (see instruction I)

☐ Under $10,000   ☐ $10,000 to $50,000   ☐ $50,000 to $100,000   ☐ Over $100,000

10. Signature	11. Title (Not necessary if reporting a personal account)	12. Date

PRIVACY ACT NOTIFICATION

Pursuant to the requirements of Public Law 93-579, (Privacy Act of 1974), notice is hereby given that the authority to collect information on TD F 90-22.1 in accordance with 5 U.S.C. 552(e)(3) is Public Law 91-508; 31 U.S.C. 1121; 5 U.S.C. 301, 31 CFR Part 103.

The principal purpose for collecting the information is to assure maintenance of reports or records where such reports or records have a high degree of usefulness in criminal, tax, or regulatory investigations or proceedings. The information collected may be provided to those officers and employees of any constituent unit of the Department of the Treasury who have a need for the records in the performance of their duties. The records may be referred to any other department or agency of the Federal Government upon the request of the head of such department or agency for use in a criminal, tax, or regulatory investigation or proceeding.

Disclosure of this information is mandatory. Civil and criminal penalties, including under certain circumstances a fine of not more than $500,000 and imprisonment of not more than five years, are provided for failure to file a report, supply information, and for filing a false or fraudulent report.

Disclosure of the social security number is mandatory. The authority to collect this number is 31 CFR 103. The social security number will be used as a means to identify the individual who files the report.

Cat. No. 12996D
415

continued

Exhibit 19-3 Form 90-22.1.

INSTRUCTIONS

A. Who Must File a Report—Each United States person who has a financial interest in or signature authority or other authority over bank, securities, or other financial accounts in a foreign country, which exceeds $10,000 in aggregate value at any time during the calendar year, must report that relationship each calendar year by filing TD F 90-22.1 with the Department of the Treasury on or before June 30, of the succeeding year.

An officer or employee of a commercial bank which is subject to the supervision of the Comptroller of the Currency, the Board of Governors of the Federal Reserve System, or the Federal Deposit Insurance Corporation need not report that he has signature or other authority over a foreign bank, securities or other financial account maintained by the bank unless he has a personal financial interest in the account.

In addition, an officer or employee of a domestic corporation whose securities are listed upon national securities exchanges or which has assets exceeding $1 million and 500 or more shareholders of record need not file such a report concerning his signature authority over a foreign financial account of the corporation, if he has no personal financial interest in the account and has been advised in writing by the chief financial officer of the corporation that the corporation has filed a current report which includes that account.

B. United States Person—The term "United States person" means (1) a citizen or resident of the United States, (2) a domestic partnership, (3) a domestic corporation, or (4) a domestic estate or trust.

C. When and Where to File—This report shall be filed on or before June 30 each calendar year with the Department of the Treasury, Post Office Box 32621, Detroit, MI 48232, or it may be hand carried to any local office of the Internal Revenue Service for forwarding to the Department of the Treasury, Detroit, MI.

D. Account in a Foreign Country—A "foreign country" includes all geographical areas located outside the United States, Guam, Puerto Rico, and the Virgin Islands.

Report any account maintained with a bank (except a military banking facility as defined in instruction E) or broker or dealer in securities that is located in a foreign country, even if it is a part of a United States bank or other institution. Do not report any account maintained with a branch, agency, or other office of a foreign bank of other institution that is located in the United States, Guam, Puerto Rico, and the Virgin Islands.

E. Military Banking Facility—Do not consider as an account in a foreign country, an account in an institution known as a "United States military banking facility" (or "United States military finance facility") operated by a United States financial institution designated by the United States Government to serve U.S. Government installations abroad, even if the United States military banking facility is located in a foreign country.

F. Bank, Financial Account—The term "bank account" means a savings, demand, checking, deposit, loan or any other account maintained with a financial institution or other person engaged in the business of banking. It includes certificates of deposit.

The term "securities account" means an account maintained with a financial institution or other person who buys, sells, holds, or trades stock or other securities for the benefit of another.

The term "other financial account" means any other account maintained with a financial institution or other person who accepts deposits, exchanges or transmits funds, or acts as a broker or dealer for future transactions in any commodity on (or subject to the rules of) a commodity exchange or association.

G. Financial Interest—A financial interest in a bank, securities, or other financial account in a foreign country means an interest described in either of the following two paragraphs:

(1) A United States person has a financial interest in each account for which such person is the owner of records or has legal title, whether the account is maintained for his or her own benefit or for the benefit of others including non-United States persons. If an account is maintained in the name of two persons jointly, or if several persons each own a partial interest in an account, each of those United States persons has a financial interest in that account.

(2) A United States person has a financial interest in each bank, securities, or other financial account in a foreign country for which the owner of record or holder of legal title is: (a) a person acting as an agent, nominee, attorney, or in some other capacity on behalf of the U.S. person; (b) a corporation in which the United States person owns directly or indirectly more than 50 percent of the total value of shares of stock; (c) a partnership in which the United States person owns an interest in more than 50 percent of the profits (distributive share of income); or (d) a trust in which the United States person either has a present beneficial interest in more than 50 percent of the assets or from which such person receives more than 50 percent of the current income.

H. Signature or Other Authority Over an Account—

Signature Authority—A person has signature authority over an account if such person can control the disposition of money or other property in it by delivery of a document containing his or here signature (or his or her signature and that of one or more other persons) to the bank or other person with whom the account is maintained.

Other authority exists in a person who can exercise comparable power over an account by direct communication to the bank or other person with whom the account is maintained, either orally or by some other means.

I. Account Valuation—For items 7, 9, and Instruction A, the maximum value of an account is the largest amount of currency and non-monetary assets that appear on any quarterly or more frequent account statement issued for the applicable year. If periodic account statements are not so issued, the maximum account asset value is the largest amount of currency and non-monetary assets in the account at any time during the year. Convert foreign currency by using the official exchange rate at the end of the year. In valuing currency of a country that uses multiple exchange rates, use the rate which would apply if the currency in the account were converted into United States dollars at the close of the calendar year.

The value of stock, other securities or other non-monetary assets in an account reported on TD F 90-22.1 is the fair market value at the end of the calendar year, or if withdrawn from the account, at the time of the withdrawal.

For purposes of items 7, 9, and Instruction A, if you had a financial interest in more than one account, each account is to be valued separately in accordance with the foregoing two paragraphs.

If you had a financial interest in one or more but fewer than 25 accounts, and you are unable to determine whether the maximum value of these accounts exceeded $10,000 at any time during the year, check item 9 (do not check item 7) and complete item 9 for each of these accounts.

J. United States Persons with Authority Over but No Interest in an Account—Except as provided in Instruction A the following paragraph, you must state the name, address, and identifying number of each owner of an account over which you had authority, but if you check item 5 for more than one account of the same owner, you need identify the owner only once.

If you check item 5 for one or more accounts in which no United States person had a financial interest, you may state on the first line of this item, in lieu of supplying information about the owner, "No U.S. person had any financial interest in the foreign accounts." This statement must be based upon the actual belief of the person filing this form after he or she has taken reasonable measures to endure its correctness.

If you check item 5 for accounts owned by a domestic corporation and its domestic and/or foreign subsidiaries, you may treat them as one owner and write in the space provided, the name of the parent corporation, followed by "and related entities," and the identifying number and address of the parent corporation.

K. Consolidated Reporting—A corporation which owns directly or indirectly more than 50 percent interest in one or more other entities will be permitted to file a consolidated report on TD F 90-22.1, on behalf of itself and such other entities provided that a listing of them is made part of the consolidated report. Such reports should be signed by an authorized official of the parent corporation.

If the group of entities covered by a consolidated report has a financial interest in 25 or more foreign financial accounts, the reporting corporation need only note that fact on the form, it will, however, be required to provide detailed information concerning each account when so requested by the Secretary or his delegate.

L. Avoiding Duplicate Reporting—If you had financial interest (as defined in instruction G(2)(b), (c) or (d) in one or more accounts which are owned by a domestic corporation, partnership or trust which is required to file TD F 90-22.1 with respect to these accounts in lieu of completing item 9 for each account you may check item 6 and provide the required information.

M. Providing Additional Information—Any person who does not complete item 9, shall when requested by the Department of the Treasury provide the information called for in item 9.

N. Signature (Item 10)—*This report must be signed* by the person named in Item 1. If the report is being filed on behalf of a partnership, corporation, or fiduciary, it must be signed by an authorized individual.

O. Penalties—For criminal penalties for failure to file a report, supply information, and for filing a false or fraudulent report see 31 U.S.C. 5322(a), 31 U.S.C. 5322(b), and 18 U.S.C. 1001.

The estimated average burden associated with this collection of information is 10 minutes per respondent or recordkeeper depending on individual circumstances. Comments concerning the accuracy of this burden estimate and suggestions for reducing the burden should be directed to the Department of the Treasury, Office of Financial Enforcement, Room 5000 Treasury Annex Building, Washington DC 200220, and to the Office of Management and Budget, Paperwork Reduction Project (1505-0063), Washington DC 20503.

*U.S. G.P.O.:1993-345-055

Exhibit 19-3 (continued) Form 90-22.1.

by all trade or businesses for cash transactions over $10,000. Using Form 8300 (Exhibit 19-4) does this. It further requires that the form be filed within 15 days after the cash is received. It also requires the filing of Form 8300 when all payments aggregate to more than $10,000. Also, the reporting requirement is imposed to any receipt of cash in connection with a trade or business whether or not the receipt constitutes income in the trade or business. Cash is defined as coin or currency of the United States or any other country, which is circulated in and customarily used and accepted as money in the country in which it is issued. Cash does not include bank checks, traveler's checks, bank drafts, wire transfers, or other negotiable or monetary instruments.

In 1986, Congress passed the Anti-Drug Abuse Act. This act subjects persons to criminal liability for knowingly participating in any laundering of money. It extended money-laundering schemes to include wire transfers. It increased fines and penalties and promoted the international exchange of information.

In 1988, Congress passed the Omnibus Drug Bill II, commonly called the Anti-Drug Abuse Act of 1988. This bill forbids financial institutions from issuing or selling bank checks, traveler's checks, cashier's checks, in connection with cash of $3,000 or more unless the person has an account. It also requires additional record-keeping requirements. Additional penalties are imposed on financial institution officers, directors, and employees. The Treasury Department is required to negotiate with foreign countries.

Schemes

Suppose a person has received income, whether legal or illegal, which the person wants to hide from his or her income or from others. The person can hide it under the mattress or elsewhere, but that would leave the person vulnerable to theft and would not get the benefit of spending or investing the money. If the proceeds are in small denominations, then the person has the problem of exchanging the small bills for larger bills. Spending large bills could cause unwanted attention to the person. Also, a large amount of bills is cumbersome to carry or transport. A million dollars in $20 bills weighs 113 pounds. The person usually starts to convert the money to readily acceptable forms, i.e., money orders, traveler's checks, etc. In many cases, the person will open up more than one bank account and make frequent deposits into them. There is usually more than one bank involved. *Smurfing* is the term used for a person making deposits into various accounts and banks on the same or subsequent days. *Structuring* is the term used for a person making more than one deposit into the same or various bank accounts at the same bank or financial institution. If the person has no legitimate source of income, then the person will want to acquire a business so that money can be run through it. The business would pay a salary or show it loaning the person money. The person may even transfer money to foreign bank accounts with bank secrecy laws.

Form 8300

(Rev. August 1997)

Department of the Treasury
Internal Revenue Service

Report of Cash Payments Over $10,000 Received in a Trade or Business

▶ See instructions for definition of cash.
▶ Use this form for transactions occurring after July 31, 1997.
Please type or print.

OMB No. 1545-0892

1 Check appropriate box(es) if: **a** ☐ Amends prior report; **b** ☐ Suspicious transaction.

Part I Identity of Individual From Whom the Cash Was Received

2 If more than one individual is involved, check here and see instructions . . . . ▶ ☐

3 Last name	4 First name	5 M.I.	6 Taxpayer identification number

7 Address (number, street, and apt. or suite no.)

8 Date of birth . ▶ M M D D Y Y Y Y
(see instructions)

9 City	10 State	11 ZIP code	12 Country (if not U.S.)	13 Occupation, profession, or business

14 Document used to verify identity: **a** Describe identification ▶ ----------
b Issued by ---------- **c** Number

Part II Person on Whose Behalf This Transaction Was Conducted

15 If this transaction was conducted on behalf of more than one person, check here and see instructions . . . . . ▶ ☐

16 Individual's last name or Organization's name	17 First name	18 M.I.	19 Taxpayer identification number

20 Doing business as (DBA) name (see instructions)

Employer identification number

21 Address (number, street, and apt. or suite no.)

22 Occupation, profession, or business

23 City	24 State	25 ZIP code	26 Country (if not U.S.)

27 Alien identification: **a** Describe identification ▶ ----------
b Issued by ---------- **c** Number

Part III Description of Transaction and Method of Payment

28 Date cash received M M D D Y Y Y Y	29 Total cash received $ .00	30 If cash was received in more than one payment, check here . . . ▶ ☐	31 Total price if different from item 29 $ .00

32 Amount of cash received (in U.S. dollar equivalent) (must equal item 29) (see instructions):

a U.S. currency $ _____ .00 (Amount in $100 bills or higher $ _____ .00)
b Foreign currency $ _____ .00 (Country ▶ _____)
c Cashier's check(s) $ _____ .00 Issuer's name(s) and serial number(s) of the monetary instrument(s) ▶ ----------
d Money order(s) $ _____ .00
e Bank draft(s) $ _____ .00
f Traveler's check(s) $ _____ .00

33 Type of transaction

a ☐ Personal property purchased
b ☐ Real property purchased
c ☐ Personal services provided
d ☐ Business services provided
e ☐ Intangible property purchased
f ☐ Debt obligations paid
g ☐ Exchange of cash
h ☐ Escrow or trust funds
i ☐ Bail bond
j ☐ Other (specify) ▶

34 Specific description of property or service shown in 33. (Give serial or registration number, address, docket number, etc.) ▶ ----------

Part IV Business That Received Cash

35 Name of business that received cash

36 Employer identification number

37 Address (number, street, and apt. or suite no.)

Social security number

38 City	39 State	40 ZIP code	41 Nature of your business

42 Under penalties of perjury, I declare that to the best of my knowledge the information I have furnished above is true, correct, and complete.

Signature of authorized official

Title of authorized official

43 Date of signature M M D D Y Y Y Y	44 Type or print name of contact person	45 Contact telephone number ( )

For Paperwork Reduction Act Notice, see page 4.

365

Cat. No. 62133S

Form **8300** (Rev. 8-97)

Exhibit 19-4 Form 8300.

Form 8300 (Rev. 8-97)   Page **2**

Multiple Parties
(Complete applicable parts below if box 2 or 15 on page 1 is checked)

Part I   Continued—Complete if box 2 on page 1 is checked

3 Last name	4 First name	5 M.I.	6 Taxpayer identification number
7 Address (number, street, and apt. or suite no.)		8 Date of birth. ▶ (see instructions)	M M D D Y Y Y Y
9 City	10 State	11 ZIP code	12 Country (if not U.S.)	13 Occupation, profession, or business

14 Document used to verify identity: **a** Describe identification ▶ ....
    b Issued by   **c** Number

3 Last name	4 First name	5 M.I.	6 Taxpayer identification number
7 Address (number, street, and apt. or suite no.)		8 Date of birth. ▶ (see instructions)	M M D D Y Y Y Y
9 City	10 State	11 ZIP code	12 Country (if not U.S.)	13 Occupation, profession, or business

14 Document used to verify identity: **a** Describe identification ▶ ....
    b Issued by   **c** Number

Part II   Continued—Complete if box 15 on page 1 is checked

16 Individual's last name or Organization's name	17 First name	18 M.I.	19 Taxpayer identification number
20 Doing business as (DBA) name (see instructions)			Employer identification number
21 Address (number, street, and apt. or suite no.)			22 Occupation, profession, or business
23 City	24 State	25 ZIP code	26 Country (if not U.S.)

27 Alien identification: **a** Describe identification ▶ ....
    b Issued by   **c** Number

16 Individual's last name or Organization's name	17 First name	18 M.I.	19 Taxpayer identification number
20 Doing business as (DBA) name (see instructions)			Employer identification number
21 Address (number, street, and apt. or suite no.)			22 Occupation, profession, or business
23 City	24 State	25 ZIP code	26 Country (if not U.S.)

27 Alien identification: **a** Describe identification ▶ ....
    b Issued by   **c** Number

Exhibit 19-4 (continued) Form 8300.

Item You Should Note

Clerks of Federal or State courts must now file Form 8300 if more than $10,000 in cash is received as bail for an individual(s) charged with certain criminal offenses. For these purposes, a clerk includes the clerk's office or any other office, department, division, branch, or unit of the court that is authorized to receive bail. If a person receives bail on behalf of a clerk, the clerk is treated as receiving the bail.

If multiple payments are made in cash to satisfy bail and the initial payment does not exceed $10,000, the initial payment and subsequent payments must be aggregated and the information return must be filed by the 15th day after receipt of the payment that causes the aggregate amount to exceed $10,000 in cash. In such cases, the reporting requirement can be satisfied either by sending a single written statement with an aggregate amount listed or by furnishing a copy of each Form 8300 relating to that payer. Payments made to satisfy separate bail requirements are not required to be aggregated. See Treasury Regulations section 1.6050I-2.

Casinos must file Form 8300 for nongaming activities (restaurants, shops, etc.).

General Instructions

Who must file.—Each person engaged in a trade or business who, in the course of that trade or business, receives more than $10,000 in cash in one transaction or in two or more related transactions, must file Form 8300. Any transactions conducted between a payer (or its agent) and the recipient in a 24-hour period are related transactions. Transactions are considered related even if they occur over a period of more than 24 hours if the recipient knows, or has reason to know, that each transaction is one of a series of connected transactions.

Keep a copy of each Form 8300 for 5 years from the date you file it.

Voluntary use of Form 8300.—Form 8300 may be filed voluntarily for any suspicious transaction (see **Definitions**), even if the total amount does not exceed $10,000.

Exceptions.—Cash is not required to be reported if it is received:

● By a financial institution required to file **Form 4789**, Currency Transaction Report.

● By a casino required to file (or exempt from filing) **Form 8362**, Currency Transaction Report by Casinos, if the cash is received as part of its gaming business.

● By an agent who receives the cash from a principal, if the agent uses all of the cash within 15 days in a second transaction that is reportable on Form 8300 or on Form 4789, and discloses all the information necessary to complete Part II of Form 8300 or Form 4789 to the recipient of the cash in the second transaction.

● In a transaction occurring entirely outside the United States. See **Pub. 1544**, Reporting Cash Payments Over $10,000 (Received in a Trade or Business),

regarding transactions occurring in Puerto Rico, the Virgin Islands, and territories and possessions of the United States.

● In a transaction that is not in the course of a person's trade or business.

When to file.—File Form 8300 by the 15th day after the date the cash was received. If that date falls on a Saturday, Sunday, or legal holiday, file the form on the next business day.

Where to file.—File the form with the Internal Revenue Service, Detroit Computing Center, P.O. Box 32621, Detroit, MI 48232, or hand carry it to your local IRS office.

Statement to be provided.—You must give a written statement to each person named on a required Form 8300 on or before January 31 of the year following the calendar year in which the cash is received. The statement must show the name, telephone number, and address of the information contact for the business, the aggregate amount of reportable cash received, and that the information was furnished to the IRS. Keep a copy of the statement for your records.

Multiple payments.—If you receive more than one cash payment for a single transaction or for related transactions, you must report the multiple payments any time you receive a total amount that exceeds $10,000 within any 12-month period. Submit the report within 15 days of the date you receive the payment that causes the total amount to exceed $10,000. If more than one report is required within 15 days, you may file a combined report. File the combined report no later than the date the earliest report, if filed separately, would have to be filed.

Taxpayer identification number (TIN).—You must furnish the correct TIN of the person or persons from whom you receive the cash and, if applicable, the person or persons on whose behalf the transaction is being conducted. **You may be subject to penalties for an incorrect or missing TIN.**

The TIN for an individual (including a sole proprietorship) is the individual's social security number (SSN). For certain resident aliens who are not eligible to get an SSN and nonresident aliens who are required to file tax returns, it is an IRS Individual Taxpayer Identification Number (ITIN). For other persons, including corporations, partnerships, and estates, it is the employer identification number.

If you have requested but are not able to get a TIN for one or more of the parties to a transaction within 15 days following the transaction, file the report and attach a statement explaining why the TIN is not included.

Exception: You are not required to provide the TIN of a person who is a nonresident alien individual or a foreign organization **if** that person does not have income effectively connected with the conduct of a U.S. trade or business **and** does not have an office or place of business, or fiscal or paying agent, in the United States. See Pub. 1544 for more information.

Penalties.—You may be subject to penalties if you fail to file a correct and complete Form 8300 on time and you cannot show that the failure was due to reasonable cause. You may also be subject to penalties if you fail to furnish timely a correct and complete statement to each person named in a required report. A minimum penalty of $25,000 may be imposed if the failure is due to an intentional disregard of the cash reporting requirements.

Penalties may also be imposed for causing, or attempting to cause, a trade or business to fail to file a required report; for causing, or attempting to cause, a trade or business to file a required report containing a material omission or misstatement of fact; or for structuring, or attempting to structure, transactions to avoid the reporting requirements. These violations may also be subject to criminal prosecution which, upon conviction, may result in imprisonment of up to 5 years or fines of up to $250,000 for individuals and $500,000 for corporations or both.

Definitions

Cash.—The term "cash" means the following:

● U.S. and foreign coin and currency received in any transaction.

● A cashier's check, money order, bank draft, or traveler's check having a face amount of $10,000 or less that is received in a **designated reporting transaction** (defined below), or that is received in any transaction in which the recipient knows that the instrument is being used in an attempt to avoid the reporting of the transaction under section 6050I.

Note: Cash does not include a check drawn on the payer's own account, such as a personal check, regardless of the amount.

Designated reporting transaction.—A retail sale (or the receipt of funds by a broker or other intermediary in connection with a retail sale) of a consumer durable, a collectible, or a travel or entertainment activity.

Retail sale.—Any sale (whether or not the sale is for resale or for any other purpose) made in the course of a trade or business if that trade or business principally consists of making sales to ultimate consumers.

Consumer durable.—An item of tangible personal property of a type that, under ordinary usage, can reasonably be expected to remain useful for at least 1 year, and that has a sales price of more than $10,000.

Collectible.—Any work of art, rug, antique, metal, gem, stamp, coin, etc.

Travel or entertainment activity.—An item of travel or entertainment that pertains to a single trip or event if the combined sales price of the item and all other items relating to the same trip or event that are sold in the same transaction (or related transactions) exceeds $10,000.

Exceptions.—A cashier's check, money order, bank draft, or traveler's check is not considered received in a designated

Exhibit 19-4 (continued) Form 8300.

reporting transaction if it constitutes the proceeds of a bank loan or if it is received as a payment on certain promissory notes, installment sales contracts, or down payment plans. See Pub. 1544 for more information.

Person.—An individual, corporation, partnership, trust, estate, association, or company.

Recipient.—The person receiving the cash. Each branch or other unit of a person's trade or business is considered a separate recipient unless the branch receiving the cash (or a central office linking the branches), knows or has reason to know the identity of payers making cash payments to other branches.

Transaction.—Includes the purchase of property or services, the payment of debt, the exchange of a negotiable instrument for cash, and the receipt of cash to be held in escrow or trust. A single transaction may not be broken into multiple transactions to avoid reporting.

Suspicious transaction.—A transaction in which it appears that a person is attempting to cause Form 8300 not to be filed, or to file a false or incomplete form. The term also includes any transaction in which there is an indication of possible illegal activity.

Specific Instructions

You must complete all parts. However, you may skip Part II if the individual named in Part I is conducting the transaction on his or her behalf only.

Item 1.—If you are amending a prior report, check box 1a. Complete the appropriate items with the correct or amended information only. Complete all of Part IV. Staple a copy of the original report to the amended report.

To voluntarily report a suspicious transaction (see **Definitions**), check box 1b. You may also telephone your local IRS Criminal Investigation Division or call 1-800-800-2877.

Part I

Item 2.—If two or more individuals conducted the transaction you are reporting, check the box and complete Part I for any one of the individuals. Provide the same information for the other individual(s) on the back of the form. If more than three individuals are involved, provide the same information on additional sheets of paper and attach them to this form.

Item 6.—Enter the taxpayer identification number (TIN) of the individual named. See **Taxpayer identification number (TIN)** under **General Instructions** for more information.

Item 8.—Enter eight numerals for the date of birth of the individual named. For example, if the individual's birth date is July 6, 1960, enter 07 06 1960.

Item 13.—Fully describe the nature of the occupation, profession, or business (for example, "plumber," "attorney," or "automobile dealer"). Do not use general or

nondescriptive terms such as "businessman" or "self-employed."

Item 14.—You must verify the name and address of the named individual(s). Verification must be made by examination of a document normally accepted as a means of identification when cashing checks (for example, a driver's license, passport, alien registration card, or other official document). In item 14a, enter the type of document examined. In item 14b, identify the issuer of the document. In item 14c, enter the document's number. For example, if the individual has a Utah driver's license, enter "driver's license" in item 14a, "Utah" in item 14b, and the number appearing on the license in item 14c.

Part II

Item 15.—If the transaction is being conducted on behalf of more than one person (including husband and wife or parent and child), check the box and complete Part II for any one of the persons. Provide the same information for the other person(s) on the back of the form. If more than three persons are involved, provide the same information on additional sheets of paper and attach them to this form.

Items 16 through 19.—If the person on whose behalf the transaction is being conducted is an individual, complete items 16, 17, and 18. Enter his or her TIN in item 19. If the individual is a sole proprietor and has an employer identification number (EIN), you must enter both the SSN and EIN in item 19. If the person is an organization, put its name as shown on required tax filings in item 16 and its EIN in item 19.

Item 20.—If a sole proprietor or organization named in items 16 through 18 is doing business under a name other than that entered in item 16 (e.g., a "trade" or "doing business as (DBA)" name), enter it here.

Item 27.—If the person is **NOT** required to furnish a TIN (see **Taxpayer identification number (TIN)** under **General Instructions**), complete this item. Enter a description of the type of official document issued to that person in item 27a (for example, "passport"), the country that issued the document in item 27b, and the document's number in item 27c.

Part III

Item 28.—Enter the date you received the cash. If you received the cash in more than one payment, enter the date you received the payment that caused the combined amount to exceed $10,000. See **Multiple payments** under **General Instructions** for more information.

Item 30.—Check this box if the amount shown in item 29 was received in more than one payment (for example, as installment payments or payments on related transactions).

Item 31.—Enter the total price of the property, services, amount of cash exchanged, etc. (for example, the total cost

of a vehicle purchased, cost of catering service, exchange of currency) if different from the amount shown in item 29.

Item 32.—Enter the dollar amount of each form of cash received. Show foreign currency amounts in U.S. dollar equivalent at a fair market rate of exchange available to the public. **The sum of the amounts must equal item 29.** For cashier's check, money order, bank draft, or traveler's check, provide the name of the issuer and the serial number of each instrument. Names of all issuers and all serial numbers involved must be provided. If necessary, provide this information on additional sheets of paper and attach them to this form.

Item 33.—Check the appropriate box(es) that describe the transaction. If the transaction is not specified in boxes a–i, check box j and briefly describe the transaction (for example, car lease, boat lease, house lease, aircraft rental).

Part IV

Item 36.—If you are a sole proprietorship, you must enter your SSN. If your business also has an EIN, you must provide the EIN as well. All other business entities must enter an EIN.

Item 41.—Fully describe the nature of your business, for example, "attorney," "jewelry dealer." Do not use general or nondescriptive terms such as "business" or "store."

Item 42.—This form must be signed by an individual who has been authorized to do so for the business that received the cash.

Paperwork Reduction Act Notice

The requested information is useful in criminal, tax, and regulatory investigations, for instance, by directing the Federal Government's attention to unusual or questionable transactions. Trades or businesses are required to provide the information under 26 U.S.C. 6050I.

You are not required to provide the information requested on a form that is subject to the Paperwork Reduction Act unless the form displays a valid OMB control number. Books or records relating to a form or its instructions must be retained as long as their contents may become material in the administration of any Internal Revenue law. Generally, tax returns and return information are confidential, as required by Code section 6103.

The time needed to complete this form will vary depending on individual circumstances. The estimated average time is 21 minutes. If you have comments concerning the accuracy of this time estimate or suggestions for making this form simpler, you can write to the Tax Forms Committee, Western Area Distribution Center, Rancho Cordova, CA 95743-0001. DO NOT send this form to this office. Instead, see **Where To File** on page 3.

✪ 368

Exhibit 19-4 (continued) Form 8300.

Business

Money laundering in businesses involves three principal methods:

1. *Balance sheet.* Balance sheet money laundering encompasses making cash deposits into a business bank account. The person writes checks using that money. The deposits are credited to shareholder loans and the checks are charged against shareholder loans. The taxpayer avoids paying income taxes on the funds in this case.
2. *Overstating revenue.* The person makes deposits into the business bank accounts and credits it to legitimate income. The person uses the funds to pay his or her own or relatives' salaries or their expenses. Another version is to purchase items with cash at a discount. The discount is not recorded on the invoice. The books show the full price paid for the item.
3. *Overstating expenses.* In this case, the person pays wages for nonexistent employees or pays for supplies or services that it never receives.

Trusts

Some criminals use trusts to hide funds or assets. It can be as simple as having an individual, such as an attorney, hold title to real or personal property in the attorney's name as "trustee." Trusts can be complex. The trustee holds income-producing property, real or personal, for the grantor. The trustee collects the income and pays the expenses for the trust property. The trustee will charge fees for this service, usually based upon the time spent in administering the trust. The trustee will file tax returns for the trust and pay the taxes. The grantor of the trust can also be the beneficiary. In some cases, the trust does not pay taxes, but passes the income down to the grantor or beneficiaries. Trustees can be almost anyone. They can be a bank or trust company, insurance company, an attorney, accountant, relative, or close friend.

The fraud examiner must view trusts in terms of hiding assets by the criminals. The difficulty with trusts is connecting the trust and its assets to the grantor or beneficiary. Trust agreements are not recorded in public records for the most part. They are generally not filed with federal or state tax authorities, except during tax examinations. Therefore, other investigative techniques have to be used. Criminals like to and want to hide ownership of real or personal property; however, they do not want to relinquish control over the property. Fraud examiners and law enforcement must look to the control factor for uncovering hidden ownership. Observing the following can do this:

1. The criminal constantly uses the property, while it is titled to a trustee.
2. Title to the property is transferred to the trust, but the liability is still retained by the grantor.
3. The grantor has inadequate income history to have allowed for such cash accumulation or asset purchase.
4. The grantor and trustee sign documents jointly for the property and related liabilities.

5. The grantor transfers property to the trust during a bond hearing after just being arrested for criminal activities.
6. The grantor is present when the purchase is made.
7. The grantor has possession of personal property titled to the trust.
8. The grantor pays rent to trust for use of trust property. Usually, the grantor pays rent either at, below, or higher than market values in the same area.
9. The grantor has to provide funds to the trust to keep it liquid or stable.
10. The grantor owned the property prior to the trust. The grantor made the transfer prior to his or her criminal activities to have future or current benefit of the property or so that the children would have an inheritance.

Nominees

A nominee is a person designated to act for another as an agent or trustee. Criminals use nominees to hide assets. In some cases, nominees are involved with the criminals in the illegal activities. Another version of nominees is called the *alter ego*. Alter ego refers to entities, corporate and business entities, that are intermixed so that their income and assets are not separable. The fraud examiner must look to the possibility of criminals using nominees and alter egos (when businesses are involved) for hiding assets. The indicators of nominees and alter egos are as follows:

1. A close or suspected relationship exists between the parties. These include:

a. Blood or marriage relationship;
b. Length of association;
c. Common address;
d. Same corporate stockholders, directors, officers, employees, attorney, accountant, etc.

2. Inadequate consideration by nominee/alter ego is given for asset purchased from the criminal. Examples include:

a. An asset transfer without a transfer of the matching liabilities;
b. Inadequate deed stamps;
c. Book value transfer of an appreciated property;
d. Use of the term "gift" on vehicle title transfers (usually done to evade state sales tax);
e. Payment of a long-term, low-interest note without adequate security;
f. Alleged consideration was for an "assumption of liabilities" by the purchaser. If so, were the assumed liabilities less than the value of the transferred property, did the criminal continue to satisfy the liabilities?

3. The nominee/alter ego does not have the ability to pay for the asset. Examples:

a. Inadequate income history reported by the nominee to have allowed such cash accumulation;
b. Interest deductions on tax returns showing large debts of nominee/alter ego;

    c.   Lack of dividend/interest income sources;

    d.   Nominee too young to have accumulated funds;

    e.   Financial statements in obtaining credit cards or applying for bank loans, opening bank accounts, making installment purchases that show inability to acquire asset;

    f.   Cosigning by the criminal that may show that the nominee's credit record or the criminal's collateral was responsible for the loan;

    g.   Lack of a "paper trail" through the bank/savings account;

    h.   Nominee who is on welfare or social security.

    4. The criminal has the ability to have paid for the asset. Examples:

    a.   The likely source of income from illegal acts;

    b.   The criminal's lifestyle;

    c.   Liquidations by the criminal prior to the nominee's purchase of an asset;

    d.   Presence of the criminal when the seller received the proceeds.

    5. There is proof of the inability of the nominee to operate the asset. Examples:

    a.   Inexperience or lack of education of nominee;

    b.   Complexity, special skill, or experience required not possessed by nominee but possessed by the criminal;

    c.   No business or occupational license by nominee;

    d.   Lack of physical strength or stamina of nominee;

    e.   Lack of zoning clearance with the nominee's alter ego location.

    6. There is proof of continued use and possession by the criminal. Examples:

    a.   Asset at criminal's address;

    b.   Insurance shows criminal as operator or occupant;

    c.   The criminal physically drives, occupies, repairs, maintains, etc. the asset;

    d.   No change of asset use after the supposed transfer;

    e.   The keys (to car, house, safety deposit box, business, etc.) in the possession of the criminal or the criminal's attorney;

    f.   The criminal uses the asset but pays no rent to nominee or pays grossly excessive rent.

    7. The criminal maintains control. Examples:

    a.   The criminal's senior status in the family;

    b.   The criminal's supervision, hiring, and firing of employees and officers;

    c.   The criminal's access and signatory authority over nominee's bank accounts;

    d.   The criminal making contracts or ordering repairs for nominee's assets;

    e.   The personal expenses or "perks" are by the nominee.

8. The nominee knew or should have known of skimming or other unclean funds. Examples:

a. Spouses and other close relatives can almost never claim ignorance, especially if they work in the business with the criminal.
b. If related corporations have the same officers, accountants, employees, etc., they are in an awkward position to allege ignorance.
c. Illegal use of incorporation is a valid ground for piercing the corporate veil or dissolving the corporation.

9. The nominee fails to observe corporate formalities.

a. Improper incorporation;
b. Under capitalization;
c. Failure to file tax returns, federal and state;
d. Acting outside corporate charter;
e. Failure to obtain various tax numbers;
f. Failure to file tax returns;
g. Failure to maintain corporate books and minutes;
h. Failure to obtain stock subscription payments from stockholders;
i. Failure to appoint officers;
j. Failure of directors to meet;
k. Loss of charter or dissolution by proclamation;
l. Failure to register in state;
m. Commingling of assets.

10. The criminal has continued financial liability in addition to the nominee's financial liability. Examples:

a. Mortgage or installment debt still in criminal's name;
b. State or local property tax records in criminal's name;
c. Utility bills (phone, water, and electric) in criminal's name;
d. Rent paid by criminal;
e. Criminal cosigned note.

11. The nominee committed perjury or has a propensity for concealment or inherent untrustworthiness. Examples:

a. The nominee makes misrepresentations either orally or on financial statements.
b. The nominee has a criminal record or pending charges.
c. A foreign corporation (offshore) loans or invests funds to the nominee or corporation.

12. The criminal has the propensity, history, or habit to use fraudulent devices. Examples:

a.   Illegal occupation of criminal;
b.   Past history of successful or unsuccessful fraudulent transfers;
c.   Lying to law enforcement.

13. Times show fraud. Examples:

a.   There is extreme haste in incorporating, in closing on real estate, or in weekend/holiday asset transfers.
b.   The transfer is prior to incorporation or while the corporation is inactive or dissolved.
c.   The transfer or sale occurs in the middle of busy or lucrative season or before contract completion and right to receive payment.
d.   Nominee acquires an asset just after the criminal obtains money from sale of a different asset.

14. There are purchase or transfer irregularities. Examples:

a.   Undocumented or unrecorded transfer;
b.   "Oral" agreement;
c.   Purchase contract signed by the criminal, but title taken by nominee;
d.   The criminal sells or conveys to nominee without:
     i.   Appraisal
     ii.   Competitive bid
     iii. Advertising
     iv.   Showing or exhibiting property to nominee
     v.   Nominee ever learning about the conveyance
     vi.   Advising mortgage holder
     vii. Cash to criminal, only a note
     viii. Written rental agreement for future use by the criminal.

15. There are use admissions of ownership by the criminal. Examples:

a.   Failure by criminal to report gain or loss on alleged sale of asset to nominee to tax authorities;
b.   The criminal listing nominee assets on financial statements given to creditors;
c.   Statements of ownership to customers, suppliers, or neighbors;
d.   Testimony in divorce proceedings as to ownership;
e.   Statements under oath of ownership on homestead exemption forms, or required contractual disclosure statements in litigation against third parties, on license applications, etc.;
f.   Statements to accountants, employees who are fired, or to spouses or relatives.

Offshore

More-sophisticated money launderers like to smuggle currency offshore and deposit it into a foreign bank account. These funds are later wired back to the United States as foreign investment in some form, e.g., loans or capital investment. Tax authorities and accountants call most of these foreign countries tax havens. Tax haven countries are those that have the following characteristics:

1. **No or low taxes.** Tax haven countries have either no or low taxes, which attract deposits and capital investments.

2. **No exchange controls.** Tax haven countries have no monetary exchange controls. A person can transfer funds in and out of a tax haven country without any interference from local authorities. Also, funds can be exchanged from one currency to another. Funds can be transferred quickly in and out of the country by electronic means. Additionally, currency can be converted to various commodities, i.e., gold, silver, platinum, etc.

3. **Bank facilities.** Tax haven countries attract many foreign and domestic banks. They encourage banks to have modern facilities and provide the services offered in other industrialized countries. Tax haven countries have banking laws that control and encourage the industry.

4. **Bank secrecy.** Tax haven countries have bank secrecy laws or customs. They do this primarily to help people conceal the fact that they have accounts in that country. Tax authorities in other countries are not allowed any information about people's bank accounts in the tax haven country. However, some tax haven countries will provide banking information if the request clearly shows violations that are not related to taxes. Some tax haven countries do not want the image of being a haven for criminals, i.e., drug traffickers.

5. **Stability.** Tax haven countries have good political and economic stability. People do not want to have bank accounts in countries that are politically or economically unstable. Why should someone deposit funds in a country that is being ravished by civil or guerrilla warfare.

6. **Communications.** Tax haven countries have good communication facilities. This is necessary for people to be able to transfer funds back and forth. Large amounts of money can be wired from one country to another very rapidly. If communication facilities were not available, then this would not be possible. Criminals have to have easy access to funds.

7. **Corruption.** Tax haven countries must be free of corruption. People do not like to make payoffs to public officials for hiding or maintaining funds in that country. However, organized crime organizations like to make payoffs to public officials for them to ignore or not interfere with their operations.

Multinational corporations use tax haven countries to avoid various taxes as well as to route funds to subsidiaries. This is legal. Avoiding taxes is legal; evading taxes is illegal. Some elements use tax havens to hide their gains or assets. Other people use tax havens for investment. The difference between hiding gains or assets and investment can be a very fine line. Some people will form a corporation offshore and deposit funds into a bank account for that corporation. A case where this is legal includes professional forms and an offshore insurance company. The professional writes checks to the foreign insurance company and expenses it on the business books. Policies are written for malpractice or liability insurance from the offshore insurance company. If a claim is made, the offshore company pays the claim. This is legal. However, it would be illegal if the funds are solely used to hide gains or assets and no claims are paid. Also, if the funds are small in comparison with the amount of coverage or claim, it would strongly indicate hiding assets, especially if no claims are made or the policy is not issued or disclosed. The ratio of premiums to the face amount of coverage should be compared with industry averages. If premiums are lower or coverage is higher than industry averages, then this indicates money laundering.

Offshore Entities

When a fraud examiner comes across an offshore entity, a determination has to be made whether this entity is legitimate. Determining the following factors can do this:

1. No payments or repayments. The subject has no evidence of making payments or repayments. The offshore entity does not loan or provide products or services without some compensation or repayments. The absence of any payments or repayments clearly indicates a shell entity.

2. Not U.S. registered. Under most states, foreign entities cannot do business in that state unless they are registered with the appropriate agency. Failure to get registered bars their legal rights in that state. If an offshore entity makes a loan to a customer, but is not registered in that state, then it does not have any recourse if the customer fails to make payments.

3. Failure to file tax returns. If the offshore entity does business in the United States, it is required to file income tax returns, even if no tax liability exists. Foreign entities are required to pay taxes on income earned in the United States.

4. No place of business. If the offshore entity has no business location in this country or in the country of origin, then this is a shell entity. Tax haven countries commonly have entities that are registered. Only the registered agent or representative is listed on the country's register. However, when the fraud examiner tries to find such entity, the entity is nothing more than a book or piece of paper in an attorney's office. It has no business location either in the United States or the country of origin.

If a financial transaction meets all or most of the above criteria, then this is a sham entity. It only serves to cover up the true source and ownership of the funds used. Many criminals and organized crime groups use this scheme to hide income and assets. In one case, a drug trafficker borrowed $800,000 from a Panamanian corporation to finance a house. The mortgage was duly filed in the county public records. The Panamanian Corporation had no business location either in the state or in Panama, nor was it registered in the United States. Further investigation revealed that the corporation was a shell. In another case, an individual borrowed funds to finance a house. The mortgage was written so that the borrower would not have to make repayments on the mortgage until 30 years later when principal and interest were due. The individual was 60 years old. Also, the individual's son was the sole shareholder of the mortgage company and a known drug trafficker. The corporation was an offshore corporation located in the Cayman Islands, which is a tax haven country. The corporation had no business location in the Cayman

Islands or the United States. These are examples of using offshore entities to cover up illegal gains or assets.

Recordkeeping

Taxpayers are required to keep records of both taxes and banking. Title 26, Section 6001, requires taxpayers to keep such permanent books of accounts or records, including inventories, as are sufficient to establish the amount of gross income, deductions, credits, or other matters required to be shown by such person on any return or information. The regulations empowered district directors to require any person, by notice served upon the person, to keep such specific records that enable the district director to determine whether or not such person is liable for tax. Taxpayers are required to keep records for at least 3 years, and in some cases, even longer. Title 31 requires more specific record keeping and retention. Congress declared that adequate records must be maintained by banks, businesses, and individuals engaging in business of carrying on as a financial institution, defined in 31 USC 5312(a) and 12 USC 1953. Individuals engaging in transactions or maintaining a relationship with a foreign financial agency have a high degree of usefulness in criminal, tax, and regulatory investigations and proceedings. In 31 CFR 103, the secretary promulgated regulations requiring records to be maintained for 5 years and filed or stored in such a way to be accessible within a reasonable period of time. A person having financial interests in foreign financial institutions is required to file the FBAR and retain records containing:

1. The name in which each such account is maintained;
2. The number or other designation of such account;
3. The name and address of the foreign bank or other person with whom such account is maintained;
4. The type of such account;
5. The maximum value of each such account.

The 5-year retention period is extended by any period beginning with a date on which the taxpayer is indicted or information instituted on account of the filing of a false or fraudulent federal income tax return, and ending with the date on which final disposition is made of the criminal proceeding.

Financial institutions must retain either the original or a microfilm or other copy or reproduction of records containing the name, amount, the nature or purpose, and the date regarding extension of credit exceeding $10,000 which are not secured by real property. In addition, financial institutions are required to keep records regarding advice, request, or instruction received or given concerning any transaction resulting in the transfer of currency or other monetary instruments, funds, checks, investment securities, or credit of more than $10,000 to or from any person with an account or place outside the United States.

Additionally, banks are required to keep customer's name, address, and identification number for all accounts opened after June 30, 1972 or certificates of deposit sold or redeemed after May 31, 1978. Also, banks are required to keep documents granting signature authority, and any notations of specific identifying information such as driver's license or credit card number. They must keep account statements showing each transaction such as checks, drafts, or money orders issued or payable by the bank or other debit items unless $100 or less, or certain checks drawn on accounts which can be expected to have drawn on them an average of at least 100 checks per year. Deposit slips or credit tickets reflecting a transaction in excess of $100 containing the amount of currency must be maintained.

Brokers, dealers in securities, casinos, and currency dealers or exchangers are required to keep records identifying name, address, social security number, and documents granting signature or tracing authority over each customer's account. A record of each remittance or transfer of funds, or of currency, checks, other monetary instruments, investment securities, or credit, of more than $10,000 to a person, account, or place, outside of the United States must be maintained. A record of each extension of credit in excess of $2,500, the terms and conditions of such extension of credit or repayments must be retained.

Businesses and individuals who are involved in cashing checks are required to maintain the name, address, and social security number of each individual to whom this service is provided. In addition, records must be maintained of each check draft, money order, cashier's check in excess of $100. The front and back of the instrument or document must be maintained or a copy retained.

Forms and Instructions

The following describes the forms used for reporting cash transactions or foreign bank accounts. They are exhibited in this chapter along with their related instructions.

1. **Form 4789.** Currency Transaction Report (CTR) (Exhibit 19-1).
2. **Form 4790.** Report of International Transportation of Currency or Monetary Instrument (Exhibit 19-2).
3. **Form 8300.** Report of Cash Payments Over $10,000 Received in Trade or Business (Exhibit 19-3).
4. **Form 90-22.1.** Report of Foreign Bank and Financial Accounts (Exhibit 19-4).

Penalties

There are penalties for not filing or for filing false forms for the above. The penalties are divided into two categories, civil and criminal. Both civil and criminal penalties for each form are summarized below.
   1. **Form 4789.**

   a. *Civil.* For any willful violation, committed after January 26, 1987, the civil penalty can be assessed upon the person or institution for the amount of coins or currency involved in the transaction, but shall be reduced by any forfeiture.
   b. *Criminal.* For any willful violation of failure to file or filing false reports shall be fined upon conviction not more than $250,000 or be imprisoned not more than 5 years, or both. If the criminal acts are committed as part of a pattern of illegal

activity involving transactions exceeding $100,000 in any 12-month period, then the penalty, upon conviction, shall be a fine of not more than $500,000 or imprisonment for not more than 5 years, or both.

2. **Form 4790.** The civil and criminal penalties for failure to file or for filing false forms are the same, both civil and criminal, for this form as it is for Form 4789.

3. **Form 8300.**

a. *Civil.* If the person or business fails to file or provide the required statement to those named in Form 8300, then the penalty is $25,000 or the amount of cash received and required to be reported up to $100,000.

b. *Criminal.* The criminal penalties for willful failure to file, filing false or fraudulent forms, stopping or trying to stop filing, and setting up, helping to set up, or trying to set up a transaction in a way that would make it seem unnecessary to file, can be a fine up to $250,000 ($500,000 for corporations) or a sentence up to 5 years, or both.

4. **Form 90-22.1.**

a. *Civil.* For failure to file or filing false reports, the penalty is $25,000 or the amount of the transaction not to exceed $100,000.

b. *Criminal.* Any person or business that violates this provision shall be fined not more than $250,000 or be imprisoned not more than 5 years, or both. In cases of a pattern of illegal activity involving transactions exceeding $100,000 in any 12-month period, the criminal penalties, upon conviction, may be a fine of not more than $500,000 or imprisonment for not more than 5 years, or both.

Terminology

There are terms used in money-laundering activities that have special meanings. These terms also define the particular scheme or purpose.

Structuring — This term is used to describe a person or persons who conduct or attempt to conduct one or more transactions in currency in any amount at one or more financial institutions on 1 or more days in any manner for the purpose of evading various cash-reporting requirements.

Smurfing — This term describes a person who goes to various financial institutions and makes deposits or obtains cashier's checks, money orders, traveler's checks, etc,. on the same day or on consecutive days.

Layering — This describes the scheme of making financial transactions to disguise the audit trail of the illegal proceeds. It involves converting cash into monetary instruments, i.e., cashier's checks, money orders, traveler's checks, stocks, bonds, etc. Layering encompasses making multiple deposits and making wire transfers or purchasing expensive assets.

Integration — Money launderers need to provide a legitimate-looking explanation for their wealth. Integration is the process of routing money into the banking system in a way to make it appear that it comes from normal business earnings. Using front companies, sham loans, and false export–import invoices commonly does this. Money launderers will purchase property at high cost with partial payment (down payment) made in cash. The purchase documents are prepared showing a lower price by excluding the down payment or "under the table" payments. Overvaluation of exports is used to justify deposits as funds from foreign sources.

Know Your Customer

The Federal Reserve Board issued a booklet, *Know Your Customer — Internal Compliance and Check Lists to Identify Abuses*, to help financial institutions guard against illegal activities that could cause heavy penalties and bad publicity. It advises financial institutions to be aware of unusual banking practices that are not consistent with the customer's business. Financial institutions must verify new customer's identity and true ownership of accounts. Internal controls must be maintained to ensure compliance and detection. This guidebook gives the following danger signs of money-laundering activities:

1. Large number of cash deposits while balance remains low and constant.
2. Large volume of cashier's checks, money orders, or traveler's checks sold for cash.
3. Large number of cash deposits to more than one account with transfers to a single account.
4. Large cash deposits from a business that is not normally a cash business.
5. CTRs are incorrect or lack important information.
6. Transactions with offshore banks in "tax haven" countries.
7. Loans or investments to offshore companies.
8. Offshore banks or companies are "shell" companies, meaning, they have no physical location.
9. Frequent wire transfers to "tax haven" countries, especially to the same person or corporation.
10. Prepayment of interest on accounts used as collateral on loans.
11. Merchants structure credit card purchases to avoid the need for approval.
12. Purpose of loan is not recorded on the loan proceeds or used for purposes not intended.
13. Loan proceeds are sent offshore.
14. Loan proceeds are used to purchase certificates of deposits, or certificates of deposits are used for loans.
15. Customer requests to be placed on the bank's exemption list.
16. Safe deposit box has heavy traffic.
17. Cash deposits are made at the same time the safe deposit box is accessed.

Summary

The federal government, as well as some states, has many laws, regulations, and forms requiring the reporting of various kinds of financial transactions by various businesses and institutions. Businesses are well aware of these laws, regulations, and reporting forms. Many have been fined for noncompliance. The fraud examiner should also become familiar with the laws, regulations, and the forms. This is one area that fraud examiners are most often called upon to unravel.

Interviewing

20

Introduction

Interviewing is an important part of a quality investigation and examination. It is important to have an initial dialogue with a person who has sufficient knowledge about the areas of interest. This person must be in a position to provide timely information, which can be relied upon. The determination of whether or not a person is knowledgeable will depend on the examiner's judgment. It is as important as any technical ability to examine documents, prepare work papers, or conduct audits.

Purpose

The purpose of interviewing is to obtain and develop information. It provides leads in developing a case. The examiner can meet, talk with, and evaluate the witnesses or victims. It later helps witnesses in remembering their statements at trials or hearings. Interviews also establish evidence. Cases are presented to a jury through the testimony of witnesses. Therefore, it is the examiner's duty to interview every witness connected with the case.

Types of Witnesses

There are three types of witnesses: the cooperative or friendly witness, the neutral witness, and the hostile or adverse witness.

Cooperative Witness

Cooperative witnesses are more than willing to give information. This is particularly true if they are also the victims. However, cooperative witnesses not only gives facts, but also mix the facts with opinions. Sometimes, they want something in exchange for whatever reason. Cooperative witnesses should be evaluated very closely. They might not be suitable witnesses on the witness stand because of biases and lack of objectivity.

Neutral Witness

Neutral witnesses have no or little interest in the case. Even though they make the best witnesses, they do not always provide all the necessary evidence. This is particularly true in cases of custodians of records. Most have never seen the subject and sometimes have difficulty in locating all their records.

Hostile Witness

The hostile witness is harder for the examiner to interview. A witness who lies or becomes uncooperative or evasive may be indicating "dishonest intent" or may have close association with the subject under investigation. The interview should be conducted professionally and with a high degree of formality. The interview should start with identification of the witness and later the identification of the subject. The hostile witnesses can be softened up by not accusing them even though the evidence is clear and convincing. The examiner should let witnesses have an "out" or offer an excuse for their behavior. Rewards for cooperation or punishment for being uncooperative should be pointed out. Under no circumstances should the examiner make any promises or guarantees. The examiner should never reveal the examiner's knowledge or lack of to the witness. The more the witness talks, the better, because more information or evidence can be obtained.

Planning the Interview

Proper planning of the interview is important. The examiner must have a general idea what witnesses know, what they can provide, and their relationship to the subject. Prior to any interview the examiner should review all the information and data relating to the case. Such information can be divided into three general categories:

1. Information which can be documented, and need not be discussed;
2. Information which may be documented, but needs to be discussed;
3. Information that must be developed by testimony.

The examiner should prepare a file that contains only data or information arranged in the order it is to be discussed or covered in the interview. The examiner should determine the purpose or goal for questioning. An outline should be prepared, in more or less detail. The outline should contain only information that is relevant and material including hearsay. Important topics should be set off or underscored, and related topics listed in their proper sequence. The examiner should keep specific questions to a minimum since they tend to reduce the flexibility of the examiner. The examiner should cover as much information as possible. The time and place can be scheduled for cooperative witnesses. The best place to interview them is at their place of business or where they keep documents. In the case of hostile witnesses, it is best to approach them unannounced. This prevents the witnesses from contacting the subject, an attorney, or disappearing. The interview outline should cover at minimum the following:

1. Name, address, employment, and contact telephone numbers;
2. Witness connection to the subject;

3.   Meetings and telephone conversations with subject;
4.   Documents furnished by the subject to the witness;
5.   Other potential witnesses;
6.   Financial dealings, including any losses;
7.   Information about the history and background of the subject;
8.   Any other material or relevant information or evidence.

Conducting the Interview

During the interview, the examiner must keep an open mind that is receptive to all information regardless of the nature, and be prepared to develop it. If the examiner isn't flexible, a great deal of time may be wasted with unnecessary questions, resulting in a voluminous statement of little or no value. Although the examiner may find it easier to adhere to a fixed pattern of interviewing, or to rely upon a series of questions or topics, rigid adherence to any notes or outline will seriously impair flexibility. The outline and data should serve only as aids and not as substitutes for original and spontaneous questioning. A carefully planned outline will provide enough leeway to allow the examiner to cope better with any situations that may occur and permit the examinee to develop leads that may arise.

Establishing good communications with the witness in the initial interview is essential because it provides an opportunity to obtain information, which may not be readily available at a later date. A skilled examiner leads the interview so that he or she obtains as much information as possible. The examiner encourages witnesses to discuss themselves, their family, hobbies, financial history, and relations with others including the subject of the investigation. After initial contact, the witness may procrastinate or become less communicative. Therefore, plan for and conduct the initial interview so as much information as possible is obtained. Let the witness talk; be a good listener. The obvious fact about interviewing is that it involves communication between two or more people. It is a specialized professional type of conversation requiring all the faculties and tools of good speech and communication.

Techniques should be developed that lead the witness into answering desired questions. The examiner should gain a clear understanding of the witness or subject's lifestyle and financial dealings. Statements made by the witness or subject may be used later as a test of their truthfulness and accuracy. Always be alert for any indications of fraud on the part of the witness or subject. Witnesses or subjects may have had unusually good or bad luck. Let them discuss their failures or successes. These are leads that are obtained in the interview and should alert you to follow up with questions to document these failures or successes. Nonresponse to specific questions should be enough to note the answer or the lack of it. Follow through on every pertinent lead and incomplete answer. Continue asking questions until all information that can reasonably be expected has been secured.

The following suggestions will help the examiner follow through and obtain answers that are complete and accurate:

1.   Use short questions confined to one topic, which can be clearly and easily understood.
2.   Ask questions that require narrative answers; avoid "yes" and "no" answers, whenever possible.

3. Question the witness about how he or she learned what is stated to be fact. The subject should also be required to give the factual basis for any conclusions stated.
4. Whenever possible avoid questions that suggest part of an answer, "leading questions."
5. Be alert to prevent the witness from aimlessly wandering. Where possible, require a direct response.
6. Prevent the witness from leading far afield. Do not allow the witness to confuse the issue and leave basic questions unanswered.
7. Concentrate more on the answers than on the next questions.
8. To avoid an unrelated and incomplete chronology, clearly understand each answer and insure that any lack of clarity is eliminated before continuing.
9. When all-important points have been resolved, terminate the interview; if possible, leave the door open for further meetings.

The witness or subject should completely answer the following basic questions:

1. Who? Complete identification should be made of all persons referred to. This includes description, address, alias, "trading as," "also known as," citizenship, reputation, and associates.
2. What? Complete details of what happened. Questions should relate to events, methods, and systems. A complete answer should be developed. Trace the event from its inception to its ultimate termination.
3. Where? Complete details regarding financial records and affairs, including their location, witnesses, clients, customers, and the like.

Recording the Interview

The principal purpose of interviews is to obtain all the facts helpful in resolving the case. Thus, it is necessary to prepare a permanent record of every interview to be preserved for future use. The methods used to record and document the interview are as follows:

Affidavit

An affidavit is a written or printed declaration or statement made voluntarily, and confirmed by the oath or affirmation of the party making it before an officer having authority to administer such oath. The procedures for taking an affidavit follow:

1. When to take an affidavit. An affidavit should be taken when an affiant presents information, written or oral, relating to his or her knowledge about the matter under investigation that has a material effect.
2. How to take an affidavit. Ideally, two examiners or investigators should be present although it is permissible for one representative to do so. One representative will swear in the affiant after the affidavit is filled out, by asking, "Do you swear or affirm that the foregoing facts are true to the best of your knowledge?" The affiant must have his or her right hand raised at the time of reply to this statement.
3. An affidavit should contain, at a minimum, the following:

    a. Name. This could contain current full legal name or any current or prior aliases.

    b. Address. Most current address.

    c. Occupation. The present occupation of the person giving the affidavit. If the information relates to a prior occupation, that should be given.

    d. Identified document. If the person giving the affidavit is presenting a document, it should be described as precisely as possible.

    e. When prepared. If a document is presented, it should be noted when it was prepared.

    f. Who prepared it. The preparer must be noted.

    g. Source prepared from. If the information contained in the document was taken from another source, state what the source was.

Memorandum of Interview

A memorandum of interview is an informal method of recording an interview. It is basically putting down on paper what the examiner learned from the interview. The memorandum of interview should be done as soon as possible after the interview when the examiner's knowledge is fresh in the mind. The examiner should have taken notes to help in writing the memorandum. The memorandum of interview should contain at least the following:

1. Date and time of interview;
2. Place or location of interview;
3. The people present at the interview;
4. Date the memorandum was prepared;
5. A summary of the conversation that took place;
6. As much information as possible about the interview and what the subject or witness said.

The examiner should sign the memorandum of interview.

Question and Answer Statement

The question and answer statement is a formal method of interviewing a witness or subject. It sometimes requires a court reporter present who will generally administer an oath and record the proceedings verbatim. If a court reporter is not used, then a tape recording is used and later transcribed. The witness is always administered an oath. The witness may be later required to read and swear or affirm to the transcribed proceedings. Even though this is a preferred method to use because it precludes witnesses or subjects from changing their testimony, it may not be admissible in court since cross-examination has not taken place. If the subject provides such a statement, then his or her legal rights should be explained before taking such a statement. If a tape recorder is used in lieu of a reporter or as a backup to the reporter, consent must be obtained on the record from the witness or subject. The question and answer statement is similar to a deposition except in a deposition, cross-examination is done by the opposing counsel or party.

An experienced reporter will be able to transcribe notes made under adverse conditions. However, if recording conditions are improved, then the reporter will be able to transcribe notes much more rapidly and with less chance of error.

The following techniques will help the reporter to do a better job.

1. **Brief your reporter before the interview.** The examiner should provide the names of the people who are expected to be present. The reporter must identify each speaker. It will be helpful if the reporter knows the witness's line of business and has a general idea of the line of questioning to be pursued. The reporter should read any correspondence or memorandums that the examiner has that would be helpful, particularly where unusual names may be involved.

2. **Control the interview.** Remind those present to speak one at a time. The reporter cannot record two voices simultaneously. This is essential even if the reporter is using a tape recorder. The machine will not encounter any difficulty in recording several voices at once, but when played back it will be difficult to understand.

3. **Open the interview in a formal manner.** Open the interview by saying, "This is the testimony of [name of witness] taken in [complete address] at [time] on [date] in the matter of [suspected crime]. Those present are [list all persons present at the interview]." This information is necessary for preparing the transcript, and, by opening in this manner, facts are accurately recorded. This formal opening also affords a built-in "warm-up" for both examiner and reporter. It also alerts all participants that anything they say after this time will be recorded.

4. **Avoid overlapping.** Overlapping is the practice of breaking in with another question before the witness has finished speaking. The transcript will have a better appearance if all parties have spoken in complete sentences. Also, it is necessary to listen carefully to the replies of your witness rather than thinking ahead to the next question.

5. **Guard against multiple questions.** The interviewer should keep questions short, concise, and to the point. The interviewer can do a lot to head off the witness who tends to ramble on without giving a specific answer. Questions should not be asked that require more than one answer or are leading.

6. **Assist your reporter with a witness difficult to record.** The interviewer may have a witness with an extraordinary rapid rate of speech or with a heavy accent or other speech peculiarity that makes it very difficult for the reporter to follow. A break of only 1 or 2 seconds in the flow of difficult language makes a world of difference to the reporter. Some helpful things that an interviewer can do in such situations follow:

a. Speak more slowly than usual when asking your questions.
b. If you have a document that you wish to show the witness, reach for it in a leisurely manner.
c. Glance at the reporter to see if the reporter is ready before you ask your next question.

7. **Remember there are no shortcuts to writing figures.** Speak slowly when giving a number with several digits. There are no shortcuts to writing figures, and they have no context. A rapidly spoken 13-digit number followed immediately by a flow of words will force the reporter to try to carry possibly five digits and seven or eight words in the reporter's head simultaneously. The possibility of error will be greatly reduced if you speak more slowly when numbers are involved.

8. **Identify documents.** If there is occasion to refer to documents, identify them specifically, such as "cash disbursement book, advertising expense column." If the interviewer says, "this book" and "that column" a reviewer examining the transcript will not be sure which documents or columns you have made reference to.

9. **Be aware of the required transcription time.** When the reporter prepares a transcript of an interview, the reporter must set it up in question and answer form, numbering each question and answer and identifying all speakers. This adds to typing time. The required transcription time for the reporter's examination is 1 hour for 5 minutes dictation at 160 words per minute. This would mean 6 hours are needed to transcribe a 30 minute interview. If examiners know the transcription time required, they will not expect to record a 6-hour interview on Monday and find a finished transcript on their desk by Wednesday morning. When a completed transcript is needed by a certain date, take this factor into consideration when setting the date of the interview.

Statement

A statement is a written record by witnesses or subjects of their knowledge of an offense that possibly took place. The interviewer should be sure that the statement is dated, and in some instances signed. A statement does not have to be sworn. Witnesses should write down everything that they have seen or heard before, during, and after the event. This helps witnesses to recall later the events in detail, even things that were not put in the statement.

The Interview

The fraud examiner should be very aware of the importance of interviews, particularly, of witnesses. Interviews are as just as important as the document evidence. Remember, especially in criminal cases, there must be both physical evidence and a witness. With no witness, the documentary evidence may not be admissible. A witness cannot only furnish evidence in the case, but also furnish leads to other evidence and witnesses. The fraud examiner should follow up on these leads. When interviewing witnesses or the subject, the fraud examiner should always take a professional attitude. The fraud examiner is only interested in getting the facts. Witnesses not only give facts, but also give opinions. The fraud examiner has to take great care to differentiate facts from opinions. Keep in mind, "you can catch more flies with honey than you can get with vinegar."

Interview Techniques

Over many decades, criminologists have developed various interview techniques. One technique is called "kinesic" interviewing which encompasses listening to the answers to questions as well as observing body movements (language), e.g., movements of head, hands, arms, etc. Certain movements by subjects can indicate deception when they answer particular questions. This method has the disadvantage of the interviewer being present with the subject. The presence of an authority figure tends to make the subject less communicative. Another method of interviewing is to have the subject or witness take a polygraph test. Similar to kinesic interviewing, the polygraph relies on body responses to answers, e.g., changes in pulse and breathing patterns. Its disadvantage is that it makes the subject feel the interviewer is intrusive and the subject becomes less informative. Also, if the subject is nervous or jittery during the whole session or has no physiological response to the questions, the polygraph test has no meaning.

Another technique is to obtain an open-ended statement from the subject or witness. The statement is analyzed to determine deception or to gather more information about an event. The subject or witness may refuse to provide a written statement, which is its disadvantage. It has several advantages over other techniques. First, the interviewer does not need to be present. In fact, it is better for the interviewer not to be present since a person does not feel threatened. Second, a questionnaire can be given to many people at the same time. This saves time and effort if many witnesses have to be interviewed. The succeeding paragraphs briefly discuss the theory and procedures of statement analysis.

Characteristics

The interviewer studies the statement for inconsistencies. This can be used for any language in which the interviewer is proficient. A truthful statement reflects reality. A deceptive statement distorts reality. The interviewer analyzes what the person has said and not what the person knows. The theory behind statement analysis is that everyone wants to give information to everyone. The more the interviewer expects the subject to talk, the higher the probability is that the subject will talk. As long as the subject is not saying, "I don't want to talk," the subject is willing to talk. The interviewer must be careful in asking questions because it might be from the questions that the subject would learn how to be deceptive. Asking leading questions is a good example of this type of questioning. The only forbidden question is a question that the person refuses to answer. The interviewer should not enter into any unnecessary argument with the subject. Also, the interviewer should not make any accusations. There is no coincidence in life, and nothing happens in a vacuum. Deception is any assertion believed or known by the speaker to be untrue with the intent to mislead. The more specific, direct, closed, and difficult the question is, the more difficult it is to lie. Statement analysis involves not only the content of a statement but also the structure of the statement. The structure is very important. Structure involves the use of pronouns, connections, changes in language, use of verbs, time frames, and unnecessary or unimportant information, and tenses.

Pronouns

The use of pronouns is important. They are objective. Pronouns are usually mentioned after a "social" introduction. Pronouns are used because they shorten the sentence and make life easier. If pronouns come before the introduction, then it is rude and impolite and might indicate a bad relationship. If the introduction is repeated more than once, then this indicates a bad relationship or that something is wrong. The use of "we" without an introduction is indicative of a bad relationship.

Some pronouns are I, you, he, she, it, we, they, my, your, his, her, our, their, me, us, him, them, myself, and ourselves. Pronouns give responsibility and possession by the speaker. When the subject says "we," that means someone was with the subject. Changes of pronouns in the same sentence indicate that there might be deception in the statement. The lack of "I" in a statement or paragraph indicates tension. Overuse of "I" is not good, because it indicates tension and possible deception. "We" is important, especially in white-collar crime when dealing with corporations and partnerships, because no one functions alone. "We" inside a statement would give an indication if the subject were relaxed or not. Was the subject tense at the time of the crime? Changes in language reflect a change in reality.

The word "with" indicates distance in reality whether in time or place. The interviewer should inquire about the relationship or events about a place when "with" is used. A bad relationship also occurs when a person changes "my" to "the." This is important in disputes about possession in arson and child abuse cases.

Connections

A connection is a phrase that connects two different links in a statement. An unnecessary connection usually replaces information, which the subject intentionally took out of the statement. Verbs, which refer to "leaving a place," are very significant. The more times "left" or the equivalent expressions are found in a statement, the more sensitive the statement becomes. Many deceptive statements start or end with "left." An answer that ends with a question mark indicates resistance, and it means that the question before the answer is a sensitive one for the person. Connections that should be identified are

> Later on
> Sometime later
> Shortly thereafter
> Afterwards
> After that
> The next thing I remember/knew

Verbs that indicate missing information are

> Started
> Began
> Continued
> Proceeded
> Completed
> Finished
> Ended

If the subject did not mention the reason for the break in an activity, then the interviewer should ask why. Failure to give a reason may indicate deception. Connections are expressions, which may indicate "missing time." This indicates that there is something the subject does not want the interviewer to know.

Out-of-Sequence Information

Out-of-sequence information might be the most important information. It is out of sequence for the reader/listener, but it is in sequence for the subject. If a person gives information, which has no connection to the question, then there is a connection. Language is not independent, but was produced by the mind. There are no coincidences in life. The basic questions for the reader/listener are

Why did the person say it?
Why did the person say it this way?
Why did the person say it this way at this specific location in the statement?
Why did the person use this specific amount of subjective time?

Out-of-sequence information is an indication that surgery was performed on the statement. The subject took out some information, but left inside the statement the effects of missing information. Out-of-sequence information is a specific case of an unnecessary link. Out-of-sequence information is an unnecessary link, but not every unnecessary link is out of sequence. A truthful story will have unnecessary links. An unnecessary link can be done by change in pronouns or vocabulary. If the sequence of events justifies the change, then the person is truthful; if not, then the person is deceptive. An unnecessary link is any link that can be taken out of the statement and the story still flows smoothly.

Objective vs. Subjective Times

Objective times are another component that is not subject to the subject's personal language. Objective times are the only connections from subjective reality to objective reality. Objective times enable the interviewer to check the subjective time used to describe different links. Many criminals put the time of the crime inside the story. If any objective time is mentioned in the statement, the interviewer should see if it corresponds to the time of the crime. If it does, then there is a suspicion that the person committed the crime. "Missing time" is time in which a person could have committed the crime. Finding missing information results in solving most cases.

Unimportant Information

Unimportant activities might be doubly important. If a person is truthful, then the interviewer must obtain the answers to the basic questions:

Why did the subject say it?
Why did the subject say it this way?
Why did the subject say it in this location of statement?
Why did the subject take the time to say it?

Verbs Regarding Communication

When a person mentions "talking" in an open statement, it means that this was an important conversation. If "we" is missing in the conversation, then the conversation resulted in an argument or disagreement. Verbs that indicate communication are *talk, speak, chat, discuss, converse, etc.* A discussion indicates disagreement or argument between the parties. Talking or chatting indicates a closer relationship between the parties.

Inquiry

The goal of an interviewer is to obtain information. The first questionnaire is an open-ended statement about an event. The first questionnaire aims to get as much information as possible about an event. This is called getting a "pure version," since the interviewer should have total belief in the statement. The second interview is conducted to get specific information. The "direct inquiry" wants specific answers to questions, and the goals are to get answers to points left out in the original version, to get a complete picture, and to determine if the person is deceptive. A direct inquiry is closed, direct, and difficult. Thus, the subject's answers become less reliable and might teach the subject to lie. The interview should not tell the subject that the subject is deceptive if the interviewer is not sure of it. If the subject is truthful, then the accusations can produce "deceptive" behavior and that will confuse the interviewer.

Questionnaire

The interviewer must provide a questionnaire to the subject(s) or witness(es). The first questionnaire should be designed to get as much information as possible and obtain a commitment by the person. The second questionnaire should be designed to address the various issues on the original statement. The first questionnaire, known as the "pure version," should comprise a small booklet, which the subject(s) will complete. It is recommended, as a minimum, that it should have the following pages:

1. **Instructions.** The first page should give the instructions to the subject as to how the questionnaire is to be completed. The subject should be advised that the subject should write answers in as much detail as possible. The subject should use a pen while writing, no typing is allowed, and the handwriting should be clear to enable reading. No corrections are allowed.

2. **Page 2.** This page should ask the subject to explain what happened during the time the event took place or to give a detailed explanation of what the person did during the time the event took place. Example: "Describe in detail your work day on [mm/dd/yy] covering the time you came to work until the time you ended the day."

3. **Page 3.** This makes the subject to be committed to his previous statement. Example: "Would you like to change any of the information you have provided?"

Summary

As one can see, interviewing subjects and witnesses is very important. It basically comprises about half the case in terms of importance. Criminal cases require witnesses to introduce evidence, physical or documentary. The most serious obstacle to obtaining information is the interviewer. The interviewer either does not ask the proper questions or influences the person to lie. In many cases, the interviewer does *not* listen to what a person says. Yet, it is easier for people to talk to a stranger than to someone they know. Also, it is not easy to lie. People usually lie by making an omission in their statement and not by commission.

Banking and Finance

21

Introduction

Fraud examiners find that their best and probably most useful evidence is various bank records. Banks maintain various kinds of records, some of which the customer does not have available. Many customers like using one or more banks on a regular basis. They want to establish a working relationship, which in turn gives a sense of security. Money launderers particularly want good relationships with bankers so that they might look "the other way" when money launderers do business. Bank records are perhaps the single most important financial source. They can provide leads to sources of funds, expenditures, personal affairs, and they may be used as evidence to prove criminal and civil violations.

Bank Services

Many banks offer all or many of the following services:

1. **Checking Accounts.** These are sometimes called "demand accounts" since the customer can make deposits and withdrawals at will. This is probably the most common service at banks. Many banks offer checking accounts for individuals, which have service charges of a flat fee or a low fee. In some areas, checking accounts are provided free to certain types of customers, e.g., elderly, minors, etc. Corporate or business checking accounts have service charges based upon account activity, and/or minimum daily balances that must be maintained.

2. **Savings Accounts.** Banks offer various types of savings accounts, often referred to as "time deposits." Banks usually offer three types of savings accounts.

   a. *Passbook.* This is a savings account that allows customers ready access to their funds, but the bank pays interest on the average balances. However, the customer cannot write checks, but must physically withdraw the funds at the bank. Banks require a minimum balance, usually, between $200 and $1,000.

   b. *Money Market.* This is a savings account that allows customers ready access to their funds. The customer can write checks against the account with some limitations. The bank pays interest on these accounts at market rates.

     c. *Certificates of Deposit.* The customer buys a certificate of deposit, basically a savings account, where the customer cannot withdraw the funds over a period of time that ranges from 3 months to 2 or 3 years. Interest is paid periodically and usually deposited into a checking account. Early withdrawals can result in penalties. Many banks will renew the Certificates of Deposit if the customer does not tell the bank not to do so.

     d. *Individual Retirement Account.* Financial institutions, banks, and savings and loans offer customers a savings plan in which individuals cannot withdraw funds without penalties until they reach age $59^{1}/_{2}$ or older. These accounts usually offer a higher return because the customer cannot withdraw it until retirement. In effect, these are tax deductible savings accounts for the customer. The bank has to file the appropriate forms with the IRS showing that the customer has an Individual Retirement Account.

    3. **Loans.** Banks make their money from making loans to customers. Many customers not only have checking and savings accounts, but also borrow funds from the bank for purchasing items. Banks will lend money provided that they have collateral, e.g., automobiles, boats, real estate, etc., from individuals. They make loans to businesses using inventory or equipment of the business for collateral. Banks do not make loans to customers unless the customers have a good credit standing in the community.

    4. **Safe Deposit Boxes.** Banks offer customers safe deposit boxes for rent. These safe deposit boxes are locked boxes in a highly secured vault. The boxes come in various sizes. Customers can use these vaults to store important papers, documents, and other valuables with safety and security.

    5. **Credit Cards.** Banks offer customers access to bank credit cards such as MasterCard or Visa. They like their customers using credit cards because they charge a very high interest rate on the use of these cards. Customers can use these cards to purchase goods and services, as well as to get cash advances.

    6. **Trust Services.** Many banks offer trust services. These services vary widely, depending upon what customers want done on their behalf. The bank, as trustee, could manage anything from simple trusts, e.g., collecting investment income, to complex trusts involving managing huge amounts of assets, investments, and income for the grantor. The grantor will probably have the bank, as trustee, provide funds to beneficiaries as set forth in the trust agreement.

    7. **Exchange Instruments.** Banks offer customers various vehicles of transferring funds:

     a. *Cashier's Checks.* Cashier's checks are bank checks. The customer purchases these checks for a small fee. Cashier's checks are usually issued for large amounts, $500 and up.

     b. *Money Orders.* Money orders are similar to cashier's checks, but they are issued for small amounts, usually $500 or less.

     c. *Certified Checks.* Certified checks are customer's checks on which "certified" is written or stamped across the front of the check. This certification is a guarantee that the bank will pay the check. Certified checks are liabilities of the bank and, when paid, are kept by the bank. However, the customer can obtain the checks by surrendering debit memorandums which the bank has charged the customer's account.

d. *Wire Transfers.* Banks can transfer funds from an internal account to another bank account at another bank by electronic means. The customer's account is charged for the amount of the transfer plus a fee. These electronic transfers can be done in minutes and can be done to any bank in the United States or any foreign country that has the ability to accept wire transfers.

Checking Account Operation

A customer goes to the neighborhood bank and opens a checking account. The customer will go through the following procedures in opening and operating a checking account.

1. **Opening.** The customer will be asked to provide the following:

   a. *Signature card.* The signature card requires full name, address, city, state, zip code, telephone number, social security number, and signatures of each person who is going to sign on the account. It is called a signature card since each person who can sign checks must sign the card.
   b. *Initial deposit.* The customer is required to make a minimum deposit. This is usually between $200 and $500.
   c. *Corporations.* If a corporation is opening a checking account, then it must submit a Corporate Resolution, which shows the corporate officers who can sign on the account. In many instances, the corporation might require that two corporate officers must jointly sign checks.

2. **Checks.** The customer writes checks (Exhibit 21-1) to various people for various purposes. The check requires the customer to complete the following items:

   a. *Date.* The customer must put the date that the check is written. However, some customers may postdate or backdate a check.
   b. *Payee.* The customer writes the name of the payee who is to receive the funds. Sometimes, customers write checks to cash in order to obtain cash.
   c. *Amount.* The customer puts the dollar amount of the check. This is written in figures.
   d. *Written amount.* The customer writes out in long hand the amount of the check. This amount should agree to the dollar amount written above. If the amounts between the figure and the written amount are different, banks usually will pay the written amount.
   e. *Signature.* The customer must sign the check. The signature must correspond to the signature that the customer signed on the signature card when the account was initially opened.

3. **Deposits.** The customer must deposit funds, currency and checks, into the checking account to cover the withdrawals. The customer must complete a deposit slip. The deposit slip requires the customer to complete the following:

   a. *Date.* The customer must record the date the deposit is made.
   b. *Cash.* The customer must record the amount of currency or coins being deposited.

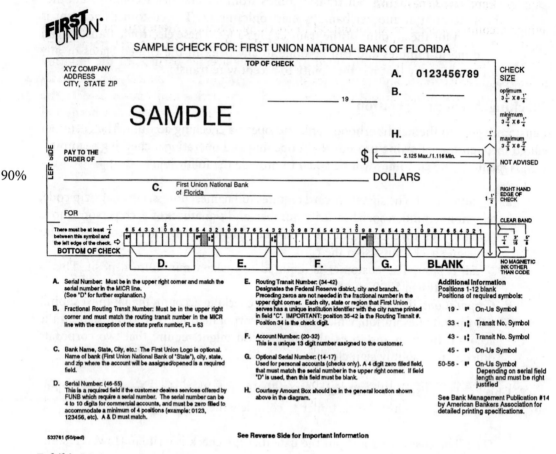

Exhibit 21-1

    c. *Items.* The customer must list every check or draft that is being deposited. This column shows from whom the check was received. Some people list the bank routing number of the customer's check while others list the name of the sender. Corporations sometimes list the customer's internal account number.

    d. *Amount.* The customer fills in the amount of the customer's check that was received and being deposited.

    e. *Total deposit.* The customer must total up all cash and checks and place the total at the bottom of the deposit slip. Some banks even want a total count of checks being deposited.

    4. **Statement.** The bank sends the customer a statement each month showing each deposit and check, and summarizes deposits and checks. It also gives the beginning and ending balances according to the bank. Customers are now obligated to reconcile their statement to their check register. For corporations, the bank statement must be reconciled to the cash receipts and disbursement journals, as well as the general ledger for that bank account. Most banks include the deposit slips and each canceled check received by the bank with the bank statement. Many banks show not only the date and amount of the check, and also the check number. In a few cases, the bank shows the payee on the check and whether the deposit is in checks or cash.

Savings Account Operation

Savings accounts operate mostly identical to checking accounts. Money market accounts function the same as checking accounts, except that they receive interest on account balances. Most interest can be computed on either the average balance, or the monthly ending balance. Passbook and certificates of deposit accounts are issued periodic statements, which show principal and interest earned for the period and year-to-date. In the case of certificates of deposit, when the term has expired, the customer must notify the bank whether the certificate of deposit is to be renewed, transferred, or refunded to the customer. If customers fail to notify the bank of their intentions, then the bank will automatically renew the certificate of deposit, which could be at either a higher or lower rate than the original rate.

Loans

Banks offer a variety of loans. They offer installment loans, home equity loans, business loans, signature loans, and mortgages. Banks earn their income from the interest on loans. A performing loan is one that the customer pays on time. A nonperforming loan is one that the customer is constantly late in making repayments or does not pay at all. Banks usually commence foreclosure proceedings when the nonperforming loan reaches 90 days past due.

1. **Installment Loans.** Installment loans are the most common loans provided by banks. They are also the most profitable. The interest on installment loans is computed on the "add-on" interest method. Interest is rebated on the rule of 78s. The "add-on" interest method is basically taking the interest rate and multiplying it by the number of years the loan is to run. The rule of 78s is basically adding the total months the loan is to run. It is rebated by the factor of adding the months remaining over the total months of the loan. This is multiplied by the total interest charged on the loan. Example:

Term:	12 months
Interest charged:	$1,000
Payoff period:	6 months has elapsed

The pay off would be computed as follows:

$$(1 + 2 + 3 + 4 + 5 + 6) = 21/78 \times \$1,000 = \$269.23$$

Note: 78 is the sum of the numbers of 1 through 12; thus, the rule of 78.

2. **Mortgages.** Banks can provide prospective homeowners with mortgages to purchase a home. Banks usually require a better credit rating and better income than other financial institutions. Banks can provide mortgages that range from 15 to 30 years. Interest rates range from prime to several points above prime. Also, banks offer both fixed rate and variable rate mortgages. Simple interest is charged on the monthly balances. Banks also charge the customer "points" for providing the loan. These points are for the costs the bank incurs in preparing and providing the mortgage. Many banks require the mortgagee to deposit funds into an escrow account for the payment of taxes and insurance. The bank uses these escrow accounts to pay property taxes and homeowners insurance directly.

3. **Home Equity Loans.** Home equity loans are loans based upon the homeowner's equity in the house. It is defined by banks as the difference between the mortgage on the property and the fair market value. Banks will loan funds up to the amount of fair market value less 10 percent and the mortgage. Home equity loans usually have an interest rate of 2 or more points above the prime rate. Most home equity loans have variable interest rates. Some banks offer revolving loans in which the loan balances can go up and down as the homeowner borrows and repays the loan.

4. **Business Loans.** Banks make loans to businesses. Inventory, accounts receivable, or equipment usually secures these loans. The loans are usually for a short term, which ranges from 1 month to a few years. Many business loans are rolled over. Interest rates range from prime and up depending upon the business credit rating.

5. **Signature Loans.** Banks will provide loans to individuals with no collateral. However, these loans are rare and are only provided to customers with a high credit rating. Interest rates range from prime and up to the maximum rate allowed by law.

Safe Deposit Boxes

Banks offer customers the renting of a box in a secured vault. Banks do not have access to this box except by court order or nonpayment of rental charges. Customers use these boxes to store important papers and documents. They are also used to store jewelry, cash, and negotiable instruments. These boxes come in various sizes. Banks maintain a log of every person who accesses the safe deposit box. It generally shows the name of the person, the person's signature, and the date and time the box was entered. Heavy access to a safe deposit box can indicate a cash hoard, especially when deposits are made on the same date.

Credit Cards

Credit cards are becoming more widespread in their use. Some businesses will only accept credit cards, while others will accept only cash or credit cards but no checks of any kind. Many businesses have electronic terminals, which can verify that the credit card is good. If it is bad, the business is supposed to confiscate the card. Most banks have a credit card division, which issues and maintains customer's accounts. When customers use their credit cards, the business establishment deposits the slips into the bank or sends them to the card issuer for payment.

1. **Credit Card Companies.** There are currently five major credit card companies. Each company has a number, which prefixes the card number, that indicates the kind of credit card:

a.	American Express	3
b.	Visa	4
c.	MasterCard	5
d.	Discover	6

American Express, and Discover require merchants to send their charge slips directly to them. The merchant is sent a draft less the fees. Visa and MasterCard require merchants to deposit the charge slips into their bank account. The bank charges the merchant's bank account for the fees. Banks become members of Visa and/or MasterCard companies who operate the system. They mail out statements to customers and collect the customer's payments. In turn, the credit card companies forward earnings (interest) to the banks. For banks, credit cards are very profitable because of the high interest charged. Even with fraud committed by either customers or merchants, banks earn more than they receive on other types of loans. The bank credit card companies publish a book, which shows the bank's identification numbers (BIN). This book is not made available to the general public.

2. **Card Numbers.** Visa and MasterCard use a 16-digit number grouped in fours. The first eight digits (on the left) indicate the type of credit card, the bank identification number, and routing number. The last eight digits represent the customer's account number.

Trust Services

Many banks offer trust services. These services vary depending upon what the customer wants. Banks have the ability to service many kinds of trusts that range from simple to complex. Fees are based upon the amount of services required to be performed. Trustees are required to file state and federal income tax returns. Some trusts are taxed upon their earnings, while others pass the income down to the grantor. The grantor is deemed to be the owner of the trust's assets. The most common trusts are

1. **Decedent's Trust.** The trustee takes control over the decedent's assets, liabilities, income, and expenses. The trustee distributes the net income and assets to the beneficiaries after the estate is probated and taxes, expenses, and liabilities have been paid. A simple version of this is called the Insurance Trust. The grantor assigns his or her life insurance policies to the trustee. The trustee distributes the insurance proceeds after death of the grantor to the beneficiaries based upon the grantor's wishes.

2. **Intervivos Trust.** The grantor transfers all or part of his or her assets to the trustee, while the grantor is still living. The trustee administers the trust assets in accordance with the grantor's wishes. The grantor can make the trust an Irrevocable Trust in which the grantor loses control of the assets. A Revocable Trust is one in which the grantor can terminate the trustee at any time and gain control of the assets.

Many criminal elements use trusts to hide their assets in order to keep them out of the reach of the government and law enforcement agencies.

Exchange Instruments

Banks offer the following exchange services for customers. Exchange instruments are basically the withdrawals of funds from bank accounts for various bank instruments.

1. Cashier's checks
2. Money orders
3. Certified checks
4. Wire transfers

Magnetic Ink Character Recognition (MICR)

MICR was developed by the American Bankers Association (ABA) as a machine language and as a standard in check design to which all banks must conform. Numeric information is printed in magnetic ink on the bottom of bank checks and other documents. This coding is electronically scanned by computers, which convert the magnetic ink notations into electronic impulses intelligible to a computer. MICR information is printed in groupings called fields. On bank checks, the first field on the left is the Federal Reserve check routing code and the next is the ABA transit number. These numbers also appear in the upper right corner of the check. The middle group of numbers shows the drawer's assigned account number at the bank. The MICR information in these two fields is imprinted on the blank checks furnished to the customer. The right field contains a control number used for processing and the amount of the check. The dollar amount of the check should be compared with the encoded amount to be sure the subject did not alter the returned check. Many banks are adding an additional field for the check number. Some place this field after the account number, whereas others place it before the account number.

Bank Reconciliation

In most cases, the bank sends a statement along with the canceled checks, deposit slips, credit and debit memorandums each month. It is up to customers to reconcile their bank account with their check register. Many banks provide the customer a bank reconciliation schedule on the bank of the statements. A typical example of a bank reconciliation is as follows:

Balance per Bank's Statement	$ _____
Add: Deposits in Transit	_____
Less: Outstanding Checks	_____
Balance per Reconciliation	$ _____

Customers will usually have to make adjustments to their check register to show current bank charges, interest earned, and any deposits or checks that cleared the bank but were not recorded. Otherwise, the customer will not be able to reconcile to the above example.

Government Securities

Banks also sell and redeem government securities. They sell U.S. bonds, bills, and notes. Bills are of very short duration, usually 60 to 360 days. Notes are short term, usually 3 to 10 years. Bonds are long term, usually 20 or more years.

Currency Transactions Reports

Banks are required to file Currency Transaction Reports with the U.S. Treasury Department whenever a customer makes a cash withdrawal or deposit, purchases a cashier's check, or makes a payment on loans of $10,000 or more.

Correspondence

Banks maintain a file of all letters to and from customers. Most bank customer correspondence relates to granting and servicing loans. However, banks maintain files of customer complaints. The bank's internal auditors review these letters to determine adherence to bank policies and internal controls.

Letter of Credit

Banks issue an official form of correspondence called a "letter of credit." A letter of credit is an official bank correspondence, which asks other banks to extend credit to the holder of the letter. The letter is generally issued to bank customers who have an established banking relationship. The customer must have an approved credit line or funds on account that can cover the letter of credit amount.

Foreign Currency Exchange

Many banks offer customers the ability to exchange foreign currency into U.S. dollars, or vice versa. Banks charge a small fee for this service. Banks must keep records of any foreign currency exchange. Currency Transactions Reports will have to be filed if the transaction involves $10,000 or more in terms of U.S. dollars.

Bank Records

Of all the sources of financial information, banks rank at the top of the list. They can provide a wealth of financial data. This data can help the fraud examiner determine the customer's lifestyle, financial patterns, and show the degree of sophistication. Examiners and investigators, when requesting and obtaining copies of bank records, should use the following checklist.

1. Records of checking accounts:
   a. Monthly statements
   b. Deposit slips
   c. Canceled checks
   d. Signature cards
   e. Debit and/or credit memorandums
   f. Deposit items

2. Records of savings accounts, certificates of deposit, or any other income-producing positive balance instruments:
   a. Ledger cards and/or monthly accounts statements
   b. Deposit slips
   c. Deposited items
   d. Transfer slips
   e. Withdrawal slips
   f. Canceled checks used for withdrawals
   g. Signature cards
   h. Items of withdrawals
   i. Debit and/or credit memorandums
   j. Interest statements (Form 1099, etc.)

3. Records of loan accounts:
   a. Ledger cards
   b. Repayment schedules
   c. Canceled loan checks
   d. Signature cards

    e. Applications, including supporting documents and escrow statements
    f. Financial statements
    g. Credit bureau reports

4. Records of credit card accounts:
    a. Monthly statements
    b. Sales drafts
    c. Payment schedules
    d. Interest schedules
    e. Applications
    f. Financial statements
    g. Credit bureau reports

5. Safe deposit box records:
    a. Applications
    b. Entry records
    c. Signature cards

6. Agreements, statements, account ledger sheets, and checks disbursed from or for any trust account established by or for the benefit of the person(s) specified

7. Wire transfer records

8. Cashier's checks or registers

9. Letters of credit

10. Cash transit letters

11. Money order records

12. Currency transaction reports, including records and source documents indicating transfer of funds prepared in compliance with currency and Foreign Transaction Reporting Act (31 USC 1051)

13. Individual Retirement Accounts:
    a. Signature cards
    b. Ledger cards and/or account statements
    c. Canceled checks
    d. Deposit slips

14. Correspondence

Security Brokers

The second most important source of financial information comes from security brokers. Securities fall into two basic markets: trading of (1) stocks and bonds and (2) commodities. Both markets operate under similar structures. The Securities and Exchange Commission (SEC) regulates the security industry. The broker is an agent who handles the public's orders to buy and sell securities, usually for a commission. A broker may be a corporation, partnership, or individual and is often a member of an exchange. A registered representative (also known as a securities salesperson or account executive) personally places customer's orders and maintains their accounts. While commonly referred to as a broker, a registered representative is usually an employee of a brokerage firm rather than a member.

Security Markets

The security markets are classified into two categories, organized exchanges and over-the-counter market.

1. **Organized Securities Exchanges.** Securities exchanges or stock exchanges neither buy nor sell securities themselves. An exchange functions as a central marketplace and provides facilities for executing orders. Member brokers representing buyers and sellers carry out the transactions. The two major exchanges are the New York Stock Exchange (NYSE) and the American Stock Exchange (AMEX), both located in New York City. While there are various regional exchanges, the NYSE and AMEX together handle more than 90 percent of the trading done through organized exchanges. If a security is to be traded on an exchange, the issue must be approved for listing by that exchange. Securities traded on the NYSE and AMEX may also be listed and traded on the regional exchanges, but no security is listed on both the NYSE and AMEX.

2. **Over-the-Counter Securities Market.** The over-the-counter securities market handles most of the security transactions that take place in the United States. The over-the-counter market does not handle the purchase or sale of securities that actually occur on securities exchanges, but it handles everything else in the way of securities transactions. Thus, securities not listed on a securities exchange are "unlisted," that is, traded over the counter. The over-the-counter market is not located in any one central place. It consists of thousands of security houses located in hundreds of different cities and towns all over the United States. These security houses are called brokers or dealers and are engaged in buying and selling securities, usually for their own account and risk. There are many more types of securities that are traded in the over-the-counter market than are traded on the national or regional exchange:

a. Bank stocks
b. Insurance company stocks
c. U.S. government securities
d. Municipal bonds
e. Open-end investment company shares (mutual funds)
f. Most corporate bonds
g. Stocks of a large number of industrial and utility corporations, including nearly all new issues
h. Securities of many foreign corporations

3. **Ownership of Securities.** There are two principal ways securities are held: in the name of the account holder and in street name. In the first instance, the customer's name is reflected on the security and the account. When securities are held in street name, they

are registered in the name of the broker. This occurs when securities have been bought on margin or when a cash customer wishes the security to be held by the broker, rather than in his or her own name.

Stock Classes

When a corporation is formed, capital stock representing the ownership of the corporation is authorized in the corporate charter. There are two principal classes of stock, common and preferred. If only one class of stock is authorized, it is common stock. The number of shares authorized can be changed by formal approval of the stockholders. Shares issued and subsequently reacquired by the corporation through purchase or donation are referred to as treasury stock. The number of shares outstanding will always equal the number of shares issued, less the number of shares of treasury stock, unless stock has been repurchased and canceled. Each stockholder is part owner of the corporation, since each share of stock represents a fractional interest in the corporation. The stockholder is entitled to a stock certificate showing ownership of a specific number of shares of stock in the corporation. If a stockholder desires to buy more stock, it is not necessary to obtain the permission of the corporation. The stockholder acquires it by purchase in the open market or privately. Conversely, if stockholders desire to sell shares, they cannot demand the corporation buy the stock. Instead, a stockholder is free to seek a buyer for the stock either in the market or by private sale. After the sale terms have been agreed upon, the mechanics of transfer are simple. The seller signs his or her name on the back of the stock certificate and delivers it to the buyer or the buyer's broker. A record of all outstanding certificates is kept by the corporation or by its duly appointed transfer agents, often a bank. The transfer agent has a record of the names and addresses of the stockholders and the number of shares owned by each. After determining that the old certificate is in proper form for transfer, the transfer agent issues a new certificate to a new owner. Most companies have a registrar. The duty of the registrar is to double-check the actions of the transfer agent to prevent improper issue of stock or fraudulent transfer.

Stock Rights

Holders of a common stock may usually subscribe (at a stated discount price) to new issues of common stock in proportion to their holdings. This privilege, known as a stock right, is usually offered to stockholders for a limited time. During this period, the stockholders may exercise the right to purchase additional shares under the terms of the offer or may choose to sell the rights. If the stockholder allows the time limit to run out without acting, the rights become worthless.

Stock Warrants

A stock warrant is a certificate which gives the holder the privilege to purchase common stock at a stated price within a specified time limit or perpetually. Warrants are often issued with bonds or preferred stock as an added inducement to investors. The stockholder may exercise the right to purchase additional shares or choose to sell the warrants.

Stock Splits

When the price of the common stock of a corporation reaches a high market value, the corporation may choose to bring the price down to a more favorable trading range. To do this, the corporation splits its shares: that is, it increases the number of shares outstanding without issuing additional stock. If, for example, a stockholder owned 100 shares which had a market value of $200 per share, a 4 to 1 stock split would increase the stockholder's shares to 400 and decrease the market value to $50 per share. Although the stockholder now owns a greater number of shares, the value of the stock and proportionate interest remains unchanged.

Dividends

A corporation may pay a dividend in cash, in stock, or in property. When a cash dividend is paid, the company, or its dividend-disbursing agent (usually a bank), sends a check to all of the stockholders whose names appear on the books of the company on a so-called record date. A dividend is a prorated distribution among stockholders and when acash dividends is paid it is in terms of so much per share. Some companies, in order to conserve cash, pay dividends in their own stock. A stock dividend has an effect similar to that of a stock split in that the stockholder's proportionate share of the ownership remains unchanged. A stock dividend is usually stated as a percentage of the outstanding shares (up to a maximum of 25 percent, above which it is called a stock split). When a corporation pays a property dividend, it is usually in the form of stock in another corporation which has been acquired for investment or some other purpose.

Bonds

When a corporation or government unit wishes to borrow money for some period, usually for more than 5 years, it will sell a bond issue. Each bond, generally of $1,000 denomination, is a certificate of debt of the issuer and serves as evidence of a loan to the corporation or governmental unit. The bondholder is a creditor of the issuer. A bond pays a stated rate of interest and matures on a stated date when the fixed sum of money must be repaid to the bondholder. Railroad, public utility, and industrial bonds are called corporate bonds. The obligations of states, counties, cities, towns, school districts, and authorities are known as municipal bonds. U.S. Treasury certificates, notes, and bonds are classified as Government securities. Bonds are issued in two principal forms: coupon bonds and registered bonds.

1. **Coupon Bonds.** Coupon bonds have interest coupons attached to each bond by the corporation that issues it. Because the corporation keeps no record of the owner of the bonds, they are called bearer bonds. On the due dates for the interest, the owner clips the coupons and presents them to the authorized bank for payment. The principal, when due, is payable to the holder or bearer of the bonds.
2. **Registered Bonds.** Registered bonds have the name of the owner written on the front of the bond. The company, or its authorized agent (usually a bank), has a record of the name and address of the owner. When interest is due, it is paid to the bondholder by check.

Types of Transactions

There are two types of transactions, long and short.

1. **Long transactions.** In a long transaction, an account holder purchases a security with the expectation that the market price of that security will appreciate or advance. Long simply means ownership of a security.
2. **Short transactions.** In a short transaction, an account holder sells a security that he or she does not own with the expectation that the market price of that security will decline. Short signifies a liability position in a security.

Records

The broker can furnish all documents relating to securities account activity. The principal documents available from a broker are as follows:

1. **Customer account cards.** This is a broker's record of the customer's account.
2. **Application for account.** This form contains basic information about the customer. Its primary purpose is to identify the customer and to be able to contact the customer when needed.
3. **Signature cards and margin account agreements.** The customer must fill out a signature card, much like that of a signature card with a bank or other financial institution. In addition, the customer must sign a margin agreement if the customer opens up a margin account.
4. **Securities receipts.** The broker keeps copies of security receipts for securities received from the customer.
5. **Cash receipts.** The broker keeps copies of receipts for funds received from the customer.
6. **Confirmation slips.** The broker keeps copies of confirmation receipts. Confirmation slips are used to confirm the customer's buys and sells of securities.
7. **Securities delivered receipts.** The broker keeps copies of receipts of securities that are delivered to the customer.
8. **Canceled checks.** The broker keeps canceled checks of payments made to the customer.
9. **Monthly account statements.** The broker issues monthly statements. These statements show all transactions for the month. Unlike bank statements, brokerage statements show the customer's holdings and their market values at the end of the month. This serves as a barometer for the customer to tell how the holdings are faring in the marketplace.
10. **IRS reporting forms.** The broker is required to keep copies of all forms that report earnings and sales of securities to the IRS.

Types of Accounts

There are two types of accounts that a customer can have with a broker:

1. **Cash.** This type of account requires the customer to pay securities in full at time of purchase.
2. **Margin.** This type of account allows securities to be purchased on credit. Margin is the percentage of the purchase price of a security that the customer must pay. The

Federal Reserve Board establishes the margin requirement. To open a margin account, there must be a minimum deposit by the customer. Stock purchased on margin must be registered in street name while in the account. If the customer's margin falls below the minimum, then the broker can liquidate the account without permission of the customer if the customer fails to bring the margin up to proper requirements.

Security Account Statements

The customer's security account statement (issued monthly) contains all transactions from the last statement date. These statements are the basic documents used to reconstruct a customer's security position. The following rules are applicable when analyzing security account statements.

1. **Buying.** The buy column will show the following entries:
   a. Bought or received. This shows whether the customer either bought the security or received the security that was previously purchased.
   b. Description. This is the name of the security.
   c. Price or symbol. This gives the purchase price per share.
   d. Debit. This is the amount of the purchase price paid by the customer including the broker's commission.

2. **Selling.** The sold column will show the following entries:
   a. Sold or delivered. This column shows whether the customer sold a security or delivered a security to the broker.
   b. Description. This identifies the security that is sold or delivered to the broker.
   c. Price or symbol. This shows the unit sales price per share.
   d. Credit. This shows the proceeds from the sales credited to the customer's account.

When a customer purchases stock, the customer has the option of taking "delivery" of the certificates from the broker or leaving them in the broker's custody. The customer usually indicates this when they open up a brokerage account.

If a customer takes delivery of the certificates, the number of shares would be noted in the sold or delivered column and the date column would show the date of delivery. In addition, there would be no entry in the price or symbol column.

If there are no entries indicating delivery of securities, the broker is, in fact, holding them and the customer is in what is commonly referred to as a "long" position. The broker will list at the bottom of the customer's statement a summary of customer's long position, that is, a listing of the number of shares of each stock being held for the customer and their market values.

Transfer Agent

The transfer agent keeps a record of the name and address of each stockholder and the number of shares owned, and checks that certificates presented for transfer are properly canceled and that new certificates are issued in the name of the transferee. In many small firms, the transfer agent is usually an attorney, a bank, or the corporation itself. In most large firms, the transfer agent is a bank. The transfer agent maintains the following information

1. Stockholder identification
2. Stockholder position

3. Stock certificate numbers
4. Number of shares represented by certificates
5. Date certificates were issued or surrendered
6. Evidence of returned certificates
7. Names of transferees and transferors

The principal documents available from the transfer agent are

1. Stockholder ledger card
2. Stock certificates

The names and addresses of transfer agents may be found in Moody's or Standard and Poor's for publicly held companies, or may be obtained from the main offices of the corporations.

Dividend-Disbursing Agent

Most large corporations distribute their dividends through agents known as dividend-disbursing agents. The dividend-disbursing agent is generally a bank and can furnish the following information

1. Stockholder identification
2. Stockholder position
3. Amount of dividends
4. Form of dividends
5. Dates paid
6. Evidence of payments

The principal documents available from the dividend-disbursing agent are

1. Canceled checks
2. Form 1099 — This form reports to the IRS dividends that were paid to the customer

It is common practice for separate financial institutions to serve as transfer agent and dividend-disbursing agent. However, a single financial institution can serve both functions. Names and addresses of institutions providing these services can be found for publicly held companies in security publications, such as

1. Financial Stock Guide Service
2. Moody's Investors Service, Inc.
3. Standard and Poor's Corporation

SUMMARY

Bank and other financial records are the most important documents for a fraud examiner. Their importance cannot be overemphasized. They should be the starting point for fraud examiners to commence their examination. Bank and other financial records will either make or break the case. Without this evidence, the fraud examiner has no case, unless the subject doesn't use banks and/or brokerage firms.

Reports and Case Files

22

Introduction

The fraud examiner has two important administrative duties to perform. The first is to obtain and maintain proper files. These files must be maintained so that evidence, statements, interviews, and financial information are readily and easily accessible. Second, the fraud examiner must prepare reports that are factual, clear, and relevant. This chapter is directed to helping the fraud examiner set up and maintain case files and prepare proper reports.

Purpose

There are various reasons why reports and files are important:

1. They give the attorney all the evidence that was obtained, so it can be evaluated regarding its admissibility and likely success in court, whether civil or criminal.
2. It helps evaluate the fraud examiner's work product in terms of thoroughness, reliability, objectivity, relevancy, etc.
3. It forces the fraud examiner to review the evidence and witness interviews or statements. If material or relevant facts have been omitted or not obtained, then the fraud examiner can go seek them out. Remember, fraud examiners will most often have to interview witnesses more than once to obtain all the facts.
4. The report should give the attorney or reviewer all the material and relevant facts. It omits immaterial information.
5. It helps the fraud examiner to ensure that all the evidence and witness statements have been obtained and are available. In quoting witnesses in the report, the fraud examiner should guard against misquoting or taking statements out of context.
6. The fraud examiner's report is a work product of the fraud examiner. It tells the reviewer what the fraud examiner has done and what the fraud examiner feels to be material and relevant. The report must be true and correct. The reviewer or attorney may uncover additional evidence and witnesses that may alter or render the fraud examiner's report invalid.

Report Characteristics

The fraud examiner's report should consist of the following characteristics:

1. **Accuracy.** The report should contain all material and relevant evidence and witness statements. Any computational schedules should be correct. Any misquotes or mathematical errors can render the report useless. Times, dates, figures, and supporting information should be reaffirmed with witnesses or subject.

2. **Clarity.** The report should use clear and simple language. The report should not use slang or technical terminology. Those reading the report usually are not familiar with slang or technical language. If slang or technical language must be used, then explain its meaning before continuing use. Witnesses may use such language in statements and interviews. The fraud examiner's report should definitely explain their meaning so the reader can understand.

3. **Lack of prejudice.** The report should only give the facts. The report should not give the fraud examiner's biases or partialities. All facts should be shown regardless of which side they favor. The U.S. Supreme Court in *Brady v. Maryland*, 373 U.S 83 (1963) better known as "Brady" held that the government's failure to disclose evidence favorable to a defendant who specifically requested it violated the defendant's due process rights because the evidence was material to guilt or punishment. In addition, a defendant is also entitled to disclosure of information that might be used to impeach the government or plaintiff's witnesses. These include, but are not limited to, payments to witnesses, immunity, any promises, witness biases, rewards offered or collected, etc.

4. **Relevance.** The fraud examiner should ensure that all relevant information is in the report. If in doubt about the relevance of information, then include it in the report. Any information that has either a direct or indirect bearing on the case should be reflected in the report. Immaterial or irrelevant information only confuses the reader and can lead to questions of the examiner's capabilities and methodologies.

5. **Promptness.** The fraud examiner should take notes during interviews of witnesses or possible subjects. These notes should be reduced to memorandums of interview or statements as soon as possible. The longer the examiner waits, the less the examiner will remember. The interim or final report should be prepared as soon as possible following the investigation. Delaying will result in the report omitting material or relevant information. It is recommended that the fraud examiner *not* work on more than three cases at any one time, unless there are extenuating circumstances.

6. **Opinions or conclusions.** The fraud examiner should never express an opinion of any kind on the guilt or innocence of the subject. The fraud examiner should never express any opinions or conclusions about a witness testimony or statements. Witness or subject statements will clearly show conflicts. Confidential informants should never be identified in either statements or the body of the report. The report should only identify confidential informants by codes or numbers. Some law enforcement agencies require "conclusions" in their reports. Actually, the conclusions are in reality recommendations. Law enforcement agencies want recommendations regarding all courses of action that are available. Conclusions or opinions of the guilt or innocence of the subject are not what they want.

Discovery

The courts have held that investigator's notes can be used as evidence in court and must be made available to the defense. Therefore, the fraud examiner should never destroy or dispose of interview notes, whether of a witness or subject. The fraud examiner does not have the right to privileged communications. However, there are two exceptions to the general rule:

1. The fraud examiner is conducting the investigation under the retainer of an attorney. In this case, the fraud examiner is working for the attorney and comes under the rules of the attorney–client privilege.
2. The fraud examiner is retained or hired by a law enforcement agency. This is considered privileged communications by the courts, especially in grand jury cases. Grand jury information cannot be disclosed unless authorized by the court.

Report Format

There is no formal or set format for the fraud examiner's report. However, the fraud examiner should identify and cover the following items.

1. **Date.** The date of the report should be when the report is finished.

2. **Retainer.** The report should be addressed to the person and entity that has retained the fraud examiner. If the fraud examiner is an employee of an entity, then the report should be addressed to the employer.

3. **Subject.** The report should identify the subject of the investigation. The subject's full name, address, date of birth, and, in some instances, social security number should be included.

4. **Case description.** The first paragraph should identify the nature of the case, such as embezzlement, kickbacks, theft, etc. It should never state that the subject committed an offense, only allege that the subject committed an offense.

5. **Investigator.** The report should identify all the investigators involved in the investigation and their respective roles.

6. **Type.** This section should identify the type of case under examination and investigation. There are basically three choices: criminal, civil, and administrative. A criminal investigation involves the potential conviction and imprisonment of the offender. A civil examination involves potential monetary damages. An administrative case involves the possibility of disciplinary action on the job such as dismissal or demotion.

7. **History.** This section should give a brief history about the subject. It should include the following items:

   a. Identifiers. The full name of the subject and immediate family members should be listed. This should include the dates of births, social security numbers, places of birth, driver's license numbers, alien numbers if applicable, etc.
   b. Health. The subject's health condition and that of his or her immediate family should be disclosed. This can have an effect of whether a criminal prosecution will or will not be pursued.

c. Employment or business history. The employment history of the subject should be fully identified. This should describe the skills and knowledge acquired from past and present employment. The employment history of the spouse may also be included if it has a bearing on the case. If the subject has operated businesses in the past or present, then they should also be identified.

d. Education. The educational history of the subject should also be disclosed. If the subject has a college degree, then this should be disclosed. More-sophisticated crimes are committed by well-educated people.

e. Residence. The subject's residence should be disclosed. This should include not only the primary residence, but also any and all secondary residences, i.e., vacation homes, relative's and friend's residences frequented by the subject.

f. Associates. Friends, close business associates, and other relatives should be identified in the report along with their specific relationships.

g. Travel. The subject's travel experiences should be disclosed in the report. This should include not only the past few years, but should go back two or more decades.

8. Evidence. This section should summarize the evidence that has been obtained to show that a crime has been committed and who committed the crime. It should identify both physical evidence as well as oral (testimony) evidence. In a large case, this should be a brief summary since many witness statements and physical evidence will be obtained which can explain it. The evidence should be categorized and indexed in a logical order. The index should contain a brief description and identify the witness and physical evidence. This can encompass large volumes of documents and witness statements or depositions. In small cases, the evidence, both oral and physical, can be summarized and referenced as attachments.

9. Intent. This section should identify the evidence, both oral and physical, that shows the state of mind of the subject. Most cases require the prosecution or plaintiff to show intent to commit fraud on the part of the subject. Intent is a state of mind. The state of mind to defraud is based upon the actions and statements of the subject. These conditions and statements should be identified and referenced to the physical evidence, statements, or depositions.

10. Defenses. This section should identify any defenses made by either the defendant or any other witness on behalf of the defendant. In addition, any evidence that contradicts the defenses should also be identified and referenced. This will help the prosecutor or plaintiff attorney be prepared for these defenses.

11. Referrals. This section should identify any referrals made to law enforcement agencies, state attorneys, or outside counsel. A copy of the referral report should be attached. If the fraud examiner is working for law enforcement, then this section is not required, since the report will be processed according to local procedures.

12. Financial data. This section should disclose the total investigative costs. This should include fees charged, investigative expenses, administrative expenses, and other direct costs that are charged the client. An itemized statement should be attached to the report. In addition to the investigative costs, the amount of the client's loss should be identified. A schedule should be attached to the report showing the details of the loss or illegal gains.

13. Recommendation. This section should express all recommendations and actions that are available. The fraud examiner should not express any opinion regarding the guilt or innocence of the subject.

Sources/Informants

The identity of a confidential informant should never be disclosed in the report. They should only be identified by a code (number or letter). Files on each confidential source or informant should be maintained. The files should contain the following:

1. **Identifiers.** There should be a profile or personal data sheet, which contains information about the source or confidential informant. Such information should include, but not be limited to, full name, aliases, address, date and place of birth, driver's license number, social security number, alien number if applicable, names and addresses of relatives, friends, and associates.

2. **Evaluation.** The fraud examiner should make notes of the confidential source or informant regarding his/her reliability. This evaluation of reliability should be objective. These notes should reflect the information provided by the informant, which should be corroborated or verified. This fact should be noted in the file. One method is to write a memorandum of interview of the informant. When the information that the confidential informant has provided has been verified or corroborated, then another memorandum to file should be prepared showing what information was corroborated and what was not corroborated. A comparison of this data will show in an objective manner the reliability of the confidential informant. The more information the informant gives that is corroborated, the more reliable the informant becomes. The converse also holds true.

3. **Financial data.** Any financial dealings with the confidential informant should be documented. The fraud examiner or investigator should obtain a receipt from the informant for any funds paid to or on behalf of the informant. Failure to get receipts can put the examiner or investigator in an awkward position in court. Also, the IRS requires receipts for any deduction taken on a tax return. Failure to have a receipt on audit will cause the disallowance of a deduction, which will result in a higher tax liability.

Confidential informants and source files should be kept in a highly secured place. The investigator or examiner should never pledge total secrecy. This can cause problems at a later date. The examiner or investigator can be jailed for failure to disclose a confidential informant when ordered by a court to disclose. Remember, the fraud examiner or investigators must keep their word for any promises that are made. Otherwise, fraud examiners will lose their credibility on the "streets." Therefore, the fraud examiner can prevent this situation by only making limited commitments.

Report Writing Mistakes

There are other mistakes in report writing besides the normal misspelling and grammar errors. Reports should always be reviewed for any misspelling and grammar errors. Other mistakes include:

1. **Opinions.** The fraud examiner should never express an opinion about the guilt or innocence of the subject. This opens up the door for the defense attorney to show bias on the part of the fraud examiner.

2. Data. Information presented in the report should be accurate. Even mistakes in small details can leave doubts about the accuracy of the report as a whole. A wrong date of birth of a subject can lead to the case being thrown out because it is not the date of birth of the subject, but someone else. This is especially true if the date is constantly used.

3. Quotes. The examiner should not misquote a witness or subject. Misquotes can lead to doubts about the examiner's reliability. The fraud examiner should always have the witness or subject repeat statements that are important. In reports, the fraud examiner should cross check any quotes made by a witness or subject.

Case Disposition

When a case has been completed, its final disposition should be noted on the report. It is recommended that a disposition report be prepared and attached to the final report. The disposition report should provide the following.

1. Fines. The amount of fines imposed by the court should be shown.

2. Prison sentence. The prison sentence imposed by the court should be disclosed.

3. Probation. The probation term imposed by the court should be shown.

4. Forfeitures and seizures. All assets that were seized and forfeited to law enforcement agencies should be delineated. Each asset should be identified that was seized by law enforcement, along with its costs or market values. Also, if these assets were sold by law enforcement, then the sale proceeds should be noted. This may be impossible to find out in some cases, e.g., autos, boats, furniture, etc., when all seized assets are pooled and auctioned off.

5. Dropped. If the case was dropped, then this should be noted. An explanation should be given for why the case was dropped. There are many reasons a case is dropped. It could be the lack of funds to pursue prosecution or a lawsuit, the lack of collectibility, insufficient evidence, subject is deceased, generation of a negative public image, and various others.

6. Judgments. In civil cases, the amount of judgment awarded by the court should be noted. Copy of the judgment should be included in the case file.

7. Restitution. If the court ordered any restitution, the case file should note this fact. Also, a copy of the restitution order should be attached to the report.

Disclosure

A log should be maintained on all people who have or have had access to the case files. This log should identify the person, date, reason for access to files, and who authorized the access. Also, the fraud examiner should issue a memorandum, which identifies only those people who should have regular access to the case files. These people are generally the case examiner(s), clerical staff, client attorney, and any other person who has a need to know on a regular basis. Staff members should be instructed on disclosure of case files and information. Cases should never be discussed or even taken outside the office. Only copies of files should be taken for witness interviews. These instructions should also be included in the memorandum. Improper disclosure can result in the case being dropped, or the examiner and client being sued. In cases involving undercover work or similar actions, this can put the examiner at risk of not being able to perform the job as planned. In criminal cases, it can put the examiner's life at risk.

Witness List

The fraud examiner or investigator should keep a witness list. This witness list should identify the name of the witness, along with the witness's title or capacity, address, both home and business telephone numbers, and should identify, in summary, the physical evidence that the witness can provide. Remember, witness files should be kept. The witness files should contain statements, depositions, and physical evidence. Some tangible evidence because of size or other characteristics may have to be kept in a separate property room. The witness file should have a note that describes in detail where the evidence is located and its description.

By using the scenario problem, the witness list shown in Figure 22-1 is presented as an example. Besides identifying the witness, it also identifies the specific exhibits that the witness will introduce in court. Each witness and exhibit is assigned a number. "W" before the number identifies the number as a witness and not an exhibit. Exhibit numbers must be associated with the witness number and name.

Witness Number	Witness	Exhibit Number	Exhibit Description
W-1	Case detective	1	Property receipt for money seized
		2	Property receipt and lab report cocaine
		3	Barclays Bank statements
		4	Gold bullion property receipt
		5	Copy of search warrant with court signatures
W-2	Public records administrator	1	100 Alpha St. Deed
		2	100 Bravo St. Deed
W-3	Life Insurance Company records custodian	1	Insurance policy
		2	Payment receipts
W-4	Furniture company records custodian	1	Purchase invoice
W-5	Cabinet Company records custodian	1	Purchase invoice
W-6	Art dealer records custodian	1	Purchase invoice
W-7	Fixture company records custodian	1	Purchase invoice
W-8	Pool and tennis contractor	1	Builders contract
		2	Payment schedule

continued

Figure 22-1 Witness and exhibit list.

Witness Number	Witness	Exhibit Number	Exhibit Description
W-9	Appliance dealer records custodian	1	Purchase invoice
W-10	Electronic store records custodian	1	Purchase invoice
W-11	Security system dealer records custodian	1	Purchase contract
		2	Payment schedule
W-12	IRS representative	1	1040 return 19X0
		2	1040 return 19X1
		3	1040 return 19X3
		4	1120 return 19X1
		5	1120 return 19X2
		6	1120 return 19X3
		7	1120S return 19X1
		8	1120S return 19X2
		9	1120S return 19X3
		10	1065 return 19X1
		11	1065 return 19X2
		12	1065 return 19X3
W-13	I. M. Balance, CPA	1	Financial statements for 19X2 store
		2	Financial statements for 19X3 store
		3	Lounge Doe, Inc. work papers for 19X1
		4	Lounge Doe, Inc. work papers for 19X2
		5	Lounge Doe, Inc. work papers for 19X3
		6	Doe Kwik Stop work papers for 19X1
		7	Doe Kwik Stop work papers for 19X2
		8	Doe Kwik Stop work papers for 19X3
		9	Real Property Co., Ltd. work papers for 19X1
		10	Real Property Co., Ltd. work papers for 19X2
		11	Real Property Co., Ltd. work papers for 19X3
		12	Work papers 1040 for 19X1
		13	Work papers 1040 for 19X2
		14	Work papers 1040 for 19X3
W-14	Bookkeeper for Suzy's Women's Clothes	1	Books and records 19X2
		2	Books and records 19X3

Figure 22-1 (continued) Witness and exhibit list.

Witness Number	Witness	Exhibit Number	Exhibit Description
W-15	First National Bank records custodian	1	Bank account records for 19X1
		2	Bank account records for 19X2
		3	Bank account records for 19X3
		4	IRA account records for John Doe
		5	IRA account records for Suzy Que
		6	Trust account for sister
		7	Trust account for brother one
		8	Trust account for brother two
		9	Trust account for parents
		10	Mercedes Benz loan documents and payment schedule
		11	Toyota loan documents and payment schedule
W-16	Credit card company records custodian	1	Credit card records 19X1
		2	Credit card records 19X2
		3	Credit card records 19X3
W-17	Utility company records custodian	1	Billing and payment schedule 19X1
		2	Billing and payment schedule 19X2
		3	Billing and payment schedule 19X3
W-18	Telephone company records custodian	1	Billing and payment schedule 19X1
		2	Billing and payment schedule 19X2
		3	Billing and payment schedule 19X3
W-19	Insurance company records custodian	1	Policy and payment schedule 19X1
		2	Policy and payment schedule 19X2
		3	Policy and payment schedule 19X3
		4	Policy and payment schedule for apartment building
W-20	Church donation records custodian	1	Receipt schedule for 19X2
		2	Receipt schedule for 19X3
W-21	Auto dealership records custodian	1	Mercedes Benz purchase document
		2	Toyota purchase documents
W-22	Apartment building tenants[a]	1	Lease agreements
		2	Payment schedule
W-23	Florida Mortgage Company records custodian	1	Mortgage documents
		2	Payment schedule
W-24	Maintenance Company records custodian	1	Maintenance records
		2	Payment schedule

continued

Figure 22-1 (continued) Witness and exhibit list.

Witness Number	Witness	Exhibit Number	Exhibit Description
W-25	Administrator, State Unemployment Compensation Office	1	Earnings records
W-26	Brokerage firm records custodian	1 2 3	Account application Monthly statements Buy and sale confirmation slips
W-27	Fraud examiner summary witness	1	Net worth schedule
W-28	Jewelry store owner	1	Gold bullion invoice
W-29	U.S. State Department Consular Officer	1	Bahamian public records
W-30	County Tax Collector records custodian	1	Property tax bills

Figure 22-1 (continued) Witness and exhibit list.

[a] Note: Each apartment building tenant is a witness along with the documentary evidence. For simplicity here, only one tenant and related evidence is shown.

The witness list in Figure 22-1 is condensed; however, this list should include the names, address, home and business telephone numbers, and business or agency name of the witness. This witness list mostly covers the evidence introduced in financial data section of the scenario problem. If witnesses can be obtained in offshore countries, then they and the evidence should be listed. In the case of offshore public records, they can be obtained by Consular Officers of the U.S. Department of State. The consular officer has the authority to introduce these documents into court. The bank records from Barclays Bank of London, England, were not introduced into evidence because a witness from that bank must be used to authenticate these records. The case detective who executed the search warrant could be used to introduce these records into court; however, the detective could not testify as to the authenticity.

The examiner should keep the witness list on a computer database. This can help the examiner's counsel or prosecutor plan and schedule witnesses for trial. Costs can be reasonable estimated for paying witness expenses, i.e., witness fees, parking, travel, lodging if required, etc.

Case Files

Case files are very important. Case files contain all of the evidence and witness statements or depositions. The two principal methods of keeping case files are originals and working copies:

Originals

Original or primary evidence and statements should be kept according to witness. A witness statement or deposition along with any physical evidence should be kept together. For trial purposes, it makes it easier for the witness to review their previous statements or depositions and examine the evidence that they provided earlier. It often takes years from the time the witness is interviewed and evidence obtained to the time the trial takes place. Both physical evidence and statements should be kept in files that are secured. Original evidence should be kept in clear plastic envelopes and properly labeled. Under no circumstances should original evidence be marked.

Working Copies

Copies of original evidence and statements should be made for use as working copies. These copies can be marked. If doing an indirect method, e.g., Net Worth or Expenditure Method, these working copies should be filed according to the method being used. In the case of the Net Worth Method, the working copies should be kept by assets, liabilities, expenses, and known or nontaxable income. In the case of specific items, the files should be kept in chronological order. This can help the examiner determine what items are missing or identify areas where more investigation is required or additional evidence needs to be obtained.

Sample Report

This section will provide a condensed version of a fraud examiner's report. Its primary purpose is to provide a guideline for the fraud examiner in preparing their investigative report. The basic elements of the fraud examiner's report follow.

1. Fraud Examiner's Memorandum
2. Table of Contents
3. Witness List
4. Schedule of Losses or Net Worth/Expenditure Schedules with references to witnesses and evidence
5. Interview Memorandums/Depositions
6. Copies or photographs of evidence

Copies or photographs of evidence will not be provided in this example. An example of a fraud examiner's report is shown in Figure 22-2.

Investigation report

May 10, 19X4

U.S/State Attorney
Any County, USA

continued

Figure 22-2 Investigation report sample.

In re: John Doe
    SSN: 000-00-0000
    DOB: 1/24/XX
    100 Alpha St
    Any City, State XXXXX
    Case #: XXXXXXX
    Criminal-Drug Trafficking and
    Money Laundering, RICO
FINAL REPORT

HISTORY

John Doe is a 24-year-old man. He dropped out of the 10th grade. He has two brothers, a sister, and parents who are still living in the area. He has not married but is currently living with a girlfriend, Suzy Que. John Doe has only had menial jobs during his career. Past employees have stated that John Doe has a talent of being a boat mechanic. John Doe is considered the "black sheep" of the family. His parents are highly educated. His father was a doctor in Cuba, but now is working as a laboratory technician. His mother is a registered nurse. His brothers and sister are continuing their education. He has been seen on many occasions with Ramon Calderone, a known drug trafficker by local and federal law enforcement. John Doe, being young, is in excellent health. He has been seen jogging, swimming, and doing heavy lifting. Doe has not worked for any employer since 19X1. He quit his last job but gave no reason to the employer as to why. The employer offered to give him a $1.00 per hour raise if he would stay. Doe refused. Doe lived with his parents up until the time that he purchased the house on 100 Alpha Street. John Doe uses pay telephones quite often. He visits his family regularly. After meeting Suzy Que, Doe has spent less time visiting his family, and more time courting Suzy. Doe does extensive travel around town and offshore. Suzy, his girlfriend, occasionally goes with Doe on his trips. It is documented that he has been to Europe, South and Central America, and various Caribbean Islands. This case was instituted because of testimony of former drug pushers in court who identify John Doe as the supplier. The former drug pushers have all been convicted and are incarcerated.

TYPE OF CASE

This is a Net Worth case. The purpose of the Net Worth is to determine Doe's alleged illegal gains from his drug trafficking and money-laundering activities. In addition, it will serve as a basis for both civil and criminal forfeitures.

EVIDENCE

Since this is a Net Worth case, most of the witnesses are record custodians who have records of transactions conducted with the subject. Some of the record custodians have personal knowledge and possible friendship with the subject. The key witness will be the summary witness, who will have to summarize the financial evidence

Figure 22-2 (continued) Investigation report sample.

introduced into court. To place the subject in the drug trafficking and money-laundering activities, witnesses will have to testify that they purchased drugs from or on behalf of the subject. Unfortunately, all the drug witnesses have been incarcerated for drug trafficking which lends them to lack of credibility. Ramon Calderone is an indicted drug trafficker who has fled the United States. It is well documented that the subject had a close association with Calderone.

INTENT

The use of the Net Worth method of proving illegal gains shows that the subject did not fully hide his illegal gains. The subject maintained offshore bank accounts to hide his illegal gains. The subject did not operate his legitimate businesses on a day-to-day basis like normal businessmen. He traveled to offshore countries where he did not have any legitimate business dealings. He made cash deposits exceeding $10,000 and the bank did not file the appropriate CTRs because of inside contacts. He made various investment purchases in cash in order not to leave a paper trail. Mortgages were obtained from offshore companies with no record of repayments. The offshore mortgage company is not registered in the United States nor does it do any other business activities. The girlfriend is known to be a drug user by her co-workers and friends. Wire-tap conversations show that the subject is involved in drug trafficking by discussing drug deals. There were many telephone calls made to offshore tax havens, many of which were to banks.

DEFENSES

The most common defenses in this type of case will be the cash hoard. In this case, the fact that the subject is young and was unable to accumulate enough cash to make the investments and expenditures that he made negate the cash hoard story. His income prior to the prosecution period was very small. His relatives were financially unable to provide the funds for the subject to make the investments and expenditures. Of course, the defense will try to discredit the witnesses who had drug dealings with the subject. The Net Worth Method of proving income will overcome these defenses.

FINANCIAL DATA

See the attached Net Worth Schedule for the illegal or unidentified gains by the subject. The fees and costs of this investigation are as follows:

Fees	$50,000
Investigation	10,000
Administrative	5,000
Total	$65,000

RECOMMENDATIONS

It is recommended that the subject be prosecuted for drug trafficking and money laundering under Federal Statutes, Title 18 USC 1956, 1963, and Title 21 USC 855

continued

Figure 22-2 (continued) Investigation report sample.

by the United States Attorney. If the U.S. Attorney declines to prosecute, then the
State Attorney should prosecute under State Statute XXXX.

Fraud Examiner

Copy to:
File
Case Detective

Figure 22-2 (continued) Investigation report sample.

The next part of the fraud examiner's report is the Table of Contents (Figure 22-3).

TABLE OF CONTENTS

1. Witness List
2. Net Worth Schedule
3. Witness Interviews and Depositions
4. Copies or photographs of evidence

Figure 22-3 Table of Contents sample.

The fraud examiner should list each witness and index each to the statements and/or
depositions in the Table of Contents. Also, copies of documents should be listed and
indexed. For simplicity, it is not done in Figure 22-3.

The next section of the report is the witness list. The witness list has been presented
in an earlier section; see Figure 22-1.

The next section shows the use of the financial loss or the indirect method. The Net
Worth Schedule (Figure 22-4) shows the account description, the witness number, evidence
number, and a brief description of the evidence. The figures have been omitted since they
are shown in an earlier chapter (see Chapter 8 for the RICO Net Worth Schedule).

John Doe

Net Worth Schedule

Account	Witness Number	Exhibit Number	Description
1. Cash on hand	W-1	1	Property receipt
2. Cocaine: 2 kilos	W-1	2	Property receipt and lab report
3. 1st National Bank	W-15	1–3	Bank account records
4. 1st National Bank	W-15	1–3	Bank account records
5. Business cash in bank	W-14	1, 2	Books and records
	W-15	13–14	Bank account records 19X2, -X3
6. Accounts receivable	W-13	1, 2	Financial statements and
	W-14	1, 2	work papers
7. Inventory	W-13	1, 2	Financial statements and
	W-14	1, 2	work papers
8. Business assets	W-13	1, 2	Financial statements and
	W-14	1, 2	work papers

Figure 22-4 Net Worth Schedule Witness List.

John Doe

Net Worth Schedule

Account	Witness Number	Exhibit Number	Description
9. Security system	W-11	1, 2	Contract and payment schedule
10. Electronic equipment	W-10	1	Purchase invoice
11. Appliances	W-9	1	Purchase invoice
12. Fixtures	W-7	1	Purchase invoice
13. Furniture	W-4	1	Purchase invoice
14. Cabinets	W-5	1	Purchase invoice
15. Paintings	W-6	1	Purchase invoice
16. Pool and tennis court	W-8	1, 2	Contract and payment schedule
17. 100 Alpha St.	W-2	1	Deed and mortgage
18. 100 Bravo St.	W-2	2	Deed and mortgage
19. Gold bullion	W-1	1	Case detective and property receipt
	W-28	1	Purchase invoice
20. Lounge Doe, Inc.	W-12	4–6	1120 tax returns
	W-13	3–5	Work papers
21. Doe Kwik Stop	W-12	7–9	1120S tax return
	W-13	6–8	Work papers
22. Real Property Co., Ltd	W-12	10–12	1065 tax returns
	W-13	9–11	Work papers
23. Mercedes Benz	W-21	1	Purchase documents
24. Toyota	W-21	2	Purchase documents
25. IRA—John Doe	W-15	4	Bank records
26. IRA—Suzy Que	W-15	5	Bank records
27. Bahama Islands residence	W-29	1	Public records
28. Mercedes loan	W-15	10	Loan documents
29. Toyota loan	W-15	11	Loan documents
30. Credit card	W-16	1–3	Credit card records
31. Accounts payable	W-13	1, 2	Financial statements and work papers
	W-14	1, 2	Books and records
32. Florida Mortgage Co.	W-23	1, 2	Mortgage documents and payment schedule
33. Business bank loan	W-15	1, 2	Loan documents
34. Purchases	W-13	1, 2	Financial statements and work papers
	W-14	1, 2	Books and records
35. Inventory change	W-13	1, 2	Financial statements and work papers
	W-14	1, 2	Books and records
36. Cost of sales	W-13	1, 2	Financial statements and work papers
	W-14	1, 2	Books and records
37. Advertising	W-13	1, 2	Financial statements and work papers
	W-14	1, 2	Books and records
38. Interest—loan	W-13	1, 2	Financial statements and work papers
	W-14	1, 2	Books and records
39. Insurance	W-13	1, 2	Financial statements and work papers
	W-14	1, 2	Books and records
40. Professional fees	W-13	1, 2	Financial statements and work papers
	W-14	1, 2	Books and records
41. Office expenses	W-13	1, 2	Financial statements and work papers
	W-14	1, 2	Books and records
42. Rent expenses	W-13	1, 2	Financial statements and work papers
	W-14	1, 2	Books and records

continued

Figure 22-4 (continued) Net Worth Schedule Witness List.

John Doe

Net Worth Schedule

Account	Witness Number	Exhibit Number	Description
43. Repairs	W-13	1, 2	Financial statements and work papers
	W-14	1, 2	Books and records
44. Supplies	W-13	1, 2	Financial statements and work papers
	W-14	1, 2	Books and records
45. Taxes and license fees	W-13	1, 2	Financial statements and work papers
	W-14	1, 2	Books and records
46. Utilities	W-13	1, 2	Financial statements and work papers
	W-14	1, 2	Books and records
47. Wages	W-13	1, 2	Financial statements and work papers
	W-14	1, 2	Books and records
48. Miscellaneous	W-13	1, 2	Financial statements and work papers
	W-14	1, 2	Books and records
49. Florida Mortgage Co.	W-23	1, 2	Mortgage documents and payment schedule
50. Utilities	W-17	1–3	Billing and payment schedules
51. Telephone	W-18	1–3	Billing, payment, and toll schedules
52. Insurance	W-19	1–3	Policy and payment schedule
53. Life insurance	W-3	1, 2	Policy and payment schedule
54. Interest—loans for autos	W-15	10–11	Bank loan documents and payment schedule
55. Income tax withholding	W-12	1–3	1040 tax return
56. Property taxes	W-13	12–13	Property tax bills
	W-30	1	Assessment and payments
57. Credit card	W-16	1–3	Credit card statements
58. Church donations	W-20	1, 2	Payment receipts
59. Trust funds	W-15	6–9	Bank records and trust agreements
60. Loss—XYZ stock	W-26	1–3	Brokerage records
61. Wages/salaries	W-12	1–3	W-2 records
	W-13	12–14	Work papers
	W-12	1	1099 records
62. Dividends	W-12	1	1099 records
	W-13	3, 12	Work papers
63. Rental income	W-12	1–3	1040 tax returns
	W-12	9–11	1065 tax returns
64. Gain—ABC Stock	W-26	1–3	Brokerage records
65. IRA—Interest	W-15	4	Bank records
66. IRA—Interest	W-15	5	Bank records
67. Tax refunds	W-12	1–3	IRS payment records
68. Sale—XYZ Stock	W-26	1–3	Brokerage records
69. Business income	W-13	1, 2	Financial statements and work papers
	W-14	1, 2	Books and records

Figure 22-4 (continued) Net Worth Schedule Witness List.

The next section of the fraud examiner's report should list the interviews and/or depositions of witness. In this case, most of the witnesses are record custodians. This section is important in that it gives the witnesses statements. These statements can be in the form of casual statements, formal statements, and depositions. Some witnesses may have more than one statement. Figure 22-5 is an example of the index of interviews and/or depositions.

Index of Interviews/Depositions

1. Case Detective	Police Reports
2. Administrator, Public Records	Interview memorandum
3. Records Custodian, Life Insurance Company	Interview memorandum
4. Records Custodian, Furniture Company	Interview memorandum
5. Records Custodian, Cabinet Company	Interview memorandum
6. Records Custodian, Art Dealer	Interview memorandum
7. Records Custodian, Fixture Company	Interview memorandum
8. Records Custodian, Pool and Tennis Contractor	Interview memorandum
9. Records Custodian, Appliance Dealer	Interview memorandum
10. Records Custodian, Electronics Store	Interview memorandum
11. Records Custodian, Security System Dealer	Interview memorandum
12. IRS Representative	Interview memorandum
13. I.M. Balance, CPA	Sworn statement and interview memorandum
14. Bookkeeper, Suzy's Clothing Store	Interview memorandum
15. Records Custodian, First National Bank	Interview memorandum
16. Records Custodian, Credit Card Company	Interview memorandum
17. Records Custodian, Utility Company	Interview memorandum
18. Records Custodian, Telephone Company	Interview memorandum
19. Records Custodian, Insurance Company	Interview memorandum
20. Records Custodian, Christian Church	Interview memorandum
21. Records Custodian, Auto Dealership	Interview memorandum
22. Tenants, Apartment Building	Interview memorandum
23. Records Custodian, Florida Mortgage Company	Interview memorandum
24. Records Custodian, Maintenance Company	Interview memorandum
25. Administrator, State Unemployment Compensation Office	Interview memorandum
26. Records Custodian, Brokerage Firm	Interview memorandum
27. Fraud Examiner	Examiner's report
28. Records Custodian, Jewelry Store	Interview memorandum
29. Consular Officer, U.S. State Department	Interview memorandum
30. Records Custodian, County Tax Collector	Interview memorandum

Figure 22-5 Index of Interviews/Depositions Sample.

Figure 22-6 is an example of a record custodian's memorandum of interview; and Figure 22-7 is an example of a witness-sworn statement.

MEMORANDUM OF INTERVIEW

Date: February 1, 19X4

Present: Records Custodian
             Case Detective/Agent
             Fraud Examiner

Place: XYZ Auto Dealership
             300 Main Street
             Any City, State XXXXX

continued

Figure 22-6 Memorandum of Interview Sample.

Mr. Paul Jones is the record custodian for the XYZ Auto Dealership. Mr. Jones has never met the subject. He only processes the paperwork that the salesmen provide when customers purchase new or used cars.

Mr. Jones provided information about the regular course of business in keeping records. These procedures are as follows:

1. The salesperson completes the sales contract and has the customer sign the contract. The salesperson also obtains a down payment or full payment.

2. The credit department gets approval from a local financial institution for financed purchases after the salesperson gets a signed contract and down payment. Once approved, the customer and the financial institution get a copy of the contract. The dealership keeps a copy of the contract. It is sent to the accounting department for processing.

3. The accounting department gets a copy of the contract for processing. The sale is recognized through the books after it has been approved by the financial institution. Mr. Jones is the controller of the dealership and the official record custodian. After the contract and sale is recognized, the contract is filed by customer name and stored.

Mr. Jones provided the following records of purchase.

1. The Purchase and Installment Sale Contract. This document shows the purchase, down payment, principal financed, rate of interest, payments, and terms.

2. A copy of the sales journal showing the receipt of the down payment.

3. A copy of the sales journal showing the payment by the financial institution.

4. A copy of the delivery receipt, which shows that the customer picked up the automobile 4 days after the contract was signed.

5. A copy of the maintenance contract and a record of service done on the vehicle while under warranty.

Figure 22-6 (continued) Memorandum of Interview Sample.

STATEMENT

I, I.M. Balance, CPA, provide the following statement about my client John Doe.

1. I obtained John Doe as a client by a referral. I don't recall who referred John Doe to me.

Figure 22-7 Statement sample.

2. I prepared John Doe's individual tax returns, 1040s, for the years 19X1 and 19X3. I obtained the data to prepare John Doe's individual tax return for 19X2, but did not prepare it because I was missing some data. I don't recall what data I was missing.

3. I prepared the 1120 federal corporate income tax returns for 19X1, 19X2, and 19X3 for Lounge Doe, Inc. These returns were prepared based upon the bank statements, canceled checks, accounts payable, inventory, and asset listings which were provided by the client. These items were processed by generating a general journal, general ledger, trial balance, and financial statements. The financial statements were used to prepare the corporate tax return.

4. I prepared the 1120S federal corporate income tax returns for 19X1, 19X2, and 19X3 for Doe Kwik Stop. These returns were also prepared based upon the bank statements, canceled checks, accounts payable, inventory, and asset listings which were provided by the client. These items were processed by generating a general journal, general ledger, trial balance, and financial statements. The financial statements were used to prepare the corporate tax return.

5. I prepared the 1065 federal partnership income tax returns for 19X1, 19X2, and 19X3 for Real Property Co., Ltd. These returns were prepared based upon the bank statements, canceled checks, closing statement, and mortgage information. These items were used to generate a general journal, general ledger, trial balance, and financial statements. The financial statements were used to prepare the partnership return. I never met the other partner, Ramon Calderone. All my dealings were with John Doe. Doe was given a copy of the return for his partner to complete his individual tax return.

6. I was retained by John Doe to do a certified audit on Suzy's Women's Clothes. This is a sole proprietorship. John Doe is the sole owner. His girlfriend and Betsy Low took care of the books and managed the store. They had about 8 to 10 employees at any one time. Suzy Que and Betsy Low received a salary to operate the business. They maintained a general journal and general ledger. In addition, they maintained accounts receivable, accounts payable, and purchase journals. I used these journals to prepare a trial balance and produce financial statements. I also made a test of the records in accordance with General Accepted Accounting Principles and General Accepted Audit Standards as promulgated by the AICPA. In addition, I prepared a Schedule C for John Doe for reporting on his individual income tax return. John Doe retained me to do the certified audit and oversee operations since he would be busy in his other business ventures.

7. I advised John Doe to obtain an Individual Retirement Account. In addition, I have counseled John Doe on taxes, management of businesses, and various investments. I advised John Doe to acquire the Kwik Stop, Inc. store. This advice was based upon the fact that John Doe wanted to supply boater's fast food items and supplies. Doe obtained a boat that he said was going to be used for this purpose. I never observed the boat.

continued

Figure 22-7 (continued) Statement sample.

8. John Doe was a friendly and personable individual. He is young and has many innovative ideas that I thought were good. He followed my advice on his business decisions. We worked well together.

I have read the foregoing statement. I fully understand that this statement is true, accurate, and complete to the best of my knowledge. I made this statement freely and voluntarily, without any threats or rewards, or promises of rewards having been made to me in return for it.

/s/ **I. M. Balance**

Witness signature   Date

Witness signature

Figure 22-7 Statement sample.

Summary

Maintaining proper files and producing reports are very important. It helps the fraud examiner and his/her clients in evaluating the case. The fraud examiner's report is the final product that is produced. It reflects the capabilities of the examiner. Sloppy reports indicate that the examiner is sloppy. It also helps the examiner. The examiner may find that evidence is missing. If so, then the examiner has to obtain it. It also helps the examiner in trial. First, it tells what evidence must be introduced into court before the summaries can be used. Second, it tells exactly what the examiner is going to testify about and gives the basis of the examiner's opinion as an expert witness.

Audit Programs

23

Introduction

Audit programs are procedures to be followed by accountants and auditors in the course of their examination of a business entity. The examiner must collect various kinds of evidence relating to the propriety of the recording of economic events and transactions. Audit programs are guidelines for the examiner in obtaining and collecting financial evidence. The auditor must collect and analyze evidence to support the auditor's attest function of the business entity's financial condition. The fraud examiner must collect and analyze evidence to uncover possible fraud by employees, management personnel, or by outsiders. While the auditor is primarily interested in obtaining evidence to support the attest function, the fraud examiner must obtain evidence that will convince a jury of peers that a certain individual(s) has committed an economic crime. The evidence required to convince a jury and to be admissible in court is much greater than to support the attest function. This chapter gives the general guidelines that a fraud examiner must follow at a minimum. The fraud examiner's judgment should always overrule any audit program.

General Guidelines

The fraud examiner, like other accountants and auditors, must have a general outline of the engagement that should be followed.

1. **Industry data.** The fraud examiner must know how the industry operates. The examiner should obtain as much data, both financial and nonfinancial, as possible.
2. **Financial analysis.** The fraud examiner should make various comparisons and analysis to identify possible fraud areas.
3. **Internal controls.** The fraud examiner must review the internal controls in order to identify problem areas.
4. **Evidence gathering.** This is the stage where the fraud examiner searches and obtains evidence of possible fraud activity.
5. **Evaluation.** The fraud examiner must analyze evidence to confirm whether fraud was actually committed.
6. **Report.** The fraud examiner must report the findings to the appropriate parties.

Industry Data

Companies that are in the same business operate and report financial and nonfinancial data in a similar manner. This is particularly true with the IRS, since their regulations set forth tax principles that various industries must follow. The IRS annually publishes industry data and statistics. There are also other governmental and publishing companies that provide industry data (see Chapter 15, Sources of Information). Comparing a business entity with others can identify problem areas, i.e., inventory, receivables, payables, sales, etc.

Financial Analysis

Financial statements should be analyzed to determine trends, relationships, and comparison with nonfinancial data in order to identify significant irregularities and unexplained fluctuations. This can help in identifying possible areas where fraud can occur. There are three types of techniques that are commonly used:

1. Ratio Analysis
2. Vertical Analysis
3. Horizontal Analysis

Ratio Analysis

Ratios are useful in determining if financial statements are reasonable (Table 23-1). Ratios can identify material fluctuations. These fluctuations must be researched for a reasonable explanation. Significant fluctuations from period to period can be a result of changing economic conditions, management strategy and policy, errors in record keeping, or fraud. The cause must be determined. Fraud could be one cause, but it is not proof that it occurred. Company ratios should be compared to industry statistics and data.

Table 23-1 Ratio Analysis

1. $\text{Current Ratio} = \dfrac{\text{Current Assets}}{\text{Current Liabilities}}$

2. $\text{Quick Ratio} = \dfrac{\text{Cash} + \text{Securities} + \text{Receivables}}{\text{Current Liabilities}}$

3. $\text{Cash Ratio} = \dfrac{\text{Cash} + \text{Securities}}{\text{Current Liabilities}}$

4. $\text{Accounts Receivable Turnover} = \dfrac{\text{Sales}}{\text{Average Receivables}}$

5. $\text{Days to Collect Receivables} = \dfrac{365}{\text{Accounts Receivable Turnover}}$

6. $\text{Inventory Turnover} = \dfrac{\text{Cost of Goods Sold}}{\text{Average Inventory}}$

7. $\text{Days to Sell Inventory} = \dfrac{365}{\text{Inventory Turnover}}$

8. Days to Convert Inventory to Cash = Days to Sell Inventory + Days to Collect Cash Receivables

9. Debt to Equity Ratio $= \dfrac{\text{Total Liabilities}}{\text{Total Equity}}$

10. Times Interest Earned $= \dfrac{\text{Net Income}}{\text{Interest Expense}}$

11. Profit Margin Ratio $= \dfrac{\text{Net Income}}{\text{Net Sales}}$

12. Asset Turnover $= \dfrac{\text{Net Sales}}{\text{Average Total Assets}}$

13. Return on Equity $= \dfrac{\text{Net Income}}{\text{Average Equity}}$

14. Earnings per Share $= \dfrac{\text{Net Income}}{\text{Number of Shares of Stock}}$

15. Gross Profit % $= \dfrac{(\text{Cost of Sales}) \times 100}{\text{Sales}}$

Gleim/CPA EXAMINATION REVIEW, Vol. 1, 11th Edition, Irvin N. Gleim, 1984. Adapted/Reprinted by permission of John Wiley & Sons, Inc.

Vertical Analysis

This method is used in comparing items on the balance sheet and income statement by reflecting all components in terms of percentages. For the balance sheet, total assets are assigned 100 percent. For the income statement, net sales are assigned 100 percent. All other items on both the balance sheet and income statement are shown as a percentage of those two figures, respectively.

Horizontal Analysis

This method is used in comparing percentage changes in the balance sheet and income statement from one period to the next. Horizontal analysis compares both the dollar amount and change percentage from year to year. Any unusual fluctuation must be investigated to determine if it is due to fraud or some other cause. It is by no means proof that fraud exists. It is only an indication that fraud may exist.

Nonfinancial Data

Financial statements should reflect what actually happened. If inventory and fixed assets are shown on the financial statements, then these assets should be observable. There is a direct relationship between financial statements and the physical goods and movement of assets. Comparing financial statement data with nonfinancial data is a good method of detecting fraud. The fraud examiner should make further inquiries when things appear out of order or sequence. Some things that should be reviewed follow.

1. If sales increase, then accounts receivable should likewise increase.
2. If sales increase, then inventory should increase.
3. If profits increase, then cash should increase.
4. If sales increase, then the cost of outbound freight should increase.

5. If purchases increase, then the cost of inbound freight should increase.
6. If manufacturing volume is increasing, then per-unit costs should be decreasing.
7. If manufacturing volume is increasing, then scrap sales and purchase discounts should also increase.
8. If inventory increases, then storage space must be available to contain it.
9. When sales increase, there are usually other expense accounts that increase in the same proportion.
10. Over-aged receivables could indicate not only slow payment by the customer, but also possible fraud. The receivable could have been received but not recorded.

Cash Flow

A cash flow statement can identify potential fraud. The cash flow statement identifies how a company uses and applies its funds and explains the net increase or decrease in cash during the period. It is particularly useful to identify problem areas. There is a close relationship between the balance sheet and income statement. The cash flow statement ties the balance sheet and income statement together in much detail. There are many cases where fraudulent balance sheets and income statements were prepared. When a cash flow statement was prepared, it was discovered that there were discrepancies. These discrepancies help confirm that the financial statements are incorrect and can identify fraudulent areas.

Cash Flow Statement

The cash flow statement can be very complicated. Its primary purpose is to explain the increase in cash accounts from one period to another. Figure 23-1 gives general steps in preparing a cash flow statement.

Cash Flow Theory

The theory behind the cash flow statement is to start with the net income from operations. The first step is to convert the net income from the income statement into the net cash flow from operations. Eliminating the noncash items on the income statement does this. The second step is to add other sources of cash flow. This is additional cash that comes from sources other than normal operations. The third step is to identify cash expenditures that do not affect current income statement operations. After the net income from operations is adjusted for noncash items, the total other cash sources are added and the other cash expenditures are subtracted from the net cash from operations. This gives the net increase in the cash accounts. This should equal the net increase/decrease in the total cash accounts. If it does not, then the financial statements will have to be further analyzed to determine the area where the potential fraud has occurred.

Net Income Adjustments

There are five types of items that will be used to adjust the net income from operations:

1. Depreciation
2. Amortization
3. Receivables
4. Inventory
5. Payables

CASH FLOW FROM OPERATIONS

Net income
Adjustments to net income
Depreciation expense
Amortization expense
Increase/decrease receivables
Increase/decrease inventory
Increase/decrease payables

Net Cash Inflow from operations

OTHER SOURCES OF FUNDS

Sales of fixed assets
Borrowing from banks, etc.
Capital investment

APPLICATION OF FUNDS

Purchase of fixed assets
Debt reduction
Dividends

NET INCREASE/DECREASE IN CASH

This should equal the net increase/decrease in cash accounts

Figure 23-1 Cash flow statement sample.

The theory for these adjustments are further explained.

Depreciation. This is a noncash expense. It is solely a journal entry by accountants to expense in a systematic method of writing off the cost of fixed assets on the balance sheet. Therefore, the depreciation expense shown as an expense must be added back to the net income from operations.

Amortization. This expense does not involve the use of cash. It is an entry used to systematically write off the cost of some tangible or intangible asset, i.e., leasehold improvements, organization costs, goodwill, and various prepaid expenses.

Receivables. Many business enterprises keep their books on the accrual method of accounting. The accrual method requires that sales be recognized when they occur and not when the funds are collected. This results in the business enterprise having an asset called accounts receivable. The IRS and the American Institute of CPAs require many business enterprises to be on the accrual method of accounting. The sales accounts have to be adjusted for noncash sales. Finding the difference in accounts receivable between the beginning and ending of the period can do this. If the receivables increase, then the net income will have to be decreased by that difference. If the receivables decrease, then the net income will have to be increased by that difference.

Payables. Payables, like accounts receivable, recognize expenses when they are incurred and not when they are paid. Again, this is the accrual method of accounting. The expenses on the income statement will have to be adjusted for noncash items. This is done by getting the difference between the beginning and ending balances in the accounts payable for the period. If the payables increase for the period, then the net income will have to be increased. Conversely, if the payables decrease for the period, then the net income will have to be decreased.

Inventory. Inventory is goods that a business enterprise has on hand that are not sold. When inventory is sold, it is expensed to the cost of goods sold on the income statement. Inventory can be purchased in a prior period and sold in the current period. This causes an outlay of cash in the prior period but not the current period. The current period has to be adjusted for inventory and cost of goods sold that does not require any cash outlay. This can be done by finding the difference in inventory at the beginning and end of the period. If the inventory increases over the period, then net income should be increased by the difference. Conversely, if the inventory decreases over the period, then the net income should be decreased by the difference.

Internal Controls

Internal control describes an entity's organization and system of procedures which provide reasonable assurance that errors or irregularities will be prevented or detected on a timely basis. The objectives of internal control are as follows.

1. Transactions are executed in accordance with management's authorization.
2. Transactions are properly recorded. This entails that a transaction has substance (existence), properly valued, classified, and recorded in the proper period.
3. Safeguard assets. This entails restricting access to assets and segregation of duties.
4. Require actual assets be periodically compared to accounting records.

Basic Concepts

There are ten basic concepts of internal controls. The first four concepts relate to accounting controls. The last six concepts relate to essential characteristics of internal controls.

Management Responsibility

Management must establish, maintain, supervise, and modify, as required, a system of internal controls for the company. It should have a proper attitude. Setting a good example for others to follow can do this. Management can issue a code of conduct, provide training, and enforce policy. If employees see management being dishonest, then they will commit fraudulent acts.

Reasonable Assurance

The costs of controls should not exceed their expected benefit. Yet, there must be controls in place that can detect fraud or other irregularities. Organizational structure that clearly defines lines of responsibility and authority can deter internal fraud. An audit committee that reports to the board of directors is an important control element. The audit committee should control both financial and operational audit functions as well as be responsible for security. The committee should never be controlled by or report to management.

Methods of Data Processing

Most business enterprises today use computers. This primarily is due to low cost of both hardware and software. Computers also save time and costs in processing financial information. Computer systems, however, provide internal control problems. Transaction trails may exist for a short period of time or only in computer-readable form. Program errors are less frequent. Computer controls may become more important than segregation of functions. It also becomes more difficult to detect unauthorized access to the computer system. There is less documentation of initiation and execution of transactions. Manual control procedures using computer output are dependent on the effectiveness of computer controls.

Limitations

Auditors should not rely entirely on internal control, even if it seems outstanding, since the best system may break down due to misunderstandings, mistakes in judgment, carelessness, collusion, and being overridden by management.

Segregation of Functions

The segregation of functions is an essential element of internal control. The basic premise is that no employee performs more than one function. The functions of record keeping, custodianship, authorization, and operations should always be kept separate.

Personnel

Personnel policies are an important ingredient for internal control system. A business enterprise should obtain reliable employees. This can be done by screening prospective employees. References should be verified regarding both competence and trustworthiness. Employees in responsible positions should be bonded. Management should supervise employees in a professional manner. It should not be overbearing, critical, intimidate, instill fear, or treat employees unfairly. This will encourage employee fraud. If management encourages team effort, ideas, gives recognition for good performances, then employee fraud is greatly reduced. Employees should be required to take vacations.

Access to Assets

Physical control over assets should be the responsibility of a custodian. This custodian should never have access to financial records. However, the custodian should maintain records of assets, listing physical description, location, and condition.

Comparison of Accountability with Assets

A control procedure of periodically comparing financial records with physical observation is an important internal control element. This should be done by an independent reviewing party. The reviewing party should not have responsibility for either record keeping or custodianship. Any discrepancies should be investigated.

Execution of Transactions

Every transaction should be authorized. The business enterprise should set up policies and guidelines that should be followed. The larger transaction should have various levels of authorization.

Recording of Transactions

There should be standardized procedures for recording transactions. These controls must ensure that fraudulent or unauthorized transactions are not recorded and ensure that authorized transactions are properly included, valued, classified, at the proper time. Any exceptions should be investigated immediately. Transactions should involve more than one employee. Proper records should be maintained. An audit trail must be maintained at all times. Audit evidence must be available for inspection and review. Source documents, i.e., invoices, purchase orders, checks, should be prenumbered and accounted for periodically.

Internal Control Checklist

The following checklist gives an outline of internal controls, which most businesses should have depending upon the size of the company (Table 23-2). For small businesses, many of the internal controls listed below are not applicable. Some of the internal controls should be used in the actual audit process.

Table 23-2 Internal Control Checklist

A. General Controls
  1. Chart of accounts (both past and current)
  2. Accounting procedures manual
  3. Organizational chart showing definite responsibilities
  4. Review of journal entries
    a. No ledger references
    b. No journal entries for ledger entries
  5. Standard journal entries
  6. Use of prenumbered forms
  7. Supporting documents for journal entries
  8. Limited access to authorized personnel
  9. Rotation of accounting personnel
  10. Required vacations
  11. System of reviews
  12. Separation of record keeping from operations
  13. Record retention policy and procedures
  14. Bonding of employees
  15. Conflict of interest policies
    a. Written policy
    b. Promulgation procedures
B. Cash on Hand
  1. Impress system
  2. Reasonable amount
  3. Completeness of vouchers

Table 23-2 (continued)

      4. Custodian responsibility
      5. Reimbursement checks to order of custodian
      6. Surprise audits
      7. No employee check cashing
      8. Physical security
      9. Custodian has no access to receipts
    10. Custodian has no access to accounting records

C. **Cash Receipts**
      1. Listing of mail receipts
      2. Special handling of postdated checks
      3. Daily deposits
      4. Cash custodians bonded
      5. Cash custodians apart from negotiable instruments
      6. Bank accounts properly authorized
      7. Proper handling of returned nonsufficient funds (NSF) items
      8. Comparison of duplicate deposit slip with cash book
      9. Comparison of duplicate deposit slip with customer subledgers
    10. Banks instructed not to cash checks to company
    11. Control of cash from other sources
    12. Separation of cashier personnel from accounting duties
    13. Separation of cashier personnel from credit duties
    14. Use of cash registers
    15. Retention and safekeeping of register tapes
    16. Numbered cash receipts tickets
    17. Outside salespeople cash controls
    18. Daily reconciliation of cash collections

D. **Cash Disbursements**
      1. Numbered checks
      2. Support for check signature
      3. Limited authorization to sign checks
      4. No signing of blank checks
      5. All checks accounted for
      6. Detailed listing of checks
      7. Mutilation of voided checks
      8. Proper authorization of personnel signing checks
      9. Control over signature machines
    10. Check listing compared to cash book
    11. Control over bank transfers
    12. Checks not payable to cash
    13. Physical security over unused checks
    14. Cancellation of supporting documents
    15. Control over long outstanding checks
    16. Reconciliation of bank account(s)

continued

Table 23-2 (continued)

17. Independence of person reconciling bank statements
18. Bank statement direct to person reconciling bank statements
19. No access to cash records or receipts by check signers

E. Investments
   1. Proper authorization of transactions
   2. Under control of custodian
   3. Custodian bonded
   4. Custodian separate from cash receipts
   5. Custodian separate from investment records
   6. Safety deposit box
   7. Record of all safe deposit visits
   8. Access limited to safe deposit box
   9. Presence of two required for access
   10. Periodic reconciliation of detail with control
   11. Record of all aspects of all securities
   12. Brokerage advice and statements
   13. Periodic internal audit
   14. Securities in name of company
   15. Segregation of collateral
   16. Physical control of collateral
   17. Periodic appraisal of collateral
   18. Periodic appraisal of investments

F. Accounts Receivable and Sales
   1. Sales orders prenumbered
   2. Credit approval
   3. Credit and sales departments independent
   4. Control of back orders
   5. Sales order and sales invoice comparison
   6. Shipping invoices prenumbered
   7. Names and addresses on shipping orders
   8. Review of sales invoices
   9. Control over returned merchandise
   10. Credit memoranda prenumbered
   11. Matching of credit memorandum receiving reports
   12. Control over credit memoranda
   13. Control over scrap sales
   14. Control over sales to employees
   15. Control over collecting-on-delivery (COD) sales
   16. Sales reconciled with cash receipts and accounts receivables
   17. Sales reconciled with inventory change
   18. Accounts receivable statements to customers
   19. Periodic preparation of aging schedule
   20. Control over payments of written-off receivables
   21. Control over accounts receivable write-offs, proper authorization

Table 23-2 (continued)

---

    22. Control over accounts receivable written off, review for possible collection

    23. Independence of sales, accounts receivable, receipts, billing, and shipping

G. **Notes Receivable**

    1. Proper authorization of notes

    2. Detailed records of notes

    3. Periodic detail to control comparison

    4. Periodic confirmation with makers

    5. Control over notes discounted

    6. Control over delinquent notes

    7. Physical safety of notes

    8. Periodic count of notes

    9. Control over collateral

    10. Control over revenue from notes

    11. Custodian of notes independent from cash and record keeping

H. **Inventory and Cost of Sales**

    1. Periodic inventory

    2. Written inventory instructions

    3. Counts by noncustodians

    4. Controls over count tags

    5. Control over inventory adjustments

    6. Use of perpetual records

    7. Periodic comparison of general ledger and perpetual records

    8. Investigation of discrepancies

    9. Control over consignment inventory

    10. Control over inventory stored at warehouse

    11. Control over returnable containers with customers

    12. Receiving reports prepared

    13. Receiving reports in numerical order

    14. Independence of custodian from record keeping

    15. Adequacy of insurance

    16. Physical safeguard against theft

    17. Physical safeguard against fire

    18. Adequacy of cost system

    19. Cost system tied into general ledger

    20. Periodic review of overhead rates

    21. Use of standard costs

    22. Use of inventory requisitions

    23. Periodic summaries of inventory usage

    24. Control over intercompany inventory transfers

    25. Purchase orders prenumbered

    26. Proper authorization for purchases

    27. Review of open purchase orders

    28. Purchasing agents bonded

continued

Table 23-2 (continued)

       29. Three or more bids or quotes

I.   **Prepaid Expenses and Deferred Charges**
1. Proper authorization to incur
2. Authorization and support of amortization
3. Detailed records
4. Periodic review of amortization policies
5. Control over insurance policies
6. Periodic review of insurance needs
7. Control over premium refunds
8. Beneficiaries of company policies
9. Physical control of policies

J.   **Intangibles**
1. Authorization to incur
2. Detailed records
3. Authorization to amortize
4. Periodic review of amortization

K.   **Fixed Assets**
1. Detailed property records
2. Periodic comparison with control accounts
3. Proper authorization of acquisition
4. Written policies for acquisition
5. Control over expenditures for self-construction
6. Use of work orders
7. Individual asset identification plates
8. Written authorization for sale
9. Written authorization for retirement
10. Physical safeguard from theft
11. Control over fully depreciated assets
12. Written capitalization and expense policies
13. Responsibilities charged for asset and depreciation records
14. Written depreciation records
15. Detail depreciation records
16. Depreciation adjustments for sales and retirements
17. Control over intercompany transfers
18. Adequacy of insurance
19. Control over returnable containers

L.   **Accounts Payable**
1. Designation of responsibility
2. Independence of accounts payable personnel from purchasing, cashier, receiving functions
3. Periodic comparison of detail and control
4. Control over purchase returns
5. Clerical accuracy of vendor's invoice
6. Matching of purchase orders, receiving reports, and vendor invoices
7. Reconciliation of vendor statements with accounts payable detail

Table 23-2 (continued)

      8. Control over debit memos

      9. Control over advance payments

    10. Review of unmatched receiving reports

    11. Mutilation of supporting documents at payment

    12. Review of debit balances

    13. Investigation of discounts not taken

M. **Accrued Liabilities and Other Expenses**

      1. Proper authorization for expenditures and concurrence

      2. Control over partial deliveries

      3. Postage meter

      4. Purchasing department

      5. Verification of invoices

      6. Impress cash account

      7. Detailed records

      8. Independence from general ledger and cashier functions

      9. Periodic comparison with budget

N. **Payroll**

      1. Authorization to employ

      2. Personnel data files

      3. Tax records

      4. Time clock

      5. Review of payroll calculations

      6. Impress payroll account

      7. Responsibility for payroll records

      8. Compliance with labor statutes

      9. Distribution of payroll checks

    10. Control over unclaimed wages

    11. Profit-sharing authorization

    12. Responsibility for profit-sharing computations

    13. Responsible employees bonded

    14. Employee benefit plans comparison with tax records

O. **Long-Term Liabilities**

      1. Authorization to incur

      2. Executed in company name

      3. Detailed records of long-term debt

      4. Reports of independent transfer agent

      5. Reports of independent registrar

      6. Otherwise adequate records of creditors

      7. Control over unissued instruments

      8. Signers independent of each other

      9. Adequacy of records of collateral

    10. Periodic review of debt agreement compliance

    11. Record keeping of detachable warrants

    12. Record keeping of conversion features

continued

Table 23-2 (continued)

P. **Shareholder's Equity**
    1. Use of registrar
    2. Use of transfer agent
    3. Adequacy of detailed records
    4. Comparison of transfer agent's report with records
    5. Physical control over blank certificates
    6. Physical control over treasury certificates
    7. Authorization for transactions
    8. Tax stamp compliance for canceled certificates
    9. Independent dividend agent
    10. Impress dividend account
    11. Periodic reconciliation of dividend account
    12. Adequacy of stockholder's ledger
    13. Review of stock restrictions and provisions
    14. Valuation procedures for stock issuance
    15. Other paid-in capital entries
    16. Other retained earnings entries

Gleim/CPA EXAMINATION REVIEW, Vol. 1, 11th Edition, Irvin N. Gleim, 1984. Adapted/Reprinted by permission of John Wiley & Sons, Inc.

Forensic Auditing

Auditing for fraud is known as forensic auditing. The accounting profession has not developed forensic auditing to the degree that it should. Public accountants, i.e., Certified Public Accountants, audit for financial statement presentation. Internal auditors examine for compliance with company policies and procedures. The Government Accounting Office audits for compliance with government programs. The IRS audits primarily for compliance with federal tax laws. However, the IRS has specialized auditors who do forensic auditing. Their numbers are few and their emphasis is tax evasion and recently has been expanded into money laundering.

Forensic Audit Phases

There are four phases of forensic auditing:

1. Recognition and planning stage
2. Evidence collection
3. Evidence evaluation
4. Communication of results

Recognition and Planning Stage

There must be some prediction that fraud exists before a fraud examiner conducts an audit. There must be some reason to believe that fraud exists; the problem must be defined. All possible explanations should be explored. Also, the examination should be planned in terms of staff, methods, place, and needs.

Evidence Collection

The second phase of forensic auditing is evidence collection. The purpose is to determine whether initial evidence of fraud is misleading and if more procedures are needed to resolve the fraud.

Evidence Evaluation

This phase determines what type of legal action should be taken, if any. Some cases will only warrant civil action, which is obtaining restitution. In other cases, criminal action may be warranted. In civil cases, the degree of evidence must be "clear and convincing." In criminal cases, the evidence must prove "beyond a reasonable doubt." When the use of an indirect method, i.e., Net Worth Expenditure, or bank deposit methods, evidence must prove "with reasonable certainty." This stage requires the cooperation of management, legal counsel, internal audit, and corporate security. If the evidence is strong enough to stand up in court, then the strategy should be planned and followed.

Communication

An audit report should be prepared and presented to management. This report should encompass a good description of the fraud, who perpetrated it, and present both documentary and testimony evidence.

Evidence Gathering Techniques

There are various evidence-gathering techniques that can be used. In most cases, a combination of various evidence-gathering techniques is required to support a case. The elements of fraud are the theft act, concealment, and conversion. The evidence-gathering techniques are designed to uncover these fraud elements.

1. **Interviewing.** Interviewing is an important evidence-gathering technique. It helps obtain information which establishes elements of a crime, provides additional leads, gets cooperation of witnesses and victims, and obtains the economic motives behind a perpetrator.

2. **Vulnerability and Internal Control Charts.** Vulnerability and internal control charts help examiners determine the best probabilities where fraud is likely to occur.

3. **Document Examination.** This technique uncovers concealment efforts of perpetrators by manipulating source documents.

4. **Employee Searches.** This technique involves examining an employee's desk, lockers, lunch boxes, etc. It is important not to violate person's constitutional rights of illegal searches. Searches are legal if conducted in a proper manner and with adequate notice. If obtained illegally, evidence can be inadmissible in court.

5. **Invigilation.** This technique involves the close supervision of suspects during an examination period. It can be effective in identifying who is committing the fraud and where it is occurring. It is particularly useful in catching fraud that is committed by independent suppliers, night watchmen, warehouse supervisors, purchasing agents, and cashiers. Its drawbacks include high cost and the possibility of low employee morale.

6. **Observation.** Observation is watching, looking, spying, or snooping to gather evidence. This evidence can be recorded on various kinds of media. This can show how the fraud is being committed.

7. **Undercover.** Undercover operations require an agent or informant. These operations should be used for major criminal acts, i.e., organized crime activities. It is important that it remains secret. It is also very dangerous for the undercover agent.

8. **Specific item.** Specific item evidence is locating and identifying specific documents which show fraud has occurred. This can be with one or more documents, i.e., altered contracts or many canceled checks.

Fraud Indicators

There are clues that indicate fraud exists. These symptoms do not guarantee that fraud exists, but can be warning signs that fraud can or has occurred. There are environmental and personal symptoms called red flags.

Environmental Symptoms

The most common environmental symptoms that encourage fraud are as follows.

1. **Loose internal controls.** If internal controls are not enforced, then the opportunity of fraud occurring is great. Fraud occurs more often when internal controls are ignored.

2. **Poor management philosophy.** If top management is dishonest, then dishonesty will flow down to employees. When autocratic management sets budgets that are impossible to attain, lower managers will have to cheat, fail, or quit. If management does not prosecute fraud offenders, even if small, it only sends a signal that the company does not deal harshly with criminals.

3. **Poor financial position.** If a company has poor cash flow, then fraud is more likely to occur. Employees are more likely to take advantage of a company when they feel insecure about their jobs or the company's continued existence.

4. **Low employee morale.** When employee morale is low, employees lack loyalty and feel wronged. Low employee morale can be the result of personal problems or can be work related. Perceived inequities at the workplace can lead to decreased employee loyalty. Some identified reasons for employee fraud to "correct" injustice are as follows:

   a. Being passed over for a raise
   b. Being passed over for a promotion
   c. Being subjected to disciplinary action
   d. Feeling that pay is inadequate
   e. Favoritism to other employees
   f. Resentment toward superiors
   g. Frustration with job
   h. Boredom

5. **Ethics confusion.** If a company does not have an ethics code, then this could lead to employee confusion. What is the line between a gift and a kickback? What is a company secret? A corporate code of conduct and policy statements should be promulgated. These

policies should address what types of gifts are acceptable, access to certain operating units, and security policies.

6. **Background checks.** The lack of a background check or the failure to exercise due care when hiring new employees can be costly. Proper screening has many benefits:

a. Results in more honest employees;
b. Acts as a deterrent to employee dishonesty;
c. Protects innocent employees from false accusations;
d. Eliminates problem employees such as substance abusers, serial thieves, etc.;
e. Eliminates poor security risks;
f. Permits honest employees to work in harmony.

Some common problems that employers encounter are as follows:

a. Previous arrests
b. Unstable work record
c. Fired from previous job
d. Employee theft
e. Mental instability
f. Drug/substance abuse
g. Personal/domestic problems
h. Health defects
i. Bad tempers

7. **Lack of employee support programs.** Job stress or personal problems can lead to fraud. An organization can help employees deal with job or personal problems. First, the company can establish employee assistance programs that confidentially counsel employees about their problems. Second, the organization can have an open door policy within the organization. Managers can encourage good employee relationships. If managers are alert, they can identify danger signs and be available to assist.

8. **General conditions.** Other symptoms that promote fraud are near-term mergers or acquisitions, regulatory problems, rapid turnover of employees, too much trust in key employees, and lack of physical security.

Personal Symptoms

There are three specific symptoms of possible employee fraud:

1. **Personal financial factor.** Employees are likely to commit fraud when they have serious financial problems. They are more likely to commit fraud as a solution to their problem. The symptoms exhibited are employees taking expensive vacations, purchasing expensive vehicles, boats, cottages, cabins, personal items, and bragging about their money.

2. **Personal habits.** Employee habits can induce fraud. Drug abuse, gambling, speculative investments, or maintaining a second household because of divorce can be a strong indication of potential fraud.

3. **Personal feelings.** Employee feelings are another symptom for committing fraud. Employees with high expectations, perception of being mistreated by management, frustration with the job, poor family or community relationships are likely candidates.

Types of Fraud

Kiting

Check kiting is a form of embezzlement. It is a form of fraud, which embezzles a bank out of funds. It involves two or more bank accounts at two or more different banks. The objective is to cover-up a check or withdrawal that is not recorded on the books by writing checks from one bank account to another bank account. When the interbank checks clear, one bank loses out by the check(s) that were cashed or withdrawn. A bank transfer schedule is effective in detecting this scheme. A four or plus column bank reconciliation would clearly uncover this scheme.

Lapping

Lapping is an embezzlement scheme in which cash collections from customers are stolen. To keep the embezzlement from being discovered the embezzler corrects the customer's accounts within a few days by posting other customer cash receipts to the account for which the proceeds have been embezzled. Lapping occurs most frequently when one individual has both record-keeping responsibility and custody of cash. Lapping will increase the average age of receivables and decrease turnover. The examiner should watch for posting of cash after an unusually long time. Also, the examiner should compare deposit slips from the bank with names, dates, and amounts on remittance advices. The examiner should investigate customer complaints.

Ghost Employees

Funds are channeled to fictitious or former employees, known as ghost employees, through phony salary payments. This should be examined closely when union members are employed. Organized crime figures use ghost employees to channel funds. A common practice is to employ people who do not work or even show up on the job. In such cases, the examiner should compare payroll files with personnel files, employment applications, tax statements, insurance and union deductions, and payroll checks. Also, the examiner should compare travel and expense vouchers to employment records and tax records.

Illegal Activities

Organized crime groups, as well as individuals, operate illegal activities. These illegal activities encompass the following activities:

1. **Arson.** This crime can result from one of several motives. One is for a nonfinancial motive and the other is for economic gain. An example of a nonfinancial motive would be a disgruntled employee. Most financial motives in arson are related to insurance claims or the elimination of competition. In case of insurance claims, the financial condition of the enterprise should be examined thoroughly to determine profitability. A losing enterprise will try to bail out by committing arson and file insurance claims. In the case of elimination of competition, the competitor will commit arson either to cause financial hardship to the victim so it may not be able to recover or to disrupt the victim's operations.

2. **Counterfeiting.** Counterfeiting involves not only counterfeiting money, but also food stamps, coupons, bonds, stocks, credit cards, and anything else of value that can be

duplicated. A key element of examining counterfeiters is obtaining the records from suppliers and vendors.

3. **Frauds.** "Con" men or women commit various kinds of fraud. Individuals, corporations, and partnerships commit it. There are many kinds of frauds. Fraud involves any means which human ingenuity can devise to take advantage of another by false suggestion or suppression of the truth. It encompasses any surprises, tricks, cunning, or any way to cheat, steal, or take anything of value from an individual or business. The victim(s) of such crimes have the documents and can testify in such cases.

4. **Gambling.** Organized crime groups, as well as some individuals, get involved in gambling activities. The most common are sports bookmaking, bingo, racetracks, casinos, and bolito (lottery). Most states have strong laws against gambling activities. In some states, gambling is legal but is highly regulated. Some states even run their own gambling, e.g., state lotteries. In Chapter 16, gambling is addressed in more detail.

5. **Illegal Alcohol.** Unlicensed production, sale, and distribution of alcohol are illegal in most states, as well as a federal crime. The primary reason for the illegal sale of alcohol is the lack of collection of sales and/or excise taxes. Another reason is that alcohol can be contaminated which could cause death if someone drinks it. This was a popular method of getting extra funds by various individuals. However, since the introduction of drugs and marijuana into our society, alcohol has become less of a concern to local and federal law enforcement. The key element is obtaining financial data on ingredients from suppliers and vendors.

6. **Loan Sharking.** Loan sharking is the illegal activity of loaning money to people at exorbitant rates of interest. Interest rates normally charged are 2 percent to 5 percent per week or day. The loan shark requires a business front behind which to conceal the illegal activities. This can be any kind of business. In some cases, the business was acquired on a defaulted loan or the loan shark has taken over the business from a legitimate owner as a front. Some of the signs of loan sharking follow:

a. The collateral for the loan is not commensurate with the amount loaned.
b. The lender requires no references or financial statements.
c. The effective rate of interest is beyond legal limits.
d. The lender has no connection with any legal lending institution.
e. The borrower has a history of extensive gambling.
f. The borrower is living beyond his or her means.
g. There are excessive losses in the stock or bond market by the borrower.
h. Finder's fees are paid for securing financing.
i. There are high rates of thefts in the business.
j. Endorsements on checks indicate payments to people with no legitimate business connection to the business.
k. Money received is in the form of cash rather than by check.
l. The paperwork and/or loan documents are skimpy or nonexistent.

7. **Narcotics.** Narcotic crimes involve the sale of any type of illegal drugs. This encompasses drugs such as heroin, cocaine, marijuana, and various synthetic or pharmaceutical drugs, whether legal or illegal. The fraud examiner must focus on the lifestyle of the drug trafficker.

8. **Prostitution.** This crime involves the sale of sexual acts for pay. Pimps are individuals who control prostitutes, determining their "johns" and the amount they can earn. Pimps usually get a big "cut" of the profits or gross receipts leaving the woman or man with little income. The prostitutes usually have to be totally dependent upon the boss — the pimp. One fraud examiner determined income by counting the towels being used. Otherwise, the fraud examiner must focus on the lifestyle.

9. **Protection Rackets.** This usually involves organized crime groups. Protection rackets encompass the charging of businesses for protection. This is like insurance, except that protection is not guaranteed. There are no benefits paid out like insurance. This is more prevalent in Asian communities today than anywhere else. The fraud examiner will have to rely on the victim(s), who, because of fear of retaliation, may not cooperate.

10. **Smuggling.** This activity involves the secret transportation of illegal goods either into or out of the country. Profits are made by the subsequent selling of those goods. The smuggler has no cost of sales or purchases. If invoices are provided, they will be false documents. If the supplier supplies invoices, then the supplier is part of the conspiracy and must be examined as well.

11. **Stolen Property.** Organized crime groups, as well as individuals, either steal or buy and then sell stolen property. The latter is called "fencing." Investigators look for the following signs of fencing:

a. The costs of purchases are unusually low.
b. Payments are made in cash.
c. There are no invoices, bills of lading, or shipping receipts.
d. The supplier cannot be identified.
e. The business owners, sellers of the merchandise, have no knowledge about the products they are selling.
f. The business has not been in existence very long.

Legal Activities

People involved in illegal activities must somehow "launder" their profits through legitimate businesses. Businesses that are most susceptible to laundering profits are the following

1. Auto agencies. These are used as fronts for stolen vehicles.
2. Factoring. Criminals use factors in laundering diverting corporate skimming from various businesses into the accounts receivable as sales or payments of accounts receivable from various businesses. This is a type of loan sharking.
3. Food products. Criminals use food stores as a way to launder money from illegal activities, as well as, skimming sales receipts.
4. Garment manufacturing. Organized crime groups use this industry to sell counterfeit brands for authentic brands of clothing. This industry is also susceptible to labor racketeering, kickbacks, ghost employees, and extortion.
5. Jukeboxes and video machines. These are used by criminals to obtain income without reporting the income to federal and state tax authorities. Also, it is an excellent vehicle for money laundering.

6. Liquor distribution. This involves stealing and selling liquor at discounts to liquor stores and bars. The profits, of course, are not reported to federal and state tax authorities.

7. Nightclubs. Since this is a cash business, it lends itself to skimming. Organized crime groups use this to operate prostitution rings and extort funds from the dancers.

8. Trade associations. This involves labor racketeering. It exploits funds from labor unions, especially pension funds.

9. Trucking. Organized crime groups use trucking to extort higher fees for transportation of goods.

10. Vending machines. Like jukeboxes and video machines, vending machines are used to obtain income without reporting it to the tax authorities. However, profits can be more readily determined by use of the Gross Profit Method.

11. Waste collections. Organized crime groups use this industry to obtain funds without paying for dumping fees and violating environmental laws. Their customers are reluctant to cooperate since they are violating environmental laws.

12. Construction. Organized crime groups use this industry to extort funds from contractors. They do this in controlling labor and using ghost employees on the contractor payroll.

13. Hotels and motels. This industry lends itself to skimming as well as money laundering.

14. Real estate. This industry is used primarily for laundering money from illegal activities as an investment for criminals. However, it is also used for selling property above market values.

15. Securities. Criminals use this industry as a front for counterfeit securities, as well as money laundering.

16. Mortgages. Criminals use this as a means of laundering money. They usually charge higher rates in order to later repossess the valuable real estate at bargain prices.

17. Entertainment. Organized crime uses the entertainment industry to skim profits and steal funds from entertainers by not reporting the actual gross receipts of which entertainers get a percentage. Also, they use this to "bust-out" which leaves owners holding the bag.

18. Credit cards. Criminals use credit cards to obtain merchandise, which is later fenced. The credit cards are usually stolen from customers or their numbers are used to make purchases. Some criminal groups steal the cards from the mail before the customer receives them.

19. Insurance. Criminals sell insurance policies for companies that do not exist. Some criminals set up their own insurance companies with the intent of not paying claims.

20. Labor. Organized criminal groups exploit various labor groups. They do this by embezzling labor union funds. The major target by criminal groups is labor union pension funds since they consist of large amounts that need to be invested so funds are available for future benefits of its members.

21. Banking. Criminals like to defraud banks either by obtaining bad loans or check kiting. Drug traffickers like to use banks for laundering their illegal profits.

Intelligence

Before fraud examiners commence any examination, they should obtain as much information as possible about the type of fraud that might be committed. This intelligence will help fraud examiners determine where they should focus their examination. If fraud examiners have intelligence that a particular type of fraud is being committed, then they can focus their efforts where that type of fraud is being committed. This intelligence can save time and money for the client since the time of investigation and examination will be cut to a minimum. Companies with internal and/or external auditors should use them to develop as much evidence about the fraud scheme as possible before a fraud examiner is retained. The fraud examiner is interested in uncovering fraud and not issuing an opinion as to a company's financial condition.

Summary

The audit program is only a guide for the fraud examiner. It helps focus the examiner to where the fraud is being committed. However, examiners must first rely on intelligence before they can start gathering evidence. If no intelligence is available, then the examiner must search for "red flags." Various types of analysis, financial and nonfinancial, can help identify those red flags. The biggest problem for fraud examiners is determining the effectiveness of internal controls. On paper, internal controls of a business look good, but when they are observed close up, they are often deficient or nonexistent.

Seizures and Forfeitures

24

Introduction

Forfeitures and seizures by governmental entities have been in existence since the American Revolution. England and the American colonies have used forfeitures to enforce customs and revenue laws. It is still used today in England, Canada, Australia, New Zealand, and the United States. Forfeitures have historically been used as a means of punishment for violation of customs and revenue laws. However, during this century, forfeitures and seizures laws have been expanded to encompass most crimes. They have been aimed at drug traffickers and other "white-collar" crimes in recent years. Forfeitures have been asserted in both civil and criminal cases. Today, forfeitures and seizures are used to deprive criminals of their illegal gains.

Federal Laws

The U.S. government has many forfeiture laws on the books. The following is a partial list of those forfeiture laws that are commonly used by federal prosecutors.

1. Title 18 — Criminal Code
    Section 492 — Counterfeiting
    Section 545 — Smuggling
    Section 981 — Civil "White Collar" Transactions
    Section 982 — Criminal "White Collar" Transactions
    Section 1467 — Obscene Materials
    Section 1956 — Money Laundering
    Section 1957 — Money Laundering
    Section 1963 — Racketeering — Criminal
    Section 1964 — Racketeering — Civil
2. Title 19 — Customs
    Section 1595(a) — Conveyances and Items Used to Facilitate Illegally Introduced Items
3. Title 21 — Drugs and Controlled Substances
    Section 848 — Continuing Criminal Enterprises
    Section 853 — Drug Felonies — Criminal

4. Title 26 — Taxation
    Section 7301 — Property Subject to Tax
    Section 7302 — Property Used in Violation of Internal Revenue Laws
    Section 7303 — Other Property Subject to Forfeiture
5. Title 31 — Money and Currency
    Section 5111 — Coin Melting
    Section 5317 — Unreported Monetary Instruments
6. Title 49 — Transportation
    Section 782 — Contraband Seizures
    Section 1474 — Civil Aircraft

(Section 881 — Controlled Substances — Civil)

Property

All kinds of property are subject to seizure and forfeiture. This includes all real and personal property, tangible and intangible property. Many states also have forfeiture laws on their books. State forfeiture laws are usually patterned after the federal statutes with some modifications. However, both federal and state forfeiture laws subject forfeitable property in the following categories:

1. **Illegal goods.** Illegal goods consist of things like drugs, cigarettes, liquor, and other personal and intangible property that has been specifically outlawed by federal or state statutes. These assets can be seized and forfeited at the point of discovery. Contraband property is usually destroyed after criminal trials of defendants.

2. **Direct ties.** Legal property, whether personal, real, or intangible, can be seized and forfeited if it can be shown that it was obtained from the proceeds of illegal activities. An example of this is when a drug trafficker purchases a vehicle (legal property) with the profits from the sale of drugs (illegal income). Also, the property used in the manufacture, distribution, and sale of contraband is also subject to seizure and forfeiture. If an aircraft was discovered with illegal contraband, then the aircraft is subject to immediate seizure and forfeiture. The connection — nexus — between the illegal activity and the assets is the key element in direct seizures and forfeitures.

3. **Indirect ties.** Illegal profits are sometimes mingled with legal sources which makes it impossible to distinguish. This is particularly true with organized crime groups which launder their illegal gains in legitimate sources. However, Congress has passed laws during this century to overcome this obstacle. Al Capone was the first subject convicted using the Internal Revenue Code. In this case, the IRS used the net worth method of determining unreported taxable income. It has been expanded, particularly under RICO and the Continuing Criminal Enterprise (CCE) to use the Net Worth and Expenditure Methods in determining illegal gains. Once illegal gains have been determined, then the forfeiture is based upon the amount of the gain.

Civil Forfeiture

Civil forfeitures are legal actions against property. These are called *in rem* actions since they are made against property and not individuals or corporations. The burden of proof is not as great as in criminal actions. Civil actions only require the government to show "clear and convincing" evidence. The rules of evidence are more relaxed. Hearsay evidence can be introduced. Opinions can be expressed. However, unauthorized searches and wire taps are not admissible. Civil forfeiture actions present a dilemma to subjects of criminal actions. If the civil actions take place before criminal proceedings, then the property owner can be compelled to produce evidence which can later be used in criminal proceedings. Also, civil forfeiture actions can be instituted while criminal actions may never be made. In addition, the property owner must establish control in addition to just having good title. The government is not required to show a direct relationship between the property seized and a specific drug transaction.

Criminal Forfeiture

Criminal forfeitures are made against a criminal who has been convicted of a crime. Criminal forfeitures are called *in personam* since they are directed against a person. The rules of evidence are strictly adhered to in these cases. Reasonable doubt or "with reasonable certainty," when the Net Worth and Expenditure Methods are used, must be established in criminal cases. All evidence introduced in a criminal proceeding can be used in any civil proceeding.

    1. **Direct ties.** Forfeitures and seizures can be made based upon direct evidence that illegal gains were directly invested in identified assets. Assets that are used in the transportation, storage, purchase, and sale can be seized and forfeited. Any assets that are used in promotion of any illegal contraband can be seized and forfeited.

    2. **Indirect ties.** In criminal proceedings, assets can be forfeited whether or not used or acquired from illegal gains. The RICO and CCE statutes provide for forfeitures based upon twice the illegal gains. This provides forfeiture of legally obtained assets as well as assets acquired from illegal activities. The RICO Net Worth and Expenditure Methods are used to determine the illegal gains.

Innocent Owner

The federal forfeiture laws makes provisions for seizure and forfeiture of property of innocent owners. The burden of proof rests upon the innocent owner to prove that he or she had:

1.   No knowledge of the illegal use of the property;
2.   Was not a party to the illegal activity;
3.   Would have prevented the use of the property in the illegal activity, if known.

Federal Guidelines

In 1987, the U.S. Department of Justice issued guidelines on Seized and Forfeited Property. These guidelines were formulated because of the Comprehensive Crime Control Act of 1984 and the Anti-Drug Abuse Act of 1986 which addressed the disposition of forfeited property. These guidelines were promulgated to:

1. Promote cooperative law enforcement efforts in drug trafficking and other investigations;
2. Ensure equitable transfer of forfeited property to the appropriate state or local law enforcement.

Use and Transfer of Forfeited Property

The U.S. Attorney General has the authority to retain any civilly or criminally forfeited property or to transfer the property to other federal, state, or local law enforcement agencies. In order for the Attorney General to transfer forfeited property to any federal, state, or local law enforcement agency, the law enforcement agency must have directly participated in the acts which led to the seizure or forfeiture. The transfer of forfeited property will be determined by the Attorney General or designee on an equitable basis. The basis will generally be on the relative contribution of the participating agencies to the investigation leading to its seizure and forfeiture. Property that is transferred to federal, state, or local agencies is to be used to increase resources for that agency. It is not to be used for salaries and regular operating expenses. If the federal forfeiture action is concluded successfully, and the property is not placed into official use or transferred to a federal, state, or local agency, it will be sold and the net proceeds of sale will be placed in the Assets Forfeiture Fund. Forfeited cash will also be placed in the Asset Forfeiture Fund. If real or tangible property is transferred to federal, state, or local agencies, the recipient must pay the liens and mortgages on the forfeited property, as well as any expenses in transferring the property.

Assets Forfeiture Fund

The Attorney General has made the U.S. Marshal Service responsible for administering the Assets Forfeiture Fund. There are two categories of reimbursements from the fund.

1. Asset-Specific Expenses. Asset-specific expenses are reimbursements for the management expenses. These take priority over program-related expenses. Asset-specific expenses are
   a. Expenses incurred for safeguarding, maintenance, or disposal of seized or forfeited property whether by federal, state, or local agencies;
   b. Payments on orders of mitigation or remission;
   c. Payments of valid liens and mortgages pursuant to court order;
   d. Equitable transfer payments to state or local law enforcement agencies;
   e. Payments for contract service relating to the processing of and accounting for seizures and forfeitures;
   f. Payments for storage, protection, and destruction of controlled substances;
   g. Case-specific expenses relating to travel and subsistence, cost of depositions, messenger services, expert witnesses, and other direct costs.

2. Program-Related Expenses. The following are program related expenses
    a. Expenses for the purchase or lease of computer equipment, and related services, at least 90 percent of whose use will be dedicated to seizure or forfeiture-related record keeping;
    b. Payments to authorized investigative agents for the purchase of controlled substances;
    c. Expenses incurred to equip any conveyance;
    d. Payment of awards in recognition of information or assistance given to an investigator;
    e. Expenses for training which relates to the execution of seizure or forfeiture responsibilities;
    f. Expenses incurred for printing training material.

Liens and Mortgages

Liens and mortgages can only be paid pursuant to an order of remission or mitigation or an order of the court. Otherwise, such amounts shall be paid from the proceeds of sale. The payment of liens and mortgages can be paid if they are beneficial to the government. Two circumstances exist for this:

1. Payment prior to the sale will improve the government's ability to convey title.
2. The property is to be placed into official use by the government.

Payments to unsecured creditors of seized and forfeited property are generally not allowed. However, in the case of a business, claims incurred within 30 days before the seizure can be paid. In addition, payments can be made for reasonable salaries and benefits of employees not believed to have been involved in the unlawful activities giving rise to the forfeiture, and not having any ownership interest in the firm. Third-party contractors of goods and services can be paid which are necessary to carry on the business activity of the firm in a regular manner. Utilities also can be paid.

Internal Revenue Service Rewards

The IRS has provision under Title 26, USC, to reward both informants and state and local law enforcement for providing information on violation of federal tax laws. Employees of the Treasury Department and individuals who are employed by other federal, state, or local law enforcement are not eligible to receive any awards. Informants can have their identity remain anonymous. Rewards are divided into two categories.

1. **Informants.** Under Section 7623, Internal Revenue Code and related regulations, an informant can receive up to 10 percent of the amount of taxes, penalties, and fines that are recovered. However, this 10 percent ceiling does not bind the IRS to fix the amount with regard to any percentage or formula. Although the law indicates that an informant may be rewarded for supplying information to the IRS, it does not bind the IRS to reward all informants. The informant must file Form 211 with either the district director of the district where the informant resides or the commissioner of the IRS in Washington, D.C.

2. State and Local Law Enforcement. Under Section 7624, Internal Revenue Code and related regulations, state and local law enforcement can get reimbursed by the IRS for costs incurred, i.e., salaries, overtime pay, *per diem*, and similar reasonable expenses, not to exceed 10 percent of the sum recovered. This is a cost reimbursement program and not a reward program. Therefore, they must meet certain criteria as follows:

a. The federal taxes imposed must be related to illegal drug trafficking or related money-laundering activities.
b. No other reimbursement has been made under federal or state forfeiture programs or state revenue laws.
c. The IRS must not have the individual already under investigation.
d. The taxes, penalties, and fines must aggregate to more than $50,000 in order to be eligible for reimbursement. This is called the *de minimis rule.*
e. Reimbursement of expenses cannot exceed 10 percent of the total taxes, penalties, and fines collected.

Summary

Fraud examiners get involved in forfeitures, therefore, they should understand the legal reasons for the forfeitures and seizures. In many criminal cases, the fraud examiner's work involve forfeitures either directly or indirectly. When an examiner determines the income from illegal activities, it is this figure(s) that can be used to determine the forfeiture, whether in a civil or criminal case. One of the primary purposes of forfeitures is to take away the profits gained from illegal activities.

Judicial System

25

Introduction

An important element that the fraud examiner should know is how the judicial system is organized and how it operates. When a fraud examiner uncovers fraud, then the examiner must know how to get a case prosecuted. To do this, the fraud examiner must know to whom the crime must be reported, what procedures must be followed, and what the policies are. The fraud examiner should be aware of how the case progresses through the legal system to its ultimate conclusion. This chapter gives the fraud examiner an overview of the judicial system in the United States.

History

The law as we know it is the outgrowth of the legal systems of England and Rome. The English jurist Blackstone defined law as "a rule of civil conduct prescribed by the supreme power of the state, commanding what is right and prohibiting what is wrong." The Roman orator Cicero stated, "The State without law would be like the human body without a mind." Legal systems, which are based upon Roman codes and customs, are commonly referred to as civil law jurisdictions, while those derived from Britain are known as common law jurisdictions. The civil law is followed in Europe, South and Central America; the common law is followed in the United States, Canada, and Australia, with the exceptions of Louisiana and Quebec, whose legal codes are based upon civil law. In addition to the civil and common law, canon law has made an imprint upon our jurisprudence system by the Roman Catholic and Anglican Churches. The law merchant, a body of rules governing medieval business affairs of the mercantile class, has also influenced modern jurisprudence.

During the early part of the fifth century B.C., the lower classes in Rome, unequally treated in the application of customs prevailing at the time, became increasingly discontented. As a result of their protests, in 449 B.C. the so-called Twelve Tables were promulgated, codifying the customs and making them applicable to all Romans. These tables remained in effect for 400 years.

By the opening of the Christian era, Rome had become a vast superstate, ruled by an emperor. During the ensuing centuries, economic and social conditions changed drastically, causing many imperial decrees and administrative orders to be added to the body of law. By the sixth century A.D., it was almost impossible to determine the law governing any particular controversy. The Byzantine Emperor Justinian began the task of clarifying and organizing this mass of Roman law. The Code of Justinian was published in 528–534 A.D. together with the Digest (excerpts from the writings of Roman jurists), the Institutes (a short manual for law students and jurists) and the Novels (a new constitution). The Code of Justinian established a legal and legislative reform that lasted until the fall of the eastern Roman Empire in the 14th century.

Interest in the civil law system was revived in medieval Italy during the Christian Renaissance period. While the Church originally was hostile to Roman law, probably because Justinian's code emphasized the secular against the clerical authority as the supreme power of the state, it soon encouraged the study of civil law and reemphasized the significance and benefits of a formal system of jurisprudence. The legal profession was then created and training in Latin and Roman law was required of all law students, who were later employed as administrators by members of royalty.

The English common law, upon which most all of our American law is founded, came into existence after the Norman Conquest in 1066 A.D. Prior to that there was no "law of England," and feudal law, with its system of manorial courts, was just in the process of creation. The ruling Anglo-Saxons governed various parts of England according to local custom, thereby eliminating any possibility of a uniform system of law. The clergy were separately governed by canon law, administered in the ecclesiastical courts (Courts Christian). Before the Norman Conquest, it was not unusual for the bishop to preside in the secular courts. After the conquest, William I introduced many administrative reforms, strengthened the feudal courts, and made real effort to separate the ecclesiastical from the secular jurisdictions.

The common law actually began under Henry I, after 1100 A.D. It developed into a system of separate royal courts, such as the Courts of the Exchequer, each court developing its own substantive and procedural law. The law was referred to then as the King's Justice, and was administered by justices appointed by the ruling monarch. In nearly all cases, these justices were members of the ruling class. In most cases, these justices were members of the clergy who exerted royal jurisdiction by a system of writs. These writs were authorizations or directions to the sheriff to summon a litigant to appear before the court for the purpose of answering a claim of a royal officer, a member of the nobility, or a wealthy patron. General considerations of fairness and equity, according to prevailing views of society, were supposed to be the foundation of legal decisions by the justices. Roman legal scholars had boasted of their enlightened maxim: *Salus populi suprema lex* (the people's welfare is the supreme law). In England at this time, the Norman trial by battle or ordeal was a frequent means of determining legal rights in both civil and criminal actions.

Writs in the King's courts were not readily available to persons of ordinary means. They were extremely costly and limited to certain types of cases. This gave rise to the establishment of chancery courts and the development of a body of law known as equity law. The rapidly growing number of writs eventually made it possible to collect them and to put them into law books, which later became known as registers. The registers were the first formal collation of legal precedents. By 1297 A.D. and the appearance of the Magna Carta, the law of the King's court had acquired the special name of common law. Publications of the King's courts, written by legal scholars, gave a yearly record of all cases argued before the courts. These yearbooks contained the common law and laid the foundation for this system's reliance on precedent. Reliance on precedent is the most significant difference between the common law and the civil law.

The English colonists in America, despite the fact that they sought to free themselves of the British yoke, brought with them the prevailing English legal system. The common law of England found its way into many local ordinances and state constitutions. Most states have enacted many statutory reforms to replace the outmoded and narrow common law concepts, to furnish a better basis for the simpler administration of the law and justice in our courts according to the needs of our growing and ever changing society. The Anglo-American systems of jurisprudence, while relying upon precedent as a guide, are notable for their ability to accept new ideas and principles by which equitable and speedy justice can be attained.

Local Law Enforcement

In the United States, law enforcement authorities have been decentralized down to the local communities. Local communities consist of municipalities that are cities or towns having their own incorporated government. These incorporated municipalities are organized into departments, which have a police department. The police department is under the control of local mayors and city commissioners. The city commission passes ordinances, which the police department is required to enforce. Also, the police departments are empowered to enforce federal and state laws. The police department operates with almost complete autonomy within its jurisdiction. The police have a great amount of discretion as to the laws that they will enforce and on whom they will impose the laws and ordinances. However, they do not and cannot enforce laws, including federal and state, outside their respective jurisdictions. On occasions, local police work with state or federal law enforcement agencies on "task forces." While on these task forces, they are granted temporary authority outside their jurisdiction.

States are divided into various counties, which have their own county governments. These county governments have a law enforcement department, usually called the sheriff's office or department. As the police department is subject to local control, it is under the control of the county commissioners and mayors. It enforces county ordinances and state and federal laws and has autonomy within its jurisdiction. In addition, it can enforce the city ordinances that are located within its county. Like the police, it has discretion regarding what laws and ordinances it will enforce and to whom it will enforce them. Sheriff departments have jurisdiction within the municipalities within their county. However, sheriff departments will usually not interfere with the police in their jurisdiction.

Officers and Deputies

Police officers and deputy sheriffs normally come from middle-class families with close family ties. Most people become police officers because they are attracted to a civil service job. Most recruits have only high school diplomas. In recent years, many local law enforcement agencies are requiring applicants to have associate and bachelor degrees before being hired. Some police departments recruit from the military because of their maturity, discipline, and training of such applicants. Since police carry weapons, wear uniforms, and are instructed into a military type of organization, police departments are sometimes viewed as paramilitary organizations. Many large police and sheriff departments have special weapons and tactics (SWAT) teams. These SWAT teams were formed to combat the more violent members of society. Members of SWAT teams are usually former military people since these tactics come from military operations.

The local police have greater contact with members of the community. As a result, they see and come into closer contact with criminals than anyone else. They see criminal acts or the aftermath firsthand. Horrible accidents and violent crime scenes cause police to become dispassionate. They view the court system as too lenient against the hardened criminal. Some police feel the bureaucracy within their department restricts them from doing their jobs. Even though corruption within a department may involve only a small number or percentage, it causes polarization of the community, those supportive vs. those critical. Some police officers constantly see criminals with high living standards, far above their own. This, in turn, causes some police officers to cross over to the criminal's side and become corrupt. Those police officers that see corruption in the local political structure may become corrupt along with it. If they try to fight it, then they lose any promotion opportunities or are transferred to menial assignments.

State Law Enforcement

All states have their respective law enforcement agencies, which are responsible for enforcing state laws. The state, unlike counties and municipalities, has more than one law enforcement agency. The states structure their agencies into specialty areas. The state police enforce traffic laws on the highways and other crimes that cross county lines. Other departments within the state have agencies that have law enforcement powers. Revenue departments have agents that go after tax evaders. The Insurance Department has agents that investigate and prosecute fraudulent claims and insurance companies. Departments of Business and Professional Regulations investigate and prosecute crimes relating to various businesses and professions. Business crimes might include improper liquor, cigarette, land, banking, and restaurant operations. Professional crimes would include investigating and prosecuting crimes relating to professional groups, i.e., medical, law, engineering, accounting, nursing, pharmacy, etc.

States generally require higher standards and education for their agents. This is mostly because the crimes they have to investigate require greater skills. A normal high school graduate would not have the skills to investigate such crimes as medical malpractice, securities and banking fraud, racketeering, criminal enterprises, insurance, and a host of others.

Federal Law Enforcement

The U.S. government has law enforcement agencies within practically every department. Since Americans do not want a national police force similar to some countries, the federal government has established law enforcement agencies within each department. Each law enforcement agency is only responsible for enforcing the laws and regulations for that department. Americans have been reluctant to have a national police force since it would pose a threat of quasi-military power. Even the military in the United States comes under civilian control.

The U.S. Department of Justice is the primary department for prosecuting criminals. Within the Justice Department, there are many law enforcement agencies. The principal law enforcement agencies are as follows:

1. The **Federal Bureau of Investigation** is responsible for investigating most federal crimes. It also investigates criminals who cross state lines to avoid prosecution.
2. The **U.S. Marshal Service** is responsible for courtroom security and going after criminals who flee from prosecution. It produces prisoners for trials and is responsible for service of process.
3. The **Border Patrol** is responsible for patrolling U.S. borders and investigating alien smuggling and apprehending illegal aliens.
4. The **Drug Enforcement Agency** is responsible for investigating and apprehending drug traffickers and other drug violations.

The U.S. Treasury Department has many law enforcement agencies. These include the following:

1. The **Secret Service** protects the president and other federal and foreign officials. It investigates counterfeiting of currency and other government obligations and credit card fraud.
2. The **U.S. Customs Service** enforces customs laws, duties, and products entering or leaving the United States. It is responsible for drug interdiction into or out of the United States.
3. The **Internal Revenue Service** enforces the federal tax law. In the 1980s, it was made responsible for enforcing money-laundering statutes.
4. The **Bureau of Alcohol, Tobacco, and Firearms** is responsible for investigations involving firearms, explosives, interstate arson, and liquor violations.

The U.S. Postal Service has a law enforcement agency called Postal Inspection. Postal inspectors investigate mail fraud and mailing of obscene and dangerous materials.

There are other federal law enforcement agencies in the other departments. The Defense Department has its investigative services. The Environmental Protection Agency enforces federal pollution laws. The list goes on.

Like the states enforcement agencies, the federal law enforcement agencies usually require higher standards and education. The crimes that federal agents investigate are sophisticated and require a high degree of knowledge and expertise in their respective areas. Each department not only trains its agents in law enforcement, but also in the laws in the respective fields.

Foreign Law Enforcement

Most countries maintain a national police agency. Some countries have a national police agency that also doubles as a military force. In Britain, police are under local control, but the home office sets nationwide standards.

Several large criminal organizations operate on an international scale. This makes it hard for law enforcement to investigate and prosecute such people. Criminals will flee from one country and seek refuge in another to avoid prosecution. Police in one country have difficulty in obtaining information and cooperation from another country. In 1923, the International Criminal Police Organization (INTERPOL) was formed for the purpose of promoting mutual assistance among international law enforcement authorities. This assistance includes coordinating and aiding international arrests and extraditions and providing a way to expedite the exchange of criminal justice information. At the present time, there are 125 members of INTERPOL. INTERPOL is not an international police agency but a conduit for cooperative exchange of criminal information to help detect and combat international crime. Each participating country sets up a national central bureau which serves as the country's point of contact with the international law enforcement community. Each country operates its national central bureau within the parameters of its own national laws and policies. In the United States, the INTERPOL function rests by law with the attorney general. The U.S. National Central Bureau (USNCB) is under the control of the departments of justice and treasury.

Agents, analysts, communicators, translators, and clerical support personnel staff the USNCB. Most employees are with the department of justice. However, other federal and state law enforcement personnel are detailed on a regular basis. With the increase of international crime, the USNCB has arranged with the states a point of contact for a full range of international services. The liaison office in that state forwards requests for investigative assistance from abroad, which requires action by the police of a particular state, to the USNCB. INTERPOL provides the following services:

1. Criminal history checks;
2. License plate/driver's license check;
3. Full investigation leading to arrest and extradition;
4. Location of suspects, fugitives, and witnesses;
5. International wanted circulars;
6. Traces of weapons, motor vehicles abroad;
7. Other types of criminal investigations.

Misdemeanor vs. Felony

In the United States, crimes are divided into two categories, misdemeanors and felonies. Misdemeanors are generally considered trivial crimes. They impose incarceration at local detention facilities and/or fines and penalties of relatively small amounts. Parking and traffic violations are considered misdemeanors. Improper use of property or authority can be classified as a misdemeanor. Misdemeanor crimes are usually heard before a county or municipal judge or magistrate. There are no juries. The judge or magistrate serves as both judge and jury. The people that are found guilty of misdemeanor crimes do not go to state detention facilities. In most cases, they only pay fines. Some states divide misdemeanors into grades according to the degree of seriousness, such as gross misdemeanors and petit or simple misdemeanors.

A felony is a crime that is or may be punishable by death or imprisonment in a state prison. The possible sentence, not the actual one imposed by the court, determines the grade of the violation of law and whether the crime is a felony or misdemeanor. Before a person can be punished, the person's acts must be plainly and unmistakably prohibited or compelled by a statute. Any and every reasonable doubt must be resolved in favor of the accused, inasmuch as personal liberty and perhaps life are at stake. This principle of strict construction does not require that a criminal statute be given a narrow meaning. The language of the law is to be given its natural, reasonable, and accepted meaning in an effort to determine the legislative intent. The law distinguishes crimes as *mala in se* (bad in themselves) and *mala prohibita* (bad because prohibited). Acts such as murder, arson, rape, and robbery, which obviously are so evil in themselves and inherently violate the mores of society, are classified as *mala in se*. Other acts, which are deemed wrong only because a specific law declares them to be wrong, are classified as *mala prohibita*.

Hearings

Hearings are informal trials before a county or municipal judge or magistrate. There are no juries. The local judge or magistrate acts as both judge and jury. These hearings handle misdemeanors, bond or bail arrangements, criminal arraignments, and small civil disputes. The federal courts use hearings for bail or bond arrangements, sentencing, and some civil disputes.

Grand Jury

A grand jury is so called because it normally has more members than the ordinary trial jury. A grand jury consists of 16 to 23 people. However, some states have statutes that mandate fewer people. Grand juries may be impaneled under either federal or state law, and classified as a "regular" or "special" grand jury, depending on the reason they are convened. A regular grand jury is so designated because it is routinely impaneled to perform the function of a grand jury and is the forum for presentation of cases developed through the normal investigative processes of law enforcement agencies. The court, often at the request of a state or U.S. attorney to investigate specific complaints or allegations of crime, convenes special grand juries. Special grand juries may be convened to investigate potential crimes involving casinos, union pension plans, and corruption in public agencies or offices.

History

It is generally agreed that the grand jury originated in England as an investigatory tool for the crown, its development usually being traced from the Assize of Clarendon, which was proclaimed by Henry II in 1166. However, its defined purpose in exercising its accusatorial and investigative function emerged as one of protecting the accused against unfounded charges rather than of furthering arbitrary prosecutions at the will of the sovereign. By the time the grand jury was brought to this country by the early colonists, it was firmly established in the common law as an important institution for the protection of citizens' rights and privileges. This historical protective function of the grand jury was incorporated into the Fifth Amendment to the Constitution as a guarantee that "no person shall be held to answer for a capital, or other infamous crime, unless on a presentment or indictment of a Grand Jury." Scholars of U.S. constitutional law generally regard the modern grand jury as being part of the judicial, rather than the executive or legislative branch of government.

404   Financial Investigation and Forensic Accounting

Rule 6, Federal Rules of Criminal Procedure

The adoption of the Federal Rules of Criminal Procedure in the 1940s established the first concise definition of federal grand jury procedural requirements. Rule 6 defines the role and procedures for federal grand juries. The following is a synopsis of Rule 6.

1. Generally. The court shall order one or more grand juries to be summoned at such time as the public interest requires. The grand jury shall consist of not less than 16 nor more than 23 members.
2. Objections. The attorney for the government or a defendant who has been held to answer in the district court may challenge the array of jurors on the ground that the grand jury was not selected, drawn, or summoned in accordance with law. They may challenge an individual juror on the ground that the juror is not legally qualified. Challenges shall be made before the administration of the oath to the jurors and shall be tried by the court.
3. Foreperson. The court shall appoint one of the jurors to be foreperson and another to be deputy foreperson. The foreperson shall have power to administer oaths and affirmations and shall sign all indictments. The foreperson is responsible for keeping a record of concurring findings of every indictment. During the absence of the foreperson, the deputy foreperson shall act as foreperson.
4. Who may be present. Attorneys for the government, the witness under examination, interpreters when needed, and for the purpose of taking the evidence, a stenographer may be present while the grand jury is in session, but no person other than the jurors may be present while the grand jury is deliberating or voting.
5. Disclosure. A grand juror, an interpreter, a stenographer, an attorney for the government, or any person to whom disclosure is made shall not disclose matters occurring before the grand jury. A violation of Rule 6 may be punished as a contempt of court.
6. Return of indictment. An indictment may be found only upon the concurrence of 12 or more jurors. The indictment shall be returned by the grand jury to a federal magistrate in open court. If a complaint or information is pending against the defendant and 12 jurors do not concur in finding an indictment, the foreperson shall so report to a federal magistrate in writing forthwith.

Secrecy

The requirement that secrecy of grand jury proceedings be maintained is one which developed gradually in English common law to protect the independence of the grand jury. Five reasons are traditionally given in modern common law for this requirement of secrecy:

1. The first is to encourage the free expression of witnesses by affording them the maximum freedom of disclosure without fear of reprisal.
2. The second is to prevent perjury by witnesses who might otherwise come forward to falsely controvert or reinforce other grand jury evidence, which they might learn about.
3. The third is to permit confidentially of the grand jury's interest in order to prevent prospective defendants from fleeing.

4. The fourth is to prevent disclosing knowledge of investigations which results in no grand jury action.
5. The fifth is to assure the grand jury freedom from outside interference.

Pretrial Procedures

After the information (complaint) or indictment has been rendered, the defendant will appear before a judge or magistrate for arraignment. The defendant's lawyer may force the prosecution by use of a writ of habeas corpus the substantive reasons for depriving the accused of liberty. Bail is also set during the arraignment. The defendant can file motions. These motions fall into two classes:

1. Motions to correct defects in the complaint.
2. Motions for judgment upon the complaint in favor of the defendant.

All motions addressed to the complaint must be made promptly. The rules of procedure governing this type of relief generally provide for specific time limitations within which such motion practice is available to the defendant.

In most states, provisions for the examination before trial of a party and of a witness were expanded and liberalized. The practice of taking the testimony of parties and witnesses is a common one. The main objective of examination before trial in all jurisdictions is to allow a party to obtain material and necessary evidence for the prosecution or defense of an action. Going on "fishing expeditions" is not permitted. Depositions must contain both direct examination and cross-examination of a witness before they can be admissible in court. The court can suppress (forbid the use of) depositions for a variety of reasons, including fraud, unfair and overreaching conduct, improper or irregular procedure in taking or returning a deposition, and evasiveness or refusal of witnesses to answer questions put to them on cross-examination.

Trial

After arraignment, pretrial motions have been ruled upon, and discovery (providing the defense all the evidence that will be used in trial) has been made, then the case is ready to go to trial. The purpose of the trial will be to determine the issues of fact. The court determines questions of law. The trial is conducted by stringent rules regarding both evidence and procedures. There are seven stages of a trial as explained below:

Jury Selection

Jury members have to be selected. Usually, there are 12 jurors who have to be selected along with one or more alternate jurors, so that if a juror becomes ill or otherwise unable to complete the trial, an alternate may be substituted for such disabled juror without any disruption of the proceedings. This selection process is called voir dire examination. Both prosecution and defense examine prospective jurors about their qualifications to serve. The objective is to determine which jurors will reach an objective verdict without any biases or prejudices. A challenge to the poll is an objection to an individual prospective juror. Such objection may be for cause or peremptory. A challenge for cause may ordinarily be either for principal cause or to the favor. Principal cause involves the legal presumption that a juror would not try the case fairly; for example, if there is a close relationship between the prospective juror and a party to the action. A challenge to the favor is merely an assertion of a suspicion rather than a legal presumption that the juror will be prejudiced in the trial of the case. The court may dismiss a juror at any time before evidence is given in the action. In a peremptory challenge, no reason need be given. Peremptory challenges vary according to the crime charged. If the crime charged is punishable by death, 30 or more peremptory challenges may be allowed. If the crime is punishable with imprisonment for life or for a term of 10 years or more, 20 challenges are normally available. In all other criminal cases, law permits about 5 peremptory challenges.

Opening Arguments

Opening addresses to the jury by both plaintiff and defendant are the next order of procedure. The purpose of counsel's opening remarks to the jury is merely to advise the jury of the general nature of the issues, which the jury ultimately will have to determine. Usually, counsel tells the jury what the counsel expects (or hopes) to prove during the trial.

Evidence by the Prosecution

The prosecution has to present its evidentiary facts. Although it is true that evidentiary facts, for the most part, are adduced by the testimony of witnesses, there are, in fact, four methods of proving a case, namely:

1. Presenting oral statements of sworn witnesses;
2. Requesting the court to take judicial notice of matters of law;
3. Offering in evidence documents that require no witnesses for their introduction;
4. Offering in evidence documents identified by the oral testimony of a sworn witness.

It is apparent that witnesses are often necessary, not only to testify to material evidentiary facts within their own knowledge, but also to identify documents which would otherwise be inadmissible in evidence. If proper identification is made and a foundation is laid for the introduction of such documents in evidence, the facts contained in them may then be used by counsel to prove the allegations of the pleadings. No unsworn testimony is admissible in courts. Defense counsel has the right and obligation to cross-examine the prosecution's witnesses.

Evidence by the Defense

After the prosecution has presented its case, then the defense presents its case. Counsel's questions must be competent, relevant, and material, and should conform to the well-established rules of evidence. Except to the limited extent permitted by specific statute, parties may not impeach their own witnesses. By that is meant that parties may not call witnesses to prove that their prior witness's general reputation is bad, that the witness is unworthy of belief, or that the witness made contradictory statements out of court. A witness must generally be asked questions that the witness can answer with evidentiary facts within the witness's own knowledge, unless the witness is called as an expert witness, in which event the witness may give opinion evidence. Leading questions are not permissible on direct examination unless the witness called by counsel is a hostile witness or an adverse witness. If opposing counsel deems a question put to a witness to be improper in form or content, counsel may object and have the court rule on such objection. Regardless of the nature of the objection, it should always be made as soon as the question is put to the witness and before it is answered. Sometimes, the witness's answer comes so fast that counsel is unable to make the objection first. In this event, if the objection is a proper one, it will be deemed timely, and the court will order the answer stricken from the record. In reality, nothing is stricken from the record.

Closing Arguments

Both sides are allowed to make closing arguments after presenting their case. Closing arguments are basically a summation of their case. They make their points in their case as previously presented to the jury. The prosecution presents its closing argument first. The defense then presents its closing argument, which is followed by the prosecution's rebuttal.

Jury Deliberations

After the closing arguments, the court will give the jury instructions regarding the law and its application to the issues involved. The law must be applied as charged, as presented to the jury by the trial court, regardless of whether the jury agrees or disagrees with it. Simply stated, the jury is the trier of the facts, while the court determines and instructs as to the applicable principles of law. It is well established in this country that the jury alone is responsible for determining questions of fact. The jury is bound only by its recollections and interpretations of the evidence adduced at the trial and not by the court's statement of fact in its charge. In fact, if the court calls material facts not in evidence to the attention of the jury, the charge will be deemed improper and a reversal will undoubtedly result.

Verdict

After the court has charged the jury, the jury will be secluded for its deliberations. The jury will take the case and decide it upon the evidence, without sympathy or prejudice, with the sole desire of eliciting the truth and establishing such truth by a fair verdict. The jury may vote either by open or secret ballot on the innocence or guilt of the defendant. The foreperson will usually count the votes. In capital cases, each member of the jury must find the defendant guilty. Any one dissension will result in a "hung" jury, in effect no verdict. Once a verdict has been reached, the foreperson will either read the verdict in open court or will have the verdict delivered to the court for open reading.

If the defendant is found not guilty of the offense(s), then he or she is able to walk out of the courtroom as a free person. If the defendant is found guilty of all or part of the charges, then the defendant will be taken to the detention facilities for further disposition. The court will order a sentencing hearing. The prosecution and defense will have to prepare for this hearing.

Plea Bargaining

Some criminals, especially those who know that they are guilty, want to plea bargain. Plea bargaining is a way of getting more lenient treatment. They know that if they go to trial and are found guilty, then they could get a harsher sentence. In areas where the courts are overloaded with cases, plea bargaining is welcomed. It reduces the time and expense of trial, and saves the taxpayer money. Plea bargaining could involve the reduction of charges from a felony to a misdemeanor. Also, it could mean that the defendant would serve less time in a local "stockade" instead of serving longer in a state prison. There are many arguments for and against plea bargaining. Plea bargaining can offer swift justice. On the other hand, it does not get hardened criminals off the streets and also does not rehabilitate criminals.

Sentencing

Prior to 1984, judges had a lot of leeway in determining sentences for convicted criminals. Sentences ranged from 2 years and up depending on the crime. However, in 1984, the Crime Control Act was passed. This act provided sentencing guidelines, which the U.S. court system must follow. It mandates the possible sentences for a particular crime. The U.S. Supreme Court, on January 18, 1989, upheld the new sentencing guidelines in *Mistretta v. United States*. These new sentencing guidelines came about because

1. A person, presumably, will not go "straight."
2. The system was unfair because of different sentences for the same type of crime.
3. The public was disillusioned with the rehabilitation process.

Prior to sentencing, the judge will order a presentencing investigation. The purpose of this investigation is to determine the appropriate sentence. Both the prosecution and defense will present their opinions and facts. The convicted criminal's background will be examined. Prior convictions for the same or similar acts will influence the judge to hand out a harsher sentence. However, the judge can be influenced to issue a lighter sentence because of family life, community involvement, and the seriousness of the offense.

At the sentencing hearing, the judge will hear arguments from both the prosecution and the defense. The defendant, also, will have the opportunity to express his or her case. In nolo contendere (no contest) cases, the judge will further ask the defendant if he or she knows the consequences of the decision not to contest the charges. Judges are not bound to give a lesser sentence if the defendant pleads out. After hearing all arguments, the judge pronounces the sentence.

Punishment

There are various forms of punishment that a judge can mete out:
1. **Jail.** The criminal will be sent to a local detention facility for a term of up to 1 year.
2. **Prison.** The criminal will be sent to a state or federal prison system for a term of 1 year or more. Most criminals would rather go to a federal prison than a state prison because

conditions in state prisons are generally harsher and more inhumane than federal prisons. Criminals sentenced 10 years or less in the federal system will go to prisons that are called "Club Fed" because they do not have the harsher rules and regulations that the state prisons have imposed.

3. **Probation.** The criminal will not go to prison or jail, but will be required to live by a set of rules, which are enforced by a probation officer. The criminal will only be allowed to do certain activities, and will be forbidden to do other activities. The probation officer is expected to help the criminal, and also to keep the criminal out of further lawbreaking activities. Another version of probation is house arrest. Criminals are not allowed to leave their home without permission. They wear an electronic device, which will alert authorities of their whereabouts or if they leave a designated area. Removing the electronic device will alert authorities that they have violated the "probation" and result in a return to jail or prison.

4. **Community Service.** In misdemeanor or minor felony cases, the judge may order the criminal to perform community services. These services include, but are not limited to, cleaning up parks, roads, and helping the elderly or children. This is done without any compensation. A specific number of hours or days is specified. This form of punishment is becoming more popular because it helps cities and municipalities in economic hard times by reducing the cost of detaining people in jails or prisons and by reducing the cost of hiring personnel to perform these functions. Another version of this form of punishment is the "half-way" house. These houses are mostly directed at rehabilitation of drug and alcohol offenders.

Summary

Forensic accountants must be familiar with the judicial system and how it works since they will be involved in the system in one way or another. It is not unusual for forensic accountants to be involved from the start to the finish. This means that they will be involved:

1. From the initial investigation,
2. To presenting evidence to a grand jury,
3. To testifying in trial, and
4. To presenting expert testimony in civil proceedings following the criminal case.

Forensic accountants are involved in all phases of the judicial system.

Criminology

26

Introduction

Criminologists study crime and justice within the social order. Sociologists study society and its social order. Some scholars think of criminology as a field of sociology whereas others view it as a field of psychology. Criminology in recent years has become a separate field of study while it has incorporated some of the theories from both sociology and psychology. Sociologists have been instrumental in helping law enforcement understand organized crime and youth gangs. Psychologists have helped law enforcement understand criminals behavior. The FBI has developed a method called "profiling." This method uses crime scene evidence to determine the psychological makeup of a criminal. It is also used by other law enforcement agencies to identify drug traffickers, serial killers, and rapists. This chapter provides an overview of the field of criminology and the basic theories.

History

The field of criminology did not emerge until the eighteenth century when an Italian, Cesare Beccaria (1764), wrote an essay *On Crime and Punishment.* An English contemporary, Jeremy Bentham wrote *Principals of Morals and Legislation* (1789). These two individuals are considered the founders of criminology. A century later, several other schools of criminology developed. One of the schools was labeled the Positivists School. This school was promoted by Cesare Lombroso and his followers, Enrico Ferri and Raffaele Garofalo. The other school was the Conflict school. This school was originated by the writings of Karl Marx in *Das Kapital* (1867–95).

During the nineteenth century, other professional groups developed theories for criminal behavior. An Austrian physician, Dr. Franz Josef Gall, formulated the theory of phrenology. Charles Caldwell promoted this theory in the United States and it was widely accepted. This theory was rebutted in 1913 by Charles Goring in his research. However, Ernest A. Hooten partially confirmed some of Caldwell's theories in 1939. In the field of psychology, Sigmund Freud had a big impact upon criminology, even though it was not his intention. Criminologists still rely on many of his theories and methodologies.

Sociologists have become involved in criminology in various ways. They are classified into four groups or schools. These schools were developed during the late nineteenth and early twentieth centuries. These theories are:

- Control
- Strain
- Cultural deviance
- Symbolic interaction or differential association

The control theories were promoted by Travis Hirschi in his 1969 book *Cause of Delinquency.* Control theories originated from Emile Durkheim in the late nineteenth century and expanded upon by Thorsten Sellin (1959).

The strain theories are also based upon works of Emile Durkheim, but they were adapted by Robert Merton (1938) for application in the United States. Other sociologists have expanded upon Merton's strain theories by developing additional theories, i.e., deprivation theories and institutional anomie theories. Anomie, according to Durkheim, means a condition of an individual or society characterized by a breakdown of norms and values.

The cultural differences theories were developed by Edwin H. Sutherland (1939) in his book *Principles of Criminology.* He was influenced by colleagues at the Sociology Department of the University of Chicago. His theories are closely related to the symbolic interaction theories by George Mead and others.

The symbolic interaction theories and the differential association theories were developed by George Mead in *Mind, Self and Society* (1934). This symbolic interaction theories is usually referred to as labeling theory or just social interaction theory.

Another school in criminology is Radical Criminology. The founder of this school was Ralf Dahrendorf, a sociologist, but was applied to criminology by George Vold in his writing, *Theoretical Criminology* (1958). Radical Criminology is closely associated with Marxist theories. Also, Radical Criminology is similar to conflict theories. Richard Quinney developed criminology theories which were closely related to Marxist ideas in his writing *The Social Reality of Crime* (1970). William Chambliss and Robert Seidman were proponents of Radical Criminology.

Schools of Criminology

There are many theories advocated in the field of criminology. These theories are classified as schools. The field of criminology has been influenced by other professions. The medical profession has made propositions that physical characteristics make criminals. This is especially the case in phrenology. Psychologists and psychiatrists believe mental disorders and processes produce criminals. Sociologists advocate social influences cause people to become criminals. Some of the criminology theories are closely intertwined. This is especially the case with Marxist theories and the conflict and radical theories. It is hard for one to distinguish the differences. The criminologists are usually more concerned with justice and human rights, whereas the sociologists are concerned with social order and harmony. In reality, the human rights and justice is so intertwined with social order and harmony that they cannot always be clearly distinguishable.

Classical School

The Classical School, founded by Cesare Beccaria and Jeremy Bentham, was based upon society which is composed of individuals. Society must impose laws to regulate the conduct of individuals within the society. Individuals form a society in order to obtain life, liberty, and happiness. This requires individuals to give up some liberties and be responsible to society for their actions and deeds. Their main concepts were:

1. Conduct is chosen by individuals within a society.
2. Punishment is a deterrent for unwanted conduct.
3. Punishment should fit the crime.

Bentham proposed his theory of "felicity calculus," which was his mathematical model of determining the amount of punishment to be imposed in order to deter an individual from committing a crime. This model was based upon his estimation of pain. The Classical School has had an influence upon the founding fathers of the United States when they incorporated the cruel and unusual punishment into the Eighth Amendment of the Constitution.

Positivist School

The Positivist School was interested in criminal behavior at the individual level. Also, the Positivist School embraced scientific methodologies more than philosophizing as the Classical School had done. The major proponents of the Positivist School were Cesare Lombroso and his followers, Enrico Ferri and Raffaele Garofalo. Lombroso studied Italian criminals. Based upon his studies, he formulated that degeneracy, called atavism, caused criminality. He also classified criminals into three categories:

1. Pseudocriminals. Involuntary crimes such as self defense.
2. Criminaloids. Predisposed to crimes because of environmental causes.
3. Habitual criminals. Criminals who chose to be because of environmental or biological factors.

Lombroso and his colleagues were proponents of criminal anthropology. In other words, heredity was the cause of criminal behavior in some instances. In America, biological causes to crime was accepted better than it was in Europe.

Conflict School

This school followed the theories of Karl Marx, a nineteenth century sociologist. Crime is considered a class struggle between the lower and upper classes for political and economic power. Crime is defined as acts of the lower class, which are prohibited by the ruling upper class. This conflict is over the control of scarce resources. Marx engenders a parasitic class of people whose interest is living off other classes, both upper and lower. This parasitic class consists of thieves, burglars, prostitutes, and gamblers.

Biological Theories

The Positivist School was the first to theorize biological causes for criminal behavior. Ernest A. Hooton, an anthropologist, conducted a twelve-year research on over 17,000 subjects. Nearly 14,000 subjects were incarcerated in jails and prisons, and the remainder were citizens. He concluded criminals have physiological differences which set them apart from the general population. He believed tattooing was done more by criminals than others. An Englishman, Charles Goring, previously made a similar study in England. He did an eight-year study on 3,000 convicts. He concluded criminals have low intelligence and this is an indication of hereditary inferiority. Charles Caldwell, a phrenologist, conducted a study of 29 women convicted of infanticide. He found most of them were poorly developed as to their sense of caring for children.

Psychological Theories

This school believes the minds of criminals are the cause of their behavior. The psychological theorists explain behavior as mental anomalies. The best known psychologist was Sigmund Freud. He conceived mental conflict was due to three incompatible elements of personality. He identified these personality elements which must be in balance as:

1. Id. This is the unconscious, which is composed of forces called instincts and drives .
2. Ego. This is part of the personality which deals with reality. This is the conscious part.
3. Superego. This is the conscience. It internalizes a person's values and norms.

From the Freudian perspective, crime is caused by the dysfunction of the ego and superego. Criminologists rely upon Freudian theories to explain the motives for criminal behavior. Freud's theories were not addressed to explain criminal behavior nor did he expect them to be used in this field.

Sociological Theories

Sociologists have developed many theories to explain normal and abnormal behavior. They have also presented theories on the causation of crime. Their basic theme is based upon external factors. These external factors involve political, economical, and ecological elements. Some of the sociological theories are intertwined. These theories can be grouped into four classifications:

1. Control
2. Strain
3. Cultural deviance
4. Symbolic interaction or differential association

Control Theory

There are many theories which can be classified as control theories. Some of these are containment and anomie theories. Durkheim was the earliest proponent of the social control theory. He believed order and conformity to rules were important for social solidarity. Criminals are individuals who will not adapt to the social norms of society. Robert Merton, as well as Travis Hirschi, formulated elements which would strengthen social bonds. They are:

1. Attachment. This refers to the individual's feelings about others.
2. Commitment. This refers to the individual's personal stake in society.
3. Involvement. This refers to the amount of time and resources the individual provides to society.
4. Belief. This refers to the individual's beliefs in adhering to society's rules.

Strain Theory

The strain theory is very similar to the control theory. Both of these theories come from the Chicago School of Sociology. Merton views society in two parts, cultural and social structures. Cultural structure refers to society's goals while social structure refers to society's means of achieving the goals. Merton proposes different ways people respond to strain:

1. Innovation. Deviant behavior is a response to blocking individual's goals by society.
2. Ritualism. This refers to individuals adhering to society's rules, but at a lower degree.
3. Retreatism. This refers to individuals who drop out of society since they are unable to achieve the goals that society wishes for them.
4. Rebellion. This refers to individuals who don't accept cultural and social structure and seek to replace them.
5. Conformity. Most people accept society's goals and the means to achieving them.

Cultural Deviance Theory

Cultural deviance theory is closely related to the strain theory. Thorsten Sellin argued that crime is caused by the conflict between cultures. The society makes laws for the majority, the middle, or dominant class. These laws can conflict with the values and norms of minority or ethnic groups who have their own set of values. In a heterogeneous society, laws represent the majority or dominant cultures.

Differential Association Theory

Differential association theory is closely associated with cultural deviance theories. The chief proponent of differential association theory is Edwin Sutherland. He suggested nine propositions:

1. Criminal behavior is learned.
2. Criminal behavior is learned through a process of communication.
3. Criminal behavior occurs in close groups.
4. Learning criminal behavior includes how to commit crimes and provides the motives and drives to do them.
5. Motives and drives come from legal definitions.
6. It's more favorable to commit crimes solely.
7. Criminal behavior varies by the frequency, duration, priority, and intensity of association.
8. Criminal behavior is learned by association with other criminals.
9. Criminal behavior does not explain general needs and values.

Symbolic Interaction Theory

Symbolic interaction theory is based upon belief that people communicate through symbols. A symbol is anything that has meaning in an individual's life. The interpretation of symbols is dependent upon each individual. Different individuals will have different interpretations based upon one's experiences. Symbolic interaction is a forerunner to labeling theory.

Labeling Theory

Labeling theory expands upon the symbolic interaction theories. It proposes that people are given various symbolic labels by interaction with people around them. These labels connote behavior and attitudes. Labeling has both a positive and negative effect. When a person is labeled as conscientious, intelligent, thrifty, trustworthy, then this implies a positive view of the person. On the other hand, if the person is labeled as lazy, dumb, or troublesome, then this implies a negative view of the person. These labels don't have to be truthful. Labeling does not only apply to individuals, but also to various minority and ethnic groups. Labeling theorists believe police, courts, and other agencies promote criminal behavior by use of labeling. Label theorists point out that crime is a matter of definition. What may be illegal at one particular time or place may not be illegal at another time or place. Gambling and alcohol consumption is illegal in many places today, yet also legal in other places in the United States today.

Critical Criminology

Radical criminology is heavily influenced by critical criminology. The major proponents of critical criminology are Ralf Dahrendorf and George Vold. Dahrendorf is a sociologist who advocated that society is divided into two classes, the domineering class and the dominated class. He applied critical theories to societal issues. George Vold applied critical theories to criminology. Vold explained crime and deviance was caused by conditions of inequality. This was made explicit by inner-city riots and political protests. Conflict theory is limited to situations where criminal acts of one group collide with another group.

Radical Criminology

The chief spokesman for radical criminology is Richard Quinney. Other supporters are William Chambliss and Robert Seidman. Radical criminology is very much Marxist oriented. It applies the social theories of Karl Marx to criminology. Quinney made six propositions concerning definition of crime. These definitions can be condensed to the premise that those in power make laws to benefit and maintain their power while restraining those not in power. Laws are ever changing to reflect changes in the political climate of society. Chambliss and Seidman also advocate that the state, even though an instrument of the ruling class, must be concerned with maintaining good relations between classes. It must balance the capitalistic society and personal interest of individuals. They point out that law enforcement is selective. Just because a law is on the books doesn't mean that it is enforced.

Scientific Methodology

Scientific methodology encompasses procedures used to search for the truth. These procedures try to eliminate human intuition and hunches and make the research more objective and verifiable. Research methodology tries to guard against the following:

1. Errors in observation. Some people fail to recognize important features of a crime scene. People have observed witnesses in court who cannot remember details of an event. Some witnesses make up observations which have contradictions when analyzed.
2. Selective observation. People only see things that they are interested in seeing. Witnesses in trials can only give facts from their observations.
3. Errors in interpretation. Everyone has some biases and prejudices. These biases and prejudices cause misinterpretations.
4. Dependence upon authority. People rely heavily on others in authority. Juries hear expert witnesses. Expert witnesses can only express opinions based upon data supplied to them. Expert witnesses have their biases and prejudices. News media reports can be slanted or biased. The headlines of one media vehicle may not be reported by another or placed in lower priority.
5. Inappropriate use of evidence. Evidence may be appropriate in one situation, but may be inappropriate in another situation. Police sometimes report more than one offender, but only arrest one offender.

Organized Crime

Many criminologists study the various aspects of organized crime. They are interested in its motives, organization, criminal activities, and individual and group profiles. In Chapter 12 different organized crime organizations have been identified along with their basic organization and criminal activities. Law enforcement is always gathering intelligence on criminal organizations and their activities. Many large city police departments as well as some states and federal agencies have units whose sole responsibility is to investigate various organized crime groups.

Organized Criminal Code

Organized criminal groups cannot function without some kind of code for its members to follow. This code is well-defined in some organizations while it is not well-defined in others. The code can vary from one criminal organization to another. Criminologist Donald Cressey made an analysis of organized crime, and he suggested the following:

1. Loyalty. Don't be an informer.
2. Be rational. Conduct business in a quiet, safe, and profitable manner.
3. Be a man of honor. Respect women and elders.
4. Be a stand-up guy. Show courage and heart. Keep mouth shut.
5. Have class. Be independent.

Rules of Behavior

Donald Cressey found three basic rules of behavior in studying the Lupollo crime family. They are:

1. Primary loyalty is vested in family; not in individual lineages.
2. Each family member must act like a man and not bring disgrace on the family.
3. Family business is secret, don't discuss outside the group.

Survival Mechanisms

Organized crime contains mechanisms which ensure the survival of the organization. The LCN has a long history in both the United States and Italy. The Triads and Yakuzas have a very long history. Even with losses from both external and internal forces, they have been able to survive and prosper. They have learned to become more sophisticated in their methods of operations and use of more professional people, e.g., accountants, lawyers, and engineers. These survival mechanisms are classified into three imperative roles. They are:

1. The enforcer. A position in the organization that provides for enforcement of its rules and the directives of those in authority. The methods can range from murder to verbal warnings.
2. The buffer. A position primarily centered on internal communication and the flow of decisions in the hierarchy. This person keeps lines of communication between leaders and followers open, forewarning of internal dissentions and problems at the street level. The buffer may settle disagreements and conflicts.
3. The corruptor. The corruptor's job is to bribe, buy, intimidate, negotiate, persuade, and maneuver into a relationship with police, public officials, and anyone who will help the family.

Predatory Crimes

Crimes that members of society fear most are predatory crimes. These are defined as "illegal acts where someone intentionally takes or damages the person or property of another." Criminologist Lawrence Cohen says predatory criminal events involve the following elements:

1. Motivated offenders.
2. Suitable targets.
3. The absence of capable guardians.

If any one of these elements is lacking, the predatory criminal event will not occur.

Legal Definition

According to law, specific criteria must be met for an act to be considered a crime and the predator a criminal. These criteria are:

1. There must be conduct (not mere thoughts).
2. The conduct must constitute social harm.
3. Law must prohibit the conduct.
4. The conduct must be performed voluntarily.
5. The conduct must be performed intentionally.
6. The conduct must be punishable by law.

Natural crime consists of acts that are repulsive to most people in society. This is "mala in se," which means "evil in itself." "Mala prohibita in se" consists of acts that are illegal by legislation or custom. "Mala prohibita in se" means "evil because it is forbidden."
Procedural and substantive criminal law draws two basic issues in law:

1. How the authorities handle matters of law and deal with law violators—the question of procedures.
2. Content of specific rules making up the body of criminal law—the question of substance.

Primitive Law

Primitive law is a system of rules and obligations in preliterate and semiliterate societies which modern legal systems are based upon. Primitive law contains three important features.

1. Acts that injured or wronged others were considered private wrongs.
2. The injured party or family typically took personal action against the wrongdoer.
3. This self-help justice usually amounted to retaliation in kind.

The Code of Hammurapi is the earliest law and covered a wide range of crimes. The four important observations are:

1. Most laws are a product of prevailing social, political, and economic conditions.
2. Some laws articulate long-established customs and traditions and can be thought of as formal restatements of existing mores.
3. Some laws reflect efforts to regulate and coordinate increasingly complex social relations and activities.
4. Some laws display prevailing ethical and moral standards and show close ties to religious ideas and sentiments.

Criminology and the Fraud Examiner

Fraud examiners should be aware of sociology and criminology. Sociology and criminology help fraud examiners understand the criminal and the motives involved. Sometimes, the examiner is questioned about personality profiles which would help distinguish those who would commit a particular crime from those who wouldn't. There is no clear-cut answer to this question. Most employees don't take a job with the view of committing a crime. Employees that commit a crime do so because of internal and external influences. The fraud examiner should be alert to all possible influences that would cause an employee to commit fraud. Some of these influences are:

1. Management committing fraudulent acts, i.e., padded expense accounts, embezzlement, skimming, using ghost employees, and a whole host of other schemes.
2. Failure to obtain a desired position or promotion.
3. Low morale by the employee and/or his or her coworkers. This can be a result of bad policies or layoffs due to bad economic times.
4. The employee has problems at home, i.e., divorce, drug or alcohol abuse, gambling debts, large medical bills, etc.
5. Employees are tempted to commit fraud if internal controls are weak and the opportunity is present.

People have daily and regular routines. Career criminals also have regular patterns. The fraud examiner should become aware of those patterns. A "bust-out" artist will open a business and "bust out" months later leaving creditors holding worthless receivables. "Boiler room" operators will operate in one location for weeks or a few months and then shut down operations. They do this to evade law enforcement. The boiler room operators move to a new location and start up operations again. "Boiler room" operators and "bust out" artists establish a regular pattern of crime. They usually remain in the same product or service since they are familiar with it. Once the pattern is determined, then the examiner can develop his case to greater degree. In addition, law enforcement can take the appropriate steps to shut down these operations with minimum effort and a greater degree of prosecution success.

Criminals have various motives for committing the crimes that they do. One major motive is greed. Other motives are to obtain power, status, etc.. The fraud examiner should be aware of the motives and patterns that criminals have mapped out.

Summary

Criminology is the study of crime and causation. Criminology has been influenced by other disciplines, e.g., psychology, anthropology, biology, and sociology. Sociology has had the greatest impact. The theories for crime and causation vary widely. These theories are classified a schools. The major schools are:

1. Classical School. This school proposes punishment should fit the crime.
2. Positivist School. This school was the first to use scientific methodology. It theorized physiology caused criminal behavior.
3. The Radical and Critical Criminology Schools. These schools advocate that societal conditions caused criminal behavior. They are closely related to the Marxist ideas.
4. Psychological School. This school believes mental processes cause criminal behavior.
5. Sociology Schools. These schools present many theories for the causation of crime based upon various social forces.

Criminologists study various criminal groups. The most common subjects are organized crime organizations. Criminologists want to learn how they operate and survive after being combated by external and internal forces. Fraud examiners and investigators need to be familiar with criminology. Criminology can help examiners and investigators understand criminals' motives for their criminal activities.

Physical Security

27

Introduction

Physical security is that aspect of security concerned with physical measures designed to safeguard personnel, to prevent unauthorized access to equipment, facilities, material, and documents, and to safeguard them against loss, damage, and theft. Loss prevention is particularly concerned with preventing loss of supplies, tools, equipment, and other materials in use, storage, and transit. Concern is not only focused on the threat of criminal activity and acts of wrongdoing by forces external to the organizational unit; it is also specifically directed toward internal causes—theft and pilferage by those who have authorized access, inattention to physical security practices and procedures, and disregard for property controls and accountability. Physical security and loss prevention measures include instructions, procedures, plans, policies, agreements, systems, and resources committed and designed to safeguard personnel, protect property, and prevent losses. Physical security helps remove the opportunity from people who want to commit fraud. An ounce of prevention is worth a pound of cure, as the cliché goes.

Responsibilities

Security is the direct, immediate, legal, and moral responsibility of all people in a business organization. However, there are officers or other personnel who have a direct responsibility for physical security and loss prevention. These personnel have different titles, i.e., Security Officer or Loss Prevention Officer. Whatever their title may be, it is their duty to

1. Manage the organization security and loss prevention program;
2. Determine the adequacy of the organization's loss prevention program and identify areas where improvements are required;
3. Develop, prepare, and maintain loss prevention and security plans;
4. Establish personnel identification and access control system(s);
5. Provide technical assistance on security matters;
6. Participate in planning, directing, coordinating, and implementing procedures for crisis management situations, which pose a threat to the organization;

7. Establish and maintain liaison and working relationships with local law enforcement and fire protection authorities;
8. Maintain good relations with other managers in the organization with specialized skills or technology in security and loss prevention.

Plans

Loss prevention and security plans should cover the following points:

1. Identify real property and structures to be protected;
2. Identify security areas;
3. Identify by location and priority the assets to be protected;
4. Assess the threat to such areas;
5. Determine legal jurisdiction;
6. Determine and identify the necessary resources: funds, staff, and equipment;
7. Establish barriers and points of ingress and egress;
8. Prescribe the personnel identification and access control system(s);
9. Identify and procure equipment that will detect and/or prevent wrongful removal, damage, destruction, or compromise of protected property;
10. Determine the number of personnel needed and prescribe their duties;
11. Establish and maintain records relating to violations and breaches of security;
12. Identify procedures for timely internal reporting of losses;
13. Identify procedures for ensuring that all losses, inventory adjustments, and surveys of property are reported to management;
14. Advise of legal and administrative procedures and remedies applicable to those found responsible and liable for losses.

Evaluation

In evaluating the need for and the type of protection required for an organization, the following factors should be considered:

1. Overall importance to the organization;
2. Importance to the business operations;
3. Ease of access to vital equipment and materials;
4. Tailoring of security measures to the organization operations and other local considerations;
5. Geographic location;
6. Legal jurisdiction of real property;
7. Aid and assistance agreements with local authorities;
8. Local political climate;
9. Adequacy of storage facilities for valuable or sensitive material;
10. Accessibility of the activity to disruptive, criminal, subversive, or terrorist elements;
11. Possible losses on the organization and their impact on operations;
12. Possibility or probability of expansion, curtailment, or other changes in operations;

13. Overall cost of security;
14. Availability of personnel and material;
15. Coordination of security personnel;
16. Calculated risk. This dictates that when there are limited resources available for protection, possible loss or damage to some supplies or to a portion of the operations is risked in order to ensure a greater degree of security to the remaining assets, supplies, and operations.

Cost of Security

Security expenditures should generally be based on the cost of the item(s) to be protected and the damage their loss could cause to the organization and to others. The cost of security is frequently greater than the dollar value of the property and material.

Crisis Situations

In evaluating the need for security protection, the possibility of injury to security personnel must be considered. This is especially relevant when addressing measures taken during crisis situations, i.e., bomb threats, fires, robberies, or natural disasters, to limit damage and provide emergency services for containment of the incident to restore the activity to normal operation. Security plans should include preventive measures to reduce the opportunities for introduction of bombs; procedures for evaluating and handling threatening messages; procedures for obtaining assistance and support by local law enforcement; procedures in the event a bomb or suspected bomb is found on premises; and procedures to be followed in the event of an explosion.

Security Considerations

Security measures to be considered when developing security plans are as follows:

1. Personnel screening and indoctrination;
2. Protection for vulnerable points/assets within the organization;
3. Security force organization and training;
4. Personnel identification and control systems;
5. Installation of security hardware, i.e., intrusion detection systems, barriers, access control systems;
6. Key and lock control;
7. Coordination with other security agencies.

Sabotage

Sabotage acts can cause destruction equal to acts of war but without fear of retaliation against the hostile war-making capability if successfully carried out. The tools and methods of the saboteur are limited only by skill and ingenuity. Readily available materials can be used to construct simple but deadly devices. The effectiveness of the saboteur is limited only by inability to gain access to targeted installations. The basic sabotage techniques are as follows:

1. Mechanical. This includes introduction of foreign objects into machinery, severing of wires or cables, removal of components, and the mishandling/abuse of equipment.
2. Arson. This includes firebombing, electrical shorting, and the use of incendiary agents.
3. Explosive. This includes use of commercial and homemade compounds, contact trip wire detonators, and timed devices.
4. Psychological. This includes such things as instigation of labor strikes, personnel disputes, distrust of supervisors, hostilities between coworkers. Organized crime organizations, particularly the LCN and the Yakuzas, use these tactics to take over businesses.

Motives

Saboteurs can be classified into two categories:

1. Internal. Internal saboteurs are employees who are often motivated by feelings of revenge, emotional disorder, disgruntlement, or use of drugs or alcohol. Offenders perform these acts to "get even" with superiors, to halt business operations, to achieve momentary fame as the "alert discoverer" of a fire or other threat.
2. External. Saboteurs outside the business organization commit sabotage because they do not like the organization's policies or political affiliations. They consider the organization "exploitative" of people in the community.

Terrorism

Terrorism is the use of tactics, principally by small groups, designed to create panic and chaos through the use of deadly force, publicity, uncertainty, and coercive acts of violence directed against specific or general targets in the general population. Generally, the goal of terrorist acts is to disrupt or destroy the bond of trust and credibility between government and the population. Acts of terrorism directed at businesses have the potential to destroy facilities, injure or kill employees, impair or delay business operations, and cause incalculable damage through adverse publicity and public perceptions of the incident.

Terrorist Methods

Terrorists use the following methods:

1. Bombs. Bomb(s) used may be of any degree of sophistication and may be placed to destroy equipment, cause fires, create casualties, etc. Depending on the bomb size and placement, the impact may range from a minor to a major crisis.
2. Ambush. Rapid ambush attacks may be employed by individuals or small groups to assassinate individuals, eliminate a group of people, or destroy or steal assets in remote locations or in transit.

3. Armed Attack. An armed assault usually involves one or more diversionary actions carried out by small groups against key personnel or critical assets with the objective of causing disruption of operations and creating adverse publicity. Hostage taking is not a usual tactic in this type of terrorist action unless the attackers are prevented from escaping.

4. Hostage Situations. A terrorist group may undertake the seizure of a specific hostage for ransom or political bargaining purposes. An armed attack scenario may be used to seize a critical asset (factory, research facility, etc.) when personnel are present in order to use both the asset and the personnel as leverage to bargain for publicity and political advantage. Care must be taken to provide for this possibility in companies that develop or produce high-technological products.

5. Sabotage. Terrorist groups may engage in the use of various sabotage methods already previously discussed.

Surveys

The security manager should conduct a security survey at least once a year. These surveys should be designed to show management what security measures are in effect, what areas need improvement, and to provide a basis for determining priorities for funding and work accomplishment.

Threat Assessments

Based upon available information, which can be obtained legally, the business organization should determine the short-, medium-, and long-term threat. Such information must be analyzed to determine what additional security measures are necessary where security requirements are inadequate. A close liaison with local law enforcement agencies is imperative.

Loss Prevention

A vigorous loss prevention program is essential. Losses of property may disrupt operations and cost millions of dollars. Losses must be minimized by application of a comprehensive loss prevention program consisting of loss analysis, proper use of available investigative resources, continuing employee loss prevention education, the application of firm corrective measures, administrative personnel action, and other loss prevention measures when necessary. As a minimum, loss prevention measures should consist of the following:

1. **Loss analysis.** To help identify trends and patterns of losses and gains, all incidents involving reportable property which is missing, lost, stolen, or recovered, reporting and investigation must be included in an ongoing program of analysis. A continuing loss analysis process should consider the types of material lost; geographic location; times and dates; proximity of personnel; proximity of doorways, passageways, loading docks/ramps, gates, parking facilities; and other activities adjacent to loss locations. Resulting analyses of loss trends and patterns will be used to balance the allocation of resources available for crime prevention.

2. **Investigative resources.** To prevent or reduce losses of property, it is essential to assign investigative personnel to loss prevention functions. A preliminary investigative capability should exist during all working production shifts (especially night shifts). Local loss analysis program data should be used to program security resources to combat losses.

3. **Loss prevention equipment.** Exterior doors in warehouses, storage buildings, office buildings, and other structures which contain high-value, sensitive, or pilferable property, supplies, or office equipment will be afforded with security protection commensurate with the value and sensitivity of the structure's contents. At a minimum, hinges will either be nonremovable or be provided with inside hinge protection, which prevents locked doors opening even if hinges are removed, and lock/hasp security systems.

4. **Employee education.** Each employee must be indoctrinated in local procedures for preventing property losses as well as responsibility for the care and protection of property under the employee's control. This indoctrination should be included in the employee's initial security education briefing upon employment and annually thereafter.

5. **Discipline.** Administrative actions should be taken against employees or others who are responsible for losses. Depending upon the circumstances, civil and/or criminal actions should be taken. Civil actions should be taken to recover losses from the responsible person. If an organization just terminates an employee for theft or embezzlement, it is sending a message to other employees that they can get away with the crime. In addition, the bad employee will go elsewhere and will probably commit the offense again.

6. **Financial responsibility.** Procedures for the issue and control of company property will ensure that strict accountability is established for persons responsible for the property that is reported missing, lost, or stolen. Recoupment action must be undertaken against an individual in which negligence or intention results in a missing, lost, or stolen property. This recoupment action is independent of, may be taken parallel with, or be exclusive of any formal criminal procedures arising from the same event.

7. **Claims.** A business organization should have adequate insurance coverage to compensate for any losses due to theft, fire, or other natural disasters. Claims should be filed as soon as possible since the insurance company will probably want to investigate the circumstances of the loss and bring civil actions against the person responsible.

8. **Criminal actions.** Examination of the facts may indicate criminality sufficient to warrant a referral to appropriate legal authorities. This action strengthens the deterrent aspects of loss prevention polices and procedures. The security manager should ensure that security portion of criminal cases are properly prepared and in sufficient detail to render them acceptable for prosecution in federal, state, or local courts. The security manager should monitor the progress of criminal issues and maintain liaison with the legal authorities.

Loss Reporting

Effective reporting of losses is basic to the determination of the scope of the loss prevention program that must be developed by the company. When reviewing property losses that are not critical to business operations and do not harm anyone is important to know whether or not the expenditure of funds on physical security will pay back in loss reductions. If real losses are extremely low, and involve only low-value and non-sensitive materials, it may be more cost effective to absorb such losses. Nevertheless, actual losses must be reported so that an accurate decision can be made by management. Steps must be taken to ensure that reportable loss and accountable individuals are identified. This can be done by matching property inventories, inventory adjustments, etc., with loss reports submitted. Historically, many audits and inspection reports have shown that not all required reports are submitted and actual losses have greatly exceeded reported losses. In each case of loss, theft, or destruction of property, efforts should be made to determine if the event involved negligence or criminality. The individuals responsible should be determined whenever possible. If an investigation is initiated, the ongoing status of the investigation will be provided during pending or supplementary reports. Incidents involving the same type or class of material are often indicative of a lack of adequate loss prevention and inventory control procedures. Causative factors should be identified and prompt corrective action initiated. Care must be taken to explain the detailed circumstances of a loss. The narrative comments should identify security problems and deficiencies related to the incident. Every report should provide details of any real or perceived security deficiency and any action taken or planned to correct such deficiency.

Area Protection

It is important to perform an analysis to determine the degree of security required. Criticality and vulnerability of security interest must be evaluated in relationship to ranking potential losses and giving the level of security to ensure the best possible protection for the loss level at efficient costs. Protective area controls are the first steps in providing actual protection against security hazards. These controls are obtained through the use of protective barriers and other security measures. All areas within a business operation must be assigned security area designations. Different areas and tasks involve different degrees of security depending upon their purpose, nature of the work performed, and the information and/or materials concerned. Areas should be designated as either restricted or nonrestricted. Restricted areas should be areas where public access is denied to both unauthorized employees and customers. Such areas can be as follows:

1. Offices where financial data are complied or sensitive information is processed;
2. Communication facilities, i.e., telephone wires, cables, and switching boxes;
3. Warehouses where inventory is kept;
4. Power stations, transformers, master valve and switch spaces;
5. Open storage areas and yards;
6. Intrusion detection systems–monitoring spaces;
7. Central storage spaces for keys and locks;
8. Cash storage spaces;
9. Negotiable instrument storage spaces.

Security Measures

Restricted areas should include measures that exclude or require the following:

1. A clearly defined area or perimeter. The perimeter may be a fence, exterior walls, building, or a space within a building.
2. A personnel identification and control system. This may include access list, entry/departure logs and identification badges. For small companies, the issuance of keys to only authorized personnel may be adequate. Larger companies may require more-sophisticated systems.
3. Ingress and egress controlled by guards or personnel within the restricted area.
4. Admission allowed only to people whose duties require access and who have been granted authorization.

Signs should be posted that tell people the area is restricted or say "authorized personnel only."

Key and Lock Controls

Businesses should establish a strict key and lock control program, which is managed and supervised by the security manager. It should include controls over all keys, locks, padlocks, and locking devices used to protect or secure restricted areas, perimeters, facilities, critical assets, and sensitive materials and supplies. The program should not include keys, locks, and padlocks for convenience, privacy, or personnel use. Examples are employee lockers, employee restrooms, and employee desks. Store managers, department heads, branch managers, etc., should be responsible for all keys controlled in their respective spaces and areas. Security locks, padlocks, and/or lock cores should be rotated from one location to another or changed at least once a year to guard against the use of illegally duplicated keys and to afford the opportunity for regular maintenance or security violations due to malfunction because of dirt, corrosion, and wear. Keys for security locks and padlocks should be issued only to those with a need approved by management and/or the security manager. Convenience or status is not a sufficient criterion for issue of a security key. A central key room should be established. Also each key custodian and subcustodian must institute a system showing keys on hand, keys issued, to whom, date/time the keys were issued and returned, and the signatures of persons drawing or returning security keys. Continuous accountability of keys is required at all times. When the door, gate, or other equipment, which the padlock is intended to secure, is open or operable, the padlock should be locked into the staple, fence fabric, or other nearby securing point to preclude the switching of the padlock to facilitate surreptitious entry by a thief or others. Inactive or infrequently used gates and doors should be locked and have seals affixed.

Parking

As a general rule, to prevent property losses, employees should not be permitted to park immediately adjacent to work spaces. Privately owned vehicles, except those driven by handicapped employees, should not be parked within 100 feet of doorways leading into or from buildings primarily used for the manufacturing, repair, rework, storage, handling, packaging, or shipping of inventory, materials, and supplies. Businesses that have many employees, more than a guard can recognize, usually 50 or more, should have employee-parking permits issued to personnel to restrict parking. A system should be in place to collect parking permits when employees leave employment.

Protective Lighting

Protective lighting provides a means of continuing, during hours of darkness, a degree of security approaching that which is maintained during daylight hours. It has considerable value as a deterrent to thieves and vandals and makes the job for them more difficult. Requirements for protective lighting will depend upon the situation. The mix between energy conservation and effective security must be carefully studied in each situation. The overall goal is to provide proper environment to perform duties, prevent illegal entry, detect intruders, and inspect unusual or suspicious activities. The following basic principles apply to help ensure protective lighting effectiveness:

1. Provide adequate illumination to discourage or detect illegal attempts to enter restricted areas and to reveal the presence of unauthorized persons within such areas;
2. Avoid glare, which handicaps security personnel or is objectionable to traffic or occupants of adjacent properties;
3. Locate light sources so that illumination is directed toward likely intruder avenues of approach;
4. Illuminate areas shadowed by structures within or adjacent to restricted areas;
5. Design the system to provide overlapping light distribution; design equipment to resist the effects of environmental conditions; locate all components of the system to provide maximum protection against intentional damage;
6. Avoid drawing unwanted attention to restricted areas.

Intrusion Detection Systems

An intrusion detection system (IDS) should be an essential element of any in-depth security program. IDS consists of sensors capable of detecting one or more types of phenomena, signal media, annunciators, and energy sources for signaling the entry or attempted entry into the area protected by the system. IDS is designed to detect, not prevent, actual or attempted penetrations. Therefore, IDS is useless unless it is supported by a prompt security force response when the system is activated.

IDS Purpose

IDS is used to accomplish one or more of the following:

1. Permit more economical and efficient use of security personnel through the employment of mobile responding guard forces or local law enforcement;
2. Provide additional controls at critical areas;
3. Substitute for other physical security measures, which cannot be used because of safety regulations, operational requirements, building layout, cost, or similar reasons;
4. Provide insurance against human failure or error;
5. Enhance security force capability to detect and defeat intruders;
6. Provide the earliest practical warning to security forces of any attempted penetration of protected areas.

IDS Determination Factors

The following factors must be considered in determining the feasibility and necessity of installing IDS equipment.

1. The type of business operation or facility;
2. Criticality of the operation or facility;
3. Threat to the operation or facility;
4. Location of the operation or facility and the location of the areas within each facility;
5. Accessibility to intruders;
6. Availability of other forms of protection;
7. Initial and recurring cost of the system;
8. Personnel and money savings over expected life of the system;
9. Construction of the building or facility;
10. Hours of operation of the facility;
11. Availability of a security force and expected response time to an alarm condition.

Types of Systems

There are basically four types of IDS systems

1. **Local alarm.** The protective circuits and alarm devices actuate a visual and/or audible signal in the immediate vicinity of the protected area, usually on the exterior and/or interior of the building. The alarm transmission/communication lines do not leave the building. Response is by local security forces that may be in the area when the alarm is sounded. Otherwise, the security force will only know of the alarm if reported by a passerby or during routine checks. The disadvantage of this type of system is that intruders know exactly when the alarm is activated and, in most cases, can easily elude capture. This type of system should be used only when guards or workers are always in close proximity to the audible or visual alarm and are able to respond to it.

2. **Central station.** The operation of alarm devices and electrical circuits are automatically signaled to, recorded in, maintained and supervised from a central station, owned or managed either in house or by a commercial firm which has trained guards and operators in attendance at all times. These personnel monitor the signals of the system and provide the response force to any unauthorized entry into the protected area. Connection of alarm equipment to the central station is usually over telephone lines.

3. **Police connection.** The alarm devices and electrical circuits are connected via telephone lines to a monitoring unit located in nearby police stations. An agreement with the local police department must be arranged prior to establishment of this type of system.

4. **Proprietary IDS station.** This system is similar to a central station operation, except that the IDS monitoring/recording equipment for all IDS systems at the installation is located within a constantly manned security force communications center maintained and/or owned by a commercial company. The security force operates and responds to all IDS activations. Connection of the alarm equipment to the monitoring room can be over telephone lines or by separate cable installed by the equipment company. This system is the preferred IDS monitoring system for medium to large organizations.

Sensor Systems

Sensor systems are divided into two areas based upon environmental use:

1. **Exterior sensors.** Exterior intrusion detection devices should be selected for the best performance under such prevailing local environmental conditions as soil, topography, weather, and any other factors that could adversely affect device performance or increase its false alarm rate. The detecting devices are designed for outside installation and are usually used in conjunction with barriers such as fences. Commonly used sensors include those that detect light beam interruption, motion, pressure, vibration, magnetic field distortions, and seismic disturbances or combinations of these.

2. **Interior sensors.** Interior intrusion detection devices should be selected and installed to provide the best reliable information to security personnel in the shortest possible time. The devices are primarily designed to operate within an environmentally protected area to overcome security weaknesses in buildings, rooms, etc. Commonly used devices include those that detect motion, light beam interruption, sound, pressure, vibration, capacitance change, heat, magnetic field change, penetration and the breaking of an electrical circuit.

Data/Signal Transmission System

This system integrates the sensors and the control/monitoring capabilities into a complete functioning IDS. The transmission medium is used to send control signals and data between all sensors, control points, and annunciator display panels. It may be wire land-lines, radio frequency, link or a combination of both. This vital system is probably the weakest and most vulnerable of the entire IDS system and requires protection.

Control and Display System

This system provides equipment for central operational control and monitoring of the IDS. Through this equipment, the security personnel are instantly alerted to the status of any protected area. This system should be located in a separate area closed off from public view. Zone numbers shall be used to designate alarmed spaces or items, i.e., buildings, room numbers, and inventory items.

Power System

Normal power to operate an IDS system is usually derived from local electrical power, e.g., the electric company. The importance of an IDS continuous function cannot be overstated. Therefore, each IDS system should have an emergency backup source of power in the event of a power failure, to ensure the continuous operation of the system. The backup power source usually consists of batteries, which should be of a rechargeable type. Power supplies should be arranged so that batteries are maintained fully charged at all times when power is available. The system should automatically transfer from AC to battery power whenever the former fails, and return to AC power upon restoration of that power.

Maintenance

Proper maintenance of an IDS system is imperative. Systems that are not properly maintained may either fail to detect intrusion or yield a high number of bogus alarms, commonly referred to as false/nuisance alarms. Systems that generate frequent false or nuisance alarms lose their credibility and demoralize security personnel to the point where alarm activations are ignored. The contracting company should develop procedures to ensure only appropriately cleared personnel install, inspect, or maintain the IDS system.

Security Audits

Each business organization should have a program to assess the degree of security within the organization. Security assessments should be done at least once a year to ensure compliance by management and employees. The assessment should cover compliance with security measures, loss prevention programs, and crisis management. Fire drills should be conducted periodically. Disaster plans should be reviewed. Management and employees should be trained or at least informed each year. Loss prevention and disaster plans should be evaluated each year.

Security Checklist

The purpose of the checklist show in Figure 27-1 is to provide a business organization guidelines for evaluating existing security measures. It is not intended to be all-inclusive. It is more appropriate for larger organizations, but many questions are relevant to smaller businesses.

1. Is there a security manager?
2. Does the organization have a security plan?
3. Does the security plan contain instructions for
   a. Fire?
   b. Natural disasters?
   c. Disturbances?
   d. Sabotage?
   e. Bomb threats?
   f. Theft?
   g. Robberies?
4. Does the security plan include procedures for
   a. Evaluating and handling threatening messages?
   b. Evacuation of personnel and customers?
   c. Suspected bomb found on premises?
   d. Reporting robberies?
   e. Reporting internal theft?
5. Does the organization have a counterespionage program?
6. Are security plans reviewed annually?
7. Has security manager established liaison with local law and fire authorities?
8. Are the basic security measures for exclusion areas in effect?
9. Are security measures in effect to protect:
   a. Electric power supplies and transmission?
   b. Communication centers/equipment?
   c. Computer and financial data and files?
10. Is there a key and lock custodian?

Figure 27-1 Business checklist.

11. Does the key and lock control program include
    a. A key control register?
    b. An inventory of keys?
12. Is the present security force strength and composition commensurate with the degree of security protection required?
13. Does the security manager inspect and brief personnel on a daily basis?
14. Does the organization have a crisis plan in effect?
15. Are security personnel available and trained in procedures to help police and fire authorities?
16. Is a pass or badge identification system used to identify all personnel in the confines of restricted areas?
17. Does the identification system provide the desired degree of security?
18. Does the identification system provide procedures for
    a. Protection for the badges and passes?
    b. Designation for areas requiring special control measures?
    c. Control of the pass or badges issued?
    d. Mechanics of identification upon entering and leaving each restricted area, as applied to both employees and visitors?
    e. Details of where, when, and how badges shall be worn?
    f. Procedures to be followed in case of loss or damage to identification media?
    g. Procedures for recovery and invalidation?
19. If a badge system is used for any security area, does the system provide for
    a. Comparison of badge, pass, and personnel?
    b. Physical exchange of pass/badge at time of entrance/exist?
    c. Accounting for each badge or pass?
    d. Location and verification of personnel remaining within the security area at the end of normal working hours?
    e. Security of badges and passes not in use?
20. Do guards at control points compare badges to bearers, both upon entry and exit?
21. Is supervision of the personnel identification and control system adequate at all levels?
22. Are badges and serial numbers recorded and controlled by rigid accountability procedures?
23. Are lost badges replaced with badges bearing different serial numbers?
24. Have procedures been established that provide for issuance of temporary badges for individuals who have forgotten their permanent badges?
25. Are temporary badges used?
26. Are lists of lost badges posted at guard control points?
27. Are badges of such design and appearance as to enable guards and other personnel to recognize quickly and positively the authorizations and limitations applicable to the bearers?

continued

Figure 27-1 (continued) Business checklist.

28. Are procedures in existence to ensure the return of identification badges upon termination of employment or assignment?
29. Are special badges issued to contractor employees working within security areas?
30. Are all phases of the personnel identification and control system under supervision and control of the security manager?
31. Have effective visitor escort procedures been established?
32. What controls are employed to control visitor movements while in restricted areas?
33. Are visitors required to display identification media conspicuously on outer garments at all times while within restricted areas?
34. When visitors depart restricted areas, are they required to turn in identification badges and is the departure time in each case recorded in the visitor register?
35. Are visitors who indicate an intention to return at a later time permitted to retain identification badges?
36. Are permanent records of visits maintained? By whom?
37. What measures are employed, other than the issuance of identification badges, to control the movement of contractor personnel working within restricted areas?
38. Have written procedures been issued and authorized for the registration of privately-owned vehicles aboard business premises?
39. What type of pass is used and where is it affixed/located within/on the vehicle?
40. Are temporary passes issued to visitor vehicles?
41. Are automobiles allowed to be parked within restricted areas?
42. Are parking areas within restricted areas located away from restricted areas?
43. Does a fence or other type of physical barrier define the parking perimeter and all restricted areas?
44. Are openings such as culverts, tunnels, manholes for sewers and utility access, and sidewalk elevators, which permit access to the restricted area, properly secured?
45. Are gates and/or other entrances, which are not actively used, locked and equipped with seals and frequently inspected by other personnel?
46. Are locks rotated annually?
47. Are all normally used pedestrian and vehicular gates and other entrances effectively and adequately lighted to assure
    a. Proper identification of individuals and examination of credentials?
    b. Interior of vehicles can be observed?
    c. That glare from luminaries does not interfere with the guard's vision?

Figure 27-1 (continued) Business checklist.

48. Are appropriate signs setting forth the provisions of entry conspicuously posted at all entrances?

49. Are "No Trespassing" signs posted on or adjacent to barriers at such intervals that at least one sign is visible at any approach to a barrier during daylight hours?

50. Are lumber, boxes, or other extraneous material not allowed to be stacked against or adjacent to the barriers or doors?

51. Do guards patrol perimeter areas?

52. Are any perimeters protected by intrusion detection systems?

53. Does any relocated function, newly designated security area, physical expansion, or other factor indicate necessity for installation of additional barriers or additional lighting?

54. Is the perimeter of the installation and security area provided adequate lighting?

55. Does a protective lighting meet adequate intensity requirement?

56. Are the cones of illumination from lamps directed downward and away from guard personnel?

57. Is perimeter lighting utilized so that guards remain in comparative darkness?

58. Are lights checked for proper operation prior to darkness?

59. Are repairs to lights and replacement of inoperative lamps effected immediately?

60. Is additional lighting provided for active doorways and points of possible intrusion?

61. Does the operation have a dependable source of power for its lighting system?

62. Does the operation have a dependable auxiliary source of power?

63. Is the power supply for the protective lighting system protected? How?

64. Is there a provision for standby or emergency protective lighting?

65. Is the standby or emergency equipment tested frequently?

66. Can the emergency equipment be rapidly switched into operation when needed?

67. Is wiring tested and inspected periodically to ensure proper operation?

68. Is parallel circuitry used in the wiring?

69. Are multiple circuits used?

70. Is closed loop used in multiple circuits?

71. Is wiring for protective lighting properly run?
    a. Is it in tamper-resistant conduit?
    b. Is it installed underground?
    c. If aboveground, is it high enough to preclude the possibility of tampering?

continued

Figure 27-1 (continued) Business checklist.

72. Are switches and controls properly located, controlled, and protected?
73. Is the protective lighting system designed and locations available so that repair can be made rapidly in an emergency?
74. Are materials and equipment in shipping and storage areas properly arranged to provide adequate lighting?
75. Does the organization employ any intrusion detection systems?
76. Does the IDS, where required or used, meet the following minimum requirements?
    a. Are balanced magnetic switches installed on all perimeter doors?
    b. Are sensors attached to window and doors?
    c. Are sensors attached to structural sections, which do not provide penetration resistance roughly equivalent to that required for the basic structure?
    d. Are IDS signals monitored at one central point, and is the guard force response initiated from that point?
    e. Are all sensor equipment, doors, drawers, and removable panels secured with key locks or screws and equipped with tamper switches?
    f. Have power supplies been protected against overload by fuses or circuit breakers?
    g. Have power supplies been protected against voltage transients?
    h. Have safety hazards been identified and controlled to preclude personnel exposure?
    i. Do IDS components meet electromagnetic interference/electromagnetic compatibility requirements?
    j. Do IDS components meet the spurious radiation requirements set by the Federal Communications Commission?
77. Do properly trained security alert teams back up the system?
78. Is the alarm system for active areas or structures placed in access mode during normal working hours?
79. Is the system tested prior to activation?
80. Is the system inspected regularly?
81. Is the system weatherproof?
82. Is an alternate or independent source of power available for use on the system in the event of power failure?
83. Is the emergency power source designed to cut in and operate automatically when normal power goes down?
84. Do trained and properly cleared personnel properly maintain the IDS system?
85. Are frequent tests conducted to determine the adequacy and promptness of response to alarm signals?
86. Are records kept of all alarm signals received to include time, date, location, action taken, and cause for alarm?
87. How frequent are nuisance alarms and what action is taken to reduce the number?

Figure 27-1 (continued) Business checklist.

88. Does the organization have a current security education program?
89. Are all newly assigned personnel provided security indoctrination?
90. Is security education training conducted for all personnel at least annually?
91. Have security personnel been trained in procedures necessary for the implementation of emergency and disaster plans for their organization?
92. Are security personnel qualified in assigned weapons if required?
93. Have armed security personnel received instruction in the use of deadly force?
94. Does the security force have its own communication system with direct lines between security and restricted areas?
95. Does the security communication system provide the security personnel with the means of rapidly apprising their superiors of problem situations?
96. Does the organization use a security dog program?
97. Have direct communications with local municipal fire and police headquarters been established?

Figure 27-1 (continued) Business checklist.

Self-Protection

Many assaults take place at either the workplace or home. Assaults in parking lots of shopping centers, office buildings, plants, etc., are becoming more prevalent. Some tips for self-protection are listed below:

1. Walk with someone. Arrange to meet other employees when entering and/or leaving the business premises. If security guards are available, you should have them escort you. This should be done when it is dark or at odd hours.
2. Stay in well-lighted areas, e.g., near curbs, lighted entrances, light poles, etc. Avoid alleys, unlighted entrances, deserted stairwells, dark rooms, etc. Avoid walking near blind spots such as columns or between cars.
3. Stay near other people or crowds. Avoid shortcuts through parks, vacant lots, or deserted places.
4. Hold a purse close under your arm with latch in, not dangling. Long straps should be around the shoulder or neck. Never set a purse or wallet on store counters, in supermarket baskets, or on car or bus seats.
5. When shopping, do not put money or credit and debit cards on counter. Put it in the hand of the store clerk. Do not flash large amounts of money.
6. Pay attention to your surroundings. Keep alert. Pay attention to anything that is unusual, e.g., people and vehicles.
7. If a driver stops to ask you questions, avoid getting near the car. Never reach in or get in a stranger's vehicle.
8. If you feel that you are being followed, then be prepared to take some action, e.g., run. If someone is following you on foot, cross the street, change direction, or vary your pace. Proceed to a lighted store or home and call the police or relative

or friend to pick you up. The police will usually escort you home. If someone is following you in a car, turn around and walk in the other direction. Record the license number and call the police.

9. When you go to your vehicle, have your key ready and check the front and back seats before entering.

10. If a you have a dog, particularly of medium or large size, and you go to a park or other recreational area, or the neighborhood store, you should take the dog with you. The presence of a medium or large dog deters criminals even if the dog has a gentle personality.

11. If attacked, scream as loud as you can. It may scare the attacker away. Otherwise, kick in the groin or on the foot and foreleg. Doing this will give you a chance to escape.

Summary

Physical security measures help remove the opportunity for employees and customers to remove inventory, assets, and supplies from a business organization premises. Therefore, it cannot be overlooked. For small business, the costs of security measures can be onerous since businesses have to balance their needs and benefits to the costs. Various electronic and other devices are making rapid advances in technology. These new and improved systems are becoming cheaper. Many businesses, regardless of size, are using various new systems. One system attaches labels that will set off an alarm if the item is not scanned at the checkout counter. In another system, clothing stores attach dye devices which will explode the dye over the clothing if the customer removes the merchandise from the store without it being scanned at the checkout counter. Each business organization will have to evaluate the various security measures to meet its particular requirements.

Search Warrants

28

Introduction

Law enforcement officers may be required to execute search warrants in order to obtain evidence. Subjects of an investigation will usually keep some inculpatory evidence in their possession, either at their residence or business premises. A search warrant authorizes limited intrusion into an area where there is reasonable expectation of privacy to search and seize certain specified evidence of a crime based on probable cause. A judge or magistrate is usually willing to issue a search warrant when information is provided by a reliable source. Fraud examiners can be used as a reliable source when they uncover evidence that other financial records are available at some identified location. Generally, evidence obtained by a defective search warrant is no longer suppressed if the law enforcement officers relied upon those defective warrants and have acted in good faith. However, search warrants may cause many motions to be filed, which can tie up a case. Also, they can trigger Fourth Amendment considerations such as staleness, overbreadth, and other issues.

Fourth Amendment

The Fourth Amendment to the U.S. Constitution, adopted in 1791, states, "The right of the people to be secure in their persons, houses, papers, and effects, against unreasonable searches and seizures, shall not be violated, and no Warrants shall issue, but upon probable cause, supported by Oath or affirmation, and particularly describing the place to be searched, and the persons or things to be seized."

Criminal Procedure

Rule 41 of the Federal Rules of Criminal Procedure contains the procedures for obtaining a warrant:

> Rule 41(a) provides for the issuance of a warrant by a federal magistrate or a judge of a state court of record within the district where the property or person sought is located, upon request by a federal law enforcement officer or an attorney for the government.

Rule 41(b) provides for issuance of a warrant to seize (1) property that constitutes evidence of the commission of a crime; or (2) contraband, the fruits of a crime, or things otherwise criminally possessed; or (3) property designed or intended to be used as an instrumentality of a crime; or (4) people, when there is probable cause for their arrest.

Rule 41(c) provides for issuance of a warrant based upon a sworn affidavit, which establishes the grounds for issuance of the warrant. If the federal magistrate is satisfied that the grounds for the application exist or that there is probable cause to believe that they exist and approves the warrant, then the officer has ten (10) days to execute the warrant. The search should be performed between 6:00 a.m. and 10:00 p.m., or the officer should be able to show cause why this cannot be done.

Rule 41(d) requires the officer taking the property to provide a copy of the warrant and a receipt for the property taken. The return shall be made promptly and accompanied by a written inventory of the property taken to the magistrate.

Rule 41(e) provides that an aggrieved person of an unlawful search and seizure may move the district court for the return of said property.

Rule 41(f) provides a motion to suppress evidence may be made in the court of the district of trial as provided by Rule 12.

Purpose

A search warrant authorizes a limited intrusion into an area protected by the Fourth Amendment. A neutral and detached magistrate may, upon a finding of probable cause, issue a search warrant. The search warrant must specify with particularity the area or premise to be searched and the persons or things to be seized. This requirement of particularity prevents any kinds of exploratory searches. The premises to be searched must be sufficiently described to enable the executing officers to ascertain and identify it with reasonable certainty. Also, the persons or things to be seized must be specifically identified without leaving any doubt. The test is whether the officer can identify the item to be seized.

Privacy Expectation

The Supreme Court has adopted a two-pronged test in determining privacy interests are protected. First, the individual must show a subjective expectation of privacy. Second, the privacy expectation must be generally recognized as reasonable. The courts have found reasonable expectation of privacy as to a person's home, a public employee's desk or file cabinets in the office, a person's luggage, and on his or her person. However, the courts have found no reasonable expectation of privacy in a warrantless installation of a pen register on a telephone or goods displayed in a store.

Probable Cause

The Fourth Amendment requires a finding of probable cause before the issuance of a valid search warrant. This protects an individual's expectation of privacy. Probable cause has been defined as facts and circumstances that will cause a prudent person to believe that an offense has been committed and that seizable property can be found at the place or on the person to be searched. Law enforcement has probable cause to conduct a search if a reasonably prudent officer, based on the facts and circumstances known by the officer, would be justified in concluding that the items sought are connected with criminal activities and that they will be found in the area to be searched.

While proof beyond a reasonable doubt is not required, some factual showing is required and not suppositions or speculations. The following have been found to be insufficient in establishing probable cause:

> Mere conclusory statement or an officer's mere notification of bare conclusions from other(s) (*Illinois v. Gates*, 462 U.S. 213);
> A officer's mere suspicion of criminal activity (*Brinegar v. United States*, 338 U.S. 175);
> Mere association with known or suspected criminals (*Ybarra v. Illinois*, 444 U.S. 85);
> An individual's mere presence at a given location (*United States v. Butts*, 704 F.2d 70).

The conclusions by an affiant may be included in a search warrant affidavit and considered in determining whether there is probable cause. Factual conclusions are a normal, necessary, and perfectly acceptable part of an affidavit. However, such conclusions must be drawn from facts contained within the affidavit and cannot be premised on the conclusory statements of others.

Magistrate

Facts justifying probable cause to search must be subjected to the scrutiny of a neutral and detached magistrate. As the Supreme Court stated in *Steagald v. United States*, 451 U.S. 204:

> The placement of this checkpoint between the government and the citizen implicitly acknowledges that an officer engaged in the often competitive enterprise of ferreting out crime may lack sufficient objectivity to weigh correctly the strength of the evidence against the individual's interests in protecting his own liberty.

An officer, in seeking a search warrant, must present sufficient facts in the affidavit to enable a magistrate to make an independent determination as to the existence of probable cause. Probable cause may be based upon hearsay information and need not reflect direct personal observations. The magistrate must be informed of the surrounding circumstances. The Supreme Court has strongly expressed preference for using search warrants because it imposes an orderly procedure and reduces the risks inherent in police actions.

Staleness

The amount of delay that will make information stale will depend upon the facts of the case. Staleness cannot be resolved by reference to the number of days between the facts relied upon and the time the warrant is issued. If the items still have a reasonable chance of being present, then the warrant can be issued even after a lengthy time. The staleness test is not designed to create an arbitrary time limitation. The test is whether or not the affidavit sufficiently establishes a fair probability that contraband or evidence of a crime would be found on the premises. The facts and circumstances of the case, including the nature of the unlawful activity, the length of time, and the nature of the property to be seized, must be considered.

Probable Cause Based on Informants

Probable cause may be based upon hearsay evidence whether in whole or in part [FRE Rule 41(c)(1)]. Prior to 1983, the court had a two-pronged test to determine an informant's reliability. First, the facts that the informant provided must show the informant is credible and reliable. Second, some of the information can be verified. In *Illinois v. Gates* (462 U.S. 213), the Supreme Court abandoned the two-pronged test and reinstated the totality-of-the-circumstance test for probable cause determinations. Elements of knowledge, reliability, and veracity were relevant considerations in the totality of circumstances. A deficiency in one element could be compensated for by a strong showing in another, or by some other indication of reliability. The Court reiterated the standard of review. A magistrate should review the evidence on the whole for substantial basis. It rejected any after-the-fact review by a magistrate for probable cause determination. One way to establish credibility and reliability is by having two informants independently corroborate each other's statements. By telling consistent, yet independent stories, the informants provided "cross-corroboration." This enhances the reliability on the application for a warrant.

Particularity

The Fourth Amendment requires that a search warrant "particularly" describe (1) the place to be searched and (2) the persons or things to be seized. The aim is to protect the privacy of citizens against general rummaging through their possessions. General exploratory searches are forbidden. The Supreme Court has interpreted this requirement to mean that the description of the place to be searched be such that the officer can easily ascertain and identify the place intended. Also, the Fourth Amendment requires particularity as to items to be seized. The purpose is to prevent general seizure of property. Only items listed in a warrant can be seized. In *Andresen v. Maryland* (427 U.S. 463) the Court expounded searches and seizures of personal or business records. It stated,

> There are grave dangers inherent in executing a warrant authorizing a search and seizure of a person's papers that are not necessarily present in executing a warrant to search for physical objects whose relevance is more easily ascertainable. In searches for papers, it is certain that some innocuous documents will be examined, at least cursorily, in order to determine whether they are, in fact, among those papers authorized to be seized. In this kind of search, responsible officials, including judicial officials must take care to assure that they are conducted in a manner that minimizes unwarranted intrusions upon privacy.

The Ninth Circuit has suggested that an affidavit should always be incorporated into the warrant. The affidavit can be used to provide further guidance to seizing agents and save an otherwise deficient search warrant. Generally, it is not a search warrant if it contains standards that guide officers in avoiding seizure of items not relevant to the case. The Ninth Circuit overturned a warrant because it was not specific enough. The warrant should have described particular items found in the possession of loan sharks and bookmakers, such as "pay and collection sheets, lists of loan customers, loan accounts and telephone numbers, line sheets, bet slips, tally sheets, and bottom sheets." A search warrant is valid if it fully describes the alleged criminal activities in connection with which the items were sought. In *United States v. Stubbs* (873 F.2d 210) the court decided the particularity issue by focusing on:

1. Whether probable cause existed to seize all items of a particular type described in the warrant;
2. Whether the warrant set out objective standards by which officers could differentiate items subject to seizure from those that are not; and
3. Whether the government was able to describe the items more particularly in light of the information available to it at the time the warrant was issued.

The Ninth Circuit suppressed evidence in the Stubbs case because the warrant that authorized the seizure of all financial records was too general. The warrant should have been more specific since there were two former employees cooperating in the investigation who knew where various documents were stored.

Places to be Searched

The Fourth Amendment requires that the warrant particularly describe the place to be searched. The Fourth Amendment does not require legal descriptions. It points to a definitely ascertainable place so as to exclude all others. The test for determining the sufficiency of a description is

Whether the place is described sufficiently enough to enable an officer to locate and identify the premises with reasonable effort;

Whether there is reasonable probability that another premise might be mistakenly searched.

There have been situations that law enforcement has searched the wrong place, even when the warrant was stated correctly. The search of an entire apartment building where probable cause was limited to only one apartment was not permitted. The courts have ruled that the name of an apartment complex or business enterprise will prevail over a street address. Also, the name of the occupant with a description of the premises will prevail over the stated apartment number or floor.

Items to be Seized

A search warrant must describe the items to be seized. The warrant must be worded in such a way to describe only those items directly related to the crime under investigation. It must be drafted so as to prevent indiscriminate seizing of both relevant and irrelevant evidence. The general rule is to describe with as much specificity as possible.

Generic Description

When the precise identity of items cannot be ascertained, then the use of generic class of items will suffice. Some courts have indicated that a general description of property will be acceptable provided the circumstances and nature of the activity under investigation are identified. The use of a generic term or general description is only acceptable when a more specific description of the items to be seized is not available. Failure to use specificity when information is available will invalidate a general description in a warrant. When there is probable cause to believe that the premises to be searched contain a class of generic items, a portion of which may be contraband, then a search warrant may direct inspection of the entire class. There must be articulated standards for the officers to follow in distinguishing between legal and illegal property. These standards may be contained in the search warrant or the accompanying affidavit. To determine that a search warrant containing a generic description satisfies specificity requirement, see if the warrant:

1. Establishes that there is a reason to believe that a large collection of similar items, i.e., evidence of a crime, is present on the premises to be searched; and
2. Explains the methods to be used by officers are to differentiate the evidence of a crime from items that are not.

Permeated-with-Fraud Concept

When a business operates in a way that every transaction is potential evidence of fraud, the "permeated-with-fraud" concept allows seizure of all business records. If the whole business is a fraud, a warrant may properly permit the seizure of everything the officer finds. To establish that a business was permeated with fraud, a pattern of criminal conduct must exist that shows the existence of a plan, scheme, or artifice. When investigating the business practices, the investigation should not focus just on a small segment of operations, but should be based upon a major portion of the business operations. The permeated-with-fraud concept does not allow for wholesale seizure of all books and records of a business. The search warrant or affidavit must accurately describe those books and records that relate to the pervasive scheme to defraud.

Plain-View Doctrine

Law enforcement officers sometimes find other articles, which they desire to seize because of their apparent connection to some criminal activity. The plain-view doctrine provides that a law enforcement officer may seize evidence when the law enforcement officer

- Is lawfully on the premises by virtue of
  Searches pursuant to warrants issued for other purposes,
  Searches pursuant to exceptions to the warrant requirement, or
  The performance of general police duties;

- Inadvertently comes upon the item;
- It is immediately apparent that the item is incriminating; and
- It is incriminating evidence.

The plain-view doctrine does not allow the seizure of material when the incriminating or evidentiary character of the material becomes known only after close inspection. Also, it does not allow law enforcement officers to examine items to expand from observation into a general exploratory search. Probable cause is required to invoke the plain-view doctrine as it applies to seizures.

Inadvertent Discovery

Inadvertence is a common element of most plain-view seizures. It is not a necessary element. However, if police failed to particularize evidence in advance with the expectation that the evidence exists, then the warrant lacks probable cause for seizure of such evidence. The second circuit concluded that where proof indicated that the police conducted a thorough investigation of a crime and the means to prove it and the search is conducted in a manner reasonable in duration and intensity, the property seized may be found to be inadvertently discovered in plain view.

Immediately Apparent Requirement

The incriminating nature of the evidence must be immediately apparent. The immediately apparent requirement ensures that the police will not use this method as a way to justify exploratory searches. Also, the police must be aware of some facts and circumstances that can justify suspicion that items are fruits, instruments, or evidence of crime. The first circuit said that the plain-view doctrine allowed evidence discovered in plain view to be lawfully seized even though the police were not originally authorized to search for it when:

- The officer's presence at the point of discovery is lawful;
- Discovery of seized items is inadvertent; and
- The evidentiary value of the item is immediately apparent to the searchers.

Affidavit Inaccuracies

A warrant may become invalidated if the supporting affidavit is inaccurate. The Supreme Court in *Frank v. Delaware* (438 U.S. 154) identified some circumstances which could mandate an evidentiary hearing. If a defendant challenges the truthfulness of statements contained in the affidavit, then the defendant is entitled to a "Frank" hearing. The defendant must show in a "Frank" hearing:

> The false statement was knowingly and intentionally made, or with a reckless regard for the truth; and the allegedly false statement is necessary to the magistrate's finding of probable cause.

The court must void the warrant if the defendant proves the allegations by a preponderance of the evidence and there is no support of probable cause.

Exclusionary Rule

The exclusionary rule prohibits introduction into evidence of any material seized during an illegal search. This rule also prohibits any derivative evidence that is the product of the primary evidence or is acquired as an indirect result of an illegal search. In *United States v. Leon* (468 U.S. 897) the Supreme Court modified the exclusionary rule for search warrants that were obtained in "good faith." The court did not want to penalize police who thought that they were acting properly in obtaining a warrant, even though the warrant failed for some technicality at a later date. The court provided the good faith factors:

- The warrants were facially valid;
- The warrants were properly approved by a neutral and detached judicial officer;
- The police relied on the magistrate's probable cause determination; and
- The officer's reliance was objectively reasonable.

The evidence will not be suppressed if the exclusionary rule is not applied. The exclusionary rule is a judicial remedy, which is designed to deter police misconduct. The appropriateness of excluding evidence must be evaluated by weighing the costs and benefits of suppression. Suppression is not appropriate if the police acted in good faith that the warrant was valid and authorized their conduct. The court defined *good faith* as the lack of disregard or conscious indifference to Rule 41.

Inevitable Discovery Exception

The Supreme Court in *Nix v. Williams* (467 U.S. 431) adopted the "inevitable discovery doctrine" as an exception to the exclusionary rule. Evidence discovered as a result of violations of Sixth Amendment rights can be admitted at trial if the prosecution can establish, by a preponderance of the evidence, that such evidence ultimately and inevitably would have been discovered by lawful means.

Independent Source Rule

The independent source rule is another exception to the exclusionary rule. It provides that evidence will not be suppressed if the government obtains the evidence from an independent and legal source.

Intermingling of Documents

Only specific and listed items in a search warrant may be seized. There are occasions where documents are so intermingled that they cannot be feasibly sorted on site. The wholesale seizure for later detailed examination of records not described in a warrant is prohibited. All items in a set of files may be inspected during a search, provided that sufficient guidelines for identifying the documents sought are provided in the search warrant and are followed by the officers conducting the search. Where documents are so intermingled that they cannot be sorted on site, the court has suggested that police should seal and hold the documents pending approval by a magistrate of a further search. If there is a need to transport the documents, then police should apply for specific authorization for large-scale removal of material to a site more suitable for searching.

Effect of Unauthorized Seizure on Valid Search

When a search is conducted and items are seized that are not specifically described in the warrant, the remedy by the court is to exclude the items that are improperly taken. The court fulfills three purposes in the following ways:

1. It erects a deterrent to illegal searches.
2. It prohibits the government from benefiting from its own wrongdoing by not using the illegally seized evidence to convict.
3. By removing the illegally seized items, it precludes itself from serving as an accomplice in the violation of the constitution.

It is permissible for federal agents to take along local law enforcement officers when executing search warrants. However, the local law enforcement officers must abide by the specifics and limitations of the search warrant.

Conforming Warrants to Technology

The search and seizure of data contained in computers and other electronic media raise various issues that must be considered. Information in computers is not evident like paper records; but must be generated by particular commands. Also, the data contained in computers may not be in readable form and may be intermingled with information that is not relevant. When it comes to computers, the question of what can be searched and seized arises. Also, the Electronic Communications Privacy Act (ECPA) imposes various kinds of restrictions and obligations on law enforcement agencies. Some of the issues that relate to computer search warrants are as follows:

Establishing probable cause
Execution or access
Segregation issues
ECPA issues
Privacy Protection Act issues
Subpoenas for computer records

Probable cause does not authorize police to search any computer found on the premises. Police must describe their beliefs that the computer was used for the creation and/or storage of financial records. The officer must determine the computer's role in the offense. Key questions are

Is there probable cause to seize hardware?
Is there probable cause to seize software?
Is there probable cause to seize data?

In developing probable cause, the investigator should evaluate the record system in operation and determine if there are any network and backup systems. Additional considerations are

Functions of the computer
Records processed and stored on the system
Programs used
Sophistication of system by users
Type of storage facilities
Media used

The seizing agent should describe the information and items to be seized as explicitly as possible in the affidavit. The seizing agent should ask for express authority to remove any hardware in order to conduct an off-site search. The agent should mention any manuals or instructions for the computer system. A "no-knock warrant" should be requested if destruction is a concern. Probable cause to seize a computer does not necessarily mean the entire computer system, i.e., all peripheral devices. The search warrant for computers needs to describe the computer system and the information contained therein in detail. For a computer not under the control of the suspect, subpoenas should be used for computerized information.

Electronic Communications Privacy Act

18 USC 2702 prohibits anyone to access stored communications and transactional records unless that person or government follows established procedures. Law enforcement must have a valid search and seizure warrant in order to obtain electronic data files. The search warrant must comply with the Federal Rules of Criminal Procedure or the state equivalent. Prior notice to the subscriber or customer is required if a governmental unit uses an administrative subpoena or summons. The court must approve and issue a nondisclosure order to prevent subscriber or customer notification. Attorney's fees and other litigation costs are recoverable by aggrieved parties if they win their case.

Privacy Protection Act

The Privacy Protection Act (42 U.S.C. 2000aa et seq.) was enacted to protect the press and certain other persons not suspected of committing a crime with protections not provided by the Fourth Amendment. The Privacy Act protects two classes of materials, work product materials and documentary materials. Work product materials are defined to mean materials that:

Are prepared or created by any person for communication to the public;
Are possessed for purposes of communication to the public; and
Contain mental impressions, conclusions, opinions, or theories of the person who prepared or created such material.

Documentary materials are defined to mean materials upon which information is recorded, and includes written or printed materials, films, video, and any mechanically, magnetically, or electronically recorded cards, tapes, or disks. Both documentary materials and work product materials do not include contraband, fruits of a crime, or materials intended for criminal use. There are two exceptions:

First, a search is permitted if the person possessing the materials has committed the criminal offense to which the materials relate.

Second, a search is permitted when it appears that the use of a subpoena or other less intrusive means of obtaining the materials would cause serious bodily injury to a human being.

Under this act, the aggrieved person may seek actual damages, but not less than $1,000 liquidated damages. Attorney's fees and other litigation costs are also recoverable.

Summary

Search warrants are a very valuable tool for law enforcement. To obtain a search warrant, the officer/agent must present all the facts so that an independent magistrate can draw the same conclusions that the officer/agent has drawn. The search warrant and the probable cause affidavit must describe in detail the specific evidence the officer/agent is seeking. Without the specificity, a search warrant cannot be obtained or, even worse, the evidence obtained from a bad search may not be admissible in court under the exclusionary rule. Law enforcement should consider the use of a subpoena or summons before considering a search warrant. The requirements of a search warrant states that the officer/agent gather more facts in order to obtain a search warrant. Particular attention should be considered when dealing with financial records and computer files. Commingling of legal and illegal documents presents a litigation hazard for law enforcement.

Fraud Examiner

29

Introduction

Accountants and law enforcement personnel wonder about the future of fraud examiners. These two professions have many common threads: a fraud examiner must be part accountant and part detective. The accountant has a good working knowledge of books and records, and the ability to analyze books and records, come up with various schedules and statements, and act as a forensic accountant in court. The detective has the ability to interview witnesses and discover evidence, and has knowledge of criminal law, especially the rules of evidence. When these elements of both the accountant and the detective are combined, the fraud examiner is formed.

Law Enforcement

Law enforcement in recent years has come to realize that economic crimes can only be solved by financial information. In order to solve economic crimes, the investigator must have a good working knowledge of financial transactions. Society today has become very sophisticated and complex in doing business. The IRS has met the needs by forming specialized groups to attack the sophisticated crimes. The FBI has formed specialized squads as well. Many big police departments have formed fraud squads to combat various types of sophisticated, complex fraud schemes. The biggest problem with law enforcement is the lack of adequate personnel and resources to combat white-collar crime. This is particularly true with shrinking budgets and the demand for more resources to combat violent crimes.

Accounting Profession

The accounting profession has not fully recognized fraud. One principal reason is the belief that fraud is the responsibility of management and law enforcement. Many certified public accounting firms have been successfully sued for failure to uncover fraud. Their main argument is that they are not there to detect fraud but to render an opinion on the "fair presentation" of financial statements. However, they do not realize that fraud can have a big impact on financial statements. It is well established that fraud has caused many businesses to go out of business because of fraud committed by employees and management.

Business

The business community for the most part has taken a laissez-faire attitude. When it finds an employee taking kickbacks or embezzling funds, it usually lets the employee go with the hope of some restitution. It fails to prosecute. When this happens, a signal is sent to other employees that they can steal and get off lightly. In the meantime, the bad employee goes to another employer and will commit the same offense. Businesses are reluctant to prosecute because of possible bad publicity. Actually, the reverse takes place. If a business prosecutes a bad employee or customer, then it sends a positive message out.

Fraud Examiner

The future for the fraud examiner looks very good. The *U.S. News and World Report* reported in its November 11, 1991 issue that forensic accounting would be one of the top 20 professions in the 1990s. In 1988, the Association of Certified Fraud Examiners (CFE) was established by the Institute for Financial Crime Prevention. This is the beginning of establishing credentials for fraud examiners. Forensic accounting has been around for more than a century, but has not been recognized as a special field of endeavor like other fields in accounting, i.e., tax planning and management services.

Association of Certified Fraud Examiners

This association has established minimum qualifications and programs for people who want to choose this field as a career.

1. **Qualifications.** The association requires candidates to have:

   a. A baccalaureate degree from a recognized institution.
   b. Two years of professional experience in fraud-related matters.
   c. Successful completion of the Uniform CFE examination.

2. **Examination.** The Uniform CFE examination tests candidates knowledge in fraud detection and deterrence. The CFE examination is divided into four parts:

   a. Investigation. This part addresses principles of interview and interrogation techniques, sources of information, report writing, case files and evidence, and covert investigations.
   b. Law. This part addresses criminal law, rules of evidence, rights of accused, privacy laws, and testifying as an expert witness.
   c. Financial transactions. This part covers accounting and auditing theory, evaluating internal controls, financial statement analysis, statistical sampling, audit evidence, and computer fraud.
   d. Criminology. This part covers crime theories; sociology and psychology of offenders; the criminal justice system; crime statistics; sentencing guidelines; plea bargains; and restitution.

Ethics

The association of CFEs has promulgated a Code of Professional Ethics. Even though this code of ethics applies to CFEs, it also equally applies to anyone who works in this field of endeavor. This Code of Professional Ethics is presented as follows:

1. A CFE shall, at all times, demonstrate a commitment to professionalism and diligence in the performance of his or her duties.
2. A CFE shall not engage in any illegal or unethical conduct, or any activity which would constitute a conflict of interest.
3. A CFE shall, at all times, exhibit the highest level of integrity in the performance of all professional assignments, and will accept only assignments for which there is reasonable expectation that the assignment will be completed with professional competence.
4. A CFE will comply with lawful orders of the courts, and will testify to matters truthfully and without bias or prejudice.
5. A CFE, in conducting examinations, will obtain evidence or other documentation to establish a reasonable basis for any opinion rendered. No opinion shall be expressed regarding the guilt or innocence of any person or party.
6. A CFE shall not reveal any confidential information obtained during a professional engagement without proper authorization.
7. A CFE shall reveal all material matters discovered during the course of an examination, which, if omitted, could cause a distortion of the facts.
8. A CFE shall continually strive to increase the competence and effectiveness of professional services performed under his or her direction.

Professionalism

The fraud examiner should possess a quality of professionalism. The characteristics of professionalism are as follows:

1. It is a specialized field of endeavor which can only be acquired by higher, formal education.
2. The profession has strict qualification standards.
3. The profession is recognized and accepted by society.
4. The profession has standards of conduct which govern members of the profession and their relationships with colleagues and the public.
5. A national organization or regulatory agency is present to promote and regulate the professional group.

The CFE is not regulated by state or federal agencies. Like most other professional organizations, the CFE must maintain and increase professional competence by continuing professional education. This has become more imperative because of the advances in technology and the increase in sophistication of economic crimes.

Diligence

Fraud examiners should be diligent in performing their duties. These duties include, but are not limited to, planning assignments, supervising assistants, avoiding conflicts of interest, obtaining sufficient evidence to form opinions, maintaining confidentiality, and avoiding any distortions.

Illegal Conduct

The fraud examiner is forbidden to participate in any illegal activities. While this seems very clear, there are times when this is not so clear cut. The fraud examiner has to be careful of libel or slander. Improper disclosure of the investigation can result in injury of a subject. The fraud examiner cannot detain any person without proper authority. Fraud examiners cannot make plea agreements. Only the court can accept plea agreements. Promises should never be made unless the fraud examiner has the authority to keep them.

Unethical Conduct

The fraud examiner is prohibited from unethical conduct. This is harder to define. The best definition would be any conduct that would discredit the fraud examiner and the profession. Such examples of this would be padding expenses, not fully disclosing all the facts, having financial interest in or with the client, using intoxicants while on duty, lending or borrowing funds from clients, misuse of title, working a case where the subject is a friend, relative, neighbor, and the like. The key to unethical conduct is how the public perceives the fraud examiner and his or her business and personal dealings. The *Internal Revenue Manual* states that agents cannot use their office for personal gain. This rule also applies to fraud examiners.

Integrity

The fraud examiner should have high integrity. Integrity consists of being honest, truthful, trustworthy, loyal, helpful, friendly, and courteous. In other words, the fraud examiner should have high morals.

Professional Competence

This relates to performance of duty. Fraud examiners should conscientiously perform their duties. They should keep abreast of current developments. Relations with associates, clients, and others should be conducted in a manner which will not cause dissension, discord, or disrupt business operations. The fraud examiner should become familiar with client's operations, respond to unusual events or conditions, and review evidence and assistants' work.

Testimony

The fraud examiner will have to testify in court on many cases. In some cases, the fraud examiner is the expert/summary witness. This is particularly true in cases involving indirect methods of proving illegal gains. The fraud examiner should only summarize evidence that is introduced into court. Opinions are admissible and sometimes required. However, no opinion as to the guilt or innocence of the subject is to be expressed. The fraud examiner should always respond to questions in examination or cross-examination, no more and no less. Answers should never express any bias or prejudice, but always be truthful.

Orders of the Court

The fraud examiner should always obey the orders of the court. Whenever a subpoena or summons is issued by any judicial body of competent authority, it should be obeyed.

Obtaining Evidence

The fraud examiner should obtain sufficient and competent evidence to render an opinion. No opinion should be expressed on the guilt or innocence of any person. Evidence should be obtained by all various means possible. This can include inspection, observation, interviews, and various other means. The evidence should be material and relevant.

Confidential Information

For all practical purposes, any information that fraud examiners obtain in the course of their assignment is confidential information. Disclosure without proper authorization and to the improper people can jeopardize a case. In the case of a grand jury, disclosure is not allowed under any circumstances, except by the court. Privileged information cannot be disclosed to anyone, not even the court. In some cases, the fraud examiner may be retained by an attorney who is representing a client and the examiner's services are for the attorney who has privileged communication status. All information that the fraud examiner obtains and analyzes belongs to the attorney. Even though the fraud examiner may retain various files and work papers and has been discharged by the client, confidentiality still remains. However, this confidentiality does not apply when an employee provides information about fraudulent acts, whether of another employee or of him or herself, since the client is the employer. Another complex situation occurs when the client is committing the fraud. The client holds the highest rank in management. The fraud examiner should withdraw from the engagement and issue a disengagement letter which should state the facts. Fraud examiners are not required to blow the whistle, but circumstances may exist where the fraud examiner is legally required to take steps. An attorney should be consulted. The fraud examiner should never let the client promulgate false or misleading reports based upon the examiner's work. Certain federal statutes require the fraud examiner to report criminal offenses to the appropriate federal agency.

Complete Reporting

The fraud examiner should always report all the facts whether they help or hurt the case. Evidence and facts are material if they can influence the report user to come to a different conclusion. An omission of facts or evidence is as much as a distortion as stretching the truth. The fraud examiner should gather all the evidence, oral and physical, whether it helps or hurts the case. The fraud examiner should never jump to conclusions.

Professional Improvement

The fraud examiner should always strive for improvements and greater knowledge. Most professionals, including fraud examiners, are required to have continuing education in order to learn new methods and techniques. Various organizations, i.e., AICPA, IIA, IMA, and ACFE, offer various seminars and programs to enhance the examiner's knowledge. In addition, the fraud examiner should keep abreast of local and national news media. They report of new schemes or variations of old schemes that are taking place in one's area. Fraud examiners should be aware of current conditions around them. When new schemes or variations of old schemes are discovered in one's locality, the fraud examiner should think and plan ways to prevent and detect such schemes.

Summary

The fraud examiner has a bright future when it comes to employment opportunities. These opportunities exist in private industry, public accounting, and government. There is the CFE certification. Fraud examiners must be aware of their responsibilities, obligations, and duties. The fraud examiner must keep abreast of current events and new technologies. For fraud examiners in the public or private sectors, they must be aware of the code of ethics. This ensures integrity and professionalism within the profession. For governmental fraud examiners, they must abide by their departmental rules of ethics and conduct. All federal agencies have their rules of ethics and conduct, which usually go far beyond those of the CFE association. For instance, many federal agencies either restrict or prohibit outside employment.

Bibliography

1. Association of Certified Fraud Examiners, Wells et al., *Fraud Examiner's Manual*, 1989.

2. Curran, Daniel J. and Renzetti, Claire M., *Theories of Crime*, Allyn and Bacon, Needham Heights, MA, 1994.

3. *Federal Civil Judicial Procedure and Rules*, West Publishing Co., St. Paul, Minn., 1996.

4. *Federal Criminal Code and Rules*, West Publishing Co., St. Paul, Minn., 1996.

5. Florida Department of Law Enforcement, James T. Moore, Commissioner, *Sources of Information*, Division of Criminal Investigations, Investigative Analysis Bureau, 1990.

6. Gleim, Irvan N. and Delaney, Patrick R., *CPA Examination Review*, Vol. 1 and 2, 11th ed., John Wiley & Sons, New York, 1984.

7. Kadish, Sanford H., Ed., *Encyclopedia of Crime and Justice*, The Free Press, 4 Vol., New York, 1983.

8. President's Commision on Organized Crime, *The Impact: Organized Crime Today*, U.S. Government Printing Office, Washington D.C., April 1986.

9. Sapire, Avinoam, *The LSI Course on Scientific Content Analysis (SCAN)*, P.O. Box 17286, Phoenix, AZ 85011-7286, (602) 279-3113, 1996.

10. *Standard Federal Tax Reporter*, Commerce Clearing House, Chicago, Illinois, 1989.

11. U.S. Department of Justice, Federal Guidelines for Searching and Seizing Computers, online at www.usdoj.gov.

12. U.S. Department of Justice, Criminal Division, *Compilation of Selected Federal Asset Forfeiture Statutes* (Rev. 7-95), Washington, D.C.,1995.

13. U.S. Department of Justice, Criminal Division, Asset Forfeiture and Money Laundering Section, *Financial Investigations Guide*, June 1998.

14. U.S. Deparment of the Treasury, Special Agents Handbook, *Internal Revenue Manual*.

15. U.S. Department of the Treasury, Tax Audit Guidelines for Revenue Examiners, *Internal Revenue Manual*.

16. U.S. Department of the Treasury, Executive Office for Asset Forfeiture, Office of Assistant Secretary (Enforcement), *Guide to Equitable Sharing for Foreign Countries and Federal, State, Local Law Enforcement Agencies*, 1993.

17. U.S. Department of the Treasury, Internal Revenue Service, *Financial Investigations*, Pub. 1714 (6-93), Catalog Number 15271F, U.S. Government Printing Office, Washington, D.C., 1993.

18. U.S. Deparment of the Treasury, Internal Revenue Service, *Search Warrants*, Document 9026 (Rev. 6-95) Catalog 148998S, 1995.

19. U.S. Department of the Treasury, Internal Revenue Service, *Sources of Information from Abroad*, Document 6743 (2–93), Catalog Number 45395E, U.S. Government Printing Office, Washington, D.C.

20. U.S. Department of the Treasury, Internal Revenue Service, *Special Enforcement Training for Revenue Agents*, Training 3148-02 (Rev. 8-84) TPDS 86837, 1984.

21. U.S. Department of the Treasury, Internal Revenue Service, Criminal Tax Division, *Forfeitures*, Document 9283 (8–94) Catalog Number 20996F.

22. U.S. Department of the Treasury, Internal Revenue Service, Criminal Tax Division, *Money Laundering from the Federal Perspective*, Document 7919 (Rev. 1-93) Catalog Number 14337A, 1993.

23. U.S. Senate, Hearings before the Committee on the Judiciary, *Organized Crime in America*, Serial No. J-98-2, U.S. Government Printing Office, Washington, D.C.

Suggested Reading and References

1. Barlow, Hugh D., *Introduction to Criminology*, 3rd ed., Little Brown and Co., 1984

2. Carson, Carl S., The underground economy: an introduction, *Survey of Current Business*, May 1981.

3. Cook, James, The Invisible Enterprise, *Forbes*, September 29, 1980.

4. Dirty dollars: Laundering Drug Cash, *The Miami Herald*, February 11–14, 1990.

5. Drugs in America, *The Miami Herald*, September 3, 1989.

6. Gugliotta, Guy and Leen, Jeff, *Kings of Cocaine*, Harper & Row, New York, 1989.

7. Kadish, Sanford, H., Ed. *Encyclopedia of Crime and Justice*, Vol. 1–4, The Free Press, New York, 1983.

8. Kleinknecht, William, *The New Ethnic Mobs*, The Free Press, New York, 1996.

9. Nash, Jay Robert, *World Encyclopedia of Organized Crime*, Da Capo Press, New York, 1993.

10. O'Brien, Joseph F. and Kurins, Andris, *Boss of Bosses*, Dell, New York, 1991.

11. Siegel, Larry J., *Crimiology Theories, Patterns, and Typologies*, 5th ed., West Publishing Co., St Paul, Minn., 1995.

12. Sifakis, Carl, *The Mafia Encyclopedia*, Facts on File, New York, 1987.

13. Simon, Carl P. and Witte, Anne D., *Beating the System: The Underground Economy*, Auburn House Publishing, Boston, 1982.

14. Spitz, Dr. Barry, Ed., *Tax Havens Encyclopedia*, Butterworths, London, 1986.

15. Ullmann, John and Colbert, Jan, *The Reporter's Handbook*, St. Martin's Press, New York, 1991.

16. Walters, Stan B., *Principles of Kinesic Interview and Interrogation*, CRC Press, Boca Raton, FL, 1996.

1.
2.
3.
4.
5.
6.
7.
8.
9.
10.
11.
12.
13.
14.
15.
16.

Appendix

Federal Reserve Districts

1. Boston
2. New York
3. Philadelphia
4. Cleveland
5. Richmond
6. Atlanta
7. Chicago
8. St. Louis
9. Minneapolis
10. Kansas City
11. Dallas
12. San Francisco

The Numerical System of the American Bankers Association

Index to Prefix Numbers of Cities and States

Numbers 1 to 49 inclusive are prefixes for Cities
Numbers 50 to 99 inclusive are prefixes for States
Prefix Numbers 50 to 58 are Eastern States
Prefix Number 59 is Hawaii
Prefix Numbers 60 to 69 are Southeastern States
Prefix Numbers 70 to 79 are Central States
Prefix Numbers 80 to 88 are Southwestern States
Prefix Number 89 is Alaska

Prefix Numbers of Cities in Numerical Order

1	New York, NY	18	Kansas City, MO	35	Houston, TX
2	Chicago, IL	19	Seattle, WA	36	St. Joseph, MO
3	Philadelphia, PA	20	Indianapolis, IN	37	Fort Worth, TX
4	St. Louis, MO	21	Louisville, KY	38	Savannah, GA
5	Boston, MA	22	St. Paul, MN	39	Oklahoma City, OK
6	Cleveland, OH	23	Denver, CO	40	Wichita, KS
7	Baltimore, MD	24	Portland, OR	41	Sioux City, IA
8	Pittsburgh, PA	25	Columbus, OH	42	Pueblo, CO
9	Detroit, MI	26	Memphis, TN	43	Lincoln, NE
10	Buffalo, NY	27	Omaha, NE	44	Topeka, KS
11	San Francisco, CA	28	Spokane, WA	45	Dubuque, IA
12	Milwaukee, WI	29	Albany, NY	46	Galveston, TX
13	Cincinnati, OH	30	San Antonio, TX	47	Cedar Rapids, IA
14	New Orleans, LA	31	Salt Lake City, UT	48	Waco, TX
15	Washington, D.C.	32	Dallas, TX	49	Muskogee, OK
16	Los Angeles, CA	33	Des Moines, IA		
17	Minneapolis, MN	34	Tacoma, WA		

Prefix Numbers of States in Numerical Order

50	New York	76	Nebraska
51	Connecticut	77	North Dakota
52	Maine	78	South Dakota
53	Mssachusetts	79	Wisconsin
54	New Hampshire	80	Missouri
55	New Jersey	81	Arkansas
56	Ohio	82	Colorado
57	Rhode Island	83	Kansas
58	Vermont	84	Louisiana
59	Hawaii	85	Mississippi
60	Pennsylvania	86	Oklahoma
61	Alabama	87	Tennessee
62	Delaware	88	Texas
63	Florida	89	Alaska
64	Georgia	90	California
65	Maryland	91	Arizona
66	North Carolina	92	Idaho
67	South Carolina	93	Montana
68	Virginia	94	Nevada
69	West Virginia	95	New Mexico
70	Illinois	96	Oregon
71	Indiana	97	Utah
72	Iowa	98	Washington
73	Kentucky	99	Wyoming
74	Michigan	101	Territories
75	Minnesota		

Index